REVISED FIRST EDITION

CHILDREN OF GIBEON

by Walter Besant

EDITED BY KEVIN A. MORRISON

Bassim Hamadeh, CEO and Publisher
Michael Simpson, Vice President of Acquisitions
Jamie Giganti, Managing Editor
Jess Busch, Senior Graphic Designer
John Remington, Acquisitions Editor
Brian Fahey, Licensing Specialist

First published in the United States of America in 2015 by Cognella, Inc.

Printed in the United States of America

ISBN: 978-1-63487-045-0 (pbk) / 978-1-63487-046-7 (br)

www.cognella.com 800.200.3908

Contents

Editor's Introduction

One of the most arresting images of nineteenth-century European visual culture is the careworn seamstress. Often depicted alone in the domestic environment that doubles as her workspace, and intensely contemplating her plight or weary and overcome by fatigue, she is an image of perplexing beauty. Despite her austere surroundings, which signify the meagerness of her life, she frequently radiates inward virtuousness. The interior illustration of this Cognella edition depicts one such seamstress, who has passed out from exhaustion.[1] As the sun begins to rise, the oil lamp that has provided the only light by which she has nocturnally sewn—an activity that caused much blindness among working-women—continues to illuminate her figure. Her limp body, partially resting on a small table, is juxtaposed with the unrumpled bed, in which she has not slept. The empty bowl from which she has presumably eaten dinner signifies the inadequacy of her diet. Its placement on an otherwise unused stool, within such close proximity, indicates that her fatigue was so overpowering that she was unable to perform the simple act of leaning over and moving the stool to support her legs. Scraps of fabric are scattered on the floor. As she sleeps, the seamstress clutches the dress that she has been sewing for a wealthy female consumer. From its position, obscuring the lower half of her body, the dress almost seems to be partially worn. But for the accident of birth, the painting seems to suggest, the seamstress might have dressed in the very clothes she is instead condemned to sew.

That one's cultural environment significantly influences—or even determines—one's fate is a central point of Walter Besant's *Children of Gibeon* (1886). Lady Mildred Eldridge, a wealthy widow from London's West End, visits a former servant and is overwhelmed by the washerwoman's struggle, as a single parent, to care for her large family. Lady Mildred offers to adopt Hester Monument's two-year-old daughter and raise the child alongside her own daughter, who is the same age. Lady Mildred renames the children Violet and Valentine so

1 Agenlo Trezzini, "A Tired Seamtress." Copyright in the Public Domain.
A Tired Seamstress by Angelo Trezzini (1827–1904). The exploited seamstress was a transnational concern in the nineteenth century.

that they, and everyone else, will remain ignorant of their true origins. Bearing an uncanny resemblance to each other, neither girl knows whether she is Beatrice Eldridge, the daughter of an heiress, or Polly Monument, a washerwoman's child. Lady Mildred promises Violet and Valentine that, when they are twenty-one, she will reveal their identities. While raising the two girls as her own, she also makes it possible for Polly's older brother Claude to receive a gentleman's education: he excels in secondary school, secures a scholarship to the University of Cambridge, and enters the legal profession. These efforts are part of Lady Mildred's grand experiment to prove that "there are, in every condition of life, children who may be trained and educated to have the manners and the instincts of the most well-bred and the most cultured."

When the girls turn twenty, they are introduced to the Monument family. While Violet shrinks in fear, Valentine, convinced that she is really Polly, relocates to working-class London, hoping to get to know her family and her people. She moves in with Polly's older sister, the fiery Melenda, a poorly treated and badly paid seamstress. Although driven to sewing out of economic necessity, Melenda is nevertheless resolutely independent. She accepts jobs from an apparel manufacturer, performing them at home, rather than working in a factory, because of the greater freedom this ostensibly provides. She dismisses all attempts, familial or otherwise, to help her, and she insults her brother Claude as nothing more than the product of upper-class charity.

Melenda shares a rented room in a tenement house with two other beleaguered working-women. Lotty and Lizzie, along with Melenda, perform a very specific task in the manufacturing of apparel. They sew buttonholes. The subdivision of labor—which by the mid-1880s was spread among a significant number of divisions, each responsible for a tiny segment of the overall product—enabled manufacturers to hire unskilled workers, often women, for a pittance. Through Melenda, Lotty, and Lizzie, Besant explores what he calls "the Law of Elevenpence Ha'penny." Manufacturers, the novel contends, have discovered that a worker's subsistence is manageable on eleven and a half pence a day.[2] Anything below this daily wage would make it impossible for the worker to survive, while anything above it would, precisely because it is unnecessary to ensure the worker's subsistence, cut into the manufacturer's profits.

Having been trained in a very small portion of the overall manufacturing process, Melenda, Lotty, and Lizzie possess no transferable skills and are unsuited for any other kind of employment. "They cannot go into [domestic] service," Besant writes, "because they know nothing, not even how to lay a table or how to dust a room; they cannot emigrate because they would be of no use in any colony; they can only sew, and, like the steam-engines which are kept going, till they fall to pieces of old age and rust, on coal and water, the sewing-girls are just as simply kept at working-power till something goes wrong with the wheels, on bread and butter and cold tea." The three women have themselves become sewing machines, working from 7 a.m. until 9 p.m. Melenda may have chosen to work outside the factory, but, Besant suggests, the home has essentially become a substitute for the factory or the small workshop.

The women are part of a vast contingent labor force variously known as sweated workers or outworkers. *Sweating* meant a form of employment that required a significant amount of hours for a minimal amount of pay in unregulated environments. A worker's home was one such location. Others included makeshift

2 One penny (plural: pence) is equivalent to one hundredth of a pound, as one penny is equivalent to one hundredth of a dollar. Victorian British currency includes pence (d.), shillings (s. or /-), crowns, and pounds (l. or £). Twelve pence are equal to a shilling, five shillings to a crown, and four crowns (twenty shillings) to a pound.

facilities, workshops, the back rooms of shops, and residential basements—"any place," James Schmiechen notes, "beyond the policing eye of the respectable artisan, manufacturer, or government inspector" (p. 3). The somewhat euphemistic phrase *outworkers* referred to everyone in the clothing and related trades who did not perform work in a factory. Because the manufacturing of apparel in the nineteenth century was cyclical, with periods of concentrated production, the capitalist found great advantage in this system. Instead of owning a factory that would then sit idle during slack periods, the manufacturer would instead employ workers as needed (Schloss, pp. 70–72).

Seamstresses were often used by artists and authors to call attention to working-class suffering because Victorian society tended to view this form of employment as essentially respectable. A narrative or image of a seamstress who performs her labor within a domestic setting was evocative because it provided a working-class figure with whom the middle classes could sympathize. Knitting and sewing, particularly as an intergenerational practice of sociability, were essential elements of middle-class domesticity. Women who worked in factories or small workshops instead of the home were viewed with suspicion. They were perceived as having betrayed their intrinsic domestic affections and, therefore, as possessing questionable moral standards. While the seamstresses of Besant's novel are all inherently virtuous because they do not appear in factories, the novel nevertheless asks whether one's residence can truly be considered a home if it functions chiefly as a place of work. Moreover, Besant suggests that Melenda, Lizzie, and Lotty unlike women who work in factories, have no opportunities to form unions that might improve their employment conditions and rate of pay.

If Melenda represents the highly independent working-woman who retains her virtue through a combination of pride and ceaseless toil, Lotty and Lizzie stand for, respectively, the physically debilitated laborer and the easily seduced dreamer of a better life. The unregulated nature of their work, with the performance of the repetitive tasks associated with sewing by hand in a stooped posture for fifteen hours a day, has taken its physical toll on all three women. Lotty, who suffers from severe back pain, is described as a "thin delicate-looking creature, about twenty-three or twenty-four years of age," with hunched shoulders and a face that is "pale and worn." Her eyes have the "patient expression which comes to those who suffer continually." Lizzie, although she too is malnourished, has the "makings of a really beautiful girl." She possesses a small "rosebud" mouth, the lips of which are generally parted, "as if the soul of the maiden within were waiting to receive the sweet and holy gifts and graces for which her eyes show her yearning." Besant notes, "It is impossible to see such a girl without longing immediately to take her away and place her where she may be in perpetual commune with things lofty and spiritual." The men who notice these same features have far more earthly considerations. Indeed, her virtue is threatened by those who would lure working-girls into sexual liaisons with promises they have no intention of keeping. To be sure, Lizzie, as well as Melenda and Lotty, are stock types. But they nevertheless represent "genuine slum dilemmas" (Keating, p. 99).

The three women live on Ivy Lane in Hoxton. Just north of central London, Hoxton was then part of the Metropolitan Borough of Shoreditch, on the outer edges of what came to be known as the East End. The borders of the East End have always been fuzzy and contested. The area only began to be represented on maps in the nineteenth century and only considered a fairly homogeneous geographical segment of the metropolis in the early 1880s (Palmer, Newland). The East End is generally thought to include various boroughs to the north of the Thames River and to the east of London—that is, not the greater urban environment but the official City of London, which is little more than a square mile, the borders of which are defined in part by the remnants of an old medieval wall. In contrast to the prosperous West End, which contained all the amenities of civilized life, the East End was one of the worst slums in Europe.

Until the early part of the nineteenth century, Hoxton was home to many affluent families. Over the course of several decades, the wealthy began relocating from central and eastern London to the West End and the suburbs of the greater metropolitan area suburbs. They were lured away, in part, by the promise of modern housing with ample amenities, situated in more desirable communities with better transportation links. Whereas the urban rich and poor had lived in close proximity to one another in the eighteenth century, an expanding consciousness about sanitation, coinciding with the marketing of socially segregated residential districts by property developers, had resulted by the early 1860s in "a dramatic geographic division of wealth: West End and East End, rich and poor" (Weiner, p. 7).

By the 1880s, prominent intellectuals and politicians became increasingly concerned about the palpable discontent among the working classes. Nascent social movements, offering critiques of capitalism and advocating political reform, were effectively taking root in the East End—such as the socialism that Sam Monument, another of Hester's offspring, propagates in the novel. The Earl of Rosebery, a Liberal who served as prime minister in the 1890s, lamented that London was becoming divided into two distinct zones, essentially realizing within its confines what Benjamin Disraeli had identified long before as a more general division of the nation into the rich and the poor. This division, Lord Rosebery concluded, had serious implications for the future of London: "I hold that it is a great and sacred responsibility, not merely for our statesmen ... but for all our leading citizens, in whatever capacity it may be given to them to lead, to endeavour to prevent the formation of those distinct nations [as exist in Continental Europe] within our metropolis" (qtd. in Weiner, p. 200). The geographic and physical separation of the classes—with areas of concentrated wealth and poverty, combined with the demographic changes taking place in the East End as a result of an influx of immigrants (to which the novel refers on several occasions)—had laid the foundation for revolution.

Addressing itself to these issues, *Children of Gibeon* was hailed by readers as a "purposeful" novel (Underhill, p. 257). It depicts government, science, religion, and socialism as equally impotent in solving the problems London was facing. Besant suggests that, in fact, only novelists—by which, of course, he means himself—can offer the kind of capacious social vision on which social unity can be based, because they "are the only true philosophers of modern times, and ought to be the only statesmen." If science, embodied in *Children of Gibeon* by a young doctor, provides an impetus for the care of the poor, it also engenders disenchantment and worldly cynicism. Religion, premised on the notion that all are the children of God, may provide greater inspiration. But its concern with the salvation of souls, Besant argues, leads to little practical change, as evinced by the assistant priest in the novel, whose labors are for naught. If socialism recognizes injustice, its advocates, such as Melenda's brother Sam, rail at "the system" and dream of a utopian future while failing, Valentine contends, to look after capitalism's individual "victims" in the here and now.

Instead of the socialist version of equality, rather uncharitably depicted in the novel as leading to a world as bleak as the one the characters already inhabit, Besant proposes a future in which the working classes can achieve cultural parity with those above them in the social hierarchy. Valentine and Claude, who become partners in efforts to bring about social unity (rather than, say, equality), conceive of an alternative revolution, unlike the commune Sam envisions, that balances individual responsibility with shared beneficence. This revolution is to begin with the recognition among the members of the middle and upper classes of a common humanity, which the affect-laden images of seamstresses invite as well. Indeed, in one passage the novel addresses directly an explicitly female reader who, but for her circumstances, might have led a different sort of life:

> My very dear young lady, you who sit at home in ease, how would you like to find yourself in food, frocks, fire, furniture, music, boots, bonnets, books, trinkets, gloves, and all the thousand-and-one things that go to make a girl's life, on sevenpence ha'penny a day? But these girls are not like you? That, I assure you, is not at all the case. It is a falsehood invented by the Devil when he invented the figment of nobility, gentry, and villain. If you desire to know what the work-girl really is, go to the looking-glass and study very carefully, not your bonnet, which is very becoming, nor your face, which is so pretty that one wishes he was young enough to fall in love with it, nor the dressing of your hair, which might be much more artistic, but the unseen self which lies behind the face. That is the working-girl as well as yourself, my dear young friend.

Lady Mildred's grand experiment of adopting Polly and educating Claude is essentially an attempt to recuperate the working class for universal humanity. The novel suggests that once those of a privileged background understand that, in one character's phrasing, "there ain't a great deal of difference between us after all; it's mostly a matter of clothes," a cultural revolution can then proceed apace, remaking the working classes in the image of the middle class.

Claude and Valentine establish an Earthly Tract Society for precisely this purpose. Offering short, pithy, and practical information, their tracts displace what Besant elsewhere calls "the education of the gutter" ("From Thirteen to Seventeen," p. 36). The most important of these tracts, on which Claude and Valentine collaborate especially closely, are included in the domestic series that is at the foundation of the society's efforts. "It began with the Tract on Wives," Besant describes the society's early development, "meaning the right treatment of a wife, with her husband's plain duties towards her; the corresponding Paper on Husbands; on Children, with a parent's duty to his offspring; on Language, the word used in its popular sense, and with special reference to the use of the Universal Adjective;[3] on the House; on Woman's clothes; on Dinners; on clean Streets; on Water; on Fresh Air; on Amusements; on Holidays; on Beer; on Pretty Things; on Dressing the Hair; on Boots; on Wages, high and low; ... on Hours of Work; and so on."

Although this revolution begins at home, its effects are nevertheless far-reaching. The change in Ivy Lane is instantaneous. It becomes a "Show Street," with the houses "as beautifully clean as a Dutch village, the blinds are white, ... there are flowers in every window, and these are clean; within, the floors are scrubbed, walls are dusted, water is filtered; the men have quite left off getting drunk; they never swear unless the situation demands strong and plain words; they do not beat their wives; the women do not scream and fly into rages; quarrelling among them is almost unknown." With a newfound respect for herself, the seamstress will enter into cooperative efforts with others like her to improve working conditions and pay for all. The diffusion of the middle-class ideal of domesticity—doled out to the working classes in simple, comprehensible lessons—"solves," according to the logic of the novel, the inequities on which social conflicts have been based.

3 A common adjective in London at the time was *bloody*, an expression of anger or loathing.

If the notion of an underlying human essence ("the unseen self") seems quaint today, or at least hopelessly problematic, and the novel's proffered solutions to sweated outwork either preposterous or pernicious (a mere change of clothes rather than a change in systems), *Children of Gibeon* nevertheless remains a vitally important historical document in understanding the social and epistemological changes occurring in the closing decades of the century. For Besant's readers, the novel represented a significant challenge to their willful blindness to the human costs of manufacturing apparel—"so great is their sympathy with those who suffer," as Besant ironically puts it, "that they cannot bear even to think of them, much less to talk about them"—and their blithe attitude toward philanthropy, "treat[ing] every painful case [of human want] with half-a-crown[4] and a basket of grapes." One of Besant's contemporaries thought the title summed up the meaning and moral of the novel most of all:

> The Children of Gibeon ... were a tribe condemned by Joshua [leader of Israel] to perpetual bondage—to be "hewers of wood and drawers of water for the congregation" [for deceiving him]. Mr. Besant knew ... that in all our back streets there are hundreds and thousands of women who are continually occupied in working out life-long sentences of toil, compared to which the tasks of the Egyptians were light, and the daily labour imposed by the slaveowner was merciful; toil coupled with miserable pay, chiefly absorbed in satisfying the rent collector, insufficient food, and deprivation of all that makes life tolerable, not to say happy. This terrible life-sentence, from which there is no escape and of which there is no mitigation, is pronounced upon these poor women at their birth: it is their punishment for the crime of being born. They have been condemned unjustly—not justly, as were the Children of Gibeon—to perpetual bondage. (Underhill, p. 257)

Following the novel's publication, "the bright light of publicity" was shown on the outwork system (*Record*, p. 12); articles were written on the sweated seamstress; and one reader established a cooperative sewing association, along the lines represented in the novel, to which Besant lent his support (Besant, *Autobiography*, pp. 246–48). With a dozen employees, a forewoman, and a directress, the association sought to establish itself as a model of improved working conditions and greater pay. While the efficacy of the resulting efforts can be debated, a comment about Besant's *All Sorts and Conditions of Men: An Impossible Story* (1882)—which inspired philanthropists to establish the People's Palace in the East End, modeled on the novel's Palace of Delight for the poor—could easily apply to *Children of Gibeon* as well. Not just a "novel with a purpose," it was a "novel with a result" (Billson, p. 619).

* * *

Children of Gibeon was serially published from January to December 1886 in *Longman's Magazine*, a periodical that catered to middle-class families, and in a three-volume edition in 1886. It was subsequently published in a number of editions in both London and New York. The text in this volume follows the 1887 edition published by Chatto and Windus in one volume. I have, however, regularized spelling and capitalization by consulting later editions. I have also silently corrected the misspelling of some characters' names in the novel

4 An English coin worth two and a half shillings or thirty pence.

and in the ancillary material. The assistance of two exceptional graduate students made this Cognella edition possible. Elizabeth Stearns helped me with formatting and proofing, and Thomas Witholt drafted many of the annotations. I am grateful to them both.

Kevin A. Morrison
Syracuse University

Works Cited

Besant, Walter. *Autobiography of Sir Walter Besant*. New York: Dodd, 1902.

– – –. "From Thirteen to Seventeen." *As We Are and As We May Be*. London: Chatto, 1903. 24–49.

Billson, Charles James. "The English Novel." *Westminster Review* 138 (1892): 602–20.

Keating, P. J. *The Working Classes in Victorian Fiction*. London: Routledge, 1979.

Newland, Paul. *The Cultural Construction of London's East End: Urban Iconography, Modernity, and the Spatialisation of Englishness*. Amsterdam: Rodopi, 2008.

Palmer, Alan. *The East End: Four Centuries of London Life*. New Brunswick: Rutgers UP, 2000.

Record [Valparaiso, Chile] 25 Apr. 1888: 11–12.

Schloss, David. "Women's Work and Wages." *Longman's Magazine* 12 (1888): 61–73.

Schmiechen, James A. *Sweated Industries and Sweated Labor: The London Clothing Trades, 1860–1914*. Urbana: U of Illinois P, 1984.

Underhill, John. "Character Sketch: Walter Besant." *Review of Reviews* (1893): 250–61.

Weiner, Deborah E. B. *Architecture and Social Reform in Late-Victorian London*. Manchester: Manchester UP, 1994.

Children of Gibeon

By Walter Besant

Contents

Prologue

Part I

Polly-Which-Is-Marla

Sit down, Hester, and let us talk. It is seventeen years since you saw me last."

"It isn't the time I grudge, my lady," Hester replied, plunging her bare arms into the soap-suds; "it isn't the time, but the things are promised, and a laundress's word is her work. If she breaks her word, it's leave the things and change the washing. And a lovely drying day."

She spoke with two pins between her lips. People of her walk in life, unless they happen to be Chinamen, always while they are standing at the wash-tub carry two pins in the corner of the mouth—they are not even safety pins; and the practice gives them for the time a curious thickness of speech.

"Let me talk and work at the same time, my lady, though it is such a long, long time since last I set eyes upon you; and a beautiful little creature you were, to be sure. Lor' a me!"

She was a woman of five-or six-and-thirty: country-bred, as you could very easily tell by the rosy hue of her cheek and by its amplitude, by her figure, full and comely, and by her breadth of shoulder. The London air—it is the fog in it, perhaps, or the smoke in it—produces in the second and all succeeding generations, a diminishing effect: it narrows and slopes the shoulders; it contracts the figure, it shortens the stature, and it makes the features small; in fact, it makes the London girl small all over, yet it does not leave her without charms of her own, as is daily testified by many. This woman was a big woman, looking still as if she was fresh from field and country lane; her forehead was lined, her mouth was drawn—but this might be due to the presence of the two pins; her eyes were limpid and full and in colour brown, something like the eyes of a hare when she is not frightened. They were set and framed in a network of lines and crows'-feet, and when she was alone they had a trick of hardening. This may have been caused by trouble, or perhaps it was only the natural result of the weekly arithmetical exercise peculiar to her profession, and worthy of a Babbage,[1] in which the good woman

1 In 1821, Charles Babbage designed what are generally considered to be the first computers, called *difference engines*, which could calculate arithmetic, as well as programmable "analytical engines" that included more complicated features.

had to enumerate, divide out, add up and make to come right, all the socks, handkerchiefs, shirts, collars, and cuffs entrusted to her care. As for her features, they were plain and even rugged. A working-woman may very naturally acquire, by the age of six-and-thirty, from her life of struggle and work, a very considerable amount of hardness. But with Hester the ruggedness seemed part of the original mould, as if Nature had left the face in the rough without the final stroke of the chisel. I do not think that Hester had ever been beautiful; but by reason of her hair, which was still plentiful, and of a warm red colour, and her limpid eyes, she may have been in her youth pleasing to look upon. It seems a fond thing to speculate upon the possible beauty of a washerwoman in the vanished days when she was young. But it has a certain interest for us, because she had children with whom we have to do, and it is a melancholy reflection that so little interest is generally taken in the past beauty of a woman, whether she be a washerwoman or a duchess.

As for her expression, it was grave and even sad at times: and when she was hanging out the clothes, or when she was ironing, or whenever there were no pins in her mouth, her lips had a habit of silently monologuising, moving in the manner of one who speaks with great rapidity, but with no audible utterance. What she said in these soliloquies one knows not; perhaps she was rehearsing the weekly returns, as, "six p'r o'socks, six; ten handkerchiefs, ten; seven shirts, seven," ... and so on; accuracy in a washerwoman being as desirable as despatch in a dentist. Or in that silent and mysterious way she may have been recalling scenes in her past history. If so, they were not pleasing scenes. Mrs. Monument's face, to those few who can read the history of a life in a face, showed unmistakable signs of trouble; anyone who knew the history of that trouble could without difficulty point to individual lines, wrinkles, and crows'-feet directly caused at various stages of it; to most of those who were ignorant of this history, and perhaps too much occupied by their own misfortunes to think much about other people's, the lines about the mouth, the wrinkles in the forehead, the set eyes, and the hardened mouth conveyed no more meaning than an inscription in cuneiform.[2] It is, in fact, only the novelist, and he only for purposes of his art, who studies the human face when it is past the time of beauty, and strives to read, with the help of what he knows, the emotions and sorrows which have left their mark upon it. It is too often, however, like reading a Greek classic with the help of an English crib, which has lost the charm of language.

"Seventeen years ago, Hester," said Lady Mildred, "I was taken to see your wedding at the village church, and I thought you the most beautiful and the most enviable creature I had ever beheld, in your white dress and your curls."

Hester played with the soap-suds and smiled. Then she frowned at her own foolishness, and then she smiled again. Since Lady Mildred was so good as to say she had once looked like a beautiful woman, it was not for her to contradict her; henceforth the memory of her wedding-day would possess another and a brighter association. But Hester, who was truthful by nature, had never been accustomed to think of herself as beautiful. Plain girls sometimes make their own consolations for themselves—notably, the comfortable assurance that as many plain girls get lovers as pretty girls—but they are never under any illusions as to their own looks. Hester, however, permitted her mind to dwell for a moment on the memory of her ruddy and rosy cheeks and white dress, and on the fashions of the year 1848, and the people in the church, and she smiled again.

2 One of the earliest systems of written expression, initially made up of pictograms.

As for the day, it was the brightest and warmest day in June ever known, and as for the year, it was in 1866. The house was one of a small row of little five-roomed cottages, irregular, picturesque,[3] with red-tiled roofs and red brick chimneys; they have now all been pulled down, not because the landlord was one of those who despise old things and love to tear down and destroy, like a First Lord of the Admiralty with the old ships, but because if they had not been pulled down they would have fallen down. Wherefore now, a terrace of little houses with bow-windows, built of grey bricks, all exactly alike and with slate roofs, stands in their place, and those who remember the former cottages fall to weeping when they pass that way. The houses stood in a strange and mysterious place, the actual and visible marge of London, looking out upon the low green levels with which Hackney Marsh surrounds the river Lea and prohibits the further march of brick. White mists lie over the Marsh in winter afternoons and autumn evenings, and make it ghostly to look upon; but it is a keen and healthy air which sweeps across the plain, a good drying air for linen, and a bracing air for children with strong lungs and sound throats. Each of the cottages stood behind a long narrow strip of garden, which was by some laid out and planted with onions, cabbages, peas, potatoes, and beans, but in more than one case was left fallow, so to speak, dotted here and there with patches of turf, and decorated with bare masts or poles instead of trees, connected by ropes, with hanging linen instead of waving foliage and blossom. It was, in fact, a convenient spot for washerwomen, and Mrs. Monument "did," single-handed, or with only occasional help, for two or three of the first families in Homerton and Hackney, sister suburbs, which melt imperceptibly into one another, and seem to differ in no other respect than that of magnitude. The fruits of her labour hung, every fine day and all the year round, upon the lines in the garden, and floated in the breeze, bulbous, spherical, wafted this way and that, with the undulations and the graces of a corpulent fairy, across the flower-beds where no flowers ever grew.

Beyond the garden the eye roamed free and unchecked across the marsh, a bare flat expanse of green turf, cut into irregular shapes by the elevated roads which cross it, deserted in the morning, but in summer evenings and on Sundays covered with the lusty youth of Hackney Wick; beyond the marsh is the Cut,[4] up and down which go majestically the barges of the river Lea: then more marsh, and then the Lea itself, narrowed by reason of the Cut, with high banks of mud and still tortuous, as if resolved to keep its character to the very end. There are two bridges over it—one a narrow footway of wood, rustic, ancient, not without beauty; the other new and broad for carts and cyclists as well as for those who go afoot. The marsh is not, it must be confessed, one of the most romantically beautiful spots upon the earth; but it lies open to all the winds of heaven; those who walk across its causeways may perhaps still get ague[5] as they used to do in the brave old days, but at least they are outside the houses, which is a very precious thing to dwellers in Hackney and its sisters. In the eyes of Mrs. Monument the marsh was chiefly delightful because all the winds which blew across it came to her drying-ground fresh and free from smut. Can Hyde Park[6] boast as much?

---

3 Originally used to describe anything visually attractive, charming, or quaint that might be represented in a painting. By the 1880s, *picturesque* referred to anything with pleasurable or appealing qualities.

4 An eighteenth-century canal made to shorten the naturally circuitous route of the River Lea in the Hackney area.

5 A fit of fever and chills.

6 Located in central London and one of the city's largest parks.

The cottage contained a kitchen or laundry, with a red brick floor, looking upon the garden. Here were the wash-tubs, and a boiler,[7] and pattens,[8] and a board to stand upon. Behind it was a sitting-room, or living-room, and above were two bedrooms. Naturally the steam of the tubs filled the whole house and ascended continually unto the heavens like the smoke of Vesta's[9] sacred fire—none of the Monument children except Polly can ever pass the steam of a wash-tub without being instantly transported back to Hackney Marsh and filled with the sense of a universal washing-day, as if the rivers and lakes of the whole world had been turned into hot and steaming soap-suds. Outside the door was a rustic porch grown over with jessamine, and within the porch at the open door stood a young lady. In the year 1866 she was four-and-twenty years of age, and in the eyes of her generation she passed for an extremely beautiful woman; her portrait may be found by the curious adorning any Book of Beauty belonging to that time. She wore a huge crinoline,[10] she carried her hair in a big net, and, after the fashion of her time, she made herself look as short of face and of limb, as dumpy of figure, as nature would allow. When one thinks of that time, and of the truly sinful waste and throwing away of feminine loveliness and grace which went on daily and from year to year, it is not pity that one feels so much as blank wonder that women could be such fools as to disfigure and transform themselves.

As regards Lady Mildred Eldridge, one would have felt a very human pity, because, in addition to her hideous crinoline, she wore widow's weeds,[11] with a vast quantity of that dolorous crape[12] which every husband who truly loves his wife ought to forbid in his will.

"And to think, my lady," said Hester, "of your remembering me after all these years!"

"I remember, Hester, how sorry I was when you left the nursery to get married. It was the first grief of my life."

The woman's face darkened.

"To get married!" she echoed bitterly. "Oh! what fools girls are! Just to get married! To leave a pleasant home full of kind ladies who'd never throw them over, and run into the arms of the first chap who comes along with a smile and promise! If it wasn't for the blessed children, I sometimes wish I had thrown myself into the cold river the morning of my wedding. Perhaps it would have been better for them too." She wrung a handful of linen as if she wished it had been her husband's neck.

"Hester!" The young widow was frightened at her old nurse's vehemence. "Hester! Tell me something about it. And why have you taken your maiden name again?"

"I changed my name to get out of my husband's way; but it was no use."

"Out of his way?"

"Yes, my lady. But never mind about my troubles. And you with your own to bear, and a widow's cap and all at your age, poor dear!"

"I have been married too," Lady Mildred replied calmly, "and I have lost my husband. But about yours, Hester?"

---

7 Similar to a kettle and used for heating water.

8 Shoes designed to protect the feet from wetness.

9 The Roman goddess of the hearth and home whose virginal priestesses ensured that her flame never died out.

10 Stiff fabric structures worn under dresses to provide the skirt with support and volume, which could drastically alter the shape of a woman's lower half. They are part of the "transformation" of the female body that Besant decries in the next sentence.

11 Plain and unassuming attire worn by widows.

12 A hard silk that was part of a widow's mourning costume.

"He is dead," the woman replied, with an obvious effort, as if it pained her so much as to speak of him. "He is dead, and I pray that my children may never hear tell of him!"

"I am sorry. Poor Hester!"

"There are some troubles." She left the wash-tub and sat down, wrapping her apron about her bare arms. "There are some troubles, my lady, that women needn't be ashamed of—such as men are born to as the sparks fly upwards—and there's some troubles that we can't think of, though we must, at times—let alone speak of. Troubles that spoil the lives of innocent children."

"There are, indeed, Hester. If these were yours, I am sorry for you."

"We came up to London," Mrs. Monument went on, "to get work. That's what he called it. Oh, fine work he got! He was a locksmith, and it's a trade which finds out a man's cleverness and leads him into temptations. Whatever his work was, there was always plenty of money, and I was happy. Oh, who could have told beforehand what was going to happen! Then my Joe was born."

"What did happen, Hester?"

"Nothing, my lady," she replied evasively; "only that I went to live by myself with the baby, and took my maiden name, and hoped never to see him again."

"And then?"

"Oh, he found me out. But he is—buried." There was just a slight pause, as if she was not quite certain whether he was actually buried or only dead, and still awaiting that rite, like one of the melancholy ghosts on the shores of Styx; though if they knew what was waiting for them on the other side they would perhaps send up word to their relations not to bury their bodies.[13]

Everybody has remarked the fondness which all well-regulated women entertain for a good round solid aphorism. It never loses its freshness for them. Therefore it was natural for Lady Mildred to remark solemnly: "Where there is no escape from evil save by death, it is better that one should die."

"Provided it's the right one," said Hester. "Because, if I'd been took, what in the world would ha' become of the blessed children?"

"Where are your children, Hester? How many of them have you?"

"Polly-which-is-Marla," replied Hester, as if the four words made but one name, "is playing among the linen—bless her!—where she can't come to no more harm than a slap in the cheek from a wet arm or a flapping skirt." She went out into the sunshine and shaded her eyes with her hand, and called, "Polly! Polly! Come to mother!"

Then there came running out from among the hanging clothes a little girl of two years. She was an extraordinarily beautiful child, though her frock was ragged and dirty, and the cap tied round her head had seen long service. Her short brown curls lay over her forehead and pressed out the cap; her deep, mysterious eyes gazed shyly at the visitor; her parted lips made the sweetest rosebud of a mouth. Two years old! This is the age when the infant passes into the child; she is still irresponsible, without morals, and void of any principles whatever; she still possesses the infantine wonder; life is still full of novelty for her; none of the gilding has been rubbed off; she is always making new experiments, and continually breaking out in new directions; she talks a most

13 The Styx was the major river separating the living world from the underworld in Greek mythology, across which souls were ferried by Charon. Besant suggests here that if those who have committed evil knew they faced eternal punishment they would not want to be properly buried.

charming language; she utters the most unexpected sentiments; and she does the most delightful things. She is a flirt, a jilt, a coquette; she is as unreasonable as the wind; she is as uncertain as the weather; she is a doll, a treasure, a joy, an idol, and a little goddess. Of such there are tens of thousands in this land of ours, and I wonder how many of us have the grace to thank God for them!

"Why, Hester"—Lady Mildred was startled at this miracle of beauty—"your child is an angel; she is a fairy. Are all your children like this one?"

"Three of them are," said Hester. "They take after their father, who was as handsome, though undersized, as he was clever. Cleverness it was which ruined him, and his good looks did him no more good than to make him wicked and false."

"What is her name, Hester?"

"The name, by rights, is Marla, but we call her Polly, because the other is an outlandish name."

"Why did you call her Marla?"

"It was her father's doing. He would have it, and as I'd my choice with Joe and Sam, I had to give way, though I blushed for shame when I told the clergyman at the font."

"Marla! It is an odd name."

"My man, you see, my lady, was fond of his book, and perhaps he found the name in one of the books he was always reading. But there—it doesn't matter now; and I always call her Polly which is handier and more natural."

"Yes—it is handier. Do you know, Hester"—Lady Mildred had the child in her arms—"it is strange! Do you know that the child is strangely like my own little girl?"

"Why, good gracious!" Hester threw up her arms in astonishment at her own forgetfulness. "To think that I never even asked your ladyship if you had any of your own! But of course you have. There's the mother in your look, plain to see. Lord! the hunger in a childless woman's eyes!"

"I have only one—a little girl—about this child's age."

"None but a woman with children of her own," Hester continued, "knows how to carry a baby right. Now, to see your ladyship with that little one!"

"Where are your other children? I should like to see them all."

"I've got four more"—Hester forgot her work and the beautiful drying day in her maternal pride—"four more. First there's Joe. He's sixteen now, and tall for his age. Apprenticed to his father's trade, and handsome, though not clever, as his father was, which gives me hopes for him. It's the stupid lads that turn out the steadiest and do the best. After Joe comes Sam, and he's seven, bless his heart! For sturdiness and appetite there isn't his equal."

"Nine years between the first and second?"

"Nine years, my lady. Because my husband—he deserted me, I told you—I came away with little Joe. But he found me out after all those years, and came back to me. And then came Sam. After Sam came Claude."

"Was that name your choosing, Hester?"

"Lord, no, my lady. I should never have thought of such a fine name for my boy. It was his father's choice. He named the boy after someone in his books—Claude something, who, my husband said, was one of the greatest men who ever lived. But he only seemed to me a rogue and a robber."

"It could not be Claude Duval?"[14] said Lady Mildred at hazard.

"I think that was the name; but I don't rightly remember. When I took the baby to church I could only remember the first name, so he is Claude, and nothing else. He is six now and a beautiful boy—more like his father than me, and as like as two peas to Polly-which-is-Marla. After him comes Melenda, who is five—another heathenish name. But it's his choice, not mine. She's like Sam, not Claude. Just after Polly was born my husband left me again—thank goodness for it."

"Do not let us talk about him, Hester," said Lady Mildred. "It only vexes you."

Just then the children came home from school. First came Sam, a sturdy red-haired child with bright eyes, and a face painfully like his mother's—chiselled hastily and with just a few strokes, rough but effective; the result being a broad forehead, strong chin, large mouth, and rosy cheeks. After him walked Claude—a pretty boy of six, who had very much the air of a gentleman in disguise, though his clothes were tolerably ragged. Last there came a little red-haired girl of five, exactly like her brother Sam. They emerged from the white curtains of drying linen and stood ranged in line before the porch.

"Here they are, my lady," said their mother, proudly reviewing her family. "This is Melenda, who's as good as gold already, and can be trusted with Polly. This is Sam. Hold up your head, Sam. It would do your ladyship good to hear that boy read. And this is Claude. He's like his brother Joe and his sister Polly. They all favour their father—in outward looks only, I hope and pray."

Lady Mildred remarked how she kept recurring to her husband, whose memory she so much detested. It was as if he was always in her mind.

"Hester," she said, "do you alone provide for all these children? Is there nobody to help you?"

"Nobody," she replied. "It's terrible hard work, to be sure; and sometimes I wake in the night and think I must break down. And then we shall all have to go to the Union[15]—you can see it from the back of the house—and me and them will be parted."

"Five mouths to be fed! It must take a great deal of washing to find food for so many."

"Yes, my lady. But there, I don't mind hard work. There's worse trouble than that for me to be afraid of—worse than hunger even for the little ones—that I dread day and night."

"Hester," said Lady Mildred, who still had the youngest in her arms, "let me help you. Let me take one of the children off your hands. Lend me this little one."

"Lend you my Polly!"

"Lend her to me, Hester. You can trust her to me. I am not a stranger to you. Let me take the child."

The mother snatched the little girl out of her visitor's arms.

"Part with my flesh and blood!" she cried jealously. "Give you my Polly!"

"If you think it would be for her good."

The woman hugged the child and pressed it closer to her heart, and shook her head. But the tears came into her eyes. "There is something on your mind, Hester," Lady Mildred persisted. "No; do not think that I want to know what it is. There is something you remember and something you dread. When you speak of

14 Claude Duval was a seventeenth-century highwayman notorious both for his robberies and his way with the ladies.

15 A workhouse where the destitute received accommodations and meager rations in exchange for their labor. The conditions of workhouses were deliberately inadequate on the theory that inmates would become motivated to provide for themselves.

your dead husband you look about you as if you feared he might be standing at your garden gate. Poor Hester! You must have had an unhappy life."

"An unhappy life—yes."

"He is dead and past our blame of it," said Lady Mildred.

"Yet something survives. The memory—"

"The memory of it," Hester repeated—"the shame of it, for me and for the children."

"If you let me have the child, I will bring her up in ignorance. She shall have no knowledge of the memory."

"Do you want to make her my young lady's maid?"

"No. She shall be brought up with my daughter—her companion; she shall be educated with her. I will provide for her. As for separation from you"—Lady Mildred remembered that if she was to bring up the child as a young lady, Sam and Melenda and Claude might not, in the course of time, be quite desirable companions—"as for separation, you shall know always how she is going on; when she grows up you shall see her again if you wish it; she shall be told about her parentage nothing more than you please to tell her. Think! You will part from the child, but it will be for her happiness, and one less to work for."

"Oh, my Polly!" cried the mother. "As if I could think it a trouble to work for your dear little mouth!"

"Think of it, Hester. Take a week, a month, to consider."

To Lady Mildred's astonishment, Hester decided on the spot.

"You shall have her, my lady. Oh, to save them from what I dread day and night, I would part with them all. Take her—take her. To save her I would consent never to meet her again till we meet in heaven. Yet—oh, let me keep her just one night—my pretty darling!—to hold her in my arms one night longer."

"Oh, Hester!" said Lady Mildred, moved to tears. "I will be like a mother to her. She shall never be unhappy if I can help it. And as for you and yours, whatever happens, you will have a friend in me and mine."

"Oh, I know—I know. But promise me one thing, my lady. Let the child never learn, whatever happens, unless I tell her—only my boy Joe knows—that my name is only my maiden name; else she'll want to know her father's name. If when she grows up she asks about her mother, tell her that her mother was an honest woman. If she asks about her father, say that he is dead and buried long ago. There are five of them. One of them knows the secret already, but he keeps it close; perhaps the three left with me will find it out, but not Polly—not little Polly-which-is-Marla. God knows I'd never part with her—never—except for that one thing, so long as I'd a finger left to work with."

"She shall be happy," said Lady Mildred, "if I can make her happy. And you shall see her again. Somehow you shall see her. You shall not altogether lose her."

In this way little Polly-which-is-Marla disappeared from Hackney Marsh, and became Valentine or Violet, I know not which—adopted daughter of Lady Mildred Eldridge, and therefore granddaughter of the Earl of Haslemere, Knight of the Garter, and daughter of the late Sir Lancelot Eldridge, Bart., M.P., F.S.A.[16] This was certainly very great promotion, and, if one may say so of a young lady of this tender age, as yet wholly undeserved.

---

16 Lady Mildred Eldridge has quite a lineage. The Earl of Haslemere is a fictional title, but the Order of the Garter is quite real; it is the oldest and highest chivalric order in Britain. Her father's titles are less impressive, although still substantial: Bart. is the suffix abbreviation for *baronet*; MP is the suffix abbreviation for *Member of Parliament*; FSA is the suffix abbreviation for *Fellow of the Society of Antiquaries.*

* * *

"Have I done well, Bertha?" asked Lady Mildred, over the two cribs in which, side by side, the two children were sleeping. Lady Mildred was a woman with many ideas, and Miss Bertha Colquhoun was the friend of her girlhood to whom she communicated them.

"They are curiously alike," said Bertha; "one might almost take them for twin sisters. As for your doing a wise thing, my dear Mildred, Time, the only infallible prophet, will disclose when the hour comes. I shall not give my decision till I hear his opinion. As for your doing an interesting thing, that is undoubted. Tell me, by the way, which is little Trix?[17] I haven't seen her since she was in long clothes; and which is the little washerwoman of Hackney Marsh?"

"Why, nobody knows except myself and my solicitor. I was obliged to tell him. I have changed nurses, and managed so carefully that nobody can so much as guess. The child with the light blue ribbon round its neck is Valentine; the other is Violet. For both of them and for all the world Beatrice is lost, as well as Polly, until October 15, 1885, when Beatrice will come of age."

"Oh!" said Bertha, disappointed at not being taken into the secret; "then I must wait like all the world, I suppose. But oh, my dear! Poor little Polly-which-is-Marla! Poor child, when she learns the truth!"

17 Trix is a nickname for Beatrice, Lady Mildred's own daughter.

Part II

The Stroke of Fate

For eight years longer those strong arms worked without rest or pause over the wash-tub. Time, who possesses an apparently double movement, like a planet, and goes round and about among us while we go straight on, frequently remarked the unchangeable character of this good woman's life, for whom none of his seasons produced either joy or pain, except so far as they brought good or bad drying days. The lines were always up, except in rainy weather, and they were always laden, for eight years, during which Mrs. Monument never flagged and never felt weary. In eight years Joe passed from a 'prentice to a workman; at the age of nineteen, like most of his fellows, he took a wife, herself seventeen; by the age of twenty-four he had five children. In eight years Sam advanced from seven to fifteen and became a pupil-teacher, being resolved to achieve the position of board school[1] master. Claude was thirteen, Melenda was eleven, and Polly, of whom from time to time the mother heard the best accounts, was, with her sister Valentine or Violet, ten years of age.

Now, after eight years, Fate suddenly interposed, acting in that decisive manner by which she has always commanded so much respect, and even fear.[2] It is, in fact, the Oriental style, in which there is no hearing of a case, or pleading, or argument, or jury, or evidence, or court of appeal, or anything at all but the Caliph, the successor to the Prophet—may his soul have peace![3] —who knows everything, and orders everything, and lo! it is done, whether it be the lopping of a head, or the extermination of a family, or the elevation of a beggar in rags to a purple robe and a seat on a white ass and the post of grand vizier. In this case, as usual, the decree

1 The Elementary Education Act (1870) established schools managed by a board of locally elected officials that provided compulsory education for children until the age of ten.

2 Fate in Greek, Roman, and Norse mythology was understood to be a trio of female entities relating to either the three periods of human life (youth, middle age, old age) or the three aspects of time (past, present, future).

3 The caliph is the head of state according to Islamic law; explorers of what was then called *the Orient*, such as Sir Richard Francis Burton, depicted these rulers as decisive, all-powerful, and quite often cruel.

of Fate was final and irresistible. Mrs. Monument began to go blind. First, she became conscious of a curious dimness of vision whereby the outlines of things were blurred; next she found that this dimness grew upon her; and finally, after the most dreadful apprehensions for the future, she sat down and folded her hands, and made Sam write a letter to Lady Mildred. She had now gone so blind that she could no longer see anything but "men like trees walking;" she would very soon cease to see them at all; then she would get to the end of her money; then, what would happen to the children?

When Lady Mildred came, in response to this letter, she was received, so to speak, by a boy who sat in the porch reading. As for the garden, it looked forlorn without the linen: the posts were there, and the fines, but there was no linen, though a most beautiful drying breeze was blowing over the marsh from the north-east, and there was a warm sun in the sky. Stranger still, there was no smell of steam or soap-suds in the house, and the stricken worker sat in the inner room, hands crossed, in the patient expectant attitude of the blind.

The boy rose and pulled off his hat. Lady Mildred by this time had quite forgotten the child who, at five years of age, had the air and appearance of the descendant of fifty dukes. His face, however, had altered little; it was now a sharp and rather thin face, marked with a strange refinement and delicacy of outline. We do not generally associate such a face with a laundry. We are wrong, of course; because in every city, court, and on every village green, and wherever humans do congregate, there will always be found some child or children with the face of refinement and sweetness, not in the least like the rough and plain faces round them. A scientific person, I believe, would call them "sports," playfully implying that nature must have her little distractions, and cannot abide for ever to be trammelled with law and rule. Perhaps, however, the scientific person would be wrong, and there may be nothing in man which is not hereditary, down to the cut of a nostril, the outline of a cheek, or the curve of a lip. If Claude's ancestors in the male line were known, for instance, we might trace every feature the boy possessed to some grandfather or great-grandmother. As for his mother's family, it is very well known indeed, and it is a most ancient and a highly honourable house, seeing that every man in it from father to son, has, from time immemorial, worn the smock-frock or leather jerkin, driven the plough, fed the pigs, sowed and reaped, and sowed again, and has presently shut his eyes and been laid under a little mound of grass in the acre of the Lord. And as for distinction, why the sons of this House fought at Senlac, where they got defeated, after unheard-of bravery, and at Cressy and Agincourt and Bosworth Field, and at Blenheim, and at Waterloo and Alma.[4] Claude has every reason to be proud of his ancestors by his mother's side. But he did not get his face from any of them, because their faces, though scrupulously honest and sometimes clean, were never either refined or delicate.

"Please, ma'am, my name is Claude," said the boy, conscious that his name was much finer than Sam's; and indeed it is a very beautiful name, and many a city knight has to put up with one much inferior.

"Claude—yes—I remember you now." Lady Mildred remembered the story of his baptism. Was he really named after Claude Duval? "Let me look at you, boy! You are like your sister—Polly. Does your mother tell you about Polly-which-is-Marla?"

"Oh, yes. A fine lady came and took Polly away. Some day we are to see her again, when she comes home for good. She won't be proud, mother says."

4 All of the battles the narrator mentions—Senlac (1066), Cressy (1346), Agincourt (1415), Bosworth Field (1485), Blenheim (1704), Waterloo (1815), and Alma (1854)—played a pivotal role in wars that helped to define England and the United Kingdom.

Then Lady Mildred left him and went to see her old nurse. She observed, however, that the boy sat down again and buried his face in his book. "You poor soul!" she said. "Tell me all about yourself, and why didn't you send for me before? And what does the doctor say?"

Presently, after the first outpourings concerning the darkened eyes—"And now," said Lady Mildred, "about your children? Is Joe doing well? And has he turned out quite as stupid as you hoped?"

"Joe's a good workman, and he's in good work at Tottenham with a plumber and house decorator. He would marry at nineteen, like all the rest of them, and now there's five innocent babies, and she two years younger than himself. But he's a good son always, though he can't help no one but himself."

"And Sam?"

"He's a pupil-teacher, and gets on wonderful. There never was a boy like Sam for getting on. He's made up his mind to rise in the world, and rise he will. Says he shall be master of a board school before he's satisfied. Think of that for my Sam!"

"Good boy! And then comes Claude—the little fellow outside in the porch."

The mother shook her head.

"I don't know what will come to the boy, nor what trade he will take to. For he thinks about nothing but books and reading. Sam reads, too; but then Sam only reads what he wants, and what will be useful to him. Claude reads everything. Oh, dear, dear! his father was just the same. Always forever with a book in his hand."

"Boys who read," said Lady Mildred, "often come to great honour. And what about Melenda?"

"She's at school yet. But she gives me a deal of trouble, my lady. I want to get her into good service, in a lady's house. But she won't go. She says all the girls at school are going to be free and independent, and earn their own living by themselves, and so will she. What do they know about it? Give me a good dinner every day, I tell her. That's the first thing. But the girls nowadays are all for freedom, even if they starve with it. There, my lady, that's enough about the children. Tell me how my Polly grows, and if she's a good girl, and pretty behaved."

It certainly was a very good thing for the Monument family that it found a friend in Lady Mildred at this juncture, when, if it had not been for her, the subsequent history of the family would have belonged to the simple annals of the workhouse. As it was, the sympathy of Lady Mildred proved of a very practical kind. First it procured for Mrs. Monument a cottage in an almshouse[5] in the Tottenham Road, where she was near her eldest son Joe, and substantial help besides, so that she would be looked after and "done" for; and as for Sam, it provided for that boy—though he never knew the fact—the means of continuing his course of study, and enabled him first to become a monitor with five shillings a week, and next a pupil-teacher with sixteen shillings a week, and then to go to a training college, and finally to get a place as assistant teacher on ninety pounds a year with a five-pound rise. And as for Melenda, it kept her at school and found her in food and clothes until she refused to stay any more. And as for Claude, I suppose the boy's pretty delicate face and intelligent eyes had something to do with Lady Mildred's kindness to the boy; but she always said it was because she found him a natural lover of learning and devourer of books. At all events, she called him one day and held a very serious conversation with him.

First she asked him what he would like to be.

5 Almshouses were a form of charity to support those who could no longer provide for themselves.

"I should like," the boy replied, reddening, "to go into a book-seller's shop. There's one in the Victoria Park Road, full of old books, where they want a boy."

"You would not be allowed to read the books. You would only sweep out the shop, put up the shutters, and run on errands."

The boy's face fell. To sit among books seemed to him the height of happiness. But to sit among books and not be allowed to read them, that would be a fate worse than that of Tantalus.[6]

"You should desire to get on, Claude. The love of reading may help you if you have the other qualities for success. Have you thought of anything else?"

No; he had no other ambitions.

"Now listen. Boys who read and are industrious sometimes get on very well. I fear it may be too late for you to do much, but you can try if you are brave."

What was he to try? Claude looked at her with great eyes of wonder.

"I will give you a good education. I will take you away from this place and have you taught as much as you can learn. You shall be educated up to your capacity, whatever that may be."

Claude felt himself, as to capacity, like unto the Great Tun of Heidelberg.[7] His colour came and went; his heart beat and he choked. What was this great happiness that was coming to him?

"When I learn that you have gone far enough, we will consider what you can do for your living. And remember"—she lifted an admonitory finger—"never pretend to be what you are not. You are the son of a working-man and a working-woman, though you will wear good broadcloth[8] and go to school with boys who may pretend to look down upon you."

Claude wondered what she meant.

"As for your mother, you will go to see her whenever you can, and you will not neglect your brothers and your sister. Your future will depend entirely upon your industry and upon your abilities. I think you will show ability, at least. If you do, remember that every avenue to success is open to you. That you will not understand at first. Say it to yourself until you do understand it. Say it when you read of any great man. Never forget it. Though you are a poor lad, you may hope for everything and dare everything. But you must not be afraid to work and to wait; you must not be afraid of fighting or of speaking out. Above all things, work. Do you understand, Claude?"

The boy's heart glowed within him. But he could not answer. His tongue refused to move. He was frightened as well as dazzled at the prospect before him.

"Will you do your best, Claude?" Lady Mildred asked in a kinder voice.

"Oh! yes, yes," said Claude, bursting into tears.

"Your best, my boy. Your hardest and your best. You will either see me or hear from me often. I shall always know exactly what you are doing and how you are getting on. Oh! child, you are too young, yet, and too ignorant, to know what a magnificent chance you are going to have. I pray that you may not throw it away. If

---

6 In Greek mythology, Tantalus was punished in the afterlife with "tantalizing" fruit and water all around him: when his persistent hunger or thirst drove him to eat and drink, the fruit rose out of his reach and the water drained away.

7 The Great Tun of Heidelberg is an enormous wine barrel kept in Heidelberg Castle of the Rhine Valley in Germany. By the Victorian era, it was no longer used as storage for wine but instead as a wondrous attraction.

8 Broadcloth is a sturdy, smooth woolen fabric.

you do, the mud into which you fall will be Malebolge[9] itself compared with the mud out of which you have been taken."

The boy understood little of these words except the great fact that he was going to learn unheard-of things; that he was no longer to wander on the Hackney Marsh, dreaming, but he was to work, something as his brother Sam was working, but with other aims, and, as he vaguely understood, with wider aims. He was to work, to fight, to wait, and to hope. In course of time success would be his. I do not know what were his ideas of success. A boy cannot frame or map out for himself a career; but he can feel that something is to be tried for and something won, and he can imagine for himself some of the glorious sensations of victory. Besides, the boy who accustoms himself to think of the world as something to be conquered, and of himself as a soldier of the future, has already won half the battle. For him there will be no false modesty. When the time comes, he will step into the front rank as one whose place is there, and that by divine right itself.

9 Malebolge was the name Dante gave in his *Inferno* to the eighth circle of Hell, reserved for those who committed fraud.

Book I

Chapter I

At Nine O' Clock

There are many delightful and desirable rooms in London; the pilgrim who is in society is continually halting on his way to rest and refresh in these Houses Beautiful.[1] But there can be no more pleasant place than that room in Lady Mildred's town house which the girls had made their own. It was on the ground floor; two windows looked through the foliage of lime, laburnum, and lilac, upon the Park, though with the road between; it had at one end a glass door opening upon a conservatory; it was always filled with the fragrance of flowers; and here the girls kept their own things—their very own—which they prized the most. Valentine had here her favourite piano, with her songs and music; the walls were hung with Violet's pictures, and there were portfolios filled with her sketches; there were cabinets full of treasures collected in their wanderings—things pretty, things ugly, things quaint, things precious, things worthless—memories of Egypt, Greece, Italy, and France and Germany—wherever the English girl is allowed to wander. It is not yet, but very soon it will become, the fashion for her to visit the States and Canada, the isles of the Pacific, Australia, India, and far Cathay.[2] Therefore the young ladies had nothing from these countries.

About seven o'clock on an evening early in July of the year 1885 the two girls were sitting together in this room, as was not uncommon with them. But it was their wont to be quiet, calm, and restful, as behoves young ladies who believe that life is always to be a long-continued and monotonous happiness in the midst of pretty things and soft cushions. On this occasion, however, they were greatly agitated. One of them, Valentine, was standing; the other, Violet, was sitting at the table. In her hand she held a pencil, and she was rapidly drawing figures on a sheet of paper.

They were about the same age, and that a youthful age; they were dressed exactly alike—they always dressed exactly alike—and for the evening. If a masculine pen may he permitted to indicate the outlines of

1 The phrase *Houses Beautiful* refers to the aesthetic movement, which sought to beautify domestic interiors on the principle that there should be no distinction between the decorative and the fine arts.

2 Cathay is an alternative name for China.

their dress, leaving details to be filled up by the imagination of experience, they wore a dainty confection of pale blue silk called, I think, surat, which fell in long folds from the waist, and was caught up at one side showing a lace petticoat, which is a pretty old fashion come back again. The throat was a little open but not much, with folds of lace about it, and there was an arrangement of ribbons and loops about the waist. They were dressed well, in fact, yet with the appearance of simplicity. Their hair was of the light brown hue which is so much beloved by the English youth. Violet's was full of curls and curves and twists, which caught the light and scattered it about as a little waterfall in a mountain brook breaks and scatters the sunshine. Valentine's hair was slightly darker in shade, not curly, but with a wave in it, and in her hair the sunshine lay and rested. They dressed their hair in the same fashion, and that not a common fashion: for it was parted at the side instead of in the middle—or as hairdressers, ignorant of Euclid,[3] say, in the centre; it is a pretty fashion if there is a pretty face for the hair to encircle, otherwise the commoner methods are preferable. Their eyes were blue in colour, but not quite the same shade of blue; for Valentine's were certainly darker than Violet's, and like the hair, they absorbed the light which Violet's received and reflected: in other words, they were deeper and graver eyes. I would not for a moment suggest that they were more beautiful; that is matter for the jealousy of a lover, and nowhere are comparisons more odious than those concerning beauty. Argument on such a subject is purely vexatious and barren, and wastes the time which should be spent in thankful hymns for the precious gift of loveliness. Always those eyes are the most beautiful which belong to the woman one loves at any moment; and, until he meets his fate, a well-regulated young man should always be in love with somebody. The girls' faces were of the oval type, but, which is a most important distinction, of the shorter oval. The longer oval, in fact, is apt to degenerate into narrowness, with perhaps the expression of a bird of prey; while the shorter form allows of strength to the chin and breadth to the forehead and amplitude to the cheek. Venus should have an ample cheek as well as a smiling mouth and kindly, gracious eyes. There may be less capacity for philosophy, but there is more for mathematics, music, and the finer feelings in the shorter than in the longer oval. A prolonged residence at Newnham[4] would be necessary in order to carry on this delightful investigation to its legitimate end. And one need not here discuss questions on which even novelists, who are the only true philosophers of modern times, and ought to be the only statesmen, might disagree; besides, these girls were neither philosophers nor mathematicians. They were only girls who had been carefully educated at home, and knew a great many accomplishments and arts, had curiously pretty customs and pleasing manners, and practised, without knowing it, the most charming graces. But they knew no political economy,[5] and they were not brought up to consider themselves bound to consider or to solve any social questions at all.

The girls were about the same height—that is to say, they were fairly tall; their carriage and bearing were alike; they looked like sisters, and were taken by strangers for twin sisters. There were, however, certain marked differences between them not immediately apparent which the stranger presently observed. Thus, Valentine was somewhat larger in person than Violet; and as to their voices, Valentine's was rich and full, Violet's was low and sweet. And as to their tastes, Valentine was a musician and a singer, while her sister painted with no mean skill, and drew, if not quite so well as Mr. Du Maurier,[6] yet well enough to delight her friends and

3 The ancient Greek philosopher Euclid is considered the father of standard geometry.

4 A college for women at the University of Cambridge.

5 A social science concerned with economics and governmental policies.

6 George du Maurier was a late-nineteenth-century novelist and cartoonist known for his satirical illustrations in *Punch* magazine.

to please herself. Yet, which is a very curious thing and only to be accounted for by the fact that everybody knew they were not really sisters, it was universally agreed by all their friends that no one could possibly mistake them for sisters. One of them—there never was any concealment of this fact—was the only child of the late Sir Lancelot Eldridge, Baronet and Member[7] for the county, who would probably have got into the Cabinet had his party returned to power in time. But they did not, and he was cut off at sixty-five, which is, for a statesman, early manhood, almost the first flush of spring promise. He left a quite young widow, Lady Mildred, daughter of the Earl of Haslemere, to take care of his infant daughter. The other girl—there was never any concealment of this fact either—was nothing in the world but the daughter of a mechanical person of the baser sort, a mere working-man. She had been adopted by Lady Mildred, no one knew why, and was brought up with her own child. Her true name, though this was not generally known, was Marla, and she had been formerly known in her own rank of life as Polly, for short. One of them, therefore, was a very considerable heiress, and most desirable in point of family connections; the other had nothing at all, and her connections were presumably most undesirable.

"No one will maintain," said the World, "that the daughter of a working-man and the daughter of a gentleman can ever stand upon the same level. Education can refine, but it cannot change base metal into gold."

Yes. Unfortunately there was a complication. No one, not even the girls themselves, knew which of the two was the heiress and which the simple working-man's daughter.

"This," said the World, "is wicked. Lady Mildred will not speak and no one knows, and there are hundreds of men only waiting to know which is which. Is it right to ignore natural distinctions? Not to know; and it ought to be such a simple thing; and yet it is not possible to tell, and it disturbs all one's ideas. Why the Eldridges have always been remarkable for the beauty of their girls. But these girls are both beautiful. And of course one ought to read old descent in a face. But here both the faces might show long descent. What man would dare to face so terrible an uncertainty? Why he might be marrying into the most dreadful family possible. Was it right, could it be right, of Lady Mildred to take a girl out of the gutter and pretend that she is a lady?"

There was once a nymph of surpassing loveliness who offered every one of her suitors a double acrostic,[8] with an alternative: either they guessed it quite correctly without the aid of any dictionary, or if they failed in any one of the lights—it was a frightfully hard acrostic, which wanted both dictionary and encyclopaedia and a complete acquaintance with the whole field of classical literature—that suitor was instantly decapitated, and so made way for another. If, on the other hand, he succeeded, this murderous young person bestowed upon him her bloodstained hand. In point of fact, though history passes it over, only one young man ever offered himself. He was the Prize Acrostic Guesser—the champion. They gave him the thing, in neat hendecasyllabics,[9] and while he was reading it they proceeded to erect the scaffold. But in the confusion and excitement which always attends a coming execution he meanly ran away. In the end this princess died unmarried. There was also another young lady, strong and staying as to wind and limb, who offered to run races with her suitors, on

7 Member of Parliament.

8 A multilayered word puzzle in which answers to given clues contain a specific letter (usually the first or last) that will reveal a hidden word when combined with the letters from the other answers.

9 A form of poetic meter during the classical period that uses eleven syllables per line.

the same terms of death or victory. But Love's Nemesis[10] came upon her too, for no one ever proposed to run with her on those terms, and she presently grew middle-aged and fat, and lamented the days of her beauty and her arrogance, and said that running races was unladylike and ought to have been discouraged long since, and it was wrong of her parents to encourage her. But it was too late, and now she leadeth apes by a chain. Lady Mildred presented herself and her two girls before society when they were twenty years of age, with a conundrum bearing much the same consequences.

She said, in fact, to the whole of the English youth, "Young gentlemen, here are two charming girls. They are natural, fresh, and innocent. I have kept them in the country for twenty years, so that they are healthy both in body and in mind. They are as pretty as most girls; they are accomplished; they are frank and they are good-natured; they are amiable, they are even clever. One is my daughter and the other is not; one is an heiress and the other is not. Fall in love, therefore, if you dare. Offer your hands if you dare. You may win a fortune or draw a blank. You may be grandson-in-law to an earl and son-in-law to a baronet, or you may find yourself surrounded by a troop of cousins with paper caps, aprons, bags of tools, sewing-machines, and with manners which generally accompany those emblems of toil. Is love worth such a risk?"

Apparently it is not in this cold and calculating age. The girls had gone through their first season, and not one man as yet had ventured.[11] This did not disturb them in the least, for they were ignorant of Lady Mildred's conundrum, and their thoughts were not bent on matrimony.

There was not wanting plenty of curiosity. There are always inquisitive persons whose imaginations are fired with every mystery, and can never rest until they know all about it. Some of these tried questioning Lady Mildred, and were coldly snubbed; some even tried the girls, who froze directly the subject was mentioned. But they learned experience, and presently grew wary and recognised the regulation smile of sympathy and the little laugh of apology with which the mystery was always approached. Some examined the various extant portraits of Sir Lancelot—that at eight years of age, that at twenty, that at forty, and that at sixty—and then furtively compared them with the two girls and sucked thereout no profit to themselves, but only more uncertainty; and others gazed upon Lady Mildred and watched her gestures, her carriage, her little distinctive mannerisms, if she haply had any, and then watched the girls, looking for some little trait in one of them—a turn of the head, a momentary emotion of the face, which might reveal the secret. There were hundreds of these indications. Unfortunately they were as remarkable in one of the girls as in the other. A mother, again, is generally found to show more tenderness towards her own child than to another, but Lady Mildred was tenderness itself towards both the girls; not the least difference could be observed in her manner towards either. Then there is the voice; but here specialists—that is to say, those who remembered Sir Lancelot—differed, because there were some who recognised in Valentine and some in Violet the tones of the late baronet's voice exactly reproduced.

And now the world was waiting. In three months Lady Mildred's daughter would be of age; perhaps the other one as well; but nobody cared about that. It would be impossible then to conceal the thing any longer.

10 The Greek goddess tasked with establishing moral balance by punishing those who committed crimes and ensuring the suffering of those who demonstrated pride before the gods.

11 The London elite typically lived in the country but returned to the city during the late spring and early summer months for a "season" of elite sociability when eligible young women would be introduced to potential suitors.

The heiress must receive her inheritance; the truth would be known; the parentage of the workman's daughter stand revealed; and the young men could come forward.

"Val," said one of the girls impatiently, "I really do believe that the evening of this day will never come."

"It is much longer than the very longest day of all the year, Violet; my dear, a longer day was never created," Valentine replied. "He belongs to both of us, absolutely and impartially, does he not?"

"That is agreed," Violet replied gravely. "He is our brother—brother to both of us."

"If we are to be proud of him," Valentine went on, "we are to be proud together. He is our own property—the property of both. If we are to be ashamed of him, we will be ashamed together."

"Ashamed of him," Violet repeated. "I suppose he will be like this." She had sketched a workman with a bag of tools in his hand, and a paper cap and an apron—a good-looking young workman. "This is the best chance for us, Val dear. But yet I don't see even in this case that we can be reasonably proud of him, can we?"

"Well," said Valentine, examining the sketch, "you have made him look respectable. Labour has its dignity. Can't we be proud of an intelligent working-man?"

"Or he may be like this." She took up another sketch showing the conventional Ælf and 'Arry[12] out for a holiday, arm in arm, roaring and shouting—they are really very rare, these two, though they certainly can be found. "Or like this"; she showed a young fellow leaning in drunken pose against a lamp-post; "Or—" here she showed a dreadful, smug young man with fat cheeks and curly whiskers, a frock coat and baggy trousers, and a smile—one of those young men who read scientific books, live on temperance principles, and are virtuous—all with ostentation.

"Don't, Violet," said her sister. "Oh, I am sure we shall not be ashamed of him. Mamma would not have asked him to come here if he were like this—or this. But possibly he is a working-man—what else can he be? We are only the daughter of one!"

"Perhaps," said Violet, "he may know which of us is his sister by some likeness to his father or his mother or himself."

"Or perhaps he may remember us. We were only two when we were taken from our—other mother; and he is three or four years older; he may remember his little sister."

"No: not after twenty years. But there may be a something—a family squint—but our eyes are straight; some people have hereditary teeth which stick out—but ours don't; or thick lips—but ours are not thick; or great ears which stick up—but yours are small and lie flat, and so do mine. Oh! there must be something, if it is only a disposition to drink."

"And then there would be no secret to tell us on the fifteenth of October. If there is anything, Vi, let us keep it to ourselves."

"I know what I should like to say." Violet sprang to her feet. "I should like to say: Brother—this is Miss Beatrice Eldridge—I am your sister. My name is Polly—Polly-which-is-Marla." For they had heard so much of the family history.

"And I," said Valentine, "should tell him that you are quite mistaken, because I have always been convinced in my own mind that I am Polly."

"There are moments," said Violet reflectively, "when I feel unheard-of possible depths."

"And there are times," said Valentine, "when I feel inconceivable basenesses."

12 A pair of ill-bred young men who appear in a variety of British stories for comedic effect or satirical ends.

"Of course, the lower classes do feel depths."

"Of course, my unworthy thoughts are my inheritance."

"Then both of us," said Violet, "must call him brother."

"And he must call us both sister."

"The two together only make one sister. Then I suppose we must let him call us by our Christian name. Fancy a carpenter in an apron addressing you as Valentine! Oh! I shall box his ears."

"Violet"—Valentine dropped her voice and blushed at the thought of the thing. "Brothers—kiss their sisters. It will he dreadful if—"

"No," said Violet, firmly. "Certainly not. No carpenter shall ever kiss me."

"Sooner or later we shall learn the truth. Till then," said Valentine, "the question must not even be raised. Besides, if one hasn't seen one's brother for twenty years, one cannot very well be expected to—oh! Violet, everybody knows the story of the beggar who became a princess, but nobody knows the story of the princess who became a beggar, and put on rags and wandered about with poor people. Do you think she was ever happy, dear?"

"No," said Violet, shuddering, "she was always miserable, and she died young, and of a broken heart."

"I don't know. Perhaps she was a great joy to the poor people, and was able to do all kinds of things for them. I think I could put on the rags, Violet dear."

"You never shall. You in rags!" Violet shuddered again. "But they might be picturesque. You shall put them on, Val dear, and sit to me in them, and I will paint you so, and send the picture, if they will have it, to the Grosvenor."

* * *

"Bertha, stay here this evening. I want you to assist at a family function which is to take place at nine o'clock."

This was in another room—Lady Mildred's drawing-room—and there were present Lady Mildred herself and Miss Bertha Colquhoun, her old friend. Twenty years had passed over their heads. The former had never married again—the latter had never married at all; as regards the ravages of time, Lady Mildred was no longer young, but she was still comely, and Bertha was of like age, but less comely, because widows wear better than spinsters. It would be unkind to say more.

"What is it, Mildred?"

"I am going, this evening, at length, to make the girls acquainted with their—"

"At last! Oh, Mildred—and you have asked me to learn the truth with them. It is kind of you."

"Acquainted with—their brother."

"Oh! But—pardon me, Mildred—is that necessary? Their brother must be, I suppose, quite a common man. Is it well to pain the poor girls with such kinds of associations? I thought they—she—had been quite separated from the family."

"You shall answer the questions for yourself at nine o'clock, Bertha. Meantime, remember that it wants little more than three months to the time when my child must learn the truth, because she will attain her twenty-first birthday."

"But why not wait to tell them?"

"Both girls know the story of Polly, but today they heard for the first time that there is a brother, and that they are to meet him this evening."

"Poor girls!"

"They are now preparing themselves, I believe, for the reception of a working-man."

"Poor dear girls!"

"And they are encouraging each other to receive him kindly. Before the truth is known to them, you see, they will have time to become fully acquainted with the whole of the other family."

"Poor Polly! Oh! Mildred, how could you!"

"Why do you pity Polly? She is as well bred as Beatrice: she is as beautiful. I shall not unmake the gentle breeding, though I take away the gentle birth."

"Still—poor Polly! Will she take her own name?"

"I do not see the necessity. She may just as well remain Valentine—or Violet Eldridge."

"I suppose the brother will come here straight from the public house, pipe and all?"

"Perhaps."

"No doubt he will. Poor girls! It is dreadful for them. After all these years of culture—of course, for one it will be only a little excitement which will pass in three or four months, and she will be able to reflect that she knew all along that she was Beatrice. But as for the other—I repeat, Mildred, poor Polly! However, you have forgotten one thing."

"What is that?"

"Why in introducing their brother you will betray the secret, because the girls will find out the truth—everybody will find it out—from his likeness to one of them. So I shall be the first to learn the secret after all."

* * *

The four ladies dined together, but it was a silent banquet. The girls, for their part, said nothing at all, but looked at each other and at the clock. At half-past eight they adjourned to the drawing-room. The brother was to be introduced at nine. The girls, as the clock drew nearer to the hour, clasped each other by the hand, while Lady Mildred and Bertha fell into silence or only exchanged a word at intervals. And oh! how slowly moved the minutes!

At nine in the evenings of early July it is not dark, but only a little overshadowed, and there is quite light enough to discern faces, which is all that is necessary for conversation. You may talk in the dark, but, as Charles Lamb[13] once remarked, it is inconvenient having to feel your companion's face for the responsive smile. As the clock struck the hour the door was thrown open.

"Mr. Claude Monument!"

The girls caught at each other and gasped. Lady Mildred rose. In the door stood a young man who looked about him with troubled eyes.

"Good heavens!" Bertha murmured, but I think everybody heard her. "The creature is a gentleman!"

Yes. He had on the outward garb of a gentleman, and he carried himself with the outward bearing of a gentleman. It was a rude thing for Bertha to say, but her mind was full of working-men, and pipes, and aprons,

13 An English essayist (10 February 1775–7 December 1834).

and the smell of beer, and she was surprised into rudeness, and she hoped that nobody would notice it. Now, there certainly was never yet in any history or in any country a carpenter, or a smith, or a working-man of any kind who ever had a dress coat to put on unless it was to go out as a waiter in the evening. Could the young man be a waiter?

"My children," said Lady Mildred, taking the young man by the arm, "here is your brother; Claude, this is your sister, Valentine and Violet."

"Good heavens!" cried Bertha for the second time, as she pressed forward and peered curiously into his face. "Why, the man is just like both of them!"

Chapter II

Which Is My Sister?

Lady Mildred touched Bertha on the arm, and they left the three together.

"Which of you," asked Claude, looking from one to the other, "which of you is my sister?"

The girls held each a hand and gazed into his face with wondering eyes, which met eyes of equal wonder. Neither of them answered, but all those wondering eyes softened and became humid. Is it a small thing, think you, for two girls to be unexpectedly presented with a grown-up brother? And that brother so desirable in outward looks? Is it a small thing for a young man, especially a young man who has been lifted from the lower to the higher levels, to be presented with a sister who has been similarly transplanted, and to outward seeming has proved equal to the change? To be sure he had already a sister, but she was Melenda, and two brothers, but one was Joe and one was Sam.

Claude saw before him two girls, beautiful exceedingly and strangely alike each other; Nature, as we have already heard, having been so good as to lend a most generous assistance to Lady Mildred. He thought of Melenda. Good heavens! if one of these was his own sister, and the other Lady Mildred's daughter—and the features of both in the soft summer twilight had the same delicacy, their eyes the same purity, their lips the same sweetness—how could one of these girls be his own sister, and the sister of Melenda? The girls, for their part, saw a young man with straight and regular features, broad forehead, resolute lips, and steady, serious eyes—a young man, somewhat slight in figure, but well shaped and of grave expression—and they were overwhelmed. This was their brother, like one of themselves they thought, the child of a London working-man. By what arts had he been transformed into a gentleman?

"Which of you," he repeated, "is my sister?"

"We do not know, Claude," said Violet, thinking guiltily of her sketches.

He turned to the other girl.

"We do not know," Valentine repeated.

"You do not know? Lady Mildred told me yesterday that she would give me a sister."

"We do not know," said Violet, for the third time; "we thought that perhaps you would recognise your sister, or might know her by some likeness to—your father, for instance."

"I do not remember my father. He has been dead a great many years. I have forgotten my sister entirely, and I was never told that Lady Mildred had taken her."

"Claude," said Valentine, "we must both be your sisters."

"I will tell you," said Violet, "Polly's history brought down to this very day. Listen. She was found by Lady Mildred nineteen years ago, and was taken from her playground, which was also the drying yard, for her mother was a washerwoman. I never see linen hanging out to dry without thinking of that day. She was playing hide-and-seek all by herself among the wet sheets, no doubt catching a dreadful cold, when she was found and carried away. She was a pretty child, and curiously like little Beatrice. Well, she was educated with Beatrice, and no difference at all was made between them, and they were called Valentine and Violet, but they knew all along that one was Beatrice and the other was Polly. They had the same masters, they learned the same things, and had the same friends. And now we are grown up and have come out,[1] and people when they don't know the story—but they are very few—think us sisters, and say there is no doubt about our descent from the illustrious house of Eldridge. It would be for some girls awkward to explain, but we are used to it, and now point out without any confusion that one of us is Beatrice Eldridge and the other is Polly—what is the name, Claude? I did not quite catch your name, which we have never been told."

"Monument."

"Monument," Violet considered the name for a moment.

"Monument. It might have been worse. Monument. Fancy being a Monument! Little Trix has grown into tall Beatrice—we are both exactly the same height. Little Polly has also grown into big Polly, which is short for Marla, her real name—we know that part of the family history, too."

Claude thought that he could perceive the least possible vein of bitterness under this bright talk, but then he was naturally sensitive about his reception.

"Don't forget, Claude," she added, "that we think quite as much about Beatrice as about Polly. Do we not, Val?"

"Quite as much," replied Valentine, gravely; "we must not be ashamed of Beatrice because she has not the same picturesqueness of birth as her sister. Please, Claude, get into the habit of remembering that Violet is really Beatrice, and that I am your very own sister. I am sure of it. Why, I actually remember playing about among the clothes. I think—but I am not quite sure—that I remember the cold I caught."

"She is quite wrong, Claude," Violet interposed. "When I shut my eyes I can really see the wet sheets, and if you want any further proof you will very soon find yourself looking to Valentine for everything which requires the instinctive impulse of generosity."

"Oh! Violet!"

"Is it possible? You do not know?" he repeated.

"We do not know," they assured him together, and for the fourth time.

"Then what are we to do?"

The girls looked at each other and shook their heads. What were they to do? The situation was embarrassing, but it was what they expected.

---

1 A girl's *coming out* refers to her introduction into adult society and subsequent marriageability.

"We had made up our minds before you came what we were going to do. You will have to treat us as if we were both your sisters, until you find out which of us it is, and after that we will consider the position again. But," said Violet, clasping her hands, "oh! the joy and comfort of having a brother so promising as you! My dearest Val, think how very, very few brotherless girls like you and me ever get such a chance as a full-grown brother given to them, and a brother too—who—looks," she spoke quite slowly and with a sigh of relief between each word, "who—looks—as—if—we—should—actually—be proud of him."

Claude blushed, but it was growing too late to see that lingering note of youth.

"You might have come home from a desert island, Claude, after you had been wrecked and been given up for lost for nineteen years. But then there would have been a sweetheart waiting for you—they always have a sweet—oh! but perhaps there is—"

"No," said Claude, laughing, "there is not."

"I am very glad, because we shall have you all to ourselves. You might have been brought to us when you were a schoolboy, and then you would have tortured and plagued us. You might have been kept back for another ten years, and then we should have been old women. Oh! it is much better as it is. You will try to like us, won't you?"

"Will you try to like me?" Claude replied, "and not expect too much of me?"

"You will tell us presently"—it was always Violet who continued to talk. She was a little flushed, and her eyes were brighter than usual, "You will tell us presently," she said, "how is it that you have become a—a gentleman." Then, as if fearing that she might have given pain, she added, "Because sons of working-men do not often look and speak like you."

"I will tell you presently," he replied. "Did you think I should come straight from a workshop?"

"This is what Violet drew," said Valentine, showing him the sketches; "we pictured the very worst you see."

"I see," said Claude, laughing. "But the sketches are delightful. May I take them? Thank you. Well, then, let us sit down, and I will tell you all about it."

So they sat down, and he, like Aeneas, began his moving tale, and they, like two twin Didos, listened.[2] When he mentioned the trade of his father and the calling of his mother, Violet begged him earnestly not to speak of those things if they were painful to him. He declared, however, and it seemed strange to her, that it was not in the least painful to him to feel that his mother had been a washerwoman. To think of one's own mother earning her bread at a wash-tub!

Claude carried on his narration into his schooldays, where he fought his way to the front and won scholarships and prizes.

"I know now," he said, "why Lady Mildred came to see me and why she fired me with ambition. Once she took me to the theatre, and between the acts asked me if I would rather be one of the actors on the stage or the author of the piece or one of the gentlemen in the stalls, because if I wished I could become any one of them. And once she took me into the Park in her carriage and showed me the great people, and asked me if I wished to be one of them, because I could if I wished. And again she took me to a court of justice, and asked me if I would like to be the counsel pleading in the case, or the judge who heard it, because it depended wholly on myself. And then to a church where there was a bishop preaching, and she asked me if I would like to be a

2 In Virgil's *The Aeneid*, the escaped Trojan hero Aeneas undergoes a series of adventures and subsequently relates some of these to Dido, queen of Carthage, who soon falls in love with him.

bishop. Always as if the highest was within my reach if I chose. So that I never felt as if the accident of obscure birth was going to be an obstacle in my way. And indeed it has not been any hindrance, so far."

"That was like her," said Valentine, "to fill you with noble ambitions."

"And besides, my mother was no longer a laundress, and I came, no doubt through Lady Mildred's promptings, to think of her courage and steadfast love and the whole life that she gave freely to her children."

"Yes, Claude," said Violet meekly.

"It was through Lady Mildred that I learned to love the hard work which was to be my ladder. I owe everything—everything—to her. And now I owe a sister." He offered, with a little shyness, a hand to each.

"And what are you now, Claude?"

"I am a barrister[3] of the Inner Temple,[4] newly called, and as yet without a brief or a client; but they will come."

"He is a barrister, Val—oh!"

"And I am a Fellow of Trinity."[5]

"Oh! Violet, he is actually a Fellow of Trinity!" They clasped hands of admiration and of joy. Could they have hoped or dreamed of such a thing?

"Now you know all. I am something of a scholar and a good deal of a student. And I have enormous ambitions, of which I will tell you another time if I may."

"Tell us everything," said Valentine; "do not have any half confidences with us. Tell us all about yourself. It is something only to know what a man's ambitions are. Remember we have some right to your confidences. We are your sisters, Claude."

"You shall have all my confidences. But do not expect too much of me. Do not be disappointed in me. As far as I have gone, it is certainly true that no one could have done much more than I have done. I am *Fabri Filius*, son of a smith, so entered in the college books. The University is open to all the world, but of course everybody understands that if the son of a working-man enters, he should justify his admission."

"You have already justified yours, then," said Valentine. "Oh! Claude, we are proud of you."

"But how am I to justify my admission?" asked Violet. "Because I am also *Fabri Filia*—that is good Latin—the daughter of the smith? Don't shake your head at me, Valentine dear, or I will call you Beatrice at once and for good. You see, Claude, Val and I have double the number of ancestors. For instance, we have four grandfathers instead of two. Two of them used to wear straw round the legs and smock frocks, and they said all day, 'Gee—who! a!' The dear old men! And as for the other two, one tied a beautiful blue garter[6] round his leg, and had a gold collar to hang round his neck, and on grand occasions he put a gold coronet on his head; and the other was a baronet, and lived in a great house, and voted solidly with the Conservatives.[7] This wealth of grandfathers naturally makes us proud. But you have no share in two of them, poor boy!"

---

3 Britain has two types of lawyers: *solicitors*, who tend to work directly with clients, and *barristers*, who are hired or instructed by the solicitor to advocate for that client in court.

4 One of four professional associations that select and train England's barristers and judges. Its headquarters in London includes a library, residential chambers, and a church.

5 An elite academic of Trinity College, University of Cambridge, who possesses certain privileges and governing rights.

6 The blue garter refers to membership in the chivalric Order of the Garter. Lady Mildred's grandfather was a member.

7 The Conservatives were one of the two major political parties in Victorian England and were committed to maintaining traditional political and social values.

Claude laughed.

"I have tried to persuade myself," he said, "that it makes no difference at all what a man's birth may have been. But of course I don't quite believe it. I am always measuring my own stature with that of my friends, and asking myself if I stand on their level as regards—what constitutes a gentleman. If I do not, forgive me and help me."

"But you do," said Valentine; "of course you do."

"Any man may make himself a scholar and a Fellow of Trinity, and even a great barrister, but I am not certain whether any man may make himself a gentleman. Do you think that after any kind of intellectual success, even the highest, a man may ever be able to say to himself, 'I am a gentleman at last; I have the instincts as well as the training of a gentleman'?"

"You have them already," said Valentine, confidently; "one can see them in your face."

"The family name is Monument," said Violet quietly.

"Quite so," Claude replied; "and the name is associated with memories. Did not Lady Mildred tell you anything about your family?"

"Nothing except my father was a smith and that my own name is Marla or Polly."

"Now tell us," said Valentine, "about the family. Have we any other relations besides yourself, Claude?"

"My dear," said Violet, "should we enquire further than is necessary? There must be cousins by hundreds. But go on, Claude."

"First there is my mother."

"Oh!" both cried out. Then their other mother was living.

"She is blind, and has ceased to work for many years. She is now in an almshouse."

"Claude, you cannot suffer her to stay there."

"She is happier there. Lady Mildred made me promise to let her stay. Do not be ashamed of the almshouse."

"Poor mother!" said Valentine; "blind and in an almshouse."

"One would much rather have heard," said Violet, "that she was the widow of a retired officer and living nicely in a villa at Southsea. But if she is happy—go on, Claude. Is our father living—in another almshouse?"

"No; he is dead," said Claude gravely. "We ought to be proud of my father. He was clever in his trade; he was sober and industrious; he was honest and respected: what more can one ask of one's father? Joe remembers him well. It is from Joe that I have heard about my father. He was but a working-man, but I am proud of him."

"We will be proud of him too," said Valentine, though as yet she saw little room for pride in a father who only possessed the very simple virtues of honesty, industry, and skill. You perceive that she was deplorably ignorant of the world, where we are constantly brought to a standstill and provoked into wrath just by the lack of these very simple qualities.

"Did Polly," Violet continued, "have any other brothers and sisters? She hopes on the whole that she did not, because it is impossible they could all be so nice as you, Claude."

"She had two other brothers and one sister. First there is Joe."

"My brother Joe. It sounds oddly at first. Joe—Joseph—Joe. I think Joseph—no, Joe—is better. We will call him Joe, Val. He is no doubt a working-man."

"He is the eldest and is a locksmith, as his father was before him. He is now six-and-thirty years of age, though he looks older."

"Is he—does he—go about with that red handkerchief round his throat that we were talking of?"

"Joe is a smith"—Claude evaded the question—"and he works for a builder and decorator. Of course he looks like what he is—a working-man."

"Things are being brought home to us, Val," said Violet. "Go on, Claude."

"He is a good-natured man and he has ten children."

"Ten children? They are our nephews and nieces. The world," said Violet, "is growing wider."

"He married, like most working-men, at nineteen. There is one good point about Joe—he is careful of his mother, whom he never forgets."

"And after Joe?"

"Then there is Sam, ten years younger. He is the master of a board school, and is unmarried. He is clever, and has read and has ideas. In fact he has too many ideas, and he holds them perhaps too strongly."

"Do you see much of your brothers, Claude?"

"No, very little. They think I have no part or lot with them any longer, and Sam resents my trying to turn myself into a gentleman. Perhaps it was absurd to try. He is unfortunately prejudiced against all the people who wear good clothes and have white hands."

"Is Sam like you to look at?"

"No, not in the least. Sam has red hair and is short. He is remarkable to look at, however, because he is always in earnest, and he looks strong."

"I think I shall like Sam," said Valentine, thoughtfully. "He seems more interesting than Joe. Every man ought to be brave and strong."

"Sam is very interesting," said Claude. "Especially when he is in a rage."

"Are there any more?"

"There is only Melenda. She is a seamstress, and she lives with two or three girls who do the same kind of work. She is free and independent, she will receive no advice and will endure no restraint, and she regards me with contempt because I am not a workman. At present I do not exactly know where she is living, because she has ordered me never to see her again. But I can find her out."

"You must find her out," said Valentine.

"In the matter of cousins now," said Violet, with resignation.

"I daresay there are hundreds of cousins, but I do not know of any. The working-people of London do not, as a rule, keep up cousinships. A family dropped down into this great city very easily gets scattered and dispersed."

"Perhaps it is as well," said Violet. "Claude, do not despise me. We knew something of all this before, of course, but only in general terms, and thus have become romantic. The plain facts are overwhelming at first. I feel shivery. It is most delightful to have a brother who is a gentleman and has distinguished himself. But—"

"Our other family," said Valentine, "seemed always so far away. And now they have suddenly become so near."

Then there was silence while a man might count twenty.

"They are not really nearer to you than they were before," said Claude. "You have not been taken to see them. You need not seek them out."

"Claude!" said Valentine reproachfully.

"You tell us we have another mother living, and you say we need not go to see her," said Violet.

"Our own mother—the only one we know," Valentine went on, "has brought you to us. She means by your means to make us known to all our unknown relations. Claude, five or six years ago she wrote us a letter—it was addressed to us both, but it was meant for Polly. 'Close beside us,' she said, 'unknown to us, are those who toil their lives away while we live at ease: they waste and expend themselves in drudgery while we cultivate both minds and soul. Do not forget that one of you belongs to them in a sense which the other does not. If, hereafter, you go among them, remember the old ties, and be full of love and compassion for them, for they are your brothers and sisters. Your brother's sin is your disgrace: your sister's shame is yours.' Violet, you remember that letter?"

"As if I could ever forget it," she replied, gravely.

"You see, Claude," Valentine explained, "the feeling that we are not really sisters has made us more than sisters. One of us is a girl—oh! so humble and so poor—and the other is so rich and so well born. And by this knowledge we are drawn together more closely than if we had been children of the same parents. Always and all day long, we have Polly with us—Polly-which-is-Marla."

"Always with us," said Violet.

"She goes with us wherever we go; we look in each other's eyes and see, reflected there, her image: the shade of Polly is always with us; she has grown up with us; she has been always like us in face and height; but when we try to picture her as she would have been if she had been left among her friends—then Claude, Violet and I cannot agree."

"I know very well what she would have been," said Violet. "I have seen her in the street. She would have a great lump of hair upon her forehead, and she would wear a grey ulster or a red crossover;[8] she would laugh very loud and she would walk three abreast—"

"Oh, no," said Valentine, "Polly would be dressed like other workgirls, I suppose, but she would be a gentle creature full of sweet and generous thoughts."

"Who would have put them in her mind?" asked Violet. "Do sweet thoughts grow in girls' working-rooms? Claude, what do you think? Could Polly be in the least like Valentine?"

It was nearly twelve when Claude left them. They had been sitting without lights at the open window looking across upon the Park. The room was full of moonlight strong enough to suppress the lamp before the house as the electric light puts out the yellow light of gas; their hearts glowed within them; the eyes of the girls were soft with sympathy and newly born love; the young man's pulse beat faster and his cheek burned, as he took their hands.

"Claude," said Valentine, "tell us—always—everything."

"He will," said Violet. "He trusts us already. Oh, Claude, you have made us so happy."

When he was gone, the two girls fell into each other's arms.

"Val," said one. "He is my very own—my brother to myself. But you may love him too."

"Oh, Violet," said the other. "That poor blind woman in the almshouse, who worked so hard. She is, I am sure, she is my mother."

8 A woman's wrap worn over the shoulders and crossed at the chest.

Chapter III

Jack Conyers

Some among us—not all—have been young. They will remember how, in one or two supreme moments, they have been carried out of themselves with a joy which can never be felt in its fullness after five-and-twenty—the intoxicating, dazzling joy in the prospect of life-long happiness.

It falls upon one, perhaps, when love has been whispered and returned: perhaps, when the first success has been achieved: more often when some kindly Prophet has foretold to trembling youth the success which his heart desireth. That Prophet shall be regarded ever after with love and gratitude, and a respect unspeakable for his gifts of discernment. Why are there so few of them? There ought to be a school of these prophets, their sole duty to prophesy, for every deserving youth, good fortune, distinction, contentment, joy, and wealth, with an eternity of happiness hereafter in the Elysian Fields.[1] Everybody feels capable of deserving, and of perpetually enjoying all these rewards and more.

There never was, in the whole history of mankind, such an occasion for rejoicing as that presented to Claude. It was the greatest thing that had ever happened to him: greater than the first scholarship: greater than his place in the Tripos;[2] greater than his fellowship: greater than his ambition.

Consider; it is a youthful instinct to impart confidence and to expect sympathy: boys, students, undergraduates, young men of every sort, in obedience to this instinct, confide greatly in each other. After examinations passed, degrees obtained, and the college walls exchanged for the wide world, which always turns out to be a coldish kind of place, young men grow less sympathetic with each other and more reticent about themselves; they exercise selection in their confidences; they even abstain altogether from talking about their personal ambitions, just as, about the same time, they cease to speak of poetry, religion, and other things which I suppose they consider too sacred for common speech. Every man makes in his heart an Adytum of the Temple[3]

1 The paradise reserved for heroes in the ancient Greek conception of the afterlife.

2 An honors division within the University of Cambridge for specialized study of a field, such as, for Claude, the law Tripos.

3 As Besant's allusion in the next sentence suggests, the adytum of a temple is its most sacred space, which is kept from the public.

which grows more full as he grows older. Only the priest is by law allowed to enter into this holy of holies, but he generally takes with him a companion, who is always of the other sex—his sister, sweetheart or wife. The sympathy of sisters, indeed, is always ready to be had for the asking, and perhaps, on that account, like everything else easily attained is less valued than it should be. Many young men, however, prefer the sympathy of other people's sisters, and this also is, to do these young ladies justice, ready as a rule when properly asked for.

Alone among his fellows, Claude had no home circle which could understand him and could follow his career, with interest. Every day since that on which he first left them seemed to separate him more and more from his own people. He had long since left off telling them, because they could not understand it, what he was doing. His mother knew nothing about Cambridge, and had never heard of Trinity, though the fame of every individual fellow of that college, as all the resident fellows know very well, is trumpeted abroad, with mighty blast, from pole to pole, and fills the round world with wonder and admiration; he knew few people; it was two years since he had taken his degree, and his old school and college friends were already scattered: among all the millions of women, old and young, which inhabit London and England, there was not one whom he could call either friend or mistress; not one to whom he could open his heart.

He was used to this isolation: it was a necessary part of his position; at school, when other boys got prizes, their mothers and sisters and all their people were present to congratulate them; when he went up to receive his prizes there was not a single person in the room whose eyes softened and whose heart glowed at the sight of his triumph. When he was head boy[4] and carried off no end of prizes, the other boys cheered and some of the spectators remarked audibly upon his singular beauty—for it was a comely lad—and he went home to his boarding-house with a cartload of books and an aching heart because of his loneliness. Even Joe, brother Joe, the plumber's man, in his working dress, would have been something. At Trinity he won an entrance scholarship and afterwards a university scholarship and a city company's scholarship, and with these helps paid his own college expenses easily, and there was no one to say, "Well done!" not even Lady Mildred, who contented herself with an expression of satisfaction, and when he concluded his student course with a fellowship, reminded him in the days of his first pride, and just as if anybody who chose could be a Fellow of Trinity, that this was nothing more than the first step. Young men, she added, may show promise by taking university distinctions, but they are by themselves of little importance. Claude must take care not to think that anything real had been achieved. Not one single person in the world to whom he could open his heart.

And now he had a sister—two sisters—one rolled out into two—both as beautiful as the day and as sweet as the roses in June, and they were proud of him. For the first time in his life he realised how well he had already done, since he could make two such girls proud of him; and he wondered how he could possibly have done it, alone, and without a single word of congratulation and encouragement on the lonely hard road he had travelled.

He stalked along the crowded pavement seeing no one, his head full of these thoughts, his chin in the air. A hand was laid on his shoulder.

Claude pulled himself together and took the other hand which was held out.

"You in London, Jack?"

---

4 In the English system, the head boy holds responsibility for representing his school or class and often for ensuring order among the other students.

"Yes. I am in London. I have been here for two or three weeks. Come to my chambers—they are close by—and let us talk."

Claude was not inclined to talk about anything except perhaps about Valentine and Violet, but he followed his friend.

"Where have you been for the last two years?"

"I have been travelling—studying—sketching. One must travel, you know."

The chambers were furnished after the modern fashion: there were cabinets with china: there were water colours: there was glass: there were skins and rugs; they were clearly rooms belonging to a man of taste.

The name of Jack goes with almost any kind of character. It suits a soldier or a statesman: a poet or a mechanician: a prince or a pauper: a hero or a humbug. It requires only one quality—that its possessor must be accepted on his own terms by his contemporaries: not that he must necessarily be popular, but he must be believed in. When Jack Conyers, in his first term, announced himself as one of the coming men, the lads about him accepted him on trust. He *was* the coming man—his manners rather than his words or his acts proved it. He had, to justify these pretensions, a good name and a good presence to begin with; he did nothing actively to encourage or to justify the belief, except perhaps that he understood the power of silence; he did not chatter, as many young men do, but when he spoke, it was slowly and quietly, as if what he had to say was worth hearing; nor was he like so many young men carried away by any enthusiasms of the hour, and he was always critical. Also, he did not laugh much, though he understood and practised the fine and subtle art of smiling, an art in which women generally excel; but Jack Conyers excelled all women. It was not exactly known who and what were his people, but it was understood that he was of good family; he had the appearance and manner of one who has money; he did not court intimacies; he dressed well, and he seemed to know London. Reading for the Senate House was, he said, narrowing to the mind which desires culture more than scholarship; therefore, he took an ordinary degree; he had a piano in his rooms, and played and sang a little; he also painted and sketched a good deal, and it was supposed that his career, of which he spoke continually, though vaguely, was to be connected in some way with art.[5]

In appearance he was of the middle height and thin. He wore a *pince-nez*:[6] his features were regular and delicate; his eyes were good, though rather hard, as if always on guard; his mouth was well formed, but the lips were too full, and his forehead was high and narrow. Not an effeminate-looking man, but evidently one who desired to appear refined and studied attitude as well as dress, and his surroundings as well as his manners. If he had been asked what he most desired to convey in his appearance he would have confessed—if he did confess—that he wished to look like a young man who is going to succeed. Claude was one of the men of his own standing who believed in him. Some there were, I regret to say, who scoffed at the name of Conyers.

The room was lit by a shaded lamp. Upon the mantelshelf there stood three small portraits side by side. They were oil sketches, and represented three girls' faces, all evidently painted by the same hand.

"You are looking at those heads," said Jack Conyers. "They are portraits—such as they are—of three women,"—he sighed—"three women—poor things!—who were so good as to complete my education."

---

5 The Senate House is where Cambridge students receive their honors degrees, the Tripos. Thus, by not "reading for the Senate House," Jack did not attempt such honors.

6 A type of spectacles, so named (in French) because, rather than being supported from the ears, they pinch the bridge of the nose by means of a spring.

"How did they do that?"

"By letting me fall in love with them. A man, I have discovered, cannot be a finished artist without a full personal experience of passion. How can he express what he has never felt? Yet, for an artist, love should be a memory rather than a living thing, and therefore each experience should be short. This was a French girl, vivacious, full of *espièglerie*; this was an Italian, the mere creature of passion;[7] this a Roumanian. Woman, as mistress or as wife, in the boudoir or the salon, should form part of every career."

Pelham or the great d'Orsay[8] could have said no more. Claude, however, asked no more questions about the portraits, though doubtless there was a whole chapter belonging to each.

"And what are you going to do?"

"I have taken a studio and I am going to begin my work."

It seemed rather a drop for the vagueness of coming greatness to take the concrete and even common form of a studio.

"As for my success—"

"Of course you will succeed," said Claude.

"I do not know. The common success—the adulation of the crowd—does not attract me. I shall never stoop to paint half a dozen pictures in a year. Perhaps one in four or five, or even ten years. The picture which I have in my mind has been growing for at least five years, during which I have filled my soul with it. The subject has been part of myself. Claude—" he raised his finger impressively; "it will be, I am assured, a great picture; there will be in it, at least, the whole soul of the artist."

Claude murmured indistinctly something to the effect that a picture with a soul in it would be indeed worthy of his friend's reputation.

"Hitherto the picture, as it exists in my mind, has been incomplete for want of one face. But I have found it at last. I discovered it in a people's concert where I was made to sing by Lady Aldeburgh—a concert somewhere near a place they call Shoreditch;[9] after the concert I talked to the girl who owns the face, which is as yet sadly incomplete; she is ignorant, but apparently open to emotions. I shall get that girl. I shall take her away from her belongings and cultivate her face. Everything shall be sacrificed to the cultivation of the face. She wants to be well fed and kept in soft silk and made dainty with fancy dresses and idleness and pretty things, and then that face will grow and develop like a rosebud. At present, I admit, it is imperfect, but it is a possibility and it will make my picture. The eyes are there, already, and they are full of possible poetry and passion."

He spoke with something nearly approaching enthusiasm.

"Can't you paint her without wanting to take her from her people?"

"No, I want her taken away altogether from the place where she lives. She must be placed wholly under artistic influence—she must be mine—my model—the slave of art."

"Wouldn't it be better, perhaps, for the girl's reputation for her to stay where she is?"

---

7 *Espièglerie* is French for *playful mischief* and, like passion for Italian women, a common romantic stereotype.

8 Both Count Alfred d'Orsay and the title character of Edward Bulwer-Lytton's novel *Pelham* were dandies and amateur artists famous for their love of women.

9 In the nineteenth century, Shoreditch, a densely populated and impoverished area in close proximity to central London, was considered part of the city's vast East End.

"Philistine![10] I want her in the interests of art. She is needed. One can't stop to think about the reputation of a girl in comparison with—"

"Don't, Jack. My own relations, you know, are somewhere about those levels, and they have reputations which they seem to value even more than the interests of art."

Jack hastened to change the subject. When you touch on the reputation of a man's possible sisters you tread on dangerous ground.

"I saw you coming out of Lady Mildred Eldridge's, but you walked so fast that I could not overtake you for ever so long. She is a friend of yours?"

"Yes, my best friend."

"I met them in Florence last winter. I was able to be of some little service to them—one of the girls sketches cleverly. They are both, in fact, pleasing."

"Thank you," said Claude, with a conscious blush; "one of them is my sister."

"What?" Jack Conyers started in his chair and dropped his cigarette. "What? One of them your sister?" He knew, like all the world, the history of the two girls in general terms, how one was an heiress and the other the daughter of a working-man.

"One of them your sister? My dear fellow, they are both—allow me to say it—both most beautiful and accomplished young ladies. You are a lucky man, and I congratulate you. Which of them is it?"

"I do not know which. My sister was adopted by Lady Mildred nineteen years ago, and the secret has been kept ever since."

"But you will find out. This is not the kind of thing which is kept hidden. There must be some points of resemblance; your father, for instance—"

"He is dead, and my mother is blind."

"At all events you are sure to find out before long."

"I daresay I shall, or else I shall be told."

"It is rather like the end of a Latin comedy."

"Yet it is only the beginning of an English comedy.[11] You know my history, Conyers. Everybody does. When men meet me for the first time they whisper to each other, 'Son of a working-man, you know.' I do not hear the words, but I read them in their eyes. That is nothing. But I have been rather a lonely man—"

"Naturally," said Conyers, trying to look as if he entirely sympathised with him, "naturally." But he was thinking which of the two girls more nearly resembled his friend.

"And I can hardly try to make you understand what a tremendous thing it is to have a sister at last—a sister who takes an interest and—and—even a pride in one."

"Well," said Jack, "for my own part I never wanted any brothers and sisters. They divide the money and they give all kinds of trouble. But from your point of view no doubt you are right. It must be a bore not to have any belongings."

Claude laughed and prepared to go.

"I have belongings, to be sure, but not of the kind which you would understand."

---

10 Someone driven by material concerns and uninterested in intellectual and artistic pursuits.

11 The final acts of many Roman (Latin) comedies and the first acts of many English comedies introduce mistaken identities that are typically resolved by the play's end.

"That is very conceivable, and I am very sorry for you. I find any other class than our own impossible to talk with and uninteresting to study. Well, I am very glad we met tonight, my dear boy. Come often—come as often as you can, and tell me when you have found your sister. Let me share your secret. Valentine or Violet—I knew that they were assumed names. Tell me when you have found out which of them it is."

"Certainly I will. Good-night."

Jack Conyers, left alone, prepared for himself and drank a lemon squash. Then he sat down and meditated with a mixture of gloom and hope in his countenance. When a young man leaves the university at two-and-twenty, resolved upon distinction and yet uncertain which path to choose—when he wanders about for two years purposeless—when he returns determined upon a career in art, as painters arrogantly call their profession, as if a novelist or a poet is not also an artist—when, further, he remembers that art is not always lucrative—that one may have to wait long before making a name, and that meanwhile no money is coming in—when, lastly, there will arise at midnight spectres of doubt which point the finger and say, "Yah! you will never succeed, even by a trick"—when, at the same time, one has conceived a way, a trick, by which to take the town by storm and has actually found the face with which to do it—there is room for the play of a good deal of mixed emotion.

Presently he saw a letter lying on his table. He took it up and looked at the handwriting and tore it open.

"My dear Jack"—he read it quickly as if to get through it and have done with it—"you have been back three weeks and you have not been to see me. Very well. Sooner or later I suppose you will come. I can wait, my dear boy. I know very well why you said you loved me, and I know all about your money matters. Go on. Within six months you will hang up your hat in my hall and be happy ever after. I shall have the money, but you shall have full liberty and a handsome allowance. I am not in the least jealous, because I am always certain of the person whom alone you love—go look at him in the glass. When you have found out that you cannot get on without me, you will repent of your negligence and come. When we settle down we will give dinners, and you shall play at being a distinguished man and I at being the appreciative and devoted wife, and we shall suit each other very well. I saw your sisters the other day. If I were you I would sometimes call upon them. Good-night, my Jack. Your affectionate Alicia."

Jack read this letter through. Then he burned it, because every word was true, and truth is best hidden in a well or behind the bars of the fireplace.

"If I could find out somehow, through Claude, which of them it is," he thought, "and I could do this without his knowing, I should have such a chance as might make me free of Alicia yet. She always had the most disgustingly coarse way of putting things, and she's getting coarser every day."

Jack's Cambridge bed-maker, who loves reminiscences almost as much as an old statesman, maintains that Mr. Conyers, though a liberal gentleman, and one who kept a deal of company, was of the sort which thinks of nobody but theirselves. Bed-makers have great experience of young men, and their opinions should be received with weight.

Chapter IV

The Haven of Rest

I should like to sing a song of almshouses—not so much of those great havens of rest with their spacious courts and old chapels and broad gardens which are scattered about this realm of England, as of the London almshouses.[1] They vary from the poor little half-dozen cottages in a row—like Lady Came's, which are so small that the residents are elected by competitive measurement, character not being so much an object as smallness of stature—to the new and stately palaces such as those at Wood Green, or the old and dignified college such as that beyond Greenwich Hospital, or that of Morden, beside Blackheath; and in wealth, from a little endowment of four shillings a week and a two-roomed cottage for four old women, to an annuity of forty pounds a year, with lodgings, coals, and light for as many old men. There are quiet and peaceful almshouses even though they stand beside noisy thoroughfares. Could anything be sweeter and more peaceful than Amyas's Houses, lying lost and forgotten behind Old Street? or than Beeman's at the back of the Kingsland Road, or the Trinity Almshouses in the midst of Whitechapel? And there are others which seem as if all the noise of the street must perpetually beat about the ears of the unhappy residents. There are some with a chapel and a chaplain and some with a chapel but no chaplain. There is a school attached to some, as at the Milburn Hospice in the Stamford Hill Road; there is a garden with some, as at Trinity Hospital, Greenwich; and a fair court with others, as at Emmanuel, Westminster. In some the almsfolk look cheerful and happy, their anxieties being ended; in others they are gloomy and grumpy, as if all their troubles were to come; in some the people are always walking about, talking with their friends, chirruping[2] with each other, and basking in the sun; while in others there is never anybody to be seen, and the old people are all hiding in their beds. In a song of almshouses, all these things and many more could be explained.

1 The opening recalls *The Aeneid* and similar epic poems that begin with a plea to the Muses for divine inspiration in the recitation of the tale.
2 Literally chirping or clucking, *chirrupping* suggests lively, pleasant conversation.

On a certain Saturday afternoon last July, a day when the sun was hot, the sky clear, and the breeze cool; when all the old men of all the almshouses between Shoreditch on the south and Tottenham on the north were out in the sun, and all the old ladies were out in the shade—for behold! this is the way of the world: the old men seek the sun because it is the source of heat, which is strength, and women seek the shade, where they can watch the sunshine and admire heat and strength—there sat in the chapel at Lilly's, which was open, one of the almswomen. She occupied the square pew, where there are cushions. She was not old, being no more than sixty or so, which is young for a colleger[3] at Lilly's, but she looked old because her hair was so very white and she sat so very still. Her eyes were closed, so that you might have thought her asleep. But she was not asleep—she was blind.

Close beside her, on one of the benches of the four long pews, her feet up, her back against the wall, sat a young girl of fifteen or so, reading a story book. She was a pretty girl, with delicate features of the London type, very capable of a quick repartee and not unaccustomed to a rough joke. The two sat in perfect silence because the old lady had been taking her afternoon nap and still felt restful, and the girl was absorbed in the book.

Lilly's is a venerable but not a splendid foundation. The name of its founder, Josiah Lilly, citizen and pewterer, is commemorated on a stone tablet let into the pediment above the great door in the middle. It consists of a single row of cottages in dull red brick, each containing two rooms, one above and one below, with a kitchen or washhouse behind. In most of the windows, which are old-fashioned, with diamond panes set in lead, there is a geranium, and in some there is a neat white blind half down, as the respectable classes of London love to have it. If any that runs will lift his eyes to read, he may observe, all round London, wherever the neat little cottage prevails, that the blinds are always half down. It is the first assertion of respectability, the first step towards gentility. The negro, with a skin like a crocodile for hardness, buys him a mosquito curtain when he intends to soar; the London housewife, when she first develops ambitions, hangs out the blind half mast down, as a kind of flag, and why one knoweth not. Nobody is more respectable than an old almswoman, so that the white blind thus adjusted is not uncommon. In front of the cottages is a narrow stone pavement, which makes a convenient walk on fine mornings, and there is a good-sized oblong patch of ground laid out as a vegetable garden, with potatoes and cabbages. It is separated from the road by a low brick wall having a wicket-gate in the middle. There are five cottages on either side of a great door under the pediment, which opens into quite the smallest chapel in this realm of England. It has a window with a semi-circular head, a door nearly of its own width, a reading desk and railed communion table, a square pew painted white with cushions and hassocks, and four long pews, also painted white and without cushions, and all of the kind which exasperates ecclesiastics, who would, if they could, take them away and substitute open benches, and so destroy the character of the little chapel. Nobody, outside Lilly's, knows whether there is a chaplain on the foundation, or if service is ever held in it, or if it is only maintained as a place of meditation and repose.

The old blind woman was Mrs. Monument. How she got into the almshouses is not known, but Lady Mildred may be suspected of a helping hand. As a general rule it is almost as hard for a poor woman to get into an almshouse as for a rich man to get into the Kingdom of Heaven. Not for want of qualified persons, for of such there is never any lack, but by reason of the pushing, fighting, and shoving over every vacancy. However she was in, and had been in for thirteen years, enjoying a time of perfect rest and quiet, though she

3 Residents of a charitable institution or "college."

was only separated from the noisy world by a low brick wall, and from absolute indigence by her cottage, her ten shillings a week, and such additions as were made by Lady Mildred, as, for instance, the attendance of her granddaughter, the girl who sat reading in the long pew, and found waiting on her grandmother a much easier way of life than any enjoyed by her friends. It was indeed a time of great peace which had come to this poor woman; of physical repose; of content and restfulness, which had settled upon her heart like the sunshine which poured this afternoon into the open door of the little temple, broadening as the sun sloped westward. She wanted nothing; her boys had turned out steady, and her daughters were respectable. To thank the Lord for the respectability of one's daughters seldom occurs to the class where this quality is assumed; but there are other circles where it is hoped for but not always found. She sat in the chapel because it was cool there, and, though only a few feet from the door were the hurrying footsteps and the roll of vehicles and the jingling of the tram, there clung about the place, as about every place of worship, however small and mean, a sense of peace and safety, like the Glory of the Lord about His house.

I know not how long she had been sitting there, but most likely since her dinner—an event which at Lilly's is of much less importance than it is at the Mansion House.[4] That function was usually celebrated at one o'clock, and now it was four. She had taken her nap and was quite awake, as one could tell by the movement of her fingers. The blind sit long and patiently; they are not great talkers, but they think continually. Conceited persons who read many books secretly believe that nobody can think who does not read. As if the book of experience ever passed through the printing-press! As if every old woman has not got enough out of her own life to occupy her thoughts for another hundred and fifty years! Why! this old woman had been young, and therefore comely; she had been a bride and a mother; she had known grievous trouble, with the helpless shame of a bad husband; she had worked single-handed to support her children; they were grown up now and doing well; she had no anxiety about them or about her own daily bread; she was growing old but without pain; her world was in darkness; her life was ended save for the things which might happen to the children, and for whatever pains and bodily disease might presently fall upon herself. To feel and to understand that nothing remains in life; that everything has been enjoyed or endured; that the work is all done; that there will be no more wages, no more promotion, no more hopes, no more rewards, no more failures; that there remains only the short downward slope which may be perhaps taken with a run and a leap—this alone must be a very serious and awful thing, though it is the common lot, and therefore, one fain would think, cannot be bad for man. Yet one would pray for a little breathing time, a short space between work and the End, in which, the tools laid down, one may fold the hands, recover and gather together scattered and long-forgotten thoughts, and meditate upon things beyond. Therefore I have always regarded with peculiar envy and admiration those to whom it is granted to spend their latter years in an almshouse. One cannot, I am sure, meditate profitably in the crowd of a workhouse.

Except that Mrs. Monument's once brown hair was now white, and her once white hands were now brown, she was unchanged since she left off her work. Her face was ruddy still—a clean, honest face with the history of the past written in deep lines and puckered crow's feet. She wore a gown of brown stuff, with a white cap and a white apron. And she sat quite composed and still, wrapped in her meditations or her memories. The girl with her feet up in the long pew was as still as herself, and if one was so accustomed to the road as not to hear its noise, the chapel was as silent as a West Indian forest. There was a foolish bee who came buzzing

4 Home and office of the Lord Mayor of London and the location for many formal ceremonies and dinners.

about the chapel in search of flowers, and finding none, got angry, and so forgot how he came in. Presently he saw the sunshine pouring in through the open door and flew out, and the place was quiet again. Next Mrs. Monument perceived that two of her fellow-lodgers were walking along the flags in front of the cottages—she knew the footsteps and concluded that certain rheumatic pains were better; and then she heard something which caused her to start and sit upright, and brought a glow to her cheek and brightness to her lips.

"Rhoder!"[5] she cried, "that's my boy's step. It's your uncle Claude. Get up, girl, and bring him here."

Then she waited in joyful expectation. There were other footsteps, whose she knew not. But she rose and left the pew and stood in the doorway.

"Mother," said Claude, kissing her.

"My son," she replied, lightly passing her hand over his face, "I did not expect you today. Who is with you? I heard girls' steps. Are you keeping company at last, Claude?"

"They are—two young ladies, mother, come to see you."

"Two young ladies! Well, ask them to the house. Rhoder, you go before and put out the chairs."

Claude led his mother to her cottage at the end of the row. There were three chairs in the sitting-room. The old lady took one—the arm-chair by the fire-place—and the two girls the others. Rhoda stood beside her grandmother gazing curiously at the visitors.

"Mother," said Claude, "you remember your little Polly?"

"Remember my dear Polly? Why, Claude, as if I could forget her!"

"We have not talked much about her lately, have we?"

"Have you seen her, Claude?" she caught his arm. "Oh! have you seen her? Lady Mildred told me you were not to see her till the time came. Tell me—what is she like?"

"I have seen her, mother. She is grown a tall and beautiful girl. She has the manners and the education of a lady. You will never regret that you gave her up."

"It was to save her from a terrible danger, my dear. I said to myself, 'Surely if one of these can be spared, I ought to spare her.' So I let her go."

"And this danger—is it over?" Claude thought she meant possible loss of work, poverty, out-door relief, or the Union, which he remembered as among the bogies of his childhood.[6]

"You are all grown up now. If what I feared were to happen—but it never can—it would not be quite so bad for you now. Sam is a great man, and you're doing something for yourself, and Melenda's in steady work—oh! yes, you could not be tempted."

"Since the danger is over, then, mother"—Claude took her hand again—"would you like to see your Polly again?"

She clutched his hand. "Claude," she said, "you have brought her. But I promised Lady Mildred—"

"Lady Mildred sends her."

"Oh!" She started up and cried aloud, holding out her arms, "My child, come to your mother. Quick! quick!"

Both the girls sprang to their feet. Claude motioned them to wait.

5 The pronunciation of *Rhoda* as *Rhoder* is indicative of a working-class upbringing.

6 Bogies are evil spirits or goblins used in stories to scare children.

"Yes, mother," he said. "Patience—patience for a moment. You do not know that Polly has been brought up with Lady Mildred's own daughter Beatrice. They are not known apart. No one, but Lady Mildred herself, knows which is Miss Eldridge and which is Polly. It is her intention that no one shall know yet. I have brought them both to you. They are called Valentine and Violet, but which of the two is your daughter I cannot tell you."

She understood not one word of what Claude was saying, but stood with her outstretched arms feeling in the dark for her child. "Give me my Polly," she cried hoarsely.

Claude led Valentine to her. "Mother," he said, "this is Valentine."

The blind woman passed her hand quickly over Valentine's face, throat, and figure. Then she threw her arms about her and kissed her a hundred times, crying and weeping over her. "Oh! my dear, my dear," she said, "your face is like Claude's. I knew you would take after him and Joe. Tell me your name. Let me hear your voice."

"I am Valentine," said the girl.

"Claude's face, but not his voice. Yet I know the voice. As for Valentine—Valentine—what do I know about Valentine? Kiss your mother, Polly. Your real name, my dear, is Marla, but oh! I have never thought of you as anything but Polly. Oh! what a tall girl you've grown! Claude's face and Claude's head, and oh! Polly—Polly-which-is-Marla"—she hugged and kissed her again—"to think that for all these years I never had you once in my arms! Oh! my dear, I've been thirsting for you."

"But, mother," said Claude, "do not be too sure. You have not seen Violet yet. Violet is perhaps—"

"Violet? Oh! I suppose she is my lady's own daughter, the beautiful Miss Eldridge, that my Polly was so like."

"Mother, you must see the other as well." Claude laid her hands upon Violet's shoulder.

"I am Violet," said the girl. But while Valentine frankly met the hungry mother's embrace, and gave back kiss for kiss, Violet stood shrinking and trembling with pale face.

The blind woman started. Then she laid her hands upon the girl's face as she had done to Valentine, but slowly and critically.

"It is Claude's face too," she said. "But whose voice was that? Speak again, you other, that I took for my girl."

"I am Valentine," said the other.

"What is it, Claude?" asked the poor bewildered woman. "They both have your face, and one of their voices, though they are different, reminds me of your father's, whom they never saw.

Tell me what it means. Oh! what does it mean? Which is my Polly?"

"It means, mother, what I told you—one of these young ladies is Miss Eldridge and one is Polly. But I do not know which."

"Will you not kiss me too?" asked Violet.

The old woman kissed her, but with the coldness induced by doubt. "I don't know," she said, "I cannot tell which of you is my Polly. And as for Miss Beatrice—"

"Oh," said Valentine, "never mind Beatrice. Only tell us what we can do for you, and if you are happy."

Mrs. Monument sat down before she made reply. They became aware that she was stiffening. The light of love went out of her face; she remembered that one of the two was Lady Mildred's daughter; what if she had poured those first kisses upon Miss Beatrice? And how could she sustain enthusiasm for half a daughter? She was chilled and bewildered.

Presently, however, she answered in measured terms. She thanked Miss Beatrice for coming to see her, which she took very kindly, and begged to send her duty to her ladyship. As for herself, she was as happy as a woman in her position has a right to expect. Like many country-bred women, Mrs. Monument held the opinion that poor people have no right to expect happiness except in small bits and irregular rations. Many people in their hearts believe that this remarkable doctrine, with the duties of contentment, resignation to injustice, satisfaction with things as they are, and unquestioning respect for everyone who wears a black coat, is laid down in the Bible and Prayer Book. Mrs. Monument went on to say that during the last winter, which had been mild, and the spring, which was short though severe, she had escaped rheumatism to a surprising extent, though there were days when her hands felt like dropping; that she was daily and faithfully attended by her granddaughter Rhoda; that she was pleased to find her boy Claude still kept on by her ladyship—she imagined that he was a kind of page or assistant butler in the establishment, though for some mysterious reason permitted to prolong his schooling indefinitely—and at this remark Claude looked at the girls and smiled without showing the least confusion. She concluded by saying that when the time came for her Polly to know herself, she hoped the knowledge would lead her to a lowly and grateful spirit, such as became one in her station; and here both girls blushed, because they understood for the first time that the child of the lowly and the humble, however she be brought up, is born to a "station."

"My dear mother," said Claude, "we are all grateful. Polly will be as grateful as you can desire when she learns the truth. Meantime we are all of us filled with a proper spirit of lowly humbleness. Valentine and Violet are both as meek as nuns; I am grateful; you are grateful; and as for Beatrice, if she is not grateful too, she ought to be ashamed of herself."

"She ought," said the girls together.

"Fie, Claude! to speak of Lady Mildred's daughter in such a manner. And she a lady!"

The girls felt hot and ashamed. Was Claude to speak of Beatrice as a stable-boy speaks of his mistress? But Claude only smiled again.

"And she a lady!" he echoed, gravely; "I had forgotten that."

"Claude, my dear," his mother went on, "if you are in good work, thank Lady Mildred for her help. But don't speak of Miss Beatrice—who is, I suppose, one of those two—those two young persons—as if she was a girl of the same rank as yourself."

"I will not, mother," said Claude, seriously.

"As for Polly—"

"Yes, dear." It was Valentine who spoke, because Violet shrank back as if she were about to receive a blow. "Yes—mother—when the time comes I hope that I shall know how to conduct myself properly and as becomes my station."

They all looked at each other. The situation seemed rather strained. "And so you worked for twenty years," said Valentine, taking the good woman's hand, "for twenty years to support your children."

"Of course I did, Miss—is it Miss Beatrice or is it Polly? Why shouldn't I? There's no hardship and no shame in having to work if you can get work to do and wages for your work."

"It is time for your tea, mother," said Claude. The kettle was singing on the hob,[7] for there was a fire, although it was the hottest month in the year, and the tea-things were laid. Then, while the two girls looked on in silence, Claude made the tea and cut the bread and butter, and Rhoda poured it out, and they broke bread together.

But the girls were silent and the old lady stiff and starched.

"Come, mother," said Claude, "one of the girls is Polly, you know."

"One of the young ladies is Miss Beatrice, Claude," said his mother, "and very good it is of her, and like my lady, her mother, to come and see her mother's old servant. I only wish I could see her pretty face."

Neither of the girls answered.

"Why, they both have pretty faces, mother; and as for Beatrice, she is so like Polly that you would never tell the difference. And as for Polly, she is so like Beatrice that you would never guess that she wasn't a lady born."

"It's play-actin', Claude," said the old woman, severely. "If I can't have my own gal to myself, it's worse than nothing. What is it to me to be told that she's dressed like her mistress and quite the lady? How can she be a lady when her mother was once an under-nurse, and then stood over the washtub on Hackney Marsh, and her father was a working-man? Don't tell me, Claude. As for her not knowing and you not knowing, that's nonsense. You might as well tell me that you've grown up a gentleman."

"I did not go so far as to say that, mother," said the Fellow of Trinity.

"No; you've got too much sense, my son. And as for Polly, if she'll quit play-actin' and behave reasonable, I shall be glad to see her any time that her mistress will spare her for an afternoon."

"Oh! Val," said Violet.

"My dear," said Valentine, kissing the poor old lady's forehead,

"We do not know. Indeed we do not know—no one knows except Lady Mildred. We will both come if you will let us, but we cannot come separately because we do not know."

She shook her head. "I do not know which of you it is, the first or the second, but you've got between you your father's voice if it's Polly, and yet it's her ladyship's voice if it's Miss Beatrice. And I can't tell which is which, for the voices have got mixed."

Then another figure appeared in the doorway. It was a working-man—there could be no mistake about that fact. He carried a bag of tools in one hand; on his arm he slung his jacket because it was hot, and he preferred to work in his shirt-sleeves; and he really had that loose red handkerchief which the girls expected to find about their brother's neck. There was also a pipe in his mouth. Quite the working-man. And perhaps in order to make it perfectly clear that he was not play-acting, whatever his sisters might be, his hands were grimed with dirt and oil. He looked in, saw the assembled company, and was astonished. Then he took his pipe out of his mouth, being a working-man of some politeness.

"Well, mother," he said. Then he kissed his daughter. "Well, Rhoder, my girl." Then he greeted Claude with a handshake.

"Admiral, how are you?"[8]

---

7 A shelf for holding things, such as a kettle, to be heated or kept warm by fire.

8 Throughout the novel, Joe playfully calls Claude by various titles of high military rank, which suggests the social distance separating them.

"This is Joe," Claude explained by way of introduction. "Joe lives in Tottenham a little up the road. On Saturdays and Sundays he never fails to come here."

"Joe's a good boy," said the old lady; "he was always a good boy to me—a good son and a good father of nine."

Joe sat on the table, which was the only place left to sit upon, and received these praises unabashed. The girls observed that he was a man of handsome features, and that if his chin was shaven, as it doubtless would be on the Sunday morning, his hair trimmed, his face washed, and his neck put into a white collar, he would be curiously like Claude, only twelve years older, or perhaps more, for sixteen years of married life with nine children ages a man, and he might have passed for five-and-forty. As for his occupation, he was the right-hand man of an eminent house-painter, decorator, and plumber of Tottenham—one of those useful citizens who lay our pipes for us, and lay them wrong; who adjust our taps and clean our cisterns, work mischief with our kitchen ranges, and never leave a house when they are permitted to enter it until there is not a screw or a sink or a tap or a pipe that is not tinkered and ruined. Theirs is a trade so lucrative that it is rapidly rising to the dignity of a profession, and before long it will probably rival the Bar in attracting the brightest and keenest of the English intellect and the flower of the Universities. Joe might not be clever after the cleverness of his father, but he understood his business, and knew how to make money for his employer if not for himself. And steady with it too, except now and again on Saturday evenings. But we have all of us some weakness, failing, or defect, a moral squint or a halting leg.

"Joe," said Claude, "I have brought your sister Polly—you remember little Polly—to see her mother."

"Oh!" said Joe, unmoved; "you have brought her, have you?"

"It is a long time since you saw her—nineteen years—and she has grown up and is a young lady now."

"So it seems," said Joe; "who'd ha' thought it?" But he seemed to take little interest in the subject.

"She has been brought up entirely with Miss Eldridge, and we do not know them apart. Polly is one of these young ladies, but we do not know which."

Joe looked from one to the other. Then he smiled. Then he passed his hand over his mouth, and the smile went into his eyes, which twinkled.

"Oh!" he said, "you don't know which of these two young ladies is Polly and which is the other. Oh! ah! And don't no one know?"

"No one but Lady Mildred."

"Oh!" Here Joe chuckled but choked. "No one don't know. That's a rum thing, ain't it, Claude?" Claude was looking at his brother, but he was thinking of the two girls and the strange awkwardness of the situation. "Rhoder, my gal, come here. Stand between them two young ladies for a minute. So! That'll do." He chuckled again and choked again. "No one don't know. That's a rum thing, ain't it? Well, if no one don't know, I don't know, do I?"

"Have you no welcome for your sister, Joe?" asked Claude.

"Tell me which she is and I'll give her a kiss"—Violet shuddered—"but I can't kiss 'em both, can I? Even Sam wouldn't have a working-man go so far as that, let alone the missus, when she come to hear of it. No, Claude, if one of 'em's my sister, she's dressed altogether too fine for me and my Rhoder and the kids. Not but what they're a pair of beauties. We workin'-men can't afford to have sisters in satin like ladies. As for the

Colonel here"—he laid a friendly hand upon Claude's shoulder—"he's a toff,[9] but we're used to him. I don't quite know how he makes his money, but he says it's honestly come by—"

"Oh!" said Violet, "this is shameful. Claude's money is nobly earned." She could endure a good deal on her own account, but was Claude to be insulted?

"Joe is quite right," said Claude.

"When workin'-men's sisters go dressed in kid gloves and silk ribbons, it's natural for people to ask how they came by the money, and not always easy to answer.[10] So, you see, I can't say as I am pleased to see Polly. As for Claude's work—"

"Claude's work," said Violet, interrupting, "is of a kind which you cannot be expected even to understand."

"Go on," he replied, grinning: "I like a girl with a cheek." He got up and replaced the pipe in his mouth, but it had gone out. "Good-bye, mother. I'll be round in the morning." He nodded to Claude. "Good–bye, Brigadier. As for you two young ladies—" He looked from one to the other, and then he turned to his daughter Rhoda. Again he smiled, and the smile broadened and his eyes began to dance—if the eyes of a working-man at six-and-thirty can be said to dance—and he laughed aloud. "Ho! ho!" he said; "and no one knows!" He swung out of the little room laughing still. He laughed across the court, and they heard him laughing as he went up the road. Now for a man to go along the queen's highway[11] laughing as he goes by himself is a strange and rather a gruesome thing.

"What is he laughing for?" asked Violet.

"Laughter," said Claude, "is produced in many ways, but especially by the unexpected. The situation is new to him, and therefore, I suppose, ludicrous."

"Joe's been a good son always," said his mother, "though not clever like Sam. Oh! Claude, if you'd only followed in Sam's footsteps. You might have been a board school master by now, like him."

"It can't be helped, mother. But it seems a pity, doesn't it? We had better go now, I think, and I'll bring Polly to see you again as soon as we are quite sure which is Polly; and then you won't be afraid of mistaking Miss Eldridge for her, will you?"

It was trying to them all except to Rhoda, when the old lady rose and folded her hands across her apron, and said slowly, because she was saying the things which are right to say, and good manners must not be hurried: "I wish you humbly good-bye, Miss Beatrice, and I send my humble respects to her ladyship. I hope my Polly will continue to give satisfaction, and I shall be glad to see her when you leave off play-actin', as of course it's your fun and you will have it. She can come in the afternoon and get back by nine. Or Rhoder'll go home, and she can sleep here if her ladyship can spare her."

---

9 A somewhat derogatory expression for someone who appears to be upper class.

10 By this, Joe implies that a working woman could only earn such finery as kid gloves through prostitution, a common form of employment for many working-women in Victorian London.

11 Any public road in England.

Chapter V

The Law of Elevenpence Ha'Penny

The girls came away from Lilly's Almshouses a good deal cast down. They had only succeeded in causing pain to the old lady and bringing shame upon themselves. Therefore they hung their heads.

"After our mother," said Valentine presently, recovering a little, "it is our duty to call upon our sister. Can we go today?"

"I think you had better not," said Claude. "For my own part a visit to Melenda never fails to make me profoundly wretched. I think you had better reserve that visit till another day."

"Does she live near here, Claude?"

"She lives about two miles down the road at a place called Hoxton.[1] "We will go on Monday. Courage!"

"We have plenty of courage," said Violet, deceiving herself more than her brother. "But somehow I am afraid we have not quite grasped the situation. Do you think my sister—Melenda—will receive us with a welcome?"

"No, I should think not," Claude replied with decision. "To the best of my knowledge Melenda is always in a rage. You know that she is horribly, shamefully poor."

"I think, Claude," said Valentine, "that we had better take your advice and go on Monday."

It was in a tenement house, and in Ivy Lane, Hoxton, that Melenda worked all day and slept at night. All the houses in Ivy Lane, or nearly all—because one is a public-house and one or two are shops—are tenement houses. They are mean and squalid houses. The doors and door-posts are black for want of scrubbing; the oldest inhabitant cannot remember when they were painted last; the windows are like the windows in Chancery Lane[2] for griminess; in most of the houses the banisters and some of the steps of the narrow stairs have been broken away for firewood; the plaster of the ceiling has long since cracked and fallen; the street is slovenly and

---

1 Hoxton had once been a relatively prosperous area in Shoreditch. Over time, the wealthier residents relocated to the suburbs, and by the Victorian period Hoxton was becoming increasingly impoverished and more densely packed.

2 A street with a high concentration of various legal services.

uncared for. But girls who can afford no more than five shillings a week for a roof and four walls sometimes have to fare worse than in Ivy Lane. They might, for instance, live in one of the courts which run out of Ivy Lane.

Melenda's room was the first-floor front. It was furnished with a broad wooden bed, one of those which are built for three at least, and have often to hold six; two wooden chairs and a round table; there was also a chest of drawers, and there was an open cupboard, the lower part of which formed a box for coals. On the hob stood the kettle, in the cupboard were a few plates and cups, and in one corner reposed a frying pan and a saucepan.

Two grey ulsters and two hats were hanging on nails driven into the door. This was all the furniture, and it would seem difficult to furnish a room for three girls with more simplicity.

There were three occupants of the room, all young, and all at work. One of them sat on the bed, the other two had the chairs beside the table. The girl on the bed was a thin delicate-looking creature, about twenty-three or twenty-four years of age; she stooped in the shoulders and had a narrow chest; her face was pale and worn, with lines about the mouth; her eyes were lustrous, and looked larger than they were in reality because her cheeks were so thin. They had the patient expression which comes to those who suffer continually. Her brown hair was thin, and was brushed simply back over her temples, and gathered into a knot; she was dressed in an old, a very old, grey stuff frock, and her shoes were long since worn into holes everywhere, sole and heel and toes. But that mattered little, because she never left the house. She sat on the bed because there was something wrong with her backbone—a twist of some kind—so that she was neither so strong nor so tall as other girls, and had to lie down and take rest whenever she "felt her back," which sometimes happened all day and all night long.

This was Lotty. She lived here, though she ought to have been kept warm, well fed, and in idleness in some asylum, or home, or hospital, partly because she knew of no such home; partly out of the deep friendship and affection which she entertained for Melenda; and partly because Melenda would never have suffered her to go so long as she could, by working day and night, provide for her.

As for Melenda, Claude's sister, she sat at the table. She was now a girl of three-and-twenty; she still preserved the red locks of her childhood. Red hair has its artistic value, and I dare say Melenda's would have looked picturesque had it been respectfully treated. But what can you expect of flaming-red hair if you treat it in London girl fashion—that is, if you cut the front part of it short, and comb a great hunch over the forehead, making a red pillow, and then roll the rest of it up in a knot behind? Such a mode might be taken as a text for the preacher and an illustration of the tyranny of fashion, which does nothing for its votaries except to make them ridiculous, and to destroy any points of beauty that they may possess. The airy, fairy, curly, dainty, delicate arrangement over some young ladies' brows no doubt suggested to the London girl the hunch of hair; but the "fringe"[3] was never intended to darken and to disfigure the face; nor was the fringe meant to be a pillow of hair; nor was it meant for thick red hair with no more curl in it than there is in a cow's tail. If Melenda had been better advised she would have brushed her hair back and disclosed to view a broad, square, and very white forehead which everyone would have respected. And then her eyes, which were as sharp and keen as a pair of electric lights, would have been set in a lighter frame. She was not pretty at all, though, like most red-haired girls, her complexion was good; her face was square; her nose was short and straight; her lips

3 More commonly referred to in the United States as *bangs*, a *fringe* is hair that has been cut to fall across the forehead at or above the eyebrows.

were firmly set; her chin strong. In stature she was shorter than the average; her shoulders were broad and her hands large; she looked a strong girl. But she was thin: her cheeks were hollow, and her figure wanted the filling out which comes of food and enough of it. Polly's sister looked always hungry: she also looked capable, strong-willed, and resolute, and she looked as if she could exhibit temper if she chose: lastly, she looked as if she often chose,

The third girl, Lizzie, was of a type which is not unusual in London and almost peculiar to the great city. It has many variations and breaks out into eccentricities of all kinds, but, speaking generally, Lizzie belonged to that class of London girls who are all eyes. They have, it is true, other features as well, but their eyes strike one first and most, because they are so large, so round, so deep, so full of all imaginable and possible thoughts, intentions, and desires. Their mouths are also noticeable, because they are small rosebud mouths, generally with parted lips, as if the soul of the maiden within were waiting to receive the sweet and holy gifts and graces for which her eyes show her yearning. It is impossible to see such a girl without longing immediately to take her away and place her where she may be in perpetual commune with things lofty and spiritual. Lizzie had her fringe too, but her hair was brown, not red: it was curly and not straight; and as she had some glimmering of taste, and did not drag a great solid lump of hair over her forehead, but had a few short curls in its place, the effect was not unpleasing. In figure she was tall but slight, and she was too thin, though she did not look quite so hungry as Melenda. Her head was small and her features possessed a good deal of delicacy. Men, who are more catholic in such matters than ladies, and can discern beauty even where the elbows stick out visibly through the sleeves, would say that here were the elements or makings of a really beautiful girl, if only she could get a fair show.

By one o'clock in the day they had already worked for six hours, because they began at seven. Six hours of almost continuous sewing seems a good day's work; one would not care to sit even over the most delicate embroidery for more than six hours a day: and this was not delicate work at all, but coarse work on coarse and heavy stuff—the stuff of which the commonest shirts are made—those intended to rasp the skin of the unfortunate native, who would so much prefer to sit in buff, brown or black, and suffer the sun to gently bake him all over. Six hours of steady sewing: no student can read with effect for more than six hours a day: no man can write for more than six hours if he care to write well: few men can dig for more or can carry burdens for more without a good spell of rest. These girls, however, were so strong and so industrious that they were going to work for seven hours longer, that is till daylight should cease; if it had been winter they would have worked long after daylight ceased. This is a really good day's work—if you think of it—from seven in the morning till nearly nine at night; this is to work with a will: to work heartily: to expend oneself without stint: to acquiesce in the curse of Adam. It is a day's work which no one but a railway director or an omnibus company dares to exact of men; if a factory were to require such a day there would be a strike, with letters to the papers, even if the men's wages were a shilling an hour. A truly wonderful day's work, only to be understood when one realises the constant presence, felt but not seen, of a Fury with serpents in her hair and an uplifted lash of scorpions in her hands, sometimes called Necessity and sometimes known as Hunger.[4]

4 In Greek and Roman mythology, the Furies were punishing goddesses, typically depicted with serpents entangled in their hair and often with whips of scorpions with which to inflict their pain.

The girls generally worked in silence, but today there had been a little outbreak on the part of Lizzie, with revolutionary sentiments. She was promptly suppressed by Melenda, who followed up her victory with a few remarks which clinched the submission but left sulkiness and a smouldering fire of rebellion.

When the clock struck one—somebody's clock in some neighbouring street—Melenda looked up and broke the silence.

"Lotty," she said imperiously, "lie down this minute."

Lotty obeyed without a word. She had been sitting up too long, and now she lay back with closed eyes, and her short breathing showed that she was suffering.

The other girl tossed her work impatiently on the table.

"One o'clock," she said. "It ought to be dinner time soon. What have we got for dinner?" she laughed derisively. "And what shall we have tomorrow? And the next day—and the day after?"

"Don't, Liz," said Melenda softly. "Don't, just now. It makes her back worse. Let her go to sleep."

"I'm not asleep," said Lotty, opening her eyes. "Don't mind me, Liz." She stretched out her hand and caught Lizzie by the wrist. "Patience, my dear."

"Patience! oh!"

"It's only since the concert that it's come on," said Melenda, looking at her companion as a physician looks upon a patient.

"Why shouldn't it be since the concert, then?" asked Lizzie,

"What have gentlemen got to do interfering with workgirls?" asked Melenda in reply.

Lizzie laughed defiantly.

"Why shouldn't he speak to me? Speaking's no harm. Why shouldn't he tell me the truth? That's no harm. Nobody else tells the truth. The clergyman don't, he says, for fear we shouldn't work any longer; and the district visitors[5] don't, for fear we should strike. And the work is crool,[6] he says, and the wages dreadful; and so they are."

"I've told you that already," said Melenda. "Sam says so too."

"And there's many better ways of living. Some girls go to theatres if they're pretty enough. And some go and get painted in pictures. He says I'm pretty enough for that, and he knows gentlemen who'd like to paint my eyes."

"Liz, he's deceiving you," said Melenda. "Paint your eyes, indeed! He takes you for a fool."

"And he says that it's no good stopping here. He says it's a God-forgotten life. He says we shall never get better money and never any easier work. Think of that, Lotty. We shall get old and die, he says, and never any pretty things to put on and always not enough to eat, and—" Here she stopped, being out of breath.

"It can't be always," said Lotty, "because there must be an end some day."

"Oh! That end!" Lizzie laughed scornfully, because the undertaker and the natural end of man's or woman's life seems so far away to a young girl of seventeen.

5 Female volunteers from the Church of England who sought to improve conditions within impoverished parishes by providing moral support or chastisement.

6 A misspelling of *cruel*, used to represent the mispronunciation of the word in Lizzie's working-class dialect.

"It won't be always," said Melenda, "because Sam says we are going to have no more rich people very soon. We shall divide everything, and after that we shall always have enough, because the people will keep their own when they have got it, and there will be no more masters."

"You're a silly, Melenda," said Lizzie, "to believe such nonsense. Besides, if it were true, what would the girls get? The men would only keep it all to themselves and spend it at the public-houses."

"Did the gentleman tell you that too?"

"Never mind what else he told me."

"Liz," said Lotty, "you haven't seen him again, have you? Oh! promise you won't talk to him any more. Oh! this is what comes of giving Concerts for the People. Liz! Liz!"

But Lizzie tossed her head, snatched her hat, and ran away, and Lotty sighed and lay back again.

"Who was the gentleman, Melenda?" she asked. "Don't let her go on talking to gentlemen. Has she seen him again? Do you know his name?"

"I do not know. We went to the concert. There was a young lady in a black silk frock, and she sang; and there was another in a pink frock, and she sang; and there was someone else who recited; and one man playing on the piano, and another on the violin. I've told you all that before. When we came away I missed Liz in the crowd, and when she came home she was all trembling like, and cried when you were asleep, and wished she was dead and buried, and told me she'd been for a walk with a gentleman, who'd been talking to her about her work and her wages, and made her discontented."

Lotty sighed, but made no reply.

"If we could strike like the men," said Melenda. "It's the only thing, Sam says. Why, if we could strike, the fine ladies wouldn't get their things so cheap; and they know it, and that's why they go about giving concerts to us and pretending to be our friends, just to keep us from throwing the work in their faces and striking. Sam says so."

"Oh, Melenda! But the ladies don't know. If they knew—"

"They do know." Melenda stamped her foot. She was in one of her rages. "They've been told a thousand times. And they don't care—they don't care—so long as they buy their things cheap. Well, we've got our freedom, Lotty; and we ain't obliged to go to their concerts, are we? And if a gentleman speaks to me, I'll let him know."

Lotty made no reply, but closed her eyes again. She had, in fact, nothing to say that could help or even console. She had never considered the subject of supply and demand, or else no doubt she might have administered solace out of those golden rules which keep wages low, hours long, and work scarce. In the old days Lotty knew a great quantity of texts which she might have found comforting, but she had now forgotten them all. Besides, no amount of texts would have brought consolation to Melenda's bosom, because that young lady was as free and emancipated from the trammels of religion as the most advanced woman in the whole school. It was, in fact, part of her independence not to attend any form of divine service, not from any animosity towards the Christian faith, but simply because all forms of worship make demands upon a girl's freedom.

There was some cold tea standing on the chest of drawers, with a loaf of bread, and some yellow substance flattered by the name of butter. Melenda cut two thick slices and poured out some tea. "Lucky we had a bit of meat for Sunday," she said. "Take your dinner now, Lotty dear."

"I am better now," said Lotty, after their feast. "If I rest for half an hour I shall be able to work again. Where's Liz gone?"

"You go to sleep," said Melenda. "As for Liz, she'll come in presently, when she's ramped round a bit."

Lotty obeyed and closed her eyes.

Then Melenda resumed her work. In a few minutes she saw that Lotty was asleep. She might have been dead, so motionless she lay and so waxen-pale were her cheeks. In sleep the closed eyes lost their worn look, and the lines of her forehead were smoothed out, and the face dropped back, so to speak, into the mould in which it was cast. Melenda carefully drew the counterpane—it was old and ragged, alas! and wanted washing—over her friend's arms and chest, and laid her ulster over her feet with tender hand and softened eyes, and then sat down again and began to stitch with a kind of fierceness. It pleased her that she could work twice as fast as the other two, and that while her friend was resting she was doing the share of both.

Meantime, in St. John's Road, close by, there walked together side by side a gentleman and a workgirl.

"You will think of it, won't you?" he asked. "It is a cruel thing for a pretty girl like you to be slaving so hard. Pretty girls were not meant to do hard work, you know. You ought to be beautifully dressed, and standing on the stage, and all the men in the house clapping because you would look so beautiful."

"I can't never leave Lotty and Melenda," the girl replied.

"Meet me again this evening. I will be by the church at nine. Will you promise?"

"I don't care," she said. "Yes, I will then. But it's no use. I won't never leave Melenda and Lotty."

There are many openings and a splendid variety of choice for a girl who insists on her independence and, therefore, refuses to go behind counters or bars, or into offices, or some other people's houses. She may become a dressmaker, a milliner, or a seamstress, she may make shirts, cuffs, collars, or button-holes: she may enter any of the various branches of the great sewing mystery: she may go into a factory—there are quantities of factories to choose from—but whatever she does and wherever she goes she may quite confidently reckon on short pay and long hours: in all probability she will be bullied by the foreman and snubbed, scolded, and nagged by the forewoman: her independence will be the privilege of sleeping in a room shared with two or three other girls, together with that of keeping any hours she pleases, and she may be certain beforehand that her poverty and her helplessness will be *exploités*[7] to the utmost by her employer as much as if she was an omnibus driver; that her whole life will be spent in bad lodgings, on slender commons, with friends of the poorest and work of the hardest: she may rely upon getting no help from anybody, certainly none from her brothers, who, poor fellows! have to pay for their clubs, their drinks, and their amusements,[8] and cannot do what they would wish for their sisters: none from the political economist to whom an ill-paid workgirl illustrates in a most satisfactory manner the beneficent law of supply and demand, ordained by the Creator in the day when He created man and woman for the advantage of the middle-man, chosen of his race, and the development of His next noblest creation the manufacturer: none from politicians, because they think that the working-woman will never be a danger to any party; none—alas!—from ladies, because their injustice is too old and stale, and the Song of

7 French for *exploited*.

8 For a fee, workingmen's clubs of the period provided members with opportunities for socialization, entertainment, and even self-improvement with reading rooms, lectures, debates, and exhibitions.

the Shirt,[9] which has been sung for forty years, is known by heart, and the sight of the sister, who never cries out or complains, is familiar, and because of that strange hardness of woman's heart towards women, which is a wonderful and a monstrous thing. Nor will the working-girl expect any help from her own class, because they have not learned to combine, and there is none to teach them, and the sharp lessons, including thwacks, kicks, hammerings, rattening,[10] and boycotting, by which the working-men were forced and driven into their union, are impossible for the girls.

Melenda chose to be a sewing machine. In this capacity she got button-holes to make with her friends. They were three really very industrious girls, and with so much industry, their rent only four shillings, and bread lower than ever it has been known before, and likely to be cheaper still, and tea and sugar always "down again," they ought to do very well indeed, and be able to buy themselves pretty frocks, and perhaps save money, and to go about with rosy cheeks, and they should every morning be ready to greet the rosy sun with a hymn of praise. That they did not do any of these things, that their clothes were ragged, their cheeks pale, their eyelids heavy, their purse empty, was due to the action of a very remarkable law in political economy—a science which most wonderfully illustrates the divine goodness and the beneficence of creation. This law has hitherto, I believe, escaped the observation of all the professors. It is the law of the Lower Limit, which will be better understood by being named after an outward and visible sign, the most obvious and best-known result of its beneficent operation. I have therefore ventured to call it the Law of Elevenpence Ha'penny.[11] It has been found, in fact, by the employers of woman's labour, who are one and all the most humane, the most considerate, and the most unselfish creatures in existence, that there is a limit of wage below which human life cannot be sustained. It is highly to their credit that they seldom try to get below this limit, which is exactly marked by the wage of elevenpence ha'penny a day. Therefore no working-woman, of those who work at home, is allowed to make more, because this would be a flying in the face of the eternal laws.[12] And it would be clearly inhuman to offer less. To be sure the women sometimes get less because they are often out of work: but the employers cannot be blamed for that. The Law of Elevenpence Ha'penny, or the Law of the Lower Limit, is the only law that humanity is called upon to obey, and the conscience of those who pay the girls at this rate of wages is calm and easy. One positively envies the conscience of the wholesale match-maker, the wholesale jam-maker, the wholesale shirt-maker, the wholesale maker of anything which may be made or sewn by the hands of women and girls. The wickedness of the men who refuse to obey this law (designed at the Creation for them as well as for women) is part of the universal depravity which causes men to think and act for themselves, without any respect for law or authority in religion, politics, morals, manners, and customs.

The Law of Elevenpence Ha'penny. As Melenda worked exactly two-and-a-half times faster than Lotty, and Lizzie one-and-a-half times, it follows that to produce an average of elevenpence ha'penny, Melenda should earn seventeenpence and five-twentieths, and Lizzie tenpence and seven-twentieths, and Lotty sixpence and nine-tenths, and that they did so shows how good a worker Melenda was. Sometimes, however, there was

---

9 Thomas Hood's poem "Song of the Shirt" (1843) describes the horrible working conditions and meager lives of the city's many exploited seamstresses. Originally published in *Punch* magazine, the poem was widely circulated through reprinting, translations, and adaptations. For the full text, see Appendix B.

10 A strategy for enforcing workers' compliance, particularly through the removal or breaking of a worker's tools.

11 An abbreviated form of "half penny," the smallest value coin in British currency.

12 The primary laws of economics are those of supply and demand, which can be used to explain the price of goods and employee wages.

less, because work has to be taken back and fetched, and there are delays in getting fresh work. At the best, therefore, these girls between them could earn seventeen shillings and threepence a week. Their rent was four shillings so that there was left the sum of thirteen shillings and threepence for everything else. That is to say, the splendid sum of sevenpence and four-sevenths apiece, or very nearly sevenpence ha'penny a day, remained for all their wants.

My very dear young lady, you who sit at home in ease, how would you like to find yourself in food, frocks, fire, furniture, music, boots, bonnets, books, trinkets, gloves, and all the thousand-and-one things that go to make a girl's life, on sevenpence ha'penny a day? But these girls are not like you? That, I assure you, is not at all the case. It is a falsehood invented by the Devil when he invented the figment of nobility, gentry, and villain. If you desire to know what the workgirl really is, go to the looking-glass and study very carefully, not your bonnet, which is very becoming, nor your face, which is so pretty that one wishes he was young enough to fall in love with it, nor the dressing of your hair, which might be much more artistic, but the unseen self which lies behind the face. That is the working-girl as well as yourself, my dear young friend.

In half an hour or so Lizzie came back, quiet and subdued, but with a rosy flush on her cheek and brightened eyes.

"I've had dinner," she answered when Melenda pointed to the tea-pot. "I've had an egg and a cup of coffee. It was given to me—by—a young girl I know."

Melenda looked at her sharply, but said nothing.

Then there was silence in the room save for the click of the needle and the thimble and the rustling of the stuff in which they were sewing the button-holes. But Melenda was disturbed and ill at ease, partly on account of Lizzie and the unknown gentleman who made her discontented, and partly because it seemed to her—perhaps the bread and butter had not been thick enough—as if a man's voice was repeating aloud, over and over again, banging and beating the words into her head, "All your lives—all your lives;" and then the voice of her brother Sam—it was a deep, rich bass—chimed in saying, "Why don't you strike? Why don't you strike?" This was not agreeable. But the time passed on, and the distant clock struck two, three, and four while Lotty still slept on and the other two worked in silence.

It was just after the striking of four that the girls heard footsteps in the narrow passage below, and voices which were not the voices of their fellow-lodgers. One of the voices said, "Will you wait below, Claude? We would rather go up alone."

And then the door opened, and two young ladies appeared. They were young ladies the like of whom the girls had seldom, if ever, seen, for they were so beautiful and beautifully dressed, and at sight of their frocks and their hats the soul of Lizzie sank within her. The District Visitor they knew, because she sometimes called and always had a fight with Melenda, but she was not by any means beautifully dressed. Also certain ladies had once or twice come into their street and gone about the houses curiously, and received sharp replies to their questions. But they were not beautiful.

"Is there a girl here named Melenda?" asked one of them.

Lotty awoke, and sat upright with a start. Lizzie stared and dropped her work and her thimble, which rolled under the drawers, and afterwards half an hour was wasted in looking for it. The owner of the name, suspecting a visit from people in the interests of church services, only looked up and nodded.

Then the two young ladies stepped forward and seized each a hand, saying softly, "Oh! Melenda, we are your sister Polly."

Alas! that Polly should have chosen this day of all days for her return after an absence of nineteen years.

Chapter VI

An Unlucky Day

Claude waited below in Ivy Lane on the shady side of the street. It was full of children playing noisily, and there were soft and murmurous echoes, poetically speaking, from Hoxton Street on the right, where there is a perpetual market. Presently he became aware of a shrill voice rapidly rising, which he easily recognised as his sister Melenda's voice.

The voice rose so loud that he could catch some of the words. And it seemed to him as if this visit promised to be even a greater failure than that to the Almshouse. At last the voice grew so shrill and the language so unmistakable, that he thought he ought to follow the girls if only to protect them.

When he opened the door he was greeted by Melenda herself with a derisive laugh.

"Charity boy!"[1] she said, pointing with her forefinger.

He had, however, heard this remark before, and now received it without emotion.

Valentine was standing at the table with flushed face and a look of bewilderment and pain. Violet was cowering in Lizzie's chair—absolutely cowering—and crying. Lotty was looking on, troubled and perplexed. Lizzie sat on the bed beside her, the work in her hands, making believe that the scene neither interested nor concerned her, and that she was wholly occupied and absorbed in her button-holes, which she handled ostentatiously, holding the garment up to the light, spreading it on her knee, contemplating it with the needle in her mouth, and in other ways proclaiming her entire unconsciousness of the Row. Yet she listened and smiled with pride when Melenda surpassed herself, and from time to time she lifted her great eyes and took in some fresh detail of the ladies' dresses. Oh! could she ever have dreamed of things so beautiful?

"Charity boy!" repeated Melenda. "Of course he brought the charity girl with him."

---

1 One who comes from poverty but has been formally educated, usually at a school for similarly impoverished boys. Used here as an insult.

Claude made no reply, which disconcerted her. And he looked at her not angrily but gravely and wonderingly, which made her still more angry.

"What is the matter, Valentine?" he asked, after a pause. "Has my sister been rude to you?"

"Yes," Melenda broke in; "I've been rude to both of 'em. I've told them the truth, and I wish they may like it and get it every day. Rude? Oh! yes, I've been rude. Don't make any error about that, Claude." She stuck—I use the word deliberately—she stuck her elbows on the table and put on her most defiant face.

"What is the truth, Melenda?" Claude asked her; "will you tell it to me as well?

The aggravating thing with Claude was that you could never make him angry by calling him names, not even by calling him a charity boy. Today, being in a rage royal, Melenda began with this supreme insult. She generally ended with it. People ought to get angry when you call them names, else there is no reason in calling names; and then, what a weapon thrown away! Not to get angry in return is unkind towards one's fellow-creatures; it betrays want of sympathy; it arrogates a disgusting superiority; it makes people who have yielded to their wrath, and slung all the names they could find, hot and ashamed of themselves. Common people, ordinary, simple, unaffected people, not stuck-up people, get very angry when they are called names, and retaliate by calling worse names immediately by return post, or they take to punching heads or jumping upon one another. Claude, for his own exasperating part, only looked at his sister with his grave eyes as if he was wondering where she was feeling the pain and what ought to be done for it.

"Let us have the whole truth, Melenda."

"The truth is that we don't want fine ladies here. We're workgirls, and we've got to earn our living, and we ain't ashamed of it. We don't want to be looked at like as if we were elephants in a circus. Let 'em go and look at somebody else. We ain't a show. Lotty ain't a clown; I ain't a jumping-horse; Liz ain't a salamander."[2]

"Don't you want to see your sister again, Melenda?"

"My sister!" she threw out her arms with a fine gesture, free and unstudied. "Oh! look at me and look at them. Listen to him—my sister! Look at my frock, and Lotty's frock, and Lizzie's frock, and look at theirs. My sister! And they can't tell which it is. My sister! If you come to that—"

"But one of these young ladies is your sister—and mine."

"It's the first I've heard of Polly being a young lady. Which of 'em is it, then? Is it her, who can't be spoken to but she begins to cry? or her"—Melenda suited gesture with her thumb to words, so that no mistake should be possible—"who wants to shake hands and to kiss? A pretty kiss!"

"They only learned a day or two ago that they had a sister. Was it unkind in them to make themselves known to you as quickly as they could?"

"Well, they're curious, and they've had their curiosity. They've seen me, and now they may go away and boast to all the swells[3] that they've got a sister who makes button-holes. Sooner they go the better. Come! they've wasted time enough already."

"You are very unkind," said Valentine. "If we were to come again when you were not so busy with work—"

"No," said Melenda, "I don't want to see either of you never again. One of you is Polly, because you say so, and I don't see why you should be proud of being my sister. Well, when Polly leaves off pretending to be a lady she may come here, and not before."

---

2 A name for someone who juggles fire.

3 A fashionable or elegant person who often believes in one's own self-importance.

"Your sister," said Claude, "can never lay aside that pretence."

"Mother hadn't ought to let her go," the girl went on; "I always said so. Why should Polly be brought up with nothing to do all her life but to sit down and to eat and drink?"

"On the contrary," said Claude, "she has done a great deal."

"Does she go dressed like this?" asked Melenda, springing to her feet, and displaying with rapid gesture the deficiencies of her scanty wardrobe, the whole of which was upon her. "Does she get up at six and work all day till nine? Does she have bread and butter and tea for all her meals?"

"Oh!" said Valentine, "if you will only let us help you. We did not come here to pry upon you—not out of curiosity—oh! not out of curiosity. We came because we wanted to know our sister."

"Now you know her then, you can go away again. I don't mind. You see what I am. Oh! I know what I'm like, and what Liz is like, and Lotty—only Lotty is different. Fine manners, ours, ain't they? Go away and laugh at us."

"Indeed there is nothing to laugh at," said Valentine.

"Then cry over us like her"—she meant Violet. "I dare say she likes crying. If a girl had said half to me that I've said to her, I'd have had her hair out of her head."

"You are cruel," said Violet; "is it our fault that Polly was taken from you?"

"Didn't say whose fault it was. It's no concern of mine. You've got my thimble, Liz. Where's your own?"

"Melenda, try to be gracious," said Claude. "Pretend to know something about manners. Make believe that Sam is here. You generally behave, you know, when Sam is present."

Melenda sniffed. "Come," she said, returning to the charge, "you were curious to see your sister, weren't you? Well, you've seen her, and I dare say you'll ask her to tea and shrimps and meet your fine friends. I'll come with Joe and Sam and some of Joe's kids if you like, to make a family party. And now you can go away and be mighty thankful that you weren't left to grow up with your mother and me. Else you'd be sitting here this moment where Liz is sitting, and working like Liz is working."

She sat down, picked up her work, and began to sew again violently.

Valentine sighed. "You shall see me again," she said, "whether you like it or not. You cannot lock the door in your sister's face. I will make you want to see me."

Melenda went on sewing without any reply.

Then Valentine turned to Lotty.

"Tell me," she said, "are you perhaps a cousin of Melenda's and mine?"

"No," said Lotty, "I'm only her friend. We've lived together for eight years, Melenda and me."

"And do you sew every day?"

"Unless we're out of work we do. It is all we have learned."

"But you don't look strong enough for the work."

"I'm stronger than I look," said Lotty, smiling. "I can do a good bit of work. It's my back which isn't strong, and makes me cough sometimes. I've got to lie down a great deal. And then Melenda works for me." She looked up shyly. "You won't mind what Melenda said, will you, Miss? She's put out today about something—something somebody said to Liz about the work, it was. Please don't mind; she's easy put out, but she's the best heart in the world."

"You'll just have to lie down again, Lotty," said Melenda, "if you talk so much."

"What is your name?" asked Valentine.

"Lotty—Charlotte East. This is Liz. Her father lives downstairs, but she lives and works with us. She's seven years younger than me. I'm twenty-four and Liz is seventeen."

"Do you like your work, my dear?" Valentine asked Lizzie.

The girl turned her great heavy eyes upwards. "No, I don't," she replied slowly.

"If you've got to do it, what's the odds whether you like it or whether you don't?" asked Melenda.

"Come, Valentine," said Violet; "it is no use staying."

"Not a bit," said Melenda.

"Have you no kind word for us at all, Melenda?" Valentine asked.

"Look here," the girl replied; "you don't belong to us, neither of you. Go away to the people you do belong to—you and Claude. They're the people that keep us girls on a shilling a day, so as they can get their dresses cheap. Stick to them. They're the people who've stolen the land and the labour and everything that's made. Sam says so. Leave us alone. Don't come here and laugh at us. I won't have it. And as for you"—she turned to Violet, who shrank back and caught Claude by the arm—"dare to come again and cry at us! If you do, I'll tear your bonnet off."

"You are behaving very rudely, Melenda," said Claude.

She sniffed again and tossed her head.

Since, however, she continued in this hard and unrepentant mood, and showed no sign of melting, there was nothing left but to withdraw, which they did, retreating in good order, as the history books say, or rolling sullenly over the border, as they also say. That is, the enemy did not shove them downstairs, nor tear off their bonnets, nor hurl things after them, nor call them names, but suffered them to retire unmolested. To be sure, they were routed; there was no possibility of mistake about that.

For at least two hours Melenda continued stitching in absolute silence, but her lips moved. At the expiration of this period she broke out into short interjectional phrases, which showed that her mind was powerfully working. "I'm glad I spoke out—did her good for once—I won't be cried at—we don't want curious ones here—teach them to keep their own places," and so forth—not original or novel phrases, and perhaps wanting in dignity, but with some fire. Then she relapsed into silence again.

It was nearly nine o'clock when it became too dark to see the work any longer, and they put it by.

Then Lizzie began to make certain preparations. She took a hat out of a drawer—a hat with a feather in it. She tied a bright coloured ribbon round her neck, and she put on her ulster, which is a workgirl's full dress for summer or for winter, only in summer there is not always a frock under it.

"Liz, dear," said Lotty, "you won't be late, will you? And, Liz—don't—oh! Liz—don't talk with any more gentlemen."

Lizzie made no reply, and disappeared.

"She's put on her best ribbon," Lotty said, with a sigh, "her Sunday ribbon. What's that for, I wonder?"

Melenda made no reply. She was thinking of her own sister, not of Lizzie.

"Oh!" she cried presently, throwing out her arms in a gesture unknown to the stage, but natural and very striking; "if she'd only come alone! But to come in a pair, and for both to sit and smile and say they didn't know which of them was Polly, as if it didn't matter what became of her—I suppose because she was a poor girl and her mother was a washerwoman, and you and me and Liz beneath their notice, and it was all pride and curiosity and looking down upon us—I couldn't bear it, Lotty, so I spoke up. I'm glad I did."

She showed her gladness by bursting into tears.

"I'd do it again. If they come again, I'd do it again. With their kid gloves and their real flowers and gold chains, and to look about the room as if we were wild beasts at a show, and a teapot a thing they'd never seen before. We don't want 'em. Let 'em leave us to ourselves. We can do our work without them, and bear what we've got to bear, Lotty, you and me together, can't we?"

"They looked sorry," said Lotty, doubtfully; "they'd got kind faces and they spoke kind."

"I don't know," Melenda went on, "which I hate the most—the one who looked as if the very sight of us made her sick and ashamed—that was the one who began to cry when I up and cheeked her; or the one who wouldn't cry, and only stared as if I was something strange, and kept saying that I was mistaken, and wouldn't get into a rage, say what I liked. Just like Claude—you can't put Claude in a rage. I believe that one must be Polly. All the same I hate her: I hate 'em both."

"I wouldn't hate them if I were you, Melenda," said Lotty.

"What's the good? They only came to see if they could help you, p'r'aps."

"They help me? Likely! I wouldn't have their help nor Claude's neither, if I was starving. As for Polly being my sister, they took her away and we've lost her."

"If it was to dress her up and make her a lady, so much the better for her. I wish somebody would take us all three away and do just the same."

"You've no spirit, Lotty. Of course it's your poor back. But you've no spirit."

Melenda put on her hat and went downstairs into the streets. She always finished the day in this manner. After fifteen hours of sewing in one room and in one position it is necessary to get change and fresh air. Therefore two of the girls roamed the streets, making of Hoxton Street and Pitfield Street and the City Road and Old Street[4] their boulevard from nine o'clock or so until twelve. The society of the streets is mixed; things are said in them which in other circles are left unsaid; but there is life and a faint semblance of joy, and some kind of laughter and light and fresh air. Melenda passed through the children playing in Ivy Lane, and the groups of mothers standing about and talking together, and turned into Hoxton Street. She avoided for once the crowd on the pavement, and trudged along in the road behind the costers' carts, for it is a street where they hold perpetual market. When she came to the end of Hoxton Street she walked on till she came to the bridge over the canal. It is a strange place. The water lies below black and rather terrible. Melenda had heard legends of girls throwing themselves into that black water when they were tired of things. There is generally visible a barge with its light and its fire. Tonight the girl's brain, as she leaned over the parapet, was full of tumult. Her own sister had come back to her, and she had driven her away with shameful words and insults. To be sure she had long forgotten the very existence of her sister. Perhaps, from time to time, she thought of her as one thinks of an old playmate gone away years ago to Australia or to the western lands, never to return. But she had come back—the little Polly—transformed into a young lady, and Melenda had used hard words.

It was nearly midnight when she got home. A few of the children were still in the court, but they were sitting on the doorstep, and some of them asleep: these were the children who were afraid to go upstairs because father was drunk and not yet gone to sleep. A few women were still talking, but most had gone home and to

4 The four streets mentioned are all close to Ivy Lane (now Ivy Street) in Hoxton.

bed. One or two of the men were singing or roaring or crying, according to their habits when drunk; but not many, because it was Monday night, which is generally a sober time. In the room on the first-floor front Liz was in bed and sound asleep. Lotty was lying on her back, watching and waiting.

"Melenda," she whispered, "they were beautiful young ladies. They meant to be kind. Don't make them cry if they come again."

"There oughtn't to have been but one," said Melenda severely.

"Go to sleep this minute, Lotty. Polly wasn't twins."

Chapter vii

After Melenda

In the evening of the same day Lady Mildred was at home. Claude's acquaintance with society[1] was limited, as may be supposed. He who is climbing must wait until he has reached the higher levels before he can think of society. Such an evening as this, with the musical laughter of girls, the continuous murmur of talk, the brightness of the rooms, the atmosphere of happiness and freedom from care, just as if everything was real, solid, and abiding, and everybody was young and happy, and was going to remain young and happy, filled Claude with a kind of intoxication and delight, and tonight he could admire his sister in one of these two girls with a sense of wonder as if it was a dream. His life had been serious—the life of one who had no chance except to succeed by his own efforts. Society, which has no serious aims, holds no place for such a man until he has succeeded: women hold no place in such a man's life until he has got up to a certain elevation.

"What are you thinking of, Claude?" Valentine asked him.

"I was thinking of contrasts and incongruities," he replied.

"The contrast of the afternoon with the evening. Yes. But if you cannot forget those things, you will begin to think that we are mocking at misery. What would Melenda think and say if she were to stand among us suddenly?"

"One can hardly imagine," Claude laughed, "anything more incongruous."

"I suppose she would ask us how we could possibly feel happy on the very day when we had seen her home and her friends. And I am sure she would not understand how we could sing and laugh and yet not forget her or cease to think of her. Society must have its incongruities—I suppose, because we must hide away so much of ourselves."

At the other end of the room was Violet in the middle of a group, talking with bright eyes and apparently the highest heart in the world.

---

1 London's social elite.

"Violet had a hysterical fit when we came home this afternoon," Valentine whispered. "Melenda was too much for her. Yet she puts on a brave face, and nobody would suspect the truth."

With her—one of her group—was Jack Conyers. As Valentine crossed the room with Claude, he glanced quickly from Violet to Valentine and then to Claude.

Strange! The girls were not only like each other, but they both looked liked Claude. It was the first opportunity Conyers had obtained since hearing of Claude's relations with Lady Mildred's daughters of making a comparison between the girls and their brother. Surely, with the portrait of Sir Lancelot at five-and-twenty, gazing upon the room from the wall; with Lady Mildred herself, present in the flesh; with the two girls, and with Claude their brother, there should be data enough to solve the problem easily. Jack Conyers, however, like everybody else who attempted a solution of the riddle, forgot one essential thing. It is this: if two girls are brought up together from childhood in exactly the same way, with the same education, the same food, the same governors, pastors, and masters, and are kept apart from other girls, and are dressed alike, they may grow very much like each other; little points of resemblance may become accentuated. Chinamen, for instance, who are a very gregarious people, present to the outward world millions of faces all exactly alike. Old married people are often observed to have grown like each other; and if you look at a girls' charity school,[2] where they live all together under one roof, and are subjected to exactly the same rules and influences, you will find that they certainly grow to have the same face.

There is, for instance, a certain reformatory[3] of my acquaintance in a London suburb. The young ladies belonging to this institution are marched in procession to church every Sunday. As they pass along the road, the admiring bystander becomes presently aware that they are all exactly alike. It is bewildering until philosophy lends its light. For the girls are like so many sisters: here a dozen twins; here a triplet or two; here more twins. Some are older, some are younger; but they are all of one family—they are apparently of one father and one mother. The Reformatory face is striking, but by no means pleasing. It looks, in fact, as if Monsieur le Diable[4] has had more to do with the girls' fathers or mothers, or both, than with other people's fathers and mothers.

No doubt it was due to the nineteen years of close association and friendship that Valentine and Violet had grown so much alike, and Mr. Conyers, had he been wise, would have looked for points of dissimilarity rather than of resemblance. But this he did not think of. Besides, the young ladies were not like the models who came to his studio: they did not sit to him; he could only study their faces furtively.

"They both look like Claude too," Jack Conyers thought, with troubled brow. "First one looks like him, and then the other. If only they wouldn't dress their hair exactly alike, there might be a chance."

Other eyes besides his own were curiously watching and comparing Claude with the two girls, for some of the people knew that the brother of one was present, and there was a natural anxiety to know which he resembled and what sort of a young man he was. Seeing that he was only the son of a working-man, it was rather disappointing to find a young man of good manners and of excellent appearance, reported to be a Fellow of Trinity who had distinguished himself, and was now called to the bar. Except that the face was somewhat like

2 A school supported by voluntary donations, which housed, schooled, and clothed a limited number of poor children within the jurisdiction of a given parish. It usually prepared them to enter various trades or domestic employment.

3 Penal institutions that sought to reform juvenile delinquents.

4 A French name for the devil in Christian theology.

the faces of the girls, cast like theirs in the oval mould, there was nothing at first sight to connect him with one girl more than with the other. So that everybody was disappointed and went empty away.

Presently Valentine sang. She had a strong and full contralto voice, which had been carefully trained and cultivated. And she had, besides, the heart of the musician. But she would not sing more than once.

"Claude," Violet whispered, when the singing ceased, "can you sing?"

"Not at all. I have no voice."

"Nor have I. That is one point of resemblance between us. Is it part of our inheritance? No voice and no fortune. Of course you can paint and draw?"

"No. I can hardly hold a pencil, and I never tried to paint."

"Oh! That is very strange, because it is the only thing I can do at all. In that respect Valentine is like you. I suppose you cannot embroider? I am clever in embroidery."

"No, unfortunately. But I can make Latin and Greek verses: that is perhaps a branch of embroidery."

"If you could make English verses I would claim this as a point of resemblance. Are you clever at sums?"

"No, not very."

"Oh! I am sorry, because I am. Now Valentine can never add anything correctly. Are you—tidy?"

"No, not at all."

"I am so glad, because I am the most untidy person in the world, and Valentine is the neatest. Her room is like a ship's cabin. Are you fond of dogs and animals?"

"Not very."

"What a pity! because I am; and I have the most lovely dogs at home—in the country you know. I would not let the poor things come to town. But Valentine does not care much for them. Do you like music?"

"Yes; but I cannot play."

"Well, I can play, I suppose, but Valentine is really a musician, not an amateur. Well, Claude, this is most exasperating, because one moment you are like Valentine and the next you are like me. Is there anything else that you can do?"

"I know one or two modern languages and a little law. And I can row a little, play cricket a little, play tennis a little—"

"We can play lawn-tennis too. Claude,"—she lowered her voice again—"never mind the points of resemblance. But, oh! it was a truly dreadful afternoon. My poor brother!"

What she meant was that if she, in one interview, found Melenda so unspeakably dreadful, what must be his own feelings about her when he had always known her?

"As for me," he replied, intelligently answering her unspoken question, "Melenda has always been my sister. I am used to her. But of course she has not been yours."

"Spare us another interview, Claude. I am selfish, I know. But I cannot bear to go there again—just yet."

"You shall not go again unless you wish, Violet. I am afraid she was—well—outspoken."

"She was—unspeakable."

This was true, and the fact is a sufficient excuse for the silence of history as regards her actual words. History, like schoolmaster Sam in his class-room, is perpetually wiping out something with a sponge. Also, like Sam, History has a board as black as Erebus itself to write upon.

"Yes;" it was Jack Conyers' voice, which was not loud but penetrating, and he was talking with Valentine. "Yes; since I saw you in Florence I have been irresistibly forced to devote myself wholly to art. Such other personal ambitions as I may have cherished are now altogether abandoned."

"Indeed! But there is nothing more delightful than art, Mr. Conyers, or more honourable, is there?"

"I shall hope to see you and your sister in my studio some happy day, Miss Valentine. My picture will not be completed and ready for exhibition for three or four years more. But my friends will be allowed to see it in progress."

"I hope we shall see it in the Academy or in the Grosvenor."[5]

He put up his hands and shuddered gently.

"Not that," he murmured; "anything but that."

"Claude," said Violet, "that is the man who paid us so much attention last winter in Florence. He really was very useful to us; and he divided his attentions equally, you see, so as to prevent mistake."

"What mistake?"

"Why, you silly boy, he might have made love to Polly instead of to Beatrice. He has had ten minutes with Valentine, and now he will come to me. Do you believe in him?"

"I knew him at Cambridge. We thought he was clever."

"He talks perpetually about himself, as if he very much wished to be thought clever; and—I don't know—but there does not seem always the right ring about him. Does there? He isn't real."

Presently Claude's turn came with Lady Mildred. She was always gracious—always a *grande dame de par le monde*[6]—but she had never been more gracious or greater than that evening, when she found her opportunity to say a few words for his own ear.

"Do you remember, Claude," she asked him, "a certain day twelve years ago when I took you to the opera, and told you that if you wished you could take your own place among the people you saw there?"

"I remember all that you ever told me, Lady Mildred."

"Well, the time has come; you may take your place. I will, if you please, place you in as good a set as anyone can desire. It helps a young man to be seen occasionally in society."

"I have never thought much of society. My ambition has always been to justify—"

"I know it has, Claude. You have more than justified what was done for you at first. Otherwise, should I have made you known to your sister?"

"But you allowed me to take them to—"

"Yes, Claude. Your sister ought to know her relations. She need not associate with them unless she pleases. Perhaps she would not quite appreciate you unless she understood what you had done. I want her to be proud of you, Claude."

"Thank you," he said.

"You think—you feel—that success and personal distinction will satisfy your soul, Claude?"

"Why," he replied, wondering, "what else is there? We are all fighting for place of some kind, and I am fighting for a front place."

"And you think you will be happy when you get that place?"

---

5 Famous institutions that exhibited art, often catering to those with conservative tastes.

6 French for *a great lady of the world*, or one of rank, grace, and dignity.

"I am sure that nothing else will make me happy. Why do you ask, Lady Mildred?"

"Be happy, my dear boy, in any way you can. Only do not be quite sure that there is no other ambition possible for you."

* * *

Claude walked away with Conyers about midnight. His friend was not quite satisfied. He had not discovered anything, and he doubted whether he had made it quite certain that he was going to be a great painter.

"Well," he said, "have you learned anything yet—the truth about these young ladies? That is, if it is not a secret of state?"

"Not a secret of state at all. Only that we do not know. Lady Mildred will tell us when she pleases."

They smoked their cigarettes in silence for a while.

"Jack," said Claude, after a pause, "about that girl—the girl you were talking about—you know—the girl with the eyes and the possible face—the girl you talked of making your model."

"I remember. What about her?"

"Don't do it, Jack. Let the girl stay. I have been quite lately among girls of her class. Such a girl might very well be my own sister. Leave her alone, Jack."

"My dear fellow, out of half a million girls—but have it your own way. There are plenty of models, though not many with such eyes. But have it your own way. As if any girl could be harmed by devoting herself to the service of art!"

"Yes," said Claude, "the same thing used to be said in Cyprus when they wanted a girl to devote herself to the service of Aphrodite."[7]

"If the girl would sit to me I would paint her. That is all. But you are quite right, Claude. It would be a pity to turn her head. She shall stay with her friends and go on with her sewing, so far as I am concerned."

---

7 Claude's suggestion here is that devotees of art could easily prostitute themselves, as did the priestesses of Aphrodite, the Greek goddess of love and sex.

Chapter VIII

Alicia

"Well, Jack, as you have not thought fit to call upon me, I have come to call upon you."

His visitor was a woman no longer in her first youth, but not yet much past thirty; of an age when one begins to say of a woman that she still keeps her good looks—a handsome woman, large-limbed and tall, with full cheek and smiling mouth; a good-tempered woman, yet one who knew her own mind and had her own way. And though she laughed, her eyes had a look in them which made Jack, who felt guilty, wish that the visit was over.

"Thank you," he said. "It has been very rude of me, but I have been getting settled. You know that I have at last taken a studio."

"Really! You may call me Alicia, you know, Jack, just as you used to do. I am glad to hear that you have begun to do some work."

"I have begun my work." There is a subtle distinction between beginning to work and beginning one's work.

"Oh! And—meanwhile, Jack?"

He met those eyes and blushed.

"Meanwhile?" she repeated. "A man can't make himself an independent gentleman quite for nothing, and you have been playing that game now for five years. And a man can't make money by painting, unless he is mighty lucky, all at once. Therefore, meanwhile, Jack, and until the money begins to come in?"

"What do you mean?" But he knew very well what she meant, because this lady knew all his family history and the exact amount of the fortune—a very little one—with which he had started, and it was no use making pretences with her: very few women are so considerate with men as to help them along with their little pretences.

"I mean, how are you going to live?"

"Like the sparrows, I suppose—somehow."

"Sparrows don't belong to clubs, and haven't a taste for claret, and don't pay a hundred and twenty pounds a year for rent. Now, I'm not going to let you take any of their money from the girls—they've got little enough, Lord knows."

"I do not propose to rob my sisters, Alicia."

"Then you will be wanting money very badly indeed before long. Besides, you never will make any by honest work. You can't paint, Jack, that is the truth, and you never will be able. What is the use of deceiving yourself? I didn't live eight years with my poor old man without learning something about pictures. Look here, now." She took up one of the small portraits on the mantelshelf. "Here's a thing! Yours, of course. Here's flesh—like putty! The eyes are not straight, and there's no more feeling about the lips than—well—and the worst of it is, you'll never learn. My old man wouldn't have given you half a crown for such a thing. No, you'll never learn, for your only chance is to begin at the bottom of the ladder, where everybody must begin. But you're too conceited for that. Oh! you're a genius, I know, and painting comes by nature, we all know that."

Jack reddened with anger. But he answered mildly, because for many reasons he could not quarrel with this plain-speaking lady.

"Really, Alicia, you carry the license of old friendship too far."

"Not a bit too far, Jack. It does you good to hear the truth. Who was this girl whose head you've got here? I seem to know her face. Some model, I suppose. She sat to you and you paid her a few francs, and now you've stuck her over your mantelpiece for your friends to see, and you pretend she was in love with you, and you brag about your conquests—" A cruelly truthful woman, because that was just exactly what Jack had done. Men like Jack Conyers always do this kind of thing. "Pretty conquests!"

"Did you come here, Alicia, on purpose to insult and wound me?"

"Not on purpose. But I certainly came to have it out with you."

She sat down, as if to contemplate the situation.

"Patience has limits. Jack, I warn you. It may seem to you easy as well as honourable to look out for a better match in society, and to throw me over if you succeed. Well, I don't think you will succeed. For you see, not many ladies, old or young, in society have got two thousand a year. And what have you got to offer them in exchange for their money, because they are not likely to give themselves away for nothing? If you haven't got fortune or family or brains, what have you got? Pretence—pretence of genius—sham and pretence. It's too thin, Jack. It won't stand washing. Besides, things will have to come out. Fancy your having to confess the little facts you have put away so carefully! Nobody in society cares where you come from so long as you can behave yourself and amuse people. All they want is to be amused; but when it comes to marrying, questions will be asked, my dear boy—will have to be answered, too. Don't look so savage, Jack. Your father wasn't much, was he? And mine wasn't in a very lofty social position, was he? And my poor dear old man made his business in the picture-dealing line, didn't he? But then, you see, I don't pretend."

"I suppose it is not a crime to desire social position," said the young man humbly. "I did not say I was trying to marry anybody. Can't I desire social position and success in my art?"

"Desire away, Jack; desire as much as you like. But how, meanwhile, I ask again, are you going to live? And how long do you think I shall let you play fast and loose with me? This kind of thing will not continue forever."

Jack murmured that he had no wish at all to play fast and loose with her.

"Look here, then," she said, "I will meet you half way. I will give you the rest of the summer. Have your fling; have your shy at an heiress.[1] The season is nearly over. I won't give you longer than the summer. Then you must come back to me for good or not at all."

---

1 Informally, a *shy* can mean an attempt.

Jack made no reply. I think, however, that in his heart he was grateful both for the length of the rope and the chance at the end of it.

"I know exactly what kind of life you desire. Your name sounds good, and you want to be thought of a good old family. You could hide the family shop, because the name wasn't over the door, and you lived at Stockwell.[2] You want to be thought a man of great refinement, and you want to be thought a genius."

"You can say what you like in these rooms, Alicia."

"I know I can. You also want all the solid comforts. As for them, I can give them to you: and some of the other things as well. You shall pretend to be a genius, if you like—I'm sure, I don't care what you pretend. I'll give you an allowance to keep up appearances with—as for its extent, that will depend on your behaviour—yes"—for Jack's face showed a disposition to be restive—"married women's property is their own nowadays, remember."

"Oh! keep your property."

"You shouldn't have made love to me, Jack, a year ago, unless you intended to hear the truth."

"You certainly make the most of your privilege."

"Oh! Jack, you have always been such a tremendous humbug. You were a humbug when you were a boy and used to brag about the great things you meant to do, and all the time the other boys walking past you easily. Then, you must become a gentleman, and must needs go to Cambridge and spend most of your little fortune there, pretending all the time that your father wasn't—"

"That is quite enough, Alicia!"

"Why, Jack, weren't the two shops side by side, your father's and mine? And didn't we go to church together? And didn't we go to the theatre together? And didn't you tell me everything? Why shouldn't we speak plain, you and me? When I married my poor dear old man, didn't I promise and vow that you and me should continue friends? You, a great man! You, a great genius! Oh no! But you can look the part, and that is something, isn't it? Good-bye, my dear boy. I don't like you so well as when you were a boy and made us laugh with your conceit, being always as conceited as Old Nick.[3] Come and have dinner with me to-night. I won't interfere with your heiress-hunting. Nobody but yourself, and a bottle of the poor old man's best claret. Good-bye, Jack. Dinner at half-past six sharp."

She lingered a moment and looked at the three portraits again. Then she burst into a loud laugh, natural, long, and hearty: "Don Juan! Conqueror of hearts! Oh! we poor women, how he makes our hearts bleed! I thought I knew the face. Why, I know them all three now. And, Jack, it is really too thin. Every picture dealer knows them. I've got 'em all at home. This one is a Frenchwoman, and sits in Paris. She's been Cleopatra and Ninon Longclothes, and anything else you please; and this is an Italian creature who's Venus coming out of the sea or a Nymph bathing—we've got her in both characters on the staircase wall. The Venus was put up at a hundred, but my old man never got his price. And the third sits for a Spanish girl, with a guitar, you know—which is stale business now—peeping behind a lattice or kneeling in church. Oh! Jack, Jack, what a terrible humbug you are!"

---

2 A middle-class suburb just outside London.

3 A colloquial name for the devil in Christian theology.

Chapter IX

Sam

There remained Sam.

After the embarrassments already twice caused by the introduction of the Duplicated Polly, Claude thought it would be best to explain beforehand. He did this, therefore, by letter, and invited her brother to meet the doubtful sister in his own chambers on the Sunday morning.

Sam accepted, but without enthusiasm. He already had one sister of whom he was ashamed, because she remained in poverty. Very likely the other would be just like her and an additional clog on his own respectability. Sam was one of that numerous tribe which dislikes the family clog. Claude, in his letter, spoke of the new sister as a young lady, but then the word Lady in these days of equality covers so wide an area. This is quite right, because why should a title so gracious and beautiful be limited to the House of Peers and the narrow class of Armigeri?[1]

Yet, everybody must not use it: it has still a distinctive meaning; it has a lower limit, except in the mind of the omnibus conductor, who employs it as a synonym for madame. Melenda, for instance, was below that limit. She could be properly described as a young girl, which is the general name for the workwoman in youth, but no one would think of calling her a young lady. One who is employed in a shop; one who has been called to the Inner Bar; one who is in the ballet; one who is in the front with the playbills, may be a young lady: but not a workgirl. Sam very naturally concluded that his other sister—the young lady—would be following such occupation, and he saw no reason for joy at the new addition to the family circle. But he was not unkind: it was only natural, after all, that Polly, on returning to the family circle, should wish to see the brother who had so greatly distinguished himself: the fame and rumour of his own rise had, no doubt, reached her wondering ears; a man's relations only really begin to rally round him when he has shown how strong and tough and brave

1 *Armigers* are those entitled to bear an official coat of arms but who are not of the nobility.

he is. Sam promised, therefore, to give up a portion of his Sunday morning to family affection. He kept that promise, and when he arrived in King's Bench Walk[2] he found the girls waiting for him.

He was not, however, prepared for the sight of two young ladies, the like of whom he had never before encountered, either for appearance, or for dress, or for manners. They do not make girls, at least not many girls, after this pattern in Haggerston,[3] where Sam's school is situated.

"One of these young ladies, Sam," said Claude, "is your sister, but, as I have already told you, we do not know which."

Sam looked from one to the other, reddening and confused. Their eyes did not say, "Is this the great and distinguished Sam?" Not at all: their expression conveyed another question, which he was quite sharp enough to read, namely, "What will Sam be like?" One after the other gave him her hand, which Sam accepted with a pump-handle movement, saying to each, "How de do?" just as if they had met after only a week's absence. Then he recovered, in some sort, the sense of himself and his own greatness, and he thought of the awe which he was doubtless inspiring, though the girls concealed it. Yet he was fain to mop his face with a pocket-handkerchief, and he said it was a hot morning, and in his agitation he dropped the aspirate,[4] about which he was sensitive, because his own was the only aspirate to be found in all Haggerston except in church, and he mopped his face again. Then he found a chair and sat down. In this position he immediately rallied and stuck his thumbs into his waistcoat armholes. This is not the most graceful attitude possible for a man, but it suited Sam better than some others would have done. He could not, for instance, stand, like Claude, with no support or background; nor could he lean gracefully over a mantelshelf. He wanted an attitude which should convey a sense of strength and of complete self-satisfaction.

"You don't know which is Polly, Claude?" he asked, looking from one to the other as if they had been a pair of lay figures.[5] "Well, I'm sure I can't remember. Never mind, my dears," he added, with a reassuring nod, "I'll call you both my sisters." Claude had used almost the same words, but somehow the effect produced was different. Violet turned away her eyes and Valentine gravely inclined her head.

Sam, as regards the outer man, which people insist on taking in evidence as regards the unseen soul, was stout and strongly built, with square shoulders. He was under the middle height, and his legs, if one must speak the truth, were short and curly. This is considered to be a sign of strength, though it is the line of beauty in the wrong place. His face as well as his legs showed strength; his forehead was broad and square; his sharp eyes were set back under thick red eyebrows; his coarse red hair rose from his forehead like a cliff; his nose, if short, was also broad; his mouth was firm, and his chin square. Never was there a stronger or more determined-looking young man. Never, certainly, if attitude and expression go for anything, was a young man more self-sufficient.

"You heard, of course," he said, amiably, "how your brother had got on in the world, and then you naturally wanted to see him. Well, here I am. Only don't look to me for a shove up. Everybody for himself, I say."

"We will not ask anyone for a 'shove up,'" said Violet, "even though we do belong to the poor."

---

2 King's Bench Walk is one of the buildings of the Inner Temple reserved for barrister chambers.

3 Haggerston is part of the Hackney borough.

4 In this case, the *h* pronounced through exhalation at the beginning of a word. Because residents of the East End typically dropped the *h*, pronouncing the aspirate was often seen as a sign of respectability.

5 An artist's wooden mannequin.

"The poor?" Sam started in his chair and turned red. "What do you mean by the poor? You belong to the working class, not the poor. The poor? Why, you are the great backbone of the country."

"Am I?" Violet replied. "Then if all the country has to depend upon—"

"The mainstay and support of the nation," Sam continued. "Don't let me hear you call the working class the poor again. One would think you came out of the Union."[6]

I am told that people in very high place are positively ignorant of rank in the middle class, and actually regard the general practitioner's lady as of no higher position than the wife of the leading draper, and the vicar's young ladies as occupying the same level as the auctioneer's daughters. In the same way it is difficult to understand that there is rank and position among working-people; so that before one gets to the poor, properly so called, one has to go very far down. They are, in fact, like the rich who continually recede the more one advances, so that one begins to suspect that there are no rich left in this realm of England.

"Very likely I did come out of the Union," Violet replied, desperately. Was there no graciousness among the Monument family? "Why should we not come out of the Union?"

"As for that," Sam continued, "I suppose you know nothing about your own family. I always said it was folly letting a girl be brought up by her natural enemies."

"Why," asked Valentine, "why her natural enemies?"

"Of course, you know nothing. Who are the enemies of the working-man unless it's the people who live upon him? Answer me that. What have your friends done for their living—eh? Answer me that." He became suddenly quite fierce, and looked exactly like Melenda. His eyes glowed like hers, and he turned upon Valentine almost wrathfully. "Of course you've been taught to look down upon the working classes and call them the poor, and that you must be good to the poor. Why, look at the way you're dressed! Should a decent working-man's sister go about with gold chains and silk frocks and kid gloves?"

"You see, Val," said Violet to Valentine, "Joe told us the same thing. We shall both have to dress like Melenda."

"Joe isn't a fool," said Sam, "though he's ignorant."

"Pray tell us all the faults you have to find with us," said Valentine. "If we know what they are, we may correct them. We have certainly been taught kindness to poor people, and we have not been taught to despise working-men. But go on."

"I don't want to find fault with you," Sam replied, more gently, "only for luxury and laziness and living on other people's labour."

"You read about the luxury and laziness in your papers, my brother," said Claude. He had been standing in the window looking on without remark. "Always verify your facts, Sam. I am sure you will not object to that rule. Ask them what they have learned. You will find that their record of work is as good, perhaps, as your own."

"Yes, I know: learning to play music and to read French and paint and make pretty things and to dress up fine. Well, I don't say it is your faults. You can't help it. I hear you've been to see my mother, and you've set her back up; and you've seen Joe, and he wants to know what it means, and what you're going to do—whichever of you it is—for a living when her ladyship is tired of you. And you've seen Melenda, and she flew out, being driven most out of her wits by hard work and being always hungry. And now you've seen me."

6 The Union Workhouse.

"Yes," said Violet. This young lady really could convey more meaning in a single word than others can in fifty. "Yes."

Claude's eyes brightened and Valentine looked anxious. But Sam observed nothing. Half tones were in fact lost upon him.

"Yes, now you've seen me. All the rest of them are proud of me, and I'm proud of myself."

"I dare say," said Valentine, because Violet smiled, which might be considered an aggressive movement. "I dare say we shall be proud of you as we are of Claude when we know you."

"Of Claude?" Sam snorted, and drew his feet under his chair. "As proud as you are of Claude? Why, do you know what I am?" He swelled out his chest and squared his elbows. "Do you know what I am? I'm the master of a board school. Do you know what that means?"

"Sam has every reason to be proud," said Claude. "When he was only a boy he resolved on making himself a master in a school, and he has done it. He taught himself mostly; I have been taught."

Sam then proceeded to give a short sketch of his own progress, showing how he had scaled Alps, levelled great rocks, crossed mighty floods, in his single-handed struggle. The story lost nothing by being told by the hero. Few stories do, which you may prove by referring to the pages of any contemporary biography. "And for the future," he concluded, "remember that you will have to deal with the schoolmaster. The working-men are the masters of the country, and we are the masters of the working-men. They are looking to us already. We are going to be their leaders."

"The House of Commons," said Claude, "will shortly be composed entirely of elementary schoolmasters."

"As soon as members are paid," Sam replied, "there will be a good many. And the more the better. The time has come when you must have men in the House who know something—not Latin and Greek, mind, but something useful. What geography do they know, now? Nothing at all. With English possessions and colonies all over the world, the members know nothing of geography. There isn't a sixth standard[7] boy who wouldn't be ashamed of the way they talk and the blunders they make. What do they know about trade and manufactures? Nothing. What do they know about the working-man? Nothing. As for us, we do know him."

"Do you influence him much?" asked Violet, innocently, so that I do not know what it was that made Valentine look alarmed.

"Not so much as we would. They won't let us teach him the truth at school. The code[8] won't let—they know very well why. We've got to waste the time teaching him things that will never be any use to him, such as spelling. What's the good of spelling to a man who never writes? And if you do write, what's the odds to a working-man whether he spells right or wrong? But we must not teach the rights of humanity. We mustn't tell the boys anything about them. It would be difficult to examine for a grant in the rights of man, wouldn't it? and dangerous for some of the Committee of Council.[9] But we know what the working-men want and what they mean to have."

"Tell us what do they mean to have," said Valentine.

---

7 The final level of elementary education that children usually reach at the age of twelve.

8 The book of regulations by the Ministry of Education.

9 The Committee of Council on Education is a division of the Ministry of Education.

"What's the use?" It was curious to mark how Sam's rugged face leaped suddenly into rage and even ferocity, and then as suddenly dropped into gentleness. He was quite gentle now, as he answered, looking with a sort of pity upon a creature so beautiful, so dainty, and so unfit for the stern realities of life.

"What's the use?" he said. "You are a young lady now and you belong to our enemies. What's the use of frightening you? Go home and enjoy yourself and eat and drink."

"But tell us," she persisted.

"I think we had better go home—and eat and drink," said Violet.

"Sam thinks his own opinions are those of all the working-men," said Claude. "It is not unusual when people think strongly. Tell them your opinions, Sam."

"They are not my opinions only," said Sam; "don't think it. Well, if you ain't afraid, I am going to tell you just exactly what we mean to do—I and my friends—with you and your friends. You don't know and you don't suspect: it's just the same ignorance that was in France before the Revolution. One or two suspected what was coming, but most thought everything was going on for ever just the same. Very well. Don't you girls go away and say afterwards that you were left in ignorance. Go home and tell your friends that the working-men of this country are going to have a republic at last; not what your friends think and call a republic, but the real thing. In a real republic every man must be equal, so we shall of course abolish the Lords[10] and all titles and privileged classes. As for the land, it belongs to the people; so we shall take the land and it shall be cultivated for the nation. And if anybody wants to be a priest, he may if he likes, after his day's work; for of course we shall disestablish the Church and take over church property of all the churches for the good of the State. There shall be in our republic no lazy parsons and ministers living on the people; and there shall be no lawyers, because there will be free justice, and every man may have his case heard for nothing by a jury, and juries will sit every day if they are wanted. There will be no masters, employers, or capitalists, but equal wages for all and the same hours of work, with extra rations for those who have got children to support. There will be free education; there will be no idlers; everybody will be a working-man. We shall take over all the railways, abolish the National Debt and the local debts. There will be no tradesmen, because the state—that is, the people—will keep the stores and distribute food and clothing. There will be no rates or taxes, because there will be no money, and labour will be the only coin, and everybody will pay his share by his own labour. There will be annual parliaments sitting every day all the year round, and nobody allowed to speak for more than five minutes. There will be, of course, manhood suffrage."

"Will women vote?" asked Violet.

"Certainly not," Sam replied, with decision. "Women can't govern. Besides, they can't be trusted to work for the public good: they would want private property restored, and they'd set up a Church and try to fix things so that their own sons should have nothing to do. Women haven't got any sense of justice."

"Delightful," said Violet. "I was afraid I might be called upon to assist in governing."

"Pray go on," said Valentine.

"There will be plenty for all and no luxury. There will be no saving money, because there will be no money to save, and everybody will have to work, whether he likes it or not, until he is sixty, and then he will be maintained by the state. All buying and selling will be in the hands of the state. The great houses will be turned

10 A reference to the House of Lords, the upper chamber of the United Kingdom's parliament, which many saw as antithetical to democracy because membership was by hereditary right or royal prerogative.

into museums; the private parks will be either cultivated or turned into public gardens. Now, do you begin to understand?"

"I think I do," said Valentine. "When is all this to be begun?"

"I don't know. Perhaps in a year or two—perhaps in ten years. We are educating the people. We shall try to keep back those who want to act at once until everybody has been taught our principles."

"Sam is a Socialist," Claude explained. "I ought to have told you that before you came."

"Why, listen to this." Sam was thoroughly roused by this time. "Here are facts for you. Claude can't deny this." He sprang to his feet and stood over Valentine with flaming eyes, breathing like a bull, and hammering his facts into the palm of his left hand with the most determined forefinger ever seen, "Look at this ..." Here followed an avalanche of facts. "What, I say, have the capitalist and the landlord done that they should get seventy per cent, of the working-man's harvest? When our men are in they will get the whole for themselves. Talk of compensation! Do you compensate a pickpocket when you take the purse out of his hands? Vested rights?[11] Rights of robbery. We shall take all—land, houses, wealth, and all—and we shall give them to the people, to whom they belong."

By this time the indignation of the prophet had touched his lips with fire, and he went on to arraign the class of those who have great possessions with extraordinary vehemence and passion, and prophesied their overthrow, like another Ezekiel.[12] Violet looked on and wondered, thinking how very much he resembled Melenda. Valentine looked on and wondered, because up to that time she had only heard vaguely of the extreme wickedness of the wealthy class, and because she could not understand at all how they were so wicked, or why they were going to be so dreadfully punished, or what this new world of the Socialist would be like. She was reassured by the attitude of Claude, who still stood at the window gravely listening, but without the least assent in his face or emotion in his grave eyes.

"And now you know," Sam concluded, "something of what is coming, not in this country only, but everywhere. Oh! yes: in the United States, which they pretend to be a land of freedom, and it's a worse country for the working-man than this, even. Perhaps it will come there first; and in France, which they pretend to be a republic—a fine republic!—and in Germany and Prussia, where they don't pretend to anything but despotism, kept up with millions of bayonets for the luxury of the privileged class. Then there shall be no more riches and no more poverty, no more rich and no more poor, no more luxury and no more starvation. If you are wise you will come over to us at once." He seized Valentine's hand and held it tightly. "Come out of it, I say, before the house falls down about your ears. Some declare that it is going to be a bloodless revolution, but I know better. There is too much to lose—money and rank and state and the easy life. Oh! yes—the easy life. They won't give these things up without a fight; they will fight to the death to defend their possessions. They will have all the shopkeepers and the merchants and the professional people on their side, and at first they will have the soldiers. It will be the working-man against the world. It will be a great and terrible struggle. There can be no revolution—it isn't in the nature of things—without fighting and rivers of blood. Come over to us, you two. I don't care which of you is my sister; you may both call yourselves Polly if you like, and I'll stand by you both. But leave Claude and leave your friends and come over to us."

"How shall we live if we do?" asked Valentine.

---

11 Established and secured rights, often of property.

12 Ezekiel prophesied the destruction of Jerusalem and the eventual restoration of a greater Israel.

"We will find something for you. Not button-holes to sew, like Melenda's work, but something that a decent girl can do. You've been educated, I suppose, in your finicking way. You know something besides looking pretty and putting on fine clothes. Perhaps it's not too late for board school teaching if you're clever enough. You are the one for school work"—he indicated Valentine; "you wouldn't be afraid, and you are strong. As for you—"

"What could I do?" asked Violet.

"I don't know. You don't look fit for much. Well, every girl can sew if you come to the worst. But there; you've heard what is coming—the greatest revolution that the world has ever seen, and the people to the front with a rush. When that rush begins—"

"A good many will be carried off their legs," said Claude.

Sam made no reply. He had worked himself up to the redhot pitch and was now cooling down. He was a little ashamed, too, because Claude remained unmoved. As for the girls, he had certainly succeeded in animating one with his dream of the people, and frightening the other by his vehemence. But he cared nothing for that—anybody can work upon the emotions of women. But Claude, who ought to have argued with him or confessed himself conquered, listened without the least sign of being moved. Yet he listened with attention, as if he had not heard it all a dozen times before. He could not complain that he had not heard the Socialist's arguments.

Sam went away. The courts of the Temple were deserted. He thought of the coming millennium, when there should be no lawyers at all, but justice should be free. As these courts were on that Sunday morning, so should they be every morning, in the glorious future of the Socialist, empty and untrodden, except by the feet of the children playing in their gardens. No more lawyers! He had no personal experience of lawyers, but yet his heart glowed within him at the prospect of their suppression. He passed under the cloisters beside the old church. Through the open doors he heard the rolling of the organ and the sweet pure voice of a boy who was singing a solo part in an anthem of prayer and praise. The very sweetness of the music irritated him, but he consoled himself with the thought that religion would shortly be entirely abolished, and that the sensitive ears of such thinkers as himself should no longer be annoyed with the singing of hymns. The Templars' church[13] would be as empty and as deserted as the chambers and courts without. He passed into Fleet Street. All the shops were closed. Why, so it should be every morning and all the year round as soon as his friends were in power. Not a single shop should be left. No more trade, no more masters, no more buying and selling for profit. So, well satisfied with the prospect, Sam went his way.

In the evening there was to be a great social gathering of a certain branch of the Democratic Federation Union,[14] at which some of the members were going to perform a play, and others were to sing and recite, and he himself was to address the meeting. It was going to be an occasion of some importance, and Sam was only sorry that he had not invited the two girls to be present. The evening would have opened their eyes. And though Sam professed to despise women, and was in no hurry to hamper himself by marriage, he did very well understand that the adhesion of two such pretty and well-dressed girls to the Cause, which is at present sadly to seek in the matter of young ladies, would greatly stimulate waverers and bring enthusiasm into the ranks. There is no leader in the world like a girl, if one can be found capable and courageous; but such a girl is rare.

"You have heard Sam's creed," said Claude; "he believes it, every word."

13 The Temple Church is a large church originally built for the Knights Templar in the twelfth century.

14 The Social Democratic Federation was Britain's first socialist party.

"After all," said Violet, "I can sew. Girls can do so much."

"And I," said Valentine, "can teach after my finicking education. But, Claude, a world with no poverty and no suffering—"

"Come," said Violet, "you must not even talk of it, Val dear, or we shall have you going over to the Socialists. Let us remain with our natural enemies, and eat and drink as much as we possibly can before we are drowned in Sam's rivers of blood. Claude, you will come to luncheon with us, won't you?" She heaved a deep sigh, which expressed some hidden emotion. "We have now seen Sam. He lives a long way off, does he not? We shall see him again, perhaps, when he is President of the Socialist Republic, and chopping off everybody's head with tremendous energy."

Chapter x

The Great Renunciation

Blessed above their fellows are those who can find relief for an overcharged mind by drawing—I do not mean the sweet copying of flower, fern, and tall grass, but the drawing of faces, heads, and figures, so that in times of oppression and affliction one can caricature one's enemy by representing him as a fool, an ass, a beast, a fox, or a serpent. This is the reason why the London School Board has thoughtfully introduced drawing into the schools, so that workgirls shall be enabled, in their afterlife, to find some relief and consolation. In the rare times of joy, in the same way, the multiplication of one's friends' portraits increases one's delight, and in times of doubt one can prevent the subject from harassing the mind by drawing likenesses of the personages concerned. Thus, it was highly disagreeable to Violet to think of Joe, with his grimy hands and smeared face and working-man's garb, as perhaps her brother. It was equally disagreeable for her to think that he was perhaps Valentine's brother. She drew him, therefore, in various positions, all more or less ridiculous, but especially that when he sat upon the table and grinned. This greatly relieved her soul. In the same way Sam, who was to her a much more objectionable character, lost half his terrors when she had drawn him triumphantly seated in the revolutionary car of Juggernaut,[1] or flourishing with zeal an executioner's axe, or calmly cutting off heads so as to make everybody the same size. But she could not draw Melenda. There are limits even to this artistic method of consolation.

Valentine had no such relief. Like Saul in his trouble, she turned to music for consolation, but found little.[2] Joe and Rhoda and the blind old lady and Sam were nothing. As connections they were not, it is true, gentlefolk, but they were such as anyone might possess without either shame or pride. Nobody in these days really thinks—though they may pretend—any the better or any the worse of a man for having brothers and cousins

1 In a Hindu ceremony for the divine incarnation of Jagannatha, an enormous cart is drawn through town and crushes whatever is laid before it.

2 In the Book of Samuel, King Saul is troubled by an evil spirit and requests a song played to soothe him.

who are carpenters or counts, baronets or bakers, Comtists[3] or Baptists, Socialists or Red Republicans,[4] Mormons or Methodists, because a man can no longer, as in the good old days, acquire fame or notoriety or disgrace by professing any trade or holding any form of belief whatever, unless, indeed, one were to go round with detonators and boxes of whitish paste, and profess himself a practical dynamiter. Sam was a very possible brother, and interesting in his self-sufficiency, his conceit, and his extreme views of politics. But besides Sam and Joe, there was Melenda. For nearly a week Valentine went about with a grisly spectre always before her eyes—the spectre of the workgirl, half-starved, overworked, resigned, in a rage, uncomplaining. When Sam proclaimed his gospel of universal plenty, she thought of the happy change it would work for Melenda and her friends; when she sat at dinner she thought of Melenda's cold tea with bread-and-butter; when she went to her own chamber at night, she saw before her those three girls crouching together on their miserable bed in the wretched room; always day and night there was present in her mind that little group of sewing girls; always the hollow eyes of one gazed reproachfully at her from the bed, saying, "Why will you still torment me so? What have I done?" and the large heavy eyes of the other raised in wonder that all women were not as she herself, the uncared-for slave of manufacturers, born to be expended in toil; and the fierce eyes of the third girl asking her how she dared in the insolence of her own luxury and happiness to mock the misery of her sister.

And then she made up a scheme. No one but Violet knew of it, and when Valentine opened up the subject she first laughed at it and then cried over it. Gautama himself did not devise a more complete thing, so far as it went. No self-tormentor in Egyptian Laura or Syrian desert or Galilean cave ever proposed for himself a thing of greater discomfort. [5]

And then she told Claude.

"It is impossible," he said at once, without the least hesitation. Every really great scheme is always declared impossible until it has been carried out, when it is perceived to have been a perfectly easy thing, and nothing to brag about. Anybody might have done it.

"Oh, Claude!" her face fell; "and I looked forward so confidently to your help."

"Let us find some other way for you."

"There can be no other way. Don't you see, Claude? There is my own sister—my sister and yours. Think how she is living; think of her miserable days. I must go and stay with her. I must help her. I daresay she will try to drive me away. Very well. I will not be driven away."

"But it is impossible, Valentine. You don't know what it is you propose to do."

The difficulties were in fact enormous. But many enormous difficulties, when faced, turn out to be like the lions which faced Christian with angry roar, and so much terrified that greatly tried pilgrim.[6] The lions are chained, and can do no harm. Or they turn out to be mere goblins, like those gruesome and shapeless and

---

3 Comtists followed Auguste Comte, the French philosopher who founded Positivism and attempted to introduce a secular religion devoted to humanity.

4 Red Republicans were members of a French political party that many of Besant's contemporaries saw as being more radical than they were socialist.

5 Siddhārtha Gautama, also known as the Buddha, gave up his life as a prince and practiced asceticism before determining that moderation was the way to enlightenment. Monks occupying *lauras*, isolated cells for seclusion in Egypt and Jordan, or caves rejected worldly pleasures just as the Buddha did during his ascetic phase.

6 A reference to the principal character in John Bunyan's *The Pilgrim's Progress*, an allegory about the trials and temptations a Christian faces on the road to salvation, including lions and goblins that attempt to scare him from his path.

nameless things which whispered horrible suggestions into the pilgrim's ear when he was nervously staggering along that valley.

"It is quite impossible, Valentine," Claude repeated. "It would kill you. Their life is not yours."

"I will make it mine. Oh, Claude! I thought I should have had your sympathy at least."

The tears stood in her eyes. All night long she had been lying awake filled and possessed by the thought. In the morning it only showed fairer and more beautiful than in the night.

"They are my own people, Claude."

"I do not know that. Besides, how are you to live among them? Will you stay with my brother Joe? or with my mother? or with Sam?"

"Neither. I intend to live with Melenda, or at least as close to her as can be managed. Where she lives I can live."

"But you have seen that Melenda lives in the very poorest way possible. Why, from a single visit it is impossible even to realise how poor and squalid is her life. Things that she does not mind at all would be simply intolerable to you."

"No, Claude. Whatever Melenda endures I can endure."

Claude shook his head.

"And then the place, and the people, and the language, and the drunkenness—oh, Valentine, it is quite—quite impossible."

"Think less of the difficulties and more of what I could do for our sister, Claude—she is our sister, you know—if I went and lived with her. Sit down and think about that. Think a little, Claude."

Claude sat down to think, and Valentine had recourse to white witchcraft.[7]

Every woman—fortunately very few women fully realise this great truth—can do with every man whatever she pleases, provided, first, that she is young and beautiful; next, that the man is a man of imagination and possessed of a right feeling for the sex; and thirdly, that she has the mastery over some musical instrument. All these conditions were satisfied in the case of Claude and Valentine.

Then Valentine began to play. First she played a solemn march with full strong chords—a march full of hope and high resolve—and she watched Claude furtively. Presently the music entered into his soul, and he was fain to rise and to walk about the room. When his step quickened and his eye brightened she changed the music, and began to play one of those songs which need no words, because, when they are played, the thoughts rise naturally to the level of the song and flow rhythmically, and great ideas take form and shape. And still she watched him. Then she changed the air again and played a simple Scotch ditty, one of those which go straight to the heart, because they came originally from the heart. When she saw that his eyes were soft and his gaze was far away, she paused abruptly in her playing, and he started.

"I will help you," he said, "if I can. I do not know what you will do for Melenda, but you shall try. At all events, you will do something for yourself."

"That is nothing. I must think of those girls, not of myself."

"But—Lady Mildred?"

"Let us get everything quite ready first, and then we will go to her with our plan complete and waiting for nothing but her consent. I think she will consent."

---

7 White witchcraft, as opposed to black witchcraft, is generally perceived to be beneficial magic.

Every scheme, even the noblest, requires machinery and service. Every drama wants to be properly rehearsed and duly mounted. The mounting of the little comedy designed by Valentine was carried out by Claude. It took him two or three days. First he went to Ivy Lane, and there, unknown to Melenda, who was sitting at work upstairs, he ascertained certain facts connected with the lodgers in the house. The ground-floor front was occupied by an elderly gentleman of unknown calling, who was reported to be perfectly quiet and harmless though dreadfully poor. The ground-floor back was inhabited by an old lady who herself assured Claude of her perfect respectability and unblemished character. If a woman's word is not to be taken for so much, for what can it be taken? As regards her profession, she got occasional employment in the funeral furnishing line. One would not, perhaps, choose this line, but it is necessary to live. Her practice, this lady further explained, in evidence and support of her great respectability, was to "go in" when the winter approached and to "come out" for the summer. In this euphemistic manner do some ladies speak of the Union. She was not by any means a nice-looking lady, and she looked as if perhaps some portions of her life had not been spent in honest industry. She also confessed, and denied not, that there were times when the possession of a little money tempted her to take a glass; but these occasions, she said truthfully, were rare, because she seldom got the money.

The back room upstairs, behind Melenda's, was occupied by a middle-aged single woman, a machinist who made trousers all day long with the help of a sewing machine, and was in even direr straits than Melenda. She accepted a bribe of five shillings and the week's rent and vacated the room, which Claude proceeded to get thoroughly washed, scoured, scrubbed, and repaired. Then he put furniture in it, and that of a kind which made the collector believe that a district visitor at least was coming to live in Ivy Lane. All this he did without the least knowledge or suspicion of Melenda.

When everything was quite ready, Valentine laid her plan before Lady Mildred. With what eloquence she pleaded her cause, with what tears and entreaties, it needs not to relate. These may be understood.

"Let me go, dear," she concluded. "Oh, let me go. I have no rest for thinking of those girls—one of them my own sister. Let me go and live with them for a little while. I am not afraid of anything that may happen to me. I shall be quite safe among them."

Lady Mildred showed no surprise; nobody is ever surprised in these latter days at any course which is proposed by daughters. She listened patiently, and bade her wait a day for her reply.

Now whenever Lady Mildred had quite made up her mind about the course she would adopt, she invariably went through the formality of consulting her friend, Miss Bertha Colquhoun. In no single case did she ever adopt that friend's advice, which was always contrary to her own opinion. Taking counsel with your friends, in fact, generally means getting an opportunity of putting your opinion into words, and of seeing how it looks. Much the same may be said as regards argument.

"Of course I knew very well," she said, "that something would happen when I brought Claude to the house and allowed the girls to visit his relations. I confess, however, that I am a little startled to find them so differently affected; for Violet is as much repelled by the poverty of the workgirls as Valentine is attracted."

"But of course, Mildred, even you will not actually suffer Valentine to go and live alone among them?"

"I do not know. Why not?"

"Alone, Mildred? Alone, and among those common people? Your own daughter—well, perhaps your own daughter—brought up as Valentine has been—would you suffer her to run the dreadful and terrible risks of such a thing?"

"What are the terrible risks?"

"Violence—insult—robbery—everything."

"No; I do not fear these at all. The principal risk is that of learning that the world is really a very wicked place. The new theory about woman's education, that she should not be kept in ignorance of evil any more than the boys, has a good deal to be said for it. Valentine will discover among these people that the world, which has always seemed to her so beautiful and so virtuous, is really full of dark places and injustice."

"Is that good for a girl to learn?"

"Why not, since it is the truth? Will Valentine be made wicked by the discovery of wickedness? I do not think so."

"And Violet? Is she to go with her sister?"

"Violet is of less courageous mould. She will remain with me, and we shall go away together somewhere—to Switzerland or the seaside."

"You would surely not go away and leave that poor girl alone and unprotected in the awful place she is going to?"

"Yes. But she will not be quite alone; there is that sewing-girl—perhaps her sister. Working-men do not generally insult respectable girls, I have learned, though they are thoughtless about them. I think she will be quite safe with her supposed sister."

"Well, Mildred, I do not see that any possible good can come of it."

"Suppose," she replied, "a girl were to learn and understand, in this or some other way, some of the worst wrongs that are inflicted on women in this city—wrongs that can only be realised by actually sharing them or witnessing them day after day; and suppose that she is a brave girl and clear-headed, as well as sound of heart—think, then, what this girl might become and what she might do in after life. My dear Bertha, think of the things you have yourself read and cried over, but never really understood—I mean the ill-treatment and oppression of workgirls. Do you suppose that women could be treated so if we made up our minds that they should not? We cannot believe that the 'Song of the Shirt' would have any meaning left at all except an ugly memory, if the women of this country once resolved that it should not. It is forty years and more since Hood wrote that song, and word for word, tear for tear, I am sure that it might be written and sung again this very day. Valentine shall learn for herself. Let her go, and let her—if it must be—suffer."

In the morning she gave judgment. There were present at this family council, besides the petitioner and Claude, Violet and Bertha. Everybody, except Lady Mildred herself, looked, for some reason or other, guilty. Bertha, because she had not risen to the level of the situation, and still looked on the step proposed as impossible for a gentlewoman; Violet, because she was ashamed of herself and her own shrinking from the life which Valentine proposed to share; Claude, because he had made all the arrangements beforehand, as if it was quite certain that consent would be obtained, and yet had made them secretly; and Valentine, because she was afraid she might be refused.

"My child," said Lady Mildred, taking both her hands, "you have thought seriously and calmly over this scheme of yours? Have you fully considered what it may mean?—that, for instance, it will colour your whole life, and perhaps sadden it; that you go alone among people of whom you know nothing but that they are rude and coarse?"

"Oh, yes," said Valentine, "I have thought of that. Claude has told me everything that will happen to me. But I feel as if I must do it."

"I shall not deny you, Valentine." Then she turned to Violet. "And you, my child?"

"No," said Violet, "I *could* not do it. I am ashamed of myself. I am a coward, if you please, but I *could* not do it." She was about to assign as the reason of her dreadful cowardice her own identity with Polly and her close connection with the Monument family, but she refrained. "Valentine sees beautiful things where I see nothing but rude manners and coarse speeches. I could not go to live among those people even if Valentine were beside me. And alone!" she shuddered.

"You shall not be asked, my dear."

"Perhaps it will not be so dreadful as it seems to us," said Valentine. "I have repeated it over and over again to myself. Instead of a beautiful home like this, a single room in a row of dingy houses; instead of the open park, a great nest of mean streets; noise instead of quiet; in place of your kind voices, there will be quarrels of women, cries of children, and bad language of men; in the place of this sweet home—" Here her voice failed her, and the tears came into her eyes, and Violet kissed her with tears of her own.

"As for your going alone," said Lady Mildred, "of course the world would disapprove, but then we need not consider much what the world may say. An Eastern lady, I believe, estimates her importance by the care taken in guarding her. We all come from the East, which accounts for a lingering of the feeling among ourselves. If we do not guard you, my Valentine, the world will say that we do not care for you."

"But I shall not say so."

"Tell us, then, exactly, what arrangements you propose to make."

Claude explained that there was a room—not a large room nor a very pretty room, but a place weatherproof—on the first floor and at the back of Melenda's room; that he had persuaded the tenant to give up this room to himself; that he had caused it to be cleaned, scrubbed, whitewashed and fumigated; that he had furnished it; and that Valentine could take possession when she pleased.

"And all before I was consulted at all?" said Lady Mildred.

Claude blushed, but did not explain that Valentine had converted him to her view, and that he had done her bidding.

"But who is to do up your room every day?" asked Violet.

Claude had no proposition to make on this important subject. But Valentine confessed, with a blush and a sigh, because this was a detail less attractive than some others in her scheme, that she would probably have to do it for herself.

"Yourself?" said Violet; "why, there are a thousand things that have to be done. Who will cook your dinner and make your breakfasts and everything?"

"I suppose I must do all this for myself. Melenda does."

"Melenda dines off cold tea and bread. She threw the fact at our heads, and reproached us with living on beef and mutton, and eating more than is good for us—you remember, dear?"

"I do not think I can live on tea and bread," said Valentine; "but I shall live as simply as I can. And I do not in the least mind boiling a kettle for myself."

"She will come back," said Violet, "with her hands as hard as a housemaid's."

"Then there are the evenings. What will you do in the evenings?"

"The days are long now. Besides, there is Melenda to cultivate."

"Yes," said Violet.

"I will not deny you, my child," said Lady Mildred. "You shall have the desire of your heart. But it must be on one or two conditions."

"Any conditions."

"Then, first of all, you will persist in the scheme for three months, even if you are lonely and unhappy, even if Melenda turns out more obdurate than you expected, and the life and companionship are far more disagreeable than you ever anticipated. You must not give it up unless you fall ill."

"I accept that condition willingly," said Valentine. "Whether I like it or whether I do not, I will stay there for three months."

"The next is that you will be completely separated from Violet and myself. We shall go quite out of your way somewhere—I do not know yet where—and stay out of your way all the summer. You will see nothing of us until next October. You will have no letters from us, nor will you write to us. That will be very hard for us, my dear, will it not?"

"It will be very hard for me, and yet I accept."

"The next condition refers to Claude. It is that he consents to remain in London all the summer, and that he sees you as often as possible—every day if he can—so that if you fall into any trouble you may always feel that you have someone at hand."

"That is a condition," said Claude, "which I willingly accept."

"He has already promised it," said Valentine.

"Then you must promise, next, that you will not try to live like these poor workgirls. Cold tea and dry bread is bad for them, but it would be far worse for you. You will live on something more substantial."

"That is a very easy condition. I am sure I do not want to live on tea and bread."

"I have no more conditions to make, my dear. But remember that it is useless to take things which one cannot mend too much to heart. And do not give away money to people; and do not believe everybody's story; and do not entangle yourself with too many friendships."

"I will try not to make too many friends," said Valentine.

"And do not give people credit for every virtue simply because they are poor and live in a single room. I dare say some of the minor vices may be found even in this Arcadia[8] of yours, my dear."

"Only untidiness at worst," said Violet sarcastically; "there cannot possibly be anything more in Ivy Lane."

"Then," said Lady Mildred, "when will you go, my dear?"

"Let me go this very day, lest I get frightened and repent in the night."

Violet went with her to her own room, where she changed her dress and put on a plain frock of brown stuff made up for the purpose, a simple hat without feathers or ornaments, a grey ulster, and a pair of Swedish kid gloves.

"Oh, Val," Violet laughed, but the tears were in her eyes, "you are as much like a London workgirl as a village maid in a comic operetta is like the real rustic. But never mind, my dear, you look as beautiful as the day and as good as any angel, and how, oh, how in the world shall I get on without you?"

Then, together, they packed a box with things absolutely necessary, and a few books, and all was ready.

8 Used ironically here, *Arcadia* is a common term for an idyllic and uncorrupted world.

"You can't be going!" cried Violet, clinging to her. "Oh, my dear, my dear, it is always you who think and say the best and noblest things. It is because you are Beatrice and I am only Polly, and she is selfish and cannot tear herself from her luxurious life. But you will be the happier of the two. I shall think of you and be ashamed of myself every day that you are gone. If we were really sisters I think I could do what you are doing. But I am only—"

"No, Violet, I am Polly, and the proof is that I am constrained by an irresistible force to go among my own people. Do you think I shall make them love me?"

"Oh, Valentine, can they help it? You will change them all. Sam, after a little of your society, will cease to yearn for his rivers of blood, and Joe will leave off grinning, and Melenda will become as gentle as a turtle-dove."

Book II

Chapter I

"I Am Your Sister"

It was done, then. Valentine sat alone in her hermitage—a single room on the first floor of a tenement house in Ivy Lane, Hoxton. She was in the middle of the great town, but she was as lonely and as far from the world as if it had been the Hermitage on the Coquet River or a cave beside the Brook Cherith.[1] She also realised with wonder how rapidly the greatest events in the world get themselves accomplished. Only two or three hours before she was torn with doubts as to whether this thing would ever be permitted, and lo! it was already done—that is to say, it was begun, because nothing in this human world ever gets itself finished.

Claude carried her box with brotherly care up the steep and narrow stair, and then looked around expectant, as the railway porter lingereth about the door of the cab. He waited, like the railway porter, for his tip, the meed of praise because he had taken no small pains,

"Tell me," he said, "tell me, Valentine, what you think of it."

"It is very small. But then I am not very big. And you have made it look pretty. I expected nothing half so pretty as this. Thank you, Claude."

"I remembered, first, a certain room in Newnham which I once saw. It was not much larger than this, and it was very daintily furnished. I hope the girl it belonged to was pretty, and that she got her first class.[2] Cleverness, you know, and beauty, and taste ought always to go together. Next I read a certain chapter about Hermits in 'Hypatia.'[3] After that, I recalled the fittings of a cabin in a little yacht wherein I sailed last year. And then I read a few chapters of 'Robinson Crusoe' and of 'Philip Quarles.'[4] This carried me a long way, and then

---

1 The Warkworth Hermitage was once a secluded chapel for monks only accessible by boat and abandoned centuries before Besant's writing. The brook named Cherith is mentioned in the book of 1 Kings in the Bible as a secluded hiding place for the prophet Elijah during an extended drought.

2 First-class honors are the highest level of academic achievement available to an undergraduate.

3 A figure of classical antiquity, Hypatia was an Egyptian mathematician and philosopher.

4 Like Robinson Crusoe, Philip Quarles was lost on a deserted island.

with just a page or two of Xavier de Maistre[5] and the help of a book on aesthetic furniture, and one visit to an artistic upholsterer, I managed to furnish your room for you. This is the result."

They were both extremely grave and serious, because, now that the thing was begun, it looked horribly beset with perils of all kinds. Perhaps this was the reason why Claude talked with a certain show of frivolity.

"Thank you, Claude." I do not know why, but her eyes became dim.

"Here is your tea service," Claude began, pointing out the things as if it was a private museum—in fact he was almost as proud of them as if he was a collector—"four cups in blue, and here is your dinner service. I hope you will like the pattern." They were ranged on the shelves of a small ebony cabinet fixed on the wall over a chest of drawers: "Here are your bookshelves; the leaves of the table can be let down so as to give you more room. I thought you would like candles better than oil, and I hope you will find this little reading-lamp useful. The view from the window is not extensive and not very nice, but I have put a box outside with mignonette in it. I know the easy-chair is comfortable, because I tried it myself. You will have no other looking-glass than this mirror over the mantelshelf. See, here is Violet's photograph, and here is mine. The old fireplace was truly disgraceful. I believe that the previous occupant, poor thing, in her extremity had eaten two of the bars. So I put in this. It is pretty, I think, and the tiles are really good. As for stores, you will find some in this cupboard—quite a big cupboard, isn't it? Here are coals, but I fear you will find your coal supply a difficulty. This is your filter, and here are your cooking utensils. Try to think if there is anything I have forgotten, or anything else at all I can do for you. Shall I come every day to sit on the stairs and peel potatoes for you?"

"No, Claude, thank you. And now you had better leave me, or else I am afraid I shall begin to cry. I am sure I shall not want anything more."

"You are not—not afraid, Valentine?"

"If I were I should not acknowledge it. But go, Claude. Today is Thursday. Come to see me on Sunday morning—not before. I think I should like to be quite alone until then. If I am in trouble I shall make Melenda help me. Good-bye, Claude. It is a beautiful thing to have a brother who will take so much trouble for one. I am very grateful. Good-bye. Go and stay with Violet this evening."

When the door was shut and she had wrestled with that inclination to cry—sustaining for a few moments a shameful defeat, but she rallied—she sat on her bed and looked about her. The room was certainly very small, yet Claude had made it pretty. The walls were of plaster, newly scraped and repaired and stained and made quite clean; the ceiling was freshly whitewashed; the little green and gold iron bed was covered with a counterpane of pleasing design; two candlesticks stood on the mantelshelf, and her lamp was on a three-cornered bracket; an embroidered cloth lay on the table, and there were flowers in a vase; there were pretty curtains to the window, of a soft stuff, pleasant to look upon and to touch, and on the floor lay a rug large enough to serve for carpet. There were only three chairs, one of them an easy chair, low, long, deep, and luxurious, in which one might meditate and rest; and the fireplace was pretty, with its tiles and its brass fender. In the cupboard she found a loaf of bread, butter, a small ham—already boiled—sugar, tea, coffee, and other things; and on the lowest shelf she discovered, and handled with some curiosity, a saucepan, a pot, a frying-pan, a gridiron, and a Dutch oven; would she have to learn the use of all these things? Besides the mirror over the mantelshelf, Claude had hung up some fans and feathers and a little picture or two. It really is a beautiful thing to have a brother who will work for one. What servant—what army of servants—would have made this

5 Author of *Voyage autour de ma chambre*, an exploration of his room in the form of an imaginative travelogue.

place so dainty and so pretty? It is a thing, in fact, which cannot be done to order. And the discovery of so small a detail as a box of matches almost brought her to tears a second time. Claude had remembered the matches! Everybody knows the dreadful carelessness of even good housemaids in the matter of matches.

It certainly seemed as if life was going to become, for a time, a much more simple thing than she had been accustomed to consider it. Here she was, in a little room only twelve feet square, surrounded by everything necessary for existence, with food and drink, shelter, bed, and clothes to wear. What else can a reasonable being want? In Park Lane[6] they had one room for sleeping, one for eating, a third for study, and a fourth for society. The things to eat were not kept in the sleeping-room, nor were the clothes kept in the eating-room, nor was the cooking done in the room reserved for society—fancy Violet "gridling" a steak in the large drawing-room! Nor was the coal cellar kept in a bedroom, nor was the pantry confused with the library. Yet here were bedroom, dining-room, drawing-room, library, kitchen, scullery,[7] and coal cellar all combined in one small chamber which Claude had made pretty for its three months' tenant.

She sat on the bed for a long time, thinking. Now that the thing was really begun, and she was alone in the house, and going to remain alone for a long time, she felt more than a little afraid. Suppose that someone were to walk in at the open door and visit her, unasked. The house door was open all day, and there was nothing to prevent any curious or impertinent person—at the thought she sprang to her feet and examined her door. Oh, prudent Claude! He had thought of this too. He had provided the door with a chain, a bolt, a lock, and a wooden bar, which could be dropped into strong iron stanchions, capable of withstanding any ordinary pressure. And besides these fortifications, she had Melenda close at hand, though as yet Melenda was ignorant of her arrival. If anything happened she could call out for her. Surely Melenda was fierce enough and brave enough for any emergency whatever.

Quite alone! There are many men who all their lives spend more than half the twenty-four hours in loneliness absolute, yet do not seem to mind it. Who can be more lonely, for instance, than the tenant of chambers, who sits in them all day working or waiting for clients, and all night reading or sleeping; and perhaps when the clerks are gone, the only man left on the ghostly staircase? Yet men live on in this solitary way, sometimes without even a club, and never complain of loneliness, and never seem afraid of ghosts. Not long ago there was a man who died at the ripe age of eighty-one, and had lived for thirty years all alone in a country house, seeing no one, and not even admitting a woman to clean up, and not taking the trouble to clean up the place himself, so that when he died the female population to a woman made haste to visit the house in order to gaze and gloat upon the dust. Yet he was quite happy. Men, in fact, live alone from the time when they leave school to the time when they marry, which is very often a long spell. They have their little distractions—their clubs, their friends, their theatres; but they spend most of their evenings and all their nights alone in their rooms. Women, on the other hand, seldom live alone: young women never. They are accustomed to go about together, to sit, work, and even study together. Valentine had never been separated for a single day from Violet. She had never been without the sense of protection with which young ladies are wrapped and clothed as with a suit of armour. Except in her bedroom, which was next to Violet's, she had never once been alone in all her life. And, needless to point out—though this is of minor importance—she had never done anything at all for herself.

6 One of the most fashionable streets in London, where many of the city's most affluent residents lived.

7 A small room adjacent to the kitchen where food is rinsed, sliced, or otherwise prepared for cooking and dishes and utensils are cleaned and stored.

Now, like Tommy Merton,[8] she was to discover that if she would eat she must work—that is, she must cook. She got up, therefore, and began to wonder if she could make herself some tea. Again, that most thoughtful youth Claude had remembered everything. The fire was laid, not with sticks—a slow and uncertain method unless you use a whole bundle, which costs a halfpenny, and is never permitted even in the most extravagant household—but with the resinous wheels, which burn fiercely and make a fine fire in two minutes. The kettle, she found, was filled with water; in the cupboard was a caddy full of tea. There was white sugar in the sugar-basin; nobody knew better than Claude that brown sugar was becoming for Polly's position, but he pretended to forget that detail. In the same way he had committed gross incongruities in the French bed, and the pretty lamp with the tinted shade, and the aesthetic table-cover. Then Valentine discovered, further, a saucer full of white eggs—not the "selected" at ten for a shilling—and two or three pots of preserves, besides the bread and the butter already mentioned. There was also a jug of milk. Where, Valentine wondered, would she get her milk for next day? Then, with a solemn feeling, as if she was setting a light to the sacred Hearth of Vesta, or propitiating the Lares,[9] she struck a match upon the magic box and set the fire-wheel crackling and blazing, and made the coals to burn merrily and to dart forth long tongues of flame, licking the bars and the sides of the kettle, and when the water presently began to sing, Valentine began to feel that she might find happiness even in living alone.

While the kettle was singing, and before it boiled over, Valentine looked out of the window over her box of mignonette. The back of Ivy Lane at this point "gives" partly upon Hammond Square, which now consists of a board school, with its asphalted pavement, where the children were playing. The great red-brick building of the school dominates the mean houses in which it is placed, much as a medieval castle used to dominate the village which clustered round it. There is, however, an important distinction. The castle was on an eminence above the village; the board school is on the same level with it. This fact alone is sufficient to prevent the board school master from becoming a proud baron. On the west of Hammond Square is the back of Hemsworth Street, and between the "backs" there are small yards which were once meant to be little gardens, but are innocent of flowers, though here and there stands a solitary tree, the melancholy survivor of the orchard, with blackened trunk and grimy branches. The yards are now used for the drying of linen, and there is always a great deal hanging out on fine days, so that at first one feels that Hoxton must be a very clean place, and therefore not far from the Kingdom of Heaven. But that is only a first suspicion, and not a first impression, for the wish is father to the thought. A closer inspection shows grubby yards, filled with rubbish, brickbats,[10] and everywhere cats, a most wonderful collection of cats, sunning themselves upon the walls; and all sleek, all well-fed, fat, and good-tempered, and probably quite certain that they are living in a picturesque country, and in the highest society, among ladies and gentlemen of the greatest refinement. Then Valentine looked across the space between the two "backs," and as she had eyes stronger than most she could see through the open windows opposite, and could catch a glimpse of interiors which filled her soul with pity. One certainly ought, under all conditions of life, and at any juncture, to be clean and to live in clean rooms; but this commandment has never been written. It is not, therefore, felt to be so binding as the others, and in time of pressure and

8 The lead character in *The History of Sandford and Merton* (1783–1789), a popular children's book, Tommy Merton is a mean rich boy who is mentored into virtuousness by a farmer's son.

9 The guardian spirits of the home in ancient Rome.

10 Pieces of broken brick.

trouble the enthusiasm for cleanliness is apt to decline. Few people have the heart to clean up when there is no work to be done, and no money to spend, and nothing to drink. And Valentine saw another thing; not only were there backyards and grimy windows, but there were courts at the back with houses even smaller than the one in which she sat. In fact, some of them were only two-roomed houses, and these houses added their little backyards and their dirt, and as she was to discover later on, their noise as well.

Valentine left her window. And then she made her tea and drank a cup, with a curious sense of unreality, because Violet's voice should have been in her ears; and it was incongruous, and like a nightmare, that she should make her own tea for herself alone in her bedroom.

After her tea she sat reading until about half-past eight, when the sun had set and the twilight was upon the ugly backs and grubby yards. And then, but with misgivings, she left her room and timidly knocked at Melenda's door.

The girls had just finished work for the day. Melenda was folding it up; Lotty was arranging herself for rest. Lizzie was stretching out her arms as Ixion[11] might have done when they took him down from his wheel and told him he might knock off for the night.

"I have come back," said Valentine.

"Oh," replied Melenda, pretending not to be astonished. But the other two gasped.

"You said that Polly might come if she came by herself. Are you glad to see me again now that I am alone?"

"Not likely," said Melenda shortly.

"I have come to stay here. I have got a room in this very house."

Lizzie opened her great eyes wider, but Melenda, who was not going to be surprised by anything, only sniffed.

"What have you done that for?"

"To be near you. We are sisters, Melenda."

"The other day you didn't know which was which. As if a girl could get lost. And how are you going to live? There's no service about here. There's a young girl wanted at the public-house,[12] I believe, but you must be pretty low down if you'd demean yourself by going there. I wouldn't, no more would Lizzie. Have you saved your money?"

"I have some money for a time." This was delicate ground, and she hastened to get over it quickly. "Claude furnished my room for me. Let me show it to you."

"Well," said Melenda ungraciously, "I can't help it, if you choose to come. You won't stay long, I suppose. Let's see the room."

They all three went with her, impelled by the strongest of feminine instincts.

Valentine had now pulled down the blind, drawn her curtains, and lit the pretty reading lamp with its coloured shade.

"Oh-h!" the girls gasped. They had never before seen a pretty room, and the prettiness of this room took their breath away. Even Melenda, who had been prepared to admire nothing, was taken by surprise. They went

11 In Greek mythology, Ixion was bound to a flaming wheel in the underworld as punishment for violating customs of hospitality while he was a guest of Zeus, king of the gods.

12 A public house is a place for buying and drinking alcohol—the long form of "pub."

round, looking at and examining everything, the easy-chair, the fireplace, the bookshelves, the table, and the pictures.

"See," said Valentine, "here is my cupboard with my stores. We will have dinner together if you will. Here are my books; we will read together every day if you like. Here is my workbox. I will work with you if you will let me. I can work very well."

"What's gone of all your fine clothes and your gold chain?" asked Lizzie, staring at the plain brown frock.

"I have not brought them here. I have only this frock and an ulster like your own." Melenda laughed scornfully. "It's nothing but play-acting, Polly. Lord! nobody would take you for a workgirl—you and your ulster! Why, it isn't ragged, and your elbows don't stick through. And where's your fringe? And you've got a collar and cuffs: and look at your fingers! I'll just tell you what you look like—nothing but a lady's-maid out o'work." She made this comparison in tones so contemptuous that for a while Valentine was confounded.

"I will pass for a lady's-maid, then," she replied, when she had recovered a little. "You won't be unkind, Melenda, will you?"

Melenda was examining the photographs on the mantelshelf. "Here's Claude," she said; "he looks a swell, don't he? What's he got a square thing on his head for? And why does he wear a black gown?"

"Claude is a great scholar. He is photographed in the cap and gown that scholars wear at the university. That is Violet, my sister."

"That's the other one," said Melenda; "her that cried. She won't come again, because I threatened to pull her hair off." She laughed grimly. "Looks a bit like Joe, somehow. But you look a bit like Claude."

"Will you let me sit with you, and go in and out without disturbing you, Melenda?"

It was Lotty who replied for her.

"Don't ask Melenda, else you'll only put her back up, and she'll answer hasty. Come without asking."

"We're workgirls," Melenda added, not a bit offended by this allusion to her temper, "and we've got our work to do, and we can't be chattering. If you won't make Liz chatter and lose her time, you may come. Lotty likes you, if I don't."

Valentine turned grateful eyes to the thin hollow-chested girl with the weak back.

"So Claude took and furnished the room for you, did he?" said Melenda. "Where'd he get the money to spend on it? I suppose you don't mind being beholden to him, do you?"

"Not a bit," said Valentine; "I am glad to be grateful to Claude."

"Humph," Melenda grunted. "He shan't help me if I know it. And he came here and took the room and all—they told me a swell had been about the place—without seeing me or telling me anything about it. He's in a rage with me, I suppose, 'cos I let out the other day."

"You called him names when he came. But he is not in a rage with you at all, I am sure."

"He pretended not to mind. Why didn't he call back then, instead of standing and looking as if he was looking through one with a bradawl?[13] Many a man would have knocked a girl down for less."

"Claude does not knock women down."

Melenda changed the subject.

"How are you going to cook," she asked, "with a finicking stove like that? The water's laid on behind, one cask for every two houses. You'll have to do all your own work yourself. Lotty'll tell you how to manage, if

13 A narrow blade for boring small holes. Thus, it is as if Claude's staring drilled straight through Melenda.

you'll ask her—she knows how to cook beautiful. You should taste her beef and onions. You can pay her any way you like. Her back's awful bad sometimes—sit down on Polly's bed, Lotty—and she never flies in a rage like I should do if my back was bad. And she isn't so proud as she ought to be. She'll take things from you."

Melenda spoke with the superiority of health and strength, but Lotty hung her head. Pride, independence, and freedom were fine things for girls with strong backs, but she was permitted to be beholden to people. It was a permission of which the poor girl could rarely avail herself. As for Liz, she gazed about her with great eyes and open mouth. The room looked to her like a little garden of Eden, or at least like Eve's Petit Trianon,[14] if she had one in that park.

"I am going to have some supper," said Valentine, pleased to have got on so well. "Here is a ham that Claude gave me, and bread and butter, and we will light the fire again and make some cocoa, if you would like to have some."

The ham looked splendid when Valentine put it on the table. All three girls became instantly conscious of a hollow and yearning sensation. Lotty turned quite white, and Lizzie clutched the back of a chair, but Melenda flew into a rage because of the temptation.

"I won't eat your ham!" she cried; "I won't eat any of your ham! Do you hear? I won't take anything from you. Lotty may, because she's weak in her back. Lizzie ought to be ashamed—she ought—if she eats any! I shan't. I shall go out for a walk. I shall take and walk up and down Hoxton Street till I'm tired. There! They are a nice lot in Hoxton Street of a night! You'll be proud of your sister, won't you? If I'd got any money to spend I'd go to the Britannier[15] or else to the Variety Music Hall,[16] and I shan't get home before midnight likely."

She made these announcements with defiance. They illustrated at once her independence, her freedom of action, and her contempt of criticism. With the light of wrath in her eyes, with her parted lips, and the lamp-light softening the effect of that lump of hair on her forehead, Melenda looked her very best. She might have been painted as an actress in a great part. But she ought to have been painted in a rage. She banged out of the room, and they heard her run downstairs. Then she ran back again.

"If you sit with Lotty," she said, while all trembled, "or if Lotty sits with you, prop her up and make her comfortable. Don't go to say that I don't look after Lotty. Don't dare to say that, or I'll serve you—"

Her eyes fell upon the photograph of Claude in the square cap and the gown, who seemed to be asking her, with grave face, if this language was becoming to a girl who respected herself. She stopped, turned, and fled.

"And now," said Valentine, "we will have some supper."

"Do ladies all live in beautiful rooms like this?" asked Lizzie, when that meal of fragrant cocoa with ham and bread and butter, served on a snow-white cloth, was finished and the things put away. She had not spoken a word, but looked about her all the time curiously and wonderingly. "Do they all live like this?"

"I suppose so," said Valentine. "This is a poor little room, but Claude has made it pretty."

"And do they all have as much ham and bread and butter as they like?"

"Yes, I believe they do."

---

14 The Petit Trianon, located at the Palace of Versailles, is a chateau adjacent to gardens and a park where Marie Antoinette could relax in private.

15 The Britannia Theatre offered cheap entertainment, often in the form of melodramas, and, unlike other theatres, served alcohol. Melenda's pronunciation ("Britannier") is indicative of her working-class origins.

16 Music and variety halls offered various performances by professional entertainers, as well as food and drink. Reformers feared they were potential dens of thieving, drunkenness, and prostitution.

Liz asked no more questions. But presently she rose and put on her ulster and hat, and went out without a word. She was no longer hungry: the sight of the pretty room and the dainty supper filled her with physical content and ease, and with a vague yearning that it might be always like this, and in her mind there echoed certain words which she could not repeat to Lotty and Melenda. "You ought to be a lady," said these words. "You ought to live like a lady in pretty rooms, and be dressed beautifully, and have nothing to do but to please someone with your lovely eyes." Why, she knew now what it was to be a lady and to live in a pretty room. She had never known before, poor Liz. And it seemed an altogether desirable and a lovely life. She went out into the street thinking how it would be to have every day such a supper, to sit in such a room, to wear such a pretty frock, and to have put away somewhere beautiful dresses and gold chains. "You ought to be a lady. You ought to live like a lady in pretty rooms, and be dressed beautifully, and have nothing to do but to please someone with your lovely eyes." Perhaps it was the devil who whispered these words in her ear continually, so that she saw nothing as she walked along the crowded street but the pretty room, with its soft-coloured light, and the sweet face of its owner, and her graceful, gentle ways. "You ought to be a lady." If she only could!

When she got home at twelve, Lotty was already asleep. Generally the pain in her back kept her awake. But now she was sleeping. There was light enough for Liz to see her thin pale face upon the pillow. Something—perhaps it was that—touched the girl's heart.

"I won't never leave Lotty," she murmured, "not even to be a lady."

When they were left alone, Valentine made Lotty lie down upon her bed and propped her up with pillows, and cooled her hot temples with eau de cologne.

"Oh," said Lotty, "it's like Melenda; but she never had any scent, poor thing." She meant that Valentine was as kind and thoughtful for her as her friend Melenda. "Don't anger her, Miss. She's a good sort if you take her the right way."

"You mustn't call me Miss. Call me—no, call me Valentine."

"Oh, but I can't, because you are a young lady. Well, then, Valentine."

"Are you always left alone in the evening?"

"Yes, always. They must go out after the day's work. I know what you think. The streets are rough. But Melenda won't get into mischief. And she's too proud to go into public-houses and drink with the men, as some girls do. And so's Liz."

"Melenda said you were not to talk much. Let me talk to you. What shall I tell you?"

"Tell me whatever you like. You've got such a soft voice. I told Melenda you were kind and didn't come to laugh at us, though you are a lady and all."

"But, my dear, ladies don't laugh at working-girls."

"Sam says they laugh at all poor people."

"Sam says what is horribly untrue then. Do not believe Sam."

"He was here the other day. We'd been out of work for three days, and Liz she'd gone to look for it at one house and Melenda at another, and I was lying down. Sam stamped and swore—he's dreadful when his blood's up—and he said, 'What do they care if all the workgirls in London starve? They're worse than the men who call themselves gentlemen, for they have listened to the workmen. They are the cruellest people in the world, and the hardest hearted.' That's what Sam said."

"Who are?" interrupted Valentine.

"The women who call themselves ladies. That's what Sam said; and then he swore again, and then he went on to say that if there had been half the tyranny with the men as there is with the women, all England would have rose. And the ladies know it, he said, and they've been told day after day; the papers, he says, are full of it; they are taught about it in the poetry books, but they do nothing; and Sam says they never will do nothing, so long as they can get their pretty things cheap, but laugh at us while we work and starve. Not that we really do starve, you know, because there's always somehow been bread and cold tea, but sometimes there's nothing more. That's what Sam says."

"It isn't true, Lotty," said Valentine. But she felt guilty, not of laughing, but of apathy. "Help me to be neither cruel nor hardhearted, my dear."

Then she was silent, thinking, and Lotty lay resting.

Presently Valentine said: "I will tell you a story, a story about myself, Lotty. Once upon a time, there was a poor widow woman, who had a large family to keep, and took in washing, but she had to work very hard. One day there came to see her a great lady who had known her a long time before, and she said to the poor woman, 'Give me your little girl, your youngest. I will take her away and bring her up with my own child, and care for her. Some day you shall see her again.' The poor woman knew that her daughter would be kindly kept, and so she let her go, and for a long time saw the child no more, because she was being taught all kinds of things, and among others to be a young lady. This is not at all easy for any girl to learn, Lotty, because it means all kinds of things besides the wearing of fine clothes; among others it means always thinking the best things and doing the noblest things, so that I am afraid that girl got but a very little way. However, after nineteen years, she went back with her benefactor's daughter to see her mother and her brothers and her sister, who was a workgirl. But they were not at all pleased to see her, and her sister made herself hard and proud, and could not bear to be helped out of the great lady's treasures, and said very cruel things and drove her away. Then the girl put off her finery and came to live in the same house with her working-sister. She came to learn how workgirls live, and what they think, and what they want, and she hoped to make her sister love her. That is all the story, Lotty."

"It isn't finished. And what does she want Melenda to love her for?"

"Oh, Lotty, love makes people happy. Suppose you had neither Melenda nor Lizzie."

"If I hadn't got Melenda," said the girl, "I should wish I was dead and buried."

Chapter II

The City of Hogsden[1]

It is best to drop a veil over the first few hours of that first night in Ivy Lane. It is sufficient to explain that the evening between eight and twelve is the liveliest time of the day for Ivy Lane; that the Adelaide Tavern then does its briskest business, that the street is fullest, the voices loudest, the children most shrill, the women most loquacious, and the "language" most pronounced. On this evening there was a drunken man in one of the courts somewhere behind the house, and somebody of one sex was beating somebody of the other sex, with oaths on the one hand and screams on the other. Suppose some step should come up the stair, and some unknown person should knock at her door. Suppose the house was quite empty except for herself. Yet Ivy Lane is not the haunt of criminals; its population is made up of honest working-men and women, whose principal fault is that they have not yet learned the virtue of self-restraint.

Towards midnight the noise began to subside, and the street grew rapidly quieter. Presently Valentine fell asleep, though with misgivings in her dreams, which would have become dreadful nightmares had she but known that Lizzie, the latest to return, had left the street door wide open for the night.

When she awoke the morning was already well advanced, which was perceptible even to a new arrival by reason of the stillness. For at nine the men are at work, and the women are "doing up" in their rooms, and the children are at school. A Sabbath[2] calm had fallen upon Ivy Lane and upon its courts to north and south. Valentine lay half asleep, thinking that she was at home, and wondering lazily why her maid did not come to call her. Suddenly she remembered where she was; she sprang to her feet, pulled back the curtains and looked abroad from behind the blind. The sun was high in the heavens, pouring down gracious floods of warmth and heat upon the linen in the yards; in the beginning of all things the sun was created on purpose to dry the linen; there seemed to be a universal calm and restfulness; from the board school at the back there was heard

1 Archaic spelling of *Hoxton*, which was used until the first half of the eighteenth century.
2 The weekly day of rest in Abrahamic traditions.

a soothing murmurous sound of many voices, and from Hoxton Street the distant roll of carts and the shouts of costers.[3] Valentine was the latest riser that morning in Ivy Lane, except perhaps those who were lying down never to get up again any more, and those who were in temporary retirement with fevers and the like.

Thankful and somewhat surprised that the night had passed with no worse adventure than that of the midnight clamour, she proceeded to make her own breakfast. She hesitated, considering whether it would be well to invite her friends in the next room. But the fear of Melenda decided her to breakfast alone. There was no milk, and she did not know where to get any more; there was no water, and she had to go downstairs and fill her own kettle, and to lay her fire, and to brush up the stove, as well as to make her own bed and dust the room. These things are not hardships exactly, but it seems more fitting somehow that other people should do them for one. What the other people think about it has never yet been made known to the world.

When Robinson Crusoe had quite made up his mind that there were neither cannibals nor wild beasts upon his island, the first thing he did was to go exploring. I have often thought how much more interesting his story might have been had there been one, only one, just one man-eating tiger on the island, so that he could have stalked Robinson and failed to catch him, while Robinson could have shot at him from places of ambush and failed to hit him; and so both the tiger and the man would have had a lively time, and the reader would have been kept awake. No doubt in Hoxton there is more than one man-eater, but Valentine never saw any at all, though she was at first horribly afraid of meeting one, and wondered what she should do if that should happen. She began that very morning, and daily continued, the exploration of Hoxton. There was indeed so much to see and to learn that she never got outside the narrow precincts of that town during the whole of her three months' stay in it.

The city of Hogsden, or Hoxton, as it is now the fashion to write the name, is not to outward view a romantic or a picturesque city; none of its friends have claimed for it that kind of distinction. It does not stand upon a rock overhanging a river, like Quebec or Durham; it is placed, on the other hand, upon a level plain beside a canal; it is not a city of gardens, like Damascus; nor a city of palaces, like Venice; nor a medieval city with old walls, like Avignon; it has no gardens left at all, except the two black patches of its two little squares; yet once it was all garden. It has no palaces, though once it had great houses; it has few associations or memories of the past, because as a city it is not yet more than a hundred years old. There is nothing at all beautiful or picturesque or romantic in it. There is only the romance of every life in it—there are sixty thousand lives in Hoxton, and every one with its own story to tell; sixty thousand romances beginning, proceeding, and ending; the stories of those who are old and of those who are growing old; of those who are children and those who are young men and maidens; of those who think of love and those who remember the days when they thought about it; of those who desire love to come and those who mourn for love departed. What more, in Heaven's name, is wanted to make romance?

It is a city whose boundaries are as well marked as if it were surrounded, like York and Canterbury, with a high wall, for it has a canal to west and north, with St. Luke's workhouse standing in the angle like the Tower of London or the citadel of breezy Troy.[4] On the east side lies the broad highway of the Shoreditch or Kingsland Road, which parteth Hoxton from her sisters, Haggerston and Bethnal Green. The southern

3 Short for costermonger or someone who sells fruits, vegetables, or fish on the street.

4 York and Canterbury are English cities with, at least partially, ancient Roman walls. Ancient Troy, also walled, had a towering fortress from which the king and queen could observe the entire city.

march is by the City Road and Old Street. It thus stands compact and complete; it is a city lying secluded and quiet, like the city of Laish.[5] Travellers come not within its borders; few, even among Londoners, wot[6] of it; foreigners never hear of it; to Americans it has no associations, and they never visit its streets; it is content with one line of omnibuses to connect it with the outer world; there is no cabstand in its precincts; it has no railway station. The newspapers do not expect to find anything of interest in Hoxton, and penny-a-liners[7] never visit it for the sake of paragraphs. Its people are quiet and industrious; folk who ask for nothing but steady work and fair wages, and have a rooted aversion to any public appearance, whether in a police court, or a county court, or on a political platform, or at a gospel revival, just as formerly they disliked appearing publicly in pillory or stocks.[8] There is no habitual criminal class in Hoxton, unless the recent destruction of rookeries[9] in Whitecross Street has driven a few of the rogues to find temporary refuge, before "chivvying"[10] begins again, in the southern streets of this city. As regards civic monuments and public buildings, there are eight churches and quite as many chapels, and some of the inhabitants have been known to visit these architectural marvels on the Sunday morning. There is the great theatre called the "Britannier 'Oxton," and the smaller or less known Theatre of Varieties in Pitfield Street; there is a splendid great school for boys and girls, where were once the country almshouses of the haberdashers; there are the Fullers' Almshouses; there are four board schools to beautify four of its streets; there are the famous iron portals of Mary Street; and there are two bridges over the canal. There are no rich residents, no carriages, no footmen; none of the flaunting luxuries which are described by travellers as existing at the West End.[11] The houses are small and mostly low; there is no doubt at all that everybody is quite poor, and that for six days in the week, all the year round, everybody works for ten hours a day at least, and sometimes more. Yet the place has a cheerful look. There may be misery, but it is not apparent; the people in the streets seem well fed, and are as rosy as London smoke and fog will allow. In the daytime the pavements of the side streets are mostly deserted, and there are not many who lounge, hands in pockets, at the corner of the street. Among the rows of small houses which speak of decent poverty there are not wanting one or two of the old houses, survivors of the time when they stood among green fields and orchards, the country residences of great merchants. The two squares in which they used to live are still left. And the streets are mostly broad, because there was plenty of room when they were built; two or three of them can even boast a double width of pavement, supposed by some, imperfectly acquainted with London, to be a luxury known only in Whitechapel Waste. And lastly, the streets, though certainly not remarkable for originality of design, are at least not all built after the same pattern, as may be seen in Bromley beyond Bow.

This was Valentine's first impression of the quarter, a first impression which might be modified but would never be quite destroyed. Since Hoxton possesses some eighty streets, it must not be supposed that she went into every one of them in a single morning. In fact she walked down Pitfield Street into Old Street, and up

---

5 In the Book of Judges, Laish is a quiet, peaceful city that was quickly conquered, in part because of its isolation.

6 An archaic word for *know*.

7 Journalists for tabloid publications were paid a penny for each written line, hence the name.

8 Both the pillory and the stock are forms of punishment that immobilized criminals between wooden boards for humiliation in public spaces.

9 A colloquial term, *rookery* was used in reference to urban slums. These overcrowded neighborhoods were often cleared out for hygienic and safety reasons. The land was also frequently appropriated, and the buildings torn down, to enable railroad extensions.

10 To harass.

11 The West End, in contrast to the impoverished East End, was and remains an affluent and prosperous area of central London.

Hoxton Street into Hyde Road and Whitmore Street, and so over the bridge which leads to Kingsland, and back by way of St. John's Road to Ivy Lane—the whole with lingering step and occasional excursions into side streets which seemed to promise something strange or curious. Not this morning only, but many successive mornings, she took this walk among streets where the people live.

She discovered, if one may anticipate, in these daily wanderings, many remarkable things and some remarkable people. Hoxton, by the circumstances of its trade, is calculated to develop character in a manner impossible for some other quarters, such as Kentish Town and Camden Town, which are cities of the little clerk. Hoxton, however, is the city of the smaller industries and the lesser ingenuities. Here they make the little things necessary to civilised life, such things as the Andamanese and the Soudanese can do very well without, but which we must have. Thus, they are workers in mosaic and in lacquer: they are cutters, fret cutters, marqueterie cutters, razor grinders, glass bevellers, and they finish brushes.[12] Some of them are hair hands, some pan hands, and some drawing hands, in the brush trade; they stitch buff, at least they say so, but it may be a dark and allegorical announcement, because one hath never heard of buff, nor knoweth what its nature may be; they gild envelopes, they emboss on steel; as regards the women they are all classified as "hands"—nothing else is wanted by a woman, not intelligence, or invention, or grace, or beauty, or sweetness—nothing but hands. There are bead hands, feather hands—who are subdivided into curling hands, improvers, mounters, and aigrette hands—mantle hands, skirt hands, bodice hands, mob-cap hands, children's pinafore hands, cape-lining hands, bead hands, butterfly hands, and tie hands, who are again divided into flat-work hands, back-stitchers, band hands, slip stitchers, and front hands; they are black borderers, braiders, and a hundred others. Besides all this, these industrious people make towel-horses, upholstery for perambulators, fancy boxes, lace paper for valentines, picture frames, paint brushes, trunk furniture, leather bags, scales, marking ink, trimmings, pipe clay, show cases, instrument cases, looking-glass backs, frillings and rush-wicks; they carve pianos, dress collars, and work in horn; they make fittings for public-houses; they dye cotton; they deal in grindery and they melt tallow; there linger still in Hoxton one or two of those almost extinct medicine-men called herbalists. Lastly, in the manufacture of annatto they are said to have no equal.[13]

These things Valentine did not find out in a single day, but in many. At first she wandered just as one wanders on a first visit to a foreign city, getting lost and then finding her way again, looking into all the shops, reading the names and the trade announcements and watching the people. And at first she was afraid; but as day after day passed and no one molested her she grew more confident.

Perhaps the least desirable of all the streets is the very one in which she had to live. Ivy Lane, by some called Ivy Street, is vexed by certain courts,[14] one of which was commanded by Valentine's window; they are inhabited by the baser sort; perhaps their presence gives a bad name to the street just as it materially increases the evening noise. Certainly Ivy Lane is not so clean as some of the Hoxton streets; its windows are unwashed; its doors want washing and painting. Yet it has both its chapel and its public-house. The former is small and plain in appearance, with a neat little pediment, a door in the middle, and a window on either side. The doc-

12 Buhl cutters and marquetry cutters are artisans of decorative brass and wood ornaments and inlays.

13 Grindery are the tools and materials of shoemakers and other leather workers; tallow is the animal fat used to make soap and candles; and annatto is a plant extract used as a spice and in red dyes.

14 Owing to London's haphazardly organized streets, courts with minimal access to a road were often formed behind and between houses. Urban reformers viewed these as magnets for disease and crime because they were cut off from public traffic and surveillance.

trine preached in it every Sunday evening is remarkable for purity. As for the public-house, very likely its beer is equally remarkable and for the same reason. But Valentine never tasted either. There are also in the street two chandlers' shops, two second-hand clothes shops, one of them filled with women's dresses, and a carver in wood. Is not that a typical English street in which religion, drink, food, art, labour and trade all find a place?

It was nearly one o'clock when Valentine returned to her lodgings. She had begun to see Hoxton. There seemed little in the place that was very depressing. A whole city at work is rather cheerful than otherwise. To be sure she had not been within the houses and she knew nothing of the interiors, which are more important from the human point of view than the outside. Very likely clergymen, district visitors, Bible women, and the general practitioner, know enough about the place to depress the most sanguine. And when she came back, she remembered all the girls who, like Melenda and Lotty and Lizzie, must be sitting within those walls stitching all day long for less than a penny an hour, and her heart fell. The cheerfulness goes out of honest labour when one learns that it only means a single penny an hour.

As she climbed the steep, narrow stair, she saw, through the half-opened door of the ground-floor back, a strange and curious thing. The occupant, an old woman, whom she had not seen before, was solemnly engaged in dancing by herself, to an imaginary audience. She shook her petticoats, pirouetted, executed unheard-of steps, capered and postured, with all the agility and some of the grace of a youthful *danseuse*.[15] Valentine was thinking of the sewing-women; the thing passed before her eyes as she went up the stair; she saw it but took no heed; nor was it till afterwards that she remembered it and wondered what this might mean.

She opened Melenda's door and looked in. Something must have gone wrong. On Melenda's brow, or where her brow should have been but for the fringe, there rested a cloud: it was a cloud much bigger than a man's hand—in fact, it treated her as if she had been a goddess of the good old time, and enwrapped and enfolded her completely, so that she was veiled in cloud. The other two seemed cowed. Lotty, sitting on the bed, hardly dared to raise her eyes. Lizzie turned her head furtively, but without so much as a smile or even a look of recognition. Both waited for Melenda to speak and went on with their work, but self-consciously.

In fact, there had been a discussion carried on with great animation by all three, mostly talking together. This method of controversy is lively, but hardly calculated to settle the points at issue. Lotty's part in it was chiefly one of remonstrance and entreaty. She had been guilty of eating some of Valentine's ham for supper, and of drinking a cup of cocoa. Perhaps it was the unusual sense of repletion which had given her a good and almost painless night, though Melenda's attitude in the morning filled her with a sense of guilt. Lizzie, on the other hand, who had no excuse, except that of hunger, for selling her independence for a plate of ham, actually gloried in the action, and proclaimed her readiness to do it again if invited, and laughed at Melenda for not taking all she could get. There were rebellious questionings, scoffs, and doubts—all put down to that concert, and the talk with the gentleman afterwards. Lizzie never used to show such spirit before she was tempted. Many bear with pride the ills for which there seems no cure; but when a way is shown, alas! Poor pride! Melenda tried argument, with reduction to first principle,[16] dogmatic assertion, and quotations from the opinions and maxims of the Philosopher Sam. Valentine and her ham were only the text. The independence of woman was the true theme.

"Do you want anything?" asked Melenda, with an ominous glitter in her eye.

15 French for *ballet dancer*.

16 A logical stance using the most basic information—that which is self-evident—to deduce other information.

"No," said Valentine, "I only came—"

"Then you can go away," said her sister; "we're working-girls, and we've got our bread to earn. We haven't taken money off of rich ladies for nothing. You can go away and eat up all the rest of the ham—you and your ham!"

"But, Melenda—"

"Go away, I say. We've got our work to do. Don't come wasting time. And Lizzie eating such a lot of supper that she couldn't be waked this morning. Go away."

Valentine meekly obeyed and closed the door. So far she had made very little way with her sister. But she caught the eyes of Lotty as she went out. They said as plainly as eyes could speak, "Forgive her, and don't give up trying."

"Oh, Melenda!" said the possessor of these eyes reproachfully.

Melenda sniffed.

"As for me," said Lizzie, "if I had the good luck to have such a sister I wouldn't turn her out of the room. I'd have better manners."

"You'd beg and borrow all she had to give, I suppose, and call that good manners?"

"I'd take anything she wanted to give, and I'd behave pretty to her."

"She ain't your sister, then. And I'm old enough to know how to behave."

This closed the discussion. And all there was for the girls' dinner—while, as Lizzie reflected, plenty reigned in the next room—was a thick slice each of bread and butter.

At Hoxton, I am told, nobody at all, not even any of the eight vicars or the seven curates—but this may be incorrect—ever thinks of dining late. Dinner at half-past seven is not possible; one ceases to think of such a thing the moment one begins to breathe the air of Hoxton. Valentine, therefore, at one o'clock, began naturally to consider the subject of dinner instead of luncheon. She had to look at it from quite a new point of view—namely, to think how it was to be provided, and how she was to use those beautiful instruments provided for her. To all right-minded and cultivated persons dinner necessarily involves potatoes; you cannot dine without potatoes. Other things may be neglected. Pickles, pudding, fish, soup, may be considered as non-essentials, but not potatoes. I have, it is true, seen a ploughboy sitting under a hedge making what he called his dinner with a lump of bacon fat, a great hunch of bread, and a clasp-knife, but he thought of potatoes; and I have seen a navvy[17] making what he called his dinner with a great piece of underdone beef cut thick, as they love it, those others, and half a loaf. But all this is merely stoking or taking in coal. Both navvy and ploughboy know very well that without potatoes there can be no dinner. There must be potatoes. Valentine had the remains of her ham and part of yesterday's loaf, but she had no potatoes. She spread her cloth, laid out these viands, which looked very much like luncheon so far as they went. What about potatoes? If she wanted them she would have to buy them. Where should she go in search of potatoes? And how was she to buy them? Do they sell potatoes by the dozen, like eggs, or by the peck, like peas, or by the pound, like cherries, or by the pint, like beer, or singly, like peaches? And how do you carry them home? Claude had forgotten one thing. He thought you could live in Hoxton without a basket for marketing. She had, it is true, an apron, but it was not one of those aprons which are designed for the carriage of things like potatoes.

17 A low-skilled, low-paid labourer, usually in construction.

Again, even if she could get over that difficulty she would have to fill her saucepan with water, for which purpose she would have to go downstairs and fetch some from the cistern, and that old woman below, who danced all by herself, might be looking out of window, and she might make remarks. And she would have to light the fire again. And lastly, if she had got her potatoes and had washed and peeled them and had put them in the pot, how long should they boil? Christmas plum-puddings, she had read somewhere, are boiled for several days and several nights continuously. But in no book had she ever read the length of time required to bring out the full mealiness of a potato. And then, when she had boiled her potatoes and eaten them, she would have all the trouble of clearing everything away and washing up. Truly, as has been already observed, certain things ought to be done for one.

She felt that she could not take all this trouble, at least for that day. Tomorrow, perhaps, but not today. She would be contented for once with a simple luncheon. She therefore cut some ham and made some sandwiches. When she had eaten these and would have poured out a glass of water, she found that her filter was empty, and the look of the outside of the cistern below did not speak well for its contents. Besides, she did not want to go downstairs. So, like Melenda and the girls in the other room, she contented herself with some cold tea remaining from breakfast, and then pretended, like the navvy and the ploughboy, that she had made her dinner. Thus easy is it to take the downward step, so narrow is the interval between civilisation—of which a modern dinner is by many considered the highest form of expression, and barbarism—in which there is no dinner, so brief is the space which separates us—I mean ourselves, gentle reader, of the highest culture attainable—from the folk of Ivy Lane.

Consider, however, the time which must be spent every day, by one who lives alone, in the mere preparation of meals and in the cleaning up. The first clean up in the morning; the fetching and carrying of water; the second clean up after breakfast; the clean up after dinner; the clean up after tea; more fetching and carrying water; always more cleaning of dishes and drying of dusters. Good Heavens! one used to wonder how the hermits of old managed to pass their days. Why, they were passed, not in holy meditation at all, for which there was no time, but in continually brushing, brooming, sweeping, washing, laying the cloth, taking it off again and putting it away, cleaning the windows, sweeping up the hearth, buying potatoes and cooking them, making the bed, dressing and undressing—the wonder is that these holy men found any time for meditation at all. Certainly they have left behind them few monuments of their life-long thoughts in seclusion. As for those who did any other work, they, like Melenda and her friends, never washed anything at all.

The dinner over, Valentine rested and read a little, and began the daily journal of her exile, passing lightly over her late skirmish with Melenda, and saying nothing—great is the power of the *suppressio veri*[18]—about the absence of potatoes, so that the impression on the mind of anyone who read those journals would be that there had been no difficulty at all as regards the dinner question. Yet she herself remembered that the question would have to be faced again; and, besides, the ham would not last forever.

About four o'clock she thought she would go to Tottenham by the tram, and visit the almshouse once more and her blind mother.

18 From Latin, a legal term for the concealment of truth.

Chapter III

On Curls and Dimples

I have always thought it a very remarkable coincidence that on the very first day of Valentine's sojourn among this strange people she should have discovered the great Family Secret—that secret which Lady Mildred thought known to no one but her solicitor and herself.

Had the discovery been made earlier, the Great Renunciation might never have been undertaken: had it been made later, it would have been prosecuted in a different spirit. Valentine, in short, on this day established her previously doubtful identity. Perhaps it is as well to know for certain who you are as well as what you are. A *homo*[1] in the abstract, male or female, cannot be expected to take as much interest in himself, or to care so much about his own views and opinions, as a *homo* who knows at least one generation of his descent, just enough to connect him with the human family. All philosophy is based upon the sentiment of family as well as individuality. Valentine, therefore, after this day, but not before, was capable of constructing a system of philosophy for herself if she wished. This in itself is an enormous gain.

"I thought you'd come back, Polly," said the old lady with much gratification. "I knew you'd come back by yourself when Miss Beatrice had enjoyed her bit o' fun with the pretending and nonsense. Well, we must humour 'em, mustn't we? Rhoder, child, you can go home. Your Aunt Polly-which-is-Marla will make my tea for me tonight. So you go home." The girl obeyed, glad to be released from the embarrassment of taking her tea with an aunt so very much unlike any other aunts she knew belonging either to herself or to her friends.

"And so you're going to stay here three months, while her ladyship goes abroad or somewhere, are you, Polly? Well now. And with Melenda too! Well, my dear, I don't know what your temper may be, but of course you can't show off before my lady, which is a blessed thing for a young girl. And how you'll get on with your sister the Lord knows, because Melenda's awful. Is she friendly?"

"Not very friendly, yet. But I hope she will be."

---

1 The genus of hominids, including modern humans.

"She's morning noon and night in a rage. First it's the work, and then it's the wages, and then it's the long hours, and she's always hungry, which makes her snappish. As for that, the last time she came you could count every bone in her body, poor thing."

Valentine made the tea and cut the bread and butter, while the old lady, pleased to have so good a listener, talked without pause about her children and her grandchildren.

"It's a real pleasure to have you back again, Polly. There's not many pleasures left for a blind old woman. And good-natured and willing with it. Well!" This is an interjection which may mean many things, and stands in turns for patience, resignation, hope, sarcasm, approbation, or even despair. This time it was accompanied by a heartfelt sigh, and stood for prayerful gratitude that so good a daughter had been restored to her. "They've taught you to make a good cup of tea, my dear, though I'm afraid you've a heavy hand with the caddy, and to cut bread and butter as it should be cut, though too much butter and the bread too thin for poor folk. I suppose you often do it for Miss Beatrice?"

"Very often," said Valentine, truthfully.

"And you don't fidget like Rhoder, who's always wanting to be off again unless she can sit in a corner and read her book. She's just like your father, Polly, terrible fond of a book."

"Was my father fond of reading?"

"Yes, my dear. He was, and that's the only good thing he ever was fond of. Never mind him, Polly. Some day, perhaps, I'll tell you all about him, but never to Claude. You can tell your daughter everything. That's the comfort of having girls, though a woman's always fondest of her boys. A son's a son till he gets him a wife, but your daughter's your daughter—as you'll find out some day, my dear—all the days of your life, though Melenda has never been the daughter I wanted."

"Then, mother, I am all the more pleased to be of use. Now—what can I do next? I've washed up the things and put them away, and tidied the table. You've got a beautiful geranium in the window, I will cut away the dead leaves. Rhoda ought to do that for you. Or shall I read to you? I'm sure you would like me to read to you sometimes."

"No, Polly," replied the old lady, drawing herself up with dignity, "you shan't do nothing of the kind. I'm feeling very well this summer; I never felt better in my life; nearly all my rheumatics has gone away and I sleep all night, and I haven't said anything that I remember to make you think I required reading. And as for years I'm sixty turned, but the youngest of them all. If I require reading I believe I can make my wants known and send for a clergyman, unless I am took sudden, which may happen to anybody, and one ought to be prepared. Perhaps allowance is made for such. No reading, thank you, my dear."

"I didn't mean religious reading exactly," Valentine made haste to explain. "However, let us talk instead, and I will attend to your flowers. Tell me something more about all of us when we were little—Claude and Melenda and me."

This she said in perfect innocency, and without a thought of what might follow.

"I will, Polly. Well, my dear, you were a fat little thing, with chubby arms and legs and curls all over your forehead, and the most beautiful little laughing face that ever was seen. No wonder my lady fell in love with you at first sight. Oh, my dear, it was a cruel hard thing to part with you, a hard thing it was."

"Why did you then, mother?"

"It was for your own good, my dear, and her ladyship promised to give you a good bringing up, which she's done, I'm sure. Besides, I couldn't bear to think of that pretty face brought to shame and tears—"

"But why shame and tears, mother?"

"Well, dear, some time or other, p'r'aps I'll tell you. Not tonight. I can't bear to talk of it nor to think of it. But some day I'll tell you, because you're Polly. But not to Claude. If you went away I thought there'd be one of them safe, for how to save them other blessed innocents I knew not. Oh, it was a great danger, Polly."

She paused and sighed, and her lips moved in silence.

"The Lord only knows," she said presently, "how I got through that time." She shuddered and clasped her hands. "Ah, my dear, it's a wonderful thing when you're old to remember what you've gone through. If the Lord sends the trouble, He gives the strength to bear it."

"You were in trouble, were you, mother?" Valentine laid her hand upon the blind woman's cheek. "Forget it—don't think about it."

"I won't, my dear. Well, when you went away the house was dull and quiet, because Claude was a grave child always, and Melenda never had your pretty ways."

"Had I pretty ways? Oh, I'm afraid I have lost them. What a pity to grow up and lose one's pretty ways!"

"And curls all over your head you had."

"Had I? And now my hair is quite straight."

"And a dimple in your cheek you had."

"The dimple is gone too, I am afraid; gone away with the curls and the pretty ways. What becomes of all these things, and where do they go to?"

"Dimples don't go, Polly, but perhaps it doesn't show as it did. Dimples never go. It is on the left cheek, my dear, and it shows when you laugh. Ah! And you were always laughing."

Then, for some unknown reason, Valentine started and flushed a rosy red.

"And you had, besides, a little brown mark, a birth-mark, on your arm, just above your elbow. You were the only one of all my children with so much as a speck or spot upon their bodies. Clean-skinned and straight-limbed children you were all, and as upright as a lance, except for that little spot on your arm."

Valentine made no reply, but her cheek was now quite pale, and she felt dizzy and was fain to catch at the back of a chair, because the walls began to go round and the solid earth to quake. This extraordinary terrestrial phenomenon, which was not noticed by any of the daily papers, nor even by the other residents in Lilly's, was entirely caused by the sympathy of the great round globe for Valentine, when by these simple words the old lady revealed the secret of her birth and filled her with strange emotions and troubled the calmness of her brain. Strange that Lady Mildred should never have thought of these little signs and proofs. But mothers, like leopardesses, know the spots upon their children which cannot be changed any more than the skin of the Ethiopian.

"On your right arm it is, Polly, my dear. Oh, I remember it very well."

Valentine made no reply.

"Where are you, dearie?" The blind woman stretched out her hands. "Where are you, Polly?"

"I am here, mother," she replied, in an altered voice. "I am here. But the heat of the day—or something—made me giddy. Wait a moment, mother dear. I will be back directly."

She went out into the open court before the cottages. After all these years of uncertainty, now she knew the truth. There was no longer any doubt.

Suppose that Prince Florestan, just before coming of age, was to discover that he was not the Prince at all, but only the son of Adam the gardener, and that Adam junior, who had always been employed in picking the strawberries, gathering the cherries, choosing the ripe peaches, shelling the peas, and cutting the asparagus for him to eat, was going to change places with him. And suppose Adam junior was suddenly to learn that he was going to eat up himself all the fruits of the earth as they came in due season, and that the former prince was to be occupied in cultivating the gardens for him? What would be the feelings of those young men?

Valentine's case was not quite this, because there never was any case quite the same as Valentine's; but it was near it. She always knew that one of the two was Adam the gardener's son, and now she knew which it was. Yet it must remain her secret. Nobody—not Claude, nor Violet, nor the blind old lady, nor Joe—must know it, partly because it was Lady Mildred's own secret and must be kept for her sake; and partly because for three months to come she was to depend upon Claude as upon a brother for protection and advice, and partly because neither this poor old woman nor Melenda must know that she was among them on false pretences.

Some girls on such a discovery would have made the most of the situation. They would have gone away and wandered with dazed eyes among the fields or beside the banks of a silver stream; they would have clasped hands and ejaculated; they would have thrown themselves in beautiful attitudes upon sofas or in easy-chairs. Most girls would do, I think, exactly what Valentine did. Like the young lady who went on cutting bread and butter, Valentine went back to the cottage and resumed her trimming of the flowers in the window. For, in fact, the dimple in the cheek, the curly hair which would not be brushed straight or lie down, the birth mark upon the arm, just below the elbow—not to speak, Valentine thought, of the pretty and caressing ways—all these belonged not to herself at all but—to Violet. Violet therefore was Polly-which-is-Marla and she was Beatrice, and Lady Mildred was her mother, and Melenda was not her sister save in the bonds of womanhood.

This was her discovery.

She was not, then, that interesting creature, the poor girl educated and brought up as a gentlewoman: she was nothing in the world but Beatrice Eldridge, the daughter of a highly respectable country gentleman, and the granddaughter of an earl. She was not a child of the people at all. Her mother was not the poor woman who now sat in darkness; nor, a more important thing still, was Claude her brother. Something of her pride was torn from her by the discovery. She had made up her mind ever since she had been able to understand at all what the thing meant, that she was the daughter of these humble people. She honestly believed it. She thought that she was returning to her own folk after many years; and now she was with them indeed, but under false pretences. If the old lady in the cottage knew the truth, first she would freeze, then she would fold her hands over her white apron, and then she would stand up like a village schoolgirl, and say, "Yes, Miss Beatrice, and my humble service to her ladyship," and Claude, if he knew the truth, would instantly lose his fraternal manner, and could do nothing more for her. Of course Lady Mildred knew that he would regard her as his sister. Why, the position would be intolerable. Melenda, for her part, would be, if possible, more *farouche*[2] than ever; Lizzie would be more shy and reserved; Lotty would be more timid; and as for all the weaker brethren in Ivy Lane, and wherever the bruit and fame of the thing might spread, and as soon as it became known that there was actually living in their midst a young lady who would in a few weeks be the

2 French for *fierce* or *wild*.

possessor of much treasure, all their worst qualities would come straight to the front with every possible form of cunning, meanness, greed, and self-seeking.

"Polly, my dearie, what's the matter? Is it the heat again?"

"I am better now, mother."

"You ain't cross, my dear, because I wouldn't let you read, are you? I'm sure you read beautiful, and you shall read if you like."

"Cross, mother! That would be a strange thing. No, I do not want to read since you don't want it. Shall I sing to you? I should like you to hear me sing."

"Why, my dear, I should like that better than reading. And then we can go on talking again. None of the other children ever had a singing voice. None of them ever went about singing as most children do. Their father couldn't sing, though he could play. All his cleverness went into his fingers."

Violet could not sing. Her voice was of small compass, and she never sang even alone or with Valentine. All her cleverness, like her father's, went into her fingers. She could play, though not so well as Valentine. She played to amuse herself; but she painted and drew professionally, so to speak.

"I can sing," said Valentine. "I will sing you a hymn, mother."

She hesitated, and then for some fancied appropriateness—I know not what, perhaps it existed only in her imagination—of the place and the time with the *motif* of the hymn, she chose an old Puritan hymn which has now dropped out of use and been forgotten, since the churches resolved to stifle the sadness of life and to simulate the voice of one who continually rejoices and is not afraid and has neither doubt nor question. This hymn had very little joy in it, save that of a faith, humble and resigned, with an undercurrent, an unexpressed feeling of sorrow, and even perhaps of humble remonstrance, that things had not been ordered otherwise from the beginning. This hymn begins with the words, "We've no abiding city here," and as Valentine sang them the blind old woman joined her hands as one who prays, and the tears gathered in her eyes.

"Oh, Polly," she cried, "my own dear Polly! To think that you should ever come back to your old mother, and to be such a good girl and all! Let me kiss you again, my dear. Melenda never had your pretty ways, poor thing! Some day—not yet—some day I'll tell you all my troubles. But you mustn't never tell Claude—mind that. We mustn't never let Claude know. You and me will keep the secret to ourselves, my dear. Come often. Come whenever you can. Oh, my Polly, you have made me so glad and happy, my dear—so glad and happy. Your voice is like her ladyship's. You've caught that by living with Miss Beatrice. But your ways are all your own—my own little Polly's soft and pretty ways."

Chapter IV

Lotty's Romance

Valentine went away with a guilty feeling, as if she had peeped into the sealed chamber: or eaten the forbidden fruit: or searched after the unlawful mystery: or inquired of the wise woman. Yet truly it was not her own seeking, but the simplest accident, which disclosed the thing. The discovery was premature. Had she been able to choose she would rather not have made it, because the only course now left to her was to go on precisely and exactly as if she had not found it out, and so she would be among them all under false pretences.

When she got home between nine and ten o'clock the market in Hoxton Street was in full swing, and the matrons of Ivy Lane were gathered together in the street, talking in knots; there was a group of men about the doors of the "Adelaide," and a crowd noisily disputing within the bar.

Was it imagination? or had there already come upon Valentine in one short hour, namely, since the discovery, a subtle change, so that she no longer regarded the people with quite the same sense of relationship? She was no longer their sister in the narrower sense. We are all of us, to be sure, brothers and sisters—the clergyman tells us so every Sunday, kindly coupling himself with the assurance, "for you and for me, brethren." But the recognition of this fact produces fruits of affection and charity in comparative scantiness. One may, besides, acknowledge the relationship, and yet be conscious of a certain natural superiority. Perhaps it was only a passing fancy. Yet there must have been some change. She had come to stay with her own individual sister: she could only now stay with the universal sister, and make believe that she was the private sister. And a great mass of miscellaneous thoughts came crowding into her mind too fast and too numerous for comfortable reception.

As for the people, they already knew Valentine, though only just arrived, as the sister of a workgirl living among them in one of their houses—presumably a shopgirl from her neat dress and respectable appearance,[1]

1 A young woman of working-class origins trained to possess the right demeanor and appearance when interacting with a store's more affluent customers. The shopgirl frequently signified the possibility of upward mobility.

and also apparently "quiet"—a quality which in Ivy Lane, as elsewhere, commands the highest respect. The women parted right and left to let her pass, and then closed in again and carried on their parliament with talk as copious and faces as animated as if they had been a conference of advanced women assembled for the purpose of destroying religion and reversing the political power of the sexes. What do they talk about, these feminine parliaments of the crossways? Indeed, no man knoweth; if any were to stay his steps and listen, that rash person would probably be treated as an intruder into the mysteries of Bona Dea. One might, it is true, imitate the reprehensible example of Clodius.[2] Foolish persons, ignorant of these parliaments and of other things, speak of streets such as Ivy Lane as dull and monotonous. How can a hive of humanity ever be dull? There is no monotony where there are, constantly happening, common to all, and talked about by all, sickness and suffering, birth and death, good hap and evil hap, and the wonderful and dramatic situations continually worked out upon the stage of the human comedy by that mysterious unknown Power, known only to man by one quality, and named accordingly by such as speak of Him as "The Unexpected." Not a day but something happens to redeem such a street from the charge of dullness. Only those places are dull where, though the human anthill divided into streets, the human ants come not forth to exchange words with each other, and one man knoweth not his brother, and each by himself selfishly eateth his own cob nuts and giveth his neighbour none, and each alone bitterly endureth his own pain. It is gentility, especially the first beginning of it, which is dull, when people separate from their fellows and refuse to partake with them of the sacrament of sympathy, whereof quiet conversation is the outward and visible sign. Kingsland, for instance, is dull, and Shepherd's Bush is dull, and Camden Town is inexpressibly dull. The man who once proposed a Palace of Delight for Whitechapel, forgot that it was ever so much more needed in Camden Town.[3]

Now, as Valentine passed through the open doorway, a man who was standing within stepped aside to make room for her and took off his hat to her. It was not until later that she realised the significance of the gesture. Everyone does not recognise the fact that the English working-man never takes off his hat to ladies. A man who does so is not a working-man. He is, or has been, among the ranks of those who do take off their hats: that is, he is, or has been, a gentleman. As Valentine went up the stairs this man went slowly into the ground-floor front. She turned to look at him. He looked quite old and was tall, but stooped a good deal. It was too dark to see much of him, but the gaslight in the street outside lit up the narrow passage. She could see that he had long white hair and a great mass of it, and that his chin was white with a week's growth of beard, for it was now Friday, and he only shaved on Sunday morning. His eyes met Valentine's in the doorway, and she remembered afterwards a strange sadness in them, which made her wonder what was the history of the man. In her own room she lit her reading-lamp, and sat down intending to follow out some of the lines of thought opened up to her by her discovery. But she remembered Lotty in the next room, and with self-reproach she went to see her.

The other two girls were out, and Lotty was lying alone. She was in much suffering to-night; her back was bad and her cough was bad; she was moaning as she lay, but in a whisper, so to speak, because when people sleep three in a bed, the habit is acquired of doing one's groans inaudibly for fear of waking the others. The

2 In ancient Rome, only women were allowed into the secret rites of the "Good Goddess" (Bona Dea) of virginity and fertility. Scandalously, Clodius broke into the rites by dressing as a woman. He was tried for and acquitted of sacrilege.

3 A reference to Besant himself, who, in *All Sorts and Conditions of Men: An Impossible Story* (1882), imagined a Palace of Delight for Whitechapel. The novel helped to galvanize support for the construction of the People's Palace in Mile End.

house was nearly opposite the public-house, and the smell of beer and tobacco with the noisy talk of the drinking men came pouring in at the open window.

"What have you eaten today?" asked Valentine.

"I am not hungry. Well, then; bread and tea."

"How long did you work?"

"The others worked all day from half-past six o'clock till nearly nine. But I had to lie down sometimes."

From half-past six till nine! Fourteen hours and a half—all the livelong day. They had been doing this for eight years, and they were going on with it all their lives, with no hope of any change or any improvement or any mitigation. It seems a heavy sentence, my sisters, for the Sin of Eve.

Valentine remembered that in her cupboard there lay a great bagful of grapes—big purple grapes from a hothouse, every one as big as a pigeon's egg, and beautiful to look upon for their delicate bloom. Claude left them there for her. Without any more talking, she got a bunch of these and began to put them one by one into Lotty's mouth, just as a nurse gives food to a little child. It was chiefly exhaustion that had brought on the pain. When she had eaten a few of the grapes it was nearly gone.

Then Valentine carried her into her own room, and laid her on her own bed and undressed her.

"You shall stay here to-night," she said, "a little out of the noise from the street. And, besides, my bed is softer than yours. I can sleep in the easy-chair. Don't dare to say a word, Lotty. Remember that I am Melenda's sister"—Oh, Valentine!—"and you have never seen me in a rage. I can get into terrible rages if I am contradicted or put out. There, now you are comfortable. Oh, what ragged stockings and shoes! I shall give you a new pair tomorrow. Melenda said you were to have whatever I gave you. And you want everything, you poor thing! And now you must eat some more grapes."

"If you could only persuade Melenda to take some," said Lotty. "But she won't, and she's getting thinner every day."

"What shall I do? How can I persuade her?"

"Don't do anything, and then, perhaps, she'll come round."

"Now, Lotty, listen to me. Tomorrow is Saturday. The next day is Sunday. I shall do all your work for you tomorrow—do you hear?—and that will give you two days' rest. And then we will see afterwards."

"You can't do my work."

"Yes, I can. Why I can do all kinds of work. Are you tired now?"

"I was tired when you came; but I am not tired now. It was the grapes. You wouldn't rather be out than sitting with me, would you? But, of course, you are a young lady. Lizzie and the City Road isn't fit company for you. Not that it's good for Liz."

"I would rather be here with you." Valentine stroked her thin cheek and soft hair. "It's better for both of us."

"Oh! you are good," said Lotty. "And please don't mind Melenda. She flies out easy, but she comes round again; and she's kind to me, and never out of temper, though sometimes my back's too bad for me to do any work at all. Then she works for both. There's not a quicker girl with her needle anywhere than Melenda."

"I will try not to mind. But, Lotty, is there nothing that can be done for you? Have you no friends anywhere?"

"No, I haven't got any friends. Father and mother were country born and bred, and I don't know where they came from. I've got no friends—only Melenda."

"Let me be your friend too." Valentine stooped and kissed the girl's forehead. "Don't be proud, like Melenda. Let me be your friend too, Lotty."

"Oh! it's wonderful," said Lotty. "Why, you are crying too, and you're a young lady. How can I be friends with a young lady?"

"Why not? And I'm Melenda's sister, you know."

Again—oh, Valentine!

"Melenda says you ought to be like herself, and a workgirl. Sam—that's her brother—"

"I know my brother Sam," said Valentine. A third time? Oh, mendacious one! But it is only the first step which gives trouble.

"Sam says there oughtn't to be gentlemen and ladies—only men and women. But then, ladies don't use language, and they don't drink. It must be a beautiful thing to be a lady, even without the fine things you had on when you came here first."

"If I am a lady, that is all the more reason for my being your friend. Tell me about yourself. How is it you are so friendless? And were you always so poor?"

"It's through father—because he failed and went bankrupt."

"Oh! is that all?" Mere bankruptcy, in the light of Ivy Lane poverty, seemed a very small thing.

"Father had a shop once in the Goswell Road, you know. It wasn't a big place, but oh! it was a most beautiful little shop, with a parlour behind and four bedrooms above. In those days we used to go to school—not a board school, but a select academy for young ladies, kept by a real lady who had been a dressmaker in a large way, but met with misfortunes—a beautiful school. On Sunday we all went to chapel, where we had a pew, and put on our Sunday frocks. I don't think there ever was a man fonder of his business and prouder of his shop than father. He'd be content to spend the whole day in it, setting out the things, sorting his drawers, and talking with his customers. And sometimes he'd go out and stand on the kerb admiring his windows, where the ribbons used to hang up most lovely. But mother she'd make him put on his hat and go out for an hour of fresh air. Mostly he'd go down Aldersgate Street and into Cheapside,[4] just to see how they dressed their windows. After a good day's takings, he'd come in and have supper and talk about bigger premises and of the time when we would be his assistants."

The romance of a small draper's shop! Yet in it were all the elements which make up romance: the hopes and ambitions of a man for himself and those he loved—the family and the home, the wife and the children—and unexpected fate impending over all with cruel and undeserved disaster. No castle with moated keep could contain better elements of romance.

"And no thought," said Lotty, "of what would happen."

"What did happen?"

"Father went bankrupt. He was broke."

"How was he—broke?"

"I don't know. The customers fell off. Everybody said it was bad times and so many out of work. It couldn't be the fault of father; nobody could be more civil and obliging. Perhaps they got things cheaper at the stores and the big shops; but father said everyone must make his profit, else how could people live? Whatever it was, the customers fell off, and then father he began to get low-spirited and anxious, and things got worse. As for

4 Cheapside was an extremely busy thoroughfare that linked the East End to central London and the West End.

mother, she'd sit and cry until he came in, and then she'd brisk up and pretend to laugh, and say things would come round, and cheer him up a bit. Oh, poor mother!"

"Poor mother!" Valentine echoed.

"That lasted a long time, and we got poorer every day. There was no more school for us, and we sent away the girl. And one day I remember—it's twelve years ago and more—father came into the back parlour, and sat down and cried as if his heart would break because there was a man in possession, and we were ruined."

"Oh!"

"That's all. They sold everything we had, and the beautiful shop that we'd all been so proud of was empty and shut up. Then we went into lodgings, and father began to look out for work. But there, he was heart-broken, and he went about as if he was silly."

"And then?"

"Why, he came home every day without finding it. Nobody, you see, is so helpless as a draper who's been bankrupt. For the other tradesmen despise a bankrupt, and it makes them think that he must drink or be extravagant. And, besides, he knows too much. They don't like to let shop-assistants learn all the secrets of the trade. So he could get no work. Then mother, she took ill with the misery, and went off her poor head, and no wonder." Lotty stopped to choke. "The parish took her, and she died."

"And what became of your father?"

"Oh! don't blame him, poor dear, because he was quite broken-hearted. And he began to drink, and then he had to be a roader[5] for the parish at eighteenpence a day—him who'd kept his own shop; and one day he took a chill from standing in the mud with his broom and his bad boots, and went to hospital, and died there."

"And then you were left alone? You and—had you any brothers or sisters?"

Lotty hesitated.

"Don't tell me more than you like, my dear," said Valentine.

"There was—one—other," Lotty replied with hesitation. "It was Tilly."

"What became of Tilly? Did she die, too?"

"Hush!" Lotty whispered. "I don't know where she is now, whether she's alive or dead. She said she wouldn't stand it, and she went away."

"What did she go away for?"

"She was a beader: she was that clever with her fingers she could do all kinds of things. Once she had very good work as a butterfly-and-bird hand, and did flat-work and slip-stitching. But there wasn't much work, and she couldn't get enough to keep her; and one day she up and said she wouldn't stand it any longer, and so, with only a kiss and a cry, she went right away—Melenda was out, else she'd never ha' let her go—and we've never seen her since. Sometimes Melenda goes to look for her, but she's never found her."

"Where has she gone, then? Where does Melenda look for her?"

Lotty did not answer this question.

"Sometimes," she said, "when I'm alone in the evening, I think I hear her step upon the stair, and oh! what I would do if Tilly would only come back, and be good again—my poor Tilly!—just as she used to be, and bear it all brave, like Melenda."

---

5 One who sweeps streets for a living.

"And then I think about Liz," Lotty went on after a pause. "Because she's discontented, like Tilly, and the hard work frets her; and she doesn't get enough to eat, and her father's awful poor, and can't help her."

"Who is her father?"

"It's old Mr. Lane, downstairs. They say he was a gentleman once, and he did something"—"did something," beautiful euphemism!—"and got into trouble. He writes letters for the German Jews at Whitechapel when they first come, and for the German workmen in the Curtain Road, where they are all furniture men. He knows a lot of languages, but he's so dreadful poor he can't give Liz anything."

"My dear, is the whole street full of terrible stories like this?"

"Well, we're poor, and I suppose there's stories about all of us—how we came to be poor."

"There is one thing you've not told me, Lotty: how you came to know Melenda."

Lotty told that story too. It was a story of two girls' friendship for each other—a friendship passing that of David and Jonathan, commonly supposed to be the leading case in friendship;[6] and how one girl who was strong stood by and worked for the other who was weak; and how for her sake she bore patiently with tyrannies, petty cheatings, bullyings, and defraudings; and how the two presently found another girl as helpless and friendless as themselves, and forced her to remain with them, and kept her in the stony path of labour and of self-respect. Quite a common story—only a wild-weed kind of story—a story which may be picked up in every gutter; so that one wonders why Valentine's heart burned within her, and why the tears crowded into her eyes and ran down her cheeks.

"You must talk no more, Lotty," she said, when her story was finished. "They are getting quieter outside and you will be able to sleep very soon. There—the grapes are within your reach. I shall do very well on the chair. Good-night, my dear. Your cough will be better now. Oh! Lotty, Lotty—I never knew there could be such dreadful troubles as these. Poor child!"

"Don't cry. Perhaps Tilly will come back."

"We must all be sisters together, my dear, and love each other," said Valentine, with some incoherence, but she had her meaning. "It is all that we can do. There is nothing else that will help us all—nothing else."

---

6 The Book of Samuel tells the story of David, killer of Goliath, and Jonathan, son of King Saul, as one of intense friendship, trust, and respect, which is demonstrated when Jonathan must choose between his father's kingdom and his friend's life.

Chapter V

A Real Day's Work

If you please, Melenda," said Valentine, presenting herself in the morning after breakfast, "I am come to do Lotty's work for her today."

Lotty was with her, looking guilty and rather frightened.

"I didn't ask her, Melenda," she explained.

"She wants a rest," said Valentine; "I mean to do it. May I work here with you, Melenda, or shall I work in my own room? It will be quieter for Lotty if I sit here."

"It is only another of their whims and fancies," said Melenda, looking at Valentine as if she was a Specimen. "Give her the work, Liz, and let Lotty lie down till she's tired of her fancy. That won't be very long, and it'll rest Lotty. Then she'll put it down and go away and forget all about the work and Lotty too. They've got nothing to do and so they're full of fancies. Here, take the work."

She ungraciously motioned Valentine to a bundle of shirts, as yet without their button-holes, lying on the table.

"Lotty must have rest, Melenda," Valentine replied, without referring to Melenda's analysis of her own character. "She wants more food and less work. Let her lie down and rest in my room because it's cooler than this." She did not add that it was much cleaner, much sweeter, and much prettier. "She shall have my dinner and I will have hers, if you like."

Lizzie, remembering the ham, chuckled sarcastically. It was her only contribution to the conversation.

"Don't be ungracious, Melenda. I have not offered to give you anything."

"You shan't, then. There!" Melenda dashed her work aside and sprang to her feet in a sudden passion. "I'll take nothing from you—nothing. Not even your cheek, nor your pride. And you shall take nothing from me. Oh! you come here and you think you can make me humble because you've got some money saved and some fine friends, and you've been brought up like a lady and taught to despise us all, and then you think you'll spite me by taking Lotty from me. You shan't have her—no." She laid her arm round her friend's neck and became immediately soft and tender. "No, Lotty dear; she wants to part us, but she shan't, shall she? All these years we've been friends and worked together, you and me, and borne such a lot and never grumbled, and she's only just come. I'll do your work for you as well as my own, Lotty, and welcome, if I have to sit up all night for it. But I can't get ham and grapes for you—work all I know—like she can." The quick tears sprang to her eyes at this consciousness of inferiority.

"She doesn't want to part you and me," said Lotty, "I know she doesn't; and you oughtn't to think I'd ever leave you. Don't be so hard on her, Melenda. Isn't she your sister and all, though she is a young lady?"

Melenda dashed the tears from her eyes. Was Lotty herself going to desert her?

Lizzie went on with her work, her head bent over the button-holes as if her friend's health, and any discussion which might arise upon it, was of no concern at all to herself. But she looked up now and then furtively, just to see whether Melenda was going to catch it or to let someone else catch it. Melenda's tears were but the drops of a short shower which comes before a thunderstorm. She stood with kindling eyes and clenched fists. She was jealous; she was so jealous that she would have liked nothing better than to have fallen upon poor Valentine and—luckily, she did not do it. But she looked so fierce that Valentine remembered what had been said to Violet about the tearing out of ladies' hair, and wondered if she was going to lose her own. She was fierce because she was jealous, and she was jealous because Lotty was visibly drawn towards Valentine, and because for the first time her own sacrifice of work and time could do nothing for her friend compared with the soft words, the grapes, and the creature comforts so freely bestowed by the new-comer.

"You shan't take her from me," she cried again, but with weakened force.

"Don't, Melenda," said Lotty. "I'm not leaving you. Oh! why are you so cruel to her?"

Melenda gave in. She said nothing, but threw herself into her chair and gathered up her work. If Lotty wanted to leave her, she must go. That is what her attitude and action meant.

"Look at her," said Valentine, taking advantage of this momentary weakness which might mean softening; "look at her pale face. Let her rest today and have good food—to-morrow is Sunday. I will go on with her work here, and you may say as many hard things to me as you please."

"I tried to do for you, Lotty—I tried my best, I did."

"You did, Melenda dear. Oh! yes, I know. But it's my back."

"Take her, then," said Melenda with a kind of sullen dignity. "Give her what you like. Give her hot roast beef and potatoes, if you like; but you shan't give none to me."

Valentine led Lotty away, and set her in her own chair with a pillow in the back, and placed some books on the table within her reach. Then she went back to the work-room.

Now, as regards the girl who was sick, she, left to herself, began first to turn over the leaves of a book which had pictures in it. It was a book of poetry. The only poetry Lotty had ever learned or read—because in the select academy poetry was not part of the curriculum—was the verse contained in the hymn-book used by the chapel where in their palmy days[1] her unfortunate family had worshipped. But it was a great many years since she had gone to any church or chapel, and the hymns were well-nigh forgotten by this time, and the hymn-book lost. Consequently, when first she looked at the "reading" and saw that it was verse, she thought it must be a hymn-book; but when she came to read the hymns in it and found she could not remember to have read anything like them in her own book, and missed all the old tags and phrases, she began to fear that Valentine

1 A family's *palmy days* means when they were successful and flourishing.

was a heretic of some kind. Of the narrow creed which had been preached in that little Primitive Christian Church some few rags and tatters remained; notably, that everybody who did not hold the Catholic Faith as expounded by the Primitive Christians was in a perilous state; and that to be a Papist, or an Anglican, or a Congregationalist, or a Presbyterian, or a Unitarian was to invite certain destruction, while even to continue in the twilight of Baptistdom or Methodism was to incur great risks.[2] It is odd how, when one's early faith is forgotten, the narrowness of it may remain, like the crust in the bottle after the wine has been poured out. So Lotty closed the book, in confusion of spirit, remembering something vague about falling from sound doctrines, and bethinking herself of some half-forgotten phrase about the wiles of Satan. These wiles had never been presented to her in a prettier form than in this dainty volume with its pictures and its poetry.

The ignorance, if you come to think of it, of London workgirls and, very likely, of workgirls everywhere, is colossal. It passeth understanding. They have no books in their rooms, not one single book, not even a Bible or a Prayer-book or a hymn-book—single-room lodgers never have any books; they read nothing at all, neither books, nor newspapers, nor journals, nor magazines, nor tracts. They have no knowledge of literature in any form. They hear nothing of the outer world: the men, for their part, may meet and discuss things with some show of knowledge, because they sometimes read a newspaper, but the girls do not; therefore they have not the least understanding of what is going on anywhere, and in all the art, science, and knowledge which we call the inheritance of the ages, they do not own the smallest share. Since, then, they are as ignorant of everything as the inhabitants of the Solomon Islands, without being anything like so well fed and so comfortable or so pleasantly clothed, would it not have been far better for all these girls if they had been born in that archipelago instead of Christian England? There at least they would have no shirts to stitch if there were none to wear, and they would have plenty to eat, even if it were only dried *bêche-de-mer*,[3] and there would be sunshine and warmth for all.

Two of these girls had been educated at board schools, where they had reached the third or fourth standard. If you wish, therefore, to know the extent of their possible knowledge, read the third and fourth standard books, and remember that they have already forgotten almost all they ever learned from those encyclopaedic works. And if they are ignorant of book-learning they are equally ignorant of all that is concerned with industry, wages, and trades. They have not the least idea that they could ever better their condition; they do not understand that they might rebel, or strike, or combine, or do anything for themselves at all. They cannot go into service because they know nothing, not even how to lay a table or how to dust a room; they cannot emigrate because they would be of no use in any colony; they can only sew, and, like the steam-engines which are kept going, till they fall to pieces of old age and rust, on coal and water, the sewing-girls are just as simply kept at working-power till something goes wrong with the wheels, on bread and butter and cold tea.

Their ignorance, however, though it was colossal, did not make them unhappy, nor did it humiliate them. The great giant Ignorance has one good point: he is, in his way, good-natured; he never suffers his victims to be unhappy or humiliated by reason of their subjection. Melenda, indeed, thought herself possessed of extraordinary knowledge, as well as of immense sagacity.

---

2 Primitive Christianity seeks to restore the church to its original form before, as some believe, it became influenced by Roman and pagan practices. Followers of this simplified approach to Christianity (as opposed to Roman Catholics, Anglicans, Methodists, and the others the narrator lists) usually worship in small numbers and do not think of themselves as part of a larger church.

3 A sea cucumber that is considered a delicacy in many parts of the world.

Presently Lotty began to look about the room and to realise slowly the way in which young ladies live—always in easy-chairs, soft and low, with flowers on the table and grapes in the cupboard, curtains to the window, books on a shelf, pictures on the wall, fans, scent on the mantelshelf, and laced handkerchiefs. How would it be to live like this always, and never do any work; never to be hungry, and never to have a pain in the back? While she was thinking of this, and wondering vaguely and asking herself if Melenda was right in saying that Valentine would soon go away and forget all about them, her eyes closed and she dropped off to sleep, lulled by the unusual sense of rest, freedom from pain, and physical ease. She had, besides, a great quantity of arrears to make up in the matter of sleep, and the morning was very hot, and there was a most delicious sense of coolness in the room and the unaccustomed fragrance of flowers, all of which reasons may serve for her excuse.

The making of button-holes is one of those occupations in which it is impossible to take an artistic interest. She who sews them is not sustained by a sense of beauty, because when you have finished and turned out your button-hole, you cannot possibly call it beautiful; it is not a thing, for instance, which you can hold up and watch while the sunlight plays among the stitches and the light and shade set off their graceful curves; besides, you have got to go straight on to make another as soon as one is finished. Nothing sustains the workwoman but the reflection that, though it takes a good many stitches to make a button-hole, so many dozen button-holes make so many pence.

The making of button-holes, however, is not difficult for a good needlewoman. Valentine received a few simple instructions from Lizzie, and then, taking Lotty's place on the bed, she began her work. The button-holes were for shirts, but these were of a coarse and common kind, made of rough material, for exportation very likely—shirts warranted to be as uncomfortable and as rasping as the monastic hair shirt.[4] In fact, I think it is very likely they were invented before the Reformation[5] for the use of monks and modern eremites,[6] and then only for the strictest and most profoundly miserable Order of Self-tormentors. They are now, I believe, used for the converts (previously shirtless) made by the missionaries. And the story of "My First Shirt" has yet to be written. So enterprising has always been the spirit of British commerce!

Valentine was clever with her needle, and could embroider as beautifully as Penelope.[7] Unfortunately she was as slow and as deliberate as that lady-in-waiting, and loved to linger over her work, and look at it, and think about it, and at times unstitch some of it. Therefore she soon perceived that Melenda turned out button-holes about five times, and Lizzie about three times, as fast as herself. Then she made haste to imitate them, and addressed her mind to the question of rapidity rather than of beauty in her work.

No one spoke: there was no other sound in the room than the click of thimbles and the rustling of the stuff. Valentine's thoughts wandered from her work, which was monotonous. This, she reflected, was the room in which three girls slept, worked, and lived. They all three lay on one bed, that on which she was sitting. It was a broad wooden bed, with a hard mattress a good deal depressed in the middle, and neither feather bed nor springs. The hot July sun was pouring in at the window, where the yellow blind, which might once have

4 Rough shirts or girdles made of goat hair and worn by early and medieval ascetic Christians who practiced penance and mortification.

5 In the sixteenth century, Christians revolted against what they believed to be the corruption and false teachings of the Catholic Church in what has come to be called the Protestant Reformation.

6 Hermits, or those who have forsaken life among human society.

7 In Greek legend, Penelope is Odysseus's faithful wife who holds more than one hundred suitors at bay for the ten years Odysseus is lost at sea by confining herself to working on her loom each day.

been white and could no longer draw up, was pinned back so as to leave a triangle of sunshine. Valentine sat in the shade, and thought she had never in her life seen so many motes dancing in the sun. The room was neglected, and wanted cleaning horribly; the grate was rusty; there was not a book in it, or a magazine, or a paper—nothing to read; there were no pictures on the wall; there were no ornaments of any kind; the whitewash of the ceiling had fallen down in one corner exposing the laths;[8] there was no carpet; the two or three cooking utensils which lay within the fender seemed to have been long unused. A place, it seemed, built with intention for the abode of grinding, wretched, hopeless poverty; a place exactly fitted for the kind of work, where there was no prospect of improvement, however zealously one worked, or of any higher pay or more regular employment.

Valentine forgot that the girls were young, and that even to workgirls there is hope, while they are young, that these troubles will pass away somehow, and give place to some unknown kind of joy.

"Well," asked Lizzie pertly, "isn't it good enough for you?"

It was at nine o'clock that Valentine began to work. At ten, or thereabouts, she became aware that she must stop, get up, and straighten herself. She did so. Melenda worked on like a machine, and took no notice at all. The other girl looked and smiled grimly. "I thought you'd give in soon," she said. "Lotty has to lie down every half-hour."

"I haven't given in," Valentine replied indignantly. Then she sat down and went on again.

In another hour her head began to reel, and she felt giddy. If two hours of button-holes produced such an effect, what would the whole day do for her? She laid aside her work, and looked up ashamed. By this time the room was very hot, although the door and window were both open, and from the street below, baked by the midday sun, there was wafted upwards a mingled perfume or incense, made up of things lying in the street; of the industries in the houses—such as the pressing of cloth, which is a hot and steamy smell; or the burning of leather straps, which is insidious, and makes one feel sick; with the smell from a fried-fish shop not far off—this is a smell which makes one sad; and the stale reek of yesterday's tobacco and beer—this is a smell which makes one sorry—from the public-house opposite.

"Do you do this every day?" she asked foolishly, because she knew very well that they did.

"Every day," said Lizzie—Melenda still taking no notice—"and all day long. Don't you like it?"

"Don't you ever stop to read, or talk, or sing, or something?"

"Sing! Oh, Lord!" Lizzie replied with infinite contempt. "Stop to sing?"

"All day long," Valentine repeated, "and never any holiday?"

"Only when there's no work. Fine ladies never think how they'd like it themselves"—Lizzie, too, was able to borrow something from the indignant Sam. "Ain't it nice to make cheap things?"

Valentine took up her work again and went on, wondering how long life could be endured if she were doomed to spend it among button-holes. Then she tried to imagine herself the lifelong companion of Melenda, and altogether such a one as Lizzie, and that she had never done anything else and never known any other kind of existence; and she wondered what she would be thinking about. But her imagination failed her, and refused to pretend any such thing, partly because the things worn by poor Lizzie were not nice to look at.

"Do you never do anything at all?" she asked presently, " except work all day and walk the streets in the evening?"

8 Thin strips of wood to which plaster or tiles can be attached for building walls and ceilings.

"Some girls go to the Britannier when they've got the money, or anybody treats them. I've never got the money, and I'm not going to be treated by anybody, no more than Melenda. There used to be the Grecian as well, but they've turned that into the Salvation Army: and there's the Theatre of Varieties in Pitfield Street, there's Collins's at Islington, and there's the Foresters in the Cambridge Road. Some girls go to public-houses and drink with the men. We won't, Melenda and me. There's talk of a girls' club, but—well, there's nothing else to do but to walk the streets at night, and you'd walk them, too, if you'd been sitting at work all day."

"And Sundays?"

"We lie abed on Sunday mornings, and go out in the afternoons."

"And on wet and cold evenings?"

"Then we sit at home, and go to bed early to save candle and fire."

"Do you never go to church?"

"Not likely!"—Liz lifted her ragged skirt. "In this?"

"Don't waste your time chattering, Lizzie," said Melenda. Then there was silence.

Soon after noon Valentine was seized with an overwhelming desire to get up and jump, or run, or leap over something.

"I must jump!" she cried, and did it.

"That's fidgets," said Lizzie. "I used to have them, but I'm used to it now."

The attack presently yielded to violent measures, for fidgets are like cramp, and must be dealt with resolutely. In reading of convicts chained to each other, and obliged to sleep side by side, I have often thought how dreadful and intolerable a thing it would be if one of them were to get an attack of fidgets and not be able to spring out of bed. Then Valentine was going to sit down again, when Melenda interposed. Lotty, she said, always rested in the middle of the day. She had better do the same and get her dinner.

"Am I not to have Lotty's?"

"Don't be silly," said Melenda. "As if you could make a dinner off bread and tea! What time did you generally have your dinner?"

"At half-past seven."

"That's supper. What did you have before that?"

"There was tea at five."

"And before that?"

"Luncheon at half-past one." Valentine began to feel guilty of most reckless gluttony.

"Oh! And what did you have at all of them?"

Valentine confessed with shame to meat at luncheon and at dinner, and possibly at breakfast.

"There," said Melenda, "it's ridiculous. You can't have dinner like Lizzie and me. Go away and get something to eat, and give it to Lotty if you like. We don't eat much here, but we're independent."

Valentine obeyed, and the other two girls went on working in silence.

Presently there was heard proceeding from Valentine's room a most curious and remarkable sound. Nothing less than the laughter of two girls, a thing which had never happened in the house in the memory of its residents. Lizzie looked up, curious and envious; Melenda suspicious and jealous.

"They're laughing," said Lizzie. "What are they laughing for?"

"She's made Lotty laugh," said Melenda, who had never even tried to work such a miracle. "What's she said to her? Lotty wouldn't never laugh at us."

The laughing continued, and Lizzie's curiosity increased, and Melenda's face grew cloudier and darker.

The old lady in the room below, sitting by herself with her funeral trimmings in her hands, thought somebody must have gone mad. Who but mad people and children ever laughed in Ivy Lane? But the laughing still went on, and her thoughts flew back to a time long, long ago, when the poor old thing herself laughed all day long—living in the Fool's Paradise which sees nothing around or before but a luminous and sunlit haze. Nobody would ever laugh, I suppose, if that haze were to be suddenly removed. Happy Paradise! Happy fools who live in it! And all to end in the workhouse during the winter, and such sewing as could be got in the summer from Mr. Croquemort of Bethnal Green. Presently she could bear it no longer, this poor old woman, but got up and put down her work, and stealthily crept out of her room and crawled half-way up the narrow stairs, her neck craned, her eyes glaring, her ear turned, to see what they were laughing at, and to hear what they were saying. She neither heard nor saw, but a strange emotion fell upon her withered old soul. The laughter of girls—light-hearted laughter!—she remembered how, long, long ago—fifty years ago—when she was nineteen or twenty, two young girls sat in a carriage on a racecourse, and laughed with handsome and gallant young gentlemen, while the pink champagne foamed and sparkled in the long glasses, and the gipsy-woman stood at the carriage-wheel, and the girls crossed her palms with gold. Then that old woman, with something like a sob, felt in her pocket and found twopence, and she went across the street to the "Adelaide" and had a glass of gin. After this she returned to her own room and fell asleep, and, perhaps, dreamed of that long past happy time of unthinking folly.

As for the laughing, it was over nothing at all but the cooking of the dinner, at which Valentine showed herself so awkward and so ignorant. Why, she knew nothing, not even the price of potatoes, or how to buy them, and she had got the very dearest kind of beef, and such an immense quantity, and Lotty had to tell her everything, even to the rolling-up of her sleeves; but she would do it all herself, and so they both laughed. And the business was no doubt as comic as the making of a pudding on the stage,[9] which is, we know, always most effective business.

And then, with the laughter, the other girls heard a hissing and sputtering, which lasted ten minutes or thereabouts, and was accompanied by an extraordinary fragrance, of the kind which used in the old days to delight those dear, simple immortal gods, so easily pleased—the incense, or perfume, namely, of meat, roasted, seethed, or fried.

Then Lizzie sat bolt upright, and said solemnly, with pale cheek, and that far-off look in her eyes which a painter might take for a yearning after things invisible and unattainable—

"Melenda, they've got—it's—it is—STEAK!"

"What does it matter," said Melenda, "what they've got?"

Lizzie was silent for another half minute. But the fragrance mounted to her brain and made her giddy, and filled her with a craving for food.

"Oh, Melenda, I'm so hungry."

---

9 In Britain, pudding is a capacious term for a variety of sweet or savory dishes. Given its ubiquity, pudding often found its way into theatrical comedy in the form of gags or pantomime performances.

"That comes of taking things. If you hadn't eaten that ham two days ago you wouldn't have been hungry now."

There was once a foolish Greek person, whose history used to be read in the "Analecta Minora"[10] when that work was put in the hands of schoolboys. He had a theory that horses ate too much, and he gradually reduced the rations of corn for his own horse, with a view to making that animal live upon nothing, and become perfectly independent of food. Just as he was upon the point of success the creature died. Melenda held much the same views.

"For shame!" she added; "where's your independence, Liz?" Just what the Greek person might have said to the horse.

"Bother independence," replied Lizzie, replying in the very words of the horse, "I am hungry."

"If you eat beefsteak today," said Melenda, "there'll be nothing but bread and cold tea tomorrow and—"

But Lizzie was gone. The perfume of the beef drew her as with ropes, and she could not choose but go.

In Valentine's room there was a white cloth spread and the dinner just ready, and Lotty, with flushed cheeks, helping to serve it, and both of them laughing.

"Come in, Lizzie," cried Valentine gaily; "there is plenty for all of us. Will you ask Melenda?"

"She won't come. Don't you go—she might fly in your face."

Valentine hesitated. Then she sat down. During dinner they talked and laughed again—actually laughed and made little jokes together. When had Lotty laughed last?

Dinner done and things washed and cleared away, they went back into the other room. Melenda was still at work, dogged and stern, with hard set mouth and resolute eyes, sick with the yearning that the smell of the roasted meat had caused, but stubborn and obstinate.

"Melenda," said Valentine, "can you live on bread and tea?"

"What's that to you? I've got to."

"Oh," she cried, "it is shameful."

"Then mend it," said Melenda fiercely; "mend it if you can. If you can't, let us alone to bear it as well as we can. We can bear it, can't we, Liz?"

Liz turned her great eyes to Valentine.

"Can you mend it?" she asked. "It is very hard to bear. Can you mend it?"

"Oh! I can do nothing to mend it. And Melenda will not let me do anything to help it."

"I thought you were going to do Lotty's work."

"She's done more already than Lotty used to do in a whole day," said Liz. "Let her rest a little, Melenda."

"No, no," said Valentine, "I shall do my day's work."

The slow minutes passed slowly. Through the open window there came the murmur and the hum of Hoxton Street and St. John's Road. It was rather a sleepy murmur, because Hoxton is not a noisy place, and there are few omnibuses and fewer cabs, and very few carts and wagons. Presently Valentine felt as if they were all three set down in some far-off place of torture, in an undescribed circle of the Inferno, condemned to work at button-holes without ceasing—button-holes for shirts which would fit nobody—like the unhappy damsels who have to fill sieves with water, and to spend their whole time—they've got all the time there is—in pouring

10 The *Analecta (Graeca) Minora* was a selection of Greek writings used in English schools to teach boys Greek and classical writings, including history, mythology, poetry, philosophy, and fables.

it in and seeing it run out again—a most tedious employment and, one cannot help thinking, with submission and respect to the court, a foolish punishment, and one can only hope that they get their Sundays at least free, in which case they are no worse off than Melenda and her friends. [11]

Presently Valentine began aloud to shape out a little apologue[12] which occurred to her.

"Once upon a time," she said, "there were three poor girls, and there was a wicked witch. The witch was always making spells for the raising of storms and bringing diseases upon good people and thwarting the work of honest people. For use in her charms she wanted a continual supply of button-holes; but why button-holes are good for magic I cannot tell you, only I believe that if you work at them long enough you can raise the—the devil. Anyhow, I know that they are most invaluable for conjuring, incantations, making people mad and miserable, and all kinds of sorcery. The difficulty with this witch was to find people who would sew the button-holes for her, because it is horrible work and tedious work, that no one would do if there was anything else to be done, and because it is work which by the laws of the country—but I think this law is an unjust one—is forbidden to be paid for at the rate of more than a farthing apiece, so that the fastest worker cannot earn more than a shilling a day at it. For a long time the witch looked about in vain. But at last she found three girls who were all so desperately poor that they were ready to take any kind of work that was offered them. It was a very heartless and wicked country, in which the rich ladies took no thought for poor girls, and did not interfere as they ought to have done, or insist upon finding them good work and fair wages, as of course they do in our own country—in England. So she offered them the work. She did not persuade them with honeyed words. She did not say 'My dears, if you will come and make button-holes for me, you shall have roast beef and pudding every day, with money to go to all kinds of beautiful places.' Not at all. She came scowling and cursing, and she threw the work in the middle of them, and she said: 'You girls; take the work or leave it. If you leave it, you will starve; if you take it, you shall taste meat once a week—on Sundays, perhaps—and live for six days on bread and butter and tea. You shall work all day long except Sundays; you shall not have any holidays; you shall waste and throw away in this dreadful work all your youth and beauty; you shall not know any pleasure or rest or fulness; you shall go hungry in body and soul. Don't think the rich ladies will interfere or help you. They care nothing for you—'"

"They don't," said Melenda, now become interested in the story.

"'They have been told about you till they are sick of hearing the story; but they will do nothing for you. So take it or leave it.' That is what the dreadful old witch said."

"Of course they took the work," said Melenda.

"Of course they did; and of course they grew every day hungrier and more hopeless. And one of them was weak, and she gets weaker. Then the other two worked harder to make up. But they couldn't quite make up; and one grew more miserable, but she worked on still"—Lizzie bent her head—"and one grew harder and more angry, and she worked the hardest of all."

"Very fine talk," said Melenda, with an intelligent sniff. "They've taught you how to talk. You talk as well as Sam almost."

11 In Greek mythology, forty-nine of the fifty daughters of Danaus, having killed their husbands, are punished in the afterlife by ceaselessly having to fill a leaking vessel. While this is comparable to some of the lesser sufferings of the damned in Dante's *Inferno*, the Danaides are not specifically mentioned.

12 A moralizing or instructive fable or allegory.

"But I haven't done yet. Suppose a messenger was to come from some rich lady to these girls—a girl like themselves—and suppose she was to offer them lighter work and better pay. Suppose she was to offer them, out of her own abundance, help of any kind—"

"The girls wouldn't be fools enough to take it," said Melenda. "They want justice. That's what Sam says. 'Take your charity away,' he says, 'and give us justice.'"

"This lady would say through her messenger, 'I cannot get justice. I am quite powerless to get justice for girls in the clutches of black wizards and witches. But I can help you three.' Melenda, suppose her messenger brought this message, would you send her away?"

"You can talk," said Melenda. "But you won't make me take your charity."

At four o'clock Lotty made some tea and brought it to them, Melenda not regarding. Then they went on working again in silence. By this time Valentine's fingers ached so that the needle travelled slowly, and her arms ached so that she could hardly hold the stuff in her lap, and her back, though she was as strong as most girls, ached with the stooping, and her head ached with the heat and closeness of the room, and her fingers were sore with handling the coarse material of which the shirts are made, and her eyes were red and inflamed.

But she would not give in.

Melenda was working as fiercely and as fast as if it was seven in the morning, and she had only just begun, and then after an excellent and invigorating breakfast. Lizzie with the quiet dull patience she habitually gave to the work, but with much greater discontent, for she had now tasted some of the joys of a lady's life. It meant, she perceived, a pretty room to live in, with soft dresses and gloves, and your hair done beautifully, and beefsteak and cocoa for dinner. "You ought," said the gentleman she knew, "to live like a lady, and have nothing to do all day but to let me paint your eyes." And when Valentine went away, which would be very soon, there would be no more beefsteak.

My brothers, think of it: the mind of man cannot conceive a greater temptation than this, when a girl half-starved and robbed of joy and doomed to the misery of work the most hopeless and the most miserable, perceives that the unattainable—the life of physical comfort and material well-being, the life she has always longed for, the life that it is natural to desire—is actually within her reach and to be had—just by signing her name to a little piece of parchment, and giving that agreement—of course after it has been duly stamped and entered at Somerset House[13]—to the Devil.

About half-past eight Lotty came in, refreshed after her long day's rest and sleep. "Oh!" she said, tearing the work from Valentine's hands; "oh! Melenda, how could you let her go on?"

For Valentine's cheek was pale and her eyes were swimming, and now she looked dazed, and trembled as she sat.

"I will not give in," she cried; but she did, because she broke into sobbing and crying, "Oh, Lotty—is it every day—all day—all day long, like this?"

"She would do it," said Melenda. "Get a little water, Liz! Quick! Don't stand gaping! It's the heat of the day. Wet her temples. That's right. Don't cry, Polly. I knew you couldn't do it. Get something out of her cupboard for her, Lotty. Some of them grapes. What can you expect of a girl like this trying to do a day's work like Liz and me?"

---

13 In the nineteenth century, Somerset House was home to many administrative offices, including the Registrar General of Births, Marriages, and Deaths.

Melenda's good temper came back to her when once she had proved her superiority. Why, when you came to try a real day's work, where was Polly, after all? Nowhere.

"You look after her, Lotty." She went on with her work, for there was still a quarter of an hour or so of daylight; but Lizzie threw down hers. As for Valentine, it was only for a few moments that the hysteria held her, and she sat up again recovered and a little ashamed of herself for giving in at the end. But—what a day!

It was Saturday evening, and the lane was noisier than usual. Presently Melenda herself thought she might stop, and they began to put things away for Sunday. It may be proved from religious statistics that button-hole makers, though they never go to church, are more open to conviction on Sabbatic doctrines than any other class of persons.[14] They would even like a Sabbatic week or a Sabbatic year—that is, a whole week or even a whole year of Sabbaths.

"I must sing," said Valentine. "I am so tired, and I ache so much that I must sing. Do you never sing, you people? How can you live without? I will sing to you."

There must be some recreation after work. Melenda and Lizzie got theirs by walking the streets; Lotty hers by resting. Valentine tried to find hers by singing.

Below in the street, the people were all outside their houses, gathered in groups talking and enjoying the cool air of twilight. To these people there happened the most wonderful thing in all their experience. Suddenly there struck upon all ears the voice of one who sang—the voice was like unto the sound of a silver clarion. The song they heard went straight to all hearts by reason of the air, for they were careless of the words; it made their pulses quicken and brightened their eyes, and the parliament of women was hushed, and the feet of all were drawn towards the house, and even the children ceased their shouting, and sat still to hear. For such singing had they never heard and never dreamed of. What Valentine sang, in fact, was a ditty called the "Kerry Dance."[15]

While she sang there came down the street, not arm in arm, because they were deadly enemies, yet walking together because they loved each other, a certain assistant priest—formerly he would have been called the curate—and a certain young general practitioner, medicine-man, doctor, a person skilled in physic, anatomy, botany, biology, and all kinds of learned things. Both were young as yet, and poor. I know not which of the two was the more pragmatic, pedantic, and conceited; whether the assistant priest, who professed to know the secret ways of the Almighty, and pretended to be entrusted with the most tremendous powers, and measured law, order, and humanity by the little tape of his little sect—he was a ritualist person and impudently called his sect "the Church": or he who knew all about bacteria and mikrokokkos[16] and evolution and protoplasm, and didn't want any church at all, and saw no soft place anywhere in his stupendous intellect where he could possibly want any religion.

"Oh Lord!" cried the doctor, who only believed in himself, and therefore generally called upon the Lord.

"Dear me!" said the assistant priest, who didn't believe in himself at all, and therefore swore by his own name.

"This is very wonderful," said the doctor, listening to the voice.

"Oh! To think of it,
Oh! To dream of it,"

14 They are, in other words, enthusiastic observers of the Sabbath but in a secular fashion.

15 A song by James Lynam Molloy, a popular Irish composer of the era.

16 Micrococcus is a common type of bacteria.

sang Valentine.

"This," said the assistant priest, "is the most wonderful thing I have ever heard. What a voice!"

He left the doctor and followed the voice up the stairs, and found himself unexpectedly in a room filled with four girls, at sight of whom he turned and fled, conscious of intrusion.

But the people in the street were clapping their hands.

Said Lotty, "Oh! it's lovely. But they want another."

Valentine laughed and sang another. The singing quite restored her. This time she sang "Phillis is my only joy."[17]

The people held their breath while they listened. When it was over Valentine shut down the window, to show that the performance was finished.

"It's all very well," said Melenda, once more conscious of inferiority; "anyone could do it if she had been taught."

"Anyone," said Valentine.

"But oh!" said Lotty; "all the same it's wonderful."

"There were four girls in the room," said the assistant priest, "and one was lying on the bed. And the one who was singing looked somehow—but it was rather dark—like a lady. I felt I had no business there, so I came away."

"Of course she was a lady," said the doctor. "Nobody but a lady could sing like that. Well; I hope she'll come again. What a mistake you fellows made when you turned the women out of your choirs. By Jove! That girl's singing would actually make the men go to church!"

What the assistant priest replied I shall not report. As he lost his temper every day with the doctor—they met every day—it would not be fair to set down in cold blood the things he habitually said on these occasions. One may, however, record briefly that he had now began with, "I *do* think"—which is the London clerical equivalent for a well-known Yorkshire idiom; sometimes he added, "I *must* say." But that was only when the controversy raged long and bitterly, and when this, or its equivalent, in nautical language, or the bargee dialect, or the London patois, was absolutely necessary.[18]

17 A song by Charles Sedley (March 1639–20 August 1701), an English dramatist and poet.

18 Yorkshire, in northern England, is known for its distinct dialect. Bargee dialect and London patois are dialects of barge workers and Londoners, respectively.

Chapter VI

Behind St. Luke's

Oh, Claude!" Valentine opened her door and came out to meet him when he knocked on the Sunday morning. "I never thought I should be so happy to see anybody! And you are ten minutes late, sir. To be sure, you have not been all alone in Ivy Lane for three days."

"The place is truly awful, Valentine. It looks even worse today than when we came here with Violet."

Certainly Ivy Lane has a way of looking more mournfully shabby and dirty on Sunday mornings in summer than on any other morning in the week; perhaps this is because there are more potsherds, mouldy crusts, bruised and decaying fruit, bits of paper, cabbage stalks, potato peelings, broken pipes, plugs of tobacco, and other drift and wreckage of life lying about on that than on any other day. It was already past eleven, but very few people were stirring, and no one had yet taken a broom in hand or thrown a bucket of water over the flags. Lizzie and Melenda were not yet dressed; Lotty was lying on Valentine's bed in restful ease, not asleep, because it is foolish to sleep in moments free from pain. She had a book in her hands, but her thoughts were wandering away to the old times of the happy days in the little shop before the custom fell off; and she was a child again with poor impatient Tilly, and her father was proud of the shop, and her mother was happy in her husband and her children. For what sins, far back in the third or fourth generation of unknown and obscure ancestors, had Fate been so hard upon this poor draper of Goswell Road and his family?

"You are still alive, Valentine, and no one has—"

"No one has offered me the least incivility, Claude, except of course Melenda, who is still unforgiving."

She looked as bright and as fresh as a young girl of twenty can be expected to look. Her long day's work had left no trace behind except a little paleness of cheek, and perhaps a little shading below the eyes; standing among those dingy houses in her youth and grace and beauty she looked as Aphrodite herself might have shown had she imitated the Father of the Gods when he went visiting the slums, and called upon Baucis and

Philemon in their squalid hut.[1] She had been waiting for Claude a whole half-hour, quite ready for him, and "with her things on"—pretty, poetical, feminine locution! To mere man, a woman's dress is the setting and frame of beauty, the mysterious accompaniment of loveliness, a thing to be regarded with wonder and respect: but to superior woman it is but a collection of "things." Such is the philosophic superiority of the sex, and so readily do they despise mere external trappings and outward show.

"It is a dreadful place," Claude repeated. "I am amazed that you dared to come here. Can you be happy in it?"

A most weak and feeble question. What is the use of asking a girl who is young, strong, beautiful, and relieved from the necessity of work, if she can make herself happy anywhere, and especially where she is entirely free? No one knows, until he has witnessed it, the happiness which the young lady, even of the best-regulated mind, feels when her movements are free and uncontrolled; and to think that, with their liberty yet to gain, women will fight for such vain shadows as female suffrage and a seat on a school board! Besides which, Valentine was going to spend a whole morning in the company of a young man charming in many respects, but especially in this, that he believed himself to be her brother.

Happiness, again, is so uncertain a quality. Nobody, except a newly engaged couple, is often consciously happy. We do not recognise happiness until it has vanished; and then we lament, yet with pride, as those who have entertained a god unawares. A truly remarkable thing that all the world should ardently desire a possession which nobody understands until it has vanished. A certain ancient philosopher, after he had made an impromptu conundrum, or a double acrostic, upon this paradox, went away and elaborated a treatise, now happily lost, on the "Folly of Praying for Happiness." I suppose that, even on this Sunday morning, Valentine would hardly have confessed to perfect happiness.

"I am going," she said, "to take you for a walk. There are no parks in Hoxton, and there are no gardens or anything. I suppose there is no place in all London so far from any open space as Ivy Lane. So we can only walk about the streets. But when we are tired, I know of a beautiful churchyard—I found it the other day—where we can sit down and rest. A good many of the people are in bed still, because it is Sunday morning. Lying in bed saves breakfast; and besides, it rests them. They get up, I believe, somewhere about dinner time. Melenda and Lizzie are in bed now, for instance. However, we shall find some of the people in the streets."

For her own part Valentine had very little desire to study the People—with a capital initial. She came to Hoxton solely in order to get acquainted with the members of her own particular family, the Monuments: and especially with Melenda Monument. But she was naturally curious about the new strange life she found there. Curiosity has led to a good many remarkable things: to the conversation with the Serpent and the tasting of the Apple; to the breaking of all laws—human and divine, moral and meddlesome, just and unjust; to the acquisition of all the knowledge that has been acquired, and to the growth and development of sympathy. She was by no means a philanthropist. Her interests, like those of all healthy-minded young people, were as yet chiefly confined to those whom she knew and loved. Her affections as yet limited her sympathies; she had no desire to deduce and to lay down general laws concerning the manners and customs or the instincts of what we feelingly call the "lower classes"—philanthropy does sometime cover such a beautiful contempt for its objects. She just began by being interested in a group of three working-girls, from whom she was rapidly

1 In Greek mythology, Zeus, the king of Gods, visits Earth disguised as a mortal and is taken in by two commoners, Philemon and Baucis. Although they have little to share, they treat the stranger hospitably and Zeus rewards them for it.

learning the one lesson most worth learning, namely, that the People are, in all essentials, exactly the same as the Other People. There are not, in fact, in this any more than in any other country, two races, but one; and the best way of acquiring an exhaustive and scientific knowledge of that one race is to sit before a looking-glass for a long time and look at it. This is really a most valuable maxim, and the sooner it is generally accepted and acted upon the better for everybody, particularly for those who are ridden by fads, fancies and old Men of the Sea.[2] Women, for some unknown reason, understand this law better than men, and it is the cause not only why they make better nurses, but also why they are harder in their dealings with the poor and needy. Those who love sweet sentimentality and the pleasures of imagination should not try to understand too many laws of humanity.

Valentine was brimful of things to talk about; but when a lady lives altogether in one room, she cannot very well use it as a *salon*. This difficulty is generally, by the ladies of Ivy Lane, on the evening when they are at home, overcome by receiving their friends upon the kerbstone[3] or by sitting on the doorsteps. Valentine, perhaps in ignorance of this custom, preferred to wander about the streets, and led Claude forth into labyrinthine Hoxton. The city has been, it is true, laid out something like an American town, with parallel streets and cross streets at right angles; but it has happily preserved some of the old winding ways which were formerly lanes between hedgerows, across fields, and among orchards of plum, cherry, apple, and pear. The lanes remain—some think that Daedalus once lived in Hoxton, about the time when Pythagoras was teaching at Cambridge[4]—but the hedgerows are gone, and houses and shops have taken their place. Valentine piloted Claude among the winding courts, but first she led him into Hoxton Street, where on a Sunday morning there is always a great market held and all the shops are open. The roadway is covered with the carts of costers, and the pavement is crowded with those who stroll idly along, content to be doing nothing except to lean against something solid, pipe in mouth and hands in pocket. Valentine led the way with the air of an old acquaintance—a two days' old acquaintance—and as one, therefore, competent to become a cicerone.[5] She showed Claude the streets branching right and left, those where every room in every house is a workshop as well as a living-room and a sleeping-room, and those where every house contains a workshop. There are no other kinds of houses in Hoxton City. In one place she showed him a mysterious court, paved and broad and clean, consisting of little two-storied houses inhabited by cobblers, repairers of umbrellas, sign-writers, feather-finishers, and the like, which is protected and beautified at either end by most magnificent iron gates, solid and splendid, richly worked, and fit for a duke's palace. How did these gates come to Hoxton?

Presently, in their walk, they came to a church, and they looked into it. The morning service was halfway through. Wonderful spectacle! There was not a single man in the church, except the two clergymen, the choir, and the churchwardens: yet everything set out in readiness for a full and enthusiastic congregation of the faithful, with a lovely row of lighted candles in staring brass candlesticks where no lights were wanted, mocking the sunshine which poured through the windows, quite an extensive choir in surplices, and two officiating

---

2 *Old Men of the Sea* are bad habits or other harmful practices, persons, or beliefs of which it is hard to rid oneself. The phrase comes from an entity that Sinbad the Sailor must confront on his fifth voyage in *Arabian Nights*.

3 British spelling of *curbstone*.

4 Daedalus was the ancient Greek inventor of legend who constructed a labyrinth to hold the monstrous Minotaur. Pythagoras, also an ancient Greek, was a philosopher and mathematician.

5 A guide who leads sightseers through institutions or sites—such as museums or places of archaeological discovery—containing items of historical or artistic significance.

clergymen, and in one snug corner a place provided with a curtain and a chair—the whole forming the simple properties necessary for a nice little confessional. Sad indeed that Englishmen should be found to scoff and to stand upright and to think for themselves, and to speak words of derision about this innocent little piece of furniture! Outside the church, benighted scoffers stood about in groups among the carts and the carrots, and even joked and actually laughed among each other; but not at the church, nor at the confessional-box, because they were perfectly, wholly, and completely ignorant and careless and indifferent about anything which might be going on within that building.

"This," said Claude when they came out, "reminds me of a procession on the stage where they have forgotten the spectators."

"It is like a concert," said Valentine, "where there is no audience. Isn't it dreadful, Claude, for nobody to go to church?"

"It doesn't seem quite as if the Church had got a strong grip of the people about these parts, does it?"

Then they left that street, and presently stood upon a bridge and gazed upon the romantic waters of the canal which parts Hoxton from Kingsland; and then along St. John's Road, which is a boulevard less popular than Hoxton Street, yet loved by the quiet and the meditative. At the end of the street stands a massive church—one of those churches built in the middle of the last century, with a vast portico of granite pillars and a white spire which is big and high and yet not beautiful. They looked into that church too. There were no confessional cribs and no candles; no one was mumbling; the clergyman, on the contrary, was speaking out plain and clear, and the service preserved something of the ancient severity. In that church there could be counted no fewer than twenty-five families—father, mother, and children—all worshipping together as they should, and making a grand total of at least a hundred and twenty people, without counting the preacher and the pew-opener. This is very satisfactory indeed, because the parish contains only seventeen thousand six hundred. One churchgoer out of every hundred and fifty! It makes one hopeful, because it reminds one of the early church in Rome, as depicted by M. Renan.[6]

Then they walked down Pitfield Street and thought no more about the people but selfishly considered each other, and Valentine narrated all her adventures, and told of Melenda's stubborn independence, and of Lotty, and of Lizzie, and her own experiment of a long day's work. Only she concealed her great discovery.

"You must never do that again, Valentine," said Claude, referring to the day's work. "Promise me you will not."

"I do not think I could. But oh! think of those poor girls working every day and all day long, and for so little! Is it just and right? Who is to blame for it, Claude?"

"The system, I suppose, is to blame—whatever the system may be. I have never considered the subject of the English Industries, except when Sam forces his own opinions upon one."

"But it concerns you, Claude; and Melenda is your—our sister."

"Why do they go on doing such work, I wonder? There are other things to do. But Melenda will not brook any interference. How can one help a girl who will not accept any help? What can I do?"

6 Ernest Renan wrote *The Life of Jesus* (*Vie de Jésus*), an influential book that depicted Jesus Christ and his time in real historical terms and not simply as mythology.

Valentine made no reply. She was disappointed. Claude did not respond to her own enthusiasm. To him it was no new thing to hear that working-girls are disgracefully paid and cruelly worked. It is, alas! no new thing to any of us. We hear about them every day, yet the thing goes on.

"Melenda might go into a shop, or she might go into some kind of service. Anything," said Claude, "would be better than what she does now. But she will take no help from me."

"You might as well put a zebra in harness as Melenda into any kind of service. Can nothing be done to get them better work?"

"I don't know. I will consult with Sam if you like."

"No, Claude, I don't want you to consult with Sam. Consult with yourself. With all your knowledge and cleverness you need not stoop to take advice of a board school master."

"My knowledge has not taught me how to deal with workgirls." Here he noticed a change in Valentine's face. "I have disappointed you, Valentine. I knew I should."

"No, Claude. But I thought—I hoped—oh! I am so sorry, Claude, for those poor girls."

"Show me, then, some way to help them."

At this point they reached the junction of Pitfield Street and Old Street. Here Valentine turned to the right, leading her companion past the old wells of Dame Annis le Clair and the Peerless Pool[7]—but they were both, unhappily, ignorant of their historical associations—past the great hospital named after the physician apostle, where certain demoniacs, unhappy ones of the earth, wait for their release from the prison of unreason—it is brought to them by a personage figured generally as a skeleton with a scythe.[8] Then they passed a church which boasts the most amazing spire conceivable. In the whole of the habitable world there is to be found none other like unto it. Country people and strangers flock in multitudes to Old Street only to gaze upon its miracle of ugliness. Travellers are said to cross the Atlantic with no other purpose than to visit this, the ugliest church in the whole world. Why not? Any street might be proud of owning the ugliest thing that ever was built, and if people willingly face the perils of the deep to visit the most beautiful church in the world, why should they not incur the same risks for the sake of the most ugly?

At the back of the church there was formerly a vast burying-ground, because when St. Luke's was built, a hundred and fifty years ago, the ground hereabouts was cheap. It is not venerable, as men generally reckon that quality in churchyards, by age, for the church itself has only baptised and buried five generations of mortal men and women. But it is venerable because here lie at rest the once aching bones of thousands who in their lives knew no rest. Here you will not find the remains of any great or illustrious men; they are all the bones of toilers; their names and histories are clean forgotten—even the histories of those whose heirs, in their pride, had the name and date of birth and death carved upon a headstone. The stones themselves still stand, ranged round the walls and within the railings, but no man readeth them any more, and if one doth perchance read them, the names, even to the oldest parishioner, awaken no memory. They have long ceased to bury in this Acre of the Lord; the funeral verses of hope and resignation are no longer heard; there is no more rattling of

---

7 Also known as "St. Agnes le Clere's Well," the spring was dedicated to St. Agnes and thought to possess healing properties. Peerless Pool was a public swimming pool converted from Perilous Pond, so named because of the drownings that occurred there.

8 Luke was a physician and apostle of early Christianity. The narrator refers here to St. Luke's Hospital, which treated the mentally insane, a class of persons some believed to be possessed by demons. The figure of Death is typically represented in Western art as a skeleton with a scythe.

ashes upon ashes and dust to dust, and they have now laid out the ground for the children's play and a place of rest and meditation for the old. The graves are levelled; the headstones are placed back two and three deep within the railings, where the garden mould covers them up within an inch or two of their deathless names, and so they stand or lean, with only the inscriptions visible, and look as if they were not churchyard stones at all, but the stone faces of the very original holders and possessors of the ground, stonily gazing without power either of spoken remonstrance or of approval upon the present use of their sleeping-place, yet so great is the power of expression in a headstone that one can plainly distinguish in some of them satisfaction; and in some, doubt; and in some, stern disapprobation. Two or three of the old railed tombs are left upon the grass to serve, perhaps, as the skeleton at the feast. As for the ground itself, it is laid out in four fair lawns, each with a round bed of shrubs and a narrow bed of flowers. In the middle the ground has been artificially lowered, and one descends by a step or two into an area where they have erected a pedestal. Why a pedestal with nothing on it should have been put up passeth man's understanding: but this is the taste of St. Luke's, and we have only to bow before it. There are, one is pleased to remark, seats in plenty; and the walks are asphalted and easy for the foot of age; and they have planted trees which will perhaps some day grow tall and be umbrageous.

This morning there were in the garden a goodly number of old men and women with a great quantity of little children. The men sat together, and the women sat together, and they talked after their kind, which is a querulous kind, because old age is a term of life only to be represented in a favourable light by those who know how to conceal things and are rich enough to make themselves comfortable. These old people hear the voice of the grasshopper continually; besides, they all have rheumatism, and they do not attempt to conceal that they hate the voice of the grasshopper and abhor rheumatic pains.

"Let us sit down," said Valentine.

"The problem of Melenda," Claude began sententiously, "is the great problem of labour. It is nothing less than the problem of the age."

"Then solve it, Claude. In the old days a knight was sent forth to kill a dragon or a loathly worm."

"Anybody could kill a dragon."

"Or to find the Holy Grail"

"If one were to find it now, people would first dispute its authenticity, and then they would stick it in a museum as an archaeological curiosity."

"But this is a task of much more interest than a doubtful relic. Is it possible, Claude, that you have never thought about Melenda and her life?"

"Seriously, Valentine, I never have. Do not reproach me with selfishness. Her own independence is one cause, and then we have always been accustomed to go each his own way. Sam goes one way, Joe another, Melenda another. The only way that I can think of to help such a girl, so fiercely independent, is to alter the system itself, and that so radically that these miserable wages shall be made impossible. And it has never occurred to me that I should try to do this. Had I the lever of Archimedes I could not do it."[9]

"Yet I think—if I were you, Claude—I think that I would try," she replied slowly.

9 Through his analysis of physics, the ancient Greek Archimedes determined that with a long enough lever, and from the right location in space, one could move even the Earth.

"I have read books and treatises on rent, production, and so forth. Everybody reads these things, especially a barrister who wants all the information that he can get from every side. But certainly not with a view of inventing or preaching any new system."

"Never mind the books, Claude. Look at the people, not the theories. Here is our own sister, Melenda. This poor thing is condemned to a life that is only better than a slave's because she thinks she has kept her independence and because she cannot be tied up and flogged. Our own sister, Claude! She is miserably fed and wretchedly clothed; she is always half-starving and she goes in pitiful rags. Her very pride and her independence make her misery cry out the louder for your help. Your own sister—our sister. And she is so brave and so fierce. Our honour is concerned, Claude; we must try; if we cannot help her any other way, we will help her by altering the system, even if we have to call in Sam, and all become Socialists. It is for Violet's sake and mine, Claude, as well as your own. How can we endure to live in happiness while she lives in such misery?"

"Yes, Valentine, yes." Claude was moved by her emotion. "You are right. It concerns me, you, Violet—all of us. And I am a selfish creature. But—what am I to do?"

"I do not know," she replied impatiently. "What is the use of education and knowledge if they cannot be used to find out things? Have you become a Fellow of Trinity and a great scholar and a lawyer only for your own advancement, Claude?"

Claude made no reply, for, you see, his own personal advancement was exactly what he had always considered the ultimate end and object of any success he might make in life. He had always put the thing to himself from this point of view; he intended to get on, to climb as high as he could, and to do the best he might for himself. He had climbed already from the washerwoman's cottage on the edge of Hackney Marsh to the Trinity Combination Room,[10] which is a good way up the hill, and he was continually thirsting for opportunities to climb higher still. When he took the prizes at school; when he carried off scholarships at College; when he stood third in the first class of the Classical Tripos, he felt himself answering the end of his existence, and justifying Lady Mildred's sagacity in picking him out from among so many. His own advancement! Why yes—his own, and no other's.

"Do not be angry with me, Claude," she pleaded. "Only this morning, before you came, while I was thinking of these poor girls, something I had read somewhere came into my mind. It was to the effect that all great things are done by strong men; each thing by one strong man, who knows what he means and is strong enough to make other men work for him. If that is true, we should be always praying for a strong man."

"I suppose we should."

"Why should not you, Claude, be the strong man?"

"Because I am not a strong man, and because my own work has been laid down for me on other lines."

"That is only your own work for yourself."

"Yes—yes, of course," he replied a little uneasily. "But then it is work which leaves no time for anything else."

Suppose you have chosen deliberately the work which seems to suit you best, and the goal which seems desirable above all others as the noblest and highest; suppose you have good reason to believe that you will succeed; suppose in fact that you are perfectly satisfied with yourself, and that suddenly you are shaken to your very centre by the information that your aims are merely personal and selfish; that you are called upon to undertake certain other work which may cause you to change your whole plan of life; that everything

10 The Trinity Combination Room is a large meeting hall located in Trinity College, University of Cambridge.

you value must be abandoned if you obeyed that call;—this was the new light which flashed suddenly upon Claude's brain on that July morning as he sat among the ashes of the obscure dead and among the houses of the obscure living. Dead and living, he belonged to them; they were his own forefathers who lay sleeping beneath his feet; they were his sisters who worked in the houses around him. He belonged to them. But never before had it occurred to him that he might work for them instead of for himself.

"Seriously, Valentine, I do not think you understand what it is you propose. Do you really mean that I should set myself to finding out a remedy for evils which have defied every professor of political economy?"

"I mean that seriously."

"But what am I, Valentine, that I should discover an answer to the questions which have baffled all the greybeards?"

"Perhaps the answer must come from the young. Oh! do you think that Paul waited till he was grey before he began to speak?"[11]

Sometimes it seems to me as if Valentine struck here upon a great and remarkable truth. We have perhaps been all along asking too much of the old. It is perhaps from the young, while their hearts are full of generous emotions and unselfish sacrifice is still possible, that an answer to all great questions may be expected. The world belongs in fact to the young; not only the world to enjoy but the world to fight; the future is in the shaping of their hands; theirs is the inheritance; they are the princes and the governors, the sheikhs and the emirs,[12] the generals and the captains. The old may go on accumulating and storing, relating and writing; that is properly their department; they are historians. As for new and great ideas, they are too much for them; when one such idea is conceived and one such great scheme is brought forth, the old philosopher, the veteran economist, the defender of vested interests, the man of sixty-year-old ideas, will very naturally bring out his watering-pot and turn the rose on to that idea, and point out the real wickedness of the world, the selfishness of man, and the unremitting watchfulness required by this project, all of which render the scheme impracticable and impossible. Then the young men will use much the same language as that employed by certain unlucky village children towards a certain prophet of old, but with a different conclusion to the story. For in my story the children would kill the bears.

"Everything," said Claude, "up to the present has been driving me farther from my own people; even, I thought, the recovery of my sister. It will be strange if she should take me back to them. Let me think, Valentine. I acknowledge the obligation, but I declare that I can do nothing. Why should I waste myself in beating the air?"

For Valentine did not see, which was clear to himself, that such an effort, to be serious, would require nothing short of a man's whole work with all his thoughts and all his strength. And even then he would most likely fail. Yet some small success might be effected. And the thing touched his honour. His own sister—not his sister in the common bonds of humanity—but the child of his own mother, was one of those who lay tied and bound by strong chains in the dungeons of Castle Famine, held there by the great bully Giant Competition. His own sister. But what could he do for her, except—and that perhaps in vain—give her all that he had? And so, like the other young man who had great possessions, he was minded to go sorrowfully away. For his own possessions were neither of silver nor of gold, but the far more precious things of knowledge and wit and

11 Paul the Apostle was a prolific writer and missionary. Fourteen of the epistles of the New Testament are attributed to him.

12 Arabic titles for rulers of small communities and of provinces, respectively.

understanding—the things which would lead him to honour and distinction and men's praise in the brave days before him.

At this point of their discourse there came ambling along the asphalte an old lady. Valentine seemed to know her, but could not recollect where she had seen her—a curious old lady to look at, because she walked delicately and gave herself airs such as might become a young and beautiful woman. There were not now remaining many traces of former beauty, but as much perhaps as one expects after seventy years of a life not devoted wholly to the contemplation of things spiritual. She was dressed in a frock which looked ridiculously girlish, and as she walked she rolled her eyes about as if to watch the effect produced by her appearance.

"Ho!" said this dear old thing, stopping before Claude and Valentine. "Ho! Indeed! The young lady of the first-floor back"—Valentine remembered her now. She was the old woman she had seen dancing all by herself: "The young lady with the new furniture"—she had inspected it through the keyhole. "I hope you are very well this morning, my dear; and I hope you are as happy as you are beautiful. Your lovely dress matches your lovely complexion, and if you didn't make it yourself, it was made in Regent Street, and cost three guineas if a penny, simple as it looks. Your pretty boots match your pretty little feet, and if they were not given to you they cost you a guinea a pair, and your gloves were four-and-six. Quite right. Quite right. Be as happy as you are beautiful, my dear—while your time lasts. Youth is the time for happiness. I was happy myself once."

Neither her words nor her appearance produced an impression of the straitest and most narrow virtue.

"I am very well, thank you," said Valentine coldly.

"With your young man. My dear, I said you had a young man. And he a gentleman. I said that nothing short of a gentleman would do for you. And he knows how a girl should be dressed, he does. Very proper too, my dear. I had the same sentiments as you when I was young."

"Let us go, Claude," said Valentine, rising.

Claude gave the old crone a coin, and she ambled away with a parting smile and a nod, very terrifying to behold.

"A reminiscence," said Claude, "or a survival of something in the theatrical way, I should say."

"If I thought," said Valentine, "that I could ever come to look like that old woman—it is not her age and her baldness and her poverty, but her terrible eyes—I would go straight into a nunnery at once and hide myself."[13]

13 Places where nuns live and worship.

Chapter VII

The Professor of Yiddish

I've been doing up the room for father," Lizzie explained. It was Sunday evening, and about nine o'clock, when Valentine came home and met her coming out of the ground-floor room. "I do it every night before I go out."

"And you sit with him sometimes, I suppose?"

"No, I ain't fit company for father. He don't want me. He was a gentleman once, and he talks proper."

"Have you got no mother or sisters, or anybody besides your father, Lizzie?"

"There's Melenda and Lotty. That's all I've got. Before Melenda taught me to sew I used to be a step-girl."

"What's that?"

"It's like this, you know. Some people—not here, but Kingsland way, over the Canal—like to have their doorsteps cleaned once a week. That's what I did for 'em at a penny a step, and sometimes three-ha'pence. When Melenda taught me to sew I gave up that. It was only a low trade."

"Where is your mother?"

"She died long ago. There's only father, and he can't do nothing for me."

If he knows how to "talk proper," Valentine thought, he might at least have taught his daughter the same art. She remembered the tall old man with stooping shoulders who took off his hat to her. Doubtless this was Lizzie's father.

"Is your father so very poor?"

"Dreadful poor," said the girl. "He was a gentleman once, but that was a long time ago."

"Do you think he would let me call upon him?"

"I don't know." She opened the door. "Go in first and ask afterwards. Father, here's Melenda's sister says may she come in?"

"May she come in?" The old man raised his head slowly and repeated the words. Then he rose and bowed, offering his chair, the only chair in the room. There was no candle, but the gas-lamp in the street outside gave sufficient light to show that the room was furnished with a wooden bed covered with a rug, a table, a chair, a washing-stand and a candlestick. There seemed to be literally nothing else at all. Strange to say, there was not even a pipe or the smell of tobacco.

"When a young lady comes to see me," he said politely, "the least I can do is to offer her a chair. Pray do me the honour to be seated."

The manner and the voice and the words of the man were inconceivably out of keeping with the squalid place in which he lived. Valentine accepted the chair and sat down, wondering who this man might be. Lizzie stood at the open door watching her father with undisguised pride. It was long since she had witnessed any of these reminiscences of polite society. "Once he was a gentleman." Why, thought Valentine, is he now a ragged gentleman, and how is it that he has suffered his daughter to grow up without any manners at all, since his own are so good?

"You have been kind to my daughter," he said, still standing. "Nobody, so far as I know, has ever before been kind to her, not even her father."

"You can't help that," said Lizzie loyally. "It ain't your fault, father."

"Therefore I thank you," he added, without noticing the interruption. "My daughter is a workgirl, and is naturally more accustomed to ill-treatment than to kindness."

"But I have done nothing for Lizzie."

"You have given her dinner and supper, and you have spoken kindly to her. It is something that the girl should find anybody to give her anything. Yesterday evening I heard you singing upstairs. You have a very beautiful voice. I could play and sing myself formerly. But it is thirty-five years since I played last.

"Have you forgotten how to play?"

"I have not played anything for thirty-five years," he repeated.

"And now you live here all alone." It was a weak thing to say, but one cannot always find epigrams, and besides, Valentine was still occupied in wondering what this strange thing might mean—the grey-headed, ragged man who lived alone in so miserable a room, and his daughter, who seemed to have nothing to do with her father except to look into his rooms once a day—a man in such a place who had the unmistakable manners and language of a gentleman, and the other who was nothing at all but the London workgirl—rough and ignorant, and ill–mannered.

"As you see," he answered, "quite alone."

He sat down on the bed, his hands joined over his knees, looking at his visitor with large and lustrous eyes. His clothes were dilapidated to the last degree—his coat in rags, the elbows in holes, his trousers patched at the knees apparently by an amateur, and his boots gaping at the toes. He was picturesque in his rags. Lying on the bed was a tattered Inverness cape, and on the table an old felt hat.

A broken-down gentleman. It was apparent in his voice, in his speech, and in his carriage. By what unlucky accident had this poor gentleman got down so low?

Girls like Valentine are not accustomed to read a man's past history in his face, but she could discern that on this man's face there was not the seal of drink and vice. It was a face with refinement stamped upon the high white forehead, and gentleness in the blue eyes which met Valentine's steadily and open, though with a strange sadness such as she had never before seen even in pictures.

"Nobody," said Valentine, "can be quite alone in the world. You must have some friends or relations."

"Most men have. But a singular accident happened to me—a very singular accident"—he raised his voice with a strange smile—"about thirty-five years ago. All my relations died suddenly. All the relations I had in the world and all the friends in one day. There is not a single person now in the whole world who ever asks if I am living: not one who cares to ask me or wishes me back again. I have passed quite away, even out of remembrance: even out of the prayers of those who once loved me. For they are all dead. They all died on one day."

"And have you made no new friends all this time?"

"None. Those who are so poor as myself make no friends. Twenty years ago I found a woman about the streets as poor and as miserable as myself. I made her my wife, and we shared our misery. Perhaps hers was lessened. Lizzie is her daughter, but she is dead. I have no friends."

"Poor man!"

"I have not complained."

"Perhaps if you were to go 'back again,' as you said, you might find some of your old friends. They did not all die, I am quite sure."

"Yes, they did. Every one. It would be odd, too, to go back to the old world just as I am now, and if they were living to offer them my hand. Sometimes I have thought of it. But there—what does it matter? As for the past, we live in the present and the past lives in us. Yes"—his voice sank—"the past never dies: every moment lives forever. That is the dreadful thing. Why, even the souls of the forgiven must go about forever with hanging heads and shameful foreheads. Always," he repeated, "with shameful foreheads."

This was the man who had "done something," Valentine remembered.

Lizzie at this point, finding the conversation just a note or two above her, went out and shut the door softly.

"You have your daughter."

"Yes. But I can do nothing for her. You wonder that she is what she is. Young lady, there is a level—I have reached it and stand upon it—which the thoughts and habits of such as yourself would turn into a hell. Better for the child of the gutter to grow up in the gutter."

"You must not call Lizzie a child of the gutter. She is your child, and she is a pretty girl, and has refinement in her face if not in her manners."

"Let her remain where she is and what she is. Then perhaps she will never understand the nature of her inheritance."

"What inheritance?"

"Lizzie is a great heiress; she will inherit the whole of my property if she ever finds out of what it consists."

"Your property?"

"The accumulations of thirty-five years, invested at compound interest in shame and dishonour." The words were strong, but he spoke quite calmly. "It is so great a property that I cannot bear to die and leave it behind me. I should like to rob her of it, and have it buried in my pauper's grave with me. It is all my own making, this property. I am quite a self-made man. When I began I had nothing of it. Yet that does not avail. I must die and leave it behind me. A man may take into the grave nothing of his labour which he may carry away in his hand. What profit hath he that he hath laboured for the wind?"

"You read the Bible still," said Valentine, starting.

"No, I read nothing. There is not a Bible or any book at all in the room: but I remember something of what I used to read. These are the words of the preacher, who said many wise things. It was he who praised the dead which are already dead more than the living which are yet alive. I too, who am yet alive, praise the dead more than the living. It must be a beautiful thing to be already dead. There the prisoners rest together: they hear not the voice of the oppressor: the small and the great are there, and the servant is free from his master."

He said all this in measured tones, and without the least passion or sign of emotion.

"You have no books. Can I lend you any?"

"No, I do not want to read."

"Do you always sit here doing nothing?"

"Always. It is my happiness to do nothing. Then I can live the past over again, up to a certain point, and I can follow the impossible future. I know," he went on, "that you would like to be helping me. Ladies who come to such places as this think they can set everything right by a few acts of kindness. I thank you, but you cannot help me. Look round the room; you see that I have reduced my life to the simplest form possible. Here is a place to lie down upon, with a rug to keep me warm; here is a roof, and here are walls; a chair, a table, a candlestick, a washing-basin—what more does a man want? I get my breakfast and my supper at a coffee-stall. When I can afford dinner I get it at a coffee-house. I neither drink nor smoke tobacco. I have no other wants than a certain amount of food and a place to lie down."

"You are a philosopher."

"No; a philosopher is contented, but I am not. I live in this wretched way because I have no choice. You are curious to learn how I live. Very well, I will tell you. It is an honest way. I know two or three languages—German and French and Italian. I learned them when I was young. I also—by accident—once learned some Hebrew. I have since learned a little Polish. I know where German immigrants congregate, and I write letters for them, especially for the Polish and German Jews—all kinds of letters, begging letters, letters asking for employment—at twopence each, or whatever I can get for a letter. They tell me their wants in their own language, which is generally Yiddish—that is to say, Polish and German and Hebrew mixed. Sometimes I do well; sometimes I do badly. Very often I do not make as much as a shilling a day. I pay three-and-sixpence a week for my room, and I can live on half a crown-fourpence a day. That is all; that is my life."

"Your present life."

"Yes, my present life. Young lady," he raised himself upright and sighed heavily, "there are some lives, some unhappy lives, across which Fate draws, right in the middle of them, a thick black line. My life has been so divided."

The thick black line meant, perhaps, some kind of failure or bankruptcy, Valentine conjectured, such as reduced Lotty's father to the profession of roader. Yet he spoke of shame and disgrace, and he was generally supposed to have "done something."

"I wish I could help you in some way," she said. "Let me try for your daughter's sake."

"You say this because you are a young lady, and generous. But I want only what I have told you—food and a sleeping-place, and obscurity. Stay, you can do something for me. Will you sing to me?"

Valentine considered a little. Then she joined her hands and sang to him. She sang, "He shall feed His flock," perhaps because it was Sunday evening.

"Thank you," said the man when she had finished. "It is thirty-five years since last I heard that sung."

"May I come again and talk to you sometimes?"

"Yes, if you please. But it is not right for you to come here. Besides, I might get to look for your coming, and that would interfere with my dream."

"Your dream?"

"While I sit here alone in the evening I am possessed by a dream. It is the dream of my old life, carried on just as it should have been. I follow myself in my dream step by step and year by year through the career which might have been mine, had it not been for that—that thick black line. If you were to destroy that dream, you would destroy my only pleasure. Then I should become discontented and dream of revenge instead. That would be bad and foolish for me; first, because I never shall get my revenge, and next, because thinking of it calls up the devil, who makes me fall into a rage and then claws at my heart and tries to drag it out of my body. One of these days he will succeed, and then the doctor will say I died of angina pectoris,[1] because it is not scientific to say that a man died of a raging devil. If it were not for that I should dream of revenge perpetually."

"Oh, but," said Valentine, in the amiable manner of one who has no enemies to forgive, "revenge is such a poor thing to desire, and besides, it never satisfies."

"I don't know," the man replied. "Simple killing does not satisfy. But something like the eternal revenge of Ugo Foscolo,[2] you know, something to go back to at intervals, and when the old rage rises again in your heart like a flame. Ah!" he clapped his hand to his heart, "it begins again." He gasped, and held his breath as one in sharp and sudden pain. Then he pulled out of his pocket a little bottle, and the room became charged with the faint scent of ether. "I must not talk any more about it. Sometimes I think that forever and forever I shall be punished for my sin by this flaming fire in my heart, and the burning desire for revenge. Well, I will not complain. Hush! Do not talk to me any more. Let me get back quickly to my dream."

She turned to go. Just then there came the sound of steps and a kind of scuffle outside the door.

It was caused by the old lady of the back room, who was being dragged, pushed, or assisted to her own room by a young man dressed in a black frock coat and a tall hat. The old lady was apparently unwilling to go.

"Is she ill?" asked Valentine.

"No; in these cases the illness follows the attack. She will be ill enough tomorrow. Come, old lady, off you go to bed."

The patient began to sing, and even Valentine, in spite of her inexperience, was able to understand that her illness was caused by nothing else than a rush of alcohol to her head. In fact, the poor old creature was tipsy. She had been spending on gin the shilling which Claude gave her in the morning. The man who was helping her got her into her room with a vigorous effort, and came out, shutting the door upon her.

"There," he said, "she's all right now. You'll hear her making a little noise perhaps, but not much, and she'll soon be asleep. Somebody has given her gin, and I suppose she'd had nothing to eat all day. The boys were chivying her about the street, so I brought her home. She will sleep it off." Then he looked into the front room. "Good evening, Mr. Lane. No more attacks, I hope?"

"I had one just now, doctor. I began to think—"

"Well, then, you mustn't think. I warned you before. If you get excited you'll just kill yourself. How's the dream getting on?"

1 The medical term for a form of chest pain often brought on by stress, which can result in a heart attack.

2 An Italian revolutionary poet praised in nineteenth-century England for his literary attacks on Napoleon.

"It is working itself out slowly, doctor. Slowly the career approaches its appointed end. A deanery has been offered him, but he has refused it. A man of such eloquence and learning can't be shelved with a deanery! A bishopric is the least that he will take. Sometimes there are thoughts about an archbishopric.[3] But I doubt whether there will be time on account of my thinking, you know, and the rages I fall into—"

"You must not fall into rages."

"The other day I seemed to hear his voice. But it was only someone talking outside with this young lady. Yet it was his own voice—exactly his own voice."

"I have warned you, remember. Good-night!"

The doctor shut the door, and turned abruptly to Valentine.

"Well," he asked, "you are the young lady that was singing the other evening. What do you think about us?"

He might just as well have asked what Valentine thought about humanity in the abstract. She replied to that effect.

"I don't suppose you have come here without an object," he went on. "You have got something at work in your brain. It is charity or religion or humanity, I suppose. Whatever it is, if you want information come to me. I know all the people about here."

He had a rugged face; his cheeks were without colour, as often happens to those who have lived always in the streets of a great city; he was neither tall nor short, rather a thin man, about thirty years of age; but he had a big head. His eyes were deep-set under shaggy eyebrows—quick earnest eyes; his forehead was square, and his nose was large, rough hewn, and distinctly ugly; his dark hair was parted at the side, and had already begun to "go" at the temple; he carried his head a little on one side habitually. It is a mode which suggests a thoughtful disposition.

"Thank you," said Valentine.

"You will want to know a good deal, I dare say. Very good then. To save you trouble." He spoke in a quick jerky way, as if he was wanted elsewhere, which was in fact always the case with him. "Do we go to church? We do not. Do we revere the institutions of our ancestors? We do not. Have we any respect for rank and dignity? Not a bit. Do we care for anything but meat and drink and warmth and ease? We do not. Are we dangerous? Not so long as we are in regular work. Do we save our money? Not a mag.[4] For whom do we vote? For the Radical, because he promises to tear things down. What is our political programme? The abolition of church and Lords. Why? Because we think it will raise wages and lower the price of beer."

"Thank you," said Valentine. "But I am not likely to inquire into the politics of the people."

"Do we, then, yearn for art? No, we do not. Do we love things beautiful? We don't even know what beauty means."

"I do not expect to find art here."

"Are, then, our morals good? They are not. Have we any virtues at all? A few. We are tolerably honest; we are generous when we have any money, and we stand by each other when we are in trouble: man by man, woman by woman, and girl by girl."

"Girl by girl?"

3 In the Anglican and Roman Catholic clerical hierarchy, a dean oversees a group of parishes that make up a portion of a diocese, while the bishop oversees the entire diocese, or a region of parishes.

4 Slang for a *half penny*.

"Because," he explained, irreverently, "there is none other that fighteth for them, as your Prayer Book says, but only they themselves. So they stand by each other. There's a magnificent example in this very house upstairs."

"Thank you very much. Good-night." She moved towards the staircase, but he stopped her.

"One minute," he said. "I mean what I say. They tell me you are staying here. It is a queer place for a young lady to take lodgings in. Got a little pocket gospel of your own to run, perhaps?"

"No, I am quite contented with the old gospel."

"Come to do good, as they call it? Well, you mean the best, I dare say. Don't do more harm than you can help. I'm always somewhere about the place if you want me. Good-night."

He nodded his head familiarly, without the usual ceremony of lifting his hat, and hurried away.

Chapter VIII

Lotty's Foolish Dream

After her two days' rest, Lotty ought in common decency to have shown some signs of improvement, if not of complete recovery. That she did not was only part of the well-known ingratitude of the poor. You may give them a lift over a bad bit, and they go on stumbling into worse bits: the sick woman basely and ungratefully develops more alarming symptoms and the man out of work continues to meet with new disappointments, so that where you began with a helping hand you must either maintain a pensioner or leave your patient in a worse plight than you found him.

I do not think that Lotty meant to be ungrateful; she would have preferred, I am quite sure, strength to weakness and health to pain, but she did have a very bad night on Sunday, and when on Monday morning Valentine looked in she found the girl in a low way. One bunch of grapes and two days' rest, and a real, not a phantom, dinner on each day, were, you see, insufficient by themselves to meet the case. Valentine thought of what the old man below had said about ladies thinking to set everything right with a few acts of kindness. Even a bunch of hot-house grapes, at four shillings a pound, is not enough to repair the mischief wrought by eight long years of privation and hard work. Valentine might as well have tried to restore her youth to the old lady on the ground-floor back with a box of violet powder. Acts of kindness are not without their uses, but they cannot actually cure disease.

Lotty was lying on her back, pale and with closed eyes. The two girls were standing by the bedside frightened.

"She's awful bad," said Lizzie. "She's been bad all night. It isn't that she's hungry, because yesterday was Sunday and there was a bit of meat. You can speak to her if you like: she isn't asleep."

"Don't try to speak, Lotty. We will carry you into the other room. It is quieter and the bed is easier. We will all three carry you." Melenda turned her shoulder with an expressive gesture. "Melenda, are you so proud that you cannot even bear to see your friend relieved?"

"Do what you like for her," said Melenda. Then she burst into tears of jealous rage at her own impotence. "You shan't do anything for me. Oh, Lotty!" she flung her arms over her friend. "I can't do anything for you, my dear, and I thought I was to do everything. I'm no use to you when you want my use the most. And now you're going to be helped by a stranger."

Valentine said nothing, and presently Melenda left off crying, and consoled herself by assuming the command in the matter of carrying Lotty.

The other room was certainly quieter and cooler, and the bed was not so hard. And then they sent for the doctor.

It was the same young man who had spoken to Valentine on the Sunday evening. But this morning he seemed rougher in his speech and manner,

"It's been coming;" he said; "I've seen it coming."

"What is it?"

"She's got to rest. Don't tell me, you girls, that she can't. Because she's got to, do you hear? and she's got to have good food."

"Rest and good food!" said Melenda, bitterly. "Oh, Lord! why don't you say she's got to have oysters and chicken and port wine?"

"Good food!" said Lizzie. But she looked at Valentine.

"Rest and good food," the doctor repeated, "and nothing to do for the remainder of her days; and that won't be long," he added in a lower tone.

"She shall have rest and proper food," said Valentine.

The sharpest sting of poverty is when you are made to feel your own impotence to relieve the suffering which wealth can remove; even to avert the death which wealth can stave off. Melenda's eyes flashed, and she made as if she would say something fierce and resentful; but she restrained herself in the presence of the doctor, though the effort cost her a good deal and the tears sprang to her eyes. "Come, Liz," she said, "we'll go back to work."

"There's only you and me now," she said presently, looking up; "Lotty won't come back any more. She won't let her come back. She'll give her grapes and beef and cocoa so that she won't want to come back. She's given her a new petticoat and new stockings already. She'll try to make her hate us just to spite me because I let her have a bit of my mind. Oh, I know for all her meek ways she's a sly one! If it's good for Lotty"—here she choked. She wished to be loyal to her friend, but it was a bitter thing that she should be taking gifts from anybody but herself. "You'll go next, I suppose, Liz. Very well then. There'll be only me left. If you want to desert me, take and go and do it. Perhaps she'll give you all your meals if you stoop so low as to take 'em."

"Don't talk wild, Melenda. Lotty hasn't deserted us. Why can't you be civil to your own sister? Why shouldn't she help Lotty? I'm glad she came here—there! I'm glad she came. Do you hear that?"

Melenda at other times would have crushed this spirit of revolt, but she was this morning too dejected, and made no reply.

"Desert us?" Lizzie went on. "Why shouldn't Lotty desert us, come to that? What can we give her? Desert us? Why, Melenda, it's so miserable that we may just as well desert each other at once, and give up trying."

Still Melenda made no reply.

"Last night," Lizzie continued, "she went and sat with father. Poor old dad! With him in his rags. Did you ever do that? And she sang to him, and Saturday all day long she worked for Lotty. You never did more. Desert us? What could Lotty do better, I should like to know? Look at this bed and the one she is lying on; look at this room and the other; look at her dinner and ours. I really wonder you should talk such nonsense."

Still Melenda made no reply. She was crushed. Her growing discontent and her newly-born knowledge of better things gave Lizzie a spirit which privation could never give her.

In this way, however, Lotty's chains were taken from her.

Day followed day, but she did not rise from the bed. Sometimes Melenda sat beside her, work in hand, gentle with her, though full of resentment against Valentine. Sometimes Lizzie sat with her. Generally it was Valentine who read to her, sang to her, talked to her, and nursed her. There are some women whose mere presence soothes a patient; whose touch drives away pain; whose voice is a sedative; who are the born nurses. Valentine belonged to them.

A little happiness, even if you do have a bad cough with it, and an aching back, and limbs which feel as if they could never move again, is a medicine delightful to take, and sovereign against many evils, especially lines in the forehead, drawn mouth, and worn eyes. Lotty's thin cheeks did not grow any fuller, but they lost something of their waxen pallor, and a faint glow appeared on them as of winter sunshine. Her hollow chest did not grow any deeper, but her shoulders seemed less contracted. Her eyes were not so weary, and on her thin lips there presently appeared once more the old smile which she had lost about the time when her father went bankrupt, and her mother went mad, and her sister said she wouldn't stand it any longer. She would never get any better; she knew this somehow, but it is not hard, when one has had so long a spell of work, just to lie passive, though the days which slip by so quickly bring death so very near. Less hard still is it when one has such a nurse as Valentine, and a doctor, who comes every day with something to charm away the aching, and for the first time, after many a long year, dainty and sufficient food. Presently sweet and pleasant thoughts began to linger in her brain; they were thoughts that came to her while Valentine read and sang. The spectre of Famine, with her dreadful uplifted scourge of scorpions, had vanished.[1] She was no longer driven to try, if only for half an hour, to hold the shirts and make the button-holes. She was no longer anxious for the future; though there was no more work for her to do, she could not starve. Valentine was with her; she could close her eyes in peace and sleep without dreaming of an empty shelf in the morning. Is it possible for us, the overfed sons and daughters of a luxurious *bourgeoisie*,[2] our eyes swelling out for fatness, who have never known a single day without its three abundant meals, and never felt the pangs of unsatisfied appetite, even to conceive of an existence such as Melenda and Lotty had lived together for eight years, with never enough to eat on any day from year to year? Why, one asks, what contentment, what resignation, even what acquiescence in life as a gift or a loan, of something precious, can there be when one is always hungry? Of the two other girls, the presence of Valentine made one daily more discontented with her lot because of that terrible temptation of which we have heard. She could any day, only by saying the word, convert herself, she was told, from a workgirl into a "lady"—the word being used to signify one who does no work for her living, and wears fine clothes and lives

---

1 The narrator's description here is not a common personification of Famine and is tied to the earlier connections he draws between Fury and Hunger.

2 The middle class.

in comfort. As for the other, it made her daily more obdurate and more angry, because she was so helpless, and it was Valentine who did everything for her friend.

"I won't be kind to her, then," she said, when for the fiftieth time Lotty besought her and expostulated with her. "I won't give in and be kind to her. Why should I? First, she comes and laughs at us."

"No, she didn't laugh."

"She said she was twins and she didn't know which she was. Do you call that laughing at us? I do. Then she comes again and thinks she can make it up with beefsteak and ham. No, Lotty; and it ain't likely."

"She came to live here of her own accord. She wasn't obliged to come. She's never cross and never unkind; she never says a hard word of anybody; and oh, Melenda, the care she takes of me! Even you, my dear, never took more care. And the nights when she sits up with me, and the things she gets for me, and, oh, Melenda, I ain't her sister, and she'd do more than this for you if you'd only let her." Melenda sniffed. That fact made Valentine's conduct the more intrusive. "And she watches every day for you to give in a bit."

"Let her watch, then," said Melenda.

* * *

"No little pocket gospel after all?" asked the doctor again. He was standing at the foot of the bed looking at his patient. He had not removed his hat—a ceremony he usually omitted in his rounds—his hands were in his pockets, and his shoulders were a little rounded, and he looked as if he despised the vulgar details of good manners. "No little pocket gospel, then?"

"None—why?"

"Because—well—because, the summer is hot and this place is noisome, and you are doing the work of a hospital nurse, and somehow you look as if you ought to be at the seaside, or in some quiet country place under the trees. And, in short, what do you do it for?"

"Why do you ask for motives? You said yourself the other day that there was only one motive, and that was pure selfishness."

"That is so. They call it religion, patriotism, benevolence, charity—whatever they please. It is all self-preservation."

"And there is no disinterested action at all possible for poor humanity?"

"There are illusions. Women do wonderful things for men whom they love, as they call it. Men call it love when they subjugate a woman and get a slave for nothing. Why women delight in being slaves I do not know."

"And so everything is an illusion."

"Everything except what you see; and sometimes that is an illusion too. When life is over, what is the past but illusion? We are born: we live and suffer: and we die: and are forgotten. That is the history of Ivy Lane, where there are eight hundred people, and two births and one funeral every week. But I don't understand you. If we ever do get a lady here, she comes and looks about her, and is disappointed because we are not more unpleasant, and then she does a kind thing or two and goes away with a feeling that the sum of poverty has been sensibly alleviated by her visit. She has seen a suffering object, which gave her pain; she has relieved her suffering for a little while, which gave her pleasure. But you—why, you have given—yourself. Well"—he changed the subject abruptly—"what do you think of the working-girl? You have got three of them to study. There are thousands just exactly like them."

"I can think of these three only and how to help them."

He answered indirectly. He took up Lotty's arm and bared it to the elbow.

"You see: a strong bone and a good length of limb. Nature designed this arm for a stout strong woman. A fair breadth of shoulder, too. Nature meant this girl to be a really fine specimen. Look at her forehead: it is broad and low—a capable forehead; and her mouth—see how fine are the lines and yet how strong; this was meant to be a very noble woman, strong in her illusions of love for husband and children. Yet, you see, a splendid model ruined."

"Poor Lotty!"

"We are always wasting and ruining fine models. This street is full of human wrecks. You've got two of them below—Mr. Lane, the letter-writer, and the old woman. What does it mean?"

"Can you tell me what it means?"

"Nature says to man, 'Learn my secrets, or I will kill you. I have no pity on anyone—I will kill you unless you learn my secrets.' Very well: some of us, the happy few who can, are always learning these secrets, and saving men from Nature's traps. But man says to his brother, 'If you are not strong enough to defend yourself against me, I will make you my slave; you shall work for me on my own terms.' I don't know whether Nature is more cruel than man, or man than Nature. Here you see"—he touched Lotty's cheek. The girl did not understand a word of what he was saying, but he was the doctor, and if he were to cut off her arms she would not dream of resistance. "Here is a case in which man, meeting no power of self-defence, has worked his wicked will, pretending that he is obeying the laws of political economy. That is to say, he turns this girl into a machine for doing what she ought not to have done at all, for longer hours than she ought to work, for less pay than she ought to receive, and for poorer food than any woman ought to eat. Nature, at her worst, would not have trampled on her worse than man has done."

"What are we to do then?"

He sat down and looked in her face blankly.

"I don't know. If I did know everybody else should know. There are only two ways of helping the working-women, and one of these, at least, is possible. The impossible way is that the ladies of the country shall unite to form a protection league for their working-sisters."

"Why is that impossible?"

"Because they don't care for their working-sisters," he replied bluntly. "You only care because you have lived among them and know what their sufferings are. Ladies deliberately shut their eyes; they won't take trouble; they won't think; they like things about them to look smooth and comfortable; they will get things cheap if they can. What do they care if the cheapness is got by starving women? What is killing this girl here? Bad food and hard work. Cheapness! What do the ladies care how many working-girls? Confess now."

Valentine would not confess.

"Well, there may be another way. It is by the working-people themselves, and that by a grand universal league, or federation, or brotherhood of labour—men and women alike—to control wages and work. I do not see why such a league should not be formed. If men can unite for one branch of work they ought to be able to unite for all."

"Why should they not?"

"Because the mass that has to be moved is so gigantic that not one prophet but ten thousand all preaching the same gospel at the same time are wanted. I wonder how it would work out."

"How would it work out?"

"We've always got to take into consideration man's greed and selfishness. However, if we got over that, first of all, a case like this would not be allowed. The league would make it impossible. The league—" he sat down and put his hands in his pockets, looking straight into Valentine's face, but as if he did not see her. "I have often wondered what such a league would do. I suppose it would become a most stupendous tyranny—everything for the general good must be. I think it would try to be just on the whole—there's somehow a natural instinct against injustice; it would be the most powerful instrument ever devised; it would control the whole government; it would go making all kinds of laws for the restriction of liberty, that is quite certain. I suppose they wouldn't let the men marry under thirty nor the women under five-and-twenty. As for the men with land and capital, and corporate bodies and companies with property, I should say the league would make itself unpopular with them. One thing, however, the league would do, and that as soon as it was established."

"What is that?"

"It would insist on this girl and her friends working half the time for double the wages."

"I don't see much difference," said Valentine, "between your league and Sam's Socialism."

"I haven't the pleasure of knowing Mr. Samuel, but there is this difference—that my league will be formed by the people for the people, and the Socialists want to impose their scheme on the people."

"Why not, if it is good for them?"

"Because, young lady, you can't improve people by any scheme or law or government at all. They must improve themselves. The best chance is when every man feels that he is part of the government. You have no idea of their obstinacy. They will neither be led nor driven nor coaxed; they will only go of their own free will. And some ways they will never go at all."

"Then I wish the brotherhood or league were formed already."

"Perhaps you and your friends would lose your property and your money."

"But we should free Melenda."

"A very good thing for her, and I don't suppose it would be very bad for you. As for me, I have got no money, and my profession brings in as it is only the wages of a mechanic—so I shall not suffer."

He got up and buttoned his coat.

"You, Lotty girl," he said, "keep quiet. I sometimes think"—he turned to Valentine again as he went out—"I sometimes think that I may live to see that great league of labour."

I know not what Lotty heard or understood of the doctor's discourse, but it may have been this which suggested a truly wonderful dream that came to her that very afternoon when she fell asleep after dinner while Valentine sat reading, and through the open window came the murmur of the children's voices in the school behind Ivy Lane. According to an ancient authority there are five kinds of dreams; and sometimes they come through the gate of horn and sometimes through that of ivory.[3] This dream came to Lotty through the gate of ivory. It was the kind described as the imagination of a non-existent thing, and yet a holy dream, and one to be

3 In *The Aeneid*, Virgil describes two gates of sleep, one of horn and one of ivory. Although the ivory gate is far more beautiful, it leads only to false dreams, while the horn gate leads to truth.

received as a gift from heaven and sent to cheer and comfort a dying girl with the vision of what might be. She dreamed that she was in a workshop—lofty, well aired, and beautiful. She was doing some kind of work—I think she was making up white linen robes for the harpers who play before the throne—and her work filled her with joy. She was quite well and strong, and without pain of any kind, and she felt a strange elasticity in her limbs. Her sister Tilly was beside her dressed in white like herself, and as she recognised her it was as if a sponge had blotted out the past, so that it should be remembered no more, and Lotty rejoiced that Tilly too should have a frock as white as any in the work-room.

Melenda was with her too, the lines gone from her face, her thin cheeks filled out, looking truly beautiful in the eyes of Lotty and her like; and Lizzie was there, also with work in her hand, but laughing and talking more than she worked. Valentine was there too, dressed just the same as herself, but she looked more lovely than all the rest; and the other one—she who had cried when Melenda spoke up; but now she was sitting beside Melenda with one arm round her neck. They were all so fond of Melenda that they could not make enough of her. There were thousands of workgirls in the room; they were all laughing and talking happily; and outside the open window stretched a great garden with the morning sun lying on it, and orchards filled with trees loaded with ripe apples. The scent of flowers came into the room; and no one was tired, no one was hungry, no one was cross or wicked. Strangest thing of all, Lizzie's father was with them, looking venerable with his long white hair brushed off his forehead. He was not in rags, but dressed like a gentleman, and he sat at a great organ. When he began to play, Valentine stood up to sing, and all the girls tried to sing too, but could not, because of the tears—tears of joy and happiness—and the memories of the cruel past, which choked them.

"Why, Lotty, Lotty!" said Valentine, "what is the matter, dear?"

"It was my dream," she replied, looking about her.

"You laughed and cried together, dear. But you have had a long and refreshing sleep, and it is nearly tea-time. This makes up for last night, doesn't it?"

Chapter IX

Showing How the Band Played

Melenda says Sam's here," said Lizzie, putting her head into the room. "If you want to see him, you'd better come at once. And, I say, you'd better look out. Melenda's in a rage, and the band's a-going to play, sharp!"

Sam Monument, from time to time, remembered that he had a sister, and went to visit her. It was not often; because since his rise to greatness, he was no longer proud of his poor relations. The few among us who have raised themselves to the level of a board school master will sympathise with Sam. Besides, it made him ashamed even to think of Melenda; and it made him rage like Scylla and Charybdis, and the Maelstrom,[1] and the rapids of Niagara, actually to see her at her miserable work. Again, there is a rule which should be carefully observed in visiting one's poor relations; but Sam had never heard of this rule; namely, always to visit them in mild and cloudy weather. The former, that one may be spared the bitterness of cold; and the latter, so that there may be no mockery of sunshine. Sam came to Ivy Lane on a splendid summer evening, when the sunshine made everything glorious that was clean and neat, and magnified the meanness of everything that was dingy and ill-kept. When Valentine opened the door he was standing with his back to the empty fireplace, which gave him the command, so to speak, of the room. Melenda was sitting by the table, her work in her lap, and the thimble on her finger; but she was not sewing: and there was a gleam in her eye which betokened another approaching triumph of temper. She looked strangely like her brother; the eyes as bright, the lips as firm, only that her own red hair was long and Sam's was short, rising from his forehead like a cliff, so that his head resembled the rounded back of a hedgehog about to defend its property.

"Oh!" he said, with a kind of snort when Valentine appeared. "You *are* here, then. Claude told me something about it. I hope you are pleased with what you have found. Ever been in this room before? Have you looked

1 In Greek mythology, Scylla and Charybdis were sea nymphs transformed into paired dangers of the sea—one a six-headed monster and the other a deadly whirlpool. The Maelstrom was also a large whirlpool from which, in Norse legend, no ship that entered it could possibly escape.

round it? Satisfied and pleased with it? Like to feel that your sister lives in it? Nice place, isn't it?" He went on without waiting for an answer. "Nice work, too, they do in it. Wholesome, well-paid work. Work to make a woman rich and happy. Something for your rich friends to be proud of, isn't it?"

The room looked more than commonly dingy. The strings of the blind were broken; the blind itself was pinned up, and a reflection of the evening sun from an opposite window fell upon the side of the room, not so much lighting it up as showing how dingy it was, and how desperately shabby.

"It don't matter much what you think, Sam, nor what she thinks. Thinking can't alter things. Those who've got work to do must do the work they can get. She can give dinners to people who haven't the independence to refuse"—Melenda tossed her head at Lizzie, who laughed defiance—"and will only be the more discontented afterwards, when she goes away. But she can't get us better work nor better wages. What's the good then?"

"What did you come for?" Sam asked. "What made you leave your friends and come down here? These people are your enemies: the working-people are the natural enemies of the people who do nothing. I told you, when I saw you first, that you've got to choose. If you like to give them up, say the word, and I'll find something for you to do. If you won't give them up, then go away back again, and enjoy yourself as long as you can, till the smash comes."

"I shall not give them up, certainly," said Valentine. "And I am not going back again just yet."

"Oh, very well. You're one of those who go tinkering up a rotten place here and painting over a bad place there, and pretending that everything is sound and healthy. I know the sort. You get some people together, and you give a concert, and call it softening the masses. You get a few pictures and hang 'em up in a schoolroom and call it introducing art among the lower orders. Yah! Art and the lower orders! Or you have tea and cakes and a hymn, and call it bringing religion home to the people. And then you go around with pennies and oranges for the children and flannel for the old women, and call it bringing the classes together. As long as you choose to stay with them, I tell you all the people are your natural enemies. Melenda here is your enemy, and so is Lizzie, and so is the girl you've got laid up in the other room."

There is a pleasing nursery fiction that accounts for many disagreeable things by a theory on the right and the wrong way of getting out of bed. Valentine remembered this, and felt quite certain that Sam, Melenda, and Lizzie had all three got out of bed the wrong way that morning. There was going to be a row, and one of uncertain dimensions. And she was invited by Melenda in order that she might assist at that row and help to make it a row royal. Therefore, she made haste with a soft answer.

"I did not come with any ambitious idea of spreading art or religion. I simply came because I wanted to know—my sister—Melenda." This was not a fib absolute, because when she came Melenda was a possible sister. But it was so far a fib that Valentine hesitated a little over its utterance.

"Ho!" said Melenda, just to show how very little way in knowledge Valentine had so far advanced.

"Partly I wanted to see with my own eyes the kind of life from which I—that is, Melenda's sister, Polly—had been taken."

"Yes," said Melenda; "to look at us as if we were black savages in a show, and to give us half a sovereign each, and then go away and forget us."

"Melenda is unjust," Valentine replied; "but she tolerates my presence, which is something, though she will not accept any service from me."

"How long are you going to stay? You can't be comfortable here?" Sam asked.

"I didn't ask her to come, and I shan't ask her to stay," said Melenda the Irreconcilable, now in her most stubborn mood, her upper lip stiffened and her eye set stormy. Perhaps she was stimulated by the example of her brother, who was of mule-like obstinacy. He called it firmness.

"I am to stay here all the summer," Valentine explained. "Then I am going back for a time. After that my plans are not yet certain."

"Humph!" said Sam. "You've taken a great deal of trouble for nothing. That's all. As for wanting to know a girl who hasn't got the spirit to raise herself out of this"—he looked round with the infinite contempt of a self-raised man—"I don't see what you expect to get by it. You've only put her tack up so far."

"That's all," said Melenda; "and it is going to keep up."

"There's one thing you might do," he went on. "You might help to make the workwomen discontented. Suppose you got hold of Lizzie here!" He laid his hand upon her shoulder. "Suppose you made her compare her frock with yours, and told her to ask why there is so much difference." Lizzie lifted her great eyes upon Valentine's frock, which really was a very neat and finished piece of work, and fitted her like a glove. Her own, she knew well, could not be compared with it. Little did Sam know of the seeds of discontent already planted in her bosom. "But that you don't dare to try. You and your friends are all for keeping them quiet. Make her feel that she hasn't got what she ought to have; then teach her why she hasn't got it—because she's robbed by your friends. Then there'll be a chance that the girls will combine to get it, and that they'll be backed up by the men. As for these girls they haven't begun to grumble."

"Haven't we?" said Melenda.

"They *believe* that there isn't more money to be got."

"No more there is," said Melenda.

"They think it is a law of the universe that they should work and live in a room like this and go in rags, and be paid elevenpence ha'penny a day."

"And find your own cotton," said Lizzie, furnishing a not unimportant detail.

"And fourpence for the workbook, which you can get for a penny outside. And if you dare to complain they make it sixpence," Melenda added.

"And be sworn at if they're Germans, and drilled[2] if they're English. We like it, I suppose."

"You're a fool, Sam," said Melenda, putting the case plainly. "You and your discontent! If you really think we like it, you're a bigger fool than you look. We didn't want her coming here, nor you neither, to teach us that it's a shame."

"Nor to tell me to look at her frock and mine," said Lizzie.

"Come then, Sam," his sister went on while Valentine kept a careful silence, "come then. Have you got anything better for us when we have got discontented? There's machine work and shirts at a penny apiece; we can get twopence a dozen for the button-holes; there's bottle-washing for five shillings a week, and cigar-makin' for the same; there's the dust-yards and the sifting at a shilling a day. Shall we change for that? There's the match-makers with the stuff that eats away their mouths—"

"Oh, Melenda!" said Valentine.

"What's he come here for, then? How can we find time to keep the place neat and tidy? Why ain't we better off? Let him show us the way then."

2 Besant depicts the practice of drilling in Book II, Chapter XXIII.

"It's better," said Lizzie, "to help people than it is to get into a rage with them. Valentine does help me and Lotty in spite of Melenda."

Melenda looked as if she might turn on the other two as well as on her brother. But she refrained. "If that is all you've got to say, Sam, you may as well go."

"Coming here," Lizzie went on, with a laudable desire to assist in the music of the band, "and swearing at us as if it was our own fault."

"I didn't swear," said Sam, in some confusion.

"You did. You always do when you come here."

"Well, then, it's enough to make a pig swear," he replied guiltily, because a board school master certainly ought not to swear. Language and temper are beneath the dignity of a profession which should be above the minor weaknesses of humanity.

"Well, Sam, please do not swear again," said Valentine, still anxious for peace; "and now—you who know so much and have had so many opportunities for studying the question from your position—your exceptional and high position, Sam—won't you sit down quietly and give us your advice?"

He did not sit down, but he took the chair from her and placed it before him, his hands on the back so that it made a kind of pulpit.

"All he's got to tell us," said Melenda, "is that it's a shame, and we ought to combine and strike."

"It's the system," Sam began. "I am ready to give you the best advice if you'll only follow it. It's the rotten competitive system—you've got to abolish that. As for you girls combining and striking, you won't do it. I told you once to combine, but now I see that women ain't educated up to combination. Combination means common sense—you haven't got it; you haven't the brains nor the courage to do it."

"We've got our independence, anyhow," said Melenda.

"And much good that does you. Independence! As if anybody is independent who's got to work for your starvation wages. You're slaves—you're white slaves. That's what you are!"

"And what are you, then, I should like to know? You've got no work to do, I suppose?"

"We cannot alter the system," said Valentine, again interposing; "at least, I suppose we cannot alter it without a good deal of trouble and delay. Meantime, don't you think you could devise something temporary for Melenda and Lizzie until you have swept away competition?"

"Who wants his help?" asked Melenda. "I tell you he can only say it's a shame. That's all he ever does say."

"I can't help them," said Sam; "nobody can help them in that way. I tell you again that it's the fault of the system. There are women by thousands no better off. If you can make your ladies leave off trying to get things cheap; if you can make your masters contented with a workman's wage for profit; if you can make the men resolve that the women shall be properly paid, and that they must strike for them and forbid them to take less; well—if you can make everybody think of his neighbour first—then you may let your system alone, because it won't matter. You can't do that, and so you must destroy the system."

"Then there seems a very poor chance for the present generation of shirt-makers. But what are you going to put in its place? And how do you know that it will be better than the present plan?"

Sam smiled with pity; girls brought up like Valentine were indeed ignorant.

"You know nothing," he replied; "I have told you already some of our scheme, but I suppose Claude laughed at it and told you to forget it at once."

"Tell me again, then, if you please."

"Very well. Now listen. We shall destroy the competitive system. What does that mean? Why that there will be no masters first, no capitalists, no landowners, no property of any kind."

"Oh! then who will pay the workmen?"

"Listen, and don't interrupt. The state will be the only employer of labour. There will be no rich people. If you have a mountain of gold it will not buy you an hour of luxury, nor will it save you an hour of labour. The stores will be kept by the state, and the food distributed daily. All will work alike and all will live alike. There will be only one rate of wages, and men and women alike will be paid, not in money, but by abundance of everything that is necessary and pleasant to life; no man will be at the beck and call of another. Think of that! Oh, we are on the eve of the most glorious revolution!" He swung his arms, and his eyes glowed. "There will dawn before long the most glorious day. Why, there will be no crime then, because every man will have all he wants, so that there will be no temptation to steal and rob; and every man will be happy, so that there will be no temptation to violence; and every girl contented and well fed, so that every girl shall keep her self-respect. There will be one offence, and only one against the state—the crime of laziness, which will be punished by bread-and-water diet. There will be one education for all; the government shall be by the people for the people; there will be no rich class, no better class, no priests, no lazy class; everybody for a certain time every day will work at something productive—but production will be regulated by committees; for the rest of the time a man will do as he pleases. Some will become artists, some will study, some, I suppose, will be preachers, some scientific men, some actors, some will write books, some will play music—the only professional men who will not be required to work at production will be doctors of medicine and schoolmasters. These, of course, will be chosen from the cleverest of the boys. The courts of justice will be administered by juries who will sit every day all the year round, every man taking his turn; law shall be open to everybody and will be free, but there will not be much left to dispute about when all property is held in trust for everybody. All the things that are now luxuries—the rare fruits and the costly wines—will be distributed to the sick and the old. Books, pictures, music, and plays will be produced for nothing at all after working hours. Every man will be taught that he must be watchful of his own rights and jealous for the community. Every man will take his turn to be a policeman. There will be no other distinctions among men than those which nature has created: for some will be strong and some weak, some will be quick and some slow. But there will be no titles, no aristocracy, no class, and no pride of one man over another. Think of it! No more poverty—no more disease from luxury or from privation, no more ignorance, no more indolence, no more vice! Think of it, I say, if ever you think of anything."

He paused, not because he was exhausted, but because he wanted, naturally, to observe the effect of his oration.

Melenda pretended that she was not listening. But she was. She listened against her will; she could not tell that the thing was as yet only a dream, and could never be realised in her own time. Sam's words filled her soul with vague hopes and a warm glow; and he looked so grand while he spoke that she was proud of him, and forgave him for his impatience and contempt. Lizzie for her part was wholly unmoved. She thought of nothing but of Sam's advice to be discontented and to compare Valentine's frock with her own. It was right, then, to be angry and to ask why she must live on slops and go in rags, and Valentine lived like a lady.

As for Valentine, it seemed to her as if in this squalid room the words had altogether a new force and meaning. In Claude's chambers she had only half perceived their significance, but here—in the presence of the two girls—they fell upon her ears like the first preaching of a new gospel. What sacrifice would be too great to bring about the state of things pictured by this young apostle? Surely there has never been since the world began any dream more generous and more noble than this of the Socialist, insomuch that there are some who think that it was first revealed to the world by the Son of God himself. It is so beautiful that it will never be suffered to be forgotten, so beautiful that mankind will henceforth be continually occupied in trying to make it a practical reality; and with every successive failure, will always be drawing nearer and nearer to the goal, until at last, if the kind gods consent, even after many years and many generations, it shall be won, and with it the Kingdom long talked of and little understood. But those who expect it in this their lifetime might as well expect the kingdom of heaven.

"Thank you, Sam," said Valentine, bringing herself back to the present with an effort. "But this is a scheme for the far future."

"No, it is for the present. Not today perhaps, nor tomorrow, but before your hair is grey it will be realised over the whole world."

"Meantime what are Melenda and Lizzie to do?"

"We've got to go on working," said the latter.

"What will you do meantime for your sister, Sam?"

"Melenda may—she may—" he made an heroic effort, "well, she may come and live with me if she'll behave."

"I shan't then, there! I won't live with anybody, and I won't behave, and I'll go in and out just as I please."

"Can you not find any better way of life for them?" Valentine persisted.

"No, I can't. There isn't any better work for girls who can only sew. You must alter the system. The work and the wages are getting worse instead of better. The worse they get, the more injustice there is, the sooner will be the end. You must begin with the beginning, I tell you. Destroy capital and abolish property. But what do you care for the people?"

"I care for this room at least and the people in it. Come, Sam, give me credit for a little humanity. I care for those of the people whom I know. Isn't that enough for a beginning? How if we were all to do as much? Perhaps there would be no need to alter the system."

"You talk like a woman. Well, then"—he picked up his hat, which he had flung on the floor at the earlier stage of the discussion—"I've made my offer. If Melenda likes to accept it, she can. If not, she will please herself. I'm going. Good-night, Melenda."

"Will you let me walk with you a little way?" Valentine asked.

"Just as you like." It seems an ungracious way of putting it, but what he meant was simple consent.

They walked down Hoxton Street, across Old Street, and along the Curtain Road, where the furniture places were closed, and the street quiet, and the German journeymen were out of sight in some hidden dens smoking pipes, and dreaming like Sam of a new world.

"You belong to the other side," he said after a while. "That is very certain. Yet I should like to talk to you; but there—it is no use, I suppose. You've been brought up in their way, and because it's an easy life you think it is beautiful."

"I only know of one side."

"That's rubbish. In all history there's always two sides: there's the tyrant and there's the slave: there's the oppressor and there's the oppressed: there's the rich and there's the poor: there's the workman and there's the master. The Lord didn't make simple man, you see, He made two classes. There were two Adams. That's what they want us to believe. The land belongs to one of them, and the duty of tilling it for nothing to the other. Oh, yes, I know the talk. There's two classes when we are quiet; there's only one class when it comes to keeping them contented. Wait till we get our turn."

"In your scheme, Sam, no one is to be lazy, no one is to shirk work, and the best men in the country will think it their highest privilege to work for all. I understand you to mean this. Yes. It is very beautiful. But how are you going to teach and to discipline the people and keep them up to the mark?"

"Oh!" Sam replied superior. "Why, the very question shows your ignorance. You don't understand the first elements of our party. Don't you see that there will be no necessity for teaching at all—that the very establishment of justice for the first time in the history of the world—free and equal justice, with no favours to any, will create such a grand universal jealousy that all injustice of every kind will be made impossible? There never has been any justice hitherto. There have been laws and lawyers, and decisions of courts have been sold to the highest bidders. But there has been no justice. It will be such a beautiful thing that everybody will watch everybody else and himself as well, to see that there is no shirking of duty. There will be an irresistible determination—but of course you cannot understand the force of the will of the people?"

"Well," said Valentine, to whom the talk about the irresistible will of the people was a new thing—and indeed it is strange that while cultivated and educated men have never agreed together to have a will of their own and to pronounce it, we are constantly told that the rough and ignorant are thinking as one man, and acting together with one consent and in such beautiful unanimity—"well, then, the will of the people, I suppose, will order everybody to be equally good, and the order will be obeyed without any difficulty. Why, it will be a return to the Promised Land. No, it will be nothing short of a return to the Garden of Eden. And, Sam, just think what a discovery you have made! The flaming sword which turns every way in the hands of the cherubim is nothing else than the competitive system."[3]

"As you like," Sam replied a little sulkily. There was just a faint hint of ridicule in Valentine's words. No prophet can abide ridicule. "I don't care what you call it. Call it what you please. Only don't pretend that you misunderstand the meaning."

"Sam, you are so strong and brave," Valentine laid her hand upon his arm, "you are so clever, you know so much, that I am sure you can help us if you think it over. Never mind the competitive system: that will take a good many years to destroy, I am sure, and perhaps it will outlast our time. Try to find some readier way to help those girls. Consider, one of them is dying slowly; we can't save her; we can only make her easier: the other two are wasting their lives in the most terrible poverty. I could give them money, but indeed it is not alms they want. Melenda will not have it. Won't you try to help them? Think, Sam, oh think"—she laid her hand upon his arm—"of their rags and their misery, and try to help them."

"I do think of their rags. Good God! Valentine, or Polly, or whatever they call you, I think of their rags and their misery for weeks together after I have seen Melenda."

"Then I wish, Sam, that you saw her every day."

"If I did I should only hate the system more and more. That other girl—she'll die, I suppose."

"Yes, she must die. Melenda is stronger. The one who will go next is Lizzie, unless something can be done."

---

3 A reference to the flaming sword in the Book of Genesis, which is held by the angels who prohibit humans from entering the Garden of Eden after Adam and Eve are expelled from it.

"There's only one thing that can be done—destroy the competitive system. Abolish property. Sweep away capital, lands, and church, and masters. Give Socialism a fair start."

Nothing more could be got out of him. A mathematician, we know, tries his theory on elementary cases; Socialism, and the ladies and gentlemen who construct, with infinite labour, constitutions, schemes, and plans for the universal good, do not. The simple case is beyond them. They are full of rage against the old system, but their indignation is expended in deepening their political convictions.

There was once another man who went down the Jericho road and fell among thieves. First there passed by the priest, just as in the former case, his scornful chin in the air: and then the Levite followed. Now this Levite did not immediately pass by, but he stopped and inquired carefully into the particulars of the case and made full notes of them, and then he went his way, and out of the notes he compiled a most tremendous oration, eloquent, fiery, and convincing, which he delivered at a meeting of the Democratic Federal Union, on the wretched system under which robbers are suffered to exist, and propounded another system by means of which there would be no more robbers in the land at all. And yet the old system goes on still, and still we see coming along the hot and thirsty road the Samaritan with his nimble twopence.[4]

"Good-night, Sam," Valentine said coldly; "I ask you for advice, and you offer me the chance of a new system. Go away and rail at competition, while we look after its victims."

4 The narrator alters the parable of the Good Samaritan in the Gospel of Luke to suggest that the Levite, the second person to fail to render aid to the gravely injured man, was not, unlike the priest who was the first to pass by, motivated by indifference or lack of compassion. Rather, the Levite, like the Socialist, was interested in changing the system rather than helping the individual. Thus it was left to the Samaritan, who was regarded with disdain by the Jews, to help a human being in dire need of assistance.

Chapter x

The Reverend Randal Smith

The assistant priest of St. Agatha's—this was the church where the morning congregation did not contain a single man—was at this time—he has just been promoted to the more independent sphere of a mission church—the Rev. Randal Smith. It was he who ran up the stairs when Valentine was singing in order to discover the secret of this strange thing.

This young gentleman became, by a gradual and natural development of events, one of Valentine's friends. Their friendship, it is true, was based upon what the doctor maintained to be the true basis of all friendship—self-interest. He first introduced himself to her in the street—there was no other common place of meeting—stopping before her and half lifting his hat. It was one of those sweet things in felt with a very broad flat brim and strings and a tassel, and he took it off with the doubtful courtesy which certain Englishmen yield to the uncertain person, as if it were a disgrace to lift the hat to any under a recognised social position. This prejudice will vanish when the board schools condescend to teach manners, and the working-man has learned to lift his hat to the working-woman.

"I beg your pardon—"

He affected the quick breathless manner adopted by many young clergymen and by some young masters in public schools. It is a manner which may mean anything, like an algebraical symbol—perhaps that is the reason why it has been adopted—but it is really understood to be a "note," or outward and visible sign, of earnestness coupled with intellectual superiority. At Toynbee Hall,[1] very oddly, it is not recognised, which makes one suspect the sincerity and the superiority of that institution.

"I beg your pardon. I think I heard you singing the other evening in Ivy Lane."

"It is very likely."

---

1 Run by a Church of England curate, Toynbee Hall was part of the settlement movement. This effort to establish interdependent communities of rich and poor drew many of the upper class to live for periods in the East End.

"I—I—have also learnt"—it was difficult to believe—"that you are the—the—sister of one of the girls who live there."

"It is possible."

He was quite a young man, not more than five or six and twenty, slight and small in stature, shaven of cheek and chin, pale-faced, insignificant of aspect. As to his creed, he professed to belong to the small and narrow sect called Ritualists, and this was proclaimed to the general world by the brim of his hat which was so broad, and the length of his skirts. By these symbols he professed the most decided views as to his own authority and the tremendous powers which he held by virtue of his office; though he was really a most simple creature, who would have been crushed, had he at all understood or realised the nature of his own pretensions, by the mere weight of them; he had never distinguished himself in any way either at school or college; he had read next to nothing, and knew next to nothing, of history, literature, or theology; his creed was narrow, bigoted, unhistorical, and intolerant; his manner was fussy, underbred, and full of little affectations. With his priestly pretensions, and his ignorance, and his fussiness, he was just exactly the kind of figure that scoffers like to put up in a pillory and pelt with epigrams, new and old, derisive laughter, mocking questions, and sneers and jeers. He was also exactly the kind of man who would not alter his course for any amount of epigrams, whether they cut like flints or whether they broke in his face like rotten eggs; and, when they took him down from his pillory, he would have gone away wondering that the world could be so sinful as actually to scoff and sniff at the sacerdotal office.

In other respects this assistant priest belonged to a kind of mortal which has never been extinct or unknown amongst us, and of late seems to have become common. It is not the cleverest kind, nor is it the most learned, the most critical, the most logical, or the most capable of argument. But it is a kind which has one great distinctive quality: it has perceived very plainly that there is a kind of life, possible to all who choose to follow it, which is an imitation, however humble, of a certain great Exemplar. In fact, no hermit, no solitary, no friar of orders grey, black, white, blue, green, yellow, buff, indigo, magenta, mauve, or alezan, ever more diligently followed that Exemplar than do the men of this kind. At the age of twenty-three, that is to say, as early as it is permitted to them, they absolutely renounce forever the world and all its delights; they give up society, culture, learning, art and pleasures of every kind; they plunge head foremost into a vast ocean, murky and cloudy, whose waves have no brightness and whose waters know no smiles; they become, in fact, assistant priest or curate, whichever they prefer to be called, in a parish of poverty; they are the slaves, all day long, of the people; they cease to have any individual life; they have no longer any pursuits.

It is a comparatively unimportant detail in such a life, that the man has a church where he must perform certain duties. Yet these take time; he has to read prayers, or to sing matins and evensong, if he prefers that way of describing the function; he marries and baptises; he has once a week to provide a discourse always full of new thoughts, powerful logic, and words which burn—at least, these things are expected. It does not really matter in the least what he preaches in places like Hoxton, because no one ever goes to church. Generally he preaches a set of doctrines which the British working-man is just as likely to embrace as he is to abandon the franchise, or to dissolve his trade unions, or to give up his beer, or to join goody clubs. But his real work is outside his church. He is the almoner of the parish;[2] he is always administering charitable funds, finding out deserving cases, and dividing eighteenpence equally among thirteen poor people; he is a professor of the

2 As Besant goes on to point out, an almoner distributes the alms, or charitable gifts, given by parishioners to those in need.

conduct of life; because weaker brethren get drunk he has to wear a nasty little blue ribbon,[3] and may not look upon the amber and the froth of the cheerful pewter; because there are so many to be helped, and so little to help them with, he lives with the greatest frugality, and gives away all that he can spare, being paid for the most part in the coin of ingratitude; he has got schools to visit; of late years he has been expected—who has neither art nor culture—to become the prophet of culture and the fosterer of art; and now, on top of all these duties, he has had imposed upon him the care of providing and devising amusement, holidays, excursions, concerts, clubs, and institutes for the young and old. He works all day long and regrets that there are not more than sixteen hours available; he is always cheerful. And for the sake of what he does and the life he leads, let us by no means laugh at this young man, but suffer him without sneers or epigrams to believe what it pleases his unhistorical soul to think he believes, so long as he does not try to make us acknowledge that he carries about in his own little waistcoat pocket, on the same bunch as his latch-key, the keys of the Gates of Heaven.

"I—I—I heard you sing," he repeated. "And I was much pleased. For an untrained voice—"

"Quite so," said Valentine gravely. But there was in her eyes a light for which there is no prettier word, I regret to say, than the word "twinkle." Nothing is more delightful than the sudden awakening to a sense of the humorous situation shown by the twinkle of a girl's bright eyes.

"But perhaps you have been trained. I beg your pardon."

"Pray go on."

"I have an institute of working-boys. It occurred to me that perhaps—perhaps—would you sing to them?"

"I do not know. Will you show me your institute?"

He led her into one of the streets which branch off right and left, and stopped at a corner house.

"This is the place," he said. "We get the working-lads here, and teach them and amuse them in the evening."

The door opened, without the intervention of hall or passage, into a good-sized room of irregular shape, fitted with benches and one or two narrow tables; at one end was a great fireplace with texts displayed above it, and at the other end was a low platform with a piano. On the walls at the end were a few shelves which formed the boys' library.

"Upstairs," said the young clergyman, his eyes kindling as he showed his beloved institute, "there are class rooms and a bagatelle-board,[4] where the older lads may smoke if they like; outside in the yard is a gymnasium. This is our common sitting and reading room where we sometimes try singing. Unfortunately I was never taught to sing or play. I can intone of course, but I cannot sing, and as for accompaniment I am trying to learn a few simple chords. Perhaps I could help out with something for you."

"Let me hear you," said Valentine.

His knowledge of the art was limited and his simple chords were few. He confessed that he rose every morning at six in order to acquire some mastery over the instrument, but as yet with small success.

"What do you do with your boys?" she asked him.

It appeared on explanation that his evenings were wholly devoted to the care of those boys, with whom he worked, read, taught, and played. While he spoke of them his face lit up, he forgot the little mannerism of speech and became natural. This was the work that he loved.

---

3 Reformed drinkers and those in support of their reform began wearing red, white, or blue ribbons in the late nineteenth century. Blue was by far the most popular choice.

4 A game similar to billiards.

Valentine felt that she stood on the threshold of a new kind of life. She went on to question him. He had other work, and a great deal of it, of a much less interesting kind. He ought to have had nothing to do but to look after the boys, whose minds he was filling with thoughts which would lead some of them whither he could not guess. But he had, besides, the church services every day, sick people to visit, poor people to relieve, a mission chapel to serve in some slum or other, addresses to prepare—an endless round of work, with no rest for a single day in the week and no hope that it would ever grow lighter.

"It is a hard life," said Valentine, wondering at the courage of those who embrace such a life.

"It is my work," he replied, lapsing into breathlessness and folding his hands, after the unreal manner of his kind. Why will they fold their hands?

Valentine thought that he belonged to those heroes who are best left unseen. There are many such, and when they die their lives read most beautifully.

She sat down and suffered her fingers to ramble over the keys thinking of this man and his life. Presently she looked up. "I will sing for your boys whenever you please."

"Thank you."

"Do you know all the people in your parish? Do you know the working-women?"

"I try to know them all," he replied, breathlessly. "It is my duty to know them all. The parish clergy are in charge of them."

"Do you ever think of them? Can you tell me how anything can be done for them?"

"If they would come to church, and submit to discipline."

"I do not speak of their religion, but of their material welfare. Can anything be done to get them better wages and easier work?"

"I do not know. It is not the duty of a parish priest to consider the subject of work."

"You are among these poor working-women all day long, and yet you have never considered the subject! Surely it must force itself upon you?"

"What would be the use? I can do nothing. I suppose there must always be poverty—'The poor ye have always with you.'"

"Oh!" Valentine cried, impatiently. "Nobody ever tries to help. I have asked a schoolmaster, and a doctor, and a scholar, and now I have asked a clergyman; and there is no help in any of them. Does nobody in the world care what becomes of the working-women?"

"The Church cares for all alike," he replied, still breathless and superior.

She bade him good-morning and left him. There was then no help to be got from man, not even from those who go continually among the people, and see their suffering and the patience of the girls every day. There are men and women working perpetually for every other possible class, but none for the workgirl. She alone is left unprotected and unheeded, and no man regardeth her.

Then an oracle came to her; the true oracle is unsuspected and unsought—sudden. You must not go and inquire at Delphi any more.[5] The voice comes to you of its own accord. It came to Valentine from an old lady. There were two of them standing on the kerbstone; one carried a loaf under her apron and the other a key.

5 Delphi was a Greek shrine at what was thought to be the center of the world and was home to the most famous oracles in ancient Greece and Rome.

They were clean and respectable old ladies. As Valentine passed them, one said to the other, "No, mum, it's no use expecting it; and if you want a thing done, you must do it yourself."

These words Valentine rightly and piously accepted as an oracle or voice from heaven.

The assistant priest meanwhile stood at the door of his institute, and watched her walking down the street with buoyant step and fearless carriage. I suppose he had seen young ladies before, but it seemed a long time, and for the space of two minutes and a half he allowed his thoughts to follow the way of most young men's thoughts in spring, though it was now full summer. In that brief interval he enjoyed in imagination a whole twelve months at least of the blessed life, the life of love and ease and happiness, with such a companion as Valentine. At five-and-twenty there are moments when all other things, and especially the Great Renunciation, seem stark staring foolishness compared with the life of love. I believe that all women in all ages have secretly entertained this doctrine, and that all men have from time to time been tempted by it. The Light of Asia experienced many such painful moments of doubt, though his biographers have passed them over.[6] We know, besides, how hermits and holy men have been wont to keep tubs of ice-cold water and deep snowdrifts ready against these attacks of the devil. A terrible thing, indeed, should a young man, after he has gone a-hermiting, meanly give it up and sneak back to his sweetheart!

Now, as Valentine walked along the street, just after she received the oracle, she encountered the very last man she would have expected to meet in Hoxton.

"You here, Mr. Conyers!"

It was, in fact, Mr. Conyers himself, and the great man appeared to be confused at the meeting. He actually blushed and stammered.

"I, yes, yes, I am here. And you, Miss Valentine?"

"I am staying with some friends."

"Yes, I remember. Your sister told me. I thought, however, you were gone to Whitechapel. Everybody goes to Whitechapel now. I am travelling about London in search of a new face for my picture. All the faces somehow seem to have been used up."

"Have you succeeded?"

"I hardly know yet."

She left him and went on her way.

"She is staying with friends." Mr. Conyers looked after her thoughtfully. "I am glad she didn't meet me five minutes ago, with that big-eyed girl. It might have been awkward. She is staying with friends—her own people. Violet told me as much, and Claude is looking after her. Is it likely that Lady Mildred would suffer her own daughter to live in such a place as this and be looked after by Claude? Lady Mildred may be liberal in her views, but she must think of her daughter's reputation. Oh, there cannot be any longer a doubt."

A sweet smile—the smile of contentment—played upon his lips. He was thinking of Beatrice Eldridge and of himself, and of a perfectly easy life, with nothing to do but to enjoy and to develop, and then slowly to ripen and to decay. "I think Valentine is better-looking than Violet," he murmured; "but with such a hatful of money, who would make comparisons?"

---

6 One of several designations of the Buddha. The phrase also appears in the title of Edwin Arnold's highly acclaimed 1879 narrative poem about the Buddha and his historical period.

Meantime the big-eyed girl, who was none other than Lizzie, strolled slowly homewards—it was her dinner hour—thinking of the words that she had heard once more and for the tenth time, because this man would not leave her alone. The temptation to have done with her hard and wretched work had grown almost to a desperate yearning for ease. It seemed to lie at her feet ready to be picked up. The more she saw of Valentine the more she longed to be even as she was. The discontent which Sam wished for all women had seized upon her, but without producing quite the effect which he anticipated. Lizzie had no desire to combine with other girls. She wished, on the other hand, to run quite away from them, and never to have anything more to do with them.

In the evening Valentine sang to the boys. There were twenty or thirty of them with the Reverend Randal Smith. She played to them first, and then she sang to them, not one or two, but a dozen rattling good songs which went straight to the boys' hearts and made them all sit with open mouths. And before she sang her last song, which was that pretty old ditty about Sally in our Alley, she made a little speech.

"Boys," she said, "you will soon be men and able to look out for yourselves. Will you remember your sisters, the girls who cannot help themselves? You will have reasonable hours and good pay; they will have to work all day long for cruel pay. It is your business to help them—I don't know how yet—but you must find out if others cannot. They will be your sweethearts. Can you bear to think that the girls you love are cruelly neglected and shamefully ill-used? Perhaps you will be able to make a union for them. Think of them. I shall come and sing to you again if I am allowed. Every time I come I will remind you of your duty towards your sisters—the girls who work. Now I will sing you a song all about one of them and her sweetheart."

Chapter XI

A Dead Man's Steps

In the multitude of counsellors, as we know, purposes are established. Hitherto, however, Valentine's counsellors had advanced her no more than those of the patriarch Job.[1] She looked from one to the other, asking in vain the questions which everyone asks when he begins to understand the simple facts. But there was no answer from any, save from Sam, and he proposed to meet the case by simply knocking down the house of cards and building it up again.

She thought of the old lady in the almshouse. Perhaps from her she might get something practical, something that would help Melenda at least, something short of Sam's universal revolution and the doctor's universal confederation of labour. It is by a natural instinct that mankind in all ages, and at every juncture have sought the advice of old women, because none are so wise as to the conduct of life, especially—which is not generally known—old women in almshouses. Their superiority is due to the happy circumstance that they have nothing to do but to observe, to reflect, and to piece together their experiences.

One must not, however, suppose that all old women know everything. Some are specialists; as, for example, those who know the art of healing and the properties of herbs. Then there are those who understand the management of man; it is a secret, and one man, at least, who has learned this secret, will never reveal it; but it is a very simple secret, the management of man in all his characters, as brother, lover, father, and husband. Some, again, are deeply versed in the treatment of tender infants. Some can read and foretell the future, plain and clear, for all inquirers, either by the cards, or by the hand, or by signs and omens, or by the appearance of birds. Some can judge, with the greatest accuracy, of character from the face, or a single feature in the face, or from the voice, or the hand, or the foot. Some can read thoughts, and can advise a man by knowing exactly what is passing in his mind. Some can charm warts and order rheumatism to vanish; and some can inform

1 The biblical figure Job suffers devastating tests of his faith. With the help of his advisers, Job tries to understand why God would allow a righteous man to suffer so much.

the inquirer exactly, and without any oracular indefiniteness, whether any proposed course of action will be lucky or unlucky. They are Sibyls[2] every one. I do not know what advice Mrs. Monument would have given to Valentine's questions, because, most unfortunately, she was prevented from putting any by a very singular occurrence.

It was this: Valentine found the old lady sitting alone, and in a strange state of nervous agitation, with shaking hands and trembling lips—in the condition known to inebriates as "jumpy."

"What's the matter, mother?" she asked. "Your hands are trembling, and so are your lips. Are you ill?"

"No, Polly, no. Oh, thank heaven you've come, my dear! I don't know myself today. When you spoke just now I actually thought it was her ladyship's voice, and I never even heard your step outside. Give me your hand, child. There! I feel safe while you are here."

"Why, mother, what is it?"

"I sent Rhoder away after dinner, because I couldn't bear her fidgets. I would rather go without my tea. And I went into the chapel; but I couldn't get any rest. And, oh, dear, dear! how glad I am you've come, Polly!"

"Well, mother, you will tell me presently when you feel a little stronger. You shall have your tea earlier this afternoon. I want to talk to you about Melenda."

"What about Melenda, Polly? She's never been the good and dutiful daughter that you are. She doesn't come to see her mother but once a month, and then she's always in a rage. She came last Sunday and tore round and carried on dreadful about you and Lotty. Never mind that. What about Melenda?"

"She is working too hard and living too low. She ought to be made to do some other kind of work. What could she try?"

"I always told her—but you might as well talk to a stick or a stone—that honest service is the best thing in the world for a young woman. What is her freedom after all? She's free to walk the streets and to get into bad company; she's free to learn bad manners, and she's free to go hungry and ragged. Well, my dear, she won't hear my advice, and—Oh, what's that?"

"It's nothing, dear," said Valentine. "But, mother, what makes you so nervous today?"

"I can't tell you, child. I can't tell anybody." It was useless to ask her for advice. The old lady was incoherent and incapable of thought. Valentine made haste to get ready the tea and to talk on indifferent things. And while she talked she saw that her mother either listened with an effort or did not listen at all, but suffered her lips to move in silence, while the trembling of her hands showed the disquiet of her mind.

When she had taken tea, which is a sedative and restorative of the highest order, the old lady felt herself stronger and breathed more freely.

"Polly," she said, "if you hadn't come today, I should have gone clean off my poor head, I should."

"Well, mother, wouldn't you be easier if you told me all the trouble? Is it anything about one of the boys? Is Joe in difficulties?"

"No, no, nothing's the matter with Joe. And I can't tell Joe, because he would only laugh at me. But I must tell somebody. My dear," she stooped forward and whispered, "I've had a most terrible fright."

"A fright? Did thieves try to break in—here?"

"No, Polly; no, not thieves. Bless you! I ain't afraid of thieves. It's far worse than that."

"What was it?"

2 Classical Greek and Roman prophets and diviners but often used in the nineteenth century in reference to any fortune-teller.

"I heard a step, Polly."

"A step?"

"Polly, I can't tell you; the young don't understand what a dreadful thing it is to hear a step you haven't heard for twenty years—a dead man's step—and to wonder why it came and what it wanted; and then to remember all the misery that step might have caused if the dead man wasn't dead. I know he's dead. I'm quite certain of that. Yet I'm terrible put out, my dear; if I hadn't told you I think I must have gone out of my senses, so shook I am today. Someone I must ha' told. I couldn't tell Rhoder, because Joe would never forgive me if I did. She's one of them who is never to know. Claude is another, and so is Sam."

"Whose step was it like, then?"

"Polly, give me your hand again. Oh, what a blessing you are to me, my dear! Your Christian name was Marla, because he ordered it; but I've always called you Polly, and I always shall. It was the step of your own father, my dear, who's dead and gone."

"My father? But since he is dead"—for the moment her thoughts turned to a certain portrait, that, namely, representing Sir Lancelot in his uniform as colonel of yeomanry cavalry proudly bestriding a gallant charger.[3] Then she remembered that, unlike any other girl in history, she had, in the mind of most people, two fathers. There are many girls who have only one father between them; but Valentine's is absolutely the only case on record in which a girl has had more than one father. "Why," she added, "it is twenty years since my father died."

"No, my dear, it is only five years. Joe brought me the news, and I cried for joy and thankfulness. Cried for joy, I did."

"Only five years? But we always thought—"

"I told her ladyship twenty years ago that he was dead. It wasn't true; and yet he was as good as dead to me and to the children; and to the world as well. I don't know whether the world or me was better pleased that he was dead to everybody. I don't know which of us prayed the hardest that he would never come to life again."

"Why, mother, what does this mean?" The bitterness of these words, and the intensity with which they were uttered, startled and terrified Valentine. What could they mean? She turned pale with a sudden presentiment of evil.

"I told Lady Mildred a falsehood. It did her no harm and I couldn't—no, I couldn't tell her the truth—her who'd known me when I was respectable, and didn't even guess what had happened. It was my secret all to myself and to Joe. There's some things a woman can't tell. As for the truth, Joe and me knew it, and nobody else, and I was then on Hackney Marsh out of the way, and there was plenty of time before me even if he should come back, and I thought to get the children put out to work so as he shouldn't know where they were nor ever be able to do them any harm, or bring shame upon them as he brought it on me."

"Do them harm? Bring shame upon them? Why?"

"You don't know, Polly. But I'll tell you now, because I can talk to you as I can't to Melenda or the boys; and oh, my dear, I feel the comfort of having a daughter I can talk to."

"Go on, mother," said Valentine.

"Well, then, my dear, if there was ever a wickeder man than your father in the whole world, Lord help his wife and children! And if ever there was a man who was more bent on wicked ways and more gloried in his wicked life, I never heard of him."

---

3 A volunteer force of landed countrymen serving on horseback in the British army.

"Where was he then, when he was dead to you and—" Here she stopped, and her cheek flamed suddenly scarlet as if she had received a shameful blow, for she understood where he was. Those who are dead to wife and children, yet living: those whose living death is a subject of rejoicing in the world, are in—

"Mother," she said, "he was in prison."

"Hush! my dear," her mother whispered, "not so loud. Yes, he was in prison. Hush! don't ever say that word out loud again. Nobody knows it but Joe and me. Joe was old enough to know when he was took. Thank God, the knowledge of it frightened him and helped to make him the sober steady man he is. No one else knows—not Joe's wife nor yet his children. They don't know. And none of the rest knows, not Sam, nor Claude, nor Melenda. Don't you tell them, Polly—don't you never tell them. Sam's that proud and set up with his grand position and his success that it would cut him to the heart, and my Claude, too, though, of course, he isn't to compare with Sam. Don't make them hang their proud heads. And Melenda, too—bless the girl—with her independence. Don't shame them, Polly, don't tell them."

"I shall not tell. Oh, mother, why did you tell me?" she asked impatiently.

"When you came here without any play actin', and leaving Miss Beatrice at home with her Mar and kind and thoughtful for your mother, my dear; oh, what a blessing it is to have my Polly back again"—Valentine kissed her and fondled her hand, penitent already for her impatience—"full of your soft and ladylike ways, my dear, which Melenda couldn't never learn, living as she does, slaving and starving, it came into my head that I must someday tell you. What's the good of having a daughter if you can't tell everything that is in your mind?"

"Tell me everything," said Valentine with a sinking heart. "Tell me everything, then, if it will relieve your mind, dear."

"I wouldn't have told you anything, my dear, if it hadn't been for that dreadful step which frightened me out of my wits almost. It was nigh upon the stroke of ten, because I heard the clock soon afterwards. I'd forgotten to lock the door; why, I often leave it ajar when I go to bed so as Rhoder can get in first thing in the morning. I was fast asleep—I must have been asleep though I dreamed I was awake, and all of a sudden in my dream of being awake I heard his step. It came over the flags within the court and walking quickly, as he always walked, stopped at my door and so into the house."

"Oh!" Valentine was trembling now because that strange horror, which we call the fear of the supernatural, is the most catching thing in the world, much more catching than measles. "Oh! and then you heard his footstep on the flag-stones?"

"Yes, and in the house; the step came into the room below. I don't know how long it lasted because I couldn't move hand or foot, and I couldn't breathe even, and my tongue was tied and I couldn't open my mouth. Oh, dear, it was last night." She stopped, overcome by the recollection of that dreadful dream.

"When I came to I got up and crept downstairs and felt about the room. But no one was there. How should there be? Blind people can't see ghosts, like other people, but they can feel them if there's one about. There was a blind woman once in the village when I was a girl, and they said the reason why she always looked frightened was that she was haunted by the ghost of her husband. He'd sit beside her bed all night and say nothing, and she couldn't see him, but she felt him there, and if all tales about her was true, it served her right. She died young, my dear, because she couldn't bear it. If one blind woman, why not two? Perhaps he came repentant. Well, I'm ready to forgive him, now he's dead; I couldn't before." Many Christians resemble Mrs. Monument in this view of forgiveness as a duty.

"You are quite sure there was no one there?"

"Neither man nor ghost was there, and the door was ajar just as I'd left it."

"And was nothing stolen?"

"No, my dear; there isn't anything worth stealing."

"It was a strange dream," said Valentine; "a strange and a dreadful dream. Did you hear the step again when you went back to bed?"

"No, my dear, not again. But I lay awake all night waiting for it, though I knew it was only a dream."

"Shall I stay with you tonight?"

"No, my dear, I am better now I've told you. I am not afraid any longer."

"Well, don't forget to lock and bolt your door."

"Locks and bolts won't keep out ghosts. And never a lock nor a bolt ever made would keep *him* out when he was alive, much less now he's dead."

"Forget your dream, mother, and tell me more about my father. Tell me all, unless it gives you pain to talk about him."

"No, my dear, it eases me, because if I don't talk about him I think about him. I almost wish I hadn't told you anything, Polly. It won't make you any happier to know that. But then I was so upset—"

"Yes, mother, it was better for you. I know now that my father's only legacy to his children was a record of disgrace which you have mercifully concealed."

"Disgrace and shame, Polly," the blind woman echoed.

Presently she went on again.

"When he came to the village first and began courting, my head was turned because he was such a handsome lad and I was such a homely one. His ways were finicking, as if he was a gentleman, and there was nothing that he couldn't do. He'd play the fiddle, which he did most heavenly, till you either laughed, or cried, or danced, just as he wanted you to do; he could do conjuring tricks, and he'd make you believe whatever rubbish he wanted; he could carve most beautiful in wood; and at his own trade, which was locksmithing, I don't suppose there was a cleverer lad in the world. Well, I never asked him what he came into our parts for, and though there was three houses broke open while he was coming and going, nobody ever suspected my James, and least of all could I suspect him. And on Sunday always in his place at church beside me with his book in his hand, so that the vicar thought he was a good young man indeed, and everybody told me I was a lucky woman. A proud woman I was, I can tell you, when I stood with my man and all the people there to see. Little Lady Mildred herself was brought to the wedding because I'd been under-nurse, and she gave me my white frock, at least her mother did, and said it was her gift, and—there—it's seven-and-thirty years ago. Joe is six-and-thirty, and you are only twenty, but close to twenty-one, being actually fifteen years younger than Joe.

"My dear," she interrupted her narrative in order to apologise for this difference, "I know it is natural there oughtn't to be such a distance between the eldest and the youngest of five. You ought to be thirty at least by now if you had your right. But I couldn't help it because your father, you see, he was generally in the place—the place, you know, where he died at last."

"You mean he was in prison," said Valentine stoutly, "and don't mind about the difference between Joe and me. I daresay I shall get to thirty in good time."

"In prison then, my dear. Now though we came to London at first to look for work I very soon found out that he hadn't got any regular work, and wouldn't take it if it was offered. Half his time he was away, saying it was country jobs which paid him well, and he'd be away sometimes a month at a spell, after which there would be a month's idleness and doing nothing. But always plenty of money and better living we had than many a gentleman's house."

"Did he have any relations?"

"No; not any that I ever heard of—some of the books here on my shelves belonged, he said, to his father; and he said his father was a gentleman, but what kind of a gentleman he was to have such a son I'm sure I don't know. Well, Polly, I lived, as they say, in Fool's Paradise; for he never got drunk and he didn't use language and he was not a striker, and though he would only work when he was obliged and left me so much alone, I loved him and thought I was the happiest woman in the world. Happy? Yes, like the innocent lambs in the fields. It was when Joe was a baby of three months that I found out the truth. He got ten years"—Valentine shuddered—"ten years. It was a bad burglary. His box of tools was in our lodgings and a chest full of stolen things, and they talked of trying me along with him, but they didn't. My dear, I never so much as suspected. Ten years! Then I took Joe and all the money that I had and went away to Hackney Marsh, and took my maiden name again, and began with the washing."

"And after his ten years he came back again, I suppose?"

"Before then; he came back with a ticket of leave, and you may be sure he found me out. I don't know how, but he did; and you might as well try to hide a rabbit from a weasel as try to hide anything from that man. He came back, my dear; and then he lived a very strange life. For he told me he had reformed, and yet he would stay away for a month at a time, and a fine reform it was. He kept quiet when he was at home and gave out to the neighbours he was a seafaring man, and he mostly wore a blue jacket. He never took any of my money and I wouldn't touch none of his, and he never had any meals in the house, but he'd sit in the parlour and read his books, and he'd smoke cigars and drink port wine like a gentleman, all by himself. Twice he went away and didn't come back for eighteen months, so I suppose he'd been took again. But after each spell back he came, and that went on, my dear, for seven long years—seven years—me asking no questions, and him telling no lies, and coming and going just as he pleased. Seven years. Sam came first, and then Claude, and then Melenda. But before you were born, my dear, though not before your name was fixed, which was Marla, as I've told you often, he was took again. It was another burglary, I know, with violence, and he got five-and-twenty years, which Joe said was as good as a lifer, and we needn't expect to see him ever again."

"Is that all?"

"That's all, my dear. And now you and me have got that secret between us, and we are never to let the two boys nor Melenda know, are we?"

"Never to let the boys know," said Valentine. "Oh, poor Claude!"

"If they never find it out it won't matter to them, will it?" said his mother. "Joe's wife and the children don't know it. Nobody knows it except you and me and Joe. Sometimes I think it's made Joe the good son he's always been to me, because we've had that secret to ourselves."

"Since he is dead—but is he dead?"

"Yes, he is dead," she replied quickly; "Joe heard that for certain. There's no doubt about that."

"Did he never write to you?"

"Never, and I'll tell you why. It was because he thought my cottage was such a good hiding-place where he could come and go as he pleased and never be suspected at all, and me living under another name. Only mind, I wouldn't have any boxes brought home with him. You see, if he'd written to me the police would have known where to look for him. Why, I've known him—oh, a dozen times—talk to the policeman over the garden palings about himself and his own burglaries as cool as you please."

"What was his name?"

"His name was Carey—James Carey. Why, my dear, you are too young to remember it, but thirty years ago the newspapers were full of his name, and the whole country was ringing with his burglaries. They wrote a life of him and sold it for a penny all over London. But of course you've never seen the book."

No. Valentine had little wish to see that biographical work. Yet there was just a touch of pride in the old woman's mention of that book.

"Look on the shelves, Polly. There are some of his books. You will find his father's name in them. At least he said they were his father's books; but who knows what his name really was, nor what was his history?"

Valentine had remarked a row of well-bound books on her first visit; chiefly, I suppose, because books are not too often met with in a Tottenham almshouse. Now she took them down and examined them. The first book was the "Divina Commedia di Dante Alighieri," in Italian; a beautifully bound copy of a scarce edition, as Valentine knew. One does not usually expect to find rare editions in an almshouse. She passed on to the next on the shelf. This was "Cupid and Psyche, English'd from the Latin of Apuleius," quarto, in calf, with the date 1741. Then came "Froissart's Chronicles," in four goodly volumes, quarto, and half-calf, the translations of Johnnes. After this came an odd volume of Hutchinson's "Durham;" then another odd volume of La Fontaine's "Contes et Nouvelles," illustrated very beautifully; then two or three volumes of Florian's works, magnificently bound. There were others, but Valentine stopped there because she suddenly apprehended the possible meaning of this thing.

If I desired to possess, and intended to show about for the gratification of vanity and the support of my pretensions to gentle birth, something solid and not to be disputed, I should not content myself with the ordinary well-known methods. I might, like some of my neighbours, invent and circulate family anecdotes which unkind friends would proceed to quote and to misrepresent in a nasty sniggering spirit. I might, also, as they do, adorn my rooms with family portraits which may be had at a reasonable figure, and are effective so long as there exists a friendly disposition to a give-and-take credulity. I might, in addition, exhibit a family pedigree, going back to the Wars of the Roses at least, and beginning with a valiant knight supposed to be connected with a very illustrious house; this, too, may be procured for a small sum, beautifully written on parchment, and adorned with shields. I should certainly stick up, wherever there was room for them, coats of mail, with trophies of spears, shields, bucklers, and pikes, all family heirlooms, and descending in the male line direct from the Crusaders and Cœur de Lion.[4] I should buy old silver mugs, and have my arms engraved upon them with the names of ancestors. These things are all useful in their way, but they want corroboration. Therefore I should proceed to search for, and to buy, old books of the sixteenth, seventeenth, and eighteenth centuries, *without names in them*, and in these books I should write the names of my ancestors in a pale brown ink, with the date of acquisition and a remark or two in Latin. Nothing is so effective as Latin. I should arrange

4 Richard I was England's king from 6 July 1189 until his death on 6 April 1199. Known as the Lion-hearted (*Cœur de Lion*), he played a significant role in the Third Crusade, one of several European religious wars.

them upon a shelf about the average height of the human eye, which is five feet seven inches, and I should say, when my friends took them down curiously, "Alas! all that I have been able to save of the old family library. You will find the names of one or two of my people there. See! here is good old Sir Simon, knighted by Queen Bess, at Tilbury." There might be jealousies and envyings, and unkind remembrance of one's grandfather and the shop; but there would be no flouts or jeers, because nothing more effectually proves the antiquity of the House than old books formerly belonging to ancestors. For modest men it is perhaps sufficient to prove that your grandfather could read Latin and Italian; therefore, books only eighty years of age might be purchased in order to serve that purpose.

Valentine opened the volumes. In each one there was a book plate with a coat-of-arms, and under the shield in each was written the name of "Francis Denison Carey." Therefore the said Francis must have known Italian and French at least, and he must have been fond of books and bindings, and illustrations, and he must have taken an interest in county history, and therefore, without doubt, he must have been a gentleman by birth.

"Were these books my father's?" she asked.

"They were all his, my dear, and his father's before him."

"Who was his father?"

"I don't know, my dear, because he never told me. I've always thought my husband must have been a love-child. He left them with me wherever he went. To be sure he couldn't take them with him when he—"

"No," said Valentine, "certainly he could not."

Even an author's works cannot follow him into that place, though they may, and generally do, accompany him to the grave.

"Then his father was a gentleman."

"So he always said, my dear. But a love-child I think he must have been. And he said that he'd got fine relations; and then he'd laugh and boast that he was bringing great honour on the family, though they would do nothing for him."

"It is strange," said Valentine. "Did he never explain how he came to fall so low?"

"No, never; and as to being fallen low he pretended he'd risen high, and couldn't own that his way of living was shameful and disgraceful. 'Why,' he said, a dozen times after he pretended to be reformed, and could talk Scripture by the half-hour, 'why,' he said, 'it's me against the world: my cleverness against your locks, and your laws, and your police. And I'm the head of them all. There's not a man in the profession but envies me and admires me. Who is there that's got into so many houses as I have? Who's defied the police as I have?' That's the way he used to go on, and as to living by honest work it was nothing but slaving for a slave driver; if he couldn't be a slave driver he wouldn't be a slave."

"And was he any the richer for his robberies?"

"I don't know, my dear, where the money went, because I never asked. But it went in wickedness, I daresay."

"Oh!" cried Valentine, stung by a sudden terror. "Suppose he wasn't dead after all; what misery to see him appear again!"

"He is dead," said the widow quietly. "It was his ghost whose step I heard. Well may he walk and be uneasy. If he wasn't dead he'd ha' been out before now. But I know very well that he's dead and buried. And, oh, Polly, I'm half sorry after all that I told you!"

Chapter XII

The Wooing of the Sphinx[1]

No intelligence, letter, or news of any kind, was to come from her own people to Valentine during her retreat. She was to be completely cut off; as much as if she had been expelled from the family circle. A hard measure, yet Lady Mildred was a wise woman, and no doubt had her reasons. Valentine was to hear nothing, whatever happened. With the exception of one episode, very little, indeed, happened. Lady Mildred and Violet went to Ilfracombe,[2] and presently Mr. Conyers made his appearance there. This was the single episode of interest. He stayed for three weeks; and he came, as was immediately apparent, with the intention of making himself, if possible, pleasing to Violet.

Ilfracombe in the season is an admirable place in which to study with thoughtfulness the character and the charms of a young lady, especially if she be not surrounded by other young ladies, and if she is permitted a certain amount of freedom, and if there are no other students of the same young lady about the place. In all these respects Mr. Conyers had the greatest possible advantages; he had the field to himself, and he was allowed every opportunity of carrying on this singularly attractive study. He walked with Lady Mildred and Violet on the Capstone Rock; he drove about the country with them; and he accompanied Violet when she went sketching; he was even permitted to go sailing with her. She had a boat of her own, and a boatman specially engaged for her own service. But there is generally a swell upon the ocean off Ilfracombe, and too often while Violet sat, rope in hand, bright of eye, and light of heart, when the white sail flew round the headlands, the young man beside her was fain to preserve silence, while his eyes assumed a fishy glare and his cheek was blanched.

"I am watching them," wrote Lady Mildred; "he may amuse Violet, but I am certain he will not touch her heart. To begin with, he is not exactly—well, there are gentlemen of many kinds, I suppose, and he knows how

1 In Greek mythology, the Sphinx was a half-woman, half-lion monster. She would pose a riddle to any young man who came across her, and those unable to properly solve it would be eaten.

2 Ilfracombe is a seaside tourist town in southern England.

to conduct himself; but he is not exactly a gentleman after our kind; I do not hear anything about his people, but I suppose they are not distinguished, or we should have heard about them. He does not ride, or shoot, or hunt; he does not know anybody, and I do not know where he comes from. He does not strike one as having lived with clever people, or well-bred people, or rich people; and I daresay he is quite poor. If he is going to succeed in his work, it may help him a little to know people like ourselves. Perhaps, as you say, Bertha, he is in hopes of marrying an heiress. Let us give him every chance then."

His best chance was when Violet went sketching, and he could carry her things and talk to her while she sat at work. He had learned from certain journals a patois criticism—every kind of patois is necessarily a debased form of the real language—and this he talked, borrowing the ideas, which are misty, of this school, as well as its tongue, and pretending that they were his own. It seems a great pity that Nature, when she created this man so ardently desirous of distinction, gave him no ideas of his own. What is genius without ideas?

From talk of art to talk of love is a natural step. Love-making, indeed, may be made, in capable hands, a most artistic chapter of life, and one to be remembered ever afterwards with feelings of the liveliest satisfaction. It is most mortifying to think that most of us throw away and waste the most splendid chances while they are in our hands, hurrying the situation, scamping the dialogue, and simply ruining the "business." Some men, for instance, have actually been known to propose by letter; while even of poets, who ought to know better, and dramatists, and novelists, not to speak of painters, all of whom should be perpetually studying situation and getting the most business possible out of every tableau, there are few who have extracted from their own love passages anything like the amount of emotion, incident, and pathos which they should have yielded.

In this case Jack Conyers made no headway at all. It seemed as if the girl, in the most innocent way possible, purposely diverted every advance into another direction. All roads in conversation may lead up to love, but there are cross lanes at every other step into which one may turn. Violet willingly walked with him and talked with him, but she showed no sign of taking the least interest in him.

By this time he had completely satisfied himself that Lady Mildred would never have allowed her own daughter to live alone or among quite poor people in such a place as Hoxton. None of the ladies of his own family would have considered such an arrangement possible—there were ladies in his own family, though he never spoke of them, and did not invite them to his chambers in Piccadilly. Of course they knew, although they certainly did not belong to quite the very best circles, what was proper and what was improper. The great middle class especially knows what is proper. It did not occur to Mr. Conyers as even possible that any young lady, much less a young lady who was the daughter of a baronet and the granddaughter of an earl, could dare to disregard those laws of propriety which are held as sacred as the decalogue by the whole of bourgeoisie.

He was so certain that he was going to risk his fate. He would make a determined effort. Somehow, although every morning he resolved upon proposing that very day, he never succeeded. He was constantly alone with the girl. Lady Mildred allowed her to go about as she pleased. He was in her boat, well off the coast with her; no one else but the old boatman within hearing; he was standing beside her while she sat and painted all the summer morning through; he was strolling with her over the cliffs to Lee, or inland, where the sea mists sweep up the narrow coombe; he sat with her on the Capstone Rock, while the waves rolled up against that great headland, and outside the harbour the pleasure-boats rolled and rocked and gave the people inside such exquisite pleasure that they all held their heads over the side and begged and prayed to be taken ashore instantly. And all the time he talked, and all the time he felt with a sinking heart that he was making no impression.

He made a last effort on the day before he came away.

"I must go back to town," he said with a sigh. "This has been a very pleasant holiday. I shall remember it all my life. But work calls."

"I thought yours was a kind of work which could wait till you chose to do it, Mr. Conyers. You have no work that you must do, have you?"

"Mine is art work," he replied reproachfully, because she ought to have understood. "Of course, therefore, I wait until it calls me."

"Oh! you wait for inspiration; and now it has come. That is why, all the time you have been down here, you have done nothing. I am only a feeble creature, but I must be always drawing. Well, and have you got your inspiration at last? And is it overwhelming?"

It seemed as if she was actually laughing at him.

"If I thought that anything concerning myself could interest you—"

"It does, Mr. Conyers. I am interested about all my friends. You are one of my friends, are you not? Besides, I am rather curious about you."

"Are you really curious about me?"

"Yes. I want to know what you really can do. You see, Mr. Conyers, we have had a great many talks about art, both in Florence and here; but I have never seen any of your work. Surely you have done something by this time. Claude tells me you used to draw very well at Cambridge."

"I will show you some day. You understand that a man may not desire to let his immature work be seen. I will tell you, in my own studio, if you let me, something of my aims, perhaps."

"As you please. But are they mysterious? If you are an artist, of course you propose to be a great artist. Claude is a lawyer, and desires to be a great lawyer."

"My ambitions shall not be mysterious—to you."

"Do not confide secrets to me, Mr. Conyers. I am the worst person in the world to keep them."

"If you are curious—that is, interested—in anyone, you like to know everything about him, do you not?"

"You mean about his family connections?"

She was thinking of her own; but the question reminded him how awkward it might be if he should have to explain certain things, and how difficult it might be to put them so that they should look really picturesque—almost everything may be made to look picturesque with proper handling, though the paternal profession and the "girls" would require delicate handling when it came to explaining and introducing.

"Fortunately, my own family connections are well known," said Violet lightly. "Claude and I come of an old family; on both sides, I believe, a family older than the Conquest."[3]

"But you do not know—it is not certain—"

"Well then, Mr. Conyers, we will leave it uncertain until October, and then, if you please, you shall show us some of your work, and explain some of your aims; though, if I were you, I should think less of the aims and more of the work."

---

3 A reference to the Norman conquest of England in 1066, which replaced native rulers with the French of Normandy and drastically altered England's culture. For a family to be older than that event would mean that one's ancestors were native English.

The most stupid man in the world could not fail to perceive that the subject must be deferred till after the coming of age. But he did something to show the disinterested nature of his passion—he went to Lady Mildred and begged for a few words with her.

"It is, briefly, Lady Mildred," he said, "that I have ventured to fall in love with one of your daughters."

"You mean Violet?" she asked coldly.

"I have not presumed to speak to her. I do not know whether she regards me with any favour at all. But I have seen her every day here—thanks to your kindness."

"And you think you are in love with her?"

"I ask only one thing, permission to take my chance; your permission to speak when you return to town. I have, I confess, but a slender fortune, though I have large ambitions. My future," he added, proudly, "is, I believe, in my own hands. It may be a distinguished future."

"Every woman desires a distinguished husband," said Lady Mildred. "But it would be a dreadful disappointment were promises not fulfilled, would it not? If you place any reliance on your genius, Mr. Conyers, it would be well to have some first-fruits ready. But indeed it is not genius that I desire for Violet so much as certain other qualities. You know the history of the two girls?"

"One is the sister of my dear friend, Claude Monument. The other is your own daughter."

"One is an heiress and the other has nothing."

"Believe me, Lady Mildred, I should be happy indeed with Violet even in the latter case."

"That is well said"—it was fairly well said—but there wanted what we call the true ring. "That is well said; and now, Mr. Conyers, as you might be tempted to tell Violet all this at once, I beg you will go away, and if you are in the same mind in October, when we return, you have my full permission to speak to her."

He went away, hardly satisfied; he returned to London. Town was quite empty, but Alicia was at home; there was always dinner for him—a good dinner—such as Alicia loved, with the beautiful claret, which she also loved, served in the great silver claret jug: dinner laid on the massive mahogany table, in the room with the huge sideboard and the pictures of game and fruit, all betokening a solid income and the substantial results of successful trading, with Alicia herself to talk about the old times before he set up for a fine gentleman and a great artist and a man of culture and sweetness, and was only a conceited handsome boy, who liked drawing girls' heads, and looked a good deal at his own face in the glass, and gave himself airs, and talked about himself to the girl five or six years older, who lived in the adjacent villa at Stockwell, and belonged to folk of like standing with himself. He liked this talking over the old times with her. She was a person of no imagination; she always laughed at his pretensions; she told him the whole truth; and she never swerved from the doctrine that there is but one thing in the world worth striving for, and that is the thing for which all good business people diligently strive—a solid income—all the rest being pure illusion.

For other distractions there was the girl at Hoxton. Something had come over this girl; a change in her manner and her talk; she had grown shy with him; the careless common talk of the streets, which formerly flowed freely from her lips, in a great measure disappeared—"it is the influence of my conversation," he said. She was now dressed better; she had a newly trimmed hat, and a new frock, and new boots; and quite suddenly she began to fill out in figure and to improve; her face was no longer promising, it was really pretty; she had more than a pair of large and expressive eyes, and she carried herself uprightly. All this was the result of Valentine's dinners, Valentine's example, and Valentine's gifts. The girl was quick to learn; she was shy with this lover of hers because she understood that the situation was serious, and she was afraid of what was before her. Melenda declared that Valentine would soon go away and forget them. She also—her name should have been Cassandra—foretold the approaching death of Lotty.[4] Then the old life would begin again; but it would be worse—far worse—because she had now learned and knew what the easier life was like. Of course she ought not to have gone on meeting him; Valentine would be very angry if she knew; and yet the future that awaited her—and then—when it began—if this man should still want her to go away and become his model, what should she say?

* * *

"Mr. Conyers is gone, Violet dear," said Lady Mildred; "are you sorry?"

"Rather. He amused us, did he not? I like talking to a downright affected man. Besides, I was pleased to watch his love for Beatrice. There is nobody he would so much like to marry as that young lady. He thinks he can deceive me into believing that he is in love with me."

"Violet!"

"But he is a wretched actor. One sees through him every moment."

"My dear child!"

"I wonder if he can really do anything? Claude says he used to draw. I dare say he has some talent. But when a man calls himself an artist, and for three whole weeks never touches a pencil, and goes out with one and looks on without offering to draw or paint anything at all—my dear mamma, I fear that Mr. Conyers is a humbug."

"He has asked permission to address you, Violet; I have given him that permission, but I have put it off until we return."

"Thank you, dear. I wonder where he comes from. He seems to know nobody. Well—I wonder what Valentine is doing now—poor Valentine! with Melenda! Mamma, I am quite, quite sure, that Beatrice—Mr. Conyers made a mistake when he gave you my name—will refuse that man."

4 Cassandra is a Greek mythological figure cursed to always tell the future truthfully yet never to be believed.

Chapter XIII

A Useless Crime

Life is entirely made up of coincidences, though in novels, which should be pictures of real life, as much is generally made out of a coincidence as if the thing was unusual. That is because, although it is common, it is dramatic. One need not be surprised, therefore, to hear that Valentine heard more about the man James Carey, and that from quite an unexpected quarter.

It was from none other than the old letter-writer, Mr. Lane.

Valentine met him one evening soon after she had received that confession at the almshouse. He was creeping along the pavement on his way home, his shoulders were stooping, his head more bowed, his coat more ragged than when first she made his acquaintance. She stopped him and offered him her hand. He did not take it, but he made as if he would take off his hat. This habit, as has been already remarked, is an indestructible proof of good breeding. Another sign is the handling of the knife and fork. A third is the pronunciation of the English language. Mr. Lane did not carry out his intention of taking off his hat, because he remembered in time that the brim was like the maiden in the ditty because at a touch it would yield. Yet the gesture moved Valentine with pity because it reminded her that the man had once been a gentleman. And how, by what cruelty or misconduct, had he fallen from the ranks?

"May I walk with you?" she asked. "We are going the same way."

They were in the Curtain Road, and it was on Saturday evening, when the furniture warehouses are all closed, and the German journeymen, if wicked report be true, are all locked up in their attics without coats, hats, or boots, so that they cannot get abroad until the Monday morning, and then they must go to work again; and cannot expect or ask to get out of doors until Saturday night.

The loneliness of Curtain Road on Saturday evening is as the desolation of Tadmor in the Desert,[1] but the smell of varnish serves to connect the place with the handiwork of man.

1 An ancient city isolated in the desert.

"Surely," replied Mr. Lane, "surely. It is long since a young lady walked with me—very long. It is five-and-thirty years."

She perceived that he walked feebly and that his knees trembled.

"I am going to take a cup of coffee, Mr. Lane. Will you take one with me?"

"You wish to give me a cup of coffee." He laughed a light, musical, but not a mirthful laugh. "It is kind of you. I will accept it with pleasure."

He had been down on his luck all day, as he presently told her in the coffee-house. Here she gave him a chop with his coffee, and thus afforded him an opportunity of displaying the little mannerisms with a knife and fork which characterise English gentlemen all the world over. His luck had been very bad, it appeared, for many weeks, so that when the rent was paid there was not always enough to satisfy the wants of the machine. This evening especially he was much run down, and the unexpected chop brought a sense of physical comfort which he had not known for a great while.

"I thank you again," he said, when he had finished. "I am sunk low indeed, for I am not humiliated by the gift of a supper."

"Do not speak of humiliation," she replied; "are we not friends and neighbours?"

"Neighbours certainly. By divine goodness. Friends?—hardly. Men like me have neighbours—the lower we sink the more neighbours we have. But friends?—no, we have no friends. Friendship begins much higher up. First comes the man who struggles and starves side by side with another in the mud; there is no end of his labour, neither is his eye satisfied with riches—for he gets none; he and his follows touch each other as they search for food, like midges flying in a cloud beside the river; but these men are not friends. Then there are work-fellows on board the same ship and in the same workshop. They are companions, but not friends. And there are the men who are engaged in the same tricks. They call themselves pals, but they are not friends. Friendship, young lady, can only be formed at a certain stage of civilisation."

"Oh! But there are such friendships as those of Lotty and Melenda and your daughter Lizzie."

"The girls club together and fight against starvation. Call them friends if you please. But—" he paused and considered. "There are some old lines in my head—

'Love seeketh not itself to please,
Nor for itself hath any care.'

Who can seek for anything but for himself when he is hungry? Starving people have no room for friendship or for natural affection. My daughter eats her bread and drinks her tea in one room—I eat my bread in another. She goes her way, and I do not ask—I have no right to ask—what way it is. Friends?—we have no friends."

"The lines are Blake's,"[2] said Valentine, somewhat astonished.

"Possibly. I have forgotten. Shall we go home?"

When they reached Ivy Lane, Valentine went with him unasked into his room.

"Will you tell me something about your dream?" she asked.

"About my dream? Oh! yes. About my dream. It is a dream which goes on continually. It has gone on for five-and-thirty years. My dream? It is my life. The rest is a vain show and shadow—a procession of days and

2 William Blake, the English poet (1757–1827). The lines are from "The Clod and the Pebble."

hours which are possessed of mocking devils, except when you come to me. And even you are part of the show and seeming. That is not my life. No one would live such a life as that. You are a dream, and Ivy Lane is a dream, and Lizzie is a dream, and all the hunger and poverty and misery are part of a dream. But what you call my dream is my reality—my life. Stay—you do not know the beginning."

"I shall guess the beginning, perhaps, if you tell me where you are at present."

"They have offered the man in my dream a bishopric. It is unusual so soon after a deanery has been refused. He is to be the new Bishop of Winchester. It was always his ambition to be bishop of the diocese in which he was born, and where there is Portsmouth with the ships and sailors. His father, you know, was a sailor—middy at Copenhagen and lieutenant at Trafalgar—so that he always loved sailors. One can understand how great an honour this invitation seems to him."

"Will he accept it?"

"Surely—surely. It is a mark of the divine blessing on his life and labours. Besides, he who desireth the office of a bishop desireth a good work. This man has always looked forward to it as to the crown of his career; yet humbly, because it brings heavy responsibilities. The consecration will take place immediately. Meantime he meditates upon his duties. Tonight he will meditate more deeply and with more spiritual advantage because I have eaten well. So closely united are soul and body."

"The beginning, as I read it," said Valentine, "is that five-and-thirty years ago you were a clergyman?"

There was, indeed, something in the appearance and carriage of the man, in spite of his rags, which suggested the clerical calling. Impossible to say exactly what was the peculiarity, but it existed.

"I was once a clergyman," he answered simply. "I dream of my own life—as it might have been."

"Please go on."

"My eldest son—I was married thirty-five years ago—has just obtained a university scholarship; my second is doing well at Winchester—my old school; my daughters are sitting with me in my study; and my wife—but she is dead." A change came over the man's face. Was his wife, then not altogether a dream?

Valentine waited to hear more.

"Five-and-thirty years ago," he said, "I was thirty, and I was married—not long married—when the dreadful thing happened to me. Good God! Why was it suffered to happen?"

"Do not talk about it. Forget it if you can and go on with your dream."

"I must talk about it. There come times when I am constrained to tell someone, even if it kills me to tell it. Last time I told it to the doctor. He came here yesterday to see me, but he only talked about you." Valentine blushed. "He is in love with you. Of course he is in love with you. Everybody must be, you know that. It was not last night that I told him, but long ago—months ago—the last time that I was forced to tell it." His face was agitated and his fingers twisted nervously. "I must tell you."

"But it agitates and pains you. Do not tell me. Talk about your dream."

"No, no—sometimes I understand that my dream is only a dream, and the real life is here, among these rags; and then I must tell someone, even if it kills me.

"He came to the village and lodged there three months, at the village inn. We all got to know him. The vicar at the vicarage[3]—that was myself—and Sir William at the house. He went about among us all, smooth-spoken and well-behaved; not a gentleman exactly, but a man who could sit with gentlemen. He came to

3 In the Church of England, a vicar is the priest of a parish.

church every Sunday; he played the violin beautifully, and I played the violoncello, and my wife the piano—it is not often that a good player comes to a village—and we had trios, I was married—yes, I had been married for six months. I should have been married before but for some college debts. I don't think there was anybody in the world happier than I was all that summer."

"Hush! Do not excite yourself; tell the story quietly."

"Tell the story—tell my story quietly? Oh! you don't know." His cheeks were white, his face was working, and his body writhing with the excitement of his story.

"But you are right. The doctor said I must keep quiet if I could. I will try. It was in the same summer that the great burglary took place at the House, and her ladyship's jewels were stolen. I have sometimes thought that, perhaps, James Carey did that too!"

"Who? What was the name?"

"James Carey was his name. James Carey."

"James Carey!" Somehow she was not surprised. There could not have been two of that name—villains both. Yet it was strange to hear about him so soon again, and in this very house under the same roof with his daughter! What new villainy was she about to hear? "When you have heard the story you will get up and go away."

"No, no—I shall not."

"It is a story of a great villain and a wretched sinner. There was a certain old debt, undischarged, which troubled me." He told his story in jerks, stalking across the room, and throwing about his arms. "The man threatened. I could pay him in three months, but he refused to wait. I was in dreadful trouble about it. The man Carey wormed himself into my confidence, and I told him. I was trustee, with another man, for a child. She had some money invested in our names. Carey showed me what to do. I ought not to have listened. I might have gone to that other man, my co-trustee; he would have lent me the money; but I was ashamed. Carey told me how to do it. Well, I was tempted and I fell—a preacher of God's judgments—and I fell. I drew a cheque—it was for a hundred and twenty pounds. I signed it with my name; Carey signed my fellow-trustee's name—out of friendliness, he said. In this way, you see, I became a forger—yes, a wretched criminal—a forger. Why don't you get up and go away? I was to draw the money and to pay it back in six months' time; no one would ever know anything about it. He was the actual forger, but I was his accomplice—his equal in guilt. Oh! I have never complained of what followed. I deserve everything, and more. I do not complain, except sometimes, that men are made so weak. Nothing that has been done to me is equal to what I did to myself. I was such a fool, too—oh, I remember. When we had signed the cheque, Carey went to the bank to draw the money for me. Well,"—he stopped and laughed—"what do you think? He never came back—he never came back with the money."

"Do you mean that he kept the money?"

"That is what he did. But I was a forger. Why, it was found out at once—I don't know how. My writing was well known; experts swore that the forgery was by me, too. My desk was found full of imitations. Carey had put them there. They found out about the creditor and his threats. There was no defence possible except that another man had drawn the money. I do not complain; but sometimes I think he was a greater villain than myself. I was only a poor contemptible wretch, born for such a lot as this."

"The man Carey," said Valentine, "is dead."

"Is he dead? Is he dead?"—he spoke as if he was disappointed—"I cannot think that he is dead. Because for five-and-thirty years I have always thought to meet him face to face. Dead! And my own course is nearly run! Great heavens! What a course!"

He gasped and laid his hand upon his heart. But the spasm passed.

"I have suffered penal servitude. I have been cut off from my fellows. All this I deserved. I have been disgraced and exiled and starved. I do not complain. But surely the other man should have had something!"

"He died in prison. He received a harder punishment than you."

"He—died—in—prison." There was consolation in the fact. "I thought that I should die before him, so as to be ready with my testimony against him when he should come before the Judge."

"Forgive him," said Valentine. "Forgive the dead, who can sin no more."

"'Their love and their hatred is now finished; neither have they a portion forever in anything that is done under the sun.' Thus saith the Book."[4]

"Then forgive him."

"No; I cannot forgive him until the day shall come when I can forgive myself. And that will be—never. Oh! men talk of forgiveness; but how can they ever forgive themselves?"

"Then do not speak of the man again. Tell me of your life since then. You found love. You have your daughter."

"Love! Do you think in such depths as mine there is room for love? I found a miserable girl in the streets, a girl as wretched as my daughter is now; as poor, as starved, as hardly worked, more cruelly robbed. I married her. Why? I suppose to save her from a little of the pain. Oh! I did not ask if the other wife was dead; all that belonged to the past life, which was gone. I married her; and perhaps she was less miserable for a while—I think she was—and then she died. I found money enough to pay some other poor wretches for the keep of the child. You know her—what she is. I have been able to do no more for her."

"Poor man! Poor child!" Valentine took his hand—the long nervous hand, thin and bony as a skeleton's.

"She is the child of the gutter, which has been her playground as well as her cradle, and will be her grave. What can you expect? Has she any of a woman's virtues? I do not know. They are not wanted in the gutter. Let her live her life out with the other gutter children, and then lie down and die. Perhaps, after she is dead she will find out why any of us were born, and what it means."

"Poor Lizzie!"

"Sometimes when the thing comes back to my memory—the prison cell—the coming out again, which was worse; the miserable life that I have led in this hiding-place—I feel as if I must ask why? But the heavens are silent. One cannot be heard up there, because of the crowd who are all crying out together and asking why?—poor wretches! You know, when Abraham communed with the Lord it was in the desert alone under the clear sky.[5] It is no use crying out among so many. Else I could lift up my voice and ask why I was born so weak and others so strong." Here his face became suddenly contorted and his eyes glared and his body bent double and his hands clenched, and he swayed from side to side as one who is wrestling with an unseen adversary. Valentine sprang to her feet, but she could do nothing. You cannot help a man in mortal agony.

The attack was over in a few moments. Presently he lay back upon the bed pale and exhausted.

---

4 The quotation, which references the dead, comes from Ecclesiastes 9:6.

5 In the Book of Genesis, God speaks to Abraham, his chosen one, and promises him a great nation.

"It was the devil," he whispered. "He always clutches at my heart when I think about James Carey. I thought he would have killed me that time."

"Do not talk. Lie quite still and quiet. Shall I bring the doctor to you?"

"No, no; it is over now. Give me that bottle. The doctor can do nothing."

She sat by the bedside and administered such words of consolation as came into her mind.

Then he sat up on the bed and began to tell her more about his life, and how, after a long period of misery and starvation, he found out the precarious way of earning his bread which he had practised ever since, and how the old life had vanished so completely that from the day when he was first put into prison he had never read a single book, nor looked in a single paper; and how, in the worst time of his trouble, his dream came to him and became a ministering angel; and he had found solace ever since in following an imaginary career of honour and distinction.

A thick black line indeed had been drawn across his life.

"What consolations," he asked, "can console for such a life as mine? There is the thought that sooner or later there will be an end of everything. 'Surely,' said the preacher, 'surely oppression maketh a man mad, and better is the end of a thing than the beginning thereof.'"

As for the other form of consolation, which sometimes does console, the poor man had lost the power of feeling it.

"You must never again," said Valentine, "even think of this man. As he is dead you may the more readily forget him. And if you do not think of him too much, you may perhaps forgive him."

"Forgive him!"

"As you hope for forgiveness yourself."

"I do not hope for anything."

"But he is dead."

"I do not know yet whether I shall meet him after death. Do not speak of forgiveness."

He fell asleep presently. It was long past midnight when Valentine went upstairs to her own room. Lotty was lying asleep; her pains had left her for the moment; she was growing daily weaker; the moonlight was pouring into the room; from the neighbouring court there came the screams of an angry woman and the oaths of an angry man. Then these subsided and all was quiet. At one o'clock Valentine heard a step on the stair. It was Lizzie, the child of the gutter, come home from wandering about the streets. Valentine thought of her father's words. Should she be suffered to be forever in the gutter? Had she any womanly virtues? Well, the girl had one virtue: she loved her friends.

Lizzie passed into her room and closed the door.

Then Valentine leaned out of the open window and thought of the great human questions—why we are born—why we suffer—why we perish—and looked into the silent heavens above. In the clear sky rode the queen of night in splendour; some of the stars were visible; she seemed to hear millions of voices around her crying aloud in the night, all asking these questions, some with shrieks, and some with sighs, and some with wonder. And she longed for the peace of the desert when on such a night as that poor old man had reminded her, the patriarch could step forth and commune with the Lord beneath the stars. Alas! the crowds of the great city would stifle such a commune at the very outset. Yet there are some—Valentine remembered—who find consolation in the faith that the heavens are not deaf as well as dumb. Else we had better all be dead, and let the great round world roll on forever by itself without the mockery of man. And some day, we must also believe, all questions shall be answered, and on that day at length men shall learn even how to forgive themselves, and shame and remorse shall be no more.

Chapter xiv

Ask Me No More

Ivy Lane, including the part now called Ivy Street, and the courts leading out of it, is estimated to contain 1,200 people, which gives, if you compute by the square mile, a most preposterous rate of population. Most of the evils of life have taken up a permanent abode there, or are efficiently represented. Poverty, for instance, is always there, but that is too common to be regarded as an evil any more than a bald head or grey hair; most people either suffer from it perennially, or get it from time to time. Destitution is always somewhere in the lane, with empty shelves and pinched faces; disease is always somewhere; drunkenness, as soon as the evening shades prevail, doth still take up its wondrous tale; repentance in the form of headache and heartache is never absent from Ivy Lane, because the people are always backsliding, and because, as the copybooks ought to enforce with greater emphasis, there is no overstepping which is not followed by its own headache; or, as another Book hath it—"The way of transgressors is hard;"[1] injustice is always outside Ivy Lane, oppressing the helpless; cheating and knavery, falsehood and treachery, craft and subtlety, everything is in Ivy Lane. Here is always the young man choosing between the broad and the narrow way; between the easy way and the rough way; generally he chooses the broad way and so gets presently into difficulties. There is the young girl with such a choice as Lizzie's always before her. There are the old men and women who feel in a blind confused kind of way that they must have made some great blunder at some time or other, else they would not now be so horribly poor. Love is always there, the love of wife and sweetheart and mother; love in all its forms, strong to save. New life is always there: every minute, or thereabouts, a child is born. And death is always there: once a week at least the black box, generally a little one, is carried down the lane.

This hive of swarming life, as soon as Valentine got over a few initial difficulties and grew accustomed to regard certain things without shrinking or terror, filled her with admiration mixed with humility. It shames us to witness the virtues of humble folk, because I suppose we are so perfectly certain that in our own case,

---

1 Proverbs 13:15.

supposing that we had ourselves to live in such a way, these virtues would be conspicuously absent. They are the humbler virtues, but useful and solid, such as patience, helpfulness, cheerfulness, and sympathy with other lives of little joy. By degrees Valentine got to know all the people. She talked with them in the streets, and sat with them in their rooms, and became, without difficulty and without money-giving, their friend. In every room there was a history. Thus, in one lay an old soldier, a Crimean veteran, full of stories, kept from starvation by a pension of ninepence a day, dying slowly of rheumatic gout, first engendered in the trenches before Sebastopol.[2] There was the woman who washed, not as Mrs. Monument was wont to wash, with a lovely drying-ground outside, but in her own room, hampered withal by a daughter of seventeen not quite right in her head—"half baked," to use the popular and feeling expression. There was the decent man, laid up for the last four months with a bad knee, and all his savings gone. There was the painter who had always been in good work until his hand "dropped"—a common misfortune in the trade when one grows elderly. There was the man whom rheumatism had seized by the fingers and the wrists, swelling his joints into huge lumps and twisting them out of shape so that he could not work. There were everywhere the women: here one down with a bad confinement; here one with a drunken husband who spent all the money in the "Adelaide"; one whose husband was out of work; one whose husband had deserted her; and one whose husband was dead, and her children crying for the food which she could not give them. Another, an elderly single woman, gaunt and thin, proud and ashamed, held out against Valentine for a long time, with something of the decayed gentlewoman in her speech and manners, and no doubt a history of her own if she chose to tell it, but she kept it to herself. As for her work—such a woman is not born for such work—she had to make trousers with the help of a machine for a delightful German firm whose daughter, though only seventeen, was told off on account of her supernatural hardness, her shrewish temper, and her fluent tongue, to bargain with the women and beat them down to the uttermost and rail at them. But yet, by reason of the beneficial Law of Elevenpence Ha'penny and despite the amiable young German, even this poor thing earned enough to keep the machine going. And everywhere a doleful and monotonous spectacle, the women and girls who toil all day with feverish energy for their miserable wage. Everywhere the life that is not life; the same slavery; the same oppression; and the same patience.

Of course these people are full of sin and steeped in wickedness; everybody says so; they are fond of drink and prejudiced against church, and avid of any little enjoyment which falls in their way; they are stiff-necked; ungrateful and never satisfied—considering that whatever is done for them they are always left with the same long hours and the same short pay, it is not wonderful that they should be discontented. All of them moreover—a thing which must be considered—belong to the class which never get any share at all in the fruit and the wine, the cakes and the ale, however hard they work; nay, the harder they work, the less they seem to get.

And there are others, beside Sam the Socialist, who are loudly asking the ominous question if this is right, that any workers, even working-girls who cannot combine and never complain, and are perfectly helpless and cannot kick, rebel, or demonstrate, and are under no law but the Law of Elevenpence Ha'penny, should always get less than their share.

"You take it too much to heart, Valentine," said Claude.

---

2 During the Crimean War (October 1853–February 1856), a yearlong siege occurred at Sebastopol on the Black Sea coast.

They were sitting beside the pretty ornamental water in Victoria Park. It was half-past one o'clock, when the Victorians are all at dinner, and the Park was like the Garden of Eden, not only for its summer beauty, but because it contained only one single pair, a man and a woman. They had been talking over these things, and Valentine was betrayed into more emotion than was usual with her.

"I cannot take it too much to heart. It is impossible." The tears crowded into her eyes, and her lips trembled. "I hoped," she added gently, but her tears rather than her words reproached him, "I hoped that you would have helped us, Claude."

She was paler and thinner than when, six weeks before, she had begun her solitary life in Ivy Lane. Her face, always serious, was now set with a deeper earnestness, and there was no smile upon her lips. You have observed the first delicate beauty of a girl who knows nothing about the world and its wickedness, whose reading, as well as her companions, has been under supervision, who has been taught to believe in everybody's goodness, who has only just begun to go into society, and who is as yet perfectly heart-whole. Well, that was now gone.

In its place was the beauty of a girl who is young, still innocent, but no longer ignorant. Such knowledge as had come to Valentine does not destroy the early beauty, but it saddens the face and makes the eyes grave. She had learned hundreds of evil things; henceforth, things which had been mere phrases, prayers which had been meaningless, would possess for her their real and dreadful meaning.

There is nothing more saddening for a girl than the discovery that the world is not only very wicked, which the most carefully shielded girl must learn some time or other, but that its wickedness, in every form, is about her and around her, at her very feet, and that she is in a sense already responsible for some of it. This knowledge of evil came to Valentine suddenly, not bit by bit and gradually, as ladies sometimes learn it, but in an overpowering cataract which was almost more than she could bear. Perhaps it would have been better, it would certainly have been easier for her, had she been kept from the knowledge. The cultured life, surrounded by hedges which are filled with rosebushes, hawthorn, eglantine, honeysuckle, and wild flowers, on one side, but set with prickly pears and impenetrable thorns on the other, so as to exclude the rough and wicked world, is far more pleasant for a girl; most of us would keep our girls in this paradise as long as we could; we think that because their frames are weaker and their limbs more delicate than our own, we ought to keep them even from knowing the wild forces and the ungoverned passions without, as if it was the body and not the soul that is threatened by those waves which break and those winds which roar. Yet Lady Mildred knew beforehand something of what Valentine would experience. She did not act without deliberation: we are all, she thought, men and women alike; it cannot be altogether bad for us to know the truth about ourselves and our brothers. Some of us still remember the old story of how the knowledge of good and the knowledge of evil go together; and there are hundreds of women who all day long wade breast-high in moral sloughs and slums, and emerge unspotted, save that some of the sunshine is taken out of their faces, some of the light from their eyes, some of the smiles from their lips.

The tears in Valentine's eyes went straight to Claude's conscience like the stroke of a whip. This girl had not been his sister so long that he had ceased to regard her with a reverence which few brothers display towards their sisters. Besides, she was entrusted to his care; and, again, he had been thinking.

"I have not forgotten my promise, Valentine," he said quickly; "I remember all that you say to me. But it is a very serious subject."

"You have really been thinking of us, Claude?"

"I have been reading as well as thinking. But, Valentine, as yet I feel powerless even to suggest anything."

"But you will never let it drop—never. Oh! Claude, I see Melenda every day."

"There is no doubt," he began, "that working-women are treated absolutely in accordance with the principle so dear to employers—supply and demand. If that is a true principle, then I suppose they ought to have nothing to complain of."

"Nothing to complain of!"

"Supply and demand means that the women have got to take the best terms they can get; in the struggle to live they undersell each other till they reach the lowest terms on which life can be supported. That is the whole case, Valentine. The employer gives the lowest wages which will be taken. There is no question of justice, or of kindness, or of mercy. They call it a law of political economy, which must be obeyed."

"Is it also a law of political economy that men who employ the women are to get rich? Who makes such laws? I suppose the manufacturers. Let us make our own laws for the women, and the first law of all, that whether the employer gets his profit or not, the girls shall be properly paid."

"We should then promptly lose the services of the employer."

"Then we would do without him."

"Women cannot combine like men. They are unaccustomed to act together. There are too many of them. And they have no public spirit."

"I have heard all this before, Claude. But first set up all your difficulties, and then you can cut your way through them."

"They could perhaps combine," Claude went on, "if they had the support of the men. How to get that? How to make the working-man feel that he must look after his sister?"

"You will teach him that, Claude."

"You are persistent, Valentine. Every day your eyes look at me reproachfully—"

"I do not mean to be reproachful."

"And yet you are reproachful. And every day the burden you would lay upon me grows heavier to look upon."

"Then take it up, Claude, and every day it will grow lighter."

"One must move the girls to act together; one must move the working-man to act for his sister; and one must move the ladies, the gentlewomen, to act for the women who work. You demand impossibilities, Valentine."

"Only a man can move the women. You must speak to them, Claude. You must speak right out—from your very heart."

"It is strange," he went on, pursuing his own thoughts without answering her, "it is strange. The oppression of the working-woman is no new thing. It has not been discovered yesterday or the day before. It has been preached and described over and over again. Never a year passes but someone writes indignantly about their treatment. It is fifty years since Hood's 'Song of the Shirt' was written, and forty since Mrs. Browning's 'Cry of the Children.'[3] Well the children have long since been released, and yet the women remain in their misery."

3 In 1842, Elizabeth Barrett Browning's "The Cry of the Children" brought to life the awful working conditions that children endured as factory laborers. The poem helped to galvanize support for Lord Shaftesbury's Factories Act (1847), which limited the

"That is because we care for the children," said Valentine, "but we do not care for each other."

"There are no women anywhere," Claude went on, "so charitable and so generous as Englishwomen; they are never tired of doing good things, they sacrifice themselves, they go about among the poor, they are nurses."

"But oh!" Valentine interrupted him, "how many thousands are there like me, who have never done anything but look for new pleasures!"

"There is a great literature upon the subject; the lines are written in blood, yet no man regardeth it. The story of the needle-woman of London is so terrible that one wonders why crusades have not been preached. As for that, a crusade has been preached, but nothing comes of it."

"It is because the preachers are women, and no one will listen to them. They want a man to preach, Claude; they want you."

"They want a stronger man than me."

"I can teach you what we women are like. I have studied myself on purpose. We are soft and luxurious; we like things to be smooth and pleasant; we never ask how things come; we think the world was made only for us to enjoy; we hate to hear painful stories; we put ugly things out of sight. You must force us to hear the whole truth: don't talk about our kind hearts; lash us with the truth about our hardness till we cry for shame and repentance."

She looked as if she herself could preach such a sermon on such a text.

"You are too bitter, Valentine."

"We want a man," she repeated, "who must be young and generous; he must be full of anger; he must be able to speak, and fearless; he must be a man who can speak to women of any class; he should be a scholar; he should know the working-women well; he should be bound to them, Claude, by more than the ordinary ties. Oh! where can such a man be found unless it is yourself? Claude, it is your sister Melenda who calls you out of her misery and her helplessness. Listen! Oh! you *must* hear her voice among them all—it is so full of rage and of madness. For what good were you taken from among them if—you—you of all men—spend your powers and your knowledge for your own ambition? Oh! Claude, if you could see the girls in their pain, too wretched even to pray"—she stopped because her voice broke down. "Claude, forgive me.

I will never trouble you again. You have your own ambition; you have chosen your own way; and all I can do is to stay among them and help one or two."

She had conquered him before, when she made him help her in the Great Renunciation by her music. She conquered him now by her tears. He took her hand and inclined his head over it, saying, "Take me, Valentine; do with me what you please. I am altogether at your service."

"Claude!" she dashed away her tears and sprang to her feet. "You mean all that you say—exactly—all that you say?"

"All, Valentine. Why, my honour is concerned; it is my sister who calls me. Which of my sisters? Is it Melenda, or is it Polly-which-is-Marla?"

She caught his hands and held them with sparkling eyes. "Only," he said, "do not expect too much. I told you at the beginning that you would be disappointed in me."

"No, never disappointed; always proud of our brother. And now, Claude, now—oh! the women have never—never had such a chance before. You will feel for these poor girls as no one else but yourself could feel

---

working hours of women and children in British factories to ten hours a day. For the text of the poem, see Appendix B.

for them. It is like taking one of themselves out of the dreadful work-rooms and giving her voice and speech and knowledge. Do you think that my mother—that Lady Mildred—meant this all along? Do you think she designed from the beginning that you were to give to the people the things she gave to you? Why, it was like a woman—was it not?—to give them through a man. But what did she intend for Polly?" Certainly, she remembered in time, Polly showed, as yet, no signs of giving back anything to her own people. Valentine ceased, therefore, to pursue this speculation, which might have carried her farther than she wished. "Oh, happy girls!" she went on, "they have found a leader at last. You will speak for them, Claude, and write for them, and think for them. Oh, to be a man and to have a great cause to fight for! And you dared—oh! you poor boy, only a month ago—you dared to hesitate between your ambition and this wonderful career that lies before you. Oh, it fills me with such joy! I cannot tell you how happy it makes me," yet she was crying. "I have been wretched because of my own helplessness. But now you are with me all the difficulties will vanish."

"As for me, I feel that the difficulties are only just beginning. You will help me to face them."

"Yes; I will help you if I can. I did not understand at first, but now I do, that this is a work which will take all your soul and all your strength, Claude; all your time—perhaps all your life. Will you give so much to your poor sisters, who will take it all and perhaps never thank you? All your life, Claude? All your life—and never to regret or to look back?"

"It is all I have to give, Valentine. I am prepared to give so much. Even to give up"—he blushed and laughed—"even to give up the woolsack, and never become Lord Chancellor."[4]

She did not comprehend—no woman could comprehend—the full extent of Claude's sacrifice. Many young men are ardently desirous of distinction or even notoriety; they will stoop to tomfool tricks if they cannot get a show by any other way. Claude, on the other hand, was possessed of the idea that he ought to justify his social promotion. It seems, if you think of it, an extremely foolish thing for a young man to be picked out and raised above his fellows if he does nothing afterwards to justify the selection. One such case have I known. The man had everything in his favour; that is to say, he was, to begin with, the son of a village blacksmith, which is an enormous advantage at the outset. You cannot get much nearer to the hard pan. Then he was a strong and lusty creature; and he was much impressed, like Claude, with the necessity for work. He did work; he worked day and night; yet, most unhappily. He was awkward and stupid, and could never acquire either knowledge or manners. He experienced as much difficulty in passing his examinations as if he had been the son of a duke; he entered a profession where brains are welcomed but are not necessary; and he has remained ever since in the lower branch of that profession on the wages of a blacksmith's assistant.

Consider: Claude had his fellowship; that is to say, a certain income for a few years longer; he could afford to wait; he had already some work, and could very fairly expect more; he could speak; he had studied law with the same intensity which he threw into all his work; and he was calmly certain that he was going to do well. There is one excellent thing about a good degree, that it makes a young man believe in himself. He who has been well up in the first class never afterwards doubts his own capacity to become lord chancellor, archbishop of Canterbury, editor of the *Times*, poet laureate, president of the College of Physicians, prime minister,—anything except ambassador. That is the one distinction which shares with the Garter the pride of being kept absolutely out of anybody's reach. These first class men do not generally aspire after the fame of

4 A senior official in the government.

Thackeray or Fielding,[5] because, in academic groves, the craft of the novelist is held in contempt, and is not yet even recognised as one of the fine arts. They do not read Lucian, Apuleius, and Heliodorus.[6] Claude therefore, who had been very near to the top, regarded any of these positions as a young athlete may regard an alpine peak. His foot may yet stand upon it. If now, at the very outset and beginning, he was to withdraw in order to work for Valentine, it would most likely be to destroy everything; and for what?

"What will you give me, Valentine, in exchange for the woolsack?"

She was *exaltée*[7] at the prospect which she saw before her, fair and glorious, because she was still very young, and because she believed greatly in this young man, who might have been, and thought he was, her brother.

"Oh!" she said, "you want nothing. It is a nobler life that you have chosen. It is a far greater thing even to try, and though you fail altogether; but you shall not fail, Claude; you shall not fail. I said that your sisters will take all that you give, and never perhaps thank you. But I will take care that they shall. And in exchange you shall have the hearts of a hundred thousand women, whose lot you will change from wretchedness to plenty. Will not that be compensation enough for you?"

When history comes to ask—as no doubt it will—how it happened that so excellent a lord chancellor as Claude Monument was lost to the country, and why he never became Sir Claude Monument, and then Baron Monument, and then Earl of Hackney Marsh, I hope this chapter will be considered a sufficient reply. No one is to be blamed, except himself, and we must not blame him greatly, because he was like his forefather when the woman tempted him, and he fell.

---

5 William Makepeace Thackeray and Henry Fielding, two leading novelists of the nineteenth and eighteenth centuries, respectively.

6 Lucian, Apuleius, and Heliodorus are ancient Greek and Roman authors considered to be some of the earliest Western novelists.

7 French for *elated* or *thrilled*.

Chapter XV

Brother Joe's Discovery

Claude's conversion, or his awakening, or his act of crowning folly, whichever you please to call it, by which he absolutely abandoned and threw away as promising a career as ever offered itself to an ambitious young man, took place on the morning of Saturday, the twenty-ninth day of August.

The date is as important as other historical dates. It marks the commencement of a new era, as will be presently seen, and it has, therefore, to be remembered like that of the Hegira or that of Martin Luther's "Theses."[1] It is also extremely important for another reason of a more private nature, and therefore, because all of us love the individual above the class, of more general interest. It is that on the very day after his conversion Claude learned a very important family secret. If he had known it on the Saturday morning his decision might possibly have been the same, but there would have been hesitations and difficulties.

He found out this important fact in a very simple way, so simple that he wondered afterwards why he had not thought of that way before. But then he had never set himself to discover a secret which Lady Mildred evidently regarded as her own, nor had he ever thought of ways by which that secret could be discovered. That kind of small-mindedness is impossible for a man whose chief desire it is to justify his promotion.

On the Sunday morning, being the day after the Great Surrender, he called upon his mother. This was not in itself by any means an extraordinary event or one calling for observation. And his mother talked a great deal about her daughter, which was also not extraordinary, because during that summer the old lady thought and talked of little else, and occupied the whole time, during every one of Claude's visits, in a running commentary on the virtues of her daughter Polly. Claude, she thought, should consider his sister more; he should take her to tea sometimes, say at the Spaniards, or Jack Straw's Castle, or North End, or High Beech, or Chingford, or to some other country place of a Sunday; she would be all the better for country air, and she was too proud

1 The Hegira refers to Muhammad's flight from Mecca to Medina, which started the Muslim era. Martin Luther's "Ninety-Five Theses" is thought to be the start of the Protestant Reformation.

to keep company with the first that offered; as for thoughtfnlness, and good temper, and singing like a bird, and never being cross, and catching a person up, or getting into rages, as Melenda did, there was nobody in the world like Polly, and what she should do when Polly went back to her place in October she did not know.

While they were still talking about her, it happened—again not an unusual thing on Sunday morning—that Joe came slowly down the road and looked in at the almshouse, and stood at the door, leaning and listening, pipe in mouth, slowly getting, in his own way, the utmost possible enjoyment out of a fine Sunday. He never said much at any time, chiefly because he was of an amiable disposition, and loved to oblige and gratify other people, and very well knew that people liked talking better than listening, and that everybody had a great deal to say on every subject. This morning he said nothing at all, but from time to time there passed over his face something broader than a smile, and something narrower than a grin. On Sundays he was newly shaven, so that the play of his lips had a chance, and his face, which during the week was always smudged, was now clean, so that his eyes had a chance. His lips, while his mother talked of Polly smiled from time to time, and his eyes danced, if a man of Joe's age can have dancing eyes. Claude observed these signs of amused intelligence, and wondered what they might mean. Presently, and soon after stroke of noon, Joe got up to go, and Claude accompanied him. They walked away together, side by side, workman and gentleman, as it should be with all workmen and all gentlemen, as well as with those who are brothers. Outside the almshouses, Joe knocked the ashes from his pipe and laughed, not aloud, but with a chuckling, bubbling, secret enjoyment.

"What are you grinning at, Joe?" asked Claude, "and what made you keep smiling while my mother talked?"

"She goes on about the gell,[2] don't she, boy? Never tired o' singin' her praises—might make a man jealous, because there's my Rhoder been with her as many years as that one weeks."

"She is very fond of her."

"Well, I ain't jealous. Not a bit, Claude. I like to hear her. It does me good to hear her go on like that, the poor old woman! It makes her happy, don't it?"

"Why shouldn't she go on, as you call it?"

"She and her Polly! Ho! ho! ho!"

"What do you mean, Joe?"

Joe stopped and looked at his brother in questioning guise.

"Why, you don't mean to tell me that you haven't found out?"

"Found out—what?"

"It don't matter to you and me; and if the old woman likes to think she's Polly, and if it makes 'em both happy, what's the odds to anybody?"

"Well but, Joe—what can you know about it?"

Joe laughed.

"As if I shouldn't know my own sister di-reckly I set eyes upon her."

"How should you know her when you haven't seen her for twenty years?"

"Brigadier, you're a scholar, and you've read a mighty lot of books. I haven't. But I'm blessed if I don't think I am as sharp in most things as you."

"Sharper, if you please, Joe. I am sure you are, in fact. But go on, please."

2 A misspelling of *girl*, used to represent the mispronunciation of the word in Joe's working-class dialect.

"Why—can't you guess now? Look here, lootenant,[3] it's this way. When father died—you've got no call to be ashamed of your father, mind—I was sixteen years old. Consequentially, I remember him, and his face too, very well, I do. You were only three or four. Consequentially you can't remember him nor his face. And he hasn't left his likeness behind. There's never a photograph of him anywheres. Now do you begin to see?"

Claude had not begun even yet to see. He had never somehow connected his father, who was the shadow of a name—but a blameless name—with these two girls.

"When I see the two young ladies, pretty and sweet-mannered like the flowers in the garden, and when I heard them going on in that pretty way of theirs about Valentine and Violet, and Miss Beatrice and Polly, and not knowing which was which, and the old woman clutching hold of the one that wasn't Polly, and then the one that was, I could ha' laughed right out. But I didn't, Claude; I just let things be, and sat as grave as a judge."

"Well, Joe?"

"Well? And didn't you see me call Rhoder and range her up alongside the two young ladies? What do you think I did that for? Why, for you to see as well as me, of course. I said to myself, 'Claude's got eyes in his head. It's easy for him to see which of them two young ladies my gell favours.' There she was—there was my Rhoder alongside the two who don't know which is which. Why, to me the likeness was just wonderful. It was most enough for a blind man to see."

"Yet I saw nothing."

"That was because you didn't think about anything but them two pretty creatures. Your head was full of 'em. As for my Rhoder, you hadn't a thought for her. Now look here, Claude, Rhoder's a very pretty gell—as pretty as most, and what's more to the point, she's just exactly like your father must ha' been when he was sixteen—as much as one sweet-pea is like another—though her grandfather couldn't exactly be called a sweet-pea. Cast your eye on Rhoder and you'll see your father over again. Then think of the two young ladies."

Claude changed colour. He began to understand now.

"Get on a little faster, Joe—do get on. Tell me everything."

"Father, you see,"—Joe did get on, but slowly—"he'd got a delicate kind of face, with what the women call speaking eyes, and a soft sort of a smiling mouth—oh! he was a good-looking chap; if you were old enough to remember what he was like, you wouldn't forget him in a hurry. Looked like a gentleman, he did. Well now, here's the long and the short of it. Rhoder has got the same eyes and the same delicate sort of a face, and the young lady she calls Polly hasn't."

"Oh!"

"But the other one has. That very same identical face and eyes she's got. Same as my Rhoder. That's why I put her up alongside for you to see. And now do you understand?"

There was no longer any room for doubt on the point. The most stupid would have understood.

"Is it possible? Are you quite sure of what you say, Joe?"

"Certain sure I am. Lord! when I see that one coming back again without her fallals[4] and pretending she was Polly come to look after her mother, I could ha' laughed again. But I didn't laugh, Claude, because mother took it mighty serious."

---

3 A misspelling of *lieutenant*, used to represent the mispronunciation of the word in Joe's working-class dialect. Like the preceding spelling of *di-reckly* (directly), it stresses the first syllable.

4 Showy decorations and finery, particularly as part of clothing.

"Joe, she does not know. Valentine really does not know."

"That's what I was in trouble about. I said, 'Either she's acting or she isn't. If she is acting, it's the best acting I ever see, and it would be a shame to spoil the fun; and if she isn't, she's a good girl, and it would be a shame to tell her when she thinks she's doing her best by her mother and Melenda.'"

"This is no acting, Joe. Valentine does not know anything, and she must not be told."

"Besides," Joe continued, "it isn't every young lady who would come and live as she's living. Not but what she's safe enough; and Melenda, though she's set her back up, wouldn't let anybody insult her but herself. I found that out first thing, Claude."

"Did you, Joe?" Claude was much touched with this act of forethought. It really was a good thing for Joe to have done, if you come to think about it.

"Lady Mildred's daughter must not be let come to no harm," Joe replied. "If it hadn't been for her, where should we all be now? So, Claude, I had a word or two with Melenda. And she knows what to do."

"Don't tell my mother, Joe. Let her find out when the time comes. Perhaps she may never find out."

"I won't tell, boy. Don't be afraid of me, captain."

"And I say, Joe, don't be offended, you know, but I hope you haven't told Rhoda or—or anybody at home."

"Tell Rhoder? Ho, ho! Claude, *do* you think I was born yesterday? You might as well tell the parish pump.[5] I've told nobody except you. Me and you know—that's enough. Polly is the other one—the one who looked out of the corners of her eyes at me—thought I was going to knock her down, p'r'aps, or say something rude, or go swearing at the ladies; or to jump upon her, very likely; wondered if a working-man was tame, and looked round the almshouses as if she was half ashamed and half curious and half amused. That one is your sister, Claude. That's Polly-which-is-Marla."

Claude began to consider rapidly the situation and its possibilities. If Valentine knew this, or was to find it out, the whole reasons for her retreat from the world would be lost, and she might as well go back again. Then the brotherly relation with himself would be at an end; he could no longer go on working with her in the same free and unrestrained manner. Why—he thought—what could be the reason for allowing Valentine to be under his care unless the maintenance of that brotherly sentiment, so that there should be no room for any other when the discovery had to be made? It was wise and thoughtful of Lady Mildred, who was always wise and thoughtful. They were always to remain brother and sister. Very well, it was strange to feel that they never could be brother and sister. Meantime, in loyalty to his benefactor and friend, the situation must be accepted now at the cost of some deception and dissembling.

"Is it possible?" he said a second time.

"As for this one," Joe went on, "that you call Valentine and mother calls Polly, she must be Miss Beatrice, I s'pose, and Lady Mildred's daughter. But, bless you, she isn't a bit proud. She sings about the place like a lark, and does up the tea-things, and dusts the room, and makes the old woman laugh, and fixes her easy and comfortable; and then she comes up to our place and sits down friendly and talks to the missus; and she's as good as a mother to Rhoder—who's afraid of her—and she buys things for the kids—boots and fruit and toys

5 The parish pump is where many locals would gather and often gossip. Therefore, to *tell the parish pump* means to tell the whole town.

and things. She's a topper,[6] Claude. That's what she is, and don't let's make no error about that. But you trust me. I won't tell. As for letting anybody know—why—there—"

He filled his pipe again and began to feel for his box of matches.

"You remember my father well?" asked Claude.

Joe's face changed curiously, and again Claude wondered. For this time it changed from sunshine to cloud, and his eyes darkened.

"Yes," he replied shortly, "I remember him very well."

"It is curious," said Claude, "that I seem to know so little about him."

"Well, Claude, there isn't much to know, perhaps. He's dead. That's about the sum of it. When a man's dead, there isn't much to say about him generally, is there? Once a man's dead, you see—why—he's dead, ain't he?"

"How was it he looked like a gentleman?"

"Can't say," Joe replied, "'cause he never told me."

"A locksmith doesn't often look like a gentleman."

"Well, I'm a plumber and a locksmith and a house decorator, and anything you please. And I suppose I don't look very much like a gentleman, if you come to that. Unless it's on Sunday morning, when I've got on my Sunday trousers and in clean shirt sleeves, and I'm a-carrying home the beer for dinner, and then I feel a gentleman down to the ground. But you always look like one, Claude. There's no doubt about you. So did father, though not such an out-and-out toff as you, captain."

"I should like to remember him."

"Should you?" Joe replied, with a strange light in his eyes. "Well, Claude, you've got no call to be ashamed of your father—remember that—though he was but a locksmith. Honest he was, and truthful—specially truthful. That's enough said about father. And don't you never talk to your mother about him, because she don't like it. Widows don't mostly, I suppose, like talkin' about their husbands. Seems natural, somehow."

As a general proposition this maxim may be disputed, but in his own mother's case, Joe was right. Mrs. Monument did not like talking about her late husband.

6 An exceptionally good person.

Chapter XVI

The Earthly Tract Society

In this informal way, merely by conversation on a bench in Victoria Park,[1] was formed a partnership which has already accomplished so considerable a work. It seems, now that we can look back from the vantage-ground of a few months' history, a natural result of Valentine's Great Renunciation and Claude's Great Surrender. And although the thing is spreading far and wide, it must not be forgotten that it was originally intended for the most obscure and the least-known quarter of London, a place quite hidden away and forgotten, concerning which nothing has ever been written, and for which nothing worthy of the chronicler has ever been attempted. Who could look for great things out of Hoxton? In that respect it may compare with a certain little city of Galilee.[2]

The complete history of this partnership will doubtless be some day written in detail. It is nothing less than a chapter in political economy, and belongs to that important section of the science which shows how tendencies have been mistaken for laws: how selfishness, avarice, greed, knavery, cheatery, and injustice have been considered the great and beneficent purpose of creation, and tricks of trade have been taken as forming part of the eternal reign of law.

It is, in fact, the story of how the supposed laws of humanity may be modified by simple acts of humanity. This, if they were indeed laws, is exactly as if the laws of gravitation could be suspended or reversed by a simple effort of the human will. And as the ideas of the partnership are spreading, and have already got outside Ivy Lane and have invaded Clinger Street, Hemsworth Road, Bacchus Walk, and James Street, and are now crossing the Kingsland Road into Haggerston, and have leaped across the canal into Islington and Dalston, and are stirring the sluggish blood of Goswell Road, it is only just to Valentine that the truth about the beginning of the New Gospel—after all only a natural outcome of the old—should be clearly stated.

1 Victoria Park played a significant role in the lives of many Eastenders. It was one of the only accessible spaces for open-air recreation available to the working classes. In addition to expansive greenery, the park also boasted a bathing pond.

2 Nazareth, a small city in Galilee, is described in the New Testament as the childhood home of Jesus Christ.

Great ideas grow quickly in the brains where they are first inspired, especially if they are assisted by a partnership of the only true kind—namely, a male and female partnership; for the masculine mind at its best is as prolific of ideas as a sunflower is of seeds or an oak of acorns. It puts them forth freely and without stint, while the feminine mind receives such of them as it catches, and nurses them tenderly while they are yet young, watching them grow, placing them in the sunshine, keeping them from east winds until they are able to go alone and need her care no longer. There have been partnerships where the reverse process has been attempted, but purely feminine ideas have proved to be weakly, sickly things, and man is never a good nurse. It does not do to fly in the face of nature. Some day there will be some such partnerships as this in art, and especially in the art of fiction, whereby for the first time the true woman may be revealed to the admiring man, and the true man to the admiring woman. As yet it has been given unto us only partially to discern the working of the feminine mind, and to understand darkly that it works on lines wholly different from our own. There are so many great ideas—just as there are so many acorns—that by this time there should be nothing left in the way of human endeavour to discover or to do. Unfortunately, just as there are so many acorns which never come to oaks, so there are so many great ideas which perish in the very inception or first beginning of them. Some are gobbled up by the pigs—those, namely, which are too generous for contemporary mankind; some fall on rocks—those, namely, which are in advance of their generation; some in ditches, where they are choked by weeds—those be they which are uttered in humble and lowly place; some fall among the crowd, which is busy in buying and selling, and so heed them not, but trample them under foot; and some fall into running streams and are carried out into rivers and so into the ocean and are lost—these are ideas which are proclaimed at the wrong time, as when, during a time of war, a man shall go about preaching peace. The loss of all these ideas is a dreadful hindrance to progress. Another is the inconceivable stupidity of that blind, deaf-and-dumb race known as the "Other People." What a world—what a wonderful and beautiful world—could we create in a year or two but for the Other People! All the wars, all the injustices, all the blunders, and all the crimes are due to the Other People. But for them we should unite, combine, agree, concert, devise, and execute such things as the world has never yet seen. It is for this long-eared race that statesmen make pledges, promises, and assurances; they have eyes which see not and ears which hear not; they are idolaters, and worship one man, one formula, one idea; and for stiff-neckedness, for continual lusting after things which they ought not to desire, they are worse than the Israelites in their most palmy days.[3]

"What next, Claude?"

"What next, indeed! What first?"

"To begin with, then, I know quantities of people in Ivy Lane. I can ask questions without giving offence. They are all friendly with me, and they don't think that I am working for them."

"I suppose nobody likes being worked for," said Claude. "Suppose the working-man were to form a society for the reformation of higher-class manners. It would be irritating to know that hundreds of men and women were going about in the West End trying to raise one—the Low Level one—to a higher level. How would you like it, Valentine, if you knew that worthy people were wearing blue ribbons solely in order to make you temperate? How should you like to be invited to tea and addresses for your moral good?"

"I should be very angry."

3 The Bible's 2 Kings 17 relates the story of the Israelites' disgrace in idolatry and "stiff-necked" refusal to turn away from their decadent and evil ways.

"So I dare say will your friends in Ivy Lane become if we let them suspect that we are working for them. Patience, Valentine, and let us get the facts."

"It is in my favour," she said, "that I do not belong to any of the well-known organisations of parish religious societies—church or chapel.[4] People do not suspect me of wanting them to do something or believe something, since I neither wear a monastic dress nor belong to the religious missions. I am not expected to rebuke nor to admonish, which makes a great difference."

She might also have explained that there were certain graces of manner peculiar to her which greatly assisted her and softened the hearts of the people and would not permit them to be brutal.

There stands a little chapel in Ivy Lane, of which mention has already been made. It is quite a modest little structure, yet proud, and justly proud, of the purity with which the Christian doctrines have always been proclaimed here to the people by faithful ministers who have never felt the least need of worldly learning. It is complete though so small; there is a gallery in it; one window with a circular head at the back and two in front. There is also a harmonium,[5] and there is a table on which a desk stands and does duty for a pulpit on Sundays. It holds at least forty people without counting the gallery. One of the first things the partners did was to engage this chapel for week-day services of a different kind. Here Valentine placed a piano, and invited all the ladies of Ivy Lane to come and to bring their babies, on certain evenings, when she gave them tea, and sang to them; and sometimes the doctor, who had a manly bass, sang too, or gave recitations; and sometimes Claude read. The women came first, because it was a new thing and pleasant; then some of them got tired of the singing and the reading, and wanted the perfect freedom of their own tongues, and returned to the open court again. But some there were—there is always a leaven[6]—who preferred the peace and the good behaviour in this chapel to the noise outside. It was from these quiet women that Valentine gathered, bit by bit, the real life of the poor. You may talk to such people for hours together without hearing anything at all, and then, quite suddenly and unexpectedly, and perhaps from the most stupid person in the world, you will get a single hint, a fact, a suggestion, which makes your heart leap up because it explains a thousand things, and shows the way clear and certain where it was formerly hidden by the bushes.

Very well; anybody can hire a hall and play and sing to people. The Kyrle Society[7] are always doing it, with admirable results. That is to say, the people are pleased, and go away, and are not in the smallest degree stimulated to learn singing and playing for themselves. If this is all the partnership and the Great Renunciation and the Surrender has been able to effect, Valentine might as well have remained among her own friends and merely married an earl or a viscount, and Claude might as well have stayed where he was and merely become in course of time lord chancellor. But there are other things, though some of them belong to a later period, after her first three months of exile were finished, and she had gone home and returned again. Besides, it is in the nature of every healthy human thing to grow and of every truly spiritual thing to grow without knowing the decay which presently falls upon things of the flesh. The purpose which began with nothing more than the

4 *Chapel* was a term used to describe dissenting, often independent, Christians (that is, those who did not belong to the Church of England).

5 A musical instrument with a keyboard and metal reed-pipes, out of which air is blown.

6 A fermenting substance added to dough to help it rise. It is used here metaphorically.

7 Founded in 1875, the Kyrle Society was an organization dedicated to beautification.

study of three working-girls, widened until it covered the whole wide and terrible subject of women's wrongs; when Valentine called for the assistance of

Claude it was in the hope of redressing some of those wrongs. But man's intellect tends to roam and woman's to concentrate; and, as the former is the stronger, so purpose grows.

"Don't you think, Claude," said Valentine one day, "don't you think that a person even in these days may get a revelation—that is, a perfectly true idea?"

"Why not? Every true thing is a revelation, I suppose. You have a new thing in your own mind?"

"Is it new? It is this—if everybody knew all that science can teach, there would be no suffering or disease, would there?"

"No, I suppose not, if science could learn new things as fast as they could teach them to the people."

"And if they knew everything in morals there would be no wicked men, would there?"

"The only original sin is ignorance. Your idea is not quite new, yet it is new enough for us. Go on, Valentine."

"It is new to me."

"Huxley has compared life to a game of chess with an invisible opponent who knows every move of the game, and takes advantage of his knowledge. If you make a false move he crushes you without the least remorse."[8]

"I did not mean anything quite so grand as that. I meant something much simpler. Such as that people ought to be clean and to keep their houses clean; they ought to take care of their own health; they ought to be temperate and thrifty; they ought to get fresh air; they ought to practice self-control—"

"All this is perfectly true. But—"

"Wait a little, Claude. I cannot put things quite like Professor Huxley. They have been told, I suppose, that they ought to do all these things. But then they have not been told why. Do you think if they knew the reasons for obeying that they would go on disobeying laws?"

"You have not said all that is in your mind, Valentine."

"Not quite. If you told me not to go across a field but round its sides I might obey or I might not. If you proved to me that I must not cross the field because there was a great shaking quagmire in the middle which would swallow me up, I should certainly not cross the field."

"I begin to perceive, my partner, that you have got hold of a practical idea."

"It came of something you said the other day, Claude," she said, blushing with the pleasure of having really thought of something.

"Of course. Adam once laid all the blame on Eve, and she has been giving him all the praise ever since."

"Well—perhaps—I do not know—things may be so connected that it would be easier to move the men in the right direction if we first endeavoured to make them more careful about their homes."

"You connect the women with the home, of course."

"Do you really think my idea, though it may not be at all new, may be worth considering? Should we begin by teaching people something? Oh! we are getting on so slowly."

"Do not be despondent, Valentine. We shall get on slowly though we give all our lives to the task. We have got to accomplish something well-nigh impossible. We have got to find out if anything can possibly be done

8 Thomas Huxley, a biologist and advocate of Charles Darwin's theory of evolution, makes this comparison in *A Liberal Education and Where to Find It* (1868).

to improve the condition of our friends. As for that quagmire illustration of yours it is almost as good as the chess comparison. But who is to make the people understand it?"

"You, Claude, of course."

Claude laughed. "Of course I can do everything. Well, I obey. The real Augean stable, I am quite sure, was Ivy Lane, and the river which was turned into it was the Regent's Canal.[9] It was, in those days, called the River of Knowledge."

It was from this conversation that the great Earthly Tract Association first had its origin. Attempts have been made, I know, to connect the foundation of this most remarkable society with other people, and many go about professing themselves to have been the founders. But the real founder was none other than Valentine; the first members were only herself and Claude; they began with the expenditure of half-a-sovereign and the printing of a single tract, which Valentine gave to her friends, the women of Ivy Lane; they wrote all the earlier tracts themselves, though it was very early in their history that the doctor joined them. Little by little more tracts were written and distributed; then they began to rewrite the first tracts, which naturally attempted too much, and they recast their original design. How the thing grew and extended itself in all directions; how people from Manchester and Birmingham and Bradford, where they are always open to ideas, heard of these tracts, and sent for them, and for more; how the tracts began to be spoken about; how wealthy people gave them money, and the sale of the tracts brought in more money, and how they were obliged to have an office and to take in clerks, and how that office is spreading into a great warehouse, and the tracts are being translated into all languages, and how it will very shortly become a vast building on the Thames Embankment—all this is history which has to be written in the immediate future when the Earthly Tract Society shall have done its work and scattered knowledge over the whole world, as the late Professor Holloway[10] scattered his advertisements, and shall have taught people in simple language the conduct of life. "If," said the original prospectus of the society, "people had taken as much pains to spread the knowledge of things in general as they have taken to spread the knowledge of one form of the Christian Faith—which they might have done, and not left the other undone—the general ignorance would be by this time as good as gone; it would have been swept away as by a mop and a bucket."

"The whole of the English-speaking world—that is to say, the educated and the uneducated—clearly understand the Christian creed as it is expounded by the Evangelical party; and this, not because the people all go to church, which they do not, nor because they read books, for they never read any book; nor because these things are presented to them in the papers, which is not the case, for the papers preserve silence on these subjects; nor is it due to their home influences, which make more for the derision of all religions than for the defining of any particular form; nor to their schools, because catechisms are no longer taught in them; but wholly, solely, and entirely to the dissemination of tracts. Would you, therefore"—one is still quoting from the prospectus—"make the people wise in the conduct of life? Write tracts, give them simple rules of life and the reasons for them. Then distribute these tracts broadcast among the people, from street to street and from house to house—keep on distributing tracts. Prepare a tract, or a series of tracts, for every virtue and for

9 In Greek and Roman mythology, the fifth of Hercules's labors was to clean out King Augeas's enormous stables, holding thousands of livestock, in one day. In order to complete this feat, he redirected two rivers through the stables and flushed them out.

10 Professor Holloway was a patent medicine and pill seller who grew famous and wealthy through his ubiquitous print advertising.

every vice, setting forth as faithfully as the religious tracts have done for many years, the true doctrine and the consequence of violating its laws."

"The first thing," said Claude, while this prospectus was under consideration, "is to write the tracts."

"That of course, Claude, you will do."

"Of course, Valentine, I am an encyclopaedia."

"You can consult an encyclopaedia. Let us begin at once."

"We will form ourselves," said Claude, "into an association. You shall be the president, I will be the secretary; we will call ourselves the Earthly Tract Society, to distinguish ourselves from the older association, which has never attempted the improvement of the world in comfort, culture, and manners. I think the name sounds well and will carry weight. And now, Valentine, let us begin to set down some of the tracts we shall want and to give them their titles."

Let no one think it an easy matter to write a tract. Many of the earlier ones, for instance, those that were first issued, proved quite useless, because they were pitched a note too high or a note too low. A tract must have a definite thing to say, and it must say that thing with great vigour and plainness, and without the least chance of mistake; the propositions laid down must be, if possible, those which are not capable of denial; and they must be stated with attractiveness. No tract, for instance, must contain a theory or anything which may be argued against. Every tract must also be short; and perhaps it is as well that there should be half-a-dozen tracts on the same subject; it is well, also, that the tract should be signed, because people like a man who is not afraid to advance his opinions. Sometimes a dialogue may prove the most useful way of presenting the subject—sometimes a fable, sometimes a story, sometimes a piece of history; in fact there is no form of literature which may not be pressed into the service of the Earthly Tract Association, except satire. This would be a perfectly useless weapon when employed against the habits of the working classes. One might as well address them in Greek or Hebrew.

The most successful of the early series were, I think, all written by the partnership, and among them, especially, were the domestic series. It began with the tract on Wives, meaning the right treatment of a wife, with her husband's plain duties towards her; the corresponding paper on Husbands; on Children, with a parent's duty to his offspring; on Language, the word used in its popular sense, and with special reference to the use of the Universal Adjective;[11] on the House; on Woman's clothes; on Dinners; on clean Streets; on Water; on Fresh Air; on Amusements; on Holidays; on Beer; on Pretty Things; on Dressing the Hair; on Boots; on Wages, high and low; in the last-named tract the working-men are first approached, but with great delicacy, on the subject of permitting their girls to take less wages than will keep a girl strong and healthy; on Hours of Work; and so on. When the doctor became associated with them he contributed the well-known tracts on certain forms of disease, and how they may be prevented; on certain elementary principles of Physiology; on Food, and what should be eaten; on Exercise; on Tobacco; and many others. It was later that the series of tracts appeared which dealt with the duties and privileges of an English subject; it was from these papers that the English workman learned for the first time, with considerable astonishment, what neither his school nor his newspaper had taught him, the prodigious extent and wonderful history of his own country, how it grew, and how it must be preserved and developed, his own inheritance in the world and what it means to be an Englishman. The latest tracts of all are those on the cooperation of men and women, and if these tracts are to

11 A euphemistic reference to *bloody*, which expresses anger or loathing.

bring about the doctor's Universal League of Labour, it will be interesting to watch that body and to consider its ways. One need hardly stop to notice the very remarkable effects of the tracts upon Ivy Lane, because they are already well known, and the place has now become a show street. The houses are as beautifully clean as a Dutch village, the blinds are white, the little chapel has become a concert and dancing-room, the Adelaide Tavern is the street club; there are flowers in every window, and these are clean; within, the floors are scrubbed, walls are dusted, water is filtered; the men have quite left off getting drunk; they never swear unless the situation demands strong and plain words; they do not beat their wives; the women do not scream and fly into rages; quarrelling among them is almost unknown; all alike have grown critical over their meat, their beer, their tea, their coffee, their bread, and their dress; every family saves something every week; and the Universal Adjective has quite fallen into contempt, though, I confess, it may still be heard in other parts of London.

More important still is the growth and development of the institution founded to run side by side with the Earthly Tract Society, that of the street committees. Every street has now its own committee, elected by the inhabitants. Up to the present time their functions have been almost entirely sanitary; but they are gradually invading the region of morals, and they are already the terror of the dustman and the dread of the vestry,[12] and the cause why landlords blaspheme. Besides, other streets have followed the example of Ivy Lane. There is, as mentioned above, a movement in Clinger Street; there is a shaking in Myrtle Row, and Bacchus Walk has already elected its committee. It is to the street committees that the Earthly Tract Society look most confidently for the carrying out of their most ambitious projects. For in morals and in sanitary measures, and in the general conduct of life, nothing can be forced on the people which the people have not resolved upon getting for themselves. But consider the possibilities of a street committee. Where would the wicked man find a home if the street committee be watchful for righteousness? Where would the Fenian and the dynamiter[13] rest their heads if the street committee refuse to receive them? What will be the fate of that landlord who refuses to keep his houses in repair? What that of the tenant who refuses to do his share of the cleaning-up work? And how long, think you, will the street committees suffer the women to live under the Law of Elevenpence Ha'penny? There will come a time—one sees it already in the close future—when the pickpocket shall find no home anywhere, and the burglar no place to store his swag and keep his jemmy;[14] when all evil-doing shall be driven out of the land, and faith, goodness, charity, hope, and the love of beauty and the desire for art shall spring up like flowers in the sunny month of June, and the men shall at last join hands and shall swear by the Living God the women shall no longer be robbed and wronged.

Moses, as we know, proceeded on the method of inculcating all his laws and precepts together—the earthly at the same time as the heavenly. But then he had a Chosen People, and even with them the result of this method did not yield results by any means so satisfactory as might have been desired. Perhaps Claude and Valentine were wise in their generation when they made their people clean first and taught the nobler truths next, and left religion to those who profess religion.

---

12 A dustman is a person whose job it is to take away refuse. The vestry is an elected body responsible for administering the affairs of the parish.

13 Fenians wanted to liberate Ireland and overthrow the English government. A dynamiter was frequently an anarchist who, as the name implies, used dynamite for illegal destruction.

14 A crowbar used by burglars.

But I am sorry to say that the assistant priest of St. Agatha's refused to assist in writing the tracts, or in their distribution, because they were not in the first place put under the protection of the Church, and because poverty and disease were treated as things which might be removed by wise treatment, and nothing was said about the duty of discipline, confession, and penance, and because the institution of Lent was left out of the programme altogether.

Chapter XVII

The Step Without

About a fortnight after that strange and terrifying dream came to Mrs. Monument, and when she had at length completely shaken off the horror of it and nearly forgotten to dread its return, it did come again, like some foul spirit who refuses to be laid. It came just as before, with the sound of a remembered footfall. There is no one single man in the whole habitable globe who is not unlike every other man as regards every single feature, detail, and particular of mind and of body. For instance, you may secure the identification of a man for life by taking an impression on wax of his forefinger or thumb, because the curves and corrugations of the skin differ with every man and are peculiar to him. Each of us is individual, and stands alone in the universe—in complete isolation—a thing curious and terrifying to consider. Most marked of all is a man's footstep, which, once recognised, can never be mistaken or forgotten. So that, when that dead man's footstep came again, Mrs. Monument was stricken with a terror unspeakable, and tenfold worse than on the first occasion. It came in the daytime, too, when such things are never expected. If the spirits of the dead walk, it is at night and in the dark, though even then it is not usual nor is it recorded of any that they walk in boots and reproduce the old familiar footstep. I have never yet heard this thing of any ghost nor have I ever yet seen any who walked in boots. There have been instances—but they are few—of daylight apparitions, but tradition and custom have established a prejudice against the mixture of sunshine with the spirit world. This is the reason why the supernatural terror—a thing quite apart from any other feeling—is so much more terrible by day than by night. A nightmare we know: not a pleasant creature, but familiar, and an old acquaintance in whatever form it comes. But a daymare—that, if you please, is a thing so uncommon and of such rare experience that it belongs to the category of nameless things which follow after the long list of devils, imps, ghosts, elves, fiends, afreets, jinns, and spectres which possess and enjoy, like peers of Great Britain,[1] their titles and ranks.

1 At the time, all peers (dukes, marquesses, earls, viscounts, and barons) were members of the House of Lords.

It was in the evening, but before sunset. The old lady had taken her tea and sent Rhoda home. She expected her daughter Polly, and she sat in her great chair beside the empty fireplace, knitting in hand, waiting with the stolid patience of the blind. The evening was warm, and, after a comfortable tea, one may sometimes experience a fuller sense of comfort than is generally the lot of mortals, and Mrs. Monument was just then completely free from rheumatism, and had no other kind of ache, pain, or disease either beginning or going on or coming to an end, which is unusual when a person reaches the age of sixty. All these causes combined made Mrs. Monument drop her eyes and her knitting, one after the other, and persuaded her to nod her head with the royal condescension[2] only to be observed at such moments, and then to let her soul lie down and be at rest, while her eyes dropped and her lips opened. Mrs. Monument was fast asleep.

She slept peaceably for half an hour. The almshouses were always quiet behind their brick wall, but today all the collegians,[3] except herself, were out basking in the sun, which is a perfect cure for everything when you can get enough of it; and the place was absolutely silent and peaceful. The continual rolling outside of carriages and carts, the tramp of the footsteps on the pavement, were audible, it is true, because they were going on all day long, and the greater part of the night, just on the other side of the wall, but no one in the houses ever heard them or noticed them, nor did they break the slumbers of the lightest sleeper, nor did they add anything to the most grievous headache.

Suddenly Mrs. Monument awoke with a cry. She started and sat upright, with pale cheek and outstretched arms, and blind eyes which rolled helplessly around.

"The step! I heard his step again."

She listened. But it did not come again. There was the rolling of the tramcar and the jingling of its bells; there was the rumbling of heavy wagons; there was the whistle of an engine on the railway; there were the steps of passengers; there was a barrel-organ; there was the whistling of a boy. But there was not the step which had awakened her. It was a single and solitary step; a step like Robinson Crusoe's impression of one—only one foot on the sand—a single footfall—a mysterious footfall—where was the other foot? Was it a one-legged Seven League Boot? Mrs. Monument sat listening for another, but no other touched her ears.

Then she sprang to her feet, and with every outward sign of terror, with trembling hands and parted lips, she began to grope and feel about the room, stopping every moment to listen, lest the step should fall again and should escape her. But she could find nothing; she could hear nothing; as for the footstep, she would have heard it, she thought, fifty yards away. Why, she had heard it once before—the footstep which had been silent for twenty years, but which she never could forget; once before it smote her ear in the middle of the night, and now in daytime, close beside her, in the very room she heard it—a soft and gentle step which she could not mistake.

She felt about the open door; she came out into the little court and stretched her hands out as if in search of space inimitable.

"It was the dream," she murmured. "It was the dream come back again. But there was someone in the room. I know there was someone in the room."

She knew it by the instinct of the blind, who feel the presence of things without seeing or touching them.

2 The monarch's bowing of the head in acknowledgement of his or her subjects.

3 Synonymous with colleger (residents of a charitable foundation or "college").

And while she stood there, a pitiful spectacle of fear and horror, the latch of the gate was lifted and her daughter Polly came into the closed garden of the almshouse.

* * *

Mrs. Monument was wrong. It was no dream. She had heard her husband's footstep, because he was standing before her, looking her full in the face. He was not dead at all, but alive. And he was enlarged; they had suffered him to go free; he was released with a document entitled, after the name of a celebrated play, the "Ticket of Leave."[4] He had called a day or two after his release to see his wife, as a husband should, after nearly twenty years of separation. She was, on that occasion, gone to bed; and so he came away. Business, that is to say, an eager and wolflike pursuit of pleasure and drink after twenty years of abstinence, kept him away for a whole fortnight. Now, his money being well-nigh spent, he called again.

* * *

A little while before Mrs. Monument woke up so suddenly and cried out, and began to carry on in so surprising a manner all by herself, there came along the road, on the east side of it, where the sunshine falls in the afternoon and evening, and where, for that charitable reason, they have planted most of the almshouses, a man somewhat advanced in years. He was dressed neatly in a sober grey tweed suit, and wore a round hat. He was slightly built, and a little below the middle height; a thin, spare man with sharp features and small delicate hands; his hair was short and quite grey, and his cheek was smooth shaven. His features were small and fine, especially his mouth; his eyes were bright and surrounded with quite a cobweb of crow's feet and wrinkles. He had something the appearance of a gentleman's servant, a butler in a great house, a hall porter in a club, or something extremely respectable in the service, and therefore he seemed out of place in a region where there are few gentlemen's servants kept, and where clubs are unknown except for political purposes. Certainly a most respectable person, with a little awkwardness about his manner of walking, as if he was a stranger to crowded streets. Presently he stopped in front of a low brick wall with a gate in the middle of it and hesitated. Then he lifted the latch, opened the gate and stepped within, where was the garden of the almshouses, and behind the garden the row of cottages.

The man turned to the right and walked straight to the last of the cottages, that, namely, which belonged to Mrs. Monument. It might have been noticed by an observant person that he walked almost noiselessly, an art which may be acquired by anybody, but it requires study and much practice. When you have acquired it you have also acquired the stealthy style, much spoken of by the better class of novelists, those, namely, whose publishers sell their productions at a penny the complete novelette. This style may be of advantage to some kinds of professional men, especially if, as this gentleman was, they happen to be burglars by profession. When the man reached the door of the cottage, which stood wide open, he looked in. Beside the empty fireplace in her chair sat an old woman with white hair, asleep.

The man looked at her curiously.

---

4 A document verifying one's parole.

"She is changed," he murmured. "I wonder if she will know me, and I wonder what she will say when she sees me? I wonder if she knows I am alive?"

He stepped inside noiselessly and looked about the little room. The woman still slept undisturbed. There was nothing in the room worth stealing if he wished to steal; nor was there anything particularly interesting to look at; but his eyes fell upon the shelf of books, and he nodded with a kind of satisfaction. So long as the books—his books—were there, he was not forgotten. On the table was some knitting work and needles in a basket, and lying with the work a torn envelope. He took this out—being an extremely curious person—and read the address upon it. "Claude Monument, Esq., 25 King's Bench Walk, Temple." It had been, in fact, left there by Valentine.

Claude Monument! He remembered now; there was a son of his named Claude—Claude Duval. The boy was living, then, or at least working in the Temple where the lawyers live; perhaps a lawyer's clerk. His own son a lawyer's clerk! Strange irony of fate! He folded the letter and placed it carefully in his pocket. It might be useful. This man was none other, in fact, than the great James Carey himself, once the acknowledged head of his profession, formerly the Prince of Burglars. And he was set loose again upon an unsuspecting world after twenty years of seclusion. When such a man as James Carey is set free the world ought to be warned. It was his step that the poor woman of the almshouses had actually heard in the evening. He had come; he had found the room dark and empty, and he had gone away again. Now he was come hack to make his release known to his affectionate family, and to look around. Twenty years of prison fare and life do not make a man inclined for honest work; and if there was any money to be got out of his wife and children, before "jobs" began to offer themselves again, he might as well get that money.

Perhaps he stepped upon a loose plank; perhaps he forgot his habitual caution—I know not—but suddenly the woman started in her sleep, sat bolt upright, and shrieked, "His step! I hear his step again!"

In an instant he saw that his wife was blind; her glaring eyes rolled over him, so to speak, as if he was not present; he saw her blindness in her outstretched hands and gestures of helplessness. The thing was quite unexpected, but with quick step and without the least noise, he crossed the threshold, stepped over the flagstones, and took up his position among the cabbage-stumps outside, where he waited and watched.

His wife was blind and in an almshouse. He had made up his mind that there would be changes. People do not stand still; the children would be grown up; perhaps they would be ashamed of their father; their mother, he knew, regarded his exploits with a most extraordinary and unaccountable prejudice. He had no doubt that she had tried to make them respectable, whereas, if he had had his way with the children, there would not have been in the whole world a cleverer or a more successful gang of plunderers, a more united and happy family, or one which lived more merrily and enjoyed more abundantly the fruits of the earth—other people's fruits, of course—in due season. Shame, that a man should not be permitted, even in prison, to direct the education of his own children in their own interests. But if they were respectable and unwilling to own their father, he must then—he had thought it all out—he must compel them to pay for his silence and suppression by a weekly subsidy. But who would have thought that his wife would go blind? He did not know what to say or how to act, and therefore he did nothing, but watched.

She came tottering to the door and stretched out her arms to the world, crying "Who is there? Who is there?"

The man made no reply. He had fully intended to present himself, and to say, "Here I am, back again. Give me all the money you have got in the place. Tell me where all the children are. I shall want money till I get back to my old work. As for repentance, don't think of it, and as for talking, stow it." This was the amiable speech he had proposed to make. But his wife was blind as well as grey, and, for some spark of humanity still lurking in his breast, he could not make that speech. While he stood among the cabbage-stumps there suddenly appeared between his wife and himself a third person—a young lady.

"Mother," she said, taking the blind woman's hand, "what is it? Oh! what is it?" For she connected the terror and the helpless hands with the strange man standing, silent, opposite to the door.

"It's the dream come back. Oh! Polly, thank God you've come, my dear! It's the dreadful dream. I heard his step a fortnight ago, in the night—once—only once—upon the stones—and again I heard it just now—once. My dear, my dear, I'm frightened out of my wits. Is it the dead come back to plague me?"

"The step again?"

"Your father's step, my dear. And something there was in the room. I felt it. Something in the room. His ghost most likely."

Valentine turned upon the man a face so full of horror, and loathing, and shame, that it actually pierced him to the heart, though his conscience was long since seared with a hot iron, and twenty years of prison had only hardened him. Yet those eyes made him shiver, and he dropped his own.

"What a strange thing!" She kept her eyes upon the man as one keeps his eye upon a wild beast. "You are sure you heard his step?"

"Quite sure. As if I could ever forget his step!" The man smiled complacently. "I heard it on the boards, falling as soft as the step of a cat. And oh! Polly—thank God you've come!" she repeated, clinging to her daughter.

"Why, mother," she replied, in a strange voice and with burning cheeks, "he is dead long ago—five years ago;" she held up a warning finger to the man. "Thank heaven! the miserable, wretched man died in his miserable, wretched prison, where he deserved to die, and was buried in the prison churchyard, where he deserved to be buried, among the thieves and rogues, his companions. Don't tremble so, mother: he is dead, we have forgotten him and all his villainies."

"Yes, my dear, yes. But your own father, my dear. Don't speak ill of your father and your mother, because it brings bad luck. And him dead too. But why did I hear his step?"

"I don't know. There is nobody here, dear," she said mendaciously, and with another warning gesture with her forefinger. "You were dreaming again. Now go back and sit down and calm yourself. As for me, I am going to get you something for your supper—a lettuce, I think. Yes, I will be back in five minutes. Go and sit down, dear. Oh! you poor, dear old thing, what a fright you have had! Sit down now. I am here, you know, and if anybody offered to frighten you, I would—I would kill him." She said this with such ferocity in her eyes that the man in the garden trembled.

She placed the old woman in her chair. Then she went outside again, and silently beckoned the man to follow her. He obeyed her, walking among the vegetables, where his footsteps were not heard.

Outside the place, Valentine took the first turning to the right, which happened to be a new street of grey-brick houses not yet finished. Nobody ever walks in unfinished streets of grey-brick houses, not even lovers, who will walk anywhere else, but not in unfinished streets, between lines of dreadful grey bricks. On Sundays the jerry-builder walks there alone and wonders how long his houses are likely to stand.[5]

Presently she stopped and turned fiercely upon the man.

"Oh! wretch!" she cried, "I know who you are. Oh! mean and skulking wretch! We thought you were dead; we rejoiced that you died, like a miserable rat in a trap, in your prison cell, and were buried in the prison churchyard."

"What do you mean?"

"Silence! Don't dare to speak. Let me think."

For she understood that the most dreadful thing in the world that could happen to them had happened. Dreadful to every one of them. To the poor old lady, to Joe, the honest and respectable Joe, who had nothing but his good name, to Sam, to Melenda, and, most dreadful of all, to Claude, and—no, no—Violet must never know, whatever else happened, whoever else suffered. She understood what this man meant, and she was filled with wrath because she was not his daughter.

"You are not dead, then; and the first use you make of your liberty is to terrify your wife. You ought to have slunk into some corner where no one knew you, and buried your shameful head there till you died. Oh! I know your story, your miserable, disgraceful story."

"You called her mother," he said, stupidly staring, "and you're a young lady, likely, or perhaps only a young lady's-maid."

She made no reply.

"If she's your mother, you must be my daughter."

Again she made no reply.

"And a precious dutiful daughter she's made you." He cleared his throat and began to pluck up his spirits. "I'll have it out of her for this. You mind that. I'll have it out of her, and I'll have it out of you, too—both of you—all of you." He stopped to swear a little—just a little—meaning to swear a great deal before he finished. "Now, then, where's your obedience? Where's your Fifth Commandment?[6]—before I take and wring your undutiful and impudent neck?"

He did use much stronger language, but that was the substance of his remarks, and the rest may be understood. He also doubled his fist and shook it in Valentine's face, but not with much confidence.

"If you dare to touch me with your little finger," said Valentine, "I will shake you to a jelly, you miserable creature!"

She was taller than this slight, small-limbed man, and a good deal heavier. Moreover, there was in her eyes a light of wrath so lurid, and on her cheeks such a fiery glow, and she looked so remarkably as if she could do it, and would rejoice in doing it, that the man was cowed. But he looked dangerous.

"Well, then, you're my daughter, I suppose," he went on sulkily. "What's your name?"

"I am called Polly," she replied, with some hesitation. "Your youngest child was baptised Marla."

"A pretty Marla you are," he said. "This comes of a girl growing up without a father's care. And how do I know what you do for a living? Marla—yes, I remember now. One forgets a many things in quod.[7] Marla

5 A jerry-builder utilizes the cheapest materials to construct shoddy housing.

6 The fifth commandment in the Hebrew Bible is to honor one's parents.

7 Another name for prison.

it was. I made up the name myself from a beautiful book about pirates and scuttlin' ships, and fighting with marlin-spikes—they don't keep them books in quod. And the other gal was Melenda. And that name I made, too. I forget how I made that name—Mile End, was it?[8] Mile End in the book?—I forget. And there was three boys—Joe was the eldest—and Sam and Claude; a pretty boy Claude was. Like me he was. I chose his name, too, after Claude Duval, the prince of highwaymen."

Valentine shuddered. Yes, Claude was like him; and so, alas! was Violet. The likeness was unmistakable.

"Come," he said, "don't go on like a she-devil. I'm back again. You can't get over that. Let's be jolly. Lord! I don't want quarrels. I never did. Your mother'll tell you that I was always a man for peace and quietness, if such was to be had with my 'bacca and my grog, or it might ha' been my port wine and my sherry wine. And you're a pretty girl, my dear, with a fine spirit of your own. There! I respect you for it. You're the girl to stand up for your mother, ain't you, now? Kiss your old father, Marla, my dear."

He made as though he was about to kiss her. Valentine—I shudder; one cannot choose but shudder—Valentine shrank back, and, with a cry of disgust, actually lifted her hand and struck the man on the cheek with so hearty a goodwill that he reeled. King Richard Lion Heart[9] never dealt a better stroke. That this wretched convict, this common felon, should offer to kiss her!

"Oh!" she cried, "if you dare to touch me, I will kill you."

The man picked up his hat, which had fallen off, and stared stupidly. That a girl should chastise her own father!

"Oh! what a pity, what a thousand pities," Valentine went on pitilessly, "that you are not dead."

He began to whine, holding his hat in his hand, and addressing the unsympathetic grey bricks and the scaffolds.

"I return home," he complained, "after twenty years. The moment I am out I hurry to my wife's humble home. I have put off the old man, and am resolved to lighten her lot and cheer her declining years, which is a shadow of things to come. I am full of repentance, and count all things else but loss, as I frequently told the good chaplain. My feet are now shod with the preparation of the gospel of peace, and I walk in love. I told him that too, and he believed it"—the man actually grinned. Then he became serious again. "As for my character, my only anxiety is to redeem it; and having been a brand ready for the burning, but now plucked from the fire, I expected treatment accordingly. And this is what I get! A daughter who calls me names, and strikes her old father. Strikes her poor, old, grey-headed, infirm, tottering father. But I offer the other cheek." He did so ostentatiously, but Valentine took no advantage of the offer. "This is the Christian spirit of my child. Take the other cheek. It may kill me. But take it. I have had my faults; I own that I have had faults; but I always loved my children. Let me go to your mother, Marla. She will receive me in a better spirit. He that loveth his wife loveth himself. Let me find out my four other dear children. There is Samuel—my son Samuel. I hope he is given to virtuous courses. And Melenda—my dear pretty Melenda. I pray that she is a Christian and a churchgoer, and all a penitent and forgiven father, who has worked out his sentence, and got a good character again, can hope to find. And there is Claude—"

"Stop!" cried Valentine imperiously.

---

8 Mile End was another densely populated area in London's East End and the location of the People's Palace, the working-class recreational facility inspired, in part, by Besant's *All Sorts and Conditions of Men* (1882).

9 Richard I was known as Lion Heart (or the Lion-hearted) for his bravery and strength in battle.

He obeyed, watching her with furtive and evil looks.

"I know," Valentine continued, after a little reflection, "that you can talk. You deceived your poor wife by your lies and your glib talk into marrying you. Let us have no more speeches. Now listen to me"—her words were brave, but her heart was beating. "Listen to me"—she took courage by the aspect and appearance of the man, who watched her like a cowed and frightened cur—"you are to go away from here—quite away to another part of London. I don't care where you go. You are never to see your wife again, or attempt to see her, or write to her, or let her know in any way that you are alive. Oh! we have thanked God so often that you are dead that we cannot afford to have you coming to life again. You are a dead man, do you hear? First of all," she repeated, "you are never to see or to communicate with your wife. Never—never."

"I hear. What the devil's coming next, I wonder?"

Meantime he had observed—he had not forgotten his old trick of observation—two or three things which struck him with wonder and made him reflect. The girl had white delicate hands; her fingers were not marked or pricked with any kind of work; her dress, which was simple, was well made, and she wore dainty well-made boots. It is only a lady who wears good boots, he thought, because he had in his old days made careful studies of the sex for professional purposes. But how in the world could his daughter be a lady?

"The next thing is that you are not to try to communicate with any of your children, or find out where they live. Do you hear? You shall not make their lives shameful for them by your loathsome and horrible presence."

"Suppose I won't promise? Why should I?"

"In that case you shall get no help. I promise you so much—not the least help from any of us. We shall keep you from your wife by main force if necessary. You may starve in the ditch and we will not help you."

I have often wondered how Valentine would have received this man had she not known the whole truth concerning Polly-which-is-Marla. One or two things are quite certain. She would not have used language of such excellent plainness; nor would she have boxed his ears; nor would she have been so unhesitating in her manner and her action.

"I only want honest work," he said with a whine. "Give me honest work and I will trouble no one. You shan't know you've got a father. I forgive you for your hard words—for your blows. Let us—oh! let us walk in love."

"I do not believe that you want work at all," said Valentine; "you did not work before you went to prison, and I do not believe that you want to begin now. You want drink and tobacco, and nothing to do. Well; I will give you what you want—on conditions. What money have you?"

He sadly replied that he had nothing; not a copper,[10] which of course was a lie. He went on to explain, forgetting that he had already said he was just out of prison, that he had spent such money as was due to him in the fruitless search after work.

"I am weary and footsore," he said, with a sigh. "Weariness I complain not of, and footsoreness is my righteous punishment."

"Lift up your foot." The man obeyed. Twenty years of prison make a man ready to obey anybody. "It is false; your boots are quite new; you have not walked about at all."

"And yet she is my daughter—my own little Marla! That I thought would have sat upon my poor knees and comforted my broken heart. And she's got a hard heart—oh! what a hard heart! I'd rather have my footsoreness than such a hard heart."

10 Coin.

"I do not want any promises or assurances from you at all," Valentine went on, "and I want no more hypocrisies. I will give you—I will give you"—she considered how little she might offer—"a sovereign[11] a week so long as you keep away. The moment you seek to find out any of your children or terrify your wife the allowance ceases. Do you hear and understand?"

"Yes, I hear. What's a sovereign? It isn't worth making a promise about. I can spend a sovereign a day and think nothing of it."

"Then earn a sovereign a day."

"If you can get a sovereign a week to give away, you can get two. I shan't ask how you get it, my dear. Lord! everybody knows that a lady's-maid—you look like a lady's-maid—generally gets opportunities." He looked so desperately cunning that Valentine longed to box his ears again. When a woman begins boxing of ears there's no saying where she may leave off—witness the case of certain czarinas and other ladies who have had command of the knout and the flagellum and the stake.[12] "Spring it to two sovereigns for your poor old father, Marla, my child."

"I will give you one and no more—but only on my own conditions. Here is the first week's money." She opened her purse and took out the golden coin. His eyes greedily grasped the fact that there were many more lying in the purse. "It is the last if you break my conditions. If you do not, I will send another next week to the address you may name."

She gave him a leaf from a pocket-book, and he wrote on it an address to some street in the East End.

"You can write to me to the almshouse; to the care of my mother. But don't sign your letter; and don't dare to address me—me—as your child."

"Who are you, then?" he asked looking at her with admiration and surprise. "Who are you, if you are not my child? A daughter of Hester Monument should be standing over a washtub. What are you?"

"That I shall not tell you. Remember that there is not one of your children—not one of them who knows the truth—who will not receive you with shame and horror unutterable. There is not one who will give you a helping hand except myself. You have your choice. Take my twenty shillings a week and go away and get drunk among the rogues and villains—your friends. If you refuse my conditions, or offer to molest any of us, you shall see how much you will get from all of us together. Go!"

There were two or three things in this speech which filled Mr. Carey with pain—especially to be told that his children regarded him with shame. Every man who becomes, whether by his own consent or not, a hermit for twenty years, builds up during his isolation an *effigie* of himself. Mr. Carey knew that he had retired amidst a blaze of popularity; the papers were full of him and his exploits; portraits were sold of him in the *Illustrated Police News*[13] and elsewhere; he knew that he stood first in the profession, which is a proud thing for anybody in any profession to say. He was the Premier Burglar. He was the gallant hero who pitted his own ingenuity and resources against all the intellect and the strength and the organisation that the richest country in the world can command. To be caught and clapped in prison was a defeat, to be sure, but there was all that

11 A gold coin with the value of twenty shillings or one pound.

12 Of the four wives of Russian czars, Anna and Catherine the Great are remembered for being particularly ruthless and cruel. Knouts and flagellums are both types of whips used to inflict pain. In this context, a stake is any post to which someone would be bound for execution.

13 A notoriously sensational newspaper of the late-nineteenth century that provided graphic coverage of crime, accidents, and supernatural occurrences.

glory—"loathing and horror"—the girl called it. This, then, was their mother's influence—their mother's; the influence of one who could never rise to the level of his greatness.

And she said he had consorted with rogues and villains. Rogues and villains—rebels when successful become revolutionists—would willingly have consorted with him, but he would have none of their companionship. He lived apart from the vulgar criminal; he consorted not with the common burglar. He worked alone, and he lived apart from his fellow-professionals.

I do not suppose that Mr. Carey expected to be received with open arms. But he did expect some show of respect—at least that respect due to his position in the walk of life he adorned. And to be received with these words of disgust and insult by his youngest daughter—it was hard to bear. Had it been her mother he would have felt it less, because she was a woman of slow imagination and contracted views, and could never understand his glory.

"Go," said his unnatural daughter.

He obeyed, and started on his way without a word.

"No," she said, "not back by that road. You will pass the almshouse, and she may hear your footstep again. Go down this road."

"I do not know where it leads to."

"I don't care. Go this way."

He obeyed, and walked slowly away, turning from time to time like an unwilling cur. Each time he turned his head he saw the girl standing in the road watching him.

When he was out of sight, Valentine returned slowly to the almshouses.

"That was a terrible dream, Polly, wasn't it?"

"A dreadful dream, mother. But I don't think it will come again. I will stay here tonight just to prevent your having it, you know. It won't come if you think someone is with you."

"Polly, my dear, it is just wonderful the difference since you came back. And, oh! the comfort of having someone that I can tell all my troubles to!"

Chapter XVIII

Le Père Prodigue[1]

The ticket-of-leave man went away obediently; and, once arrived in the main road, he began to think—that is to say, to devise wickedness. This girl, who said she was his daughter, if he could only, in some way or other, get her under his thumb. She was a most beautiful girl; she was possessed of manners which would make anybody think her a lady; she wasn't afraid—heavens! what could he not do if he had such a girl to work for him? There was once a professional in his own line, a cracker of cribs[2]—he had read this story somewhere in the old days when he used to read so many books—who had in his power, and at his orders, such a girl, whether his daughter or his mistress he knew not. She went into the finest society and kept her eyes about her, and put this fortunate professor on to what she observed, and helped him to get into houses, unlocking doors for him, slipping the bolts at night, pulling up shutters, and opening windows for him. And all the time pretending she was a lady. Mr. Carey remembered this beautiful story, and dreamed of the wonderful time he might have if Marla would only be such a daughter to him. And he dreamed as well of the great and glorious reputation he might make for himself; much greater and much nobler even than his first glory, which was now, he already perceived with sorrow, well-nigh forgotten. In fact, the burglar, like the singer and the actor, is liable to a swift oblivion. His works do not, like those of the poet and the sculptor, live after him, and there is little to keep his memory green, except a few pages, perhaps, in the Newgate Calendar.[3]

---

1 The chapter's title, translated from French, means "The Prodigal Father"—a reference to the parable of the prodigal son in the New Testament Gospel of Luke.

2 The phrase *a cracker of cribs* is slang for *a burglar of small houses*.

3 The *Newgate Calendar* was a popular publication that described the executions of criminals. It eventually included more detailed accounts of criminal activities and legends, as well as poetry and notes written in honor of, or even supposedly by, criminals awaiting execution.

From daughter to son is a natural step. Mr. Carey began to think of his son as well—there was another daughter; but he had heard nothing about her, and three sons, all men now; one of them, he knew, was a workman of some kind; as for the other two, what were they? She dared to make conditions about her measly sovereign, did she? He was not to show himself to any of his children. Why—hang her conditions! He would do as he pleased. He would go and see his children if he pleased. The working-man, he reflected, would certainly be married, and as certainly would have no money, except perhaps the price of a pint, which is neither here nor there. Besides, he had not yet found out where this son lived, nor where the second lived. There remained the third, his youngest son, Claude, who lived in the Temple. He only knew about the Temple that it is a place much frequented by lawyers, a tribe whom he naturally disliked, and ranked in the same class with policemen, detectives, and judges. His son was employed there in some capacity; a clerk, no doubt. Every profession, of course, preferred to their father's! He took the stolen envelope out of his pocket. "Claude Monument, Esquire, 25 King's Bench Walk, Temple."

"It's a chance," he said. "Perhaps the boy has got some money. I'll risk it."

He had been drinking since he left his daughter, and the brandy and water, perhaps, gave him the courage to break the conditions and so endanger the weekly sovereign. However, he did break those conditions, and yet he did not lose his allowance, as you shall hear.

* * *

About ten o'clock that evening Claude was sitting alone in his chambers. He was neither reading nor writing, but the lamp was beside him, and a book was on his knees, and he was looking into the fire, for the evening of early autumn was chilly. Outside, the Temple was very quiet. There are only a few now who continue to live there, and these were out of town; I think that in all these courts Claude was the only living person except the policeman. And there was a silence almost as absolute as that which fell upon the place after the suppression of the great order and the burning of the grand master and his knights.

He was thinking about the strange work in which he was engaged; and upon Valentine, who thought she was his sister, but was not, and of her glowing cheeks and kindling eyes, and the voice which moved him like the notes of some great organ playing mighty music. He was thinking, too, that it would not lead to peace of mind if he should continue to think of those eyes and that voice.

In the midst of this silence—he heard no warning footstep on the stairs—there was a single knock at his door.

He wondered who could be his visitor so late and so unexpected. It was a stranger; an elderly man, thin and spare, with grey hair, who stood at his door.

"I beg your pardon humbly, sir," he said, taking off his hat; "I am come in hopes of seeing a boy, sir, a boy named Claude Monument, who works on this staircase. Perhaps he is in the housekeeper's room on the basement."

"Can't you read? There is the name on the door."

The man read and looked surprised.

"I am Claude Monument. What do you want with me?"

"You Claude Monument? You?"

It was rather dark in the passage where Claude stood, but the gas-lamp on the staircase showed Mr. Carey that his son was not quite what he had expected.

"Is your master out of the way, young man?" he whispered.

"What do you mean?"

"Your master. Is he out of the way?"

"My master?"

"Can you take me where we can have a quiet talk together—you and me—without his asking questions? It's for you and me together, you know."

"Who are you?"

"I've something important to tell you—something joyful. But, I say, you can't be Claude Monument? Why, you're dressed like a gentleman."

"Who are you?"

"Well, that is just what I have come to tell you."

Claude hesitated. "These are my own chambers," he said.

"Good Lord! Your own chambers!" The man was amazed. "Your own chambers! Your own! How the devil—and the gal looked like a lady. Quite time I called and inquired. Look here, young man, if you live here, and if you are alone, take me inside. I've got something to say; something—ah!—something you'll be pleased to hear. But we ought to be quite alone. It is a family secret, young man—a family secret, and it mustn't be talked out loud."

"Come in, then." Claude admitted the man and shut the door, not without some presentiment of coming evil. A presentiment never does any good, being in this respect like the cold wind before the rain; it comes too late for a warning, and no sooner is it felt than the evil thing is upon one. Yet it is a comfort somehow to feel afterwards that one had a presentiment. Men bitten by rattlesnakes have often been consoled in their last moments by this thought.

"Now," said Claude, leading his visitor into the room, and shutting the outer oak, "who are you, and what do you want? I don't remember to have seen you before."

There was only a reading-lamp on the table, but the lamp was covered by a shade, so that the room was comparatively dark. The man had taken off his hat, and was now holding it awkwardly in both hands as if he wasn't used to a hat of that kind; indeed, he had worn one of quite a different shape for twenty years. Claude saw that he was grey-headed and smooth-cheeked, and that he was a man of slight build.

"Now then," he said, "go on with your important news."

The man cleared his throat.

"Are you really and truly, young man," he asked, "Claude Monument?"

"That is my name." Claude owed no man ought, so that the man could not possibly have come for money. Perhaps he was a beggar of the more complicated kind, a book hawker, or one who touts for subscriptions. But beggars of this kind ply their trade by day. He felt uncomfortable.

"You are the son of Mrs. Monument who used to live beside Hackney Marsh, and—if one may speak of it to a swell like yourself—took in washing, being a poor but honest woman."

"My mother was a washerwoman," said Claude.

"Well," the man went on, "I don't understand it. You look like a gentleman, and the other"—here he checked himself—"And you live among the lawyers."

"I live among the lawyers."

"I've seen 'em in court—many times, takin' their characters[4] away from unfortunate men. I've seen 'em and heard 'em." He added a short but impressive prayer relating to their final doom. "And you live here! Lord!" his eyes swell out with fatness, "and look at me without a mag."

"Who are you, then?"

Claude snatched the shade from the lamp. The man was decently dressed; he did not look like a beggar; yet he was certainly trying to get something out of him. As for the man's knowing something of his family history, everybody knew that. Wherever he went, on his first introduction, or on the first mention of his name, there followed the whisper, that he had often actually heard, and more often saw on the lips of those who uttered it. Your own experience of the world, dear reader, will supply the words.

The man did not reply. He was looking about the room, which had a certain appearance of wealth—that is to say, there were easy-chairs, pictures, half-a-dozen silver cups won at scratch fours and other sports; and there were a few "things," as collectors say; there were books—heaps of books—and curtains, and carpets, and all the things which go to make a young man's chambers look handsome and well appointed. On the mantelshelf were two large photographs of two girls. The man recognised one of them. "That's Marla," he murmured; "The other, I suppose, is Melenda." Then he turned sharply to Claude.

"Are all these things your own?"

"Certainly."

"And you leave your mother in an almshouse! And the other one"—he checked himself again, though the situation was absolutely incomprehensible.

Claude reddened, but he kept his temper.

"What has that to do with you?" he said. "Get to your business."

"Young man, you leave your mother there—blind, too—among paupers, without a sixpence to bestow upon any deserving relations and friends who might happen to call—"

"Get on with your business."

"If such is your treatment of your mother, how would you treat your unfortunate father?"

Claude laughed.

"For heaven's sake, man, tell me what you want, or I shall turn you out of the place."

"If your unfortunate father was to come to you, not having seen you for twenty years—if he was standing before you poor and destitute, as I might be now, but happy in his mind through repentance; all his old pals scattered, and nothing left him in the world but his hopes of heaven and his good resolutions for the path of righteousness, which wraps a poor man as with a garment, and keeps off of him the cold wind of poverty: and with his clear conscience and his term worked out and his ticket in his pocket, afraid of no man, whether policeman or magistrate—would you treat that father with scorn, and send him, like you sent your mother, to an almshouse for the remainder of his days?"

---

4 A necessary document for employment in Victorian England, a character is written documentation of a person's qualities and behavior.

"Can you do nothing but ask questions? Now, man, come to the point or leave the place. As for my father, you may keep his name out of it, because he has been dead for twenty years."

"Suppose he wasn't dead," he whispered hoarsely, looking Claude full in the face, but only for a moment, for his shifty eyes dropped again. "Suppose your father wasn't dead, after all?"

"I cannot suppose anything of the kind."

"Who told you he was dead?"

"I don't know. I have always been told he was dead."

"Did they never tell you where and how he died?"

"No; I never asked."

"And did they tell you what was his trade?"

"My father was a locksmith, and clever at his trade."

"He was. Correct, young man. There wasn't a finer locksmith in all London either for making a lock or for picking one—or for picking one, mind—which made his fortune and his name. There wasn't a cleverer man at his trade in all England—ay, you may throw in the United States as well, though he never practised in the States. He was the envy and the pride of all such as followed the same trade. A locksmith! And so that's all you know about it. Lord! To think that children *could* be so bad brought up. So you think your father was a low mechanic, do you? That's what they told you. And that he's dead. That's what they told you. Well, it's like them. It's all part of the same treatment. Made you ashamed of your own father; called him a mechanic, did they?"

"This is very strange." Claude by this time felt a profound uneasiness in the presence of this man, who looked at him so curiously and asked so many questions and gave no answer to any. "Can't you tell me who you are, and what you want?"

"Directly—I will directly. So he was a locksmith, and clever at his trade, and he died somewhere. Nobody knows where; none of his children ask after him; no one cares about him; they have even dropped his name and taken their mother's."

"What? Dropped his name?"

"Young gentleman," he went on slowly, "I've got a most important communication to make. Give me something to make it on."

"Here are paper and pens."

"I want drink, man. Good Lord! I've been off of it for twenty years, and I've only just begun again. Give me something, I say, to make it on."

Claude gave him some whisky. He drank half a glass of the spirit neat, and then a tumblerful mixed in equal proportions.

"That's what I call something to make communications on. Now then, I'll sit down, I think."

He sat down. "A most comfortable chair too. You swells know how to make yourselves comfortable, don't you? And to think that you're a swell, and your mother in an almshouse! And your father out on his ticket of leave!"

"What!" Claude started. "Say that again, man. What do you mean by that?"

"A dozen times I'll say it, young man. Your father, I said, out on his ticket of leave, I said. Out—on—his—ticket—ticket, you know—ticket—of leave, leave, you know. For the unexpired part of his term. That's what I mean."

Claude did not call him a liar; he only gazed stupidly at him. "I will say it a hundred times more if you like," contmued the stranger. "Your father—"

"No! don't say it again. Don't—don't dare to say it again."

"Why, you are not ashamed of it, are you, mate? You can't be ashamed of it. A ticket of leave is a very honourable thing to have. Only well-conducted convicts, and them as can stand fast in the faith and can be trusted, and are favourably reported on by the good chaplain, ever get a ticket of leave. My good chaplain thought very high of me when I came away. Continue in prayer, sez 'ee, and watch in the same, he sez."

"Your chaplain? Yours? Are you a convict, too?"

"Look here, young feller, don't speak as if convicts was dirt beneath your feet. Very likely you'll be one yourself before long. Most chaps are sooner or later. Convict! Yes, and why not? I've served my eighteen months, and my two years, and my five years, and my five-and-twenty, and by this time I ought to know. Convict? Why, there's many and many a better fellow in than out, let me tell you. As for yourself, with your swell clothes and your pictures and all, I should think you must be in before long. It's a neater turn-out than ever I could show, though I was looked up to as the head of the profession, and there wasn't a man in it but would have worked under me and proud. But I worked alone. No one knew where I was, nor where I was going next. Yet I never got so far as to rooms in the Temple among the lawyers theirselves. What's *your* lay, mate? Is it genteel fakin? Is it sport? Is it races, or cards, or what—that keeps such chambers as these?"

Claude felt dizzy and sick. He could not reply.

"You may tell me, my boy, because you see"—again he lowered his voice and dropped his eyes—"you see, Claude, it's a long time since you saw me, and o' course you can't be expected to remember me. But I am your father. Nothin' else than that, my son."

"You? My father? You?"

The man crossed his legs in his chair and grinned. He had told his secret, and he was bolder.

"Yes, Claude, I'm your father. I couldn't get out to see you very well, and none of you ever come to see me. Of course, if you'd known I was alive you'd have come regular and as often as they let you. Give us your hand, my boy. You're a well set-up lad, and I'm proud of you."

"My father? You?" Claude repeated; but he did not take that proffered hand.

The ticket-of-leave man swore a great oath as loudly as if he had been a Norman king. Then he assured Claude again, and with much greater emphasis, that he really was his parent.

"Look here, boy," he went on, "you ought to be proud of your father. But they've never told you about me. Now I've got a surprise for you—a joyful surprise. Your mother, you see, never took any honest pride in my profession, and ran away from me, she did, when she found out what I was. Ran away and took her maiden name again, and told all her children they were Monuments. It wasn't hard to find where she'd gone to, which I did first thing when I came out. Bless you, it was the most convenient thing in the world for me, that little cottage by the marsh! If ever I was wanted, and when it was convenient to lay by for a bit till people got unsuspecting again, I could go and lay by there. The neighbours, they thought I was in the seafaring line, which accounted for my coming and going as I pleased, and many's the hiding-place I've made in that cottage unknown to that honest woman. She was too proud to take any of my money—well, I had all the more to spend, and I had no pals to stand in with, and so I lived like a fighting-cock, travelled first-class like a gentleman, and stayed at the best hotels and drank champagne like the out-and-out swell I was. But I never got to lodgings like this. I wish now I'd thought of that."

Claude stared at him, and listened without saying a word. "Well, at last, there I was—five-and-twenty years. So she told you all I was dead; and she never told you who her husband was, nor where he was. My son, I am no other than the great Jem Carey, of whom you've heard o' course."

Claude's face showed no emotion at all on hearing this intelligence.

"Jem Carey. Why, man, you can't pretend you never heard of Jem Carey? The King of the Burglars they called him; Prince of Housebreakers, some of 'em said. His name was in all the papers, and the country rang with his noble name. Jem Carey—why, you must have heard talk of Jem Carey?"

"Unfortunately," said Claude, "I have never heard of him before."

"Oh Lord!" said Mr. Carey, properly disgusted. "And you the boy that I destined for the profession from the beginning! I said to myself I must have a successor. One of my boys shall be brought up to his father's business. And I had you christened Claude Duval a purpose, after the most dashing highwayman in history."

Claude for the first time in his life actually wished that he could exchange his Christian name for another—Samuel, for instance, or Leviticus, or anything.

Mr. Carey contemplated his son with a doubtful eye. There was no kindling of joy or of glory in Claude's aspect, but on the contrary a steady look of pain and dismay.

"Won't you shake hands then?" He held out a forgiving and paternal hand.

"No," said Claude, "I will not shake hands."

"Very well." The man put on his hat. "I will go away now. I shall come again when you have got your swell friends round you. I will introduce myself to them as a ticket-of-leave man and your father."

"You will do as you please."

Mr. Carey hesitated. "Will you give me something to help me on my way?"

"Nothing. Be good enough to go."

"Your father is starving."

"That is not true. You are just out of prison. You must have some money. Go."

"I come back after twenty years of quod, and I find my boy a swell, and this is how he treats his repentant father." He looked as if he was trying to cry.

"You can go. I have nothing for you. Take yourself and your history and your prison cant"—he shuddered with shame—"out of my chambers. You have my address. You can send me yours. Whatever we do for you—if we do anything, remember—will be done on the condition that you keep yourself out of the way of everybody."

"I'm going. I am sorry I came to such an unnatural son. But I have other children. Yes, they will be kinder to their father. They will be Samaritans, if it's only twopence."

Claude made no reply.

"There's my boy Joe, my eldest. No doubt he's a married man now, and his wife and children will be pleased to see the poor old man, and to take him in. And there is Sam. I can very easily find out Sam if I like. I think Sam will be glad indeed to see me. And then there's my wife in the almshouse. Poor old woman! she hasn't got any money, but she'll share her crust. And—then there's the two girls. Vey likely those are their pretty likenesses." He pointed to the two photographs. "The girls look the right sort, don't they? Which of them two, now, is Marla, and which is Melenda?"

Claude took the photographs and laid them on their faces. It was intolerable that this man should so much as look at them.

"Stay," he cried. "You shall not even try to make yourself known to—to my sisters. Do you hear? Do you hear?"

He would have seized the man by the collar, but a certain filial piety—a filial repugnance—prevented him. It is impossible for anyone to shake his own father by the collar, however badly he may turn out. Valentine, it is true, had boxed Mr. Carey ears, but then she had her secret, and knew that he was not her father; and besides, he had offered to kiss her.

"Good heavens!" Claude cried, looking at the man with a kind of despair. "They said you were dead. We thought you dead. We believed—we were told—that you were an honest man. You ought to have been dead long ago."

"Ought I?" The man grinned. "That's a question of opinion. Why, I mean to live for thirty years more. Prison is a very healthy place, my dear boy, whatever you may think, though they do cut the diet close. I feel as young and as fit as if I was twenty-five instead of sixty. I mean to live to ninety, and I shall very likely come here a great deal. Thirty years more I intend to live. We shall see each other very often, my son. Oh! very often indeed, Claude, my boy."

Claude made an effort and refrained, even from bad words. "You heard what I said about—your daughters."

"Explain yourself more clearly, my son. I am afraid you presumed to give orders to your father. Whereas you will read in the Epistles, 'Children, obey your parents in all things.'"

"I said that you must not attempt to find out your daughters."

"Why not, my son?"

"Because your very existence is a shame and a disgrace to us; and because they are happy in believing you to be dead."

"Is that all?"

"No. Because they have never been told, poor things, that their father is a convict."

Mr. Carey put his hands in his pockets and whistled.

"Look ye, my lad," he said; "suppose I want my girls? Consider a father's feelings. However, I am a peaceful man; I am always open to reason. What will you give me?"

Claude hesitated. It was clear that this man would have to be bought off. But at what price?

"I don't know," he replied; "I must consult my brother."

"Is he a swell, too? Hang me if I understand it!"

"No; he's a locksmith by trade."

"Then I shan't wait for Joe's opinions. I'm one of them who stick to their rich friends. I stay where the money is. Now, there's money here. If you and me don't come to an understanding—" Here he interposed a long parenthesis full of all the words he had not been allowed to use in prison. It treated of his son's behaviour to him and the revolting nature of that unfilial loathing which Claude exhibited towards him. This, he said, he must and should revenge, unless an understanding was come to. "Then I go straight to the almshouse—I know where it is—and I'll frighten the old woman into fits; and to-morrow I'll find out Melenda and Marla, and introduce myself to their fine friends."

Ten minutes later Mr. Carey walked down the stairs. He was richer by thirty shillings than when he mounted those steps. He had also the assurance that this sum would be continued to him as a weekly allowance so long as he observed two or three simple rules. These were, in point of fact, the same as had already been made by Valentine. He was not to make his existence known, or to force himself upon his wife or any of his children, especially either of his daughters. Should he break these conditions, Claude assured him, in the most solemn manner, he should never receive another farthing from himself or from any of his brothers and sisters.

The parent replied that his sole desire was to live virtuously and to retrieve the past in the eyes of the world; gentlemen who are penitents of this description always assume that the world is following their career with the greatest interest, and yet they continue in a retiring modesty about their own antecedents. He also said that he should strive to find some quiet corner in London where there were none of his old associates, and only pious men. Here he should perhaps be enabled, by his son's assistance, to open a small shop in the good-book line. He had thought of conducting an open-air service on Sundays for penitents like himself. As for telling any of his family that he was alive, or being wishful to force his company upon them, nothing could be farther from his thoughts. Claude might trust him. It was not a great thing for a father to ask the confidence of his son. Thirty shillings was little enough for the mere necessities of life. But he would make it do. He deserved no more. Fortunately he never drank; that habit he had given up; he illustrated the remark by taking another glass of whisky and water. He had read a great deal of the Bible while in his cell. Among the things he remembered were the gracious words of Paul, Corinthians—.

"That is enough," said Claude. "Here is your first week's money. I shall send your next to this address. No; don't dare to come here for it. I do not want ever to see your face again."

"They'll never tell each other," Mr. Carey murmured, going softly down the stairs. "They'll be ashamed to tell each other. And they're good, between them, for two pound ten a week. This is a good day's work—a very good day's work."

Chapter xix

In the Churchyard

When the man left him, Claude remained standing, and mechanically listened for his footsteps on the stairs; they were as light as the steps of a girl and as noiseless; but he heard them on the gravel in the court below. Then they ceased, and he lifted his head and breathed a sigh of relief. He was alone. Something to get rid of such a presence, though one knows full well that it will come again. Over his mantelshelf there was a cabinet adorned, among other things, with a small square of looking-glass. In this Claude caught, as he turned his head, a glimpse of his own face. He shuddered and crimsoned with shame—for he recognised, unmistakably, the features of the man who had just left him. Only for a moment, then the resemblance disappeared; but he had seen it; he was the son of that man.

He took up the photographs of the two girls which he had laid upon their faces while the man was with him. The same resemblance flashed across Violet's face in the same strange and sudden manner, disappearing instantly. It was like the evidence of an unwilling witness "Behold!" said the picture, "I am none other than that man's daughter."

He was, then, the son of a convicted felon, a burglar, a ticket-of-leave man, an habitual criminal; not, as he had formerly thought, and often proudly stated, *fabri filius*, the son of a smith; not the son of an honest man whose memory he cherished with filial pride and admiration; but the son of a man who had spent most of his life in prison; he had been all his life going about under false pretences; his very name was false; it was Carey, not Monument at all; James Carey, his father, was a most notorious and celebrated evil liver, and his own very Christian name was chosen for him in honour of an illustrious thief. His father was a burglar and a convict—the one goes very naturally and fitly with the other. If a man's birth were a mystery, and if he were tempted to pry into the secret in the hope of turning out a baron or an earl, and were then to find out that his father was not a nobleman at all, but only a rogue, there would be little pity for that man. Because, given an unknown father, and remembering that there are more rogues than barons in the world, the chances are in favour of the less desirable connection. But when a man has all his life rejoiced in the honour of his father, and been as proud of him, though he was but a locksmith, as if he had been a baronet, and now has without any fault of his own such a father sprung upon him suddenly, that man is very greatly to be pitied. He needs all the pity and all the sympathy that the world has to offer. It is one thing indeed to have it whispered that you are self-made, son of a working-man; and another thing to hear it whispered, each whisper ringing in your ears like the blast of Fame's Trumpet[1] echoed from pole to pole, that you are the son of a—*convict*.

Claude heard that whisper already. The room was full of the echoes of that whisper. They rang from wall to wall, from floor to ceiling. "Son of a convict—son of a thief—son of a rogue!"

"I will emigrate," he said, "I will take another name—I will go to some far-off colony where no one will know who I am."

A foolish resolve. Because there is no colony, near or far off, which will receive any man without knowing all about him; who was his father; what he has done; why he has left his native country. He may keep these things secret if he pleases. Probably they will be found out for him. In either case, he will enter no better society than can be found at a bar or in a saloon. He will be a *déclassé*.[2]

London is the only possible place for such concealment. He who travels, as the poet tells us, may change his sky but not his mind. He may also change his name, but never his history—that is unchangeable and indestructible—and that, whatever it may be, good or bad, these honest colonials insist upon knowing before they admit him to their society.

Claude, ignorant of this fact, remembered immediately that he could not emigrate, because it was impossible for him to leave his people. He thought of the misery which might come to them; to his mother; to his brother Joe; to Sam, proud, like himself, of his honest father; to Melenda—to Valentine first, and to Violet next. He remembered their defenceless condition. Could he be so cowardly as to leave them? Could he go away and leave them to the tender mercies of this—creature? One must not under any circumstances speak evil of one's father; one should not, if possible, even think evil of him. Therefore it is providential that there exist certain neutral words which carry reproach by the manner of expression rather than by any accusation conveyed in themselves. Thus—"this"—gasp—"*creature*," "this"—gasp—"man," "this"—gasp—"woman." Moses said, when he broke the tables of stone, "this"—gasp—"*people*." We can use such words—gasp and all—without breaking any commandments—blamelessly, and for the relief and solace of the soul.

He stood in his silent room for an hour at least, trying to look the thing in the face, and failing altogether. Then a thought—a feeble thought at best—struck him. Joe it was who said his father was dead. What if the man was an impostor? Why did Joe say he was dead? What reason could there be for Joe making up a story? He forgot for the moment the evidence of the looking-glass and the photographs, catching, as men in trouble do, at a straw. He would go at once and consult Joe. His mind was so troubled with the burden of this horrible discovery that he actually forgot that it was already midnight. He seized his hat and sallied forth with intent to get to Tottenham.

He walked down Fleet Street where there were plenty of people about, especially late journalists; up Ludgate Hill which was still awake; and along Cheapside, where the stream of life was still running, but in a narrow thread. At the bank there were the last omnibuses with a great shouting and a crowd. But Cornhill was

1 In Greek and Roman mythology, the goddess or spirit of Fame was depicted and described as blowing loudly on a trumpet as she proclaimed a person's good deeds. However, Fame could easily change into her other persona: Rumor and Scandal.

2 French for someone who has been reduced in social status.

quiet. Whether the streets were noisy or quiet, crowded or empty, made no difference to Claude, who strode on, wrapped in his gloomy thoughts. Then he turned into Bishopsgate Street and began the long straight walk which leads past Shoreditch and along the Kingsland Road and the Stoke Newington Road to Tottenham.[3] The road was nearly deserted now, and long before he reached Tottenham the last belated resident was safe in bed. Nobody awake, he thought, except the policeman and the burg— perhaps he remembered, with a natural shudder, his own father, getting his hand in again, after many years' total abstinence from the jemmy.

As he walked along the silent road there followed him two voices, speaking in his ear at either side. They kept on repeating the same words, and those very disagreeable words, such as "Your father is a convict and a thief…Honour thy father that thy days may be long in the land … He has spent most of his days in prison … The fathers have eaten sour grapes, and the children's teeth are set on edge … He is a most notorious and even historical rogue … Unto the third and fourth generation … The most wicked man, probably, that at present lives … That which is crooked cannot be made straight … A lawless and impenitent villain … His seed shall be destroyed among the children of men …"[4] And so on—one at each side. To stifle these voices he began to think of a certain work on the mystery of pain, written by a learned physician who persuaded himself that he understood all about it. With pain may be considered shame and all kinds of evil. Everybody, said the learned physician, should bear it cheerfully if anybody else is relieved or helped by it. But who was benefited by the fact that Claude's father was a rogue? And who, to put a plainer case, can help another man by having a toothache? This doctrine Claude perceived would not help his own case. And then he suffered the voices to go on again.

When he arrived at Tottenham and stood at the door of Joe's house, with its closed shutters and drawn blinds, he realised for the first time that it was the very dead of night, in fact, at two o'clock in the morning, when sleep is at its soundest. He might knock up his brother, but what excuse could be made to wife and children for this unusual disturbance? Or he might go straight home again, which would be absurd after coming all that way. Or he might walk about until morning, which was not far off; or he might find a place where he might sit down and gnash his teeth.

Not many years ago Tottenham was a small country town full of pleasant lanes, spacious houses, leafy orchards and splendid gardens, with memories of Isaac Walton, and the High Crown and the famous arbour—"the contexture of woodbines, sweetbriar, jessamine, and myrtle"—and the Seven Sisters, and many goodly mansions inhabited by great London merchants, and of Quakers fiery for the faith and abounding in good works.[5] The Quakers have mostly gone; the big houses are mostly pulled down; rows of streets lie to right and left, ugly with grey brick and mean design and monotonous uniformity. Claude strolled about these new streets, slowly and wearily. His first excitement was wearing off; besides, he was feeling tired. Presently he took by accident a road which led him past the new houses and into the region of old Tottenham—such of

---

3 Claude's path takes him from central London to the east, then to the north, finally reaching the suburb of Tottenham almost seven miles away.

4 These quotations are all from the Old Testament and relate to Claude's fear that he will pay for his father's sins, although, notably, the proverb about sour grapes is referenced in two books as one that should no longer apply to the children of Israel. See Exodus 20:12; Jeremiah 31:29 and Ezekiel 18:2; Numbers 14:18; Ecclesiastes 1:15; and Psalms 21:10.

5 Izaak Walton was a seventeenth-century English author most famous for the *Compleat Angler*, a treatise on fishing. The subsequent quotation, in part about the loveliness of Tottenham, is extracted from that work. The narrator elaborates on this reference to Tottenham by evoking a former stand of trees called the Seven Sisters and the High Cross, which sat atop a tall structure in the area.

it as still exists. He was in a lane with walls on both sides—they were old red-brick walls with stonecrop and wallflowers on top, but these details escaped him in the darkness; beyond the walls were trees, and beyond the trees were gardens, and the night air was heavy with the scent of a thousand flowers—the flowers of early autumn when the mignonette is still sweet, and the honeysuckle and jessamine still blossoming. The lane led him, he perceived, to the church, which stood, a dark mass with a black tower, outlined against the sky among the white tombstones. He opened the gate and stepped within the churchyard.

Tottenham Church has a very good churchyard, full of interesting monuments of unknown people, and in the daytime you might wander there for a long time and learn quantities of history just hinted at in the bald disjointed way common to tombstones. You might, I say, under happier conditions, but you cannot, because they have stuck up rows of spiky iron railings beside the path, so that no moralist, unless he have very long legs, shall ever be permitted to get any good out of the churchyard at all. It is an abominable, unchristian custom. What should we say if the catacombs of Rome, or the cemetery of Aries, were to be closed for ever, and so the messages and lessons of the dead to the living were to be read no longer? What if they were to hang curtains before all the tablets in Westminster, and rub out the inscription of Eshmunazar?[6]

This, however, if you come to think of it, is exactly what the bright intelligences of Tottenham have done for their folk. At Waltham Abbey, too, this same thing has been done, and at St. Giles's in the City, and I dare say in hundreds of churchyards. There are, again, two splendid yew trees in the churchyard which ought to be surrounded by benches for the old folk to sit upon in summer evenings; but they are now within the spikes and there is no bench round either of them, and so another opportunity is lost until, in good time, there may haply come a vicar with a touch of poetry and sentiment, and a feeling for the dead; and then the spikes will be taken away, and the benches will be put up, and the tombstones will resume their solemn lessons to the living.

Claude was more desirous of resting than of reading the monuments; it was too dark to read, and, besides, he was not in a moralising, but rather of an accusing and rebellious mood. He stepped over the spikes, however, being tall enough and long enough of limb, and finding a flat stone, sat down upon it and tried to think connectedly, which he had not as yet been able to do. It is something in every case of trouble, just to put the facts plainly. Three or four hours ago, he explained to himself, as if there was somebody inside him who was very stupid, he had suddenly come into possession of the most undesirable thing in the whole world, a thing absolutely impossible to get rid of, or to forget, or ever to put away and hide—namely, a disgraceful and shameful father. Try to think, you of the majority whose fathers have lived blameless lives and left an honourable record behind them—put it to yourselves—what it would have been to you, had they, like Claude's father—you will find a difficulty in finishing the sentence.

When your doctor discovers that you have got a disease which he will never be able to cure, which you will have to carry with you to the grave, a burden which will never fall off your shoulders, you presently, when the shock is over, fall to inquiring after the various methods employed by the faculty for alleviating the horrid thing, just as the man who has to carry a knapsack is always trying to adjust the confounded straps into the most comfortable position possible. Claude began already to adjust his straps. It was a horribly heavy burden which was laid upon his shoulders. It was a burden with which he could no longer venture among his friends; it would render impossible for him the only life which he thought worth having—the life of culture among

6 Eshmunazar was an ancient Phoenician king whose sarcophagus was excavated in 1855. The sarcophagus is a particularly significant artifact because it contains an impressive twenty-two-line inscription with information about the king.

men and women of culture. It could not be hidden away or disguised; it was like a humpback. How could such a burden be alleviated? There seemed but one way. It was the way already adopted by Valentine. His father must be bribed into effacing himself. No one must be permitted to know of his existence or to see him except Claude himself. He must bear the burden alone; he must keep the secret to himself. Perhaps when his father—he kept on saying "my father" to himself, in order to bring the Thing home more completely—when his father quite understood that his only chance of getting money was to keep quiet and out of the way he would do so. If he disobeyed, why then—Claude ground his teeth—then he might do his worst; and then—poor Violet! —poor Valentine! He sprang to his feet in an agony of wrath and shame, for in such a case he could do nothing for them, nothing at all, but sit down with them in sackcloth and ashes, and remember that this was only the first generation and that there were yet two or even three to follow, with the sins of their grandfather to drag them down as they strove to climb upwards.

The annals of our ancestors are for the most part forgotten, so that it is only in great families, whose history is preserved and handed down to posterity, that the tragedies, the disgraces, and the shames are remembered. To do the great families justice, they seem rather to rejoice in the desperate villainies of their ancestors. But the evil deeds of the rude forefathers are for the most part vanished into oblivion, no longer remembered, no more talked about by the second and the third generations, though they may, in their poverty and obscurity, be suffering for those sins. Who remembereth that the great-uncle of the family baker—himself a very worthy man—was hanged? Who careth that the respectable family solicitor had a grandfather by the maternal side sent to Botany Bay?[7] What difference does it make to the vicar that his father's sister—the thing having been carefully concealed—ran away with the groom? All these stories are clean forgotten and out of people's minds; so that the sins of the fathers do not seem always to pursue the generations which come after. Yet there are some hereditary disgraces which nothing but the waters of Lethe can wash away.[8] Where is that benevolent stream? In what region, in what unknown corner of the earth does its current flow? How shall we find it so that we may make that which hath been vanish away and become as if it had never been? There is a way—religious men tell us that way—by which things may be forgiven; but I have never yet heard any method by which they can be forgotten.

I suppose it was somewhere about two o'clock in the morning when Claude sat down upon the tombstone, his mind torn by these and a thousand other thoughts, which took shape in the twilight and flitted before his eyes like ghosts in the deep shadows of the place. The headstones became faces which mocked and jeered at him; he saw the figure of himself wandering in the dark shadows with downcast eyes and bowed and shameful head; the shades of Valentine and Violet fell at his feet, weeping and sobbing for shame and disgrace; his brother Sam stood before him with clenched fist, grinding teeth, and helpless rage in his eyes; Melenda turned away in humiliation from her friends and hid her proud face; and his mother wept because the thing she had concealed so long from her children had come to light at last. The night was not dark, but there were black depths beneath the trees and in the recesses of the church; there was such a dim suggestion of light as

7 Australia's Botany Bay was a British penal colony for convicted felons.

8 In Greek mythology, the river Lethe flowed through the underworld and caused anyone who drank it to forget everything of their past.

is favourable for a procession of ghosts. Presently there arose a young moon in the east;[9] the sky was clear and the air was quite still. The silence fell upon his heart, but it did not soothe him. The dead men lying around him tried to whisper comfort in his ear—"We have lived; we have suffered; we are dead. Our suffering is over; yet a little while and no shame or disgrace can touch you—your lot shall be with us." Yet the words brought no consolation. Then the still soft air of the night lay upon his cheek and murmured gently—"Live out thy life. This thing can do thee no harm; go on as if it had never been." And again, "Bear it alone and bear it with brave heart, for the sake of those who might be crushed beneath the burden." But these words failed to comfort him. And again—we are a scoffing and an infidel generation; but in all times of sickness, sorrow, or any kind of adversity, there are certain words which rise up in the mind of every Englishman, though he believe in nothing at all but his own infallibility. They come out of an old book which it is a fashion with some to dishonour, to neglect, and even to deride—so in Claude's mind there arose and lingered certain words which need not be set down concerning strength and trust, and presently he lifted his head and saw the grey dawn spreading in the east, and heard the birds twitter in the trees around him. Then he got up—the air was cold—and he shivered. It was light enough now to see things clearly outlined in the chill morning light. He tried the handle of the door of the great south porch—by great good fortune it was open. Within there is a bench on either side—he thought he would sit down there. But he tried the handle of the church-door. Wonderful accident! That, too, was open, and he stepped within the church. It was fast growing lighter; the painted windows—the lower windows are all painted in Tottenham Church—were beginning to show a glow of colour, and a pale light shone in the clerestory windows, making the bays and aisles and columns mysterious and ghostly. Then the windows grew brighter, and the colours warmer, and presently the east sprang suddenly into splendour when the sun rose and the colours fell upon pillar and on wall, painting in crimson, blue, and gold the figures of Ferdinando Heyborne and Richard Kandeler and Eliza his wife.[10] With the daylight the ghosts and devils of the night fled shrieking, and Claude stood upright, facing the splendid sunshine, and remembered that he was a man, with a man's work before him, and a man's duty to bear, and his burden to endure, and his honour in his own hand, and that the past was dead. Wherefore—I do not explain the phenomenon, but I state it—while his strength and courage came back to him, and he felt once more the power of his will, and peace returned to his soul, his eyes overflowed with tears, and he sat down and hid his face in his hands, and then—he fell fast asleep.

It was nearly eight o'clock when he awoke and went out of the church. The business of the day, so far as concerned the birds in the gardens round the churchyard, was already pretty well over, because the sun, who gets up about half-past five at this season of the year, was already nearly halfway towards high noon. It was too late, moreover, to see his brother, who would now he on his way to the workshop, or perhaps already deranging somebody's pipes, laying the foundations for an attack of typhoid, or for a boiler explosion, or an overflow of

---

9 After his death, Besant was criticized for this inaccuracy: "In the 'Children of Gibeon' Walter Besant has caused a new moon to rise in the east at two o'clock in the morning. The most casual observer has, without doubt, noticed that the new moon appears in the western sky, and sets from the moment it becomes visible" (John Preston Beecher, "The Inaccuracies of Authors," *Saturday Review* [September 1901]: 363).

10 In the parish church of Tottenham, one of several marble monuments commemorates four related figures: Richard Candeler, a justice of the peace, with his wife Eliza, along with their daughter Anne and her husband Ferdinand Heyborne, who was a composer and Groom of the Privy Chamber under Queen Elizabeth I.

the bath, or an escape of gas—for Joe was really clever in his own line. But that mattered nothing. Now, he was not going to tell Joe or anyone else at all. It should be his own secret.

"I wish, however," he said, "that I had a clothes-brush. And my boots would be all the better for a little attention. I'll go and see my mother."

She was already dressed and in her arm-chair. To his astonishment Valentine was there too. The fire was burning brightly, the kettle was singing, the cloth was spread, and she was making the tea, looking fresh and bright enough to raise the spirits of a man going in for a competitive examination.

"That is the step of my boy," cried the old lady, while he was yet afar off.

"Claude!" cried Valentine. "You here at this hour?" Claude stooped and kissed his mother.

"Give him a kiss, Polly," she said, in the quick peremptory tone with which she ordered her daughter about. "Can't you kiss your own brother, child?"

Valentine blushed but obeyed—that is to say, she offered her hand as a substitute for her cheek.

"Suppose," said Claude, when he had paid this knightly homage—"suppose I had got up early in order to walk here and have breakfast with you, mother? But how is it you are here too, Valentine?"

"I stayed with mother all night because her nerves were a little shaken, and I did not like her to be alone."

"We're glad to see you, my dear. Polly, go and buy two or three eggs and a bit o' bacon. The boy must be hungry. Have you got any money, child? Now, run, my dear; make haste."

Valentine nodded to Claude, and laughed and ran upon her errand.

"She's a real good girl, Claude," said the old lady. "That's what she is, mind: there's nobody like Polly. Don't you let her be put upon by Melenda. She's got a heart of gold, and she thinks of everything. Last night I had a dreadful fright—oh! a most terrible fright, and it put me all of a shake—"

"What was it, mother?"

"My dear, I thought I heard a footstep—it was a footstep that I knew, and the second time I heard it—the step of a dead man—your father, Claude. It was only a dream, I know; because Polly, she came in a minute or two afterwards, and she said there was nobody. But it gave me such a shake as I never had before; I haven't felt like myself ever since. But Polly, she don't mind staying here."

"What time was it, mother?"

"In the evening, about eight o'clock. Polly stayed all night with me because I was afraid."

"And you—you heard nothing more, did you?"

"No—nothing more. It was only a dream, you see. But it gave me a terrible turn. When a person is blind, she feels these fancies more than most."

"Don't think any more about it," said Claude. It must have been the step of his father; but how was it that Valentine saw no one? And how could his father have got his Temple address?

Then Valentine came back with her purchases.

"You don't look well, Claude," she said. "You have dark rings round your eyes and you are pale. Have you been walking too far before breakfast? or have you been working too hard?"

"I am very well—but I thought you were looking pale, Valentine. There is nothing the matter, is there?"

"What should there be?" she answered with the approved evasion.

Involuntarily they watched each other, both thinking of the dreadful secret they knew and would keep from each other. And once Claude met Valentine's eyes, and he felt, wondering, that they were full of pity.

Why did she pity him? Yet, if she knew,—oh! how greatly would she pity him? He could not mistake that expression, which would be read and understood by the merest beginner in the art of thought-reading. Why did Valentine pity him? She knew nothing.

"Eat your egg while it's hot, my dear," said the old lady, pleased to have her boy with her. "You were always a famous boy for an egg. Polly, my dear, cut his bread and butter thick. And plenty of sugar in his tea. What a boy he used to be for sugar, to be sure! Claude, it's twelve years and more since you had your breakfast with your mother. If I could only see you—oh! dear, dear—if I could only see you with my own eyes as I used to see you, eating hearty as you used to eat. I suppose you've grown out of bread and dripping—Polly, is the bacon kept hot for him? Don't let him say we sent him away hungry. I hope the loaf is to your liking, my boy! I wish we had some jam for him. Cut him a crusty bit, Polly. He used to like the crust. You and me can eat the crumb"—and so on, because her boy was at breakfast with her; and because, as women use, she made a king of him, and of herself and her daughter she made his slaves.

Claude ate and drank, being hungry after his night in the open, and he tried to laugh and joke. Between him and Valentine—each saw it and thought it hidden from the other—stood the spectre of a grey-headed man, with cunning eyes and smooth face, holding out his hands for more, and threatening to turn all their innocent joy into mourning and all their pride into shame!

Chapter XX

The Lady with the Parasol

There are some institutions, some kinds of wickedness, some classes of men, some modes of suffering, which seem, to people of the gentle life, outside the possibility of any connection with themselves. They belong to another kind of creature, only outwardly resembling them. The prison, for example, is an institution only known to most of us by hearsay: those kinds of sin which bring upon us the man in blue, are such as we think we shall never commit—the disgrace, shame, and remorse of crime, are among the emotions which we shall never feel. This way of looking at life is, of course, misleading, because everything becomes possible when one is tempted.

Valentine had learned already that the girl Polly, whom she personated, was the daughter of a dead convict: she learned now that the dead had returned to life, and was prepared to heap coals of unspeakable disgrace upon everybody connected with him, unless she could stave him off. And in Ivy Lane, under the same roof, were the man's daughter and the man's chief victim; for there could not be, even in Mr. Carey's remarkable career, another instance of wickedness quite so bad as the case of Mr. Lane; and every night, also in Ivy Lane, sharing the same bed with his own daughter, was his victim's daughter. There cannot possibly be any misfortune much worse to bear than a disgraceful father. A foolish father, a spendthrift father, a miser, a brute, an evil liver, a selfish father—these are common, and have often to be endured. But to have such a father as James Carey, Prince of Burglars, that is indeed a cross not often laid upon suffering humanity. To be sure he was not Valentine's father; but she felt as if, but for the accident of Violet being Polly, he might have been. When she went home in the morning the little room upon which this evil spirit might at any time intrude his detestable presence if he found out the place, seemed like an oasis of rest, with its flowers and pictures. Lotty was lying on the bed, now her permanent abode; her eyes were closed, but she was not sleeping, and she welcomed Valentine's return with a smile of affection which went straight to her heart, and filled her eyes with tears. When one is in great trouble even a little thing will sometimes do this.

"My dear," Valentine said, kissing her, "have you had a good night? I was obliged to stay at Tottenham."

"I am always having bad nights now. Melenda's been sitting up with me—I've been dreadful bad—I'm glad it wasn't you again."

"But Melenda was working all day—she must not sit up all night."

"She liked doing it—oh! Valentine"—Lotty held out her thin hand to take Valentine's—"she is always half starved—we were all half starved till you came—and now work is slack: and what will she do, poor thing? And she's harder and more independent than ever!"

"What can I do for her?" She thought of a danger almost worse than starvation. "Lotty, we are all in terrible trouble."

"Not you, Valentine—you haven't got any trouble, have you?"

"Yes, I have, Lotty—but don't talk about it."

"And I'm such a burden to you! Oh! if I could get better. I'll show you, and Melenda too, as soon as I get better."

"Yes, dear—don't think of yourself as a burden, Lotty. The trouble has nothing to do with money."

"Melenda's jealous," Lotty went on. "But she's not so jealous as she was—she doesn't sniff any more when she looks at your pretty things. In the night, when she thought I was asleep, she began to cry—she kept on crying. Do you think she cried about the work being slack? I never saw her cry before, except when she was in a rage!"

Valentine turned her face away. There was reason enough for Melenda's crying in Lotty's hollow cheeks and lustrous eyes, in her weakness and her bad nights.

It was the doctor's morning. He called, and gave his patient a few directions. Then Valentine followed him down the stairs. He replied to the unspoken questions which he read in her eyes:

"I think, exactly and truthfully, that she may last perhaps till the spring. That's all there is to think."

"Poor Lotty!"

"When the weather gets chilly you might send her to Ventnor or somewhere, if she can travel, and so prolong her life a little—it's my business to prolong life. But"—he pointed to the direction of Melenda's room—"is that kind of thing worth living for? Perhaps there is something beyond, and perhaps there isn't. I'd rather take my chances on the other side, if I were Lotty, than stay here. Not that she will be asked—poor girl!—which she'd rather have."

"She is happier now; she seems to forget the past miseries. It is something for her to have sufficient food and to rest."

"And when you go away, what is to prevent all the miseries coming back?"

"The past shall never return, for her or for the others, doctor, if I can help it. We may be powerless against the system which makes slaves of these girls, but we can do something for one here and there!"

"I believe you are the Countess of Monte Cristo![1] I hear the same story about you wherever I go. I wonder if your ladyship keeps millions in the cupboard?"

"No; my millions are not there."

"Has your ladyship a sister called Melenda?"

---

1 The doctor refers to Valentine as a female version of Alexandre Dumas's title character in *The Count of Monte Cristo* (1845–1846), who has an enormous fortune hidden away, and in various disguises, helps friends in financial distress while also seeking revenge against enemies.

"Perhaps."

"You are not well this morning," said the doctor, changing his tone; "you've got a black ring round your eyes, and your cheeks are white. What's the matter with you?"

"I am in great trouble," said Valentine, "but I cannot tell you what it is."

"Well—anyhow, don't vex your soul about the women. We'll get the Labour League some day and work wonders; see if we don't. The men shall rule it, though—it's good for women to be ruled by men."

Then Valentine sat down and waited, curious to learn what the convict would do next.

The convict behaved exactly as might have been expected of him, only with greater promptitude; for the very next day, Valentine got a letter from him, addressed to the almshouse, stating that, by a most unfortunate accident, he had lost the sovereign she had given him and was now penniless, but full of trust that his daughter would see her repentant father through.

She made no reply to this letter. Two days afterwards there came another. A most magnificent chance occurred, he said, by which, for thirty pounds down, he could secure a tobacconist's shop, a going concern, with a connection in the newspaper line. Only thirty pounds wanted to establish himself in a Christian way for life! He would give up her allowance altogether in consideration of the thirty pounds.

Valentine read this letter carefully. The man was certainly feeling his way. As for giving him the money, that, of course, was out of the question. Her only chance with him, she thought, was to make him understand clearly that he would get nothing if he did not comply with the conditions. She resolved on seeing him again, though with misgivings. She wrote to him, therefore, telling him to meet her in the gardens at the back of St. Luke's, on Saturday morning at twelve.

Mr. Carey kept the appointment. He came, however, half an hour before the time, and he was accompanied by a girl. She was dressed soberly and respectably. She wore a thick veil and carried a parasol with a black lace fringe—one of those instruments by means of which ladies can observe others without being themselves observed. They are adapted for modest curiosity, or for curious modesty, or for anything in the detective and secret search line.

"She isn't come," said the man, looking about. "Very well, then, she'll come directly. All you've got to do is to sit here and wait till she goes out. Then you get up and follow her, and find out where she lives and come and tell me."

"That's right, daddy," said the girl, grinning.[2] "It isn't the first time I've done that! Oh, isn't it beautiful to see them walk right away, unsuspecting, and me on the other side of the road, quiet and takin' no notice, and generally a good bit behind, till they get home? And next morning some of us calls, and the game begins!"

"Never you mind about the next morning," said Mr. Carey; "that's my look-out. You just find out where she lives—that's what you're paid to do!"

"Very well, daddy." This girl will, no doubt, some day be taken on in the detective service;[3] but at present she is the confidential employee of a small, modest, and retiring syndicate, for whom she finds out all kinds of secrets connected with houses and their private interests; shops, shopmen, and clerks, religious professors

---

2 *Daddy* is slang for any older man in charge, an appellation particularly in use among the working classes.

3 In Victorian London, as now, some detectives worked within the police force and others, including women, outside it. Detectives benefited from familiarity with crime and criminals and some of the most famous early detectives, in fiction and reality, were former criminals.

and their private characters, gambling and betting clubs and their associates. When, after infinite pains, lies, pretences, and inventions, chiefly by the aid of this clever young lady, they have got possession of a secret, they begin to *exploiter*[4] it for their own purposes; that is, they sell the secret or their own silence and sometimes make considerable sums of money, and on the whole, when the young lady is active and has been fortunate, they do very well indeed. Sometimes, however, they get into prison.

"Well, daddy," said the girl, "I found out about the old woman's sons for you, didn't I?"

"I don't say you didn't. You were paid for it handsome. But it's been no use to me yet."

Mr. Carey left her on the seat and began to walk up and down the asphalte walk, with one eye suspiciously turned upon the policeman, much as a partridge, even out of the season, may regard a man with a gun.

Valentine arrived presently, only a few minutes late. Mr. Carey perceived, from a certain look of contumacy in her eyes, that she was likely to give him trouble. He held out his hand, however, in a fatherly and forgiving spirit.

"You have written to me," she said, rudely refusing to take it; "you have written two letters to me. One contained a falsehood about losing the sovereign I gave you, the other also contained a falsehood about a shop."

"No, gawspel[5] truth—not a falsehood; and it's a most beautiful chance. I shall never get such a chance again. The shop is next door but one to a chapel, too. Oh, how handy for the means of grace!"

"I told you the other evening, and I tell you again, that you will have no more money from me than the pound a week I have offered you; and if you break my conditions, you will have nothing at all. Now do you understand?"

"Well, my dear, I thought you'd say that. Most of 'em do, till they feel the screw a bit. Then they talk reason."

"Nothing. That is all I have to say to you. Now you may go."

"Look here, my girl," he tried to bluster; but somehow the girl's face, or the near presence of the policeman, abashed him, and he spoke in little more than a whisper. "Look here—your father's a ticket-o'-leave man, and your name isn't Monument at all, but Carey; and you're the daughter of a convict and a burglar, and you're ashamed of it. That's what you are. Very well, then, it's like this: you're ashamed of it more than a pound a week, and you've got to pay up accordingly."

"You shall have nothing more."

"P'r'aps you can't lay your hands on thirty pound all at once. Lor, I don't want to press you, and p'r'aps I can help you to get it off of somebody that has got it. There's a lover or a husband about—oh, I know. And he mustn't never know, must he? Husbands and lovers mustn't know about the ticket-o'-leave men, must they? P'r'aps you're married and there's babies. Very well, then, naturally you don't want the babies never to learn about the great burglar, though p'r'aps when they're old enough they may be glad to crack a crib and thankful of the chance. But there's a prejudice against burglars, ain't there? You'd give a great deal not to have your father in your house, wouldn't you? Why, there, we're agreed already."

"I suppose I must hear what you have to say."

"Why, of course you must. Very well, then." He coughed and looked at her with some hesitation, because he was wondering how far he might go, and what figure he might name, and he considered her dress and external appearance carefully before he spoke. The gloves decided him, though perhaps the boots helped. It

4 French for *to exploit*.

5 A misspelling of *gospel*, used to represent the mispronunciation of the word.

is only the really prosperous who have both good boots and good gloves. Mr. Carey, an old student of human nature, remembered so much. "I want more than thirty pound—I want a hundred—"

"Do you?"

"A hundred pounds. I'm ready to take that money, partly in valuables and partly in gold—partly today and partly the day after tomorrow."

"You must ask someone else for the money then."

"I shall ask my wife. At the almshouse."

"You cowardly villain! Then you will get nothing!"

"I shall ask my sons then, one after the other. I know where they are, all of them."

Valentine changed colour. The man had already found them out then!

"You see, my pretty," he went on, with a mocking grin, "your father isn't quite such a fool as you thought him—not quite such a fool. And he's been making a few inquiries. Joe works for a plumber; most respectable Joe is; and Sam's a schoolmaster, highly thought of; and Claude's in the Temple, where the lawyers live. As for you, my pretty, you—with your lover or your husband—I haven't found out yet, because I haven't tried. But I shall find out as soon as I do try. All of 'em will be delighted to see me, though they have cast off their father's name, and I dare say your lover will be as pleased as Sam and Joe will be pleased when I show up."

The girl recovered her presence of mind.

"You will do just exactly as you please," she said quietly. "You have heard what I had to say."

"And you shall do just exactly as I please," he replied with a rough oath. "A hundred pound. That's my first and last offer. I ask no more and I take no less. I don't ask you where the pound a week comes from, do I? Very likely it's the housekeeping money, or it may be out of the till. Who the devil cares where it comes from?"

She made no sign, standing with folded hands, and eyes which looked as if she had not heard.

"It's so easy done," he went on. "It isn't as if I wanted anything dangerous or difficult. I'll take all the danger myself! There's lots of ways—there's a cheque and a signature—I shouldn't want any more than that. You get me a signed cheque, and I'll alter the amount—I know how to take out the writin' and put in fresh. There's a door left unlocked at night p'r'aps—or there's just the little straight tip where the valuables is kept; or maybe there's the least bit of help when the till's got to be cleared! Mind you, my dear, I don't value no lock nor bolt ever invented, not a brass farthing. You needn't be a bit afraid of me—not one bit. Money or money's value—it's all the same to me. Just turn things over in your mind, Marla, my dear, and you'll come to reason, I'm sure."

"Oh!" said Valentine, "surely this man is the most wicked wretch in the world!" Nothing ever astonished Mr. Carey more than his daughter's plainness of speech. She had even boxed his ears; and he shrank from her in cowardly terror lest she might do it again. Now, it is not often that a man can boast of a daughter who has both boxed his ears and called him names. Such daughters are rare. Even King Lear's elder daughters did not reach this level.[6]

"Now," she said, facing him with a resolution which he admired, "listen to me again. I will give you no money except this pound a week. Remember, that as for getting you a hundred pounds—begging it, borrowing it, or stealing it—I will have nothing to do with it. And if you dare to show yourself to my mother or my

6 In Shakespeare's *King Lear*, the titular character's two elder daughters profess their love for him and he, in turn, divides his kingdom between them. They subsequently treat him and his retinue wickedly and eventually turn him out of their homes.

brothers, you shall have nothing more from me at all. Do you hear? Nothing! And this I solemnly swear to you, because I suppose you will not believe a simple promise."

His eyes dropped, and he made no answer. Then he began to protest that he wanted nothing but an honest livelihood, and to show his repentance, throwing in the scripture phrases which reeked so frightfully of the prison, when she interrupted him again:

"There is one thing I might do for you."

"What is that?"

"I might send someone to you who would make you an offer"

"What kind of offer?"

"So much a week, if you would go abroad and stay there."

"What! And leave London, when I have only just come out?"

"Yes, you would have to leave England. It would be a liberal offer."

"Leave England? And at my age? Never!"

"You have heard what I had to say. Now go. Leave me here. Take your detestable presence out of my sight!"

Mr. Carey obeyed, with mental reservations about the future, and the revenge he would take on this unnatural child. He had yet, however, to discover where and how she lived, and why she was so anxious to keep the knowledge of his existence from her brothers.

As for Valentine, she felt inclined to communicate to the policeman in the gardens certain new ideas as regards the penal system. It ought to include, she would have told him, provision for the incarceration of such a man as this for life. He should be allowed such special luxuries as tobacco, rations of drink, and permission to keep his gas alight till—say ten o'clock at night. But he should never be allowed to go back to the world for a single day. The place of his incarceration need not be called a prison, perhaps, but a penitents' retreat, or some such name, so as to soften the apparent cruelty of the sentence. She did not, however, communicate these ideas to the policeman; but she left the garden and walked away. The girl with the parasol and the black fringe round it got up from the seat and went out after her slowly. The policeman looked on and noted the circumstance. First, one girl comes to the garden with a man. Then another girl comes. Man converses with that girl. First girl waits. Then second girl goes away alone. First girl follows second. There was a little game up. But he was on duty in the garden, and he could not follow and observe.

Valentine was a very easy person to follow and watch, because she walked quickly, looked neither to the right nor to the left, and was so absorbed in her own thoughts that the woman might have walked at her very elbow without attracting her suspicions.

She crossed the City Road and walked along the street until she came to Hoxton Street, when she turned to the left. The girl followed. Valentine went on nearly to the end of the street, when she turned into a mean and shabby street. The girl stood at the corner and watched. There was a public-house in the street. Perhaps she was going there, but she was not. She entered a house exactly opposite the public-house. The spy stood at the corner, with one eye on the house, and waited, looking at the shop windows for a few minutes. She could not be living there—that was absurd. Young ladies cannot live in such a place. Presently, however, as she did not come out, the spy turned into the street, and as there was no one about of whom she could ask any questions, she went into the public-house and "took" something,

"Isn't there a young lady," she asked the potman, "as comes and goes in the house opposite?"

"There is just," replied the young man, who had taste. "And what do you want with her? Because, you see, if you mean any harm to her, you'd best clear out of Ivy Lane."

"I mean harm? Why, bless the man, I worships the ground she treads on. A sweet lady! Where does she live when she's at home?"

"Why, there."

"Oh! Does her husband work, then?"

"Her husband? She ain't got no husband!"

"Oh! Then how does she live?"

"Go and ask her yourself," he replied.

The girl looked into the house. It was only a mean and shabby tenement house; she belonged, then, to poor people. What was the little game of the old man—her new friend—with this young person?

But that was no concern of hers. It was something vile and wicked, of course, because she knew all her companions were vile and wicked. She went away, therefore, and faithfully narrated what she had observed.

Mr. Carey was greatly puzzled at this unexpected discovery.

His daughter, who permitted herself such airs, and talked as if she had thousands, and looked like a lady in every particular, wearing the most beautiful boots and gloves, actually lived in a mean street of Hoxton, the meanest and also the most virtuous part of all London—a place in which he should be ashamed to be seen. And she lived in a single room, with those gloves and those boots. What could this mean?

"Pity, my dear," he said, "that you couldn't find out how she makes her money. For money there is."

"If you'd told me what you wanted, and why you wanted it, I might have found more. All you said was, 'Find out where she lives.' Well, I have found out, and a potboy who told me nearly bit my head off for asking about her."

"What is she, then?"

"Well, I think she's one of them which go about with Bibles, and fake up excuses for making the people virtuous. There's no end to their dodges. They're getting as artful as you and me pretty well. One of 'em collects rents in a court close by here. It's an Irish court, too. But, bless you, she ain't afraid, and they won't harm her. Well, I s'pose that young lady is up to some game of that sort, daddy. And what game you are up to with her I should like to know."

Mr. Carey shook his head. He was conscious of so heartfelt a dislike to all forms of religion, virtue, or morality, that he thought it must have been transmitted to his descendants. Besides, a woman to do this must be a lady to begin with, and his daughter Marla was only the daughter of a washerwoman. I am sorry to say that he placed a bad construction on the matter, and concluded that she was engaged, for purposes of her own, in some genteel game which might be spoiled by the discovery of her father's profession, and of his return to its active exercise. "But," he murmured, "I'll have that hundred pound yet."

Chapter xxi

A Friendly Father

For a whole fortnight Mr. Carey refrained from molesting either of his children, graciously consenting to receive twenty shillings a week from one and thirty shillings from the other. The reason for this modest retirement and simple content was simply that as yet he had made few friends—it takes time for a professional gentleman of distinction to find out congenial spirits of his own lofty level—and therefore he had met with no temptation for the display of that hospitality which formerly was one of his most delightful qualities. Besides, he had not yet overcome the strangeness of the world, which had changed a good deal during his twenty years of seclusion, even to the language of the fraternity, and this, I understand, undergoes a complete change in twenty years. Book language lasts, it is true, but the slang of rogues, like the dialect of a savage tribe, is always changing from generation to generation. Mr. Carey found that the old patter, that spoken by himself in the early sixties, was unknown, and even provoked laughter among the new generation; and it distressed him that he was completely ignorant of the new idioms, and was slow to understand the back slang, the rhyming slang, and the so-called theatrical slang which are now current in thieves' land. Consequently he sat apart and stayed his soul with flagons, tobacco, and books. Fifty shillings a week was enough for his simple wants. Therefore it was in pure devilry and with the deliberate intention of vexing and shaming his son Claude that he paid a second visit to the Temple. The door was shut; nevertheless, Mr. Carey opened it with the help of a simple instrument which he always carried about him. When Claude returned about midnight he heard, while yet upon the stairs, the scraping, not unskilful, of a fiddle. Such a sound is strange in King's Bench Walk. Outside the door he recognised that the fiddle was being played in his own chambers, and on opening the door he discovered that his father was the musician. He was sitting in a chair playing merrily; in his mouth was a short pipe, a bottle of wine, half finished, and a glass stood on the table.

"Glad to see me, Claude?" he asked, nodding and grinning. "I thought you would be, so I came round. It's a goodish step from Whitechapel, isn't it? I told you I should step in sometimes. Well, you were out, so I let myself in. It's not a bit of good locking a door to keep me out, bless you. Lord, there isn't a lock in the whole country that will keep me out, and so, my son, I've been making myself comfortable."

Claude groaned, and his father, with a smile of satisfaction and a brightened eye, for the sight of his son's disgust and humiliation affected him with a singular joy, went on with his conversation, which was a monologue.

"I picked up this fiddle on my way—bought it in Houndsditch for a sov,[1] which you'll have to hand over, my dear boy. Have you got the money about you or shall I put one of these pretty mugs up the spout? I suppose they're real silver. Thank you! It is a very good fiddle for the money, but my hand is a little out. There's no fiddling allowed in the jug. I'll play you something Claude." He played correctly, and with some feeling and an old-fashioned lingering among the notes, as if he loved them every one, Balfe's air "Then you'll remember me."[2] After this he played "My pretty Jane," and "Tom Bowling."[3]

"There, boy," he said, laying down the fiddle, "can you do that? Not you. Can you take the fiddle, and play a hornpipe, and make the boys dance whether they want to or not, and draw their hearts out of the women, and the tears from their eyes? That's what I could do when I was a young man. As for the girls, a man who can fiddle like me can do what he likes. Ah, Lord! To think of the old days! Can you do it? Not you. What can you do? How do you live, I say? What is your lay, now? Where do you find the money for all this?"

Claude made no reply.

Then the man filled and lit his pipe, and drank two more glasses of wine. It was Burgundy, and he seemed to appreciate it. But the wine did not warm his heart apparently, for his eyes had a devilish look in them as they fell upon Claude's face—the look of one who considers evil day and night—the look of one who took pleasure in contemplating his victim's shame, and revenged himself at the same time for the loathing of his own presence. He already hated his son, who showed so clearly the humiliation caused by his return, and yet bore with him, and did not, as he might have done, shove him violently down the stairs. He hated him, and he rejoiced in his power of humiliating and disgusting him more and more.

"Look ye, Claude," he said, with a full, round, and sonorous oath; "you may keep your trade to yourself, if you please; you're afraid of my getting a hand in it, I suppose. But you won't keep your old father out of your rooms; I shall come here for company and for drink—I shall come here whenever I choose. It's rather lonely where I have got my pitch, and they're a low lot about now, compared with the old pals, and there's not many of the new men that I care to know. Why, there was a man last night pretended never to have heard of the great Jem Carey. The profession has gone down: it's gone very low indeed. Any man calls himself a burglar when he's once learned to crack a crib, and to carry a revolver in case he's heard upon the stairs. As if I ever wanted pistols!—as if I was ever heard!—as if anybody ever heard or caught me in a house! Ah! Claude, it was a great misfortune for you when your father was lagged. You'll never understand with them prejudices of yours what a misfortune it was. You've got a quick eye, and a light tread, and clean fingers. You would have equalled your father almost; you couldn't surpass him. And I'd always made up my mind what to do with you. And now it's

1 Sovereign (a gold coin worth one pound).

2 Michael William Balfe (15 May 1808–20 October 1870), an Irish composer.

3 The first is an eighteenth-century song by English composer Charles Dibdin (c. 4 March 1745–25 July 1814). The second is an early nineteenth-century song by librettist Edward Fitzball (1792–27 October 1873) and composer Henry Rowley Bishop (18 November 1786–30 April 1855).

come to this—a black coat and a tall hat—talk like a swell—lodgins among the lawyers—actually among the lawyers—my own son—Jem Carey's son—among the lawyers!—and something genteel in the book-making line. Well, as I was saying—this bottle's 'most empty; go and get me another. It's cool stuff, and carries a man along better than brandy. As I was saying, the profession is clean ruined by revolvers; it's getting low; there's no pride in a neat job. But there, nothing good ever came from America yet. I am getting old now, and I doubt if I shall ever do much more, my boy; but it's heart-breaking to find yourself forgotten after all that's been done. As for work, why should I work anymore, when I've a beautiful, dutiful, affectionate son to keep me, not to speak of a wife and two daughters, and two other sons, every one of whom deserves nothing so much as to welcome back the fond father they have lost. He is a ticket-o'-leave man; he is repentant, and is open to the tender influences of awakening grace, and understands at last the Christian virtues and has cast off the works of darkness. The good chaplain says so, and the chaplain ought to know, because he's always converting such a lot of wicked sinners, and a giving of 'em the best of characters. It's a contrite spirit—oh!—and a broken heart!"

"For heaven's sake," said Claude, "it is past midnight, drink what you want and go."

"I shall go when I please. Now, about this family of mine. Thirty bob[4] isn't enough, my son!"

"I shall give you no more."

"Very well, then, I shall think about trying the rest of them. Perhaps altogether they would make it forty. As for the girl who lives in Ivy Lane, Hoxton"—Claude started—"dressed like a lady, though where she gets her money from is what I do not yet know—"

"Who told you about her?"

"Never you mind. Who told me about you, and about your mother, and about Sam and Joe? I know all about the family; there's Joe—he isn't worth calling on, because he's only a working-man with a family of eight. Sam, again, he's only a poor miserable schoolmaster." (It must be remembered that Mr. Carey went into his hermitage before the passing of the Elementary Education Act, and, therefore, did not appreciate the present position of the schoolmaster.) "He's got the parson over his head to bully him, and make him go to church and look humble. He's got nothing but his miserable salary. There's no use in worrying Sam. And your mother's in an almshouse and blind. If I go to see her perhaps they'll send her away out of the place, 'cos she isn't a widow, and make me keep her. I don't want to keep her. And there's the other girl—Melenda—and as yet I don't know where Melenda is. So you see, Claude, there's only you and your sister Marla. One of you two I must see sometimes, and I shall. Which shall it be? All I ask, Claude, is—which shall it be—you or her? Come, now."

"If you thrust yourself on her"—it was clearly Valentine of whom his father spoke—"I swear that I will stop my money altogether, and you can do what you please."

"Don't you think it just possible, my dear son, that your sister Marla has got friends who would rather not know about her father? Don't you think she would come down as handsome as you've done—you and your thirty bob!—just to keep these friends from knowing? Therefore, Claude, which of them is it to be?"

"It seems as if I can't keep you out of my chambers if I tried."

"No, my boy—you can't. Take your oath of that." He took his two or three times over, with a glass of Burgundy to each, just by way of setting an example.

4 Thirty shillings.

"But if you force yourself on Val—on your daughter, I shall do my very best to dissuade her from giving you anything."

"Thank ye. You're a dutiful boy, ain't you? And suppose I force myself upon both of you?"

Claude made no reply at all.

"Eh!" he repeated; "suppose I force myself upon both of you?"

"Then," Claude replied, "there will be only one thing for us to do. My sisters and I will all go away—out of the country—somewhere—anywhere, out of your reach. Sam and Joe shall have the task of protecting my mother. You may be very certain," he added grimly, "of the reception you will get from both Joe and Sam."

"Nice boys, both," said their father. "They won't turn up their noses as if they were gentlemen. A pretty kind of flash gentleman you are!"

"Very nice boys they will be," said Claude, "when they hear who you are and what you want. They will astonish you by their nice behaviour. I fancy I see Sam before he flings you into the gutter for pretending to be his father, the honest locksmith. Why! we might all pretend that you are an impostor. I wish I had begun that way!"

"No, you don't, Claude." But he looked uneasy. Suppose these sons of his should all pretend not to believe in him, there might be considerable trouble and difficulty before him. "Don't think of that."

"Yes, I wish I could see Sam's face when you go to him. Go to him, by all means. Or go to Joe, and then you will find out how dutiful your sons can be, and how deeply your eldest son respects and loves your memory."

"You can talk, young 'un, if you can do nothing else. So can I. Never mind Sam and Joe; you and me will do. I will stick to you, my boy—"

"As the leprosy stuck to Naaman—"

"Quite right, Claude—always quote the scriptures. Didn't Joe never tell you about me? Joe was—how old was Joe when I was last lagged? He was sixteen. Oh! Joe knows all about it. I saw him in court when I was tried. It was a beautiful trial, and it would have done your heart good to hear how my counsel bowled 'em down, one after the other. At one time I thought I should have got off altogether. But it wasn't to be. There was a providence in it, as our chaplain said. It brought me to a knowledge of the truth. Be not, then, ashamed of me, a prisoner!" The man displayed a horrid aptitude in quoting the Book most read in prison. He took the more pleasure in it because it caused such peculiar pain and disgust to his son. For this reason the historian passes over most of these flowers of speech.

"Joe," said Claude, "thought so highly of your profession and your career that he concealed everything from us, and bade us, on the other hand, be proud of our dead father—he said you were dead, because he wished and hoped that you were dead. We were to be proud of our father, on account of his character for honesty and straightforwardness. His character! Good heavens!"

Mr. Carey laughed; but his eyes looked more wicked.

"That was not well done of Joe. When I quarrel with you, Claude, I shall pay Joe out for that. I shall go to Joe's house and introduce myself to his wife and children and shall tell them the whole story. It will please Joe when he comes home in the evening, won't it?"

Claude said nothing.

"And it will please you, my son, when I tell you that I have already begun practice again. Yes, in a small way—not in a low and mean way, mind you, but in a small way only. I knock at the front door and tell the maid that the back bedroom is afire. She rushes upstairs, and I then step in and help myself. Twice today I did that trick."

"Oh!"

"Then I got a book and a pencil, and I pretended to be the gas company's man, and went downstairs to examine the meter."

"For heaven's sake, stop!"

"These rooms would make a beautiful fence. I'll bring the things here, Claude."

"You shall not." Claude's eyes showed this man that he had gone too far. He laughed, and took some more drink.

"You're capital company, Claude, if you'd drink more. That's the pity of it, you can't drink. Sit down, my boy, and let us drink together."

"Drink together?"

"If you won't drink then, and if you won't smoke, you'll just have to listen."

This ghastly night wore itself out at last. The man drank, smoked, and talked. He talked with extraordinary volubility. He seemed perfectly careless whether Claude were listening or not. It was sufficient for him that he was awake. He talked, with deliberate design, on all those topics which he knew would most humiliate his son; of his crimes, bold and successful; of the changes and chances of his profession which were constantly landing him in prison; of his last burglary, when he made a splendidly daring attempt at a great lady's jewels, and would have got them had it not been for a lout of a country policeman, who accidentally stopped him, and whom he very nearly killed in the fight which followed; of his trial for burglary and violence and his long sentence; of his prison life, and his dodges with the doctor and the chaplain.

Claude stood on the hearthrug, without replying. The man talked on for several hours, during which Claude endured an agony. The clock struck four. Then the man rose slowly. The drink he had consumed seemed to have made no impression whatever upon him; he was not "disguised," his speech was clear, his bearing steady. But he looked more wicked, as if the wine had brought out upon his forehead with greater clearness the Name of the Beast or the Number of his Name.[5]

"I shall go to sleep," he said. "You are capital company, Claude, my dear boy. I knew you would be. I shall come very often." The bedroom door was open. He stepped inside, threw himself upon the bed, without any preliminary undressing, and fell asleep in a moment.

Claude sat down with a sigh of relief. But he was too tired for any further load of shame, and he fell asleep in the chair.

When he awoke it was nine o'clock, and his laundress was in the room. He remembered his guest of the night, and hastened to look into the bedroom. But the man was gone. He had taken his fiddle with him.

* * *

"Valentine," said Claude, later in the day, "I have something to tell you."

---

5 In many denominations of Christianity, the end of the mortal world will be marked by the return of Satan, whose name, mark, or number will be written on his forehead. Satan's followers are also thought to be similarly marked.

"You have had something to tell me for the last fortnight. Are you going to tell it now? What is it, Claude?" She laid her hand on his arm, and looked into his face with the sisterly affection which was not counterfeited. "Do you think we do not take notice when you look ill and worried? What is it, Claude?"

"Have I looked worried?"

"You poor boy! There has been a line an inch deep across your forehead, and your eyes have had a distressed look, as if there was something you could not understand."

"I don't understand it, Valentine. It is a part of the mystery of evil. But you—are you worried, too? Life here is too much for you. I wish to heaven the middle of October was come."

"I am always troubled about the girls," she replied, mendaciously. "But I am very well. Tell me something of your own trouble."

"I cannot, Valentine. Someday, perhaps, but not yet. I am a coward, and I am afraid to tell you. What I have to say now is, that certain things have come to my knowledge within the last week or two, which have made me realise, in quite a new sense, how I belong to the very lowest of the people."

"Why, Claude, you have found some mare's nest!"[6] She laughed, but she felt uneasy. Could he have learned the truth? "You have discovered, perhaps, that you have cousins very poor. What does that matter?"

"It is not their poverty"—and then she knew that he must have learned the story of his father's life. Who could have told him? Not the old lady! Was it Joe? Why had Joe told him?

"It is not their poverty, Valentine. I have only just learned from what dregs—from what unspeakable depths—I have been rescued—all of us have been rescued—you with us, if you were Polly."

"Oh, Claude, do not talk like that! Dregs—depths—why these things are beneath your feet! What can it matter, now, what your relations were? You cannot be ashamed of what they are!"

"No; but of what some of them were. Would it not matter if some of them were criminals, Valentine?"

"No, Claude," she replied stoutly, "not even then!"

"Nay," said Claude sadly, "it would matter a great deal. Such a thing as that would lay upon me a new obligation. I should have to atone and to make such reparation as may be in my power. You asked me once if I was ready to give all my life, if it were called for, to the work we have attempted. Why, Valentine, *it is called for*! The old life—the life I used to long for—the life of honourable work and distinction—I need make no further question about giving it up; it has already become impossible for me. It is not any longer a question of choice. Do not ask me why; but I can never again even sit down with the men who have been my friends. I must leave the Temple. I shall come to live here. Oh! I will hide nothing! If people say, 'There goes the son of a—of a—d'"

"Of a locksmith, Claude," Valentine interrupted quickly; "remember what Joe told you. Remember what Sam and Melenda believe. Think, if not of yourself, of Violet and of me."

She knew now—she was quite certain—that, in some way or other, Claude had discovered something, if not all, of the truth.

"I do think of Violet and of you," he replied; "heaven knows that. If it were only myself concerned, I could bear it lightly. But suppose Violet should find it out? And how am I to keep the truth from her?"

"I believe," said Valentine, wise with the wisdom of books, "that nothing is ever so bad as it seems to the imagination beforehand. Therefore, I daresay Violet and I will be able to bear it, whatever it is. Women are really much stronger than men, in many ways, though you are so conceited over your superior intelligence!"

6 A fanciful illusion, something that does not exist, or a more general misconception.

"You do not ask me what it is that I would conceal."

"No; I am contented to wait. Meantime, Claude, conceal nothing if you please. I do not ask you to conceal things; but parade nothing. My poor boy! Yet, if this trouble should give us a stronger champion, we ought to be glad that it has come upon us. Clear up that clouded brow, Claude. Let us see the old light in your eyes."

Chapter xxii

The Doctor Speaks

The doctor is in love with you."

This information was conveyed by no higher an authority than the ragged old man below; but it is information of a kind which is not readily forgotten, even though—as the newspapers in the last century used to say of the King of Sweden's movements—it wants confirmation. It is of the kind which makes a girl pensive. Whatever the answer she intends to give when the question shall be put to her, the knowledge that it will be put, and probably very soon, greatly raises the aspirant in the young lady's esteem. It makes him interesting; it also makes her expectant and watchful.

Valentine remarked, first of all, that the doctor attended his patient with a regularity amounting to zeal; this in itself could not fairly be considered a symptom. But he stayed longer than was necessary, and he always made his visit the occasion of conversation with herself. This, again, taken by itself, is not a symptom, because Valentine was the only young lady living within the boundaries of the doctor's round; in fact the only lady he had ever known in all his life, and she was without doubt a very pleasing young lady, and it was natural that he should like to talk to her: one would not wish to draw conclusions of love from mere attraction. Presently, however, she became aware of a change in his talk; he began to speak of himself. Now this, as everybody knows, is an infallible symptom; he told her of his own position, his prospects, his history, and his opinions. He wanted, quite naturally, because he was so much interested in her, to interest her in himself. So far he succeeded, because he really was an interesting man. None of the physicians in the West End whom she had met were at all like this young physician of Hoxton.

"Of course," he said, one day, "I don't pretend to be a gentleman; don't think that—I've got nothing to do with gentility, and I don't know the manners of society. I am just a Mile Ender—the old man keeps a shop there, and I could have become his partner if I had chosen, with a tidy income and a nice smug, comfortable life—chapel twice on Sunday, and a hot supper on a Saturday night, and all—"

"What a pity to have missed the hot suppers!"

"Yes; it's cold supper with me, every day of the week."

"Why did you give up the shop?"

"When I was a boy, I unluckily got hold of some scientific books, and I began to read them. Nothing seemed worth looking at after that, except science. I was lost to trade from that day."

"And so you became a doctor?"

"Member of the Royal College of Surgeons, doctor of medicine in the University of London, general practitioner in this genteel neighbourhood. This is the end of my scientific ambitions. London Hospital is not so very far from Mile End, and it seemed to me as if the only way into the scientific life was through the hospital. A good many scientific men have begun that way, so why not I? I had never heard of the scientific schools or of university and King's and South Kensington, you see, and the old man had never heard of them either. So I became a medico. Well, I've got the scientific life I asked for—medicine is called scientific, I suppose—and it isn't exactly the kind of life I fancied, which is always the way. You ask the Fates for what you want, and you get it; they give it to you, and then it doesn't turn out what you thought it was going to be."

"But you've got the most beautiful, the most unselfish life in the world!"

"Have I? Ho!" he grunted in derision.

"The most beautiful and the best; you are everybody's friend; you go about carrying health and recovery in your hands."

"Well, my hands are certainly occupied a good deal in making pills and compounding draughts, and there's only a measly boy, besides, to help carry those pills and bottles. So I suppose you're right. If I'd stuck to the shop I should have been measuring yards of stuff on the counter. Making pills or measuring calico, it doesn't seem much of a choice to offer a man. But the calico for money."

"Money!" This girl, who had so much, naturally held money in the deepest contempt. "Money! what does such a man as you want with money? What would you do with money? Money cannot advance science."

"There is a sense of freedom without money, isn't there? A man with empty pockets isn't tempted to buy things, and doesn't nourish extravagant desires, and can't give anything to anybody."

"The work you do for them actually doesn't want money."

"There you go," replied the doctor. "For them! Hang it, can't a man be allowed to do something for himself? Here I am, with the wages of a mechanic, doing twice a mechanic's work! I used to be ashamed, at first, of taking their half-crowns from the poor devils—I beg your pardon—from the others, and where is the life of science I longed for?"

"Why, you have it—you must be learning something new every day!"

"Oh! the action of drugs and the symptoms of disease—yes, to be sure, whatever advances man's knowledge is good, I know," he went on impatiently; "of course even this is better than standing behind a counter with a yard measure and pair of scissors. But I wanted to advance knowledge—not my own, but the world's. I had ambitions—but you don't know; women never understand."

"We sometimes understand a little," she replied, humbly.

"See here." He pointed to the sick girl, who lay with closed eyes, as if she was asleep. "This is the great mystery which men are always searching after, and have never found. I wanted to be one of those who search. Some day it will be discovered, and then we shall be like the immortal gods. Meantime, what are we? One after the other, for all of us in turn, the steady flame begins one day to dwindle; then it burns low; sometimes it goes on flickering for a long time. Then it goes out. Birth, growth, decay and death. Why? We cannot tell. We are surrounded by a great black cloud, which we keep pushing back farther and farther; and it is always rolling in again. Whether it is close around us, or whether it is pushed far away, we never succeed in getting through it or looking over it. And beyond it—silence! The generations pass away, and one after the other, we all ask the same questions, and have to lie down unanswered."

"What is the use of asking questions which cannot be answered?"

"The use! The use! There's all the use, not for asking but for looking. Those who keep on searching find at last. All the secret mysteries of life will be found out, sometime or other: and yet you think I ought to be satisfied with such work as this, while others are able to search." He put on his hat and went away, without the usual ceremony of leave-taking. He was a very rude and unpolished person; but somehow he was in earnest. Any man in earnest is always sure of forgiveness, whatever his social sins may be.

"I've been thinking," he said, a day or two later, "about your notions of an unselfish life. I can't feel any reality about it. A man must work, but he ought to choose his own work. And every man must work for himself. Would you have a man really satisfied with being a general practitioner in Hoxton?"

"If there is no choice, isn't it wisest to find out all that there is in his manner of life that is noble and generous, and so be contented with it?"

"I don't want nobility and generosity. I am a selfish creature; every man is, whatever you may pretend. Very well then. I want everything that I can't get—leisure, books, instruments, money to work with. What do I care about other people? If I cared about other people I should be contented, and then my life would be just a selfish indulgence. Let me have all I want for myself first. I will think about other people afterwards."

"As it is, you can't have what you want, and therefore you have made the best of it, and begun to think of other people first."

"Then, suppose I wanted"—he rested his chin in the palm of his left hand and his left elbow on his left knee, with his left leg crossed over the right—it is a meditative attitude—and he looked thoughtfully in her face. "Suppose I wanted to make love?[1] Life is an incomplete kind of thing without it. Incomplete with it, for that matter; but still—"

"You said the other day that men and women cheat themselves with the unreal sentiment that they call love."

"So I did. But sentiment may have its value."

"And you said that man's love was another name for his desire to obtain a slave."

"So it is. But there might be women for whom one would reverse the situation."

"And you despise women."

"That is true, in a way—perhaps a little more than one despises men. So would you if you were a G.P. But there are women one cannot despise. With these a man would willingly exchange the illusions of love."

"Be patient, doctor; perhaps your day will come. Meantime, though you are such a selfish creature, you do a good deal for these poor people, to gratify your own selfishness, no doubt."

"In the way of business. I take their half-crowns all the while."

"Yes, I know how much you will get from the poor woman you sat up with this morning until four."

1 To woo or to court.

"Way of business," he repeated. "I wonder who serves out the lives; I suppose they are served out by someone. So many hundreds told off for general practitioners; so many for starving needlewomen; so many for drunken husbands. One, just one, for Miss Valentine Eldridge."

There was certainly very little reason why this young doctor should look cheerfully on life. His practice was larger than is comfortable; and the larger it grew the poorer he became, which is a truly wonderful result of success. He was paid in shillings and half-crowns; he lived in a small house, with an old woman to look after him, and she looked after him badly. He made up his own medicines and dispensed them with the aid of a boy; he walked about the streets all day and sometimes all night; he made his meals and took his rest when he could; he had no time for reading, and his thirst for knowledge was very great. Tantalus[2] was, I believe, a young and very successful general practitioner in a poor neighbourhood, who ardently desired leisure for study and research.

He had no society; and the assistant priest of St. Agatha—Mr. Randal Smith—was his only friend, and they quarrelled every time they met.

"Smith," he said one evening when he found time for a pipe and a glass of beer (of course Mr. Smith didn't smoke, and sported a blue ribbon as proudly as if it had been the Order of the Garter)—"Smith, did you ever turn your attention seriously to the question of love?"

Mr. Randal Smith's pale face flushed. "My work," he said, proudly, "compels the celibate life."

"Don't talk more ecclesiastically than you can help. Mine compels the celibate life as well, because the income isn't more than enough for one! But I don't brag about it. Why can't a man go on through life without falling in love? Why does he ever want to hamper himself with a woman? She doesn't probably know anything; she doesn't care for the things he cares about. Very likely she's a fool! He can never be so free when he is married as when he was unmarried."

"Perhaps," said the assistant priest, "she has qualities which he desires to possess."

"You don't fall in love with a pretty face—at least, only a fool does that—nor yet with a pretty figure. I'm an anatomist, and I know all about the pretty figure. It's a fine piece of machinery, I confess; but it is a great deal too delicate for the work we expect of it, and it is always getting out of order. You can't fall in love with a machine, or with the case they've made for it."

"No"—Mr. Randal Smith saw his chance to make a point—"you fall in love with the soul."

"Ah! that's your department. I never saw a soul in the dissecting-room; never heard of anybody who did. All I know is, that there are no diseases in my knowledge which are caused by the soul, so that it can't form part of the body!"

"It doesn't," the other man replied, still getting the best of it. "That is why you fall in love with it."

Whatever it was that the doctor loved, it was called Valentine, and it had a very charming face, with eyes which spoke all kinds of possible things, and especially a most beautiful sympathy, so that this young doctor felt that he could talk about himself and his own thoughts all day long with her, and that neither of them would get tired. He, at least, would not. Men vary in their expressions of love; but a strong and masterful nature generally takes this form and demands perfect sympathy from the object of its passion. So that the

2 A figure in Greek mythology condemned to stand for eternity in a pool of water over which were tree branches with low-hanging fruit that were just out of his reach.

doctor was partly right in calling love the desire to get a slave for oneself. The thing called Valentine with which he was in love, also had a pretty figure, a graceful manner, and a highly pleasing voice.

He spoke at last. It was in the beginning of October, a week before her furlough was to expire.

"You are actually going away in a week?" he asked.

"Yes; for a little while. You will come every day to look after Lotty while I am away, will you not?"

"I will do what I can for her—or for you. Before you go"—it was in Valentine's room, but they had got into the habit of talking freely before Lotty, who seemed to take no notice of what was said by these two—"before you go, I should like you to know—just for the sake of knowing—not that it will do any good, but still you ought to be told—that there are two men in love with you."

"Oh! Why should you tell me that?" she answered, with a natural blush.

"They are not much to boast of—only Hoxton men; but still—men."

"Don't go on, doctor."

"I must now. One of them is Randal Smith. He confessed it last night when I taxed him with it, after beating about the bush awhile. He's been in love with you, he says, for a long time. Of course, he can't look at things straight, and he pretends that it's out of gratitude to you for singing and talking with his blessed boys—the humbug! But he won't tell you, because he's got to be a celibate for the good of the Church—ho! ho!—and because you won't submit to discipline! That's what he calls confession, and penance, and Lent."

"Poor Mr. Smith! I shall always think the better of myself, because there never was a more unselfish man, I believe."

"As for the other man—will you guess who that other man is?"

She met his eyes with perfect frankness and without a blush.

"Do you mean—yourself?"

"Yes, I do. I don't at all understand why, but it is so."

"It is a part of the general pretence and unreality of life, perhaps."

"No, it is as real as—as neuralgia,[3] and as difficult to shake off. I don't know who you are, but I know what you are. Smith doesn't want an answer. Have you, by any chance, got one for me?"

"Only, that a woman ought to be proud, to think that two such men like her. Will you go on liking me, both of you?" She offered him her hand, but he did not take it.

"I said love, not like," he replied, grimly. "Well, you've said what I knew you would say, only you've said it more kindly than I expected—or deserved, perhaps. Yet, I don't know. If a man loves a woman he can but tell her so, even if she's a royal princess. That'll do." He rose and stooped over Lotty on the bed.

"Feel easier this morning, don't you? That's right. Had a good night? Pretty good. Don't talk much. Let Melenda come and talk to you, but don't you talk. Very well; now keep quiet. We shall soon be—quite well."

"Doctor!" It was Valentine, as Lotty closed her eyes again and lay as if she was asleep.

"Quite well," he repeated, with a kind of defiance. "Asleep and well. What could be better for her, or for any of them, come to that, poor things!"

The tears came to her eyes, but she said nothing.

"Her sorrows will soon come to an end. You have made her happy, in spite of them. Now I'll go. Forgive me."

---

3 A sharp pain caused by nerve damage.

"There is nothing to forgive, believe me."

"I was bound to tell you, once, before you went away. I shall never speak of it again—you know it, and that is enough."

He looked in her face once more, from under his shaggy eyebrows, and pressed her hand. Then, as he left her and went his way, at the bottom of the stairs he tumbled over a couple of cats which were sleeping on the lowest step in the sun. I am sorry to say that he swore at those cats aloud. I have said that he was a rough and a rude young man. When he cursed those cats, he cursed his own fortune as well. Valentine heard the words and forgave them, understanding the cause. As for the cats, they knew the doctor very well, and retired with precipitation and wonder, asking each other what in the world could be the matter with a man whom they had known and respected since kittendom, as a constant and tried friend of cats. There are a great many cats about Ivy Lane—cats have taken the place formerly occupied by oyster-shells in poor neighbourhoods—but the doctor had never before kicked a single one of them. Therefore they were naturally hurt and surprised. One more illusion gone.

"Valentine," Lotty whispered, "you are going away in a few days. I heard all that you said."

"Yes, dear, but only for a day or two. I shall come back. Do not be afraid."

"The doctor loves you. Everybody loves you, except Melenda. And I shall soon be quite well. Oh, I know now what he means. I understand things much better now than I did before you came. Oh! before you came. If I could but see Tilly once more before I am quite well—and asleep."

"Lotty—Lotty—my poor child."

"Don't cry, Valentine. Perhaps Melenda will give in when I am—asleep and well—because we have been such friends, her and me. And you've been so good to me. You'll be patient with Melenda, won't you?"

Chapter XXIII

How Melenda Was Drilled

When Melenda carried back the bundle of finished work to the shop she generally returned with the money and another bundle, if work was abundant and she was lucky, by noon, or one o'clock at latest. On this occasion, which was a certain morning towards the end of September, she did not return at the usual time, nor did she indeed come back until past seven o'clock in the evening, when she appeared at Valentine's door with empty hands.

"They've drilled me," she said, with a catching in her breath. "They've drilled me all day long."

"Oh! Melenda!" It was a bad day with Lotty, and she was reduced to a whisper. "Oh, Melenda!"

"And they haven't finished yet. Don't tell Liz, but it was all along of her button-holes. She's got dreadful careless lately."

"What is drilling?" asked Valentine. "Melenda, you look frightfully pale."

Melenda was a brave girl, and strong, but the day's work, whatever it was, had been too much for her; and now she sank into a chair and threw her hat upon the floor. Her cheeks were white, but her eyes were hot and angry.

"I'm tired, that's all. So would you be; and I'm hungry, too. No, I won't have anything out of your cupboard. There's some cold tea and some bread and butter in the other room."

Valentine brought them to her; it was the first time that Melenda had accepted any service from her. But in taking the food from Valentine's hands she preserved her independence because it was her own bread and butter.

"What is drilling?" asked Valentine again.

"Last time they drilled her," whispered Lotty, "she went off directly she came home, and we had dreadful trouble to bring her round. Don't go off, Melenda dear."

"I ain't going off; I'm better now. Don't tell Liz it was her fault."

The trouble came upon Melenda through Lizzie's *laches*,[1] not her own. It is not everybody that can bear a glimpse of the better life. That which poor Lizzie got caused her the most poignant envy and discontent. Very soon Valentine would go away and leave them. Then the bread for dinner would reappear, and the dainty meals which Valentine had given her would be a memory of the past to embitter the present, and the stockings and shoes and "things" with which Valentine had replenished her scanty wardrobe would wear out, and there would be no money to get any more. Let us do the child justice; she thought, too, how the cheerful face, the kindly voice, the evening song, the lips that never uttered a harsh word, would go too, and the lodgings return to their former condition when they were all comparatively satisfied, because they knew no better. "This is the way," she said to herself, "that ladies live at home, and this is the way we live," and always in her ear the voice whispering, "Come with me, and you shall live like a lady." The good food which Valentine provided her, the comparative ease—because now that Lotty was off their hands they were able to get along with less work—the better clothes that she wore, the greater attention which she paid to Valentine's example, and therefore to neatness and cleanliness, had made poor Lizzie by this time a really pretty girl. When Valentine came she was a girl with possibilities; now she was a girl with realities; her figure filled out and rounded, her cheek fuller and of a healthier hue—her eyes brighter. She represented, in fact, like any other animal, the advantages which result from good and regular feeding.

But these things made her, as well, careless in her work, and Melenda was drilled, therefore.

"But what is drilling?" Valentine repeated.

"I got there," said Melenda, eating her bread and butter ravenously, "at half-past nine this morning. I thought I'd be in good time. So I was. The clerk—it's the fat-faced one with the whiskers—he took my work and passed it in. Presently, he calls me and he says, 'You stand there,' he says. 'They'll send down your money and your work presently,' sezee.[2] Then he grinned, and the other girls who were standing about the shop for their turn, they looked at each other, and they whispered, 'You poor thing! He's going to drill you.' Of course I knew that. And so he did."

"Oh!"

"Drilled you?"asked Valentine, for the fourth time.

"Now I'm better," said Melenda, finishing her bread and butter. "Coming home, Lotty, I thought I should ha' dropped."

"But tell me what they've done."

"Lord! you don't know anything, and you've been here nearly three months. You're real ignorant, Valentine." Melenda, in her own opinion, knew everything. "It's like this, you know. If the work isn't so good as it ought to be, they just drill us. Well, we can't help it. A girl hasn't got any rights, Sam says, because she can't fight for herself, and nobody cares to fight for us. The men they stand up for the men, and the women stand up for the men, but they don't care for other women. Sam says so. As for the ladies, what odds is it to them if we are all drilled to death?"

"But what is it?" Valentine asked; "how do they do it?"

"They don't do anything. They just tell you to stand and wait, and they keep you waiting. If you go out, you're told when you come back that the work's come down and been given to another girl. You've just got to

1 French for *slackness* or *negligence*.

2 A misspelling of *says he*, used to represent the mispronunciation of the phrase.

wait for your money and for the new work as long as they choose to keep you. Sometimes they've drilled a woman for five or six days, and her with babies at home crying for their food. What do they care?"

"Oh! but it is impossible. Have you been kept standing all day long? Actually standing all day? And without food? Have you had nothing to eat?"

"Not likely," said Melenda; "neither dinner nor tea."

"Melenda," said Valentine, "you must let someone help you. Oh! my dear, it is a shame! It is horrible."

"I won't, then," Melenda cried fiercely. "I said I wouldn't, and I won't. I've always been independent, and I always will be." It was her formula of consolation, and though it was no more than a fetish,[3] it never failed.

"Independent! Oh, Melenda—what independence!"

In the morning Melenda went again to get her money and her work. Again the clerk ordered her to stand aside and wait. She was to be drilled a second day, a punishment which marked the gravity of her offence.

Melenda obeyed with an angry spot in either cheek. Some of the women about the place whispered to her that it was a shame. It was all that the women could do. "It is a shame," they whispered low, so that the men should not hear. The whole history of woman seems somehow contained and summed up in those four short words, "It is a shame."

If you think of it, the chivalrous sentiment and the Christian sentiment and the humanitarian sentiment, all combined, have done but little as yet to remove the truth and force of those four little words. Everywhere the woman gets the worst of it. She is the hardest worked, and has to do all the nastiest kinds of work; she is the worst paid; she is always bullied, scolded, threatened, nagged, and sworn at: she has the worst food; she has the lion's share of the trouble and the lamb's share of the pleasure; she has no holidays; she has the fewest amusements. Even in those circles where women do not work and are never kicked, she has the worst of it. Beautiful things have been written about womanhood, damsels, and gracious ladies. Girls do, in fact, enjoy a brief reign while they are wooed and not yet won. And after that the men take for themselves everything that is worth having, save only in those well-appointed and desirable establishments where there is enough to go round for man and wife too. But for the great broad lower stratum of the social pyramid, there is but one sentence that will express the truth. You will hear it from the lips of women and girls wherever working-women and girls meet together; on the pavement and outside the shops it is cried aloud; in the shops and work-rooms it is only whispered; one short sentence, in four short words, "It is a shame."

All day long to stand and wait. It seems a cruel thing. And very likely at home the children crying for their bread, or sitting empty and hungry at school, while the figures swim and reel upon the blackboard, and the teachers wonder how children can be expected to learn when they have had no breakfast and no dinner. To be made to stand and wait from half-past nine in the morning until seven in the evening. And women, my Christian brothers, are not really so strong as men, though we treat them as if they were capable of far more endurance than we ourselves ever give to our own work. It seems cruel; but then, consider, drilling is punishment. There must be punishment. And the very nature and essence of punishment is that it is unpleasant. In the good old slavery times women were tied up to the post and lashed, which hurt them a good deal, and even inflicted deep flesh wounds and caused indelible scars. But these heal up; the pain of being drilled for three or four days in succession is certainly a great deal worse than the pain of being lashed for three or four

3 A fetish is an object that one believes to be endowed with mystical properties and thus, by extension, anything that is irrationally venerated.

minutes, and the injuries it inflicts on a girl are not skin and flesh injuries and do not heal up, nor can they be forgotten in a day or two. Quite the contrary; these injuries last a whole lifetime, and sometimes lap over to the next generation. There must, however, be punishments in every trade; how else are you to get work done properly? You cannot fine a woman whom you have already engaged according to the strictest principles of sound political economy on the Law of Elevenpence Ha'penny; you are not allowed by foolish modern laws to flog her, not even to correct her with a cane, nor to box her ears, nor to kick her; it is no use turning her off, because the next girl will be no better; you may not put her in the stocks or the pillory; you may not duck her: civilisation, humanity, Christianity, and political economy agree together in forbidding all these things. But they agree in allowing an employer to pay starvation wages to his girls, and by way of punishment, when he pleases, to drill them. It is a small and miserably inadequate kind of punishment. Let us pity the poor employers; they have nothing else left.

On the third day she went again.

Again she was told to stand aside and wait.

Again she obeyed, and prepared submissively for a third day of patient suffering.

Only one hundred and fifty years ago, when maid-servants or workgirls committed any fault, it was customary to beat them with sticks. As it was the custom no one took much notice. One of the sights of London was Bridewell Prison, where visitors and idlers went to see the women flogged. Sometimes, again, the women were placed in pillory and so exposed to the derision of the multitude. It seems barbarous to us when we read of these things. We have now, no doubt, cast away forever such barbarities. Of course we have—we are now so considerate and kind to women that we never overwork them, never pay them wretched wages, and are constantly careful that other people shall treat them with equal consideration. This is an age of humanity. We even go too far in our resolution that there shall be no cruelty. If a schoolmaster flogs a boy we invent stories to stimulate and goad the public wrath. We say that the schoolmaster has even cut the boy's toes off in the zeal of his *argumentum baculinum*.[4] We will have no boys whipped, no donkeys kicked, no dogs or cats ill-treated; and it is commonly reported that the cases of the fox, the hare, the rabbit, the weasel, the stoat, the pheasant, the partridge, and the grouse, are shortly to be taken into serious consideration. Wherefore it is absurd to suppose that there can be any cruelty in drilling.

Girls who are drilled do not cry out, to begin with, nor do they write to the papers. They know very well that, if they do venture to complain, they will get no more work. Besides, if it were cruel, if it were not for their own good, it would not be done. Like many other necessary chastisements, however, drilling has its disagreeable side. Those girls, to begin with, who habitually work sitting all day, feel extremely uncomfortable after standing for a couple of hours. The discomfort increases to the point of pain, and from pain to torture if it be prolonged sufficiently. When the torture does begin, the girl feels first of all grievous pains in her limbs; she shifts her weight from one foot to the other, her feet swell, her back and shoulders ache, her head becomes an aching lump of lead; she is nothing at all from head to foot but a collection of aches and pains; there is no part of her which does not give her pain; every bone is aching, every muscle is drawn, every joint is swollen, and you may observe, if you take the least interest in a girl who is being drilled, that, after an hour or two, her cheeks have become flushed, her lips tremble, her hands are shaking, and her eyes are unnaturally bright.

4 From Latin, the *argumentum (ad) baculinum* is an appeal to force, or a threat of force.

There is another thing. Workgirls do not generally breakfast off anything richer or more substantial than bread, or bread and butter. At stroke of noon they are ready for their dinner, which may be bread with a piece of fried fish—it is cheap and very nourishing dipped in oil, as the Beni Yakub[5] love it—and sometimes of bread and butter with tea. At one o'clock, if this meal has not been provided, they are desperately hungry; by two or three, they are faint and sick with hunger. By the evening, if they have had nothing since breakfast, they are devoured by that pain which was once poetically and happily likened unto the gnawing of a wolf at the intestines by a man whose name has been forgotten, but who had personally experienced this pain, and had also been chewed by a real wolf—I think it was in Epping Forest, about the time of King Athelstane.[6] This man, who lived to a great age, and now lies buried in Greenstead churchyard, beside St. Edmund's oaken church, always declared that he greatly preferred the real animal to his imitator.

All day long the people came and went in the shop, each one about his own business, nobody regarding so insignificant a thing as a young workgirl standing still and submissive; no one, indeed, knew or guessed or cared to think that here was a girl who was aching in every bone and sick and faint with fatigue and hunger, waiting for money due to her and for work promised her, who had so waited two days and was now waiting the third day. And the hours when one is being drilled move on so slowly. They go too slowly in the city for those in the ranks of clerkdom; far too slowly for the youngsters who want to be off and away, using up the last of the autumn evenings upon the bicycle in the roads about Leyton and Wanstead; far too slowly for the young man who longs for the evening, when he may walk and talk with the girl who is going to marry him as soon as he reaches the income of a hundred and twenty pounds; too slowly for him who is already married and now draws two hundred, and has a house at Leytonstone, with a garden and children five. But the hours went much more slowly to Melenda than to any of these. The fat-faced clerk already mentioned—he with the whiskers—went on with his work and from time to time turned his eye upon Melenda. Because it was the custom, he thought nothing of the punishment. Just in the same way, when the Romans nailed a man on the cross, the thing was so common that none of the passers-by gave a thought to his agony. He hung up there, over them, sometimes enduring his agony for two or three days, while everybody went on below just as if the man were lying on a bed of roses. The soldiers on guard rattled their dice and told their stories and sang snatches of song; the boys played with their knucklebones and quarrelled and fought at the foot of the gibbet;[7] the women carried their fruit to market on their heads, and hardly looked up; the happy lovers passed hand in hand beneath the man who would love no more, and on whose drooping head were the dews of death; the scholars walked by disputing. There was a man being slowly done to death upon the cross—well, it was the custom. This clerk was like the Romans; I daresay he knew that drilling was painful, but it was the custom. The girl had left at home, very likely, brothers and sisters who were waiting for the money and the work, and were, meantime, without food: perhaps he understood in his dull and unsympathetic way that hunger is an extremely painful thing. But it was the custom. He was only doing his regular work. He was no more moved than the Roman soldiers, or than the schoolmaster is moved by the sad face of a boy kept in, or than the beadle

5 Literally the Sons of Jacob, the Beni-Yakub were one of the wandering tribes that became the Jewish people. The term is used here to refer to Besant's Jewish contemporaries.

6 King of England from c. 924 to 939.

7 A post to which executed criminals would be chained and displayed. It is used here to refer to a post for crucifixion.

was wont to be moved when, in the days of his now lost magnificence, he walked, gold-headed staff in hand, beside the wretch who was being admonished at the cart tail by the nine-tailed vengeance. It was the custom.

Out of so many workgirls, there are always so many careless girls; therefore so much drill, so much starvation. It was nothing but the necessary discipline of the establishment. The clerk was really a very kind-hearted person, who would not willingly give anyone pain. He spoke with the greatest abhorrence of the ruthless Russian and the tyrannous Turk; if he had any money to spare he would subscribe to all kinds of virtuous and benevolent things, such as the Cruelty to Animals Society; and as for vivisection,[8] words fail him when he even thinks of it. One is anxious that this gentleman, who is still comparatively young, should not be misrepresented, and therefore it should be added that he is a member of a surpliced choir, in which he sings tenor, and that he belongs to a guild, and sometimes is allowed to put on a long cassock, which makes him completely happy. The chiefs of the establishment have houses at Buckhurst Hill, Stoke Newington, and Finchley.[9] They are all most kind-hearted men. If their children were kept waiting for breakfast a single quarter of an hour, they would turn every servant—man Jack and maid Jill—out of doors; if any of their own girls were kept without food for a whole day, they would fall into apoplectic fits. It is needless to say that they are diligent at church and chapel; they approve of all good works; on the question of discipline they speak vaguely; on that of woman's wage they cling manfully to the great sheet-anchor of trade—the primal law—the most beautiful and most beneficent of all laws—that of supply and demand. Theirs, you see, is the demand; the girls furnish the supply. In the evening the chiefs, who make a succulent luncheon at one, go home every man to a handsome dinner at half-past seven, picking up something on their way at the fish and game shop outside Broad Street Station. At the moment when their gongs proclaimed the serving of dinner, Melenda would be allowed to go home to her bread and tea.

I believe that a two-days' drill is considered severe. Melenda's case must therefore have been very serious indeed, for she was drilled the third day, and perhaps it was intended that the drill should go on for a day or two longer, but an accident, the nature of which you will learn immediately, prevented the continuance of the punishment. It was not that Melenda "went off," or fell down, or flew into a rage and delivered her mind and was consequently excited. She did none of these things. She stood perfectly quiet and waited. The clerk began to think that punishment had gone far enough, but it was not by his orders that girls were drilled. That was done in a department upstairs, which took about as much human interest in the girls as a board of magistrates laying down rules for prison diet, or a board of guardians ordering a costume for workhouse girls, or the Admiralty[10] issuing orders for the British sailor.

Valentine it was who ended her punishment for her.

When they found that Melenda did not return by the noon of the third day, Valentine declared that the thing should no longer be endured.

It was nearly one o'clock. Melenda stood alone in a kind of corner, out of the way of the people who kept coming and going. She now hoped for nothing but for the stroke of seven—still six long hours distant—and stood swaying herself gently from side to side, to ease some of the pains which racked her limbs. When she saw Valentine at the door she changed colour, and was ashamed. This was indeed, she reflected, a beautiful

8 A surgery typically performed on living animals to determine how the organs operate.

9 Buckhurst Hill, Stoke Newington, and Finchley are all London suburbs and home to the middle and upper classes.

10 The board responsible for directing the royal navy.

kind of independence—independence to be justly proud of! Valentine looked about the place, saw Melenda standing in her corner, and then addressed the man who seemed to be in office. It was, in fact, the clerk whom Melenda called "him with the fat face."

"Is it, pray," she asked, "by your orders that girls are tortured in this place?"

"I don't know what you mean," he replied.

"Is it by your orders, then, that the workgirls are drilled, as you call it?"

"No, it isn't. The orders come from upstairs."

"Will you tell me where I can find the chief partner of the house?"

"Oh! come," said the clerk, laughing, "that's too good, that is! You don't expect him to bother his head about a workgirl, do you?"

"Will you take me to him?"

"Well, no—I won't, if you come to that. It's more than my place is worth."

"Will you tell me his name?"

"Why, of course; all you've got to do is to read the name on the brass plate at the door."

He dimly perceived, through the fog of daily routine and custom, which clouded a perhaps otherwise fair understanding, that here was a young lady and that there was going to be a row.

There was, but not much; because you really cannot expect the senior partner in so great a House to trouble himself about a mere insignificant London workgirl. You can't sell a workgirl as you can sell a roll of silk; you can buy her, it is true, and you can buy her cheap, and you can use her up quick; you can drill her if she is careless; you can pay her the wages of competition—in some confusion of ideas, Valentine thought these must be the wages of sin turned the other way about. All this an employer can do with a workgirl, but he cannot sell her; so that he has naturally no direct interest in her, except to get as much work out of her as he can while she lasts. And this, of course, he does.

In ten minutes' time Valentine reappeared. With her was an elderly gentleman of benevolent aspect.

"You shall see for yourself," she said, indignantly. "You cannot disclaim the responsibility for abominable cruelties committed in your name. You shall deny them if you can!"

"Cruelties! Really, my dear young lady—cruelties in my house! It is absurd. Let us see these cruelties." He looked at her card—"Miss Valentine Eldridge."

"I am a daughter of Lady Mildred Eldridge," she said, instinctively getting at a weak place. "Now, sir, will you please to tell me whether it is by your approval or by your orders that this girl has been ordered to stand here for three days, from half-past nine in the morning till seven at night—nearly ten hours each day—without being permitted to leave the place or to sit down for three whole days? To stand all day without food from nine until seven! Would you dare to use your own daughter so?"

"Really, this is very—"

"For three days! Oh!" Valentine was now so indignant that she said more than was wise. "Do you understand at all what it means to stand for ten hours in one place? Do you understand what it is to go without food for a whole day? Do you know that she has been kept from the money owing to her all this time? You have, I suppose, the right to pay her starvation wages and to overwork her. Have you the right to torture her?"

"One moment, Miss Eldridge." He called the clerk and retired up the shop in conversation with him.

"I hear," he said, presently returning, "that the girl was not told to stand, but to wait; there has been nothing to prevent her sitting down, or going out for dinner or tea, had she chosen; her work was kept back for three days as a slight—a very slight and inadequate—punishment for very culpable negligence. Under these circumstances I trust that you will recall the harsh expression." He spoke with great dignity, but his cheeks were red.

"I will not. Your excuse is a miserable prevarication! It is false that the girl could sit down or go out. She has been deliberately tortured. You make a practice of torturing the poor helpless women you employ."

"At all events, it shall not occur again with this girl. She shall receive whatever money may be owing to her and she may go. We will strike her name off our books," said the senior partner. "Since discipline is construed into cruelty, and kindness into torture, you had better, Miss Eldridge, take your *protégée* elsewhere. I am sorry I cannot help her any longer."

Nothing could have been grander than the way in which he delivered himself of these words. He took off his hat and retired. It was not until he was gone that Valentine found any reply, and then it would have been unequal in dignity to that of the manufacturer.

"Now you've lost your work altogether," said the clerk. "Lord, what a fuss to make about a day's drill."

"Will you find a chair for the next girl you drill?" asked Valentine.

"Well, Miss," he replied—mindful of the senior partner's words—"I told her to wait; I didn't say stand! Is it my fault that there was no chair?"

"We are always made to stand," said Melenda. "Never mind—there's other places!"

They went away, Valentine feeling miserably guilty. She had fallen into a rage, and before a man known all over London for active benevolence, and she had gone to his private room and accused him of cruelty and of torture, and of underpaying his girls and overworking them. Valentine, for once in her life, showed—to put it mildly—an immense capacity for indignation. She startled the good old man, and when she offered proof of her words, he could not choose but follow.

He had a dinner-party that evening, and I think he must have been feeling uncomfortable, in spite of his grave and dignified language, because he talked a good deal about the question of women's wages. They were necessarily, it was agreed by all, ruled by the state of the labour market first, and the production market next. And there was only one feeling, that it was most desirable to find some way in which the wages of women and girls could, without violation of political economy, be improved. He did not tell the drill story, because there were one or two awkward points about it. Besides, this young lady certainly had friends, and her friends might write to papers. Now, there is nothing in the whole world which men of all ranks, classes, trades, fortunes, or professions, dread more than the publication of "trade customs"; because, somehow, from the fee of a barrister down to the bill of a plumber, so many delicate questions can be raised, and so many awkward questions may present their sharp and spiky points; and it is not enough to feel, as we do feel, that we are all in the same boat. This makes it, in fact, worse, because if anyone in his wrath should happen to bore a hole in the boat on account of another man's sins, down we all go together. The benevolent senior partner could not get out of his mind the white face and trembling limbs of the girl he had been drilling. They made him feel actually uncomfortable. Besides, he was afraid of the newspapers. Perhaps, however, nothing more would be said about it.

"You've got my work took from me, Valentine," said Melenda, not ungraciously. "Never mind—you gave it him hot! He didn't like it, though he bounced it off. There won't be much more drilling done there for a month or two. But, Lord! it isn't him you should blame. He don't know nothing about it. It's upstairs where the orders for drill comes from!"

Chapter XXIV

Melenda Is Vanquished

Thanks, therefore, to Valentine's well-meant, but perhaps injudicious, interference, there was now no work to do, and the girls were idle. Of the two evils, compulsory idleness, with no money and therefore no food; or compulsory drudgery, with very little money, and very little food; perhaps the latter is the lesser, though workgirls differ in opinion. Lizzie, leaving the care of the future to Melenda, went rambling about the streets, appearing regularly at meal times in Valentine's room; if she loved anything it was idleness, and as she could now get well fed without doing any work, she was contented with the present, and not anxious to begin again at the button-holes.

Melenda it was who went seeking work, and, as generally happens in such cases, found none. There were already, as she very well knew, far more seekers than work for them. This is the hopelessness of women, that there are so many who seek for work and will take it at any terms. There are, for instance, those who ought not to take it at all, such as girls of the better sort who live at home and will do work for any wretched pay in order to earn a little money for dress; then there is the married woman, who will take work for any pay in order to buy a pair of new boots for her boy: these crowd the shops side by side with the women whose very livelihood depends upon their work, and are obliged to take whatever work and whatever pay is offered.

It was a slack time, too, and perhaps the history of Melenda's late dismissal was noised abroad to her discredit among establishments which reserve the right of torture. However that may have been, Melenda got no work. She was greatly magnanimous. She never charged Lizzie with the carelessness which brought on punishment; more than this, she did not suffer Valentine to feel that she had been indiscreet in her treatment of the chief partner. And she was too proud to complain, and so sat in misery and hunger alone in her room, except when she sat by Lotty's bedside. Why was she so long in getting well, when she had plenty to eat and nothing to do, and rest for her poor back? Yet she showed no signs of getting better, and only spoke in a whisper, and grew daily thinner and more wasted.

"Melenda's got no money at all left now," said Lizzie, after four or five days of this vain and fruitless seeking. "Yesterday there was twopence: today there is nothing, not even a loaf."

She made this remark as if it was a matter of quite small importance. At a certain depth, the fact of being penniless and out of work is not so uncommon as to excite either wonder or compassion. Besides, there had been penniless times before, and they had pulled through somehow.

But Valentine hurried to Melenda's room. She found her sitting beside the table; there was nothing at all on the plate where the loaf was wont to stand; the lid of the teapot was off; there was no work on the table; the room was quite neat and tidy. Now for a workwoman's room to be tidy means that there is no work. The girl's eyes were set hard, and when she saw Valentine at the door they became harder. "What do you want here?" she asked. "I haven't asked you for any help, and I won't—I'll starve first."

"Oh, Melenda, you are starving already! You have starved because you were so proud. My dear, if you will not accept, will you at least borrow?"

"No, I won't have anything from you."

"You have had a great deal from me already. Take a little more."

"What have I had from you?"

"You have taken for your friends what you refused for yourself."

"Lizzie may do what she likes. As for Lotty—" Her voice broke down, and the tears came into her eyes. "I've done what I could for her. All I could do I've done; I'd ha' worked my fingers to the bone for her. But that wouldn't ha' done her any good. We've been friends for eight years."

"You have, indeed!" said Valentine.

You know and have read how in certain wild parts of the Earth, where the policeman and the Ten Commandments which he guards are both unknown, and the choicer blessings of civilisation have not yet arrived, and even Lynch is as little studied as Coke upon Blackstone, men join hands and become sworn friends and allies against all the world. But, as in our modern times the word "friendship" has come to mean so weak and feeble an alliance that your friend will not hesitate to stab you in the back with an epigram, or to ruin your fondest hopes for his own advantage, it has been found necessary to make use of another word. These men in the wild places are therefore brothers. We ourselves—we of civilisation and slang—when we mean that a man is a real friend, call him affectionately a pal. It is expected of a pal that he will stand by one both in public and in private. This differentiates him from a friend.

Workgirls, however, are friends, not sisters or pals. Like the men in the wild places of the earth, where every stranger is an enemy, and every creature one meets is a wild creature, they stand hand in hand; everybody is an enemy; those who employ them rob them; those who sell them food rob them; they are robbed in their rent, they are everywhere and in everything robbed, stinted, and starved. Political economy is dead against them—who can stand up against professors? They are weak of body and have no power of speech; they are as dumb sheep, for they do not even bleat in complaint, but together—two and two—they are strong in patience: together they can suffer, together they can bear the life which we of the Christian brotherhood have assigned to them in these happy and religious days of charity, faith, and hope. In this Saturnian age,[1] when we are all brothers and sisters in love and sympathy, standing together hand in hand, they can find something like contentment among the potsherds and the mouldy crusts.

1 A mythological era referred to as the *golden age*.

"It's me, after all, that she could have done without," Melenda went on, "and you that's done everything for her."

"You have taken this service from me for her sake," said Valentine; "my dear, take another service—for her sake—I do not say for your own."

"You want me to take your food and your money. I won't, then; I'll starve first! I am starving! Oh, there's a pain like a knife inside me! Go away and laugh at me!"

"Oh, you are too proud! Melenda, would you disturb poor Lotty's last days? Will you let her die in sorrow because you are so hard?"

"Her last days?" Melenda sprang to her feet. "What do you mean?"

"I mean that she is dying. She may last a week, or even three months, but she is dying. Nothing can save her now. Oh, Melenda, your friend is dying!"

"Lotty dying? Lotty dying!" she sank into her chair in despair. She knew already that Lotty would never recover. But between going to die and actually dying there seems so wide a space.

"She will very soon pass away from us, my dear; away from the crowded street and her life of toil and pain. Would you keep her? You would not wish that she should stay. She is going to some better land. While she lives, Melenda, my sister, let us make her happy. She can only be happy if she knows, when her eyes are closed at last, and she has no more pain to bear—that you and I will love each other, for her sake—for her dear sake, Melenda."

"Lotty—dying!" she murmured, as if she had not heard.

Then Valentine threw herself at her feet and caught her by the hands.

"Oh! my dear—my dear! Do the thing—for her—which Lotty most desires. 'If only,' she said this morning, 'if only Melenda will leave off being hard-hearted.' The doctor has told her that she will die, and she is not afraid, poor dear. But she is troubled for your sake. Forget your angry thoughts and angry words, Melenda; they shall be as if they never had been spoken. Try to believe that I love you. My poor, proud, brave girl, you have suffered so much and have been so strong. Let love break down your pride!"

The tears fell fast on Melenda's hands.

"What's the use?" she cried, "oh! what's the use? Lotty's dying, and I am all alone. You are a young lady; I don't believe you are my sister Polly at all. Sam says it's the other, because she's like Joe's Rhoder. How can you love me even if you are Polly? Look at your clothes, and look at me."

"My clothes! What have clothes to do with it? Do you think I have watched you every day for three months and seen how brave you are, and how you have worked for Lotty, and how patient you have been with Liz, and your resolution, and—and everything"—she could not refer to evenness of temper, but there are always some points which must be omitted—"and not love and admire you?"

"Oh! what's the use?" cried the girl; "I'm always cross and ill-tempered, even with Lotty." She slipped one hand from Valentine's grasp, and passed it over her streaming eyes.

"Try me, dear," said Valentine.

She threw her arms round poor Melenda's neck, and kissed her a dozen times. "I told you when I came," she said, "that perhaps I was your sister Polly. Perhaps I am not after all. Polly or not, we are sisters, you and I, always sisters. Shall we promise?"

"If—if you like," said Melenda, with such sobs and tears as become the vanquished; "if you like."

"Then, my dear, sisters must do everything they are told to do by each other. You will order me and I will order you. First, I am going to dress you."

Melenda was conquered.

Valentine ran into her own room, and came back with a bundle of things.

"Do you think I am going to have my own sister go about in such shocking rags as these any longer? Take off your frock this minute, and—oh, the ragged petticoat! Here is one of mine, and a frock, and a pair of my own stockings. Everything has got to be changed. You are not quite so tall as I am, but the frock is short for me. There, my dear, the stockings fit you like a glove. You and I have both got such small feet, which is almost a proof that I am Polly, after all. The frock is a little loose in the waist—that is because you are so thin—but you will fill out very soon now. Oh! my dear, what sticks of arms you've got! Mother says she can count every rib in your body, and I am sure I could. That comes of eating so little. Today you shall have chops, and tomorrow steaks, and you shall never—never—never go back any more to your horrid cold tea and bread and butter, mind that. Now there's your hair. Do you know, Melenda, you have got much finer hair than most girls? See what a colour it has! Artists would give anything to paint that beautiful red-gold hair. What a pity you cut it in the front! You will have to let it grow again. Why, it hangs down below your waist. Now sit quite steady, my dear, and I will dress it for you nicely, so as to hide the nasty fringe."

With true artistic feeling, Valentine carefully combed back the fringe, and plaited a braid of the thick red hair to hold it back in its place, and rolled up the great mass of hair behind. When it was completed the effect was wonderful. For the first time there was displayed a broad and white forehead—for the first time Melenda's eyes showed at their best—strong and steadfast eyes, deep set, though now red with tears; for the first time her face looked as Nature intended it to look, not beautiful, but clear, capable, and trustworthy. In the grey dress which Valentine gave her, with a red handkerchief in front, with a white collar and white cuffs, and her hair dressed in this new fashion, fringe hidden and forehead displayed, no one could have taken her for the ragged workgirl of that very morning.

"Oh! good gracious!" Melenda cried, when Valentine completed her operations by bringing her the looking-glass.

"There," said Valentine, "you look like—like a professor of mathematics," she added with a little hesitation; certainly Melenda in her new dress had the air of great capability. "Exactly like a professor of mathematics, and you ought to be at Girton College.[2] There isn't a Senior Wrangler[3] anywhere who could look so clever if he tried his utmost. Nobody would believe that I had such a beautiful sister. Come, dear, we will go to Lotty."

"Lotty, here is Melenda; we are friends, as sisters ought to be. I have been dressing her. Now you are not to talk, but you may whisper, if you please, that you are glad. What shall we do with her?" She went on talking because Melenda was blushing like a bride in her new character of Melenda the vanquished, and the tears were very near the surface. "What shall we do with her now that she has no more work to do? As for the old work, that is done with. There shall be no more button-holes. First of all, Melenda has got to nurse you, Lotty, hasn't she? That will be work she will like, and perhaps now she is at your bedside, Lotty dear, you will get well soon. Oh! and she has had no breakfast yet. Here is a box of sardines, and here is bread. I will make some fresh tea

2 The first residential college at the University of Cambridge open to female students.

3 The student who achieves academic supremacy among Wranglers—those granted first-class degrees in mathematics—at the University of Cambridge.

in a minute. Eat at least half the sardines before you say a single word: mother says you never did eat enough. Now isn't the flat kettle a capital thing? Here it is boiling already. Why, how in the world could Lotty and I enjoy our breakfast and dinner when we thought of your bread and tea? There! Now I push the table closer so that you needn't move out of your chair, and oh! Melenda! don't begin to cry again, or we shall all of us—"

It is a pitiable thing that three young women cannot feel unexpectedly happy without crying over it. Perhaps, in Melenda's case, the sight of the food which she had refused so often was an outward and visible sign of her changed frame of mind; a holy sacrament and token of a solemn covenant, meaning reconciliation and affection. She was not one to go back upon her word: she was vanquished: her independence was gone. If Lizzie had been the girl concerned, we should have added that she was hungry. But with Melenda that circumstance mattered nothing. She was always hungry; she had been hungry for eight years; she was hungry day and night, and except sometimes on Sunday, all the week through. However, she bowed her head and took her breakfast, and choked over it, while Valentine recovered slowly.

No one, unfortunately, noticed Lizzie.

She stood looking on with wonder and jealousy and a certain fear. Melenda was dressed like a young lady—a young lady of a shop. Her hair was brushed back, she was no longer a workgirl: no workgirl wears a white collar and cuffs, no workgirl was ever yet known to have her hair so dressed. Therefore, Lizzie, who had a quick, if not a logical mind, jumped at once to the conclusion that when Valentine went away—Melenda had always insisted that she would soon go—she would be left behind, alone. No one wanted her; no one took any notice of her; she was not Valentine's sister! And Lotty was going to die; they would both be gone, and she would be left quite alone.

She stepped out of the room, put on her ulster and her hat, and descended into the streets, her poor little brain in a tumult of envy, jealousy, and apprehension.

"And now," said Valentine, cheerfully, "you will stay and nurse Lotty, won't you? If there was anything you would rather do than that, you should do it. But I know there is nothing. Here is her medicine and the glass. Don't let her talk too much, but you may talk to her. Tell her about the man at the factory, the chief partner, you know, and how he pretended you could have sat down if you pleased, the old humbug! Let her go to sleep if she can, and if she is thirsty, here are her grapes, and don't go into your own room till I give you leave. Obey your sister, my dear!"

Presently they heard footsteps on the stands and in the other room. But Melenda obeyed. The steps came and went, twice or three times. When, in the afternoon, Valentine took Melenda back into her own room, the place was transformed; they had scrubbed the floor and cleaned the windows, washed the woodwork of the door and cupboard, they had pasted up the paper where it had fallen, they had put up a new blind and pretty curtain, they had brought new chairs—the old wooden bed was gone, and a new iron bedstead was in its place, with new sheets and blankets. There were flowers on the table—even the rusty grate was cleaned up and polished; and a piece of carpet lay upon the boards, which were hardly yet dry.

"There!" said Valentine; "This is an improvement, isn't it, my dear? The past is quite gone; let us make the future as unlike it as we possibly can, so that we shall never be reminded of it."

"But my work!" said Melenda, feebly.

"We shall find work. Do not be troubled about work."

Thus was Melenda subdued, dressed, and promoted. In the morning she was a young girl, in the afternoon she was a young person. Students of modern English will recognise the distinction. The next step is, of course, that to the rank of a young lady, which is obtained by getting employment in a shop, or behind a bar, or in a show. There is not any other promotion open to working-women beyond and above this rank of young lady. They are never, never by any chance, made duchesses or countesses, or anything. This is, no doubt, a shameful wrong, but it is not yet felt; and until an evil has become a crying evil, and a cry has become a bitter cry, and a thing that is felt and acknowledged to have become a disgrace to the country, we are resolved not to mend it or to mind it.

In the evening, Melenda went out, as usual, by force of habit. The street market was in full swing; the roadway as well as the pavement was crowded with people—women with baskets, men loitering along with pipes in their mouths, everybody making rough, good-natured jokes; the boys whistling, the men at the barrows and stalls shouting; everything going on just as usual. Strange! These things amused her no longer—and the people seemed not to know her; they did not chaff her, nor did the boys push her, nor did the young men address her with words of impudent familiarity. Quite the contrary. They made way for her, as if she had been a young lady. And for the first time in her life, she did not like the crowd. She left the street, therefore, and went back to her own room. It looked so pretty, and so much like Valentine's, especially when she lit the lamp with the coloured shade, that she wondered how in the world she could have gone on so long in such a grimy den! Thus easy is it to take an upward step. And may every young girl speedily become a young person, like Melenda, if not a young lady!

When Lotty fell asleep, Valentine came to talk with her. They had such a talk as made the girl's heart glow within her. For Valentine spoke of a divine future, in which the women who work—yea, the very lowest and poorest, such as she and her friends had been, shall work in happiness, not in misery, for a wage which will keep them in comfort, and for hours which will give them leisure; when there shall be no drilling, and driving, and swearing and abusing! And when there shall be time to look about and enjoy the world, while yet the pulse is strong and the blood runs swift; and when women who work shall be able to read books as well, and to learn music, and to visit green fields and forests.

"My dear," said Valentine, "remember that the time must come. Perhaps we shall not see it, but let us help its coming while we live. The future belongs to those who work. But the girls cannot do much by themselves—they must have two things—the help of the working-men, and that of the women who do not work."

Then she accused herself, and her own hardness of heart—her apathy and selfishness, in having lived for one-and-twenty years without so much as thinking of the women who work, and, with herself, she accused all those women who do not work and do not think. "Why," she said, "it is forty years since the most generous hearts in England showed a way, and preached it as if it were a new gospel—yet I think it is only a part of the old; the men have followed it, but not the women. Oh! Melenda," she cried, "it needs nothing but determination that the women shall have the proceeds of their labour. And we are too lazy and too indifferent to care for them."

These were stirring words, such as Sam would use. Melenda understood very little of what they meant; but they rang like words meant to put people in a rage, and therefore she liked them.

"We will start our co-operative work here, Melenda. You shall be the forewoman, when you have learned a little more. Oh! there will be plenty of work for you; we shall work together, and Claude will work with us.

I shall want you to give me more than I can give you—all your time, all your cleverness, all your skill. Why, what can I give you, my dear, in return? And then, when we are quite ready with our workshop and our girls, we shall go to the ladies, and tell them what we are going to do, and ask them if they will come to us instead of going to the shop; and perhaps the shops will come to us instead of going to the factory. There must be some sympathy, somewhere in the world. But yet, after all that has been said and written about it, we seem only just beginning. Claude says that the history of all great things is the same: first it is the man who finds the truth and preaches it to deaf ears, and dies; and then the little school of disciples which survives him and preserves his teaching; and afterwards, the martyrs, and the preaching to the four winds of heaven, and to a great, stupid world, which will hear nothing, in spite of its long ears; till, little by little, the words begin to take effect, and produce their fruits!"

The doctrine of co-operation was difficult for Melenda to grasp. She only understood, of work, that it must be "given out" in the usual manner and by the customary machinery of clerks. There are many points of distinction between the masculine and the feminine mind: as that the woman is not happy unless she is quite sure and certain, and that the man gets along very comfortably under a sense of uncertainty; also that any man who disagrees with a woman is, to her, an utterly contemptible person, while to a man, he is only a person with a curious mental twist. But the most distinctive of all these points is, that a woman never invents anything, or wants to change anything, or to improve any methods or ways of doing things. In order to illustrate this proposition, consider the common housemaid, the common household cook, and the household nursemaid; the first of these has never been known to show the smallest invention in the laying of a fire, nor the second in constructing a dish, nor the third in dressing a baby.

Melenda, therefore, could not at first understand how the Golden Age may be restored. Few, indeed, are those whose imaginations can overstep the bounds of custom and sally forth into the world where women are actually paid for labour, at a price which is not ruled by competition. In that world, if work is slack, there will be savings to fall back upon; there shall be no grinders[4] and drivers, and no woman shall be able to undersell another. In that world will spring spontaneously all those beautiful virtues, which can only flourish in physical comfort, sufficiency of food, and freedom from anxiety. And in that world, the girls will refuse to marry early, and the men will not ask them.

"But they will always try to beat us down," said Melenda, incredulous of any Golden Age.

4 Employers who pay extremely low wages for labor-intensive work.

Chapter XXV

Lizzie's Temptation

Lizzie went down into the streets unperceived, and with a sense of having been driven out. To such girls, who are perfectly conscious of their poverty and their personal insignificance, there is no greater pleasure than "notice," and therefore no greater blow than neglect. She was jealous—she had taken Valentine's dinners for nearly three months—she had never shown any pride about accepting presents; yet no fuss was made over her. And the moment Melenda gave in, there was as much rejoicing as there is over a sinner who repents. Melenda, the penitent, was caressed and cried over, while no one took the least notice of herself.

Besides, Melenda would not be a workgirl any longer, that was quite clear; no workgirl could be dressed in that way, and Valentine was her sister. And Valentine was going away. Melenda always said that she would go away and forget them, and Melenda was never wrong. She said so herself, which proved the truth of the statement, and Lizzie always believed her; well, then; now that Valentine and her sister were friends, they would go away together.

And Lotty was going to die.

Everybody was agreed that Lotty was going to die; she knew it herself, and talked about it. It is strange how quickly a girl may become accustomed to the contemplation of approaching death. The shadow hangs over the house; everybody feels it, the sick and the well, the patient and the nurses. Day follows day and the shadow remains or becomes deeper, but Azrael[1] lingers, and when he comes at last, though his terrors have vanished, the surprise remains that the end should be so soon.

Lotty would die. Lizzie knew that she might linger on. Would Valentine leave her and forget her? She ought to have perceived that this was impossible, but she did not perceive it. In her trouble and perplexity, the foolish girl pictured herself nursing her friend through her last days and then left alone, without even Melenda. What should she do? Who would find for her the work—hard work, but better than none—that

1 The Angel of Death in some Abrahamic religions.

Melenda had hitherto found? How was she to live? She had no other friends in the world—her father counting as nothing—except the two girls. They had been sufficient for each other; and now the little circle was going to be broken up. Then, again, who would share a room with her? To the London workgirl, the thought of sleeping all alone in a room is full of terrors. If it was dreadful to think of the night, how much more dreadful to think of the day! For the last two months she had been as happy as the unwonted sense of physical satisfaction which comes of good and abundant food can make a girl; it makes an enormous, an inconceivable difference. She knew, Melenda said so, that it would not last, but she was satisfied with the present. If you give ever so little happiness to these poor girls, starved of joy, they blossom like flowers in sunshine. Now she was like the butterfly who feels the first chill winds of autumn and knows that summer and sunshine are over.

To the butterfly there is no other chance or hope. For Lizzie there was what seemed to her ignorance not only a chance, but a certainty. It was a letter—the last of a dozen letters—received two days before. She had read it a dozen times at least and knew it now by heart, yet she read it again a dozen times.

It was nothing less than a love letter. The man who wrote it had told her over and over again the same thing, yet words which are written seem to mean more than things which are said. He loved her and he thought about her day and night. That was what the letter said. But he had told her so day after day, walking beside her; he whispered it to her in the crowded streets; he had told her so in the quiet side streets—there are side streets in Hoxton, where, but for the children, who do not count, and are besides sometimes in school, and the costers, who are not always bawling, there reigns a perennial silence; he had taken her hand in his and kissed her, telling her so, not in a rough way as working-lads use, but daintily, and yet with a curious coldness as if it wasn't quite true. It was not quite true, but he told her this because he wanted her; and besides, it was nearly true, for the girl had grown wonderfully pretty. He really did, as he told her, desire above all things to get that face and those beautiful eyes into his own studio. Lizzie knew very well that her face and her eyes were beautiful; she did not know how much her beauty had grown since Valentine found out and provided for her an infallible remedy against the dreadful disease known to girls as "falling off." The remedy consists solely of a good dinner taken daily, with a reasonable breakfast and a hearty supper. It is sovereign for colouring the cheeks, brightening the eyes, putting in dimples here and there, and filling out the figure. So that Lizzie, who had been nothing but a thin, hollow-cheeked, and hollow-chested girl such as may be seen by thousands, only with large and beautiful eyes, was grown, in three short months, tall and well proportioned, of good carriage, with soft and dreamy limpid eyes and a mouth that looked as if it might smile, but could seldom laugh, and a face of infinite possibilities. In her speech, too, she had amended, being an imitative animal. But her ulster still covered a ragged frock and her hat was shabby to the last degree. This lover of hers went on to assure her that he wanted to do nothing all his life but paint her face and eyes—the hands, he reflected, but did not say so, would have to be chosen from another model; but he could not even begin until she made up her mind to give up her present life, and to trust herself entirely to him. Was she afraid of him? Well, you see, Lizzie was afraid of him. He was a gentleman. Workgirls are horribly afraid of gentlemen, though they pass it off with cheek and chaff; and though in every workshop there is a tradition that once there was in it a girl as poor as themselves, whom a most beautiful gentleman, young, handsome, and passing rich, picked out from all the world, and loved her better than he could have loved any number of countesses, and married her, and made her happy ever after. They tell the story, but they forget altogether how horribly dull it was for that girl after her marriage, with nothing to talk about, and none of her old friends, and the best company manners to be carefully maintained all day long. And naturally, they do not understand how dull it was to the unfortunate young gentleman, and how devoutly he wished ever afterwards that he hadn't done it, but had taken up instead with even the least desirable of the countesses. Lizzie, however, found this gentleman lover horribly dull company. She had nothing to say; absolutely nothing. She was afraid of him and of his cold polished manner.

Was she afraid to trust him? It was a most eloquent letter. That could hardly be the case; she should have everything that the heart of a woman can desire; she should lead the softest and easiest of lives; her only duty should be to sit to him; her days should be full of light, sunshine, and art. Here Lizzie felt that fear again; for what was it that he was always talking about? What was this precious art? She knew nothing about art; she cared less. One evening her friend took her to the Bethnal Green Museum,[2] where she saw big vases and paintings. He said that was art, but it made her yawn. She would have to make him do without art. She should, the letter went on to assure her, be always dressed in the finest and the prettiest. Her hands, which were now spoiled by rough work—making button-holes in thick coarse shirts does really pull the fingers into all sorts of shapes—should grow white and delicate as a beautiful woman's hand should be.

There was never yet devised by the subtlety of man or evil spirit a more terrible temptation than this which falls in the way of such girls as Lizzie. Fortunately for man, no such temptation is possible for him, though he is often enough tempted to enact the part of the serpent; else the lot of humanity would be far more wretched than it is. It is a temptation which assails a girl partly through her womanly pride of beauty and love of admiration; partly through her natural desire to escape the hard life which has been her lot and to enjoy the easy life of which she has only caught a glimpse; and partly through her youthful desire to enjoy the sunshine and to have a little play, and to gather some of the flowers of the spring.

Even if Lizzie had been less ignorant; even if she had known what would have followed; even if she had seen, as in a map, the years of her life stretching out before her—even if she had seen herself sinking deeper and deeper into misery—yet think what a temptation! Even if she had been restrained by religion—but she had no religion; or by education—but she had not been educated; or by love and respect for her friends—but Lotty was dying and Melenda would be taken from her, and then she would have no friends.

There is no such temptation in all the world, unless it be the temptation to steal for one's starving children. Against a life of penury and privation, a lot of plenty; against hard work, idleness and leisure; against the fierce anxieties and struggles of competition, ease and freedom from any anxiety.

Alas! Lizzie, left alone, was not strong enough for such a temptation.

Let us bring out the woman who gives way to the place of stoning.[3] Tear the veil from her face and make her stand before us trembling, crying, full of shame and terror and despair. The matrons, of course, are armed with the largest and the sharpest flints. But see—the men sit down and refuse to throw a single stone. Even the employers of women and the manufacturers, and those who are governed by the Law of Elevenpence Ha'penny, refuse. And the women are ashamed to begin. Then she steals away unharmed. And always in the city within its grey walls, almost in sight of the place of stoning, sit Lizzie's friends, sewing button-holes as she did, making shirts, machining men's coats, rolling cigars, fashioning match-boxes, sorting paper, confecting

2 The Bethnal Green Museum was a collaborative effort between the private citizens of the East End, who funded the construction of the building, and the West End's elite, who donated the artworks and artifacts that constituted the collection.

3 According to ancient Jewish law, a person who had committed a particular crime was brought outside the city to be stoned to death.

jam, all starving, all hollow-eyed, all sad of heart and heavy of limb, and all getting their elevenpence-ha'penny a day, when they are in luck. And in the midst of all the serpent, twined about the branches of the apple-tree, continually whispers to those who are young and pretty and will listen, his soft and mellifluous promises.

Lizzie suffered the temptation to assail her all day long. She wandered about the streets, now buffeted and beaten by the tempter, who reviled her for her stupidity in resisting; now contemplating with shrinking terror the picture which he held up before her imagination of a wretched girl alone in a wretched room, with no work, no money, no food, no friends, no light, alone in the world. How could she go on living so?

"Why," said the tempter. It was not the serpent actually visible, but a memory of certain words which had been said to her by the man who followed her and wrote to her those letters. "Why, what do you know in this God-forgotten place of what is done at the other end of the town? There are girls, not half so pretty as you, whose photographs are sold in every shop and put up in every window. They can get what they please to ask at any theatre, just for going on the stage to be looked at. Why, you want nothing but a little better dress to outshine them all."

Then she remembered how he took her into one of the little draper's shops, of which there are so many everywhere, and picked out a bright-coloured kerchief, one of the cheap things in jute which look so pretty. "Take off your hat," he said.

She took it off, and with a dexterous hand, which showed practice upon more than the mere lay figure, he twisted the kerchief round her neck, and over her shapely head, so as to let the curls of her fringe play about the folds and to set off the singular beauty of her eyes with a frame rich and full of colour. "Look," he said, showing her the looking-glass. Then he took off the thing. "Put on your hat. Look now."

She shuddered, because it seemed to her as if all her beauty lay in the crimson handkerchief.

"Don't think," he went on, outside the shop. "Don't think that I shall let you go upon the stage. I shall keep you all to myself. The world shall only see you in the exhibition of my picture. I can wait for you a little. But don't try my patience too long. As soon as you are tired of privation and toil, come to me."

She ought to have put the thought behind her; it should have been treated as a thing impossible to be even considered. But this she did not do.

Late in the afternoon she went into a small stationer's shop, the place where her letters were received for her, the only letters she ever had from any one. Her mind was made up. She would struggle no longer. After all, she would be better off than some, because he was a gentleman.

For a penny she bought a piece of note-paper and an envelope, the shopwoman kindly allowing her to use the counter and her own pen and ink for nothing. Here she wrote a letter in reply. It was the first time she had ever answered her letters, which always proposed a meeting, so that they could be answered by word of mouth, and her answer hitherto had always been a hesitating "no." It was a very short letter, because she had never written a letter before in all her life, and, perhaps, she will never write another. It was also spelled in a manner disapproved by the great Butter,[4] and disallowed at spelling bees, but the spelling we may alter.

"Lotty," she said, "is going to die. Melenda is going to be took away. She's got a new frock, and her fringe is brushed back. So I shall be all alone. I can't stay all alone. So I will come to you tomorrow. Tell me where you will meet me. —Your friend, Lizzie."

---

4 Presumably the narrator refers to Nathaniel Butter, a seventeenth-century publisher of the first edition of Shakespeare's *King Lear*, as well as one of the earliest English-language newspapers, who played a leading role in standardizing grammar and spelling.

She addressed and posted the letter—this took her last penny. It was then two o'clock. He would get it in two or three hours. She would have an answer the next morning. Now when she had irretrievably promised this thing, because nothing is so hopelessly past recall as a letter dropped in a post-office, she felt strangely agitated. She was afraid to go home. Like Eve, she wanted to hide herself. She had no more money, and was getting horribly hungry, but she was afraid to go home. Her eyes, she thought, would tell the tale of what she had promised. They would guess it from her cheeks, which were burning. If they guessed it, what would they say? If they actually found it out, how would Melenda rage, and how would Lotty cry, and how would Valentine look at her with grave eyes, full of pity and of wonder, under which she would sink to the earth in shame? When principle and religion fail, you see, the opinion of one's friends may still be useful.

It was quite late, nearly eleven o'clock, when she got home. Her father's candle was burning, and she opened the door and looked in. He was sitting in his chair, motionless and abstracted, as he sat every night.

"Can I do anything for you, father?" she asked. It would be the last time she would ever do anything for him.

"Is that you, Lizzie?" he replied, shaking his head as one who rouses himself. "No, my dear, thank you. Why should you do anything for me? I've never done anything for you, have I? And now, I never shall. You ought to have had a better father, child!—"

"Never mind, dad; it isn't your fault that you're so dreadful poor."

"It is my own fault, I suppose, that I have a daughter to share my poverty. Never mind, child. You have found a friend at last."

"If you mean Valentine, then you're wrong. She's going away. She's going to take Melenda with her and Lotty's got to die."

"If she is going away, she will come back. She has been here this evening. You will have no more trouble, Lizzie. As for me—the bishop is very ill. His sons are sent for. I do not know what will happen; but you can do better without me. There will be no more slavery for you, child."

There would not, she thought; but what he meant she knew not.

"The Lord," he went on, "cursed mankind with the curse of labour; the profit of the earth is for all. The preacher said it. Yet there is the work of the wicked and the work of the just. And there is a vanity, saith the preacher, that is done upon the earth; but there be just men to whom it happeneth according to the work of the wicked. That was not quite your father's unhappy case, my daughter, but something like it. And as for you, your toil has been for the wicked man. Henceforth it shall be for the righteous woman. That will be your happiness."

She could not understand one word. It was his wont to speak in this kind of allegory, and generally she did not try to understand. But this evening; of all evenings, after what she had done and promised, what did he mean?

"Never mind the preacher, father. What do you mean?"

"She will tell you herself. Go, child. I told you that the bishop is dangerously ill."

Lizzie hesitated. It was the last time that she would see her father. She felt sorry for him, with his long grey hair and feeble limbs and his dire poverty. She lingered a moment. It was cruel to leave him, but she could do nothing for him, nor he for her. She shut the door and went upstairs. Melenda was in the room. Gracious!—what had happened? She was reading a book, rather ostentatiously perhaps, but it was the first time for eight years, and Melenda felt that the thing gave her dignity; and by the light of a most beautiful lamp covered with a most beautiful red-coloured shade; and there were white curtains to the windows, and a carpet on the floor, and a bright new bedstead. Lizzie gasped. "What does it mean, Melenda?"

"Lizzie," said Melenda, who was not at all the kind of girl to practise virtue passively, and was an ardent missionary, whatever views she might adopt; "Lizzie, it's time you cured yourself of walking the streets till midnight. It isn't respectable."

"Well, Melenda, only last night you were out yourself. What's up now? You and me are respectable, I suppose, though you have combed back your fringe. What's come to the room?"

"She gave us all these things. They are all from her, and they're all for you and me, Liz. I'm not ashamed any more to take her presents, and I don't care if you do throw them in my teeth, after all I've said. I've given in. They're for you and me. Everything's new, even new sheets to the bed."

"For you and me? Isn't she going away then?

"Yes, she's going away in a day or two."

"And ain't you going with her?"

"No, you and I are going to stay and nurse Lotty. The doctor says as soon as possible she's to go to the Isle of Wight,[5] he says, and she may last through the winter, with care, he says. You and me will take care of her."

"And where's the money and the work to come from?"

"She'll find the money and the work too. Oh, Liz! such a fool I've been! She's full of thought for us; she's the best girl in the world! Sam says the other is Polly, because she's like Joe's Rhoder. But I don't care—I shall never care about the other—the one who cried!"

"It's all for you—she doesn't care about me."

"Yes, she does, she cares as much for you as for me, which shows that she can't be Polly. Don't get jealous, Liz, there's a good girl. Let's be happy while we can, and have no more tempers! I know I have a bad temper—but then we've all been so hungry, and Lotty's been so bad—poor Lotty!"

She paused and wiped away a tear.

"She's got a new frock for you, Liz. She's been talking about you all the afternoon, and after tea she took a cup down to your father, with a plate of meat, and talked with him, and told him what she was going to do for you—and came upstairs crying! Why, you didn't think we should go away and leave you all alone, did you, Liz? Well! I wouldn't have thought that bad of you—never—I wouldn't! You know she's coming back again, and then we are going to set to work—somehow—to make a business like the men, or co-operate somehow—I don't know how. It's the ladies themselves who are going to manage it. She says if the ladies had made up their minds years ago, we should all have been paid fair wages by this time. But they'll do it now, or else she'll know the reason why; and there's to be no more drilling, and plenty of work for everybody, and good wages—that's what she says." It was not exactly what she said, but it was near enough. "Not," said Melenda, descending again from the imaginative to the practical, "not but what they'll go on trying to beat us down, if they can."

Lizzie made no reply, but proceeded to go to bed. And then, whether through the strangeness of the new bed, or her hungry condition—for she had eaten nothing since breakfast—or the discovery that she had been wrong in her assumption, she lay awake half the night; and when she fell asleep, it was only to dream that

5 A small island off the southern coast of England. It is one of the sunniest and warmest places in the country and would, therefore, have been an ideal place for recuperating, especially during London's cold and damp winter months.

Melenda was pursuing her with a long stick in her hand, and an infuriated countenance—and that Lotty was weeping and Valentine pointing the finger of scorn, and all Ivy Lane looking on, while they cast her out.

Chapter XXVI

No Defence

"This," said Valentine next morning, "is our last day but one together." They were all at breakfast—Melenda with them for the first time.

"But you won't be gone long," said Melenda.

"No; I shall come to see you nearly every day, until I come to live with you again."

There was something the matter this morning with Lizzie. She would eat nothing, and, when Valentine said she was coming back again, she took up her cup of tea and choked over it, which was strange, because Valentine's departure for two or three days hardly seemed to offer an adequate cause for this emotion.

"I do not know when I shall be able to live here altogether, but that is what I shall try to do. Then we will get more ladies to come here, and we will make our own society in Hoxton. Instead of everybody living together, all in one part of town, we ought to separate, and make settlements in different parts of London. Then there would be a chance for better things, and art, perhaps, and culture." Sometimes Valentine would talk in this unintelligible fashion, but the girls listened without laughing at her, which would have been rude, or questioning her, which would have been uninteresting. "As for you, Lotty dear, I shall come to see you as often as I can. I am only going to Park Lane, which is not more than two or three miles from here, though they think it is two or three hundred miles by distance, and several centuries by time. But then they are dreadfully ignorant in Park Lane."

"Why didn't you tell me yesterday?" cried Lizzie, with a sudden outburst of passion. "Oh, if you'd only told me yesterday morning!"

"My dear child, does it matter much? I am very sorry, if it does matter, that I did not tell you yesterday."

"If you'd only told me!" she repeated; "if you'd only told me!" What was the matter with the child?

"Since it is the last day but one, and tomorrow I shall have a great deal to do, and Lotty has had a good night, cannot we go somewhere together? Melenda can leave Liz to look after Lotty. We will go to Tottenham first, and spend the day with mother, if you like, and look at green fields and the River Lea—shall we?"

"I can't look after Lotty," said Liz, with burning cheeks. "Oh, you mustn't go away and leave Lotty by herself."

"Where are you going, then?"

"I'm going—I don't know where I am going!" She sprang to her feet and ran into the other room.

"Stay here, Melenda dear," said Valentine. She remembered the doctor's warning, and ran after the girl. "Lizzie!" she cried, catching her by the arm, "you must tell me what you mean—where are you going? Why can you not look after Lotty? Does Lotty know why?"

"No, no, you mustn't tell Lotty; please don't never tell her!"

"Does your father know?"

"He won't ask after me—he won't miss me. Don't tell father. I must go!"

"Then I shall go with you; I shall not let you go out of my sight all day long."

Lizzie sat down. The eyes that she feared were upon her, and, as she expected, they were full of grave reproach.

"Where are you going, Lizzie?"

"I thought I was to be forgotten and left alone. What is it to you? I ain't your sister, like Melenda. You don't care for me like you do for Lotty. If I'm left alone, with no work, I shall starve. Let me go; it's nothing to you."

"It is everything to me, Lizzie. Do you think we do not care for you? Why, after all these years, when you have worked with Melenda and Lotty, ever since you were a child, do you think they do not care for you? Tell me, what folly is it that you have committed?"

Lizzie hung her head guiltily.

"I know that you have been seen more than once, walking with a gentleman. What did he say to you?"

"He wanted me to go away and be his model. He wants to paint my face and eyes. Well, then—what's the harm?"

"If there is no harm, why didn't he come here and ask you openly, before Melenda and Lotty?"

"Oh!" The girl began to cry. "I said I couldn't never leave Lotty and Melenda. I told him so twenty times—I told him so; but he wouldn't take 'No' for his answer. And he knew where to meet me, and sometimes, before you came, when I was dreadful hungry, he'd give me a chop for dinner. But I wouldn't take his money. Oh! don't tell Melenda; I think she'd beat me, she'd be in such a rage. And don't tell Lotty, because she'd cry."

"Lizzie, you've been worse than foolish! But there is something more to tell."

She felt those eyes, greatly superior, upon her, and she confessed the whole.

"Then he began to write letters to me. Oh! beautiful letters; and the day before yesterday there came another; here it is."

She drew forth the letter, of which we know, from her pocket and gave it to Valentine.

"Am I to read it?" she opened and read it through. "My dear, it is the letter of a bad man—a wicked and deceitful man. What he says is false. It is false that you are the most beautiful girl in the world. Oh, what nonsense! there are hundreds and thousands prettier than you, in this place only. It is most wicked to flatter a girl in this extravagant way. And how can he love you? He calls himself a gentleman, I suppose; he is a man of education; and you, my poor child—what do you know, and how could you talk with a gentleman so that he should pretend to fall in love with you?"

It will be remarked that Valentine had not yet learned everything; and that, as regards the science and practice of love, she was still in that happy state of ignorance where it is believed and accepted as a maxim that a gentleman cannot possibly fall in love with a girl below himself in the social scale. Most young ladies believe this, even after their brothers have got engaged to barmaids.

"You don't love him, Lizzie? You can't love a man, you know, unless you are his equal, and can understand him!" Which also proved that she was as yet inexperienced in the ways of love and in the workings of the human heart, which does sometimes refuse, if history hath not lied, to recognise the artificial distinctions of birth, wealth, and education.

"You don't love this man," Valentine repeated.

"I don't know. I am afraid of him."

This confession was really, though Valentine did not know it, a most extraordinary and almost unique instance of a girl in Lizzie's class being able to explain or disclose her mind at all. Most girls are absolutely unable to detach even one of the fine, confused variety of feelings which agitate their minds when a wooer comes to them. Lizzie was flattered by the praise of her beauty; she was honoured by the admiration of a gentleman; she was tempted by the offer of the "easy life"; she knew that her lover was handsome, well dressed, and of good manners. But she was afraid of him. I suppose the reason why she confessed that fact to Valentine was that fear, of all the contending forces in her brain, was the strongest. "I'm afraid of him."

"Why, then, there is not much harm done," said Valentine, with a sigh of relief; "if you are afraid of a man you cannot love him. If a girl loves a man," she went on, like the philosopher on the seashore, picking up shells and feeling after knowledge in the unscientific, pre-Baconian method; that is, without the making of experiments—"If a girl loves a man, I suppose she is attracted by him; she cannot, certainly, be afraid of him; she must long to talk with him, and to hear him talk. Do you long to talk to this man?"

"No; I can't understand what he says. It is all about art, and what people should do for art. He says we must all give ourselves to art—I don't know what he means, but he is always saying it."

"Then of course you are not in love! Well, go on. You have something more to tell me. Where were you going just now?"

"I thought you were going away with Melenda, and Lotty was dying, and I should be alone. I couldn't live all by myself, and there is no work."

"Yes, my dear, you were very foolish. You ought to have trusted your friends. But you know better now. Now go on, and tell me all."

"I'll tell you, only don't tell Melenda and Lotty—I'm afraid you will tell them."

"No, I will not let them know if it can possibly be avoided. But you must tell me the whole truth."

Confession is said to bring in some troubles the greatest relief possible, especially to the feminine mind. But as yet the apostle's injunction has never been perfectly carried out, only partially even by the Wesleyan Methodists, who, I believe, are supposed to confess to one another in open meeting of the church members—but I doubt the fulness and reality of their confessions. As for confession in the ecclesiastical way, in a hole and corner in the dark, and through a square aperture in the wall, and to an unknown man beyond, that, to an outside heretic, does not seem to meet the apostolic precept. Lizzie found in full confession the greatest relief. She poured out the whole story, down to the very words of his letters. Besides, she was in a great fear that the gentleman would make her keep her promise, even if he had to drag her away; and Valentine was like a strong fortress of protection.

"And he'll be waiting for me—and perhaps he'll come to fetch me—and what shall I do? And what will Melenda say?"

"Poor child," said Valentine. "It was a dreadful temptation, my dear. Never tell anybody this—keep it buried and forgotten. I will help you through. But never, never speak to a gentleman again."

They went together to the stationer's shop, where the letter was lying for Lizzie. Valentine opened it. First there was a banknote for five pounds in it, and then a brief letter, directing the girl to buy, with the money enclosed, a few necessary things, and to meet the writer at the gates of St. John's Church that morning at twelve. Valentine kept the greater part of the letter to herself, because it contained references to beautiful eyes, which might have weakened Lizzie's repentance. After a surfeit of sweets, more sugar is undesirable. There were also expressions of contempt for her recent work, which were as well left unsaid. Then Valentine began to consider what was best to be done.

"Come home with me," she said; "let me bring you safe home first. My dear, you are like a deer escaped from the eagle's clutches, or a lamb from the wolf. He would have torn you to pieces with his cruel teeth. Hold my hand tight, you poor silly child, and thank God that you told me everything and were stopped in time!"

Lizzie made no reply, and they walked back, hand in hand, and both with hanging head and flaming cheeks, for the cloud or shadow of shame was upon both their hearts, and one of them thought that her dream was come true—that the very children of Ivy Lane were going to call out upon her, and that Melenda was waiting for her with wrathful eyes and scornful words and cruel blows.

"Come in here," said Valentine, as they entered the house; "come into your father's room. It is a wretched room, is it not? He is miserably poor. You would have left him to his fate, in his poverty and his old age, without one friend to help him and not one to love him and to console him. He is ill—any sudden excitement or sorrow will kill him. If he were to learn that you had left him and run away to strangers, and to your own ruin, he would most likely die from the shock. You would have killed him! From this you have been saved. Upstairs, Lotty is on her death-bed. The end may come to her any day. If she were to learn that you had left her without a word of farewell, and run away, the end would come very quickly. You would have killed her, too. From this you have been saved!"

* * *

Let us leave them together.

We generally think that the priest, because he hears no end of confessions, and knows such a quantity of wickedness, makes the best admonisher unto godliness. In the same way, the solicitor, who becomes intimately acquainted with all possible forms of roguery, or the police magistrate, or the schoolmaster, or the police-man himself, or even the professor of roguery standing in a neat uniform at the treadmill, ought to be good admonishers. For my own part I think that the grave and serious remonstrance, with womanly tears and sympathy and kisses, of an innocent girl might, with such a girl as Lizzie, be worth the admonitions of a hundred priests. And it is to be hoped that the words which poor Lizzie heard that day may sink into her heart and bring forth fruits of righteousness.

* * *

It was an hour later when Valentine and Lizzie went upstairs. There were signs of recent tears in Valentine's eyes, and Lizzie was crying and sobbing still.

"Oh, Lotty!" she cried, throwing herself upon her knees and clasping her hands—"But you must never know—"

"This foolish girl," said Valentine, "actually believed that we were going to leave her all alone here! I have been scolding her; but we must forgive her, because she is so sorry for her want of confidence. Melenda dear, don't say a word to her about it. Lotty, you will forgive her, won't you? And you must keep her here all day—it shall be her turn to nurse you."

At twelve o'clock, Valentine kept Lizzie's appointment for her. She had no other directions than to meet an unknown gentleman at the gates of St. John's Church at noon. This, however, was most likely a sufficient indication, because gentlemen are not common in the streets of Hoxton at any hour, and a gentleman waiting about a street corner is easily distinguished. She arrived at the trysting-place a few minutes after the hour, and there was already a gentleman standing on the broad pavement, outside the railings. A man, at least, was there, dressed like a gentleman. He was, no doubt, the wretch who had written those letters. There could not be two gentlemen, each with an appointment for the same time, in the same place—and in such a place! A hansom cab was waiting close by, evidently for him and for his victim.

The girl's heart beat fast. She would have liked to say something, but she could not trust herself. The man was looking in the opposite direction, but he turned as she neared him. Good heavens! It was none other than Mr. Conyers.

"You!" she cried.

"Miss Valentine!"

"You? Oh! is it possible?"

She remembered now, that she had met him once before, nearly on the same spot. He was confused then; he looked more confused now.

She had no doubt, not the least doubt, that he was the man whom she had come to find.

"You are waiting for someone," she said. "You have got a cab waiting, too!"

He made no reply.

"You are waiting for my friend Lizzie. I have brought you back the bank-note which you sent her. She will not keep the appointment."

He took the bank-note.

"I asked her," he said, "to let me paint her face."

"I have read the letters," Valentine replied, "in which you asked her. They are in my hands. Go—"

Mr. Conyers was a man of considerable impudence; but there are times when the most brazen impudence must break down. No living man, for instance, could stand unmoved before the scorn unutterable, the condemnation unpitying, of a young lady, for such a thing as this man had attempted. He made no reply. There was nothing, absolutely nothing, that could be said. She had read his letters.

"Go," said Valentine, pointing to the cab.

He turned and got into his cab without a word of explanation or excuse. She had read his letters! After that, what room was there for defence?

Chapter XXVII

Alicia

"To Russell Square,"[1] he shouted to the driver.

It was in Russell Square that Alicia lived, in one of the largest and finest houses, full of the most solid furniture, and crammed with pictures—pictures in every room and on every wall, as one might expect of one who was the widow of a dealer in pictures. Jack Conyers hated the house, and the furniture, and the pictures, because they all belonged, somehow, to the life from which he had vainly attempted to escape. Those game and fruit pieces in the dining-room, those landscapes in the drawing-room, those portraits—not family portraits—on the stairs, the massive furniture, all alike spoke of money and of trade, and he desired to belong to the world of money without trade.

Well, that was over now; the morning's work had effectually demolished any chance of that; he must think about it no more.

And after making everything ready for the grand coup! Violet was certainly Beatrice. He had established, in his own mind, so many points of resemblance between her and the portraits of Sir Lancelot, and so many between Valentine and Claude, that he had no doubt at all on the subject. And now to be caught, actually caught, like an offending schoolboy, by one of the two girls concerned, in such a business as a love affair with a workgirl—a thing so unworthy of a man of light and sweetness and culture;[2] so common, so philistine, so vulgar, and so low! And his very letters read—the thought of those letters made his cheeks to flame and his nose to feel hot. And that the thing should be discovered on the eve of his great coup only three days before the disclosure of the secret! But the damning thing was the fact of the letters—Valentine said that she had read all his letters. If it had not been for the letters he would have brazened it out. What business had she to read letters not addressed to herself? But women have no honour. They were, in fact, letters of the kind which

1 A garden square in Bloomsbury where many affluent Londoners lived.

2 A reference to Matthew Arnold's *Culture and Anarchy* (1869), which posits "sweetness and light," or beauty and ideas, as the essential components of human perfection.

cannot possibly be explained away or forgotten or forgiven—letters to a common working-girl, dressed in a shabby old ulster and ragged frock, who called him "sir," unless she plucked up courage to utter some delicate street joke, some cry of the gutter. Now there is this curious and dangerous quality about such letters that, whether a man addresses himself by love-letter to a shirt-maker or to a countess, incontinently he gets carried away by the enthusiasm of beauty and the magic of imagination, and becomes extravagant. Therefore, Jack's letters to poor Lizzie might have been written to Violet, so high pitched and so serious they were. And, apart from this other side of the matter, which was bad enough in all conscience, this unhappy young man felt that he had made himself ridiculous. No doubt Valentine would show those letters about.

A good morning's work. The best house on his list closed to him. Worst of all, if Alicia heard of it most likely she would be lost to him as well.

Alicia was out. Jack waited for her; and while he waited he wrote a short note to Lady Mildred. It was not a pleasant note to write; but it was better to withdraw of one's own accord than to be kicked down stairs.

"Dear Lady Mildred," he said: "When I spoke to you at Ilfracombe and opened, as I then thought, my whole heart to you, I did not know, nor could I possibly foretell, that I had made the most terrible mistake. This is the case, however, and I have no other hope than to throw myself on your mercy and ask for forgiveness.

"I have long loved another lady, and I have now learned that in certain conclusions I had too rashly drawn, concerning her affections, I was wrong. Fortunately, I have said nothing to Miss Violet on which I can reproach myself. Again I ask your indulgence, and remain, dear Lady Mildred, yours very sincerely, John Conyers."

Not a pleasing letter to write. But it had to be done. Better to preserve the appearance of walking out than to be turned out. I do not think it likely, however, that he will ever call upon Lady Mildred again!

Alicia returned rather late, and hungry for luncheon. She was a lady who was always hungry for luncheon.

"You here, Jack? I expected you about this time. Let us have lunch, my dear boy—you've got such a long face that I know exactly what you've come to say. You shall have some fizz, to give you Dutch courage! Don't be more ceremonious than is necessary. I should like it best if you would just say, 'Alicia, my dear, I've concluded to come down.' But I suppose that won't do for you—it isn't grand enough?"

They had luncheon together at the great mahogany table, among the pictures of game and fruit. How in the world can a man ever become a leader of art, culture, and the higher criticism, who sits daily among these pictures, and has married the widow of a picture dealer?

"Now, Jack," said the widow, "will you have a cigarette, or will you talk without tobacco? I don't mind, you know?"

Jack proceeded, with some solemnity, to put his case in the most favourable light possible. He said, but the lady laughed aloud while he spoke, that he must appear to have acted an unworthy part; he could not, in fact, understand his own blindness; for three months he had been as one who struggles against the overpowering force of conviction; he had tried to persuade himself that his happiness lay elsewhere. "This illusion," he concluded very gravely, "this illusion, Alicia, has now been dispelled."

"Has the young lady refused you, then?"

"No! My proposal for the young lady has been made—I confess it—and it lies still in her mother's hands. She is the daughter and heiress, Alicia, of the late Sir Lancelot Eldridge—"

"What does it mean, then, Jack?"

"It means, Alicia, that I have returned to my allegiance, to my first love"

"Oh!" She received the information doubtfully, because there was a lack of ardour in the bearing of her suitor. His words were ardent, but his manner was cold.

"I have reason to believe that the kindness of Lady Mildred might—I only say might, Alicia, because I do not venture to claim any positive knowledge as to the young lady's feelings—might be equalled by the kindness of her daughter—"

"Oh!"

"I have, however, written to Lady Mildred; you shall see the letter, here it is." He drew it forth and gave it to her. "You see, it is a free withdrawal—"

"Jack!" she read the letter quickly, and kept it. "Are you quite, quite straight with me?"

"Perfectly, Alicia. I have never been anything but straight with you."

"And it isn't money?"

"You mean that I have not much left. That is quite true, I have nothing to conceal from you. But it isn't money. There is plenty, at all events, in that young lady's hands, far more than there is in yours. But it isn't money, Alicia, I am not so mercenary as you think, and I have given up this other girl wholly for your sake. Forgive me, Alicia! Perhaps, some day, you will take pride in me—"

She laughed gently. "Ah, Jack! you always said that. Well, let me see. I know where you were. Down at the seaside with one of those girls—"

"The daughter and heiress —"

"Trying to get round her. Then you came back to town. I thought you were afraid of catching the wrong one, which would be catching a crab, wouldn't it?"

"I have always known which is the real daughter—"

"Have you? I thought nobody knew. Well, now, I will post this letter myself, to prevent accidents. Jack," she said, looking straight in his face, "there was once a man like you, with no money of his own, you know, who married a woman with a tolerably good fortune. He thought, as soon as he was married, that he could do what he liked, and so he began to carry on shameful, as if his wife hadn't common feelings. She let him have his head for a bit, and then, when he'd quite got accustomed to the best of everything and couldn't live without it, she turned him into the street, where there is no claret and no champagne. So that poor man caught a Tartar,[3] didn't he?"

"What has that to do with me?"

"Oh! nothing, of course; and I'm sure you'll never give me cause to allude again to that unfortunate creature, who now walks the streets between two pretty boards! I don't mind the portraits of the models—your three beautiful conquests, you know—and I don't care a bit about Miss Eldridge, because I am quite certain she wouldn't have had you. But there is something worse than either. There is a certain little girl at Hoxton, the workgirl, Jack." He started and turned pale. What did she know? "You've been seen walking with her; not once, but half-a-dozen times. Now, you know, I am not going to stand that! It isn't likely."

"She was going to let me paint her face, Alicia—"

"Well, you'll paint somebody else's face—your own, if you like; it's red enough now. No, Jack, no more visits to Hoxton, if you please. I wonder if it is reckoned good form for a gentleman—your father and mine

3 Someone or something that is surprisingly difficult or unexpectedly strong.

weren't gentlemen, but they wouldn't have done that—to meet a ragged little creature like that, in her dinner-hour, and turn her silly head with nonsense? I wonder what men are made of? You told her she was pretty, I suppose?"

"I am sure I don't want to meet the girl any more. These girls, Alicia—don't imagine that I was really turning the girl's head with any nonsense—often require a great deal of persuasion before they will consent to sit—"

"I dare say," she replied, with an incredulous sniff. "Well, Jack, I'm a fool to forgive you, and I shan't trust you too much. Most women would give you up altogether after finding out all I've found out. But when we're married—mind— You may kiss me again, if you like."

Jack obeyed her, but not as if he liked it much.

"As for playing the distinguished man, I think you will find it a precious deal easier in Russell Square with me than in Park Lane with your Eldridges! We're an easy-going lot, me and my friends, and we will just take you on your own estimate, however big it is; and if you like to talk art and aesthetics when my friends come to dinner, why this is just the house to talk it in. Wasn't all the money made out of art? I don't say we shall understand you, but that doesn't matter a bit, and they'll think all the better of you if they don't, particularly as they all knew your poor father! You'll look well, and you'll talk well, and you'll be very careful, my dear boy, very careful indeed, not to turn up your distinguished nose at my friends because there may be a letter wanting here and there, or because their money, like mine, was made in the shop. If you do, there will be pepper. As for your father—"

"That is quite enough, Alicia—we understand each other thoroughly. We shall make ourselves perfectly happy, and you shall have your own way in everything."

"I mean to, Jack. As for getting into society, I am not anxious to know people who despise honest trade. But if you like to bring them here, you can. They won't dare to show their contempt for the shop, I think, in my house. If they do—but never mind, my dear Jack, you are going to lead the most comfortable life in the whole world. And you don't deserve it a bit; and I shall tell all my friends—who wouldn't tell a fib for the man she loves?—that you are really almost as clever and distinguished as you look!"

Chapter XXVIII

"Return, O Shulamite!"[1]

So, at last, dawned the morning of Valentine's last day in Hoxton—the last day comes, if one waits long enough, of everything.

Her last day. She awoke before daybreak, and watched how the dawn—a pretty sight—gradually revealed in all their beauty, the board school and the back yards and the courts commanded by her window. There were no larks singing in the sky or swallows flying about the eaves to welcome the sun, perhaps because the season was too late for larks and swallows; nor was there any autumnal splendour of wood and coppice for the sun to shine upon and to glorify; but there were cats and there were sparrows—and gradually there arose a murmur of life, and dirty blinds were pulled up or pinned up, and the mortals behind them got themselves dressed in their work-a-day clothes, and the day's labours began. For most of them such dreary, weary, monotonous, and unprofitable labours!

Her last day. She looked round the little cell where she had spent three long summer months, a willing prisoner—and now she loved the place. On her bed lay the sick girl, who had taken so many nights' rest from her. When first she came there was no sick girl to care for, nor had she any single friend—who now had so many—in the whole place. There were her household gods—all the things which Claude had given her for what she thought would be a three months' picnic, but proved to be the prelude to a lifelong work—they were no longer new; the frying-pan, never very strong—man, mere man, cannot know how to choose a frying-pan—was now battered out of shape; it had fried quantities of chops, steaks, eggs, kidneys, and bacon. The saucepan and the kettle, both showed—because they had boiled with enthusiasm—the black and respectable garb of labour. The first freshness was gone from the colour of her rugs and curtains. The mignonette in the window-box, which had been all the summer so great a solace to her, was now reduced to three scentless stalks. The summer was over, and the air, when she opened the window, blew fresh and cold; and as for her

1 The chapter's title refers to the final line of the Song of Solomon 6, which sings of the Shulamite as the perfect woman.

face, as she looked in the glass and wondered what Violet would say, it seemed to have grown longer, though that could hardly be, and graver. In the past three months how much had she learned and how much had she seen!

Her last day! She was going home—to the real home; in what Sam called the camp of those who are the natural enemies of the working-classes, where no one has to work, and the days flow on in idlesse all; where there is abundance, where there is music, where there is art, and where there is the magic of poetry; where the girls are wrapped in soft silks, and kept from hearing how the workwomen cry aloud and cry in vain, and how they suffer in patience, hand in hand, with no one to help them or to care whether they live or die. But their cry, and the memory of their sufferings, would never leave her. She knew that she could no longer remain in that camp; she must come back again! She must return to the world where the women suffer. Everybody who once visits that world must go back to it. Those who work in it never want to leave it. Only three months ago: why—Claude was then her brother; what was he now? How could they go on working together when he should find out the truth? Three months ago they were both children of an honest workman, dead long since, and now Claude's father was not dead at all, but a shameful, horrible, lying creature, who was going to bring misery upon all of them unless she could keep him silent and obscure. That silence, at any cost, she would procure and pay for—Claude must never know or suspect, and Violet must never know or suspect.

She would come back again, not as a visitor, but to live. That was now her firm resolve. She was as bent upon it as a novice is bent on taking the vows. But she would no longer live in her single chamber. That was not necessary. Enough for three months to have been housemaid, cook, parlourmaid, and lady's-maid all in one; enough for honour to have carried water upstairs, swept her own room, cooked her own dinner, boiled the kettle, made the bed, and cleaned the window. In one respect only she differed from the old woman below her—that she put out her washing. Now the old woman never had any to put out. For the greater part of the time her bed had been occupied by a girl in a consumption, so that she had to sleep as she could, on a chair, or a bed made up of three chairs. One must be a Moravian missionary[2] before one can contemplate without a shudder a continuance of this way of life. She was coming back, but it would be to a home of her own, where she could live somewhat more as she was accustomed to live. Her house should be in Hoxton—she was resolved upon that, but it would not be quite in the midst of those who habitually get drunk on Saturday nights, and commonly use coarse imprecations, and when in liquor knock down and kick their wives. Even the fellows of Toynbee Hall do not actually live in the very courts and lanes of the Whitechapel Road and Commercial Street. No doubt they will do so when, by their efforts, these courts have become courts of the Great King; at present they seclude themselves in their college, each man with his own room aesthetically furnished for the pleasure of his soul, and removed somewhat from noise and stress and struggle of the common life. We may, in fact, give ourselves up, "like anything," for our fellow-creatures, who will very likely give up nothing, not even a humble little vice or two, in return; but there are some hours in the day which should be kept apart and consecrated, even by the most thorough Renunciator, for the recreation and refreshment of his soul. All the monks, hermits, and recluses on record made the great mistake that they did not provide such hours of rest. The gain, for example, in the way of spiritual elevation would have been inestimable if the Holy Fakeer, Simon Stylites, had let himself down by a rope ladder, once a day, just to enjoy in the cool of the evening the

2 The Moravians were a small organization thought to be particularly zealous and influential in their work as Christian missionaries.

conversation of the damsels and gossips in the bazaar;[3] and think of the difference it would have made to the saint who used to swing all day with the hook in his back, if some kind friend had taken that hook out of him every day, at the going down of the sun, so that for a couple of hours at least he might have smoked a pipe and had a chat beneath the village banyan.[4] To what pinnacles of spirituality might not the Fakeer Simon and the hooked saint have risen! But they failed. Simon got no higher, spiritually speaking, than the top of his pillar, and the other holy man never got outside, so to speak, of his dangling hook, because they were always attached to these foolish things. And now their sayings, if they ever said anything, and their discoveries, if they ever made any, in theology and morals, are quite lost and forgotten, just for want of that little daily intermission and rest, which would have brightened them up and inspired them with words of wisdom.

These general reflections applied to Valentine mean that too much Hoxton for those who have the best interests of Hoxton at heart is bad for Hoxton.

When Valentine went down stairs, she found her friend the letter-writer starting on his daily round among the German immigrants. There had been recently quite a large importation of Polish Jews who were making a little Yiddish Poland for themselves up a court. I think they had brought with them a great many barrels of native dirt, so as to feel home-like; and were now living on charity, in the begging of which the scribe was making an unusual harvest. He was doing so well that he had bought a new pair of second-hand boots; like a tax-gatherer, he carried his ink in one waistcoat-pocket and his pen in another, while his writing-paper lay in a shabby old leather case, which perhaps was once brown, but now was black with age. He greeted Valentine with cheerfulness, though the bishop at the moment was lying grievously ill, and his family were gathered at the palace, and three physicians were in consultation.

"But suppose the bishop dies," said Valentine; "then your dream will be finished."

"Yes," he answered, with his soft and gentle smile. "Yes, if the bishop does not recover, my dream will be finished indeed; for I am the bishop, you know. You are leaving us today?"

"Tomorrow morning. I have got, where I am going, another mother and another sister. Do you not think it is time I went to see them?"

They were standing in the court, between the little chapel and the open space on the south side, where two or three houses have been pulled down. The old man pointed with his stick to Melenda's window, which was open, showing the new clean blind and the new curtains; next, he passed that stick slowly before all the houses comprehensively and severally, meaning to include them all; and then he pointed to the little children swarming about the place like tadpoles in a pond; and, lastly, he indicated the women, bustling about their daily tasks. He did this solemnly and slowly, as one who hath a thing to say and thus delivers his soul.

"Do you know," he asked, after performing this ceremony, "do you know what they are saying, all of them, at your departure?"

"What are they saying?"

"They are saying, 'Return, O Shulamite!'"

---

3 The Christian saint Simeon Stylites lived as a hermit atop a pillar and abstained from food or drink for more than a year. Muslim or Hindi mendicants, known as fakirs, similarly engage in extreme forms of asceticism and detachment from the material world.

4 Some ascetics would endure different forms of deprivation, such as of sleep, by inserting a hook in the flesh of the back, attaching it to a pole, and thereby suspending themselves in the air.

He walked away slowly, with his rounded shoulders, his long grey hair and his ragged coat; an old man who ought to have been taken right away and forbidden to work anymore; who should have been provided with all kinds of things that are pleasant to old men—with books and sunshine and warmth and companionship. In a well-ordered state this will be done for all the old men alike, from saint to sinner, from duke to ditcher. But nothing can ever be done now for this individual poor old man, and you will presently discover why.

"Return, Shulamite!" The words lingered in her ears; the sweet old words of love and yearning.

Did they want her to return? Had she done anything to anybody during her three months that they should want her to come back to them, or that they should miss her presence among them?

There is a sense which lies dormant with most of us. It may always be awakened, and, once roused, it never leaves us. Let us call it, if you please, the sense of humanity. It is not philanthropy, nor benevolence, nor sentimentality; it is a thing much fuller and wider than any of these. Peter got this sense when he had the vision of the great sheet.[5] It is the sense of the universal brotherhood. Some of the French Republicans were filled with it when they first began to shout their cry of equality and fraternity.[6] Some of the Socialists are filled with this sense: it has nothing to do with religion or with creed: the lives of the saints are full of the stories of men who have had this sense strongly developed; the lives of the sinners, which have yet to be written—would that I could attempt that stupendous task!—will also be found quite full of such stories. Saint or sinner, it matters not; the sense of humanity may be found in either. One may be a peer and have it; one may be a beggar and have it not. Those who have it, and have developed it, are like mathematicians, when they resolve all plane forces to two, and all forces in space to three, for they presently resolve humanity into the simple pair—the man and the woman or, to be practical, since in the world there are no planes, but everything is of three dimensions, into the man, the woman, and the child. It is a sense by means of which one is enabled to separate the man from his clothes, whether they are rags or gowns of office, and from his sins, whether they be those which society allows, or those which are not recognised; and—which is a dark saying—it destroys respect and yet builds up reverence. Valentine had discovered this sense; she had awakened it in Claude; she saw it in Sam, in the doctor, and in the assistant priest.

When the letter-writer had passed out of Ivy Lane Valentine remembered the old woman who lived below her and got drunk whenever she could. She was not at all a nice old person, but Valentine thought she would see her before she departed—it would be neighbourly. So she knocked at her door and went in. This morning she looked very dreadful, because she had been tipsy the evening before, and had got a bruise round one eye, and the other was red; her lips were tremulous and her cheeks blotched; also she wore no cap, which was an error in art, because her head was bald in patches. Queen Venus, when she is old and bald, ought at least to wear a cap. And she was muttering over her work, which, as has already been stated, was intimately connected with approaching funerals.

"Well, my dear," she said, cheerfully, "and how is the sweet young gentleman? And how long are you going to stay here?"

---

5 In Acts 10 of the New Testament, Peter has a thrice-repeated vision of a blanket set before him on which are depicted all kinds of animals, including those he considers to be "common" and unclean by Jewish law. God tells Paul that because these animals come from Him, they are clean. Peter infers from this that so, too, are people of different races, tribes, and nations. He concludes that the old laws separating Jews from other nations must be unjustified.

6 The two main ideals, along with liberty, of the French Revolution.

"I am going away tomorrow. I came to see if I could do anything for you before I go."

"There, now! I said there'd be a wedding when I saw you in St. Luke's graveyard with him. A sweet young couple indeed. Ah! it does an old woman's heart good to let her eyes fall on such."

"But I am not going to be married."

"Well, my dear, it won't matter much how you arrange it. And there'll be another match soon, unless I'm mistaken, with Liz upstairs—there's another pretty one for you—and her young gentleman. Oh! I've seen them together too."

"Is there anything I can do for you before I go?"

"Well," said the old woman, "I daresay he's given you some money. He looks the sort to be free of money."

"I tell you I'm not going to be married."

"I didn't say you were, my dearie. But if you've a shilling upon you to spare, I'd thank you for it. Get all you can, my dear, get all you can while your time lasts."

She looked detestably cunning and inconceivably wicked. Valentine, however, found a coin for her.

"The air's getting fresh now," the old lady went on, "and the nights are cold. When it's too cold to sit without a fire and to sleep without blankets, I've got to go back to the 'Ouse. It's warm there, if it's nothing else. You think it's hard, but wait till you're as old as me, my dear, and see if you don't come to it as well. Make yourself happy while you can. It's no use saving; spend and enjoy all you can get while you are young, my pretty. When you're old you'll have the remembrance of it, and it'll make you feel happy just to think that you didn't let the good times slip past. Don't forget me next year if I'm spared to come out. Oh! it does one good in such a place as this, even to see a pretty girl with a proper frock on. But there, you won't be pretty when you come back here. Lord! what a figure I had once! And I can tell you about the time when I had a house of my own!"

Valentine left her at the commencement of these recollections. Eve, in age and decay, long after she had eaten, not one, but all the forbidden apples within reach, and longed for those out of her reach, may have looked so and talked so. A curious case for the spiritual physician. Next year she will be "out" again, for these old women are tough and long lived; and perhaps for many years she will continue to be alternately "in" and "out" and to exist as an example and a warning for the young. This dear lady, too, ought to be taken away and carefully cherished, with warmth and good food, and the semblance of liberty. Not that she would ever repent her of her sins, or wish the memory of the past to be other than it is, or get a gleam of light into her darkened soul about a better life. A better plan, perhaps, would be painless and sudden extinction. But the old lady, who, I suppose, would have to be consulted, for form's sake, is not yet educated to the point of perceiving how much her disappearance would benefit mankind. The subject opens a wide field for speculation, for there are so many among us who might with advantage be painlessly and unexpectedly extinguished.

Valentine proceeded on her way down Ivy Lane calling at the houses where she had friends, that is to say, at nearly every house. The children ran after her as she went, catching at her hands and hanging to her skirts. That means nothing, because children are so foolish as to trust and love everyone who is kind to them. "Come back soon," they cried; "Come back soon." Then from the children Valentine went to see her friends the workwomen in their rooms. She knew, by this time, dozens of them, which is not difficult in this thimble-and-thread-land, where there are so many thousands always at work. The women paused in their work for a minute to bid her farewell. There was the young tailoress of nineteen with two babies and a husband out of work, and her mother who looked after the babies, while she worked from seven in the morning till ten at night, for eight shillings a week, less the cost of coal and candle, soap and cotton. She was a handsome, capable-looking girl, with square chin, fresh lips, and strong eyes. She looked up and laughed a welcome, and when Valentine bade her farewell, she cried, but not for long, although a whole hour's crying would only have cost her a penny and one-fifteenth. "But you'll come back soon," she said. Then there was the woman who lived on the ground-floor, working all day long for bare life, with her daughter; there was the old lady with the imbecile husband, who worked for both; there was the girl who ought to have been married some years before, and there was the girl who ought not to have been married for some years to come; they all stopped to bid her farewell and to say "Come back soon," and then returned again to their breathless and headstrong flight from the Fury of Famine, who pursues them continually with a scourge of knotted cord, or a flagellum loaded with lead, such as that with which the Romans corrected disobedient slaves. Then there were the older women with their great families—Nature, very oddly, when the horn of plenty is quite empty, always fills it with babies. How bravely they work, these mothers! And how their faces harden, and how early the lines gather round lips and eyes! Surely, as the girls murmur when the drilling begins, surely, "it is a shame!"

And from them too, from every room into which Valentine had found her way, from every court there came the cry, "Come back soon"—"Return, O Shulamite!" Strange how the words lingered in her ear and repeated themselves—words sometimes will, just as if they followed one about or were echoed within the recesses of the brain.

At the door of the Boys' Institute, she met the Rev. Mr. Randal Smith. He was looking pale and overworked, because he had been in London all the summer; and besides, had given away his money, and had none to go on holiday with; and his long coat and broad-brimmed black hat were shabby because he could not afford new ones, and he looked faded, and dejected, and boyish, and without dignity.

"I know you are going," he said, gloomily. "The doctor told me."

"I am coming back again."

"It is wonderful that you stayed so long. We shall miss you, though you never come to church."

"Not to your church."

"Oh! what a power for good you might be if you chose! Why, you might bring all those boys of mine to church: they would follow you. It's the only thing for them—church discipline and confession. I know you laugh at us; but there is nothing except the confessional for getting a hold over the people and putting the priests in their right place."

"Well, Mr. Smith, if you will confess to the doctor, I dare say he will confess to you. Will not that satisfy you? Never mind your confessional, tell me about yourself. You look pale—you want a holiday."

"I cannot get one, unfortunately."

As Valentine considered this young man she remembered that it was for some such life as this, without the choral services, that Claude was giving up his career. What if he should weary of it?

"Tell me," she said, "you who work so hard and do so much for the boys—are you contented with your life?"

"I am quite contented with it. I ask for nothing better."

"That is a brave thing to say. Would you, if you had the chance, exchange it for an easier life and a larger income?"

"Not now," he replied, sturdily. "When I grow old and feeble I should like a stronger man to come here."

"Do you think that everybody engaged in such work as this continues to be as satisfied and contented?"

"I think so. We must not desire anything beyond the work that we are set to do."

"Do you never wish," Valentine continued, "for opportunities of distinction? Are you never ambitious?"

"I have no other ambition," he replied, with an ecclesiastical tag and a return of the breathless manner, "than to be a faithful servant." In fact, he had no desire for distinction at all, probably because in quite early life he understood that he was neither sharp nor clever.

"And do you never," she asked, "do you never think of love or marriage?" She was asking all these questions in the interest, so to speak, of Claude, and she suddenly, but too late, remembered what the doctor had told her. This young man had been thinking about love. "Forgive me," she said, hurriedly, because he blushed and trembled and looked about for the earth to swallow him; "forgive me, Mr. Smith, I ought not to have asked you that question."

"It—it doesn't matter. Thank you," he said, "it's of no consequence."

"I was only wondering," she explained, "whether in such work as yours there never comes a sense of weariness, as if it was all no good and one might as well be living like the rest of the world."

"There is no weariness of the work. Sometimes, perhaps, sometimes one thinks of a life—with—with love in it." His eyes dropped, and he blushed again.

"No weariness in the work. That never palls, does it?"

"Well," he was really a truthful young man, "there are the church services. It is no doubt the best discipline possible for a man, and of course we say matins and evensong for the whole parish, but as nobody ever comes to hear them, one sometimes feels as if there were too many services."

"So I should think."

"It is a weakness of the flesh which I hope to overcome in time."

She touched his hand and left him with a pleasing and rather uncommon mixture in her heart, composed of admiration, respect, and pity in equal parts, and just as one adds to a claret cup a little sprig of borage, or a strawberry, so she added the merest dash of contempt. His life was so hard—he was so contented, so courageous, and so unselfish—he was so patient—he thought so little of himself—he was so free from any ambition except to be, as he said, a faithful servant—he accepted with so much meekness the tiresome and useless things which wasted his time and dragged him from his real work, the daily chanting of services which nobody attended, the weary iteration of litanies in an empty church and the fripperies which this poor ignorant lad took for the true religion of the past, the present, and the future; a religion in which, he thought, there was to be no singing except of Gregorian chants; and no sunshine except through painted windows; and no attitude for the laity *in sæcula sæculorum*, except of continual genuflexion before a close-shaven man in a cassock and a cope, and a biretta cap, surrounded by boys in white surplices, with pots of incense.[7]

7 From Latin, *in saecula saeculorum* means "for ages of ages" or for all eternity—used to emphasize the obligation of the laity, or the non-clergy, in offering permanent fealty to the priesthood.

Chapter xxix

The Last Evening

"You must spend this evening with us, Claude," said Valentine; "it is my last evening, and we are going to have tea in Melenda's room. Besides, I want you to say all sorts of kind things to the poor girl."

"Your last evening! A good deal has happened, Valentine, since you came here first."

"Yes, a great deal has happened. But, Claude, we must get those lines out of your forehead and the depression out of your eyes." See how readily men betray their trouble.

"You will not do that easily, Valentine," he said, with a forced laugh. "The fates are too strong even for you."

She was now quite certain that the trouble of his soul could only be caused by some knowledge of his father's history, but she could not learn how much he knew.

"You do not regret your choice, Claude."

"I had no choice," he replied gloomily; "I thought I had. But I had not. There are some men, Valentine, who are condemned to obscurity from the very beginning; they can only be happy when they are unknown and forgotten."

Claude was more than usually gloomy because he was suffering from an acute attack of a complaint not described in any book on medicine. Celsus and Galen ignore its symptoms.[1] It has no name, but it is caused by family or paternal shame. His excellent father, who found in the torture of his son a truly delightful amusement, and concluded that the daughter, who lived in Hoxton, was not worth following up so long as she paid her weekly sovereign, now visited his chambers at all hours, having a master-key which he had made for himself. He borrowed Claude's clothes; he drank his wine; he sat there and fiddled all day along; he smoked tobacco there; he opened all the desks and drawers and read all the private papers—even those verses with which every young man loves to comfort his soul, and the letters from his friends; he came in the morning and stayed all

1 Prolific writers on medicine in the first and second centuries, whose works make up a substantial portion of contemporary medical knowledge.

day; he came in the evening and stayed all night. Claude might give up his chambers, but the man would follow him, and what would be the end? He demanded money perpetually, and always got some, if not all that he asked, by the exercise of a very simple threat. If he did not get it he would go to his daughters. He had even begun to take away things which were portable and might be pawned, such as the silver mugs, those volumes which were expensively bound, and the pictures; honestly, however, giving his son the pawn tickets.

Claude made no objection at all. Let the man go on; let him strip the place; let him do what he pleased, so that he remained unknown to the rest of his family.

Claude forced himself, however, to assume a pretence of cheerfulness, and stayed with Valentine. They all had tea together in Melenda's room. It was a quiet party; Melenda, to begin with, was shy, and as yet a little awkward in the performance of her new character as Melenda the amiable. Yet she looked the part. The new dressing of her hair changed her face, her eyes were no longer fierce; two days only of good food had taken the hungry look out of her face; she was in repose, and she was afraid of her brother, who, however, said nothing about the great and startling transformation—not even to offer a word of congratulation, being quite absorbed in thought about other things. As for Lizzie, she was still under the influence of repentance, and not without fear that her lover might himself come to the house, and insist on her promises being kept. Moreover, the shadow of death rested upon the place, and in the next room lay one who patiently awaited the summons.

The autumn day was already closed, for in the middle of October the sun sets at five; the curtains were drawn, the lamp was lit, the fire burning, and Melenda in the newly-born joy of her own humiliation, thought the room looked almost as lovely as Valentine's; and after tea they sat round the fire, Valentine holding Melenda's hand in her own.

About seven o'clock they heard steps upon the stairs, and there appeared at the door no other than Joe himself, accompanied by his daughter Rhoda, and Sam.

"Mother told us," he said, "that you were going away tomorrow. Why, what in the name o' wonder has come over the place?" For Melenda's room, he perceived, was transformed into a lady's bower.

"It is only that Melenda and I are friends at last," Valentine explained. "Come in, Rhoda dear; come in, Sam."

"And so I thought I'd come. Well, I shouldn't ha' known the place, Melenda, I shouldn't really—nor you neither, I shouldn't—and I brought Rhoder along with me, and we went out of our way to fetch Sam. Look at your Aunt Melenda, my gal; now she's something like. I never knew you were so well worth lookin' at, Melenda." Melenda blushed and laughed.

"Sit down, Joe," said Valentine. "Rhoda, you take my chair. Sam, you must sit on the bed, unless you like to stand."

So, for the first time since the departure of Polly into the aristocratic world, the whole of this remarkable family, counting Valentine as Polly, were gathered together. The vicissitudes of families have furnished many subjects for the moralist and the storyteller, as well as for the genealogist. In every house there are those who have climbed or are climbing, and those who have gone under and are still going lower. Down goes Jack, and with him his whole detachment. Up goes Dick, and with him his sons and his daughters and his grandchildren. But it is rare to find so much variety in one group and one generation. It is not usual, for instance, for a Fellow of Trinity to have one sister a needlewoman, and another a young lady; nor is it a general thing for a plumber's man to have one brother a board school master and one a Cambridge scholar. It is also unusual, Claude reflected, for any family to have a father with so remarkable a history as their own.

"You're going away," Joe repeated slowly, looking still at Melenda, whose changed appearance fascinated him. "You're going away." It is the place of the elder brother to give utterance for the family on all occasions of importance, and on every *conseil de famille*.[2] Joe accepted his responsibility, and was always ready to perform his duties as head of the family, though Claude might be a gentleman, and Sam had achieved greatness. "You're going away tomorrow; well, you've done a deal o' good to us since you came. Mother, she'll miss you more than a bit. We left her cryin', didn't we, Rhoder? And so will the girls here—they'll miss you terrible, won't you, Melenda? Lord! It's wonderful. You look just exactly like a girl out of a shop, quiet and respectable, instead of going about in rags, and flying in one's face like a wild cat. And you'll miss her too, Liz; and as for that poor girl in the next room—your own room too!—what in the world will she do without you?"

"But I'm not going away for long. I am coming back. I am going to live in Hoxton; so is Claude."

Sam grunted.

"There was two of you came first," Joe went on slowly. "You said then as you didn't know which of the two was Polly. As for the other one, she hasn't come again, has she? Very well; first, we don't need to say much about you before your face, do we? No. When you go away, whether it's for short or for long, there's some you've left behind who'll remember you, ain't there, Melenda?"

"She knows there is," said Melenda.

"Well, and about the other one now. If it should happen"—he said this very slowly, so that there might be no possibility of any mistake—"I wish to say—for all of us—that if it should happen to come to pass that the other one was to turn out to be Polly after all, and not you at all; and that you should turn out to be her ladyship's daughter, Miss Beatrice—which it may be for aught I know—why, I want to give you a message for the other one."

"Yes, Joe, what is the message?"

"It is a message from all of us; from Melenda, and Sam, and Claude, as well as from me. It's to tell her not to be ashamed of her family, because her father was a man with such a character for truth and honesty as very few men can boast, and a clever work-man as well—" Oh, Joe!—Claude and Valentine glanced involuntarily at each other. "That's what I've always told Claude. Don't let her be ashamed of her father; and as for us, why we don't expect her to come and live with us as you've done; we don't ask her, nor we don't expect her. We know that she's a young lady accustomed to live among young ladies, and we're on'y plain working-people. It's enough that you've come. We haven't harmed you, have we? You've heard a bit of rough talk now and then; perhaps you've seen a bit o' rough ways, and found out a deal of things you never suspected before, I dare say; but our people haven't harmed you—our people never will harm any respectable girl. If she'd wanted us, she'd have come to us with you. So you tell her that she's a sweet young lady to look at, and we like to think of her pretty face, but we shan't take it amiss that she don't come to us, because she is not one of us. Don't forget to tell her that—not one of us has got anything to ask of her or to take of her." Sam snorted, and Melenda tossed her head. She had surrendered to one and not to both. "She needn't be a bit afraid that any of her relations will ever seek her out, or intrude upon her, except Claude, and he's a gentleman. I don't see that she's any call to be ashamed of us as honest and respectable people, ain't we, Melenda? and one of us has worked himself up

2 French for *family council.*

noble, hasn't he, Sam? As for her father, you tell her again that he was one in a thousand—ah!—as one may say, one of a thousand for honesty."

With the repetition of this colossal falsehood, Joe paused. Then he added a few words of personal application, just as a clergyman winds up his discourse.

"As for you," he said, "whether you are Polly, or whether you are not, you're a lady, and such we are glad to see. You can't come too often nor stay too long. You don't want to poke your nose into the working-man's affairs, as some ladies do; you don't think your duty lays in giving advice gratis; you don't want to manage folk as if they were Sunday school children; you don't come the temperance gospel nor the blood and fire hallelujah over us; you don't look at us as if we were specimens in a museum; you don't sniff and make believe as if you were sorry for us all when there's a little mess about the place; when a chap's in trouble or down in his luck, you don't wait for three weeks while the case is gone into; you don't talk about us as if we working-people were the poor, and everybody else was the rich. Sam does that when he gets into a rage, but it don't amount to more than slashing into the system. Sam thinks he can make us all rich and happy with a new system. Lord! there ain't a great deal of difference between us after all; it's mostly a matter of clothes. Look at Melenda, now you've smartened her up. She ain't so pretty as you, but now she's dressed and quiet, she looks as nice mannered, almost."

"Thank you, Joe," said Valentine. "If it should be as you think, and Violet should prefer her present life, which is possible, I will tell her what you say. If it should not be so, why, all the more reason for my coming back to live among my own people, and to be proud of my brothers. Oh! Joe, I do think you are the best fellow in the world." For that brave sticking out for his worthless father, so that the brothers and sisters might never be ashamed, and never even suspect the truth, went straight to her heart.

"And now we'll go," said Joe. "Come, Rhoder. Good-bye, Miss Eldridge." He took her hand respectfully, not fraternally, and she clearly perceived that he knew her secret.

Then Melenda and Lizzie went to look after Lotty, and the three who remained began to talk.

"And what are you going to do when you come back?" asked Sam. "You can't do any general good, though you may do something for these three girls. Nothing can be done of any real use until the system is changed, and we've begun by putting the land on a proper footing. That's at the bottom of all."

"You shall settle that, Sam," said Valentine. "Meantime we shall take the world as it is, and go on tinkering in our small way, until your revolution sets everything right for ever after."

"What's the use of arguing with a woman?" Sam asked, turning to Claude. "Here we are, working up for the grandest change the world has ever seen—the change that is going to give the people their own back again—and she keeps on at us because we don't stop to make a fuss about the workwomen."

"We cannot expect you, with such a magnificent scheme in your head, to think about your sisters, Sam, can we?"

"It will all come in time. I am thinking about them, I tell you. When we've abolished rent and competition, and interest, and capital; when we've nationalised the land, and prevented anybody from getting rich, and made everybody work, I suppose women's wages will be as good as men's; that is, they will all be alike, and they'll mean a good living to everybody—won't that satisfy you?"

"Perhaps, when it comes. But, Sam, how long it is in coming? And suppose we don't like it when it does come? Suppose you only make it more possible for selfish men to use the labour of others, and for strong men to trample on the weak?"

"You are talking nonsense. You don't know the very first beginnings of our revolution."

"Claude, have you nothing to say?"

Claude hesitated. Things had grown terribly real with him of late, and he spoke slowly and with sadness. "I do not suppose," he said, "that some men are born with saddles fitted to their backs, and others with spurs on their heels. And I think that Maurice[3] was right when he taught that the reign of universal competition is not exactly and altogether the Kingdom of Heaven. And I do not believe that the Lord is always on the side of the man who is making money."

"Very good," said Sam. "Why, this is just as I would begin myself."

"But I am certain there is no system, or institution, or code of laws, whatever, which can be imposed upon a people, unless they are ready for it, and desire it for themselves. You will never live to see your dream realised, Sam, because it will be always impossible to make the men of ability, who are the only men to be considered, desire a system in which they themselves shall not be able to do good to themselves first. If it were established tomorrow, it would fall to pieces the next day, for want of incessant and universal watchfulness. I think we had better take the world as it is, and use the materials lying ready to our hands."

"Oh! the world as it is," Sam repeated, "with the Lords and the Church, the parsons, and the landlords, and the manufacturers, and the capitalists!"

"With all of them—just as it is—let us take it as it is. Meanwhile there is a revolution going on of which you know nothing. It is a movement which will be perhaps one of the greatest things that the world has ever seen." He did not mean the Earthly Tract Society. "Men and women who have learned all that science and art and history and philosophy can teach them, are returning to the soil and to the gutter from which their fathers sprang. They come back laden with treasures, which they long to lavish among the people. This is to practise the Christianity which you advanced thinkers despise. Consider another thing, Sam. It is not only that these missionaries will live among the people and teach them all kinds of things, but they will bring the fierce light of publicity to bear upon their ways and their wants. Do you think that any employer in the world would dare to pay his working-women as Melenda has been paid, and to treat them with the cruelty of drilling as she has been treated, if he knew that his name and his rate of pay and his treatment of woman would the very next day be paraded in the public press? The power of publicity has only just commenced. The journalists as yet only half understand their own power. Why, these men and women are going about actually setting up electric lamps in dark places. Let us try to bring this light into all the workshops, so that no kind of grinding and tyranny shall be overlooked. You know what the Russian student said at the grave of his dead comrade, while the police stood by ready to arrest him for a word; 'My brothers,' he said, stretching out his arms, "Light! We want more light." With light, everything may come; even some of the universal unselfishness, Sam, which your generous heart thinks possible. At least, the first steps will be taken when the people begin by themselves to resolve that justice and equity shall be meted out to all, even to the London working-girl. And as for systems, the force of opinion is stronger than any system. Opinion is the will of the people; let us get opinion on the side of the girls. And then—Light—more Light."

3 John Frederick Denison Maurice, more widely known as F. D. Maurice (29 August 1805–1 April 1872), the Christian Socialist.

Chapter xxx

The Bishop's Deathbed

It was about nine o'clock when Sam left them. He was angry, because he could not convince them, and because his brother was so very near the gate of truth, and so very perverse in his refusal to step in. And yet, said Sam to himself, logic, justice, equity, reason, natural religion, the laws of the universe—everything cries aloud that there is no gospel but Socialism. All men are born equal—every man with two legs and ten fingers, and no possessions at all, not a scrap of purple velvet,[1] and not a shovelful of land; no spurs on his heels, and no saddle on his back; no crown on his head, and no chains on his wrists: for everyone the same inheritance, namely, the whole of the round world and all that therein is, that is, as much of it as, divided among the x inhabitants, in equal portions, constitutes his share. Every man must work every day for the general good, he must eat at a common table—why should one man have cutlets à la Soubise, and another, cold pig? He must share in all the luxuries that are attainable by every one: if there be other luxuries which are not enough to go round, they may be divided among the sick and the aged; why should one man drink champagne and another vin bleu? This is Sam's position, and, really, it is impossible to dislodge him from it. He is impregnable, because he is perfectly right. Against him, however, is a force with which he and his friends have never reckoned; it is sometimes called human nature. It is, in fact, the simple, unarmed, naked, natural man, who, alone, is a match for a host, armed with all the weapons of logic, and reason, and right, because of his selfishness, which is a whole armour in itself. He wants all he can grab for himself, and he will go on grabbing all he can. He derides equality; he holds that the spoils are for the strongest; and on this principle he is resolved to live, and so will continue to live until the Kingdom of Heaven comes to change all, and make his position disagreeable. Such being the habit, custom, resolution, and attitude of the natural man, the Socialist may rage furiously, but he will rage in vain.

1 Purple velvet is a signifier of royalty. Velvet was historically an expensive fabric, and purple an expensive dye.

"I must go, too," said Claude, taking his hat; "I am glad they came tonight. Alas! the summer is over, tomorrow morning you will be gone. Good-night, Valentine, and farewell."

"Why a solemn farewell, Claude?"

"Because the past can never be repeated—"

"Nothing is ever repeated; but things can be continued. If you are going to walk, let me walk a part of the way with you. Oh! I am not afraid of returning alone, no one ever molests me. I am just a shop-girl going home, you know, after business."

They went out together. The streets were crowded, because it was fine, and a Saturday night. Even Pitfield Street and East Road, which are considered quiet thoroughfares, were filled with costers' carts, and with folk who came out to buy. The City Road was noisy with multitudinous footsteps, and a good half of Old Street was blocked with the overflow of White Cross Street, where there is held every day and every evening, the noblest costers' market in the whole of London, not even excepting that of the Whitechapel Road. The space is more limited; but then, the very narrowness sets off the variety and cheapness of the goods displayed. Many costers' markets there be in this great town: one would not willingly do injustice to Clare Market, to the New Cut, to the High Street, Marylebone, or to Leather Lane; but that of White Cross Street outshines them all.

"These faces haunt me," said Valentine, as they moved slowly through the crowd. "I shall carry home with me a ghostly crowd of faces. How many thousands of faces have I seen here, and none of them alike? The noise is nothing; one does not remember noise, but the faces—the faces remain; they are always with me."

"If the faces were all boiled down into one by repeated photographs, what sort of a face would it be?"

"Not into one face, Claude; there must be two faces; those of the working-man and the working-woman. I think the man's face would show a certain sluggishness and a good deal of self-indulgence, and in his eyes one would discern a sense of humour; the woman's face would show patience and suffering, and her eyes would be sharp with indignation; they would have no humour in them. Whatever they might turn out they would not be bad faces."

The English face, compounded of many races, is seldom, in fact, a bad face; it is good-tempered to begin with; it is independent and self-reliant; there is a love of justice in it; there is strength in it; there is capability in it; there is the possibility of wrath in it; such wrath as makes the Englishman, when his blood is roused, the most dangerous animal in the world—witness the savagery of our soldiers in India not quite thirty years ago; yet the devil faces which one sees in Paris, when the people are out in the streets, are never found in White Cross Market. To watch the English face is to learn trust in the English people.

"You will cease to think of your troubles, Claude," said Valentine; "you will think of these men and women instead, won't you? It will be best for you; and I am sure it is best to let the dead bury the dead."

"I wish to heaven I could. But suppose the dead refuse to be buried?"

She said no more. Perhaps he had found out even more than she had feared. Presently they reached the end of Old Street where it runs like a broad river into Goswell Road and Aldersgate Street, and here Valentine stopped.

"Good-bye, Claude," she said; "come to see us at home tomorrow evening. I am going home again. Oh! I have had the strangest, the most beautiful summer that ever any girl had, and all by your help, Claude. How can I ever thank you enough? I wonder if you can understand at all what it has been to me—this revelation of men and women, whom we dare to call common men and women? I am like Peter after the Vision and the

Message, which only came to him three times. But my Vision and my Message, Claude, have been repeated to me daily for ninety days."

"And as for me, Valentine," he replied huskily, "I can never tell you; I can never even try to tell you what the summer has been to me."

He pressed her hand and she left him. She was not, you see, his sister; that he had known all along, and now she would find out the truth, and it was impossible that they should continue together in the old relations. What more? He loved her. Who could help loving her, who was so winsome, so loyal, and so brave? He had always loved her, ever since the day when he found out that she was not his sister; and for her sake he had given up all his ambitions, yea, even the ambition of the chancellor's woolsack; and there were moments when it seemed possible, but the appearance of his father made that and everything else impossible; and now, he should never be able to tell her, even in the after years, what she had become to him. How could such a man as himself, with such a family record, dare to connect himself, even in thought, with such a girl?

He stood at the corner of the street watching her light figure speeding quickly along the pavement. Now, either because his heart was so full of love that he could not bear to let the girl go out of his sight, or because a divine admonition came to him—they do come sometimes and interfere strangely with the fortunes of men, though generally we disregard them, so that rogues triumph—Valentine had not got thirty steps before he felt constrained to turn and follow after her. He did so, keeping a few yards behind her, and not losing sight of her for a moment.

The light figure moved swiftly among the people who crowded the pavement, through the men who lounged hands in pocket, and the women who pushed basket in hand. They made way for her to pass, no one offering her the least familiarity. Some of them, perhaps, knew her by this time. She passed through the crowd and crossed the street to the north side where there were fewer people. Presently she stopped, and Claude watched her while she talked to a girl. I know not what she said, or whether she gave the girl anything, but when Valentine left her that girl went away quickly, and in exactly the opposite direction, which seemed as if she had changed her mind about something. In the City Road she stopped again, to talk with another woman who had a baby in her arms. She did give that woman something, and she, too, turned and walked away in another direction, which leads one to believe that she proposed to go home and put the baby to bed. One of these days we shall have a female police in addition to the present highly efficient masculine force.[2] They will be called probably the female persuasives, rather than the female force. They will carry no clubs or revolvers, and they will be horribly dreaded by all kinds of sinners. When you have crossed the City Road and engaged, so to speak, with Brunswick Place, you are already within the limits of Hoxton itself, and if you are so happy as to live in that City of Industry, you are among friends, and almost at home; therefore you will naturally, as Valentine did, begin, at this point, to walk more slowly.

Claude still followed her, as far as the western entrance of Ivy Lane in St. John's Road. There he would have left her and gone his way, but for a thing which awakened his suspicions. St. John's Road is not better lighted than any other of the less important London streets, where they blindly follow the custom of our ancestors, and plant the gas lamps—each with a glass top artfully designed to let all the light mount upwards to the sky and so be lost—at the same intervals as were thought good in the old days of oil lamps. The conservatism of the official mind is a truly wonderful subject for contemplation. The street was, however, well enough lighted

2 Women were not allowed to join the London police force until the early twentieth century.

for Claude to see a figure waiting about on the pavement, opposite to Ivy Lane. There were plenty of people walking, but this man was evidently waiting, and when Valentine turned into Ivy Lane, this man crossed the road and followed her.

He followed her at a distance of three or four yards—Claude wondered what it might mean. Then he passed under the gas lamp at the entrance of the street, and Claude saw his face. Heavens! It was the face of his father! What could he want with Valentine, except to break his promise, and molest and frighten her? It was his father, and by a lurch of the shoulders which betrayed him, his father, it was certain, had been drinking.

Claude quickened his step, his first impulse being to stop the man; but he checked himself, because to do so would certainly cause a row in the street. He would wait till Valentine was in her own room. He kept close behind, therefore, ready to interfere for her protection.

The street was pretty full of women, talking, though it was past ten o'clock and the evening was chilly: there were also a good lot of children, shouting and playing. Valentine passed through them, with a word of greeting and a fair good-night for each. The crowd parted right and left and made a lane for her, because they knew her; they parted again for Mr. Carey, because the crowd always does make a respectful lane for a man who has been drinking. But for Claude they did not make way, and he had to force his way through, and the children got about his feet, so that the chase drew ahead of him, and he was unable to prevent what most he dreaded.

On the ground-floor Valentine found Mr. Lane's door wide open, and his candle burning. She looked in and nodded pleasantly.

"You are feeling well to-night?" she asked.

"Never better, never better," he replied stoutly. "Business has been good this week. I think they are beginning to find me out at last. It is strange, too, because I am very near the end of my dream."

"I hope not. Can't your dream last a little longer?"

"I've got no control over it. You don't expect me to alter the decrees of Fate. The good bishop is on his deathbed—I am certain he can never recover. The children are with him. The prayers of all the churches in the diocese have been offered for him. Many there are who live on, long after sixty-seven: mostly they are men who have only cumbered the ground, whose lives should be an eternal shame to them—men like me—unprofitable dogs. Men like the bishop are generally called away early, before the allotted span. Well, he will go to his own place. But as for me, what shall I do when he is dead and buried?"

"Indeed, Mr. Lane, I do not know. You will have to find some other amusement for your evenings."

"Amusement? For me?" He shook his head; and she left him.

Then the old woman who lived at the back came out of her den.

"There's been a gentleman asking for you, my dear," she said—"not a young gentleman: oh, no!—an elderly gentleman—quite the gentleman—with a pipe in his mouth, and a little in liquor: and most pleasant in his manners, and liberal and generous."

"A gentleman for me?"

"Yes, my dear, and very anxious he was to know your ways, and asked a many questions!" (she did not add that he had begun by giving her a florin[3]) "about what you do with yourself, and who gives you your money. But I was very careful—oh! I am very careful indeed, my dear—I didn't let out nothing about the young gentleman. For, thinks I, very likely he may be one of the jealous sort!"

3 A silver coin worth two shillings.

"Oh!" said Valentine impatiently, "what have I to do with any elderly gentleman?"

"I do hope there's not going to be any trouble about the young gentleman. P'r'aps it wasn't jealousy, and to be sure, I have known, more than once, the lawyers to step in at the last moment and stop it, when the banns[4] was on the point of being put up, so to speak, and the wedding-ring bought. Mind, my dear, don't you give up the letters—don't give up a single line of writing—make 'em pay for the letters, if it's five hundred pound—Here he is again—don't forget about the letters. He do look like a lawyer a bit, come to look at him, don't he?"

It so happened that Mr. Carey, at the very beginning of this evening, and when he had not yet taken more than two or three glasses, had begun to consider the problem of his daughter, and why she lived in Ivy Lane, and where she got her money from, and by what steps she had come to look like a lady, and what a beautiful thing it would be for himself if he could by any means entrap her, and make her his confederate and partner. Such things have been done; but first it is necessary to know a little of a girl's history. He drank another glass or two, then he resolved that he would himself pay a visit to Ivy Lane and find out what he could. It was a beginning, and he would trust no one but himself. So he came and began, Valentine being out, by pumping the old lady, who willingly told all she knew, which was little to the point. Then he waited for her return.

"Well, my dear," he began, cheerfully, "well, Marla, my gal, I've found you out at last—eh? You didn't expect me, did you? Well, this is an agreeable surprise for you, because, my dear, I'll take the liberty, being your father and all, of asking what it means, and how you make your money? It's my duty to see that my children are living honest, and my pleasure to advise them in their courses."

"Go away!" said Valentine.

The old woman stopped at the foot of the stairs to watch. Was he a lawyer? Was it a jealous one?

"Go away!" Valentine repeated. The man laughed. The drink had given him courage. Otherwise he would have obeyed.

In the front room the dreamer started and looked round: he had heard a voice he knew.

"Come," Mr. Carey whispered—"let us talk it over friendly. Give me a kiss, my dear."

He laid his hand upon her shoulder. Valentine shrank from him with a cry. Melenda heard her—flew from her room, and sprang from the top to the bottom of the stairs with one bound, and stood before her.

"Now, then, who are you?" she cried. "Don't you be afraid, Valentine. It's only some man who's been drinking, and come to the wrong house! I ain't afraid of any man, drunk or sober—don't you mind. Your very last night, too!"

"Now, don't you put your oar in, young woman. You'd best stand out of the way, you had!"

"Go out of this," said Melenda firmly, "or I'll show you the way."

"Well," he went on—"if this don't beat all!" He steadied himself, because the drink made him just a little heavy in the head, and just a little uncertain in his speech: "They ought to be proud of me—everybody else would be proud of such a man—you'd be proud, you would, my dear—you look like somebody I knew once—you do, indeed—it's a most remarkable likeness! There isn't such another man as me in all London. Why, you wouldn't believe it, from the conduct of that skittish little devil there, that I'm James Carey—the great James Carey. Everybody has heard of James Carey! They used to call me the King of the Burglars. I'm King James the First—his Gracious Majesty King Carey. His Royal Highness and Right Reverend King Carey!"

"Go away!" said Melenda, "or I'll tear you in pieces!"

4 A public announcement of an intended marriage.

She hadn't torn anybody to pieces for some time; she had not even enjoyed the luxury of a rage royal, since the last day of the drilling. Now she looked fierce enough for anything. But then a hand was laid upon the man's shoulder—

"Come away," said Claude—"come away without a word!"

"It's the boy," said the man, with such a gush of horrid blasphemy only possible after a wretched man has swallowed compulsory doses of scripture for twenty years. "It's the adjective boy![5] What's he doing here? Oh! you think you'll get rid of me, do you? The allowances are to stop, are they?" He addressed Claude, because between him and Valentine there stood a tigress with flashing eyes and thirsty talons. "You'll stop yours, will you? Well, we'll see to that, my young swell, and whether you'll rather pay down, or let me own up—pay down, my boy, or let me own up." He had not drunk so much but that he was perfectly coherent in his speech, but the drink made him foolhardy.

"Go!" said Claude.

"I shall not go." He raised his voice and added a volley, copious and eloquent, of those flowers of language which are so abundant in Ivy Lane as to pass for weeds. "I shall stay," he concluded, "all night if I like."

By this time a little crowd was gathered round the door, expectant of a row.

Then there happened a strange and wonderful thing. The door of the ground-floor front opened, and there came forth, slowly and unsteadily, the old man whom they all knew, the harmless old man who had lived among them so many years, and had held speech with none. He carried in his one hand a lighted candle. The other hand, raised to his shoulder, trembled and clutched and closed. His face was perfectly white, as white as the face of a dead man. His long limbs trembled with extreme weakness; his head was bent forward eagerly; his eyes were glaring. It was actually the face of a dead man with living eyes, which gleamed with light supernatural.

"Oh!" he said, with a deep sigh of satisfaction, "at last I have found mine enemy. I was dying—but I heard his voice. The bishop"—he turned to Valentine—"The bishop is dying. And I was dying. But I knew I was not to die till I had seen him once again." He looked round him as one might look who was taking a last farewell of earth, and he gave his candle to Valentine as one about to die upon the scaffold hands the last thing he values to the last friend beside him.

"No man," he said, solemnly looking about him, "hath power in the day of death; neither shall wickedness deliver them who are given to it." Then a very wonderful change passed suddenly over his face. It became the face of a young man: the change which sometimes falls upon the face of one who is nearly dead fell upon this man's face before his death. Valentine saw it and knew that she was looking upon the man as he had been, save for his white hair, thirty–five years before, while he was yet in honour and respect. Mr. Carey saw it too—and staggered as if struck suddenly.

"You?" he said, "you? I thought you must be dead long ago." He became instantly sober, as half-drunken men sometimes do. Then as the long lean figure turned towards him with outstretched arms, he quickly stepped out of the house and fled, running through the people. After him, with long swift strides, followed Vengeance, long deferred. It seemed as if no one noticed them, for no one ran after them, and no one cried after

5 In his autobiography, Besant notes that he represented in *Children of Gibeon* the daily life of the working poor "so far as they can be offered without offensive and useless realism" (p. 247). Besant refuses here to write *bloody* ("It's the bloody boy!"), which was regarded as "the universal adjective." His readers would have readily understood his meaning.

them. They passed through the crowd unheeded, and as if unseen. When Claude thought of this afterwards it seemed to him a thing beyond and above the natural. Though the streets were full of people, this strange flight, this strange pursuit, attracted no attention at all, no more than if they were invisible. But he who fled was filled with a wild and dreadful terror, that which falls upon the heart when some long-forgotten crime springs into light, and escape is impossible, and the time of forgiveness is past. And he who followed after was filled with such gladness of rage and satiated revenge as filled the heart of Fredegonde, when, after many years, she saw Brunehaut about to be dragged at the heels of the wild horse.[6] The fugitive ran in vain, for at his heels, though he knew it not, there followed Death, before whom all fly in vain. He was in the shape of an old man, striding with long steps, bareheaded, his grey hairs flying behind him, in rags, with panting breath, white face, and outstretched arms.

There is a place beyond St. John's Road where a bridge crosses the canal: and beyond the bridge there is a way down to the bank. It is a dark and narrow way. The man ran down here—thinking that he might so escape. But he did not. As he reached the tow-path the avenging hand was laid upon his shoulder. He turned and faced his enemy. Of what should he be afraid? A poor, old, trembling man who had been starving during all the years which he himself had spent in prison, well cared for and well fed. He looked so decrepit that James Carey laughed aloud and forgot his terror. He had been afraid because he had been drinking. That was all. Afraid of a silly old fool too weak to harm a girl.

"Man!" cried Mr. Lane, seizing his enemy with both hands and shaking him by the coat collar, "Man! give me back my ruined life." James Carey would have laughed again, but that his enemy's face became distorted as by sharp and sudden pain—for once more, for the last time, came that clutching and tearing at the heart—and that his enemy's legs trembled and his body swayed to and fro, and they were on the water's edge, and the decrepit hands, strange to say, held him like a vice. Then there was a staggering and a struggle on the gravel: and a cry of agony and terror, and a splash in the water ... and ... and ... why, Mr. Lane had got back his life, and, with it, had already learned, one hopes, why such misery and such weakness as his had been permitted even for such an infinitesimal period of time as thirty-five years. When the victim recovered his life, what did his tempter and oppressor recover?

* * *

"Who was it?" asked Melenda, when they were gone.

"A drunken man," said Valentine.

"But he seemed to know you. And Claude knew him. And what had he done to Lizzie's father?"

"I do not know," said Claude; "but I know this of him, that he is a bad man. Do not ask any more, Melenda."

"Well," said Melenda, "he's gone at any rate. Come upstairs, Valentine."

She left them and went back to Lotty. The old woman, feeling the florin burn in her pocket, stole out gently, and made for the public-house opposite by a circuitous route, namely, half down Ivy Lane and back again, so that she should not seem like going out expressly for a drop of gin. She would only have two twopenny goes and drink up the rest on the morrow—Sunday. And on Monday she would go "in" again for the winter. Oh!

---

6 Fredegund and Brunhilde were two sixth-century Frankish queens who engaged in a forty-year feud, leading to assassinations and a civil war, over the murder of Brunhilde's sister.

this florin was a blessed windfall indeed, because now she would be able to go back to the House with some of the resignation which accompanies recent gin. The crowd at the door had dispersed, disappointed; there are always more disappointments than real rows; things seldom come off in all their possible fulness.

"The man is gone, Valentine," said Claude. "Do you know who he is?"

"Yes, I know him. Something terrible will happen. The other man—Lizzie's father—will do him a mischief; they are old enemies. Oh, it is more wickedness."

"If there is to be more trouble," said Claude, "somebody must be here to meet it for you. Go upstairs, now, Valentine. Good-night."

Valentine obeyed. She did not ask Claude how he came to be there; it was natural that if she was in any danger he should be there to protect her. Nor did she ask Claude how he came to know the man.

Meanwhile, Claude shut the street door, and sat down on the stairs and waited. They were very uncomfortable stairs to sit upon, being steep and with narrow steps. The candle left in the room beside him went on burning until midnight, when it went out suddenly after just one flicker in the socket. Then the stairs were in perfect darkness, but the front room was lighted by the gas lamp in the street. Outside, the talk of the people grew languid, and finally ceased altogether, and the shuffling of their feet was heard no more; the children left off shouting and crying and went away to bed; the public-house shut up, and the men in the bar dispersed noisily; there was an occasional step of a belated resident, and then nothing but an echo of steps from Hoxton Street, or the distant shouting of some drunken man.

Claude sat on his uncomfortable perch for two or three hours, and then he remembered that there was a chair in the next room. He changed his position, but he did not allow himself to sleep. Strange! that the old man did not return. Had something happened? His mind was agitated and full of foreboding.

In the middle of October the nights are long: the sun does not rise until after six. Claude waited and watched through the whole of that long night, for seven long hours. Neither of the two men came back. As for one, he was probably in the Temple asleep on Claude's bed, or drinking and smoking and fiddling through the night. But the other—Lizzie's father—where was he?

And what would come of it all? What would be the end? As for Valentine, in a few hours she would be safe; in two days more she would know that she was not this man's daughter at all. She knew who he was: she said so. How did she know it? How much did she know? There was plenty to occupy his thoughts all through the night.

The morning broke at last—Sunday morning. At the first streak of daylight Claude went out into the court, as if expecting to find there some traces of the missing pair. The air was keen and clear; Ivy Lane, as the light grew stronger, looked inconceivably disreputable, shabby and dirty, with the wreckage and rubbish of a week lying about, the cabbage-stalks, bruised plums, rotten apples and pears, the shreds of paper and potsherds. Well, Valentine was going away: she was no longer to be considered: he was free, so far as she was concerned. He would go to Joe and tell him all; between the two their mother would be protected; he would give nothing more to his father, and as for his real name and the family history, let them both be proclaimed upon the housetops, with all the infamy and the shame of it, if needs must.

"Thank God," he murmured—"Valentine is not his daughter!"

A little before eight, there was already some stir among the younger and hungrier residents; the elders lie in bed as long as they can on Sunday mornings, and when the bell of St. Agatha's was calling upon a deaf and stiff-necked people to get up and come to early celebration, and the assistant priest was hastily robing himself for that lonely function, and the shops in Hoxton were getting swept out and garnished for the Sunday morning market, Valentine came downstairs.

"You here already, Claude?" she asked, surprised.

"Why, Valentine, you did not suppose I should go away and leave you unprotected, would you?"

"You have actually been here all night? You have been watching for me? Oh, Claude! it is too much!"

"Nothing is too much for you, Valentine. Don't think of me, but tell me—what do you know of this man? Why does he come here? Why did he follow you?"

"What do you know, Claude?"

"I know all that there is to know: the whole shameful business."

"And I, too, know all that there is to know. Do not pain yourself to speak about it. I have known the whole story for a month—Joe and the mother both think he is dead."

"But how did you come to know him?"

Valentine told her tale, briefly; and passing over one or two passages, especially that in which she was constrained to box the man's ears.

"I bought his silence," she concluded—"I sent him money every week. But I knew that some time or other it would be found out. Claude, be brave—let us take Joe into our confidence and devise something that will keep him from the others."

"I bought him, too," said Claude—"but I will give him no more money. Thank heaven, you are out of his reach, and so is Violet: she must never know. As for the others—"

"Let us persuade him to go away, Claude. He may be bribed."

"He will never go away as long as there is a house left in England that he has not robbed."

There are so many houses in London alone, that the prospect opened up was more stupendous than the mind of man can well take in. And to think, besides, that new houses are always being built.

"At least, Valentine," Claude went on, "you are going home this very day. Go at once—if you go now you will find them at breakfast—if you stay here, there may be, I know not, some terrible tragedy. I feel as if anything may happen! Why has not that old man been home all night? And they were enemies, you say. Go at once, Valentine, before any scandal happens which may involve your name. So much, at least, we owe to Lady Mildred. I will get you a cab. Have you anything to pack?"

She obeyed. There was nothing that she wished to take away. She transferred the care of Lotty to Melenda, kissed the girls, promised to return in a day or two, and hurried away, with the sense that something was going to happen.

Claude remained, watching in Mr. Lane's room, all the morning. Presently Lizzie came downstairs to see her father, and appeared neither astonished nor alarmed to hear that he had not been home all night. He had slept out before, when he had work to do. Claude told her nothing of what he knew or suspected. He must have gone down Whitechapel way she said, among the German Jews, who regard not the Christian Sabbath when they want work done.[7]

At one o'clock the "Adelaide" opened its hospitable doors, and the old lady of the back ground-floor crossed the court, and proceeded to spend what was left of her florin. In half an hour she came out, with trembling lips

7 For Christians, the holy day of rest is Sunday, whereas the Jewish Sabbath is Saturday.

and glassy eyes, and returned to her own room, where she flung herself upon the floor heavily, the door wide open, careless of the world, to sleep off the last drink she would get for six months, at least.

At two, Claude thought he would wait no longer. Perhaps his father might have gone to the Temple.

He had not—no one was there, and there were no traces at all of his presence. Nothing had been taken away, no tobacco was on the table, and there were no empty bottles. This was very strange. Surely something must have happened!

Chapter xxxi

Home Again

Claude withdrew from Ivy Lane. Heavens! without Valentine how desperately mean and squalid the place appeared! Even Melenda and Lizzie, now neat and "respectable," were incongruous amid such surroundings! As was Ivy Lane without her, so would be his whole life without her.

He stayed in his chambers all that Sunday afternoon, expecting a visit from his father. But there was no visit. What was he doing? And why had not the old letter-writer returned? All day he sat in the quiet rooms looking over the empty courts, while his feet were drawn as by a magnet towards the west of London. Persons who are afflicted with a constant drought are drawn to public-houses as by strings; but lovers towards their mistresses by ropes and hawsers. When it grew dusk he went to his club with a sense of safety because he could not be disturbed there, and after dinner he repaired to the house where he fain would be all day long.

"I am very glad to see you again, Claude." Lady Mildred welcomed him with unwonted warmth. "You have been a brother indeed, and more than a brother, to Valentine. She has told me all that you have done for her. And now, before you go to see the girls—Violet is very well and is longing to see you again—sit down and tell me something about your summer. I am afraid you have been a prisoner, from your own point of view. I want to know exactly what it is that Valentine has done. All I can get from her, except by parenthesis, is an enthusiastic account of what you have done. But you are looking ill, my dear boy; ill and worried. Is anything troubling you?"

"Yes; one or two things are troubling me a great deal. I will tell you about them afterwards."

Then he began to talk about Valentine's life among these poor folk of Ivy Lane, and because it was a really fine theme, and he had been watching the subject of it closely for three long months, during which he had thought of nothing else but the girl and her courage and her patience, he spoke eloquently and even with burning words. It was a rare spirit indeed which has persevered until Melenda was conquered, which had saved Lizzie and nursed Lotty. And if Claude's lips were touched with flame, and his eyes glowed, it was not only because he loved the damsel, but also because he admired her deeds.

Lady Mildred listened and watched him curiously, as if trying to read something unexpressed—something between the lines.

"And your own part in all this, Claude; you have not spoken of yourself."

"Oh! my part. I am Valentine's servant; her vizier." But he hesitated and dropped his eyes, because he would have to confess that he had deliberately thrown away all those gods which formerly he had worshipped.

"More than a servant, Claude, I think. What is this I hear about your self-sacrifice?"

The young man blushed. Nobody likes to be suddenly accused of such a virtue as self-sacrifice, which is at once rare, difficult of attainment, and much admired.

"It seems to me a very serious thing, this that you propose, my dear boy," Lady Mildred went on. "You have always been ambitious from the very beginning. Nobody has begun better than you; none of your contemporaries has a better chance. There is, I am assured by those who know, a really splendid prospect before you. Think well before you throw it away. There is a successful practice before you; in course of time, perhaps, a seat upon the Bench[1]—even in the future a peerage—anything is possible for such a man as you—including, if you are wise enough to wait until success is assured, such a marriage, with such connections, as will advance your children as well as yourself. Wealth and distinction are as certainly within your grasp as can be humanly predicted, and you propose to throw them away. Are they things, then, of no value to you? Claude, if you have consented to this sacrifice only to please the whim of a girl, I cannot, I must not allow it to be carried into effect without remonstrance."

"Valentine has no whims—she has purposes. But, indeed, even if it was at first by her entreaties that I consented to change the plan of my life, that no longer remains the only reason. My old plans are abandoned of necessity—there is not left to me any choice but a life of obscurity."

"Why have you no choice?"

"Do you remember, Lady Mildred, how, long ago, you took me to Westminster Abbey to hear a great preacher, and to see the tombs of great men?[2] and to the courts of law to look at the judges and hear the barristers: and to the Academy[3] to see the pictures—and to the theatres to see the play?—and how, everywhere, you fired my imagination by telling me that this, and this—and everything, was in my reach, if I desired it, and chose to work for it. You made me the most ambitious of boys. Besides, I had to justify things—certain things—my education."

"You have nobly justified those things, Claude!"

"There never seemed to me anything in the world worth living for, except distinction and success. And now I have to give up all."

"Why, Claude?"

"I cannot pretend that it is for the sake of my own people—for unselfish motives—I thought I might pretend that, until a fortnight ago. And I cannot pretend that it was for love of a girl, though there is nothing in the world I would not do for Valentine's sake."

"Claude!"

1 The Queen's Bench is one of three divisions of the High Court of Justice in England. It is reserved for the highest-ranking judges.

2 Westminster Abbey is part of the Church of England. It has been the location for royal coronations since 1066 and the burial site for seventeen monarchs as well as a number of Britain's leading figures in politics, literature, medicine, and other fields.

3 Royal Academy of Arts.

"No, Lady Mildred, she is not my sister—she thinks she may be, but I know better—my brother Joe told me the truth. He recognised Violet's resemblance to her father and his own daughter, and I love Valentine. One moment, please. I can no longer think that I am giving up my ambition for her sake. I am only a man who must live in obscurity; I am condemned to it because I am overshadowed by a great social disgrace."

"What disgrace, Claude? What possible disgrace can have fallen upon you?"

"It has become impossible that I should continue to live any longer among gentlemen. I can no longer pretend to associate with them. I must not, for common decency's sake, sit with them or talk with them; I ought not to have come here even, without letting you know the truth before I came. But I only found it out three or four weeks ago. It is my father"—he stopped short with cheeks aflame, for it was a most horrible thing to put into words—"my father is not dead, as I always thought, and as you were told. He has been in prison all these years; he is not an honest man, as my brother Joe always declared; he is a liberated convict: he is at large, with a ticket of leave."

"Oh! Claude! my poor boy, is this true?"

"Yes. He first made himself known to Valentine, whom he took for his own daughter; she stood between him and my mother, who does not know—yet. She bribed him to silence: I know all now. Valentine had a terrible time with him. Then he broke her conditions and came to me, unknown to her, to my chambers, to the Temple. I daresay he is there at this moment, drinking and smoking. He takes my money: he pawns my things: he comes at all hours of the day and night. Now you know, Lady Mildred, the trouble that has fallen upon me."

"My poor boy!" she repeated.

"If I do anything or succeed at all, he will be at my elbow, selling his own silence. He takes a delight in the shame he inflicts upon me. He is, I firmly believe—though he is my own father—the worst man that lives. Oh! can there be," he cried, with a despairing gesture of shame and pain, "can there be—is there anywhere, in this great city, a man nearer to the gutter than myself? Now you understand why I must go away and hide myself. If I do any work it must be for the people from whom I sprang—if only in atonement—it must be work that will never be spoken about. Is it for me to have ambition? Is such a man as myself to ask for distinction? Why, if I were a judge tomorrow, I might have to try my own father. My only friends should be the men like myself, whose fathers are in the gaols[4]—the sons of the burglars and thieves of London. And now, Lady Mildred, you understand, do you not, why I am not ashamed, since I have told you all this, to confess that I love Valentine. For a man so fettered and held in bonds might as well love a princess. All day long I hear my father's voice, that mocks at everything honest and true; all day long I say to myself, 'Go back to the slums and work for those who are like yourself, children of the gaol-birds and the outcasts;' and at night I lie awake, waiting for the sound of his footsteps in my room."

"Claude, my poor boy!"

"I trust only that Violet will never learn the truth. As for the others, sooner or later they will learn it, I suppose. One cannot always keep such a man back, and very soon he will have taken all the money I have."

"Violet shall never know if I can prevent it. And as for yourself—"

"As for me, my course is clear. What other men do for a few years and of free choice, able to take up and lay down as they please, I must do all my life, and by compulsion. And as for Valentine, I shall go on being her

4 Jails.

servant. You will trust me, I know you will trust me, never to let her suspect, by any word of mine, that I regard her other than a sister. I have endeavoured—I have always hoped and endeavoured—to be a gentleman."

"Thank you, Claude," she pressed his hand with both her own in a kindly and motherly fashion. "You learned very early, my dear son, the instincts of a gentleman—there is nothing finer in the world than to be a gentleman—and I have always trusted you and always loved you. Oh! my poor boy, I am so sorry for you." For the first time Lady Mildred kissed him. She laid her hands upon his shoulders and drew his face to her and kissed him on the forehead, while her eyes were full of tears.

Claude turned his head to hide his own. "I am glad," he said, "that I have told you. I can bear it better now that you know."

"Yes, it is better to tell things to people who love you. As for Valentine, she will always love you—as your sister. I am sure of that. It is good for a young man to love a girl, if she is worthy of him, though he can never win her. Go on loving my daughter, Claude, and, if you please, believe her to be everything that a woman can be, this side the Gates of Heaven.

"And now," she added, "forget your troubles. We will all take counsel how to bribe this man into voluntary exile. You shall be protected somehow. And Violet shall never know; and now go and make the girls happier, Claude. They are longing for you."

* * *

It was immediately after this that Lady Mildred explained some of her views on the situation to her friend and confidante.

"My dear Mildred," said the latter, "I cannot believe that any good can come of a girl going to live by herself among the scum."

"The scum, Bertha, rises to the top."

"Then the grounds, or the settlings of society, with the drunken and disreputable people, unprotected. Think of the wickedness she must learn."

"Yes, I suppose that Valentine knows already much more wickedness than both of us put together. It is strange to think of it. Yet the knowledge does not seem to do her any harm. She is as sweet as ever and as good, though she looks more womanly. I dare say Eve looked more womanly after she had eaten of the tree of knowledge of good and evil, but she would look guilty as well, which my child does not."

"No, poor thing!"

"When you and I were born, Bertha, our fathers mostly called the people the mob, or the common people, or the lower orders, or the lower classes. They laughed at their ignorance, and expected one thing only of them—respect. Things are changed."

"They are indeed!"

"We cannot afford to laugh at the ignorance of the people anymore, because we have given them all the power, though they don't know yet that they have got it; but they will find out very soon, and then—"

"Oh, Mildred! don't say there is going to be a horrid revolution, and that we shall all be swallowed up."

"We have had a long rope if we are to be swallowed up. But I am not afraid of the English people. And as for the revolution, it has been quietly going on all around us for a hundred years. They will take away class power, and curtail the power of land and capital, Bertha, but they will not guillotine us. We are an orderly people, and do not want to murder each other. But the more we, of our set, learn what working-people want and think, and how they judge things, and the more they, for their part, learn what we think about things, the better it will be for all of us, and the safer. Valentine has learned things which she will never forget. Do you think that if there were many girls like her, the workmen of this country could be made, by any stump orator, to look upon rich people as their natural enemies?"

"I like the old ways best," said Bertha. "Let the working-man go his way, so long as he behaves himself, and let us go our way. But what will you do about Claude? Of course, if Valentine should turn out not to be his sister after all, they cannot go on together as they have done."

"That will be for Valentine to determine."

"But, my dear, the young man might so far forget himself as to fall in love with her."

"It will be Valentine's business. She will do as she pleases."

"Would you? But you could not let your daughter marry a young man who has such family connections—a workman brother and a working-girl sister?"

"My dear, I think a woman can never do better than marry a distinguished man. I married Sir Lancelot because everybody said he was distinguished. He has been dead nearly twenty years, and everybody has clean forgotten him, so that, I suppose, there are certain kinds of distinctions which don't last. But as for Claude, I am sure that he will distinguish himself in a way that does last. If one of the girls—the one who is not his sister—were to marry him, she might advance him."

"But of course they will both love him merely as a brother, which is a safeguard."

"I don't know. The true sisterly feeling does not grow up in three months. It wants the long years of childhood."

"We have said nothing about Violet," said Bertha, after a little.

"What about Violet?"

"I mean about her future, if she should be Claude's sister."

"Violet in any case will remain with me. She has the artistic temperament, which naturally dislikes rude realities and shrinks from rough people. Artists are full of emotion and sympathy because they are quick to see; yet they are generally touched with a kind of selfishness of their own, which also belongs to the temperament. Now Valentine is not an artist; she neglects the rags, whether they are picturesque or not, and looks for the man below them; she will go back to the rags and roughness, but Violet will remain. Claude will go with Valentine, sister or no sister, and Violet will stay with me."

"And now I am quite sure," said Bertha quickly, "that if Valentine had not been your own daughter, you would not have sent her on this quixotic errand."

"You will know tomorrow."

"Yes," Bertha repeated, "I am quite sure. You would never have incurred the terrible responsibility of risking another person's child. Yes. You are a clever woman, Mildred, but I have discovered your secret at last. Well, the son of the soil goes back to the soil. That is wonderful, considering what he must remember about the place. It is not wonderful at all that Violet should refuse to return, though she cannot remember anything, because she can imagine. But it is to me inexplicable that Valentine should have wanted to go down there at all, and still more wonderful that she should want to return there."

* * *

"Here is Claude at last," cried Violet, "Claude at last! Oh, Claude!" She gave him both her hands and would have liked nothing better than to kiss him on both cheeks. "How glad I am to see you again, and Valentine again! Is it really you? Sometimes I thought it was all a dream and that there never was any Claude. You have made Val thin, Claude, and you are thin yourself. And she has been having grave fits and telling me dreadful stories about working-girls, poor things."

At that moment, Valentine was not grave at all. To be back again in the old home atmosphere; to put on again a dress that was not the plain grey or brown stuff she had worn for three months, but the same dress, or something like it, in which Claude had first seen her, a sweet and dainty confection of white, with lace; and to be again with Violet, filled her with happiness. To Claude she was always more than mortal. And now she was more than a goddess. And she was laughing. Alas! had he ever once succeeded in making her laugh during the whole three months that they had been together every day? Could this really be the same girl who only twenty-four hours since was shrinking in terror from his—his father—Violet's father?

"I think it must have been a dream," Valentine said, "unless, perhaps, everything is a dream. The summer, in that case, is only just going to begin; it is still June and we are considering where we shall go. It is like the last scene in the opera which is the same as the first, and the heroine wakes up to find that it has all been a dream.[5] I suppose there is not any such place as Ivy Lane, is there, Claude? Was there ever a tall old man with grey hair named Mr. Lane? He had a daughter in my dream called Lizzie, and there was a girl named Melenda, and another named Lotty—poor Lotty."

"And another pretending to be Polly-which-is-Marla," said Violet. "No, dear, it isn't a dream, and I have had the most dismal time you can possibly conceive. She looks much too pale, Claude. Do you think she has had enough to eat? O! Val, how could you live three months by yourself, and among those horrid people? I hope my relatives behaved with tolerable decency towards you. Did Melenda tear the clothes off your back? Did Sam make you a Socialist? Did Joe treat you civilly? Tell me, Claude, were they nice at all?"

"Melenda is now my dearest friend," said Valentine. "You would not know her if you saw her now."

"Oh!" The little interjection implied that Violet had no desire to know that young lady more intimately. "And she has done everything for herself, Claude. Do you think you ought to have permitted it?"

"I am rather ashamed now," said Valentine, "of having a lady's maid."

"She has actually cleaned her own windows and washed her own cups and saucers. Yet she hasn't spoiled her hands. Why do all housemaids have red hands, then?"

"I confess that I did not really like cleaning up. But it is soon done, and it gives very little trouble."

"That depends upon the person," said Violet; "to me it would give all the trouble in the world. I want everything provided for me, clean, bright, pretty and finished, just as if things grew so, and would always remain so. I don't want to know who made them—no doubt, unpleasant people—or how they came. I like to have everything made for me, brought to me, and presented to me, as a matter of course, just as if I were a princess by divine right,[6] and oh! if I were a princess, how fervently I should believe in divine right!"

"My dear, you will always have everything just exactly as if you were a princess."

"Instead of a—"

5 Likely Georges Bizet's *La jolie fille de Perth*, which is based on a novel by Walter Scott.
6 Divine right holds that monarchs are chosen by God and therefore unquestionable rulers.

"No, Violet, you shall not say it. The strange thing is the way in which mistakes are made and young princesses get mixed up and served out wrong. Now I am certain that Melenda was meant for a despotic sovereign. She would have made an admirable czarina in the days when they chopped off heads without trial. And Lizzie was born, I am sure, to be a fashionable young lady."

"And what about that other girl who looked delicate and was lying down?"

"She is dying, Violet," said Claude gravely.

"Poor thing! I suppose there is always somebody dying there. We must send her grapes, Val dear."

Violet belonged to that large school of philanthropists who would treat every painful case with half-a-crown and a basket of grapes. And so great is their sympathy with those who suffer that they cannot bear even to think of them, much less to talk about them.

"There is tragedy as well as comedy at Hoxton," said Claude.

When they fell to talking again in a lighter strain, and they were so happy at being together again that they talked the greatest nonsense imaginable. Claude forgot his troubles and laughed with them, though, for all three, the tears were close behind the laughter, just as in the pools which are sometimes geysers, the bubbles on the surface show the agitation of the waters below. As for Valentine, this return to an atmosphere of peace, where there could be careless talk, was like the wandering down a green glade, beside a little brook, with the birds singing and the flowers at her feet, after a long sojourn in the hot and thirsty sands. She had never appreciated it before. This possibility of careless talk, as if there were no misery in the world that she could cure or cause, or that concerned her.

An atmosphere of peace. It is, if you think of it, the choicest possession of the easy classes. Yet they share it with the shepherd on the hillside and the gamekeeper in the woods. Those who live in crowded streets and narrow courts, in tenement houses or in model lodgings, can never breathe this atmosphere of peace. All around them is the buzz and humming of their fellows—not a peaceful murmur as of bees, but an angry, dissatisfied, suffering sound, made up of groans and oaths and lamentations, as well as of the laughter of children and the shouts of those who play.

And Claude was wondering whether the Valentine of this evening could be really the same girl who, twenty-four hours before, stood in the doorway shrinking with terror from a half-drunken and unrepentant convict who called himself her father. In his inexperience, he made no allowance for reaction. One is never so completely *folâtre*[7] as on the day after a period of great anxiety. Gentlemen, for instance, who have been locked up for a short term are said to exhibit a larklike blitheness and vivacity at the "friendly lead" which follows their release.

Then Claude wondered, looking at the two girls, how he could ever have entertained the least doubt as to the real Beatrice. For he saw now that the face of Violet was Joe's face, and his own face, and his father's face. And her voice was Joe's, and his own, and—his father's; a soft and sweet voice in her, and in the men a low and musical voice. How could anyone have ever doubted? To be sure, when he saw Violet for the first time he had not yet seen his father, and he thought less about Joe than about Melenda and Sam. Now Violet was not in the least like Sam and Melenda, who, as we know, "favoured" their mother.

Authorities are divided as to whether at its best the masculine or the feminine countenance is the more perfect from the artistic point of view. Yet one would have liked, in the days when there was the strongest

7 French for *playful.*

feeling on the subject, to have said unto Zeuxis:[8] "Just figure for me in undying colours the most beautiful girl-face that exists anywhere around the shores of the Mediterranean." English girls about that time were still in the rough, somewhere among the Hercynian forests.[9] "Next, paint me the same face in its masculine form, and then the same face as a child, as a boy, as a girl, and as an old man, and as an old woman, so that in every age we may have the most perfect type of beauty." I think that Violet would have done very well for the first type and Claude for the second. Horrible to think of the same face grown old and marked with the seal that stamps the prison-bird! His own face, Claude clearly discerned, and his father's face, were both so plainly drawn in Violet's, that he wondered how there could ever have been the slightest doubt. But very few, of those concerned, had had the pleasure of making Mr. James Carey's personal acquaintance.

---

8 A fifth-century Greek painter.

9 An enormous section of woodlands described in ancient Greek and Roman geographies of Germany, which some Victorians viewed as the ancestral origins of the English people.

Chapter XXXII

The Finding of the Inquest

When Claude went back to his chambers, he was disappointed in not finding them already occupied by an elderly gentleman with grey hair and a fiddle in his hand, and a pipe in his month. He fully expected to find that gentleman in occupation; he expected to hear him fiddling as he went up the stairs; in fact, he had made up his mind while walking home what he should say to him, and he arranged a dramatic scene, short but very effective. He would begin by saying, firmly and calmly, "You have broken the conditions. I shall therefore discontinue your allowance. You will get no more money from your supposed daughter; and I will take care that the others shall give you nothing. If you attempt to worry my mother she shall be taken out of the almshouse, and placed under proper protection." At this point his parent would probably break out into that rude eloquence which is known in Ivy Lane as "language."

Then Claude would go on—"I will, however, allow you twenty-five shillings a week, on the condition that you go out of the country to Guernsey, or Jersey, or somewhere." A certain amount of filial piety (how much filial piety ought to be expected towards a father who turns out so badly?) would suffer him to be regardless of the language, but he would be firm in refusing to give him anything, except on that one condition. Filial piety, he was sure, was consistent with starving a parent into submission, so long as submission is good for his children. This reduction of obstinacy once effected, one might again consider the Fifth Commandment and its bearings on the case, and how one might contrive to scrape together, somehow, in obedience to the injunction, a little, if ever so little, honour for one's father; just as the toper squeezes the empty bottle and the miser skins the flint.[1]

Somehow these previously arranged dialogues and dramatic situations never come off as they are intended, so that one always has to fall back upon impromptu words and unforeseen tableaux.

---

1 A *toper* drinks alcohol, usually to excess, while a miser will save money in any way possible.

His chambers were empty; the windows were dark; there was no one in King's Bench walk, except the ghosts of the dead lawyers, who have long since driven away the ghosts of the Knights Templars, and now walk nightly in wigs and gowns, a merry troop, laughing and telling each other the old circuit stories of which barristers are never tired; the stairs echoed to no other footsteps than his own; no one waited for him on the landing: there was no one in the room.

Well, his father had only postponed his visit, that was clear; he would come in the night, or next day, or the day after, because no more money would be sent to him, and he must sooner or later come to terms, because he had no means of getting any. That he would go to Tottenham appeared unlikely, because there was nothing to be got out of a poor old almswoman. There was, indeed, another possibility, which Claude did not take into account, as it was a thing quite outside his own experience. He forgot that his father had a profession—not, it is true, one of the learned professions, but yet a profession which requires the greatest dexterity, a brain full of resource, an eye keen to watch for opportunity, vulpine stealth, and that kind of natural aptitude which, when applied to the arts of poetry, the drama, and fiction, we call genius. What was there to prevent Mr. Carey from resuming the active practice of that profession? This, indeed, conducted with the greatest caution, and, if necessary, supplemented by an occasional levy upon his son and daughter, was the scheme of life contemplated by the enlarged captive. He nourished thoughts, also, of a second course of public glory; he would again be the head of the profession. Fate, as too often happens, prevented the accomplishment of this design; otherwise, the end of Mr. Carey's history, and of this story, would have been different.

Then Claude, with dismal forebodings of a nocturnal visit, went to bed. The Temple was perfectly quiet; there was no noise from the river, which by day is not at all a silent highway, and none from the Embankment; there were no steps on the gravel and in the court below. He lay awake waiting for the soft footfall which he knew and dreaded, or for the light click of the burglar's key unlocking his door; once or twice he thought that the man must be actually in his rooms, and he got up and looked into his keeping room in order to satisfy himself. Two or three more such nights as this and he should go mad; when at length he did fall asleep, worn out by the long vigil of Saturday night and by his own anxieties, it was to dream that his father stood by his bedside threatening that he would never leave him, that he would remain with him night and day, all the rest of his life, that he would never be out of his sight or out of his thoughts for a single moment.

That dream will in a way be fulfilled; Claude will never cease to have his father with him; he "can never" be out of his thoughts. Yet this nightmare will not come true in the sense in which it was first understood.

All the morning he remained in his chambers, expecting this visitor, or at least a letter or some kind of message, if only a threatening message. None came at all. The very silence itself was threatening, and all the more because its threatenings were as vague and uncertain as the distant roll of thunder.

In the afternoon Claude resolved to wait within no longer. He would go to Tottenham and satisfy himself that his mother had not been molested.

She had not. He found her walking with her granddaughter Rhoda, in the sunshine on the flags. She was quite calm and undisturbed, there was no reason for asking her any questions.

Her husband had not been near her, that was certain, since the day when Valentine bought him off. But for her part she asked a thousand questions about Lady Mildred, and how her daughter had been received, and when she would come back again to see her mother.

"I wouldn't stand in her light, Claude, not if I was never to see her again." Like all blind people she spoke of seeing her friends just as if she still had the use of her eyes. "And if she's happy she must not think too much about me. Not but that she will, for she's that affectionate in her nature that she loves all that loves her and thinks about them day and night. Give me a loving-hearted girl, Claude. Why, as for you she loves the very ground you tread upon." Claude started and blushed; one need not blush at being loved by one's sister, but only Rhoda saw the blush, and she was selfishly thinking about her own little ambitions, not about Claude at all. And therefore, though she observed some evidence of emotion, she did not connect it with any cause. "If you were her sweetheart, my son, she couldn't love you better. She'll sit and talk about you all day long, she will, and never get tired; and makes me tell her again and again, just like as if she was a little girl again, how you took to your book when you was only a little boy, and how you were sent to a grand school by her ladyship, and how you got all the prizes and brought them here for me to see and feel their beautiful leather covers. Oh! she's a good sister, Claude, as well as a good daughter."

"I suppose she loves Joe and Sam quite as well."

"Not she, then. She's uppish you know, and Joe, he's a good boy, but he's only a working-man, you see. He hasn't got your fine ways; and as for Sam, he's hardly civil with anybody, is he?"

"I am glad you think she loves me, mother," said Claude, meekly. "But then, of course, it's natural to love her brother, isn't it?"

"Of course it is, my dear. You don't make half enough of her, Claude. As for talking about her, you never do. Nor about yourself either, lately. You've got to be silent, my dear boy. There isn't any trouble, is there? You haven't got caught by some artful hussy, I hope?"

In Mrs. Monument's view, if one of her sons fell in love, he must be caught by an artful hussy. Such is the opinion which women in certain circles entertain as to girls and their wiles. To be sure, a mother is difficult to please in the matter of daughters-in-law.

"No, mother, there is no artful hussy in the case, I assure you. And as for loving Valentine, I am certain no brother in the whole world loves his sister so much. I can say nothing too good for her. Never dream that I do not think about Valentine, mother."

"That's well said, Claude. That's a brave boy. Brothers don't generally care about their sisters, more's the pity. If they did there'd be many a poor girl saved from trouble."

Then Claude went to Ivy Lane, getting there about six o'clock, just before dark. It struck him that the street was unusually animated for the time of day, and he might have guessed that so many people would not have been gathered together at six in the evening without some cause. However, he passed through them, and so to the house. The front room was still empty, and from the position of the chair, which was exactly where he had left it, it seemed as if no one had been there since he left it. Therefore the old man had not yet returned. He looked into the back room; this also was empty. In fact the old lady, who could no longer do without a fire, had that very morning changed her residence for the winter and gone where, whatever may be their faults, they do keep up a good fire, namely, to the House; and was already dressed in the blue and white check which forms the neat and tasty uniform of the place, and had consumed in gin the last twopence of Mr. Carey's florin, and was looking forward with resignation to six or seven months of temperance and regular hours.

Claude went upstairs. Melenda's room was open, but no one was in it. Melenda herself was sitting in Valentine's room, with Lotty, who was asleep.

She ran to meet Claude with some signs of agitation. "Oh, Claude!" Melenda came out hurriedly, "I am so glad you are come again. Something dreadful's happened. Hush! I don't want Lotty to hear."

"What is it?"

"It's Lizzie's father. He's dead."

"How did he die?"

"I don't know. It was this morning that a policeman came and asked if there was a man lived here named Lane, and we called Liz, and she said yes, and he was her father; and he said, 'Then your father's dead,' he said, 'and you'd better come along o' me,' he said; and she went. And I can't leave Lotty, and there's nobody in the house but us two. Oh! dear. I never thought we should miss Valentine so soon."

Outside the house the people were talking together in knots of two and three. They spoke in low voices, as people talk in the presence of the dead.

Now, while Claude looked about him for someone to ask or to advise him, there strolled leisurely into the street none other than his brother Joe.

"You here, Joe?"

"Why, colonel," said Joe, slowly, "I sez to myself when we knocked off today, I sez, 'There's Melenda with that sick girl, and the young lady gone, and p'r'aps they want a bit o' help or advice.' So I came down the road in the tram, and here I am."

"Well, Joe, it strikes me that we shall all want as much advice and help as we can get before very long."

"I beg your pardon, sir"—one of the women detached herself from the group and accosted Claude; "you knew the poor old man, sir. I've see you here with the young lady."

"Yes, I knew the old man; what has happened?"

"They picked him up in the canal, and they've got him at the Stag's Head in the Canal Road. Lizzie's gone there too, for the inquest."

Found in the canal! Claude felt sick and dizzy. How did the man get there? and in whose company was he last seen?

"What's the matter, young 'un?" asked Joe, surprised. "What makes you so white in the gills?"

"Come with me, Joe; I'm afraid we shall find out soon enough."

In the parlour of the Stag's Head, on the great table dented and battered with a thousand hammerings of pewter pots at friendly leads and the emphasisings of a thousand toasts at lodge meetings—for a lodge of the Ancient Order of Buffaloes met here—and club meetings, there lay a shapeless heap, covered over with a white sheet. A policeman sat in the room, not for fear of those who break in and steal, but out of respect to what was under the sheet. In a far corner—as far as she could get from the table—sat Lizzie, looking scared and frightened.

"Oh!" she cried, "you've come at last—I knew you'd come. Don't go away, please. There's to be an inquest directly, and I've got to give evidence. Oh! I am so frightened."

"Don't be afraid, my gal," said Joe; "we won't go away till you've done."

"Father's dead," she whispered.

"I know," said Claude. "But, Lizzie, is there no other place than this for you to wait?"

"There's only the bar, but it's full of men drinking, and they keep asking questions."

"How was it?"

"I don't know. They are there—under the sheet. You can look if you like."

"Who are they?"

"Why, the other—I don't know who he is. They found them together."

"If you knew the deceased, either of you," said the policeman, "you might give evidence. The jury are called for half-past seven."

He laid back a corner of the sheet and showed the face of the dead man. It was perfectly calm and peaceful; the lips had dropped into a smile; the eyes were closed in what looked like the sleep of a child. The long white hair lay upon the pillow on which they had placed his head, as if reverent hands had disposed it to the best advantage, so as to serve as a frame for the beautiful waxen mask of a face. The poor old scribe had got what he demanded of his enemy; he had got back his life. What more could he desire?

"Oh! isn't father beautiful?" Lizzie whispered. "He was a gentleman once, before he got into trouble. Don't he look like a gentleman again?"

He looked perfectly peaceful and happy. He looked like one who had spent his life wholly in the contemplation of things saintly and the working of things holy. The dead bishop lying on his bed could not look more holy. But there was more beneath the sheet.

The policeman rolled back the sheet a little farther and discovered a second head. There was, as Lizzie explained, another body found with her father's. It lay upon its side facing the first. The limbs were writhing when they were fixed in death: the face was distorted, wild, and full of horror, with open and staring eyes which still seemed to see something inexpressibly terrible and fearful. The right hand of the first corpse held the coat collar of the second as if dragging an unwilling and conscience-stricken prisoner to justice.

This was Claude's father. A terrible death after a shameful life. The thought that it was his father, whatever the life, whatever the death, touched him with such pity as one might feel for one who was not a disgraceful father. All was finished now, the persecution, and the extortion, and the dread. No more to be feared from him. Only room now for the thought of what he might have been.

"That's just how they were found," said the policeman, "only this one's left hand, you see, was clutching the other side of the coat collar as well, but the hook tore the collar. No one saw them roll in: no one seems to know how they fell in. Looks like a quarrel, don't it? But they're both oldish men, and the one with the grey hair looks near seventy. Men of seventy don't quarrel and fight, do they? Not as a rule, says you. The young woman here is ready to identify her father, but no one seems to know anything about the other man. Looks respectable, doesn't he? Got new boots, and good boots too, and new clothes. Here's his hat"—too well Claude knew that hat! "It was picked up on the bank. Oldish man, but he looks as if he'd got a good bit o' life left in him still: wiry kind o' face, isn't it? Didn't like tumbling in, seemingly. Was it one tried to push the other in? Were they in drink? Nothing in their pockets; not a penny; only a scrap of paper in this one's pocket with the name of Lane, Ivy Lane, Hoxton, on it. Not a penny: at least that's what the bargees say who pulled 'em out. 'Tain't likely there would be a penny after they'd had the run of the pockets." Claude thought of asking whether there had not been found a watch and chain—his own watch and chain, in fact—but he refrained in time. "Why, man alive," said the policeman to Joe, "haven't you ever seen a dead body before?"

In fact, Joe was gazing with open mouth and hanging hands; his cheeks were white, and he seemed unable to tear his eyes from the sight before him. Just so, Claude felt, he must himself have appeared when first his father announced himself in his chambers. In the feeling and beautiful language of our ancestors, Joe "was confounded, and his jaws stuck."

"Why, Joe," said Claude, "what's the matter? Sit down, man, and don't look at them any longer." He covered the bodies again with the sheet. "Nothing at all in this man's pockets. Nothing in his pockets. No letter, or card, or address. Why, perhaps you will not be able to identify him."

"Perhaps not," said the policeman. "As for this one, we know him through his daughter."

"We know him too," said Claude. "We are come to do what we can for his daughter."

"And as for the other, why, very likely he'll never be identified at all; there's a many bodies that never do. They are country people, for the most part, and they get into bad company and mischief; or they're foreigners perhaps, and it's bad company with them, too; and no one asks after them, and when they don't come back to their hotels, presently their boxes are opened and sold, and nothing said."

"Very likely he will never be identified at all," Claude repeated, slowly and with emphasis, looking at his brother. "Joe, do you feel better? We both know this girl, who is very respectable, and there will be no difficulty in identifying her father, at any rate."

Joe retired to the bar, where he had a glass of brandy neat,[2] and tried to pull himself together, but with small success. For he had seen his father again. After all these years, he remembered him instantly—and his father was dead.

As regards his former statement concerning his father's death it had been, of course, fabricated and invented by himself without the least authority. He made that statement for the ease and satisfaction of his mother. When a man of over forty goes into compulsory retirement for a period of five-and-twenty years, which is equivalent to twenty years at least, one may be justified in supposing that he will never come out again; though, from time to time, Joe asked himself what would happen if his father were after all to come out and to find his way to the almshouse, and what his own missus would say, and what Claude and Sam and Melenda, from all of whom the truth had been carefully hidden, would say. Once the fiction was invented, Joe satisfied his conscience, which was not more than reasonably tender, by the assurance that his father could never live to complete his sentence.

He had lived, then, and he had presumably received his ticket of leave, and he was out. How long he had been out, or what he had done since he came out, what friends he had made, who knew his secrets, Joe knew not. His father was out of prison, and he was dead; he was discovered drowned like a rat in a ditch. Suppose the policeman were to ask him if he knew the body. Suppose they were to seize him and put him in the witness-box, what should he say? Why had he come there with Claude?

Presently the jury came and the inquest was held. They were mostly householders who kept small shops in the neighbourhood; they came rather sulkily, but they went through the business conscientiously, and as if they had experience of coroners' inquests, and how they should be conducted.

The court was held in a dingy room—the bar-parlour—after the jury had viewed the bodies. Claude and Joe stood in the doorway and looked on. The witnesses were called; the two boatmen who deposed that they saw a hat lying on the towing-path, and the marks of the trampling of feet, or some kind of struggle, on the gravel; that they dragged the canal, and almost immediately pulled up the two bodies locked together in a deadly embrace just as they now lay upon the table; one man holding the other as if he were trying to shove

2 Brandy without ice.

him under—that they searched the pockets and found nothing except in one pocket, writing materials with a name and address; both men were very clear and decided upon that point; that they had called the nearest policeman, who also searched the pockets and found nothing. The policeman, in his evidence, did not express surprise on this point. Then they put up Lizzie, who identified her father as one who lived by writing letters for Germans and Poles, especially Polish Jews; he was very poor, she said, and as for the other man, she had never seen him, and her father was one of those who have no friends. It was fortunate, Claude reflected, that Lizzie had not been present at the disturbance on Saturday evening.

He might himself have given evidence. But to what effect? That he was a barrister and a Fellow of Trinity: that one of the dead men was his own father, a ticket-of-leave man and a notorious evil liver, whom he was himself supporting on certain conditions; that this convict broke one of these conditions on Saturday evening, and forced himself upon a young lady, the daughter of Lady Mildred Eldridge, whom he took for his own daughter; that at sight of the other man, now also lying dead, he broke away and fled, and the other ran after him, and that they were no more seen. This was a strange story to tell in this bar-parlour before the Hoxton jurymen. Further inquiry would be demanded, and Valentine herself would have to give evidence, and then there would be a beautiful case for the papers.

Joe, too, might have given evidence. He stood in terror that he should be called upon to do so. His evidence would at least have satisfied the police that one of their worst offenders was gone to another Court of Justice. He listened with open mouth and pale cheeks. When the coroner charged the jury, he trembled and shook: when the verdict was returned, he gave a great gasp of relief.

As for the summing up of the coroner, nothing could be more simple. These two men, he said, were evidently drowned together. They might have been quarrelling, but there was nothing to prove it; they might have been drinking together, which seemed much more likely, because they had not apparently robbed each other, neither having anything to lose. One of the men—the one identified—was very old and feeble; the other was well advanced in life. The one identified appeared also to be quiet and respectable. Men of that age do not certainly go out and fight when they are sober; the very unfrequented nature of the place where they were found pointed perhaps to the theory of drink. One slipped, perhaps, and dragged the other in with him; or one was drowned in an attempt to save the other. As for the uncalled-for remark of the bargemen that it looked as if one was trying to shove the other under, that was a conclusion formed without any facts to warrant it, and they might just as well consider that it looked as if one man was trying to pull the other out. The jury without any delay found a verdict of "Found drowned"; and to this verdict every man affixed his name and seal.

The case was over. No one now will ever know, except his two sons, when and where James Carey died: and they know no more than that he was drowned.

As they walked away, Joe, who had taken a second glass of brandy after the finding, and yet looked pale and trembled, began to explain things.

"You saw that I was took aback, young 'un, by the sight of them two bodies?" he began.

"Yes, I saw that, Joe. Very much took aback you were."

"Well, now, don't you tell the mother what I'm going to tell you. Don't you let on to no one, Claude, and I will tell you the truth, and why I was took aback. Which I do not deny it."

"I will not tell anybody, Joe. Go on."

Claude perceived from his brother's anxious face as well as from the general situation, that Joe's imaginative and creative faculties were about to be called into play, on a larger and more active scale than usual.

"Well, then, it's like this. Father, you know— "

"Who died so many years ago."

"Yes, him. Who died so many years ago, poor old chap! I don't think, Claude, I ever quite got over the blow of his death; for, says I, though but a youngster at the time, where in the world shall I ever find another father who'll be such a honest and respectable father as him who's been took? But what you never have been told, nor any of the others, is, that father had a brother. That's where it is. Yes, he had a brother—a twin-brother—just exactly like himself: same age, same height, same hair, same coloured eyes. So like him that you might have taken them two for each other. People have been known to make that mistake; and once he—the twin-brother, I mean—got off, because he got fifty people to swear he was handing round the plate at chapel at the very time that the burglary was committed—namely, churchtime. But, bless you, it was father, not him, that carried round the plate! They wouldn't ha' trusted him with a plate if there was only twopence in it. Besides, he never went to church nor chapel. If they had a trusted him with the plate, he'd a sneaked it, money and all."

The narrator felt that he was really getting on splendidly.

"Well, Joe?"

"Well—father—you know—father—he was just about as steady and as honest as they make 'em. Once they gave him a silver mug for his honesty, and it was put into the Sunday papers. I remember that very well."

"Yes, Joe, I think I remember something of it, too."

"You can't very well, Claude—that is, you can't remember much of it, because it was before you were born. But you go on being proud of your father. You stick as tight as wax to your pride, my boy."

"I will, Joe—I will. I'll be just as proud of him as if he had never had a twin-brother at all."

"Well, as for that precious twin—that other chap—he was a reg'lar bad 'un. He was so bad that father never let him come into the house where, he said, honesty alone should shake a leg." Claude laughed, but begged his brother to continue. "Whatever good there was about father was bad about that other chap. If one was sober, the other drank like a fish; and if one was a steady workman, the other one never did a day's work in his life; if one got silver mugs for good character, the other was always going off to quod for roguery. He was a burglar too, and proud of it. Father got at last not to speak to him—wouldn't own to him—wouldn't help him—wouldn't have nothing to say to him. But it made no difference, whether father argued with him or whether he walloped him it was all the same. A reg'lar confirmed bad 'un, he was."

"I suppose he got into trouble pretty often, didn't he?"

"He did so, Claude. He got into trouble a heap of times; he was 'most always in trouble, and at last he got a long sentence. I thought he must be dead, Claude, I did indeed. And what struck me all of a heap, sudden-like, when I see that body was to reckonise that it was nothing else in the world but the body of that—very—same—twin-brother. There! Now you know why I was took aback. I thought he was dead ever so long ago. And if I'd had to give evidence I should ha' had to say that he was father's twin-brother—a ticket-of-leave man, Claude"—his voice dropped—"on'y a ticket-o'-leave man."

"That was very strange, Joe. Hadn't we better keep this story to ourselves? There are always bad hats in every family, and it does no good to talk about them, does it? Besides, considering we've had a father who is such a credit to all of us that we are never tired of talking about him, what does it matter about this uncle—this twin-brother?"

"Right, lad, right," cried Joe, brightening up. "What does it matter, after all? We won't tell Sam, will we? Nor yet Melenda, nor yet my missus and the young 'uns. There's no need to let 'em know now, and him dead and all, that then father's twin-brother was such an out-and-out regl'ar bad 'un."

Joe's readiness of invention thus extricated him from a great difficulty, and he has ever since congratulated himself upon his resource and the fertility of his imagination, which enabled him so readily to make Claude believe in the existence of the twin-brother—the out-an'-outer, and in the exemplary character of his father.

It is the privilege of the parish to bury, at the expense of the ratepayers, such persons as die poor or friendless within their borders. The parish funeral is not a costly matter; the parish undertaker does not generally retire from business with a large fortune; and things are not always ordered at these functions with as much solemnity as the relations might desire. Therefore it was felt to be a kindly act when Claude undertook to provide the funeral expenses for both these poor men. He "followed" in person, accompanied by Lizzie, who was supported by Melenda. Joe did not appear. Thus, the hawk and the pigeon, the wolf and the lamb, lay down in death, side by side, together.

In such a case as this, the words of the funeral service produce upon the bystanders something of an incongruous effect. Did Mr. James Carey really entertain the sure and certain hope spoken of by the chaplain at the last moment when his soul came bubbling up to the surface of the dark canal? Did he hear that voice that cried, "Blessed are the dead which die in the Lord"?[3] Pity that prayers for the dead are not encouraged by the church; one would have preferred, for such a funeral service, a few words of supplication in the deepest humility on behalf of a sinner most horribly unrepentant, together with a word of thankfulness on behalf of those from whom his death had averted so much misery and disgrace.

Claude gave to each of the girls a wreath. "Lay yours," he whispered to Lizzie, "on the stranger's coffin. Say 'I have forgiven.'"

Lizzie did as she was told, thinking it was part of the service.

"Lay yours on Lizzie's father, Melenda," he whispered her. "Say, 'Forgive the father for the daughter's sake.'"[4]

Melenda, too, did as she was told. She knew that there was a mystery and that it was Valentine's secret. Therefore she made no search into it, and never spoke of it, and no one, now, knows the complete history of James Carey and Mr. Lane except Claude and Valentine, and, as we have seen, even they do not know all the concluding chapter.

---

3 Revelation 14:13.

4 A phrase from Samuel Richardson's *Clarissa* (1748), whose titular character clings to her virtue despite the shenanigans of her family and the sexual violence perpetrated against her by Robert Lovelace, a suitor.

Chapter xxxiii

Coming of Age

Never was there any coming of age which more nearly resembled a funeral. The daughter of Sir Lancelot Eldridge should have attained her majority in her own country house; there should have been joy-bells and treble bob-majors, Venetian masts[1] with streamers and flags, bands of music, bouquets for everybody, dances on the village-green, treats for the children, sports and athletics for the young men, a great ball at the house and half the county invited to it, and, to crown the whole, the heartfelt, outspoken rejoicings of an affectionate, grateful loyal, contented, industrious, respectful, and scrupulously clean tenantry and peasantry. We all know how respectful, loyal, and affectionate are the peasantry and tenantry of England, Scotland, Ireland, and Wales.

The family solicitor came, a young gentleman of thirty or so, accompanied by his junior partner, who was not quite so young by forty years or so, and carrying a great box of papers. They arrived at about eleven, and were taken into the library. The girls heard their steps, and felt somehow as one feels when the undertaker calls.

Claude was with them, and the conversation languished, because one of the three was anxious, and two were stricken with a sense of guilt. These were the two who had already discovered the secret. When Lady Mildred came to them, she found the two girls sitting hand in hand, and Valentine with hanging head and burning cheeks. She looked at them for a moment with troubled eyes; then she held out her hands, and they sprang to their feet, and fell upon her neck, one on each side, and I think that all three were crying—those tears which flow freely and readily from women's eyes and express every emotion, whether of joy, or sorrow, or sympathy.

---

1 Treble bob-major is a type of composition for bell-ringing, and Venetian masts are large poles decorated with spiraled colors and, occasionally, flags.

"My dears," she said, "I thought it would be easy to tell you. It used to seem a small thing that I should have some day to say to one of you, 'My dear, you are not my daughter.' But it is not a small thing, children; it is a very hard thing. I have done, I fear, a grievous wrong to one of you, because Beatrice must have her own property; and Polly must have her brother, and you will no longer be equal."

"Beatrice can give Polly half her fortune," said Valentine.

"Polly can never take any of the fortune," said Violet. "But Claude can still be brother to both of us."

Valentine made no reply to this proposition. That was because she had known for three months that he was not her brother. This kind of knowledge entirely changes one's views as regards fraternal affection. She knew, by this time, that a brother cannot be shared. He is one and indivisible, like a strawberry.

"My other daughter," Lady Mildred went on, looking straight between them, "forgive me for bringing you up in ignorance. At first when I took you from your mother, I thought chiefly of helping a very poor and heavily-burdened woman. I thought little about the child's future. Then, when I placed her beside my own little girl, and saw how pretty she was, and how winning, and how dainty, I thought how it would be to bring both up together, and not to let either know which of the two was the gentlewoman, and how it would be curious to watch them both, and I wondered whether birth would show. My dear children, what has been shown? Why, that there is no difference—not the slightest difference—between you. You have proved that there are, in every condition of life, children who may be trained and educated to have the manners and the instincts of the most well-bred and the most cultured. But I, for one, never doubted. Just so, among ourselves, the well born and the well educated, there are men who are clowns in manners and hogs in taste. Not the slightest difference between my two girls. Nobody can pretend that there is. Yet, the moment the truth is declared, the world will cry out that they knew it all along, and always said so, and it never had been any secret which of the two was of gentle birth. No one, as yet, has ventured to say that one of you is less gracious, less generous, less well-bred, less a gentlewoman, than the other. There is nothing in the world so good as to be gentle, and one of you, my dears, is as gentle as the other. And your brother Claude, my dear Polly," she added, still looking between the two, "is as gentle as yourself. One of you must learn that you do not belong to gentle blood. I trust she will learn it without regret and without false shame. If Beatrice will divide what is in her power to share, and Polly will accept it, I shall be very glad. But if not, one of you is an heiress and the other has nothing. Nothing? Oh, yes, my children, she has our love, the love of Beatrice and myself, and she will always be, in all things, my daughter and her sister; and she has more than Beatrice, because she has a brother of whom she may be justly proud. Patience, Claude! I will give your sister to you in a few minutes!"

Nobody moved—nobody spoke—while Lady Mildred paused to collect herself. Then she continued, still looking between the two girls and holding them each by one hand.

"As for you, Beatrice, you become today mistress of your father's house, estates, and fortune; you have a great many acres of land, which used to mean a great many thousands a year, but they do not mean so much now; you have investments which have been accumulating for you; you have houses—this very house is yours—with all that is in it. You have become today a person of very great importance; you will be courted wherever you go, for your fortune, and you will be told that it is for your beauty and your cleverness. You will be assailed by all kinds of persons who want money; there will be plenty of people ready to assure you that you have all the virtues. No one can possibly have a more difficult position than an heiress, my dear. I am very sorry for you, and I am sure you will thank me for keeping you so long from knowing the truth. It is a grievous misfortune, my child, for anybody, and especially for any young man or young woman, to be rich. I do not think anyone should be allowed by law to be rich until he is at least fifty years of age, and I doubt whether most people are ready to take upon themselves the burden of wealth, even then. Perhaps sixty is too soon for most."

"Violet." She kissed her, and the girl started and turned quite pale, and trembled. "Let me give you to your brother. Claude, she is your sister. This is little Polly-which-is-Marla. Valentine, let me restore you to your own name. You are henceforth Beatrice, only daughter of Sir Lancelot Eldridge."

"Oh! no, no!" said Valentine, "I will never change my name; I shall always be Valentine."

"Claude," cried Violet, "I was perfectly certain of it, always, from the very beginning; I remembered the wet sheets and the clothes-lines; I am sure I did; my own brother! You would rather it had been Valentine—you are disappointed in your sister; I am very sorry, for your sake."

"Indeed, Violet—indeed I am not disappointed." He did not say, though it was in his mind, that he was very glad it was not Valentine; nor did he—though that too was in his mind—inform her that her father was lying dead at that moment in the parish mortuary. He kissed her solemnly, and rather awkwardly, on the forehead; it takes time to learn how a sister should be kissed, and, in fact, there are many ways: the simple chaste salute on the brow is much in use as a formal acknowledgment of relationship, especially when people are no longer young; a common way is for the brother to kiss his sister on both cheeks, one after the other, while he holds her head in his two hands. But this is only for quite young people, and when brother and sister do really love each other. A girl's lips must always, of course, be left for her lover. They are sacred.

"Valentine has had you all to herself for three months," she said, blushing at his embrace: "you must think of her already as your sister—not of me at all. But it is my turn now, Claude. Let us try to be a good deal to each other; I am selfish, and I hate—oh! how I hate—rough things; I can never go to Hoxton. But the world is not all Hoxton, is it? There are other places and other things; you won't be always pulling people out of the mire and getting into a rage about injustices and workgirls, will you?"

"No, Violet; we will try to be a good deal to each other." But his eyes wandered from her, and rested upon Valentine.

Then Violet, in her quick way, turned to Valentine, still holding Claude's hand tightly. "My dear, who should be Beatrice if not you? If it had been me," she added, with more feeling than grammar, "I must have abdicated in your favour. As for sharing your fortune—"

"You shall," said Valentine; "of that I am fully and absolutely resolved."

Then Violet turned to Lady Mildred. Her eyes were very bright and her cheeks flushed.

"You have kissed me so often when I was Violet," she said; "kiss me now, when I am only Polly—Polly-which-is-Marla. We will go and live together, Claude and I, the children of the gutter; we will live somewhere, but not in Hoxton—not in Hoxton. I will set up my easel and paint. Perhaps I shall be able to sell my pictures, and I shall sign them Marla Monument, or Polly Monument, or Polly-which-is-Marla Monument, whichever Claude likes best. As for the fortune, I would die rather than take any of it. Sometimes you will let me come and see Valentine, won't you? I couldn't live without seeing her sometimes—just to tell her how the princess likes the rags. We have often talked together about the princess and the rags."

"Oh, my dear—my dear!" cried Lady Mildred, distressed. "You do not understand. You are never to leave me, you are always my daughter—my Violet. Everything is exactly as before, only that I have given you a brother."

She had also, Claude reflected, given her a large and very interesting family. But no mention was made of them on this occasion.

Then Lady Mildred drew Valentine away and left the brother and sister alone.

"I must confess to you, my brother," Violet said, "I must tell you the whole truth, if you despise me for it. Claude, I have always feared this day. Ever since I learned the story of Polly's parentage, I have had a presentiment. Oh, it was a certainty that I was the Polly, and not Valentine at all. Don't despise me too much, Claude. I was so selfish that I longed for it to be otherwise. I longed to be Beatrice, not for her money, but for her family. Don't hate me more than you can help, Claude. I loathed the thought of going back to these poor working-people. When Lady Mildred told me that you were coming, I pictured a workman, and I was crimson with shame. Don't despise me more than you can help, Claude. Then sometimes, when we went about together, I have seemed to hear all the women whispering—you know how kind women can be to each other!—and saying, 'What right has this common girl among us? Let her go back to her own people.' Why, let me confess it all, I have even prayed that I might be Beatrice. And all the time, Valentine was so unselfish and so ready to meet her—other people—Claude," she clung to him and looked into his eyes for some sign of forgiveness. "Don't—don't despise me too much."

"There is no question of despising, my sister." He should have kissed her again at this point, but he was unused to sisters and did not know how such a step would have been received. "I have known the secret for three months, Violet. Do not speak of forgiveness."

"You have known that Valentine was not your sister? And yet—"

"And yet I have pretended. Finish your confession, if you have anything more to say, and then you will be happier."

"Well then—when we actually went to see them—when we talked with Joe and with Melenda, oh! and with Sam, it was dreadful. It was more than I could bear. I can never go again to face Melenda and hear her dreadful abuse. You will not ask me to go there again, will you, Claude? I will go to see my mother—sometimes—with Valentine, but not the others—not just yet. Perhaps in a year or two, one might be able to see Sam or Joe, one at a time, you know, and for a few minutes. Valentine will take me, perhaps, because she is not afraid of them. But not Melenda."

"You shall never go, Violet, unless you wish to go. They do not expect you to go. Valentine has a message for you from them. You shall stay here, my sister, and live on in your world of art and things beautiful. Only, don't let it become an enchanted land. Remember that outside there are always the men and women who work."

* * *

"Mother," said Valentine, an hour later, when the family solicitor had put the papers back into the box and gone his way with the junior partner; "mother, I have a confession to make to you."

"What is it, dear?"

"Only that I knew the secret from the very first day. Claude's mother told me."

"Why, she is blind?"

"Yes; but she told me about the dimple in her cheek and the mark on the arm, which Violet has. But Claude never knew or suspected. That would have spoiled all. It was the thought that I was his sister which made him so ready to work for me, and so thoughtful."

"It might have been so, Valentine; it was so proposed by me; but, most unfortunately, you see, Claude discovered the secret about the same time. His brother Joe told him. And Joe seems to have found it out from Violet's resemblance to her father. So, after all, the only one kept in the dark has been Violet."

"Oh, is it possible? Could Claude know? Yet he always behaved exactly like a brother; and I thought—"

"Yes, dear; you were both acting a deceitful part all the time. Yet it was a very good thing for you that Claude played his part so well, without speaking of yourself, because it secured the services of an honourable and very deserving young man for you. It was unfortunate for him, because he naturally—I am not blaming him for it, mind—it was quite natural that he should fall in love with you."

"Oh, mother!" Her cheek flushed quick.

"And, of course, considering his birth and relations, even if it were not for this miserable story of his father, which he has told me, and which Violet must never be suffered to learn, he clearly understands that he must never speak to you on the subject."

Lady Mildred paused, but Valentine made no reply. Her cheeks were crimson and her lip trembling.

"I have talked the matter over with him. Claude is honourable and reasonable, as I expected he would be. My dear, he is a gentleman, though his father is a convict and a ticket-of-leave man and his mother was a washerwoman. Claude is a gentleman. Be quite easy in your mind, my child. He understands the position perfectly."

"The position?"

Lady Mildred went on slowly as if she was considering every word carefully, and watching her daughter as if she was looking for the effect of her words.

"You need be under no misapprehensions about his behaviour, and I am sure you will meet him half way, and continue in your old friendly relations, just as when you each thought the other filled with brotherly and sisterly affection. The dreadful disgrace that has befallen him in this monstrous father of his need not make much difference for you."

"Disgrace? For Claude? What disgrace can attach to him because his father is a wretch?"

"My dear, the world would consider it a disgrace. To be sure, the world never knows more than half the facts, and never makes allowance. And as regards your future relations with Claude, you will find him quite willing always to be your servant. All his life, since you have accepted his services."

"My servant? Claude?"

"He is really a *very* loyal and honourable boy. I am proud of my share in him. I have studied him for twelve years now, and have learned to think better of him every day. There is nowhere a young man who has greater command of himself, or, I believe, greater abilities, or is more trustworthy. He has assured me—and you may accept that assurance fully—that neither by word nor look will he ever make you feel that he has ventured to love you."

"Oh, mother, I cannot bear it!"

"That is arranged, then. You like him and you trust him; you have proved him true; you have already accepted his services; you have taken from him his profession and his career—in fact the future of distinction which awaited him; you have plunged into work which may very likely fail, and perhaps keep him in obscurity all his life. So that I think you are really bound to be friendly towards him."

Valentine tried to speak, but she could not. The tears stood in her eyes, and her voice failed her.

"Of course, he has done all this out of pure love for you. It is quite right that you should know this. You, of course, my dear, must look for a very different kind of alliance. Sir Lancelot's daughter may take any place. Your birth, your fortune, and your beauty, my child, entitle you to be ambitious, and I do not doubt that a very good position indeed will be yours. The mere idea of a young man with such connections presuming—but Claude does not presume. He is a very good boy, poor fellow! and it will always be pleasant for you to remember, even when you are married and have other duties, that you possess what very few women have—a truly loyal and faithful servant working for you among the poor; always humble and obscure, for your sake; desiring nothing better, for your sake; contented to have sacrificed himself and everything—all for love of you!"

"Oh, mother!" she fell sobbing at her mother's knees. "You kill me. You kill me!"

"Why, Valentine—why? Beatrice, my dear, what is it?"

"Because—because—how can you talk of my marrying—any other man?" she whispered the last words, burying her face in her hands.

"Do you mean it seriously, my daughter?" Lady Mildred smiled, unobserved by her child—"do you mean that you can actually love this young man? My dear, remember what you are, and what he is;—the son of a convict, actually the son of a disgraceful felon, a professional thief and rogue, a man who was convicted and sentenced to twenty-five years' penal servitude for burglary with attempt at murder—and his mother only a washerwoman—his brother a plumber or locksmith, or whatever he calls himself, and his sister a working-girl of the very lowest kind; and all their friends, no doubt, such as one may expect. This would be a very pretty family connection for Sir Lancelot Eldridge's daughter, not to speak of myself! Am not I to be considered? Is there to be an absolute ignoring of rank and birth? Are we to have no pride at all in our family? Why, there never was anybody prouder of his family than Sir Lancelot!"

"Claude is—Claude," Valentine replied; "what do I care about his family? Besides, they all know me, and I know them, and they love me—and I"—she murmured softly—"oh! I love Claude!"

"Then, my dear," said Lady Mildred, "I withdraw my opposition. Make your own choice—marry whom you please. You will have your faithful servant still, whether you marry him or not. But there is one dreadful difficulty in the way."

"What difficulty?"

"I am afraid it is an insuperable difficulty. Claude will never break that resolution of his—he will never speak to you of love. Oh! my poor child, you will—actually—have—to ask him yourself!"

Chapter the Last

Valentine Speaks

She would have, sometime, to speak to her lover, who would never speak to her. This is a thing which a girl does not forget in a hurry. It was not until the end of the year, the very last day in the year that she did speak, and then she was constrained by a force strong enough to break through her womanly reserve.

They were at Bournemouth,[1] whither, in late October, Valentine brought the dying girl and her friends. A change to Bournemouth would not save her; no change of place and air would save her, any more than a change of climate would save the poor wretch over whom the great car of Juggernaut has passed, crushing bones and grinding limbs. All the year round this great car of ours moves slowly onwards, crushing the limbs of hapless women, and pounding and beating them to death. Some of us have eyes to see them writhing beneath the wheels, and each says to each—of those, that is, who do have eyes to see—that it is not his fault. No; it is nobody's fault, but perhaps someday the working-men as well will receive eyes to see their suffering, and ears to hear their cries, and then they will perhaps try to find the remedy which we have failed to find. Not all of them have the good fortune that befell Lotty in being taken out of the noise and the dirt, the privation and the hunger, for just a few weeks, a brief holiday, after her eight years' suffering, of peace and rest. Happy girl! To be lapped in love and plenty, though all her bones were broken and though life was ebbing rapidly away. Happy girl! To forget, before she died, the existence of the sweater and the manufacturer; to feel no more the weight of that accursed Law of Elevenpence Ha'penny, even though the day was swiftly drawing near when there would be set up, in the green churchyard upon the hillside, among the multitudes of white marble crosses, one more to mark the resting-place of an obscure girl slowly and cruelly done to death. Yet no one's fault. No, it is no one's fault.

1 A seaside town in southwest England.

When first Lotty came she could be wheeled about a little in a chair; the sun was still warm at mid-day, the yellow leaves were still on the trees, there were still flowers in the great garden of the town; they could watch the sea, mysterious, wonderful, to girls who had never seen it before; and listen to the plash of the water upon the shore and breathe the fragrance of the pines. But very soon the sun lost his warmth even at noon, and the days grew short and cold, and Lotty went out no more.

Then she sat in a warm room where Valentine ministered to her and Melenda nursed her day and night, her mind filled with sweet thoughts and gentle hopes, which she had never known before Valentine came to her, so that her death-bed was indeed to her an opening of the gate of life. The whole of the dreadful past was clean forgotten; she remembered no more the long and weary days with the never-ending click of needle and thimble, and the slow creeping hours, the dull pain in her back, the hunger of the time, the sleepless nights, when she longed to moan aloud but would not, for fear of disturbing the girls asleep in the same bed with her. Ivy Lane was far away; it receded farther every day; the girls had never been there; it was a dream; always she had been sitting in this soft chair, and lying on the soft bed, eating grapes, while Valentine read to her or made sweet music for her, or while she gazed through one of those twelve gates, which are never shut by day or night, into the wondrous city.[2] And always Melenda quiet and subdued, and never in a rage, and Lizzie contented and happy.

There came a day—it was the last day of the year—when the poor child was to feel her pain no more. She was lying with a smile upon her lips, and in her soft and tender eyes as they rested on Valentine or on Melenda lay love unspeakable. They all knew—she knew herself—that she was dying. At the foot of the bed stood Lizzie weeping without restraint, and at the head Melenda dry-eyed, self-contained, sat holding Lotty's white long fingers. She would cry when she could do nothing more, but not till then.

"Dear Lotty," whispered Valentine, bending over her, "your troubles are nearly over now."

Lotty made no reply. Her heavy eyes rolled slowly round till they rested on Melenda.

"There is no more sorrow, dear," Valentine went on, "nor any pain left for you. Perhaps you will see us all again soon: Melenda, and Lizzie, and me."

The dying girl made answer none. In her last moments she was back again, in imagination, among the shirts and button-holes.

"Never mind what they said, Melenda dear," she murmured, her eyes wandering as if there was something she did not quite understand. "Them Germans do swear awful and call dreadful names, but never mind what they said: don't get into a rage; what does it matter so long as they give us the work?"

"Lotty, there is no more work: it is all done," said Valentine, "all done and put away—and paid for," she added. "Oh! it is paid for, with this."

"The room gets hot, doesn't it, in the afternoon, and the days get longer and longer. Oh! Melenda, it's you who do all the work. It's my back, dear—I must lay down again. Give Lizzie my bread and butter, dear, when she comes in. I don't want any dinner when I'm laying down. Poor Liz, she's always hungry, isn't she? Don't be hard on Liz, Melenda. Think of Tilly."

Melenda clutched her hands and set her lips; but her eyes were dry.

2 The twelve gates of Jerusalem as described in the New Testament's Book of Revelation.

"When Tilly comes home again, Melenda, we won't be cruel to her and drive her away, will we? Let us take her back again, and pretend we don't know. Oh! Melenda—she was so dreadful poor, and she was always an impatient one. She wasn't brave and strong, like you."

Valentine stepped back, so that the girl's eyes should fall on no one but her old companion.

"I haven't done much work lately, have I? because I've been so bad, but I feel better now. There's no pain in my back today, and I shall soon be quite well. The doctor said so—and Valentine—who is Valentine? Melenda"—her eyes were full now of a vague yearning as if after something unknown—"Melenda, we've been friends, haven't we?—we've always been friends."

She closed her eyes and her hands dropped. Melenda kissed her, breaking out into passionate cries and weeping. But Lizzie stopped crying, and laid the limbs straight, and folded the arms across her breast. For Lotty was dead.

* * *

When Claude came in the afternoon, Valentine led him into the room where the dead girl lay.

"See," she whispered. "This is the beautiful face she was meant to have. You can discern it now, though the cheek is so thin. Did you think our poor Lotty could ever have been half so pretty? Her face was smirched and spoiled by our cruelty and neglect and apathy, not by any sins of her own, poor child! Since she ceased to work she has grown daily more beautiful—and now she is dead. As the doctor said, what better thing could befall her? Oh! Claude, we have been Christians for nearly two thousand years, and we can say still that the best thing for thousands among us is to die."

"Are we Christians?" he replied. "Have we, even yet, begun to understand what Christianity means?"

Presently they left the chamber and went out together upon the cliff. It was a still afternoon, with a clear sky and no wind, and in the west there was a glorious winter sunset. When the sun had quite gone down there arose a splendid afterglow, red and rosy, high in the western sky, and reflected in the ocean, full of consolation and of hope; and below their feet the quiet waters lapped upon the shore. Behind them, in the east, there was a blackness in the sky that could be felt.

"Claude," she whispered, "we are still in the presence of the dead. This place is like a church; and—oh! I can speak at last."

"Speak, Valentine. What is it you would say?"

"My mother tells me you have confessed things—things about me. And that you said foolish things about your father's sins and your own—inheritance. And that your lips were sealed."

"They were not foolish things, Valentine; they were real things. How could such as myself ask you to share with me my inheritance of shame?"

"Oh, Claude! Have I not shared it already? Can I ever cease to share it? Forget that foolishness. Besides—you are—yourself. We are not brother and sister; you have known that all along, and so have I. There lies a great garden at our feet, where we can work—if we work together—always together. Claude, have I said enough? Oh! do not ask me to say more."

He took her hand and kissed it. He bent his head and met her lips and kissed them. But he could not speak for awhile. Presently he found a voice.

"Oh, my queen!" he murmured. "Oh, my mistress! Oh, my lady and my love!" She raised her head, while the red light in the west filled her eyes and made them wondrous.

"Hand in hand, Claude, all our lives."

So, almost beside the girl's dead body, these lovers were betrothed.

The afterglow died in the west; the last day of the year was over; the past was done; but in their hearts there sprang the new light of another day.

Appendices

Appendix A

The Economic and Geographic Divides of Victorian London

From Charles Booth, "Condition and Occupations of the People of East London and Hackney, 1887," *Journal of the Royal Statistical Society* 51 (June 1888): 276–339.

[Charles Booth (1840–1916) was a prominent social investigator whose magnum opus is the seventeen-volume *Life and Labour of the People in London*. This work began in 1889 with a one-volume inquiry into the lives and occupations of residents in London's East End. The following extract is from an article, published a year earlier in the *Journal of the Royal Statistical Society*, in which he documents some of his initial findings. Booth focuses here on the neighboring areas of Bethnal Green and Shoreditch and concludes by referencing Besant's novel, which was published while Booth was conducting field research.]

If we consider London north of the Thames as a semi-circle of which the City is an enlarged centre, the district I am describing forms a quadrant, having for its radii Kingsland Road running due north, and Cable Street (continued as the East India Dock Road) running due east. Between these lie the Mile End Road (continued as the Bow Road to Bow), while a similar division more to the north may be made in the line of Hackney, dividing the quadrant into three equal segments, but the route to Hackney is deflected by Victoria Park, and no street exactly occupies the line ... The district also includes Hoxton—lying to the west of Kingsland Road—and Wapping, and the Isle of Dogs, formed by bends in the river, lying to the south of Cable Street and the East India Dock Road—but is otherwise co-extensive with this quadrant. The City itself has a radius of nearly a mile, and outside this London extends to the north and east from 3 to 4 miles. The greatest extension is at Stamford Hill, where the boundary is 4 ½ miles from Southwark Bridge, and the least at Bow, where it is 3 ½ miles from the same point. There is, however, less difference than these figures would seem to show in the actual extension of London, for from the City to Bow the entire space is built over, whereas at Stamford Hill and Clapton there are still some open fields, and further south and east the Metropolitan boundary includes the marshy land, unbuilt on, which skirts the river Lea. A circle drawn 3 miles outside the City boundary practically includes the whole inhabited district; and this may be divided into two parts—an inner ring of 1 ½ miles ending at the Regent's Canal, and an outer ring of similar width extending to Stoke Newington, Clapton, Homerton, Hackney, Old Ford, Bow, Bromley, and the East India Docks. The line of the Regent's Canal, which very closely follows the curve of the inner ring, marks a real change in the character of the district. Slight as this obstacle might be supposed to be, it yet seems to have been sufficient to gird in the swelling sides of London. It is also to be noted that it is in itself a girdle of poverty, the banks of the canal being, along nearly its whole length, occupied by a very poor population.

The inner ring consists of most of Shoreditch, Bethnal Green (excepting the Victoria Park end), all Whitechapel and St. George's, Wapping, Shadwell, and Ratcliffe, with the inlying portions of Mile End, all tightly packed with buildings, and crowded with inhabitants, except so far as occupied by business premises. Space and air are everywhere at a premium—the largest scale map shows as open spaces only a few churchyards and old burial grounds. A similar condition of things extends along the river bank, over Limehouse and Poplar proper, which lie within the outer ring, but the rest of this ring, consisting of Bow, Bromley, the outermost parts of Mile End and Bethnal Green, and the whole of Hackney, shows a different character. Not only are there some large spaces open to the public—Hackney Downs, London Fields, and Victoria Park—but the map begins everywhere to show more ground than buildings. The streets are wider; the houses have gardens of some sort; and in the houses themselves fewer people are packed. In the inner ring all available space is used for building, and almost every house is filled up with families. It is easy to trace the process. One can see what were the original buildings; in many cases they are still standing, and between them, on the large gardens of a past state of things, have been built the small cottage property of today. Houses of three rooms, houses of two rooms, houses of one room—houses set back against a wall or back to back, fronting it may be on to a narrow footway, with posts at each end and a gutter down the middle. Small courts contrived to utilise some space in the rear, and approached by archway under the building which fronts the street. Of such sort are the poorest class of houses. Besides the evidence of configuration, these little places are often called "gardens," telling their story with unintended irony. But in other cases all sentiment is dropped, and another tale about their origin finds expression in the name "So and so's rents"—not houses, nor dwellings, nor cottages, nor buildings, nor even a court or a yard, suggesting human needs, but just "rents."

Another sort of filling up which is very common now is the building of workshops. These need no new approach, they go with, and belong to, the houses, and access to them is had through the houses. Some are even arranged floor by floor, communicating with the respective floors of the house in front by a system of bridges. These workshops may or may not involve more crowding in the sense of more residents to the acre, but they, in any case, occupy the ground, obstruct light, and shut out air. Many are the advantages of sufficient open space behind a house, whether it be called garden or yard, for economy, comfort, and even pleasure. Those of us who have seen no more, have at least obtained a sort of bird's-eye view of such places from the window of a railway carriage, passing along some viaduct raised above the chimnies of two-storied London. Seen from a distance, the clothes lines are the most visible thing. Those who have not such outside accommodation must dry the clothes in the room in which they eat, and very likely also sleep; while those, more common, who have a little scrap of yard or stretch ropes across the court in front, still suffer much discomfort from the close proximity to door and window of their own and their neighbours' drying garments. From the railway, there may be seen, also, small rough-roofed erections, interspersed with little glass houses. These represent hobbies, pursuits of leisure hours—plants, flowers, fowls, pigeons, and there is room to sit out, when the weather is fine enough, with friend and pipe and glass. All this goes when the workshop invades the back yard; and as to sanitation and health, I need hardly point out how essential is sufficient space behind each house.

Worse again than the interleaving of small cottage property or the addition of workshops, is the solid backward extension, whether for business premises or as tenements, or as common lodging houses, of the buildings which front the street; and finally we have quarters in which house reaches back to house, and means of communication are opened through and through, for the convenience and safeguard of the inhabitants in case of pursuit by the police.

The building of large blocks of dwellings, an effort to make crowding harmless, is a vast improvement, but it only substitutes one sort of crowding for another. Nor have all blocks of dwellings a good character in any respect. All these methods of filling up have been, and some of them still are, at work in the inner ring. Different parts show different characteristics, but this one is common to the whole district.

In Bethnal Green are found the old weavers' houses, with large upper room, now usually partitioned off to make two or three rooms or accommodate two families. In some cases the houses had originally only one room on each floor; and each floor, partitioned, now accommodates its family. In several cases a family (not weavers) have taken such a room, and while living in it themselves, let a weaver stand his loom or looms in it, getting rent for each loom. Weaving still lingers, but is undoubtedly dying out, and furniture making takes its place. To some of these weavers' houses there are still long gardens, and when these are in front they are often utilised for storing costers' barrows; but mostly the gardens have been built upon.

Of Shoreditch, or rather Hoxton, which is the most characteristic part of Shoreditch, I am tempted to quote from a description by Mr. Besant, which will be remembered by all who have read "The Children of Gibeon." There is, he says, nothing beautiful, or picturesque, or romantic in the place, there is only the romance of life in it, 60,000 lives in Hoxton, every one with its own story to tell. Its people quiet and industrious, folk who ask for nothing but steady work and fair wages. Everybody quite poor; yet, he says, and says truly, the place has a cheerful look. There may be misery, but it is not apparent; the people in the streets seem well fed, and are as rosy as London smoke and fog will allow.

Contrasting with this, the northern and western part of Hackney, divided from Hoxton only by the canal, is almost entirely a middle class district. The old streets of De Beauvoir Town, or the new ones of Dalston and Upper Clapton, are alike of this kind, and in the old roads running through the new districts large and small houses are pulled down, and those of medium size erected.

Appendix B

Literary and Social Contexts

[The following contains a selection of material on the novel's literary and social contexts. *Children of Gibeon* refers directly to Thomas Hood's and Elizabeth Barrett Browning's poems focusing on the appalling conditions of employment that many women and children faced in the first half of the nineteenth century. Both "Song of the Cheap Customer," written by Tom Taylor but published anonymously, and "A Dream of Unfairly-Treated Women (A Long Way After the Laureate)," which has remained anonymous, appeared in *Punch*, the era's most influential magazine, which also published Hood's poem. "Song of the Cheap Customer" lays the blame for the suffering of needlewomen on customers who seek the best quality for the cheapest price. "A Dream of Unfairly-Treated Women (A Long Way After the Laureate)" continues the protest against unfair pay and poor treatment. The title plays on "A Dream of Fair Women" by Tennyson (the laureate to which the poem refers). The two selections by Harry Quelch, which were published in *Justice*, provide insight into how historical subjects committed to socialism, somewhat uncharitably depicted by Besant in the form of Sam Monument, viewed the sweated trades.]

1. Thomas Hood, "Song of the Shirt" (*Punch* 5 [July-December 1843]: 260)

With fingers weary and worn,
    With eyelids heavy and red,
A Woman sat, in unwomanly rags,
    Plying her needle and thread—
        Stitch! stitch! stitch!
In poverty, hunger, and dirt,
    And still with a voice of dolorous pitch
She sang the "Song of the Shirt."

"Work! work! work!
While the cock is crowing aloof!
And Work—work—work
Till the brain begins to swim;
Work—work—work
Till the stars shine through the roof!
It's O! to be a slave
Along with the barbarous Turk,
Where woman has never a soul to save,
If this is Christian work!

"Work—work—work
Till the brain begins to swim;
Work—work—work
Till the eyes are heavy and dim!
Seam, and gusset, and band,
Band, and gusset, and seam,
Till over the buttons I fall asleep,
And sew them on in a dream!
"O! Men, with Sisters dear!
O! Men! with Mothers and Wives!
It is not linen you're wearing out,
But human creatures' lives!
Stitch—stitch—stitch,
In poverty, hunger and dirt,
Sewing at once, with a double thread,
A Shroud as well as a Shirt.

"But why do I talk of Death?
That Phantom of grisly bone,
I hardly fear his terrible shape,
It seems so like my own—
It seems so like my own,
Because of the fasts I keep,
Oh! God! that bread should be so dear,
And flesh and blood so cheap!

"Work—work—work!
My labour never flags;
And what are its wages? A bed of straw,

A crust of bread—and rags.
That shatter'd roof—and this naked floor—
A table—a broken chair—
And a wall so blank, my shadow I thank
For sometimes falling there!

"Work—work—work!
From weary chime to chime,
Work—work—work—
As prisoners work for crime!
Band, and gusset, and seam,
Seam, and gusset, and band,
Till the heart is sick, and the brain benumb'd,
As well as the weary hand.

"Work—work—work,
In the dull December light,
And work—work—work,
When the weather is warm and bright—
While underneath the eaves
The brooding swallows cling
As if to show me their sunny backs
And twit me with the spring.

"Oh! but to breathe the breath
Of the cowslip and primrose sweet—
With the sky above my head,
And the grass beneath my feet,
For only one short hour
To feel as I used to feel,
Before I knew the woes of want
And the walk that costs a meal!

"Oh! but for one short hour!
A respite however brief!
No blessed leisure for Love or Hope,
But only time for Grief!
A little weeping would ease my heart,
But in their briny bed

My tears must stop, for every drop
    Hinders needle and thread!"

With fingers weary and worn,
    With eyelids heavy and red,
A Woman sat in unwomanly rags,
    Plying her needle and thread—
        Stitch! stitch! stitch!
    In poverty, hunger, and dirt,
And still with a voice of dolorous pitch
Would that its tone could reach the Rich!—
She sang this "Song of the Shirt!"

2. Elizabeth Barrett Browning, "The Cry of the Children" (from *Blackwood's Edinburgh Magazine* [August 1843]: 260-62.)

Do ye hear the children weeping, O my brothers!
    Ere the sorrow comes with years?
They are leaning their young heads against their mothers,
    And *that* cannot stop their tears.
The young lambs are bleating in the meadows,
The young birds are chirping in the nest,
The young fawns are playing with the shadows,
The young flowers are blowing toward the west;
But the young, young children, O my brothers!
    They are weeping bitterly!
They are weeping in the playtime of the others—
    In the country of the free.

Do you question the young children in the sorrow,
    Why their tears are falling so?
The old man may weep for his to-morrow
    Which is lost in long ago.
The old tree is leafless in the forest—
The old year is ending in the frost;
The old wound, if stricken, is the sorest—
The old hope is hardest to be lost!
But the young, young children, O my brothers!
    Do you ask them why they stand

Weeping sore before the bosoms of their mothers,
In our happy fatherland?

They look up with their pale and sunken faces,
And their looks are sad to see;
For the man's hoary anguish draws and presses
Down the cheeks of infancy.
"Your old earth," they say, "is very dreary—
Our young feet," they say, "are very weak!
Few paces have we taken, yet are weary—
Our grave-rest is very far to seek.
Ask the aged why they weep, and not the children;
For the outside earth is cold—
And we young ones stand without, in our bewild'ring,
And the graves are for the old.

"True," say the young children, "it may happen
That we die before our time!
Little Alice died last year—her grave is shapen
Like a snowball, in the rime.
We look'd into the pit prepared to take her—
Was no room for any work in the close clay!
From the sleep wherein she lieth none will wake her,
Crying–'Get up, little Alice! it is day!'
If you listen by that grave, in sun and shower,
With your ear down, little Alice never cries;
Could we see her face, be sure we should not know her,
For the smile has time for growing in her eyes.
For merry go her moments, lull'd and still'd in
The shroud, by the kirk-chime!
It is good when it happens," say the children,
"That we die before our time.

Alas, the young children! they are seeking
Death in life, as best to have!
They are binding up their hearts away from breaking,
With a cerement from the grave.
Go out, children, from the mine and from the city—
Sing out, children, as the little thrushes do!
Pluck your handfuls of the meadow-cowslips pretty—

Laugh aloud to feel your fingers let them through!
But the children say—"Are your cowslips of the meadows
Like our weeds anear the mine?[1]
Leave us quiet in the dark of the coal-shadows,
From your pleasures fair and fine!"

"For oh," say the children, "we are weary
And we cannot run or leap.
If we cared for any meadows, it were merely
To drop down in them and sleep.
Our knees tremble sorely in the stooping—
We fall upon our faces, trying to go;
And, underneath our heavy eyelids drooping,
The reddest flower would look as pale as snow.
For, all day, we drag our burden tiring,
Through the coal-dark, underground—
Or, all day, we drive the wheels of iron
In the factories, round and round.

"All day long, the wheels are droning, turning—
Their wind comes in our faces!
Till our hearts turn, and our heads with pulses burning,
And the walls turn in their places!
Turns the sky in the high window blank and reeling—
Turns the long light that drops adown the wall—
Turn the black flies that crawl along the ceiling—
All are turning all the day, and we with all!
All day long, the iron wheels are droning—
And sometimes we could pray,
'O ye wheels,' (breaking out in a mad moaning)
'Stop! be silent for to-day!'"

Ay! be silent! let them hear each other breathing,
For a moment, mouth to mouth;
Let them touch each other's hands, in a fresh wreathing
Of their tender human youth;
Let them feel that this cold metallic motion
Is not the life God giveth them to use;
Let them prove their inward souls against the notion

1 A commissioner mentions the fact of weeds being thus confounded with the idea of flowers. [Note by EBB]

That they live in you, or under you, O wheels!—
Still, all day, the iron wheels go onward,
As if fate in each were stark;
And the children's souls, which God is calling sunward,
Spin on blindly in the dark.

Now, tell the weary children, O my brothers!
That they look to Him, and pray
For the blessed One, who blesseth all the others,
To bless *them* another day.
They answer, "Who is God that He should hear us,
While the rushing of the iron wheel is stirr'd?
When we sob aloud, the human creatures near us,
Pass unhearing not—at least, answer not a word;
And *we* hear not (for the wheels in their resounding)
Strangers speaking at the door.
Is it likely God, with angels singing round him,
Hears our weeping any more?

"Two words, indeed, of praying we remember;
And, at midnight's hour of harm,
Our Father, looking upward in the chamber,
We say softly for a charm.[2]
We say no other words except *Our Father!*
And we think that, in some pause of angels' song,
He may pluck them with the silence sweet to gather,
And hold both within his right hand, which is strong.
Our Father! If he heard us, he would surely
(For they call him good and mild)
Answer—smiling down the steep world very purely—
'Come and rest with me, my child.'

"But no," say the children, weeping faster;
"He is silent as a stone,
And they tell us, of his image is the master
Who commands us to work on.
"Go to!" say the children; "up in heaven,
Dark, wheel-like, turning clouds are all we find!

2 The report of the commissioners represents instances of children, whose religious devotion is confined to the repetition of the two first words of the Lord's Prayer. [Note by EBB]

Do not mock us! we are atheists in our grieving—
    We look up for Him—but tears have made us blind."
Do you hear the children weeping and disproving,
    O my brothers, what ye treach?
For God's possible is taught by his world's loving—
    And the children doubt of each!

And well may the children weep before ye—
    They are weary ere they run!
They have never seen the sunshine, nor the glory
    Which is brighter than the sun!
They know the grief of men, but not the wisdom—
    They sink in the despair, with hope at calm—
Are slaves, without the liberty in christdom—
    Are martyrs by the pang without the palm!
Are worn as if with age; yet unretrievingly
    No joy of memory keep—
Are orphans of the earthly love and heavenly—
    Let them weep—let them weep!

They look up with their pale and sunken faces,
    And their look is dread to see;
For you think you see their angels in their places,
    With eyes meant for Deity.
"How long," they say, "how long, O cruel nation!
Will you stand, to move the world, on a child's heart,
Trample down with a mail'd heel its palpitation,
And tread onward to your throne amid the mart?
Our blood splashes upward, O our tyrants!
    And your purple shows your path—
But the child's sob curseth deeper in the silence,
        Than the strong man in his wrath."

3. Tom Taylor, "Song of the Cheap Customer" (*Punch* 7 [1844]: 255)

Hurrah for cheap clothing! I want not to know
    How the work or material was got;
If the article's good, and the figure is low,
    For the *wherefore* I care not a jot.
Make me out to encourage oppression and vice,

On my beggarly meanneass enlarge;—
Ha! I get a whole suit at one half of the price
A respectable tailor would charge.

Hurrah for the Saxony coat superfine,
Which I buy for about two pounds ten!
If Theft furnished the cloth, 'tis no business of mine,
If Starvation the stitching,—what then?
Hurrah for the trousers of beat kerseymere,
And the gay satin vest at thirteen!
To employ any tradesman, although he is dear,
All because he is honest,—how green!

And hurrah for the shirt for whose purchase I pay
From a couple of shillings to three,
Wrought by famishing Need at a farthing a day;
What on earth can that matter to me?
All I want is to dress at the smallest expense,
In as stylish a way as I can,
Like a practical, straightforward, plain, common sense,
Economical, provident man.

That to clothe me the skinflint and swindler combine,
Is a fact I don't ponder about,
And that thousands in hunger and wretchedness pine,
I regard their employers' look-out.
To procure all my goods at the lowest of shops
Is the course that I mean to pursue;
Then hurrah for low tailors and sellers of slops!
Be they Heathen, or Christian, or Jew!

4. H. Quelch, "Sweating," from *Justice* (11 Sept. 1886)

The sweating system has been so often described and so frequently and justly denounced, that we may take it for granted that most of our readers at any rate know what is meant by the phrase. As generally understood, though it has found few defenders, little or nothing has been done to destroy this system, mainly because people generally have regarded it as a question to be settled by those immediately concerned, as a matter only relating to a private contract by two individuals, namely the sweater and the sweated, and involving no question of public interest at all. This, however, is not so. The system of sweating has entered very extensively into our public services, very much to the detriment of the quality of the goods supplied to our troops, both at home and on foreign service, and it would be scarcely going too far to assert that the scandals which have lately arisen with regard to the inferiority of the weapons supplied to the troops, and the general jobbery said to pervade both the fighting departments, is to a very considerable extent due to the widespread development of this system. Some time ago an agitation was started by a number of well-meaning ladies on behalf of the women employed in the Army Clothing Factory at Pimlico. Considerable indignation was roused against the manner in which these women were being treated and the way in which the labour of others was used against them to reduce their wages by sub-contracts, etc. Yet though their case was clearly made out nothing apparently came of the agitation. Either because the forces against which they had to contend were too powerful, or because those who had taken up the work were dismayed by the task before them. These women, however, are by no means the only sufferers. A glance at the working of this system of sweating will be sufficient to show its pernicious effects upon everybody concerned, except the sweaters. A certain order has to be executed, it may be for military accoutrements, belts, fleeces, harness, or what not. A contractor engages to supply them at a certain price; his may or may not have been the lowest tender. We will assume that the persons responsible for giving the order got the lowest price quoted that could be obtained, though it is by no means to be taken for granted that this is generally the case. However that may be, this contractor does not even employ the people who make the goods he contracts to supply, still less make them himself. He finds a number of other men to contract to get these things made for him; these are the sweaters. He may or may not supply the raw material to be worked up. That is immaterial. What is of the utmost importance to him is that the work should be done as cheaply as possible, everything else is subservient to this, as the lower the price he pays the sweaters the larger is the amount of his profit. It is therefore to the interest of the sweaters to engage to work up the goods at ruinously low rates. This they do, frequently engaging to supply goods at prices which would leave them absolutely no profit at all if the people who did the work were even reasonably well paid. But the sweaters do not forego their profit on that account. That the sweated should be reasonably well paid is quite outside of their calculations. Their profit depends upon these being very badly paid indeed, and they therefore grind them down to the very lowest subsistence. During the past week in Bermondsey one of these sweaters has kept men at work for forty-four hours for the magnificent sum of twelve shillings and twopence. In this particular case three men only are employed in the sweater's den. The rest of the work is taken away by others, mostly women who do it at home. One of the men has served about fourteen years in the army, and is now about thirty-four years of age. A man in the prime of life with the full use of all his faculties, with all his wits about him, and with a technical knowledge of his work, being, as he himself expresses it, "not a dunce at the game," can and does by working hard for four and forty hours earn this enormous sum of twelve shillings and twopence. The others, the women and children who do the greater part of the work at their own homes are even worse paid. And it is of course the competition of these for the work which enables the sweaters to force down the wages of the men to such a miserable level and to reap the splendid profits which they themselves manage to secure through the misery of the people whom they rob and murder.

A short time ago a meeting was held by some of the men employed by these sweaters with a view to forming a society for their own protection, but they were all so miserably poor that they found it impossible to properly start the society, far less keep it going. But this is not their question alone, it concerns all of us, and this particular phase of it concerns every taxpayer as much as it concerns every working man, seeing that one of its consequences is the defrauding of the nation for the benefit of a few blood-suckers, by supplying to the army accoutrements which fall to pieces when put to the use for which they are presumably intended. But the larger question is a class question and one which concerns every member of our class.

"Labouring men and labouring woman
Have one glory and one shame,
Everything that's done inhuman
Injures all of them the same."

And that system, which, whether applied to private or public enterprise, crushes down the workers in the way this sweating system does, is the enemy not only of the people immediately concerned, but of the whole labouring community, all of whom are, whether they know it or not, injured by a wrong committed against one of their number.

5. H. Quelch, "The House of Terror," from *Justice* (23 Oct. 1886)

Over a hundred years ago a bourgeois writer dilating upon the idleness and extravagance of English workmen and bewailing the fact that they were able to get a living by working only four days a week, urged the propriety of compelling them to work six days a week for a bare living, and, as a means to that end, suggested the providing of "ideal workhouses," which should be "houses of terror" for the indigent poor, in which they should be compelled to work so hard, for so many hours, and for such a small return, that they would only too be glad to accept any terms that might be offered them outside. These "houses of terror," which then only existed in the imagination of a malignant enemy of the producing class, have a very real existence in fact for the worker of today. The progress of discovery and science, the development of "labour-saving" machinery in all branches of industry, the adaptation of such resources of civilisation as steam and electricity, gun-cotton and dynamite, to the production of wealth, have but rendered the position of the worker more precarious, the conditions under which he works more intolerable. So far from being able to secure a living with four days work a week he has considerable difficulty in obtaining the barest subsistence with the work of six. His position is one of absolutely helpless dependence upon the goodwill of the capitalist who employs him. And behind it all, enforcing this position of helpless dependence upon him, is that "house of terror," the workhouse. A Workhouse only in name, a prison of the vilest kind in point of fact. Poor people will endure any hardship, accept any conditions that may be offered to them by their exploiters, rather than resort to what is represented by the eulogists of commercialism to be a refuge provided by a benevolent bourgeoisie for worthless and workless proletarians.

Scarcely a week passes now but we hear of the death by starvation of some workless worker who has preferred even that bitter termination to his or her struggle for existence to incarceration in one of our modern bastiles. This fact is most pleasing to the capitalist vultures who live and thrive on the poverty and misery of the proletariat, and the workers, poor fools, are constantly being congratulated upon the commendable pride, which impels them to prefer death to pauperism, even when it happens, as it did in Rotherhithe last week, that this involves the sacrifice of their helpless little ones. In this case the man, who was a large builder, had been out of work for three months, and his six children had in consequence been frequently without food, and it was a common occurrence for them to have nothing but water and a piece of bread during the day. In the end one of the children, aged nine, succumbed to this prolonged starvation.

How gleefully must the advocates of "laissez-faire" have rubbed their hands and smiled over this example of the success of their endeavours to teach the working man the virtues of self-reliance and frugality! This man had not applied for parish relief. No, because he probably knew that if he had, he would have been told by the chairman of the Board of Guardians, with a self-satisfied smirk, that he could "come into the House" if he liked, but that no out-relief could be granted. This offer is always made, and made only because it is known, that in the majority of cases it will be rejected with scorn, upon which the chairman will remark, in a somewhat deprecatory, but still self-satisfied tone, "we must keep down the rates, you know."

If the people would only take them at their word and go into the "House" *en masse*, this state of things would soon be altered. The rates could not bear the strain that would be thus thrown upon them, and means would have to be devised for providing useful work for those who today are compelled either to starve or become a burden on their fellows, simply in order to maintain a reserve army of labour for capitalist exploitation. People who pay poor-rates should understand this, that these rates, a considerable proportion of which are paid by very poor people, are not paid to maintain the poor for their own sakes, but simply to bolster up a vicious system of society. And that the present rigorous administration of the poor law is due to no desire to relieve the rates at the expense of the health and lives of people who, given opportunity, could maintain themselves in decency and comfort, but in order to place these people, as it were, bound hand and foot, at the tender mercy of the capitalists.

6. "Dream of Unfairly-Treated Women (A Long Way After the Laureate)" (*Punch* 98 [1890]: 59)

I read, before my eyelids dropt their shade,
  A leader on weak women and their woe,
In toil and industry, in art and trade,
    In this hard world below.

And for awhile the thought of the sad part
  Played by them and of Fate's ill-balanced scales,
Moistened mine eyelids, and made ache mine heart,
    Remembering these strange tales

Of woman's miseries in every land,
  I saw wherever poverty draws breath
Woman and anguish walking hand in hand,
    The dreary road to death.

Those palled sempstresses of Hood's great song
  Peopled the hollow dark, not now alone,
And I heard sounds of insult, shame, and wrong,
    And grief's sad monotone,

From hearts, like flints, beaten by tyrant hoofs;
    And I saw crowds in somber sweating-dens,
With reeking walls and dang and dripping roofs—
        Fit scarce for styes or pens.

Death at home's sin-stained threshold; honour's fall
    Dislodging from her throne love's household pet,
And wan-faced purity a tyrant's thrall,
        With wild eyes sorrow-wet.

And unsexed women facing heated blasts
    And Tophet fumes, and fluttering tongues of fire;
And virtue staked on most unholy casts,
        And honour sold for hire:

Squadrons and troops of girls of brazen air,
    Tramping the tainted city to and fro,
With feverish flauntings veiling chill despair
        And deeply-centred woe.

So shape chased shape. I saw a neat-garbed nurse,
    Wan with excessive work; and, bowed with toil,
A shop-girl sickly, of the primal curse
        Each looked the helpless spoil.

Anon I saw a lady, at night's fall
    Stiller than chiseled marble, standing there;
A daughter of compassion, slender, tall,
        And delicately fair.

Her weariness with shame and with surprise
    My spirit shocked: she turning on my face
The heavy glances of unrested eyes,
        Spoke mildly in her place.

"I have long duties; ask thou not my name
    Some say I fret at a fair destiny.
Many I have to tend; to make my claim
        Some venture: we shall see."

"I trust, good lady, that in a fair field,
The case 'twixt you and tyranny will be tried,"
I said; then turning promptly I appealed
To one who stood beside.

She said, "Poor pay, and plenteous fines, and worse,
Made me rebel amidst my mates' applause.
To insubordination I'm averse,
But have I not good cause?

"We are cut off from hope in our hard place,
Sweet factory? Ah, well, *our* sweets are few.
We strike for justice. Man might show some grace
I think, Sir; do not you?"

Turning I saw, ranging a flowery pile,
One sitting in an entry dark and cold;
A girl with hectic cheeks, and hollow smile;
Wired roses there she sold,

Or strove to sell; but often on her ear
The harrying voice of stern policedom struck,
And chased her from her vantage, till a tear
Fell at her "wretched luck."

Again I saw a wan domestic drudge
Scuttering across a smug suburban lawn;
Tired with the nightly watch, the morning trudge,
The toil at early dawn,

And then a frail and thin-clad governess,
Hurrying to daily misery through the rain.
Toiling, with scanty food, and scanty dress,
Long hours for little gain.

Anon a spectral shop-girl creeping back
To her dull garret-home through the chill night,
Bowed, heart-sick, spirit-crushed, poor ill-paid hack
Of harsh commercial might!

These I beheld, the world's sad woman-throng,
Work-ridden vassals of its Mammon-god,
Their destiny to creep and drudge along,
And kiss grief's chastening rod.

And then I saw a spirit surface-fair,
A Mænad-masked betrayer, base, impure,
But with sin's glittering garb, and radiant air,
Gay laugh, and golden lure.

It smiled, it beckoned—whither? To the abyss!
But of that throng how many may be drawn
By the gay glamour and the siren kiss
To where sin's soul-gulfs yawn?

How many? No response my vision gave.
Make answer, if ye may, ye lords of gain!
Make answer, if ye know, ye chiders grave
Of late revolt, and vain!

Dream of *Fair* Women? Nay, for work and want
Mar maiden comeliness and matron grace.
Let sober judgment, clear of gush and cant,
The bitter problem face!

Appendix C

Working-Class Domestic Interiors and Middle-Class Domesticity

[This section begins with an extract from John Ruskin, who provides perhaps the quintessential Victorian definition of the home. According to him, the ideal home provides shelter for the family, particularly the man who must leave regularly to confront the brutal confusions of the world. The ideal wife and mother, who radiates domesticity, tends to the hearth. The subsequent extracts document the ways in which working-class domestic settings fell far short of this ideal. They also provide a glimpse into the historical context informing Besant's depiction of the Earthly Tract Society, which Valentine and Claude created to disseminate knowledge about middle-class domesticity among the working classes.]

1. John Ruskin, from "Of Queens' Gardens," *Sesame and Lilies: Two Lectures Delivered at Manchester in 1864*

... I want you to feel, with me, that whatever advantages we possess in the present day in the diffusion of education and of literature, can only be rightly used by any of us when we have apprehended clearly what education is to lead to, and literature to teach. I wish you to see that both well-directed moral training and well-chosen reading lead to the possession of a power over the ill-guided and illiterate, which is, according to the measure of it, in the truest sense, *kingly;* conferring indeed the purest kingship that can exist among men....

There is, then, I repeat—and as I want to leave this idea with you, I begin with it, and shall end with it—only one pure kind of kingship; an inevitable and eternal kind, crowned or not: the kingship, namely, which consists in a stronger moral state, and a truer thoughtful state, than that of others; enabling you, therefore, to guide, or to raise them....

Believing that all literature and all education are only useful so far as they tend to confirm this calm, beneficent, and *therefore* kingly, power—first, over ourselves, and, through ourselves, over all around us, I am now going to ask you to consider with me farther, what special portion or kind of this royal authority, arising out of noble education, may rightly be possessed by women; and how far they also are called to a true queenly power. Not in their households merely, but over all within their sphere. And in what sense, if they rightly understood and exercised this royal or gracious influence, the order and beauty induced by such benignant power would justify us in speaking of the territories over which each of them reigned, as "Queens' Gardens." . . .

We cannot determine what the queenly power of women should be, until we are agreed what their ordinary power should be. We cannot consider how education may fit them for any widely extending duty, until we are agreed what is their true constant duty. And there never was a time when wilder words were spoken, or more vain imagination permitted, respecting this question—quite vital to all social happiness. The relations of the womanly to the manly nature, their different capacities of intellect or of virtue, seem never to have been yet measured with entire consent. We hear of the mission and of the rights of Woman, as if these could ever be separate from the mission and the rights of Man;—as if she and her lord were creatures of independent kind and of irreconcilable claim. This, at least, is wrong. And not less wrong—perhaps even more foolishly wrong (for I will anticipate thus far what I hope to prove)—is the idea that woman is only the shadow and attendant image of her lord, owing him a thoughtless and servile obedience, and supported altogether in her weakness by the pre-eminence of his fortitude.

This, I say, is the most foolish of all errors respecting her who was made to be the helpmate of man. As if he could be helped effectively by a shadow, or worthily by a slave!

Let us try, then, whether we cannot get at some clear and harmonious idea (it must be harmonious if it is true) of what womanly mind and virtue are in power and office, with respect to man's; and how their relations, rightly accepted, aid and increase, the vigour, and honour, and authority of both.

And now I must repeat one thing I said in the last lecture: namely, that the first use of education was to enable us to consult with the wisest and the greatest men on all points of earnest difficulty. That to use books rightly, was to go to them for help: to appeal to them, when our own knowledge and power of thought failed; to be led by them into wider sight, purer conception than our own, and receive from them the united sentence of the judges and councils of all time, against our solitary and unstable opinion.

Let us do this now. Let us see whether the greatest, the wisest, the purest-hearted of all ages are agreed in any wise on this point: let us hear the testimony they have left respecting what they held to be the true dignity of woman, and her mode of help to man.

And first let us take Shakespeare.

Note broadly in the outset, Shakespeare has no heroes;—he has only heroines. . . . In his labored and perfect plays you have no hero. . . . Whereas there is hardly a play that has not a perfect woman in it, steadfast in grave hope, and errorless purpose: Cordelia, Desdemona, Isabella, Hermione, Imogen, Queen Katherine, Perdita, Sylvia, Viola, Rosalind, Helena, and last, and perhaps loveliest, Virgilia, are all faultless; conceived in the highest heroic type of humanity.

Then observe, secondly,

The catastrophe of every play is caused always by the folly or fault of a man; the redemption, if there be any, is by the wisdom and virtue of a woman, and, failing that, there is none. The catastrophe of King Lear is owing to his own want of judgment, his impatient vanity, his misunderstanding of his children; the virtue of his one true daughter would have saved him from all the injuries of the others, unless he had cast her away from him; as it is, she all but saves him. . . .

Observe, further, among all the principal figures in Shakespeare's plays, there is only one weak woman—Ophelia; and it is because she fails Hamlet at the critical moment, and is not, and cannot in her nature be, a guide to him when he needs her most, that all the bitter catastrophe follows. Finally, though there are three wicked women among the principal figures,Lady Macbeth, Regan, and Goneril, they are felt at once to be frightful exceptions to the ordinary laws of life; fatal in their influence also in proportion to the power for good which they have abandoned.

Such, in broad light, is Shakespeare's testimony to the position and character of women in human life. He represents them as infallibly faithful and wise counsellors,—incorruptibly just and pure examples—strong always to sanctify, even when they cannot save.

Not as in any wise comparable in knowledge of the nature of man,— still less in his understanding of the causes and courses of fate,— but only as the writer who has given us the broadest view of the conditions and modes of ordinary thought in modern society, I ask you next to receive the witness of Walter Scott. . . .

. . . [I]n his imaginations of women . . . with endless varieties of grace, tenderness, and intellectual power, we find in all a quite infallible and inevitable sense of dignity and justice; a fearless, instant, and untiring self-sacrifice to even the appearance of duty, much more to its real claims; and, finally, a patient wisdom of deeply restrained affection, which does infinitely more than protect its objects from a momentary error; it gradually forms, animates, and exalts the characters of the unworthy lovers, until, at the close of the tale, we are just able, and no more, to take patience in hearing of their unmerited success.

So that, in all cases, with Scott as with Shakespeare, it is the woman who watches over, teaches, and guides the youth; it is never, by any chance, the youth who watches over or educates his mistress. . . .

. . . I will ask you whether it can be supposed that these men, in the main work of their lives, are amusing themselves with a fictitious and idle view of the relations between man and woman;— nay, worse than fictitious or idle; for a thing may be imaginary, yet desirable, if it were possible; but this, their ideal of women, is, according to our common idea of the marriage relation, wholly undesirable. The woman, we say, is not to guide, nor even to think, for herself. The man is always to be the wiser; he is to be the thinker, the ruler, the superior in knowledge and discretion, as in power. . . . Are . . . these great men mistaken, or are we? . . . .

But how, you will ask, is the idea of this guiding function of the woman reconcileable with a true wifely subjection? Simply in that it is a *guiding*, not a determining, function. Let me try to show you briefly how these powers seem to be rightly distinguishable.

We are foolish, and without excuse foolish, in speaking of the "superiority" of one sex to the other, as if they could be compared in similar things. Each has what the other has not: each completes the other, and is completed by the other: they are in nothing alike, and the happiness and perfection of both depends on each asking and receiving from the other what the other only can give.

Now their separate characters are briefly these. The man's power is active, progressive, defensive. He is eminently the doer, the creator, the discoverer, the defender. His intellect is for speculation and invention; his energy for adventure, for war, and for conquest, wherever war is just, wherever conquest necessary. But the woman's power is for rule, not for battle,—and her intellect is not for invention or creation, but for sweet ordering, arrangement, and decision. She sees the qualities of things, their claims and their places. Her great function is Praise; she enters into no contest, but infallibly adjudges the crown of contest. By her office, and place, she is protected from all danger and temptation. The man, in his rough work in the open world, must encounter all peril and trial:—to him, therefore, the failure, the offence, the inevitable error: often he must be wounded, or subdued, often misled, and *always* hardened. But he guards the woman from all this; within his house, as ruled by her, unless she herself has sought it, need enter no danger, no temptation, no cause of error or offence. This is the true nature of home—it is the place of Peace; the shelter, not only from all injury, but from all terror, doubt, and division. In so far as it is not this, it is not home; so far as the anxieties of the outer life penetrate into it, and the inconsistently-minded, unknown, unloved, or hostile society of the outer world is allowed by either husband or wife to cross the threshold, it ceases to be home; it is then only a part of that outer world which you have roofed over, and lighted fire in. But so far as it is a sacred place, a vestal temple, a temple of the hearth watched over by Household Gods, before whose faces none may come but those whom they can receive with love,—so far as it is this, and roof and fire are types only of a nobler shade and light,—shade as of the rock in a weary land, and light as of the Pharos in the stormy sea;—so far it vindicates the name, and fulfils the praise, of home.

And wherever a true wife comes, this home is always round her. The stars only may be over her head; the glowworm in the night-cold grass may be the only fire at her foot: but home is yet wherever she is; and for a noble woman it stretches far round her, better than ceiled with cedar, or painted with vermilion, shedding its quiet light far, for those who else were homeless.

This, then, I believe to be,—will you not admit it to be?—the woman's true place and power. But do not you see that to fulfil this, she must—as far as one can use such terms of a human creature—be incapable of error? So far as she rules, all must be right, or nothing is. She must be enduringly, incorruptibly good; instinctively, infallibly wise—wise, not for self-development, but for self-renunciation: wise, not that she may set herself above her husband, but that she may never fail from his side: wise, not with the narrowness of insolent and loveless pride, but with the passionate gentleness of an infinitely variable, because infinitely applicable, modesty of service—the true changefulness of woman. . . .

II. I have been trying, thus far, to show you what should be the place, and what the power of woman. Now, secondly, we ask, What kind of education is to fit her for these? . . .

The first of our duties to her—no thoughtful persons now doubt this,—is to secure for her such physical training and exercise as may confirm her health, and perfect her beauty: the highest refinement of that beauty being unattainable without splendour of activity and of delicate strength. . . .

. . . [Y]ou have first to mould her physical frame, and then, as the strength she gains will permit you, to fill and temper her mind with all knowledge and thoughts which tend to confirm its natural instincts of justice, and refine its natural tact of love.

All such knowledge should be given her as may enable her to understand, and even to aid, the work of men: and yet it should be given, not as knowledge,—not as if it were, or could be, for her an object to know; but only to feel, and to judge. It is of no moment, as a matter of pride or perfectness in herself, whether she knows many languages or one but it is of the utmost, that she should be able to show kindness to a stranger, and to understand the sweetness of a stranger's tongue. It is of no moment to her own worth or dignity that she should be acquainted with this science or that; but it is of the highest that she should be trained in habits of accurate thought; that she should understand the meaning, the inevitableness, and the loveliness of natural laws; and follow at least some one path of scientific attainment, as far as to the threshold of that bitter Valley of Humiliation, into which only the wisest and bravest of men can descend, owning themselves for ever children, gathering pebbles on a boundless shore. It is of little consequence how many positions of cities she knows, or how many dates of events, or how many names of celebrated persons—it is not the object of education to turn the woman into a dictionary; but it is deeply necessary that she should be taught to enter with her whole personality into the history she reads; to picture the passages of it vitally in her own bright imagination; to apprehend, with her fine instincts, the pathetic circumstances and dramatic relations, which the historian too often only eclipses by his reasoning, and disconnects by his arrangement: it is for her to trace the hidden equities of divine reward, and catch sight, through the darkness, of the fateful threads of woven fire that connect error with retribution. But, chiefly of all, she is to be taught to extend the limits of her sympathy with respect to that history which is being for ever determined, as the moments pass in which she draws her peaceful breath; and to the contemporary calamity, which, were it but rightly mourned by her, would recur no more hereafter. She is to exercise herself in imagining what would be the effects upon her mind and conduct, if she were daily brought into the presence of the suffering which is not the less real because shut from her sight. She is to be taught somewhat to understand the nothingness of the proportion which that little world in which she lives and loves, bears to the world in which God lives and loves;—and solemnly she is to be taught to strive that her thoughts of piety may not be feeble in proportion to the number they embrace, nor her prayer more languid than it is for the momentary relief from pain of her husband or her child, when it is uttered for the multitudes of those who have none to love them,—and, is "for all who are desolate and oppressed."

Thus far, I think, I have had your concurrence; perhaps you will not be with me in what I believe is most needful for me to say. There *is* one dangerous science for women—one which they must indeed beware how they profanely touch—that of theology. Strange, and miserably strange, that while they are modest enough to doubt their powers, and pause at the threshold of sciences where every step is demonstrable and sure, they will plunge headlong, and without one thought of incompetency, into that science in which the greatest men have trembled, and the wisest erred. Strange, that they will complacently and pridefully bind up whatever vice or folly there is in them, whatever arrogance, petulance, or blind incomprehensiveness, into one bitter bundle of consecrated myrrh. Strange, in creatures born to be Love visible, that where they can know least, they will condemn first. . . .

I believe, then, with this exception, that a girl's education should be nearly, in its course and material of study, the same as a boy's; but quite differently directed. A woman, in any rank of life, ought to know whatever her husband is likely to know, but to know it in a different way. His command of it should be foundational and progressive, hers, general and accomplished for daily and helpful use. Not but that it would often be wiser in men to learn things in a womanly sort of way, for present use, and to seek for the discipline and training of their mental powers in such branches of study as will be afterwards fittest for social service; but, speaking broadly, a man ought to know any language or science he learns, thoroughly, while a woman ought to know the same language, or science, only so far as may enable her to sympathise in her husband's pleasures, and in those of his best friends.

Yet, observe, with exquisite accuracy as far as she reaches. There is a wide difference between elementary knowledge and superficial knowledge—between a firm beginning, and a feeble smattering. A woman may always help her husband by what she knows, however little; by what she half-knows, or mis-knows, she will only teaze him.

And indeed, if there were to be any difference between a girl's education and a boy's, I should say that of the two the girl should be earlier led, as her intellect ripens faster, into deep and serious subjects; and that her range of literature should be, not more, but less frivolous, calculated to add the qualities of patience and seriousness to her natural poignancy of thought and quickness of wit; and also to keep her in a lofty and pure element of thought. I enter not now into any question of choice of books; only let us be sure that her books are not heaped up in her lap as they fall out of the package of the circulating library, wet with the last and lightest spray of the fountain of folly.

Or even of the fountain of wit; for with respect to the sore temptation of novel-reading, it is not the badness of a novel that we should dread, but its over-wrought interest. The weakest romance is not so stupefying as the lower forms of religious exciting literature, and the worst romance is not so corrupting as false history, false philosophy, or false political essays. But the best romance becomes dangerous, if, by its excitement, it renders the ordinary course of life uninteresting, and increases the morbid thirst for useless acquaintance with scenes in which we shall never be called upon to act.

I speak therefore of good novels only. . . .

Without, however, venturing here on any attempt at decision how much novel-reading should be allowed, let me at least clearly assert this, that whether novels, or poetry, or history be read, they should be chosen, not for what is *out* of them, but for what is *in* them. The chance and scattered evil that may here and there haunt, or hide itself in, a powerful book, never does any harm to a noble girl; but the emptiness of an author oppresses her, and his amiable folly degrades her. And if she can have access to a good library of old and classical books, there need be no choosing at all. Keep the modern magazine and novel out of your girl's way: turn her loose into the old library every wet day, and let her alone. She will find what is good for her; you cannot: for there is just this difference between the making of a girl's character and a boy's—you may chisel a boy into shape, as you would a rock, or hammer him into it, if he be of a better kind, as you would a piece of bronze. But you cannot hammer a girl into anything. She grows as a flower does,—she will wither without sun; she will decay in her sheath, as a narcissus does, if you do not give her air enough; she may fall, and defile her head in dust, if you leave her without help at some moments of her life; but you cannot fetter her; she must take her own fair form and way. . . .

Let her loose in the library, I say, as you do a fawn in a field. It knows the bad weeds twenty times better than you; and the good ones too, and will eat some bitter and prickly ones, good for it, which you had not the slightest thought were good.

Then, in art, keep the finest models before her, and let her practice in all accomplishments be accurate and thorough, so as to enable her to understand more than she accomplishes. I say the finest models—that is to say, the truest, simplest, usefullest. Note those epithets; they will range through all the arts. Try them in music, where you might think them the least applicable. I say the truest, that in which the notes most closely and faithfully express the meaning of the words, or the character of intended emotion; again, the simplest, that in which the meaning and melody are attained with the fewest and most significant notes possible; and, finally, the usefullest, that music which makes the best words most beautiful, which enchants them in our memories each with its own glory of sound, and which applies them closest to the heart at the moment we need them.

And not only in the material and in the course, but yet more earnestly in the spirit of it, let a girl's education be as serious as a boy's. You bring up your girls as if they were meant for sideboard ornaments, and then complain of their frivolity. Give them the same advantages that you give their brothers—appeal to the same grand instincts of virtue in them; teach *them* also that courage and truth are the pillars of their being: do you think that they would not answer that appeal, brave and true as they are even now, when you know that there is hardly a girl's school in this Christian kingdom where the children's courage or sincerity would be thought of half so much importance as their way of coming in at a door; and when the whole system of society, as respects the mode of establishing them in life, is one rotten plague of cowardice and imposture—cowardice, in not daring to let them live, or love, except as their neighbours choose; and imposture, in bringing, for the purpose of our own pride, the full glow of the world's worst vanity upon a girl's eyes, at the very period when the whole happiness of her future existence depends upon her remaining undazzled?

And give them, lastly, not only noble teachings, but noble teachers. You consider somewhat, before you send your boy to school, what kind of a man the master is;—whatsoever kind of a man he is, you at least give him full authority over your son, and show some respect to him yourself; if he comes to dine with you, you do not put him at a side table: you know also that, at his college, your child's immediate tutor will be under the direction of some still higher tutor, for whom you have absolute reverence. You do not treat the Dean of Christ Church or the Master of Trinity as your inferiors.

But what teachers do you give your girls, and what reverence do you show to the teachers you have chosen? Is a girl likely to think her own conduct, or her own intellect, of much importance, when you trust the entire formation of her character, moral and intellectual, to a person whom you let your servants treat with less respect than they do your housekeeper (as if the soul of your child were a less charge than jams and groceries), and whom you yourself think you confer an honour upon by letting her sometimes sit in the drawing-room in the evening?

Thus, then, of literature as her help, and thus of art. There is one more help which she cannot do without—one which, alone, has sometimes done more than all other influences besides,—the help of wild and fair nature. . . .

. . . Suppose you had each, at the back of your houses, a garden, large enough for your children to play in, with just as much lawn as would give them room to run,—no more—and that you could not change your abode; but that, if you chose, you could double your income, or quadruple it, by digging a coal shaft in the middle of the lawn, and turning the flower-beds into heaps of coke. Would you do it? I think not. I can tell you, you would be wrong if you did, though it gave you income sixty-fold instead of four-fold.

Yet this is what you are doing with all England. The whole country is but a little garden, not more than enough for your children to run on the lawns of, if you would let them *all* run there. And this little garden you will turn into furnace ground, and fill with heaps of cinders, if you can; and those children of yours, not you, will suffer for it. For the fairies will not be all banished; there are fairies of the furnace as of the wood, and their first gifts seem to be "sharp arrows of the mighty;" but their last gifts are "coals of juniper."

And yet I cannot—though there is no part of my subject that I feel more—press this upon you; for we made so little use of the power of nature while we had it that we shall hardly feel what we have lost. Just on the other side of the Mersey you have your Snowdon, and your Menai Straits, and that mighty granite rock beyond the moors of Anglesea, splendid in its heathery crest, and foot planted in the deep sea, once thought of as sacred—a divine promontory, looking westward; the Holy Head or Headland, still not without awe when its red light glares first through storm. These are the hills, and these the bays and blue inlets, which, among the Greeks, would have been always loved, always fateful in influence on the national mind. That Snowdon is your Parnassus; but where are its Muses? That Holyhead mountain is your Island of Ægina; but where is its Temple to Minerva?

Shall I read you what the Christian Minerva had achieved under the shadow of our Parnassus, up to the year 1848?—Here is a little account of a Welsh school, from page 261 of the Report on Wales, published by the Committee of Council on Education. This is a school close to a town containing 5,000 persons:—

"I then called up a larger class, most of whom had recently come to the school. Three girls repeatedly declared they had never heard of Christ, and two that they had never heard of God. Two out of six thought Christ was on earth now (they might have had a worse thought, perhaps), three knew nothing about the crucifixion. Four out of seven did not know the names of the months, nor the number of days in a year. They had no notion of addition beyond two and two, or three and three; their minds were perfect blanks."

Oh, ye women of England! from the Princess of that Wales to the simplest of you, do not think your own children can be brought into their true fold of rest while these are scattered on the hills, as sheep having no shepherd. And do not think your daughters can be trained to the truth of their own human beauty, while the pleasant places, which God made at once for their school-room and their play-ground, lie desolate and defiled. . . .

III. Thus far, then, of the nature, thus far of the teaching, of woman, and thus of her household office, and queenliness. We now come to our last, our widest question,—What is her queenly office with respect to the state?

Generally, we are under an impression that a man's duties are public, and a woman's private. But this is not altogether so. A man has a personal work or duty, relating to his own home, and a public work or duty, which is the expansion of the other, relating to the state. So a woman has a personal work or duty, relating to her own home, and a public work or duty, which is also the expansion of that.

Now the man's work for his own home is, as has been said, to secure its maintenance, progress, and defence; the woman's to secure its order, comfort, and loveliness.

Expand both these functions. The man's duty as a member of a commonwealth, is to assist in the maintenance, in the advance, in the defence of the state. The woman's duty, as a member of the commonwealth, is to assist in the ordering, in the comforting, and in the beautiful adornment of the state.

What the man is at his own gate, defending it, if need be, against insult and spoil, that also, not in a less, but in a more devoted measure, he is to be at the gate of his country, leaving his home, if need be, even to the spoiler, to do his more incumbent work there.

And, in like manner, what the woman is to be within her gates, as the centre of order, the balm of distress, and the mirror of beauty; that she is also to be without her gates, where order is more difficult, distress more imminent, loveliness more rare.

And as within the human heart there is always set an instinct for all its real duties,—an instinct which you cannot quench, but only warp and corrupt if you withdraw it from its true purpose,—as there is the intense instinct of love, which, rightly disciplined, maintains all the sanctities of life, and, misdirected, undermines them; and *must* do either the one or the other;—so there is in the human heart an inextinguishable instinct, the love of power, which, rightly directed, maintains all the majesty of law and life, and, misdirected, wrecks them.

Deep rooted in the innermost life of the heart of man, and of the heart of woman, God set it there, and God keeps it there. Vainly, as falsely, you blame or rebuke the desire of power!—For Heaven's sake, and for Man's sake, desire it all you can. But *what* power? That is all the question. Power to destroy? the lion's limb, and the dragon's breath? Not so. Power to heal, to redeem, to guide and to guard. Power of the sceptre and shield; the power of the royal hand that heals in touching,—that binds the fiend, and looses the captive; the throne that is founded on the rock of Justice, and descended from only by steps of Mercy. Will you not covet such power as this, and seek such throne as this, and be no more housewives, but queens?

It is now long since the women of England arrogated, universally, a title which once belonged to nobility only; and, having once been in the habit of accepting the simple title of gentlewoman, as correspondent to that of gentleman, insisted on the privilege of assuming the title of "Lady,"[1] which properly corresponds only to the title of "Lord."

I do not blame them for this; but only for their narrow motive in this. I would have them desire and claim the title of Lady, provided they claim, not merely the title, but the office and duty signified by it. Lady means "bread-giver" or "loaf-giver," and Lord means "maintainer of laws," and both titles have reference, not to the law which is maintained in the house, nor to the bread which is given to the household; but to law maintained for the multitude, and to bread broken among the multitude. So that a Lord has legal claim only to his title in so far as he is the maintainer of the justice of the Lord of Lords; and a Lady has legal claim to her title, only so far as she communicates that help to the poor representatives of her Master, which women once, ministering to Him of their substance, were permitted to extend to that Master Himself; and when she is known, as He Himself once was, in breaking of bread.

And this beneficent and legal dominion, this power of the Dominus, or House-Lord, and of the Domina, or House-Lady, is great and venerable, not in the number of those through whom it has lineally descended, but in the number of those whom it grasps within its sway; it is always regarded with reverent worship wherever its dynasty is founded on its duty, and its ambition co-relative with its beneficence. Your fancy is pleased with the thought of being noble ladies, with a train of vassals. Be it so; you cannot be too noble, and your train cannot be too great; but see to it that your train is of vassals whom you serve and feed, not merely of slaves who serve and feed *you*; and that the multitude which obeys you is of those whom you have comforted, not oppressed,—whom you have redeemed, not led into captivity.

And this, which is true of the lower or household dominion, is equally true of the queenly dominion; that highest dignity is open to you, if you will also accept that highest duty. . . . [W]hether consciously or not, you must be, in many a heart, enthroned: there is no putting by that crown; queens you must always be; queens to your lovers; queens to your husbands and your sons; queens of higher mystery to the world beyond, which bows itself, and will for ever bow, before the myrtle crown, and the stainless sceptre, of womanhood. But,

1 I wish there were a true order of chivalry instituted for our English youth of certain ranks, in which both boy and girl should receive, at a given age, their knighthood and ladyhood by true title; attainable only by certain probation and trial both of character and accomplishment; and to be forfeited, on conviction, by their peers, of any dishonourable act. Such an institution would be entirely, and with all noble results, possible, in a nation which loved honour. That it would not be possible among us, is not to the discredit of the scheme. [Ruskin's note.]

alas! you are too often idle and careless queens, grasping at majesty in the least things, while you abdicate it in the greatest; and leaving misrule and violence to work their will among men, in defiance of the power, which, holding straight in gift from the Prince of all Peace, the wicked among you betray, and the good forget.

"Prince of Peace." Note that name. When kings rule in that name, and nobles, and the judges of the earth, they also, in their narrow place, and mortal measure, receive the power of it. There are no other rulers than they: other rule than theirs is but *mis*rule. . . . There is not a war in the world, no, nor an injustice, but you women are answerable for it; not in that you have provoked, but in that you have not hindered. Men, by their nature, are prone to fight; they will fight for any cause, or for none. It is for you to choose their cause for them, and to forbid them when there is no cause. There is no suffering, no injustice, no misery in the earth, but the guilt of it lies lastly with you. Men can bear the sight of it, but you should not be able to bear it. Men may tread it down without sympathy in their own struggle; but men are feeble in sympathy, and contracted in hope; it is you only who can feel the depths of pain; and conceive the way of its healing. Instead of trying to do this, you turn away from it; you shut yourselves within your park walls and garden gates; and you are content to know that there is beyond them a whole world in wilderness—a world of secrets which you dare not penetrate; and of suffering which you dare not conceive.

I tell you that this is to me quite the most amazing among the phenomena of humanity. I am surprised at no depths to which, when once warped from its honour, that humanity can be degraded. I do not wonder at the miser's death, with his hands, as they relax, dropping gold. I do not wonder at the sensualist's life, with the shroud wrapped about his feet. I do not wonder at the single-handed murder of a single victim, done by the assassin in the darkness of the railway, or reed-shadow of the marsh. I do not even wonder at the myriad-handed murder of multitudes, done boastfully in the daylight, by the frenzy of nations, and the immeasurable, unimaginable guilt, heaped up from hell to heaven, of their priests, and kings. But this is wonderful to me—oh, how wonderful!—to see the tender and delicate woman among you, with her child at her breast, and a power, if she would wield it, over it, and over its father, purer than the air of heaven, and stronger than the seas of earth—nay, a magnitude of blessing which her husband would not part with for all that earth itself, though it were made of one entire and perfect chrysolite:— to see her abdicate this majesty to play at precedence with her next-door neighbour! This is wonderful—oh, wonderful!—to see her, with every innocent feeling fresh within her, go out in the morning into her garden to play with the fringes of its guarded flowers, and lift their heads when they are drooping, with her happy smile upon her face, and no cloud upon her brow, because there is a little wall around her place of peace: and yet she knows, in her heart, if she would only look for its knowledge, that, outside of that little rose-covered wall, the wild grass, to the horizon, is torn up by the agony of men, and beat level by the drift of their life-blood.

Have you ever considered what a deep under meaning there lies, or at least, may be read, if we choose, in our custom of strewing flowers before those whom we think most happy? Do you suppose it is merely to deceive them into the hope that happiness is always to fall thus in showers at their feet?—that wherever they pass they will tread on herbs of sweet scent, and that the rough ground will be made smooth for them by depth of roses? So surely as they believe that, they will have, instead, to walk on bitter herbs and thorns; and the only softness to their feet will be of snow. But it is not thus intended they should believe there is a better meaning in that old custom. The path of a good woman is indeed strewn with flowers; but they rise behind her steps, not before them. "Her feet have touched the meadows, and left the daisies rosy."

You think that only a lover's fancy;—false and vain! How if it could be true? You think this also, perhaps, only a poet's fancy—

"Even the light harebell raised its head
Elastic from her airy tread."

But it is little to say of a woman, that she only does not destroy where she passes. She should revive; the harebells should bloom, not stoop, as she passes. You think I am going into wild hyperbole? Pardon me, not a whit—I mean what I say in calm English, spoken in resolute truth. You have heard it said—(and I believe there is more than fancy even in that saying, but let it pass for a fanciful one)—that flowers only flourish rightly in the garden of some one who loves them. I know you would like that to be true; you would think it a pleasant magic if you could flush your flowers into brighter bloom by a kind look upon them: nay, more, if your look had the power, not only to cheer, but to guard them—if you could bid the black blight turn away, and the knotted caterpillar spare—if you could bid the dew fall upon them in the drought, and say to the south wind, in frost—"Come, thou south, and breathe upon my garden, that the spices of it may flow out." This you would think a great thing? And do you think it not a greater thing, that all this, (and how much more than this!) you *can* do, for fairer flowers than these—flowers that could bless you for having blessed them, and will love you for having loved them;—flowers that have eyes like yours, and thoughts like yours, and lives like yours; which, once saved, you save for ever? Is this only a little power? Far among the moorlands and the rocks,—far in the darkness of the terrible streets,—these feeble florets are lying, with all their fresh leaves torn, and their stems broken: will you never go down to them, nor set them in order in their little fragrant beds, nor fence them in their shuddering from the fierce wind? Shall morning follow morning, for you, but not for them. . . .

Will you not go down among them?—among those sweet living things, whose new courage, sprung from the earth with the deep colour of heaven upon it, is starting up in strength of goodly spire; and whose purity, washed from the dust, is opening, bud by bud, into the flower of promise. . . ? . . .

. . . Oh—you queens—you queens! among the hills and happy greenwood of this land of yours . . . in your cities, shall the stones cry out against you, that they are the only pillows where the Son of Man can lay His head?

2. Alice Lewis, from "Housing of the Poor in London," *Economic Review* (1900)

Meanwhile, much can be done by individual effort to alleviate the present distress by helping to remake the homes of the people; for it is possible to purchase whole blocks and streets, which are at present noisome slums, and to establish a beneficent rule over them by the extraordinary powers belonging to a landlord. And for this purpose women have special aptitudes. We need not forget the warning, "Tis good to have a giant's strength, but tyrannous to use it as a giant;" but in this work, among the decivilized sections of society, a good despotism is for a time the only cure. Women are born rulers, if we may accept Ruskin's authority. Not every man aspires to be a king, but every woman aspires to be a queen; and it is this tendency towards rule that makes her of use in a London slum. In such a quarter no rule worthy of the name exists at all but every man does what is right in his own eyes, be it to break every panel in the doors of his rented house, or all his own furniture, or his wife's head, or to keep his neighbours awake all night by a horrid din.

Women's peculiar work has always been keeping house; it is now almost an instinct, and house management is only house-keeping on a large scale. Instead of one house to keep clean, wholesome, and happy, some of us have two or three hundred; instead of one dispute to settle among the children, we may have a score to settle among the tenants; instead of £10 house-keeping money, we may have £100. We may have a staff of workmen to look after instead of a staff of servants, and we may be held responsible for the wholesome condition and moral tone of our tenants, workmen, and houses as for the welfare of our own house, children, and servants. And for this wider sphere of work we need the same qualifications—orderliness, power of rapid judgement, eyes that see, perception of character, economy in buying, knowledge of sanitation, and, above all, the capacity to exercise a firm rule which will fit itself to the needs of the human creatures for whom we are working.

3. L. T. Meade, from *A Princess of the Gutter* (1895)

I had never seen stairs which were like those we now ascended. They were slippery with dirt, black with dirt, falling to pieces with dirt and neglect. The greater part of the banisters had long disappeared; the windows, which were originally made to give light, were choked with filthy rags; there was not a scrap of glass in the two we passed. Here and there on the stairs was a hole over which we had to leap to keep ourselves from being hurled into some unknown abyss of horror below … I pushed the door boldly open and went in. Was this a room? Was any one in Christian England expected to pay coin of the realm for such a den? The attic in question was very small; it was also very low; it had a sloping roof which contained one tiny window. This window was begrimed with smuts and tightly shut. The sun beat pitilessly on the sloping roof. The air of the room was foul in the extreme. Fiery beams of strong light came in through the tightly shut window. The atmosphere must have been considerably over ninety.

4. Octavia Hill, from "Blank Court; or Landlords and Tenants," *Macmillan's Magazine* (1871)

In many of the houses the dustbins were utterly unapproachable, and cabbage leaves, stale fish, and every sort of dirt were lying in the passages and on the stairs; in some the back kitchen had been used as a dustbin, but had not been emptied for years, and the dust filtered through into the front kitchens, which were the sole living and sleeping rooms of some families; in some, the kitchen stairs were many inches thick with dirt, which was so hardened that a shovel had to be used to get it off; in some there was hardly any water to be had; the wood was eaten away, and broken away; windows were smashed; and the rain was coming through the roofs. At night it was still worse; and during the first winter I had to collect the rents chiefly then, as the inhabitants, being principally costermongers, were out nearly all day, and they were afraid to entrust their rent to their neighbours. It was then that I saw the houses in their most dreadful aspect. I well remember wet, foggy, Monday nights, when I turned down the dingy court, past the brilliantly lighted public-house at the corner, past the old furniture outside the shops, and dived into the dark, yawning, passage ways. The front doors stood open day and night, and as I felt my way down the kitchen stairs, broken, and rounded by the hardened mud upon them, the foul smells which the heavy, foggy air would not allow to rise, met me as I descended, and the plaster rattled down with a hollow sound as I groped along. It was truly appalling to think that there were human beings who lived habitually in such an atmosphere, with such surroundings. Sometimes I had to open the kitchen door myself, after knocking several times in vain, when a woman, quite drunk, would be lying on the floor on some black mass which served as a bed; sometimes, in answer to my knocks, a half-drunken man would swear, and thrust the rent-money out to me through a chink of the door, placing his foot against it, so as to prevent it from opening wide enough to admit me … [I]t is there not so much a question of dealing with houses alone, as of dealing with houses in connection with their influence on the character and habits of the people who inhabit them. If any society had come there and put those houses into a state of perfect repair at once, it would have been of little use because its work would have been undone again by the bad habits and carelessness of the people. If improvements were made on a large scale, and the people remained untouched, all would soon return to its former condition. You cannot deal with the people and their houses separately. The principle on which the whole work rests is that the inhabitants and their surroundings must be improved together. It has never yet failed to succeed.

5. Andrew Mearns, from *The Bitter Cry of Outcast London* (1883)

Whilst we have been building our churches and solacing ourselves with our religion and dreaming that the millennium was coming, the poor have been growing poorer, the wretched more miserable, and the immoral more corrupt; the gulf has been daily widening which separates the lowest classes of the community from our churches and chapels, and from all decency and civilization … It is perhaps scarcely necessary to say of the hundreds of thousands who compose the class referred to, that very few attend any place of worship … Constantly we come across persons who have never been to church or chapel for 20 years, 28 years, more than 30 years; and some persons as old as 64 never remember having been in a place of worship at all. Indeed, with the exception of a very small proportion, the idea of going has never dawned upon these people. And who can wonder? ...

[Excerpt from a section entitled "The Condition in Which They Live"]

We do not say the condition of their homes, for how can those places be called homes, compared with which the lair of a wild beast would be a comfortable and healthy spot? Few who will read these pages have any conception of what these pestilential human rookeries are, where tens of thousands are crowded together amidst horrors which call to mind what we have heard of the age of the slave ship. To get into them you have to penetrate courts reeking with poisonous and malodorous gases arising from accumulations of sewage and refuse scattered in all directions and often flowing beneath your feet; courts, many of them which the sun never penetrates, which are never visited by a breath of fresh air, and which rarely know the virtues of a drop of cleansing water. You have to ascend rotten staircases, which threaten to give way beneath every step, and which, in some places, have already broken down, leaving gaps that imperil the limbs and lives of the unwary. You have to grope your way along dark and filthy passages swarming with vermin. Then, if you are not driven back by the intolerable stench, you may gain admittance to the dens in which these thousands of beings who belong, as much as you, to the race for whom Christ died, herd together. Have you pitied the poor creatures who sleep under railway arches, in carts or casks, or under any shelter which they can find in the open air?

You will see that they are to be envied in comparison with those whose lot it is to seek refuge here. Eight feet square—that is about the average size of very many of these rooms. Walls and ceiling are black with the accretions of filth which have gathered upon them through long years of neglect. It is exuding through cracks in the boards overhead; it is running down the walls; it is everywhere. What goes by the name of a window is half of it stuffed with rags or covered by boards to keep out wind and rain; the rest is so begrimed and obscured that scarcely can light enter or anything be seen outside. Should you have ascended to the attic, where at least some approach to fresh air might be expected to enter from open or broken window, you look out upon the roofs and ledges of lower tenements, and discover that the sickly air which finds its way into the room has to pass over the putrefying carcases of dead cats or birds, or viler abominations still. The buildings are in such miserable repair as to suggest the thought that if the wind could only reach them they would soon be toppling about the heads of their occupants. As to furniture—you may perchance discover a broken chair, the tottering relics of an old bedstead, or the mere fragment of a table; but more commonly you will find rude substitutes for these things in the shape of rough boards resting upon bricks, an old hamper or box turned upside down, or more frequently still, nothing but rubbish and rags.

Every room in these rotten and reeking tenements houses a family, often two. In one cellar a sanitary inspector reports finding a father, mother, three children, and four pigs! In another room a missionary found a man ill with small-pox, his wife just recovering from her eighth confinement, and the children running about half naked and covered with dirt. Here are seven people living in one underground kitchen, and a little dead child lying in the same room. Elsewhere is a poor widow, her three children and a child who had been dead thirteen days. Her husband, who was a cabman, had shortly before committed suicide. Here live a widow and her six children, including one daughter of 29, another of 21, and a son of 27. Another apartment contains father, mother, and six children, two of whom are ill with scarlet fever. In another nine brothers and sisters, from 29 years of age downwards, live, eat and sleep together. Here is a mother who turns her children into the street in the early evening because she lets her room for immoral purposes until long after midnight, when the poor little wretches creep back again if they have not found some miserable shelter elsewhere. Where there are beds they are simply heaps of dirty rags, shavings or straw, but for the most part these miserable beings find rest only upon the filthy boards. The tenant of this room is a widow, who herself occupies the only bed, and lets the floor to a married couple for 2s. 6d. per week. In many cases matters are made worse by the unhealthy occupations followed by those who dwell in these habitations. Here you are choked as you enter by the air laden with particles of the superfluous fur pulled from the skins of rabbits, rats, dogs and other animals in their preparation for the furrier. Here the smell of paste and of drying match-boxes, mingling with other sickly odours, overpowers you; or it may be the fragrance of stale fish or vegetables, not sold on the previous day, and kept in the room overnight. Even when it is possible to do so the people seldom open their windows, but if they did it is questionable whether much would be gained, for the external air is scarcely less heavily charged with poison than the atmosphere within.

Wretched as these rooms are they are beyond the means of many who wander about all day, picking up a living as they can, and then take refuge at night in one of the common lodging-houses that abound. These are often the resorts of thieves and vagabonds of the lowest type, and some are kept by receivers of stolen goods. In the kitchen men and women may be seen cooking their food, washing their clothes, or lolling about smoking and gambling. In the sleeping room are long rows of beds on each side, sometimes 60 or 80 in one room. In many cases both sexes are allowed to herd together without any attempt to preserve the commonest decency. But there is a lower depth still. Hundreds cannot even scrape together the two pence required to secure them the privilege of resting in those sweltering common sleeping rooms, and so they huddle together upon the stairs and landings, where it is no uncommon thing to find six or eight in the early morning.

That people condemned to exist under such conditions take to drink and fall into sin is surely a matter for little surprise. We may rather say, as does one recent and reliable explorer, that they are "entitled to credit for not being twenty times more depraved than they are." One of the saddest results of this over-crowding is the inevitable association of honest people with criminals. Often is the family of an honest working man compelled to take refuge in a thieves' kitchen; in the houses where they live their rooms are frequently side by side, and continual contact with the very worst of those who have come out our gaols is a matter of necessity. There can be no question that numbers of habitual criminals would never have become such, had they not by force of circumstances been packed together in these slums with those who were hardened in crime. Who can wonder that every evil flourishes in such hotbeds of vice and disease? Who can wonder that little children taken from these hovels to the hospital cry, when they are well, through dread of being sent back to their former misery? Who can wonder that young girls wander off into a life of immorality, which promises release from such conditions? Who can wonder that the public-house is "the Elysian field of the tired toiler?"

Appendix D

The Lady Visitor

[This section contains a selection of materials on district visiting. Initially an eighteenth-century parochial activity that involved middle- and upper-class women going to the houses of the poor to save their souls, the practice expanded in the nineteenth century to include the dissemination of sanitary knowledge and tips for household management and childrearing.]

J. LL. Davies, from his lecture "District Visiting" (1855)

District Visiting, indeed, is not a new work for ladies to undertake; but, on the contrary, one of the most common and familiar of all benevolent occupations....

... There is no reason why gentlemen also should not visit, nor why others of both sexes who would not be called ladies and gentlemen should not be joined with them.... But I shall ... confine my remarks to the case of ladies only, visiting as they do now, and as they may do any day, in the poorer parts of London.

Let me, then, endeavour to trace, first, the true principle of such District Visiting, or, in other words, to discover how Visitors ought to regard their own work....

... Let me then suppose a lady, as one of yourselves, to look around her, with her eyes open, and in an honest conscientious spirit. She knows that, not far from her own house, there are multitudes of poorer persons dwelling, made of the same flesh and blood as herself, objects, according to her creed, of equal divine care with herself.... She sees that there is much in their lot, to which she would shrink from being herself reduced. She is aware of the hard toil to which they are compelled: she cannot be blind to ... the physical discomforts, the dirt, the coarseness of the whole exterior life, which seem inevitably attendant on the condition of poverty.... She thinks within herself, "I have certainly been made to differ, in many points, from those poorer women—, Why?" She has some leisure, perhaps a good deal of it. She has been told, indeed, that she ought to fill up her time, say in cultivating her mind; but she finds cultivating her mind rather dry work; she is conscious that many of her hours might be reclaimed from some sort of idleness or other, to which they are carelessly abandoned. She has knowledge, position, cultivation, above the working multitude; and she discovers that these combine to give her *influence*, that she wields a certain power, even without intending it, over poorer persons with whom she comes in contact. "Might it be," she asks herself, "that the few have received these advantages on which they pride themselves so much—cultivation, refinement, influence,—expressly in order that they may *use* them, that through them they may be better able to serve the many?". . . She dwells on this thought: she finds out that she can, in various ways, help and encourage those who have not her advantages; she finds she always learns something and breathes a fresher life herself when she is trying to help others. Would it not be a blessing if she could really *work* to serve, by fellow-help, the poor about her? She becomes convinced on inquiry and reflection that the class to which she belongs is separated more than is good for either from the class whose disadvantages have touched her; she suspects that at this present time the separation is greater, the chasm more uniform and *smooth*, than it has been in former times. She longs to do what she can to close the gap, to show that she holds every special advantage on the tenure of being the more useful to those who are without it.

Observations and feelings more or less resembling these, must have been called forth in all women of the easier classes who have any desire to be useful among the poor. They suggest, as it seems to me, the elementary principle of that kind of District Visiting which we are now considering. . . .

Then, of course, the question arises, How is she supposed to set about it? . . .

. . . First, there is the difficulty about *intrusion*. The most delicate, that is, the most womanly, women shrink from forcing themselves upon the acquaintance of others just because they are poorer. They are afraid that this reluctance of theirs may have its counterpart in the disgust with which an intrusive visit would be met by those who have not lost all sensitiveness and self-respect. . . . But the true inner delicacy of the Visitor will not be impaired, if she can say to herself, 'I do not go intrusively to make my calls. I do not want to gratify any vulgar curiosity. I am not going to lecture the poor from a high vantage-ground on their improvidence, their ingratitude, and the other vices attributed to them. I have no desire to pry into anything which they may wish to conceal from me. But as a Christian, with certain heavy responsibilities, I am going quite humbly to see whether these my neighbours will do *me* the service of letting me serve *them*. . . .'

Charles Kingsley, "Speech in Behalf of Ladies' Sanitary Association" (1859)

Let me begin by asking the ladies who are interesting themselves in this good work, whether they have really considered what they are about to do in carrying out their own plans? Are they aware that if their Society really succeeds, they will produce a very serious, some would think a very dangerous, change in the state of this nation? Are they aware that they would probably save the lives of some thirty or forty per cent. of the children who are born in England, and that therefore they would cause the subjects of Queen Victoria to increase at a very far more rapid rate than they do now? And are they aware that some very wise men inform us that England is already over-peopled, and that it is an exceedingly puzzling question where we shall soon be able to find work or food for our masses, so rapidly do they increase already, in spite of the thirty or forty per cent. which kind Nature carries off yearly before they are five years old? Have they considered what they are to do with all those children whom they are going to save alive? That has to be thought of; and if they really do believe, with some political economists, that over-population is a possibility to a country which has the greatest colonial empire that the world has ever seen; then I think they had better stop in their course, and let the children die, as they have been in the habit of dying.

But if, on the other hand, it seems to them, as I confess it does to me, that the most precious thing in the world is a human being; that the lowest, and poorest, and the most degraded of human beings is better than all the dumb animals in the world; that there is an infinite, priceless capability in that creature, fallen as it may be; a capability of virtue, and of social and industrial use, which, if it is taken in time, may be developed up to a pitch, of which at first sight the child gives no hint whatsoever; if they believe again, that of all races upon earth now, the English race is probably the finest, and that it gives not the slightest sign whatever of exhaustion; that it seems to be on the whole a young race, and to have very great capabilities in it which have not yet been developed, and above all, the most marvellous capability of adapting itself to every sort of climate and every form of life, which any race, except the old Roman, ever has had in the world; if they consider with me that it is worth the while of political economists and social philosophers to look at the map, and see that about four-fifths of the globe cannot be said as yet to be in anywise inhabited or cultivated, or in the state into which men could put it by a fair supply of population, and industry, and human intellect: then, perhaps, they may think with me that it is a duty, one of the noblest of duties, to help the increase of the English race as much as possible, and to see that every child that is born into this great nation of England be developed to the highest pitch to which we can develop him in physical strength and in beauty, as well as in intellect and in virtue. And then, in that light, it does seem to me, that this Institution—small now, but I do hope some day to become great and to become the mother institution of many and valuable children—is one of the noblest, most right-minded, straightforward, and practical conceptions that I have come across for some years.

We all know the difficulties of sanitary legislation. One looks at them at times almost with despair. I have my own reasons, with which I will not trouble this meeting, for looking on them with more despair than ever: not on account of the government of the time, or any possible government that could come to England, but on account of the peculiar class of persons in whom the ownership of the small houses has become more and more vested, and who are becoming more and more, I had almost said, the arbiters of the popular opinion, and of every election of parliament. However, that is no business of ours here; that must be settled somewhere else; and a fearfully long time, it seems to me, it will be before it is settled. But, in the meantime, what legislation cannot do, I believe private help, and, above all, woman's help, can do even better. It can do this; it can improve the condition of the working man: and not only of him; I must speak also of the middle classes, of the men who own the house in which the working man lives. I must speak, too, of the wealthy tradesman; I must speak—it is a sad thing to have to say it—of our own class as well as of others. Sanitary reform, as it is called, or, in plain English, the art of health, is so very recent a discovery, as all true physical science is, that we ourselves and our own class know very little about it, and practise it very little. And this society, I do hope, will bear in mind that it is not simply to seek the working man, not only to go into the foul alley: but it is to go to the door of the farmer, to the door of the shopkeeper, aye, to the door of ladies and gentlemen of the same rank as ourselves. Women can do in that work what men cannot do. The private correspondence, private conversation, private example, of ladies, above all of married women, of mothers of families, may do what no legislation can do. I am struck more and more with the amount of disease and death I see around me in all classes, which no sanitary legislation whatsoever could touch, unless you had a complete house-to-house visitation by some government officer, with powers to enter every dwelling, to drain it, and ventilate it; and not only that, but to regulate the clothes and the diet of every inhabitant, and that among all ranks. I can conceive of nothing short of that, which would be absurd and impossible, and would also be most harmful morally, which would stop the present amount of disease and death which I see around me, without some such private exertion on the part of women, above all of mothers, as I do hope will spring from this institution more and more.

I see this, that three persons out of every four are utterly unaware of the general causes of their own ill-health, and of the ill-health of their children. They talk of their "afflictions," and their "misfortunes;" and, if they be pious people, they talk of "the will of God," and of "the visitation of God." I do not like to trench upon those matters here; but when I read in my book and in your book, "that it is not the will of our Father in Heaven that one of these little ones should perish," it has come to my mind sometimes with very great strength that that may have a physical application as well as a spiritual one; and that the Father in Heaven who does not wish the child's soul to die, may possibly have created that child's body for the purpose of its not dying except in a good old age. For not only in the lower class, but in the middle and upper classes, when one sees an unhealthy family, then in three cases out of four, if one will take time, trouble, and care enough, one can, with the help of the doctor, who has been attending them, run the evil home to a very different cause than the will of God; and that is, to stupid neglect, stupid ignorance, or what is just as bad, stupid indulgence.

Now, I do believe that if those tracts which you are publishing, which I have read and of which I cannot speak too highly, are spread over the length and breadth of the land, and if women—clergymen's wives, the wives of manufacturers and of great employers, district visitors and schoolmistresses, have these books put into their hands, and are persuaded to spread them, and to enforce them, by their own example and by their own counsel—that then, in the course of a few years, this system being thoroughly carried out, you would see a sensible and large increase in the rate of population. When you have saved your children alive, then you must settle what to do with them. But a living dog is better than a dead lion; I would rather have the living child, and let it take its chance, than let it return to God—wasted. . . .

It is in the power, I believe, of any woman in this room to save three or four lives—human lives—during the next six months. It is in your power, ladies; and it is so easy. You might save several lives apiece, if you choose, without, I believe, interfering with your daily business, or with your daily pleasure; or, if you choose, with your daily frivolities, in any way whatsoever. Let me ask, then, those who are here, and who have not yet laid these things to heart: Will you let this meeting to-day be a mere passing matter of two or three hours' interest, which you may go away and forget for the next book or the next amusement? Or will you be in earnest? Will you learn—I say it openly—from the noble chairman, how easy it is to be in earnest in life; how every one of you, amid all the artificial complications of English society in the nineteenth century, can find a work to do, a noble work to do, a chivalrous work to do—just as chivalrous as if you lived in any old magic land, such as Spenser talked of in his "Faërie Queene;" how you can be as true a knight-errant or lady-errant in the present century, as if you had lived far away in the dark ages of violence and rapine? Will you, I ask, learn this? Will you learn to be in earnest; and to use the position, and the station, and the talent that God has given you to save alive those who should live? And will you remember that it is not the will of your Father that is in Heaven that one little one that plays in the kennel outside should perish, either in body or in soul?

James Begg, from *Happy Homes for Working Men, and How to Get Them* (1866)

The general principle is, that the family system, like the Sabbath law, being an institution of Paradise, is essentially connected with the permanent wellbeing of man. No mere extension of barrack accommodation will therefore cure the evil which exists. Man must not only have a covering, but a HOME. God made men in families; and it is upon the right maintenance and ordering of these little kingdoms that the peace and social order of all the great kingdoms of the world depends. The idea of Home, with all its delightful associations, its concentrated power and far-reaching influences, is as certainly of Divine origin as the existence of man himself....

Taking this as our starting point, the first step necessary is to bring suitable houses into existence in sufficient numbers.... The whole structure of human society is built on the family system, by the wise appointment of God. A comfortable home is the centre of that system. Where that system is maintained in purity and comfort, we may expect general peace and happiness. Where, on the other hand, that system is set aside, and numbers of the people are huddled into miserable habitations of one apartment, social purity and happiness are equally impossible. This one broad fact goes far to explain all the filth and fever of our towns, as well as much of the profligacy of our rural districts; and until it is boldly grappled with, no real social progress on a national scale can be expected.

Benjamin Ward Richardson, from his lecture to the Fourth Congress of the Sanitary Institute of Great Britain, "Woman as a Sanitary Reformer" (1880)

... Adam had no paradise in Paradise itself, until Eve became the help meet for him. How then, in a world which is anything but a paradise, shall we transform it into anything like one till the Eves lend us a hand, and, combining their invincible power with ours, give us the help that is essential to success?... [T]he human being is neither perfected in thought nor in action, until the two natures are blended in thought and action. The man invents, the woman applies the invention; the man conquers nature, the woman makes useful the victory; the man discovers, the woman turns the discovery to due and faithful account; the man goes forth to labour, the woman stays at home to watch the centre common to them, and tend the helpless there.... And, because the natures and dispositions of both are not equally perfect, they have so much the more need the one of the other, since what one lacketh the other hath.

www.ingramcontent.com/pod-product-compliance
Lightning Source LLC
Chambersburg PA
CBHW081354090726
47908CB00011B/2671

* 9 7 8 1 6 3 4 8 7 0 4 5 0 *